HISTORY OF MEDIEVAL CANON LAW
Edited by Wilfried Hartmann and Kenneth Pennington

---

*Canonical Collections of the Early Middle Ages (ca. 400–1140):
A Bibliographical Guide to the Manuscripts and Literature*

Papal Letters in the Early Middle Ages

The History of Western Canon Law to 1140

The History of Byzantine and Eastern Canon Law to 1500

*The History of Medieval Canon Law in the Classical Period,
1140–1234*

*The History of Medieval Canon Law in the Late Middle Ages,
1234–1500*

The History of Courts and Procedure in Medieval Canon Law

*A Guide to Medieval Canon Law Jurists and Collections, 1140–1500
(http://faculty.cua.edu/pennington/biobibl.htm)*

The History of Byzantine and Eastern Canon Law to 1500

The History of Byzantine and Eastern Canon Law to 1500

Edited by Wilfried Hartmann and
Kenneth Pennington

The Catholic University of America Press
Washington, D.C.

Copyright © 2012
The Catholic University of America Press
All rights reserved
The paper used in this publication meets the minimum requirements
of American National Standards for Information Science—Permanence
of Paper for Printed Library materials, ANSI Z39.48-1984.
∞

LIBRARY OF CONGRESS CATALOGING-IN-PUBLICATION DATA
The history of Byzantine and Eastern canon law to 1500 / edited by
Wilfried Hartmann and Kenneth Pennington.
  p. cm. — (History of medieval canon law)
Includes bibliographical references and indexes.
ISBN 978-0-8132-1679-9 (cloth : alk. paper)
1. Canon law—Eastern churches—History.   I. Hartmann, Wilfried,
1942–   II. Pennington, Kenneth.   III. Title.   IV. Series.
KBS132 .H+
262.9´815—dc23
                                                      2011036469

Contents

Acknowledgments   vii

Abbreviations   ix

1. The Formation of Ecclesiastical Law in the Early Church   1
   Susan Wessel

2. Sources of the Greek Canon Law to the Quinisext Council (691/2): Councils and Church Fathers   24
   Heinz Ohme

3. Byzantine Canon Law to 1100   115
   Spyros Troianos

4. Byzantine Canon Law from the Twelfth to the Fifteenth Centuries   170
   Spyros Troianos

5. Sources of Canon Law in the Eastern Churches   215
   Hubert Kaufhold

Index of Councils and Synods   343

General Index   345

Acknowledgments

The editors are particularly pleased to present this volume of the History of Medieval Canon Law because no other book in any language covers the rich history of canon law in Eastern Christianity. As will become clear to the reader, from the perspective of the contemporary world canon law in the East presents linguistic difficulties and ironies. The difficulties are the number of non-Western languages that are necessary to explore the field, in addition of course, to the mother language of canon law, Greek. The irony that will strike today's readers is the fact that many basic texts of Eastern canon law are preserved in languages other than Greek: Arabic, Syriac, Coptic, Armenian and others. We only know a number of texts in their Arabic guise.

As will be clear from the notes, this volume owes many debts to previous scholars and their scholarship. It will also be clear that this particular volume reflects the long tradition of Greek and German scholars' interest in Eastern canon law. Today that tradition is still alive and well at the Max-Planck Institut für Europäische Rechtsgeschichte in Frankfurt am Main. The European authors of this volume all benefitted from sojourns in Frankfurt.

This volume, like the others, is an international effort and has had international support. The now defunct Werner Reimers Stiftung in Bad Homburg, Germany supported this project in the early 1990s. The National Endowment for the Humanities, the Gerda Henkel Stiftung, and the Alexander von Humboldt Stiftung gave generous support over the past twenty years. The editors' universities, Syracuse University, The Catholic University of America, and the Universität Tübingen, provided crucial financial and scholarly support as well. The bulk of this volume was originally written in German and Greek. The editors are grateful to the translators who helped turn these chapters into English. Steven Rowan (University of Missouri, St. Louis) translated the chapters of Heinz Ohme and Hubert Kaufhold. The editors revised Rowan's translation with the help of Ohme and Kaufhold. Father Panayiotis Papageorgiou (Famagusta, Cyprus) translated the Troianos chapters. Ruth Macrides (then Edinburgh and now Birmingham), John Erickson (emeritus St. Vladimir's Orthodox Theological Seminary), and David Wagschal (St. Vladimir's) reviewed the translation and made suggestions for bibliographical additions. The editors revised and reworked the English translations. They are completely responsible for the final form—and infelicities—of these chapters. They must also thank Martina Hartmann for contributing her expertise to this volume.

Some editorial decisions for this volume were difficult. The most basic question was which system of transliteration should be used for proper names for a volume with so many different languages. For the most part we have tried to follow standard English usage in the scholarly literature. However, we have not imposed uniformity, and we have respected the wishes of our authors.

Wilfried Hartmann and Kenneth Pennington
Munich and Washington, D.C., 2010

Abbreviations

Abh.	Abhandlungen (Akademie Heidelberg, Göttingen, Munich)
ACO	*Acta conciliorum oecumenicorum* 2, ed. E. Schwartz and J. Straub (Straßburg-Berlin 1914–1984), second series ed. R. Riedinger (Berlin 1984–)
AHC	*Annuarium historiae conciliorum*
AHDO	*Archive d'histoire du droit oriental*, Brussels
AKG	*Arbeiten zur Kirchengeschichte*
ANRW	*Aufstieg und Niedergang der römischen Welt. Geschichte und Kultur Roms im Spiegel der neueren Forschung*, ed. H. Temporini and W. Haase (Berlin–New York 1972–)
BISA	*Bibliographia Iuris Synodalis Antiqui*, www.uni-bonn.de/bisa/
BKV	*Bibliothek der Kirchenväter* (Kempten-Munich 1911–; 1st ed. Kempten 1871)
BSAC	*Bulletin de la Société d'Archéologie Copte*, Cairo
BZ	*Byzantinische Zeitschrift*
CC	*Le canoniste contemporaine*
CE	*The Coptic Encyclopedia*
ClavisG	*Clavis patrum grecorum*, ed. Maurits Geerard (6 vols. 1974–1998)
CSCO	*Corpus Scriptorum Christianorum Orientalium*
DDC	*Dictionnaire du droit canonique*
DSAM	*Dictionnaire de spiritualité, ascétique et mystique*
DThC	*Dictionnaire de théologie catholique*
EEBS	Ἐπετηρὶς Ἑταιρείας Βυζαντινῶν Σπουδῶν (Athens 1924–)
EEC	*Encyclopedia of the Early Church*, ed. A. Di Berardino (Cambridge 1992)

EKA	*Ekklesiastike Aletheia*
EKEID	Επετηρίς του Κέντρου Ερεύνης της Ιστορίας του Ελληνικού Δικαίου της Ακαδημίας Αθηνών (Yearbook of the Research Centre for the History of Greek Law—Annuaire du Centre des Recherches de l'Histoire de Droit Hellénique, Athens 1948–)
EOMIA	*Ecclesiae Occidentalis monumenta iuris antiquissima canonum et conciliorum interpretationes latine*, ed. C. H. Turner (Oxford 1899–1907)
FM	*Fontes Minores* 1–8, ed. D. Simon; 9, ed. L. Burgmann (Forschungen zur byzantinischen Rechtsgeschichte 1, 3, 4, 7, 8, 11, 14, 17, 19; Frankfurt 1976–1993)
Fonti	Codificazione canonice orientale. Fonti
GCS	Die griechischen christlichen Schriftsteller der ersten drei Jahrhunderte (Leipzig 1897–1941, 1953–)
HOr	*Handbuch der Orientalistik*
JA	*Journal Asiatique*
JAC	*Jahrbuch für Antike und Christentum*
JÖB	*Jahrbuch der Österreichischen Byzantinistik* (formerly Jahrbuch der Österreichischen Byzantinischen Gesellschaft)
JSSt	*Journal of Semitic Studies*
JTS	*Journal of Theological Studies*
KLCO	*Kleines Wörterbuch des Christlichen Orients*, ed. H. Kaufhold (Wiesbaden 2007; 2nd ed. of KWCO)
KWCO	*Kleines Wörterbuch des Christlichen Orients*, ed. J. Aßfalg with Paul Krüger (Wiesbaden 1975)
LACL	*Lexikon der antiken christlichen Literatur*, ed. Siegmar Döpp and Wilhelm Geerlings (Freiburg 1998)
LMA	*Lexikon des Mittelalters*
Muséon	*Le Muséon*
NGWG	*Nachrichten der Gesellschaft der Wissenschaften zu Göttingen*. philologisch-historische Klasse (Berlin)
NPNF	(A Select Library of Nicene and Post-Nicene Fathers of the Christian Church, Second Series, Volume 14; New York–Oxford 1905, reprint Grand Rapids, Michigan 1956, 1983 and Peabody, Massachusetts 2004)
OCA	*Orientalia Christiana Analecta*, Rome
OCP	*Orientalia Christiana Periodica*
ODB	*The Oxford Dictionary of Byzantium*, ed. A. P. Kazhdan, et al. (3 volumes. New York 1991)
OLP	*Orientalia Lovaniensia*
OrChr	*Oriens Christianus*
OrSyr	*L'Orient syrien*

ParOr	*Parole de l'orient*
PatrOr	*Patrologia Orientalis*, Paris
PG	J.-P. Migne, *Patrologiae cursus completus*. Series Graeca
POC	*Proche-Orient chrétien*
PTS	*Patristische Texte und Studien* (Berlin 1963–)
RAC	*Reallexikon für Antike und Christentum* (Stuttgart 1950–)
RE	*Real-Encyclopädie der classischen Altertumswissenschaft*, ed. A. F. Pauly and G. Wissowa (Stuttgart 1893)
REA	*Revue des Études arméniennes*
REB	*Revue des études byzantines*
RECA	*Real-Encyklopädie der classischen Altertumswissenschaften*
ROC	*Revue de l'orient chrétien*
RSO	*Revista degli Studi orientali*
SB	Sitzungsberichte (Berlin, Munich, Vienna)
SC	Sources chrétiennes
SOCC	*Studia Orientalia Christiana*. Collectanea, Cairo
ST	Studi e testi
TU	Texte und Untersuchungen
VV	*Vizantijskij Vremennik*
ZDMG	*Zeitschrift der Deutschen Morgenländischen Gesellschaft*
ZKG	*Zeitschrift für Kirchengeschichte*
ZNW	*Zeitschrift für die neutestamentliche Wissenschaft und die Kunde der älteren Kirche*
ZRG	Zeitschrift der Savigny-Stiftung für Rechtsgeschichte
Kan. Abt.	Kanonistische Abteilung
Rom. Abt.	Romanistische Abteilung
ZTK	Zeitschrift für Theologie und Kirche
ZvglR	Zeitschrift für vergleichende Rechtswissenschaft

Short Titles

Alivisatos, κανόνες = H. S. Alivisatos, Οἱ ἱεροὶ κανόνες καὶ οἱ ἐκκλησιαστικοὶ νόμοι. 2nd ed. (Athens 1948).

Almazov, *Neizdannye kanoniceskie* = A. Almazov, *Neizdannye kanoniceskie otvety Konstantinopoloskago patriarcha Luki Chrysoverga i mitropolita Rodosskago Nila* (Zapiski imperatorskago novorossijskago universiteta; Odessa 1903).

Beck, *Kirche* = H. G. Beck, *Kirche und theologische Literatur im byzantinischen Reich* (Munich 1959).

Beck, *Nomos* = H. G. Beck, *Nomos, Kanon und Staatsraison in Byzanz* (Österreichische Akademie der Wissenschaften, Phil.-hist. Kl. SB 348; Vienna 1981).

Beneševič, 'Monumenta Vaticana' = V. N. Beneševič, 'Monumenta Vaticana ad ius canonicum pertinentia', *Studi bizantini* 2 (1927).

Beneševič, *Sbornik* = V. N. Beneševič, *Kanonizeskij Sbornik XIV. Titolov So Vtoroij Cetverti VII. Veka Do 883 G.* [= The Canonical Collection of 14 Titles from the Second Quarter of the Seventh Century to 883] (St. Petersburg 1905).

Beneševič, *Synagoga* = V. N. Beneševič, *Ioannis Scholastici Synagoga L Titulorum ceteraque eiusdem opera iuridica* (Abhandlungen der Bayerischen Akademie der Wissenschaften, 2nd series 14; Munich 1937; reprint Munich1972).

Beneševič, *Syntagma* = V. N. Beneševič, *Syntagma XIV titulorum sine scholiis secundum versionem paleo-slovenicam adjecto textu graeco e vetutissimis codicibus manuscriptis exarato* (Russian). St. Petersburg 1906. Reprint Leipzig 1974.

Beveregius = G. Beveregius (W. Beveridge), Συνοδικόν *sive Pandectae canonum* (Oxford 1672) 1–2.

Bonefidius = E. Bonefidius (Bonnefoi), *Juris orientalis libri III* (Geneva 1573).

Christophilopoulos, Δίκαιον = A. P. Christophilopoulos, Δίκαιον καὶ Ἱστορία (*'Justice and History'*; Athens 1973).

Cotelerius = J. B. Cotelerius (Cotelier), *Ecclesiae graecae monumenta* 1–3 (Paris 1677–1686).

Darrouzès, *Documents* = Jean Darrouzès, ed. *Documents inédits d'ecclésiologie byzantine* (Archives de l'orient chrétien-Institut Français d'Études Byzantines 10; Paris 1966).

Darrouzès, 'Dossier'/ *Documents* = J. Darrouzès, 'Dossier sur le charisticariat', in *Polychronion: Festschrift Franz Dölger zum 75. Geburtstag*, ed. P. Wirth (Heidelberg 1966) 150–65.

Dimitrievskij, *Opinsanie liturgitseskich rukopisej* = A. Dmitrievskij, *Opisanie litrugitseskich rukopisej* 1 (Kiev 1895; reprint Hildesheim 1965).

Dölger, *Regesten* = F. Dölger, *Corpus der griechischen Urkunden des Mittelalters und der neueren Zeit. Reihe A: Regesten, Abt. I. Regesten der Kaiserurkunden des oströmischen Reiches von 565–1453*; 2. Teil: *Regesten von 1025–1204* (Munich-Berlin 1925; reprint Hildesheim 1976); 3. Teil: *Regesten von 1204–1282*, 2nd ed., ed. P. Wirth (Munich 1977); 4. Teil: *Regesten von 1282–1341* (Munich-Berlin 1960); 5. Teil: *Regesten von 1341–1453* (Munich-Berlin 1965).

Dölger, *Regesten* = F. Dölger and A.E. Müller, *Regesten der Kaiserurkunden des oströmischen Reiches*, 1.1: *Regesten 565–867*, edited by J. Preiser-Kapeller, A. Riehle, and A. E. Müller (2nd ed. Corpus der griechischen Urkunden des Mittelalters und der neueren Zeit A 1.1; Munich 2009).

Funk, *Didascalia* = F. X. Funk, *Didascalia et Constitutiones Apostolorum* (Paderborn 1905; reprint Turin 1964).

Grotz, *Die Entwicklung* = Grotz, *Die Entwicklung des Bußstufenwesens in der vornicaenischen Kirche* (Freiburg 1955).

Grumel-Darrouzès, *Regestes,* **or Laurent,** *Regestes,* **or Darrouzès,** *Regestes* = *Les regestes des actes du Patriarcat de Constantinople;* 1: *Les actes des Patriarches,* and 2 and 3: *Les regestes de 715 à 1206,* ed. V. Grumel and J. Darrouzès (Paris 1989); 4: *Les regestes de 1208 à 1309,* ed. V. Laurent (Paris 1971); 5: *Les regestes de 1310 à 1376,* ed. J. Darrouzès (Paris 1977); 6: *Les regestes de 1377 à 1410,* ed. J. Darrouzès (Paris 1979); 7: *Les regestes de 1411 à 1453,* ed. J. Darrouzès (Paris 1991).

Hanson, *Search* = R. P. C. Hanson, *The Search for the Christian Doctrine of God* (Edinburgh 1988).

Harduinus = Jean Hardouin, *Acta conciliorum et epistolae decretales ac constitutiones summorum pontificum.* Volumes 4–6 (Paris 1714–1715).

Hefele = C.-J. Hefele, *Conciliengeschichte* (9 volumes. Freiburg im Breisgau 1873–1890).

Hefele-Leclercq, *Histoire* = C.-J. Hefele and H. Leclercq, *Histoire des Conciles* (Paris 1907–).

Herman, Introductio = E. Herman, Introduction in I. Croce, *Textus selecti ex operibus commentatorum byzantinorum iuris ecclesiastici* (S. Congregazione per la Chiesa Orientale, Codificazione canonica orientale; Fonti, ser. 2, fasc. 5; Vatican City 1939) 7–35.

Honigmann, *Trois mémoires* = E. Honigmann, *Trois mémoires posthumes d'histoire et de géographie de l'Orient chrétien* (Brussels 1961).

Joannou CCO/CSP/CPG = Périclès-Pierre Joannou, *Discipline générale antique (IIe–IXe s.),* 1.1: *Les canons des conciles oecuméniques (IIe–IXe s.),* 1.2: *Les canons des synodes particuliers (IVe–IXe s.);* 2: *Les canons des pères greques,* 3: *Index* (4 volumes; Codification canonique orientale, Fonti, Série 1; Rome-Grottaferrata 1962–1964).

Kanonika 6 = *The Council in Trullo Revisited,* ed. G. Nedungatt, M. Featherstone (Kanonika 6; Rome 1995).

Katerelos, *Die Auflösung* = E. Katerelos, *Die Auflösung der Ehe bei Demetrios Chomatianos und Johannes Apokaukos* (Europaische Hochschulschriften, 23, 450; Frankfurt am Main 1992).

Katsaros, Ιωάννης Κασταμονίτης = V. Katsaros, Ιωάννης Κασταμονίτης, Συμβολή στη μελέτη του Βίου, του έργου και της εποχής του (Thessalonike 1988).

Kaufhold, *Väterlisten* = H. Kaufhold, 'Griechisch-syrische Väterlisten der frühen griechischen Synoden', *Oriens Christianus* 77 (1993) 1–96.

Kiousopoulou, θεσμός = A. Kiousopoulou, Ο θεσμός της οικογένειας στην Ήπειρο κατά τον 13ο αιώνα ('The institution of the family in Epiros in the 13th century'; Forschungen zur byzantinischen Rechsgeschichte, Athener Reihe 4; Athens 1990).

Lauchert = Friedrich Lauchert, *Die Kanones der wichtigsten altkirchlichen Concilien: Nebst den apostolischen Kanones* (Sammlung ausgewählter Kirchen- und dogmengeschichtlicher Quellenschriften 12; Freiburg im Breisgau 1896).

Laiou, 'Contribution' = A. Laiou, 'Contribution à l'étude de l'institution familiale en Epiru au XIIIème siècle', *FM* 6 (1984) 275–323.

Leunclavius (J. Löwenklau), **JGR** = I. Leunclavii, *Iuris Graeco-Romani tam canonici quam civilis tomi duo* (Frankfurt a.M. 1596; reprint Farnborough 1971).

Menevisoglou = P. Menevisoglou, Ἱστορικὴ εἰσαγωγὴ εἰς τοὺς κανόνας τῆς Ὀρθοδόξου Ἐκκλησίας (Stockholm 1990).

Milasch = N. Milasch, *Das Kirchenrecht der morgenländischen Kirche*, trans. A. R. von Pessic (Mostar 1905).

M-M, Acta = F. Miklosich-J. Müller, *Acta et diplomata Graeca medii aevi* I–VI (Vienna 1860–1890; reprint Athens [no date] and Aalen 1968).

Mortreuil = J. A. B. Mortreuil, *Histoire du droit byzantin ou du droit romain dans l'Empire de l'Orient* 1–3 (Paris 1843, 1844, 1846; reprint Osnabrück 1966).

Ohme, *Quinisextum* = H. Ohme, *Das Concilium Quinisextum und seine Bischofsliste* (AKG 56; Berlin–New York 1990).

Ohme, *Kanon* = Heinz Ohme, *Kanon ekklesiastikos: Die Bedeutung des altkirchlichen Kanonbegriffes* (Arbeiten zur Kirchengeschichte 67; Berlin–New York 1998).

Ohme, *Konzil* = Heinz Ohme, *Concilium Quinisextum: Das Konzil Quinisextum* (Fontes Christiani 82; Turnhout 2006).

Oikonomides, *Byzantium* = N. Oikonomides, ed., Τὸ Βυζάντινο κατά τον 12ο αιώνα: κανόνικο δικαίο, κράτος και κοινωνία (*'Byzantium in the 12th century: canon law, state and society'*; Athens 1991).

Opitz = H. G. Opitz, *Urkunden zur Geschichte des arianischen Streites 318–28* (Berlin 1934).

Ortiz de Urbina = I. Ortiz de Urbina, *Nicée et Constantinople* (Histoire des conciles oecuméniques, 1; Paris 1963) [German Translation, *Nizäa und Konstantinopel* (Geschichte der ökumenischen Konzilien, 1; Mainz 1964).

Oudot, *Patriarchatus* = I. Oudot, *Patriarchatus Constantinopolitani acta selecta I* (Rome 1941).

Papagianni, Οἰκονομικά/Νομολογία = E. Papagianni, Τα οικονομικά του εγγάμου κλήρου στο Βυζάντιο (Forschungen zur byzantinischen. Rechtsgeschichte, Athener Reihe 1; Athens 1986); Η νομολογία των εκκλησιαστικών δικαστηρίων της Βυζαντινής και μεταβυζαντινής περιόδου σε θέματα περιουσιακού δικαίου ('The jurisprudence of the ecclesiastical courts of the Byzantine and post-Byzantine periods with regard to issues of property laws') 1 (Forschungen zur byzantinischen Rechtsgeschichte; Athener Reihe 6; Athens 1992).

Pedalion = Pēdalion tēs noētēs nēos, tēs Mias Hagias Katholikēs kai Apostolikēs tōn Orthodoxōn Ekklēsias (3rd ed. Zakynthos-Zanthe 1864; reprint Athens 1957, 1982 and several other dates).

Pieler, 'Rechtsliteratur' = P. E. Pieler, 'Byzantinische Rechtsliteratur', *Die hochsprachliche profane Literatur der Byzantiner* 2, ed. H. Hunger (Handbuch der Altertumswissenschaft 12.5.2; Munich 1978) 341–480.

Pitra, *Iuris* = Jean Baptiste Pitra, *Juris ecclesiastici Graecorum historia et monumenta* (2 volumes, Rome 1864–68).

Pitra, *Spicilegium* = Jean Baptiste Pitra, *Spicilegium Solesmense complectens SS. Patrum scriptorumque ecclesiasticorum anecdota hactenus opera selecta e graecis orientalibusque et latinis codicibus*, 4: *In quo monumenta tam Africanae quam Byzantinae Ecclesiae proferuntur et illustrantur* (Volume 4, Paris 1858; reprint Graz 1963).

Pitsakis, Το κώλυμα γάμου = K. Pitsakis, Το κώλυμα γάμου λόγω συγγενείας εβδόμου βαθμού εξ αίματος στο βυζαντινό δικαιο (Athens-Komotini 1985).

Rhalles-Potles = Georgios A. Rhalles and Michael Potles, eds., Σύνταγμα τῶν θείων καὶ ἱερῶν κανόνων (6 volumes; Athens 1852–59, reprint Athens 1966).

Ritter, *Konzil* = A. M. Ritter, *Das Konzil von Konstantinopel* und sein Symbol (Göttingen 1965).

Routh = M. Routh, *Reliquiae sacrae* (Oxford 1846).

Rudder = D. Cummings, trans., *The Rudder (Pedalion) of the Metaphorical Ship of the One Holy Catholic and Apostolic Church of Orthodox Christians = or, All the sacred and divine canons . . . as embodied in the original Greek text for the sake of authenticity and explained in the vernacular by way of rendering them more intelligible to the less educated* (Chicago 1957).

Schminck, 'Zur Entwicklung' = A. Schminck, 'Zur Entwicklung des Eherechts in der Komnenenepoche', in Oikonomides, *Byzantium*.

Schneemelcher, 'Bibel III.' = W. Schneemelcher, 'Bibel III. Die Entstehung des Kanons des Neuen Testaments und der christlichen Bibel', TRE 6 (1978) 22–48.

Schwartz 'Kanonensammlungen' = E. Schwartz, 'Die Kanonensammlungen der alten Reichskirche', ZRG, Kan. Abt, (1936) 1–114; (reprint Gesammelte Schriften 4; Berlin 1960) 159–275.

Schwartz, *Bußstufen* = E. Schwartz, *Bußstufen und Katechumenatsklassen* (Schriften der gelehrten Gesellschaft zu Straßburg 7; Strasbourg 1911) (reprint Gesammelte Schriften 5; Berlin 1963) 274–362.

Schwartz, *Athanasius VIII* = E. Schwartz, *Zur Geschichte des Athanasius VIII*, NGWG.PH 1911, 367–426 (reprint Gesammelte Schriften 3, Berlin 1959) 188–264.

Tanner = Norman P. Tanner, *Decrees of the Ecumenical Councils*, 1: *Nicaea I–Lateran V*, 2: *Trent to Vatican II* (2 volumes; Washington, D.C.–London 1990).

Tiftixoglu, 'Zur Genese' = V. Tiftixoglu, 'Zur Genese der Kommentare des Theodoros Balsamon', in Oikonomides, *Byzantium*.

Troianos, Δημήτριος ο Χωματιανός = S. Troianos, Δημήτριος ο Χωματιανός κατά θεοδώρου του βαλσαμών: Είναι γνήσια τα τέκνα από ιερολογημένη μνηστεία; Πρακτικά Διεθνούς Συμποσίου για το Δεσπότατο της Ηπείρου (Arta 1992); 'Kirche und Staat. Die Berührungspunkte der beiden Rechtsordnungen', *Ostkirchliche Studien* 37 (1988).

Troianos, Πηγές = S. Troianos, Οι πηγές του βυζαντινού δικαίου (*The sources of Byzantine law*; Athens 1986 reprint 1999).

Turyn, *Codices graeci vaticani* = A. Turyn, *Codices graeci vaticani saeculis XIII et XIV scripti annorumque notis inscripti* (Vatican City 1964).

Abbreviations

van der Wal–Lokin = N. van der Wal and J. H. A. Lokin, *Historiae iuris graeco-romani delineatio: Les sources du droit byzantin de 300 à 1453* (Groningen 1985).

Voel-Justel = G. Voellus and H. Justellus, *Bibliotheca iuris canonici veteris* 1–2 (Paris 1661).

Wenger, *Quellen* = L. Wenger, *Die Quellen des römischen Rechts* (Österreichische Akademie der Wissenschaften. Denkschriften der Gesamtakademie, 2; Vienna 1953).

Wohlmuth = J. Wohlmuth, *Dekrete der ökumenischen Konzilien I*, Paderborn 1998.

Zachariä von Lingenthal, 'Nomokanones' = K. E. Zachariä von Lingenthal, 'Die griechischen Nomokanones', *Memoires de l'Academie Impériale des sciences de St. Pétersbourg* 7.23.7 (St. Petersburg 1877) = K. E. Zachariä von Lingenthal, *Kleine Schriften zur römischen und byzantinischen Rechtsgeschichte* 1–2 (Leipzig 1973–).

Zahn = Th. Zahn, *Geschichte des neutestamentlichen Kanons* 1–2 (40 1888–1890, reprint Hildesheim 1975).

Zepoi, JGR = J. and P. Zepos, *Jus graecoromanum*, 1–8 (Athens 1931; reprint Aalen 1962).

The History of Byzantine and Eastern Canon Law to 1500

I

The Formation of Ecclesiastical Law in the Early Church

Susan Wessel

Understanding the development of ecclesiastical law in the Eastern empire prior to the Council of Nicaea (325) involves several assumptions.[1] First is the conviction that eastern canon law can be profitably differentiated from its counterpart in the West. Especially for this early period, however, there is little material to prevent one from doing precisely that, because nearly all of the extant sources are of an eastern provenance, and even those that were written in the West were composed originally in Greek (the most obvious exception being the early western councils, which shall be omitted from this account). Second, few would quarrel with the fact that a body of ecclesiastical law gradually came into being whose development can be understood and traced as a linear unfolding or even pro-

---

1. Although a great deal of scholarship exists for each of the sources mentioned here, very little has been written on the general development of ecclesiastical law prior to the Council of Nicaea. See Jean Gaudemet, *Les sources du droit de l'église en Occident du IIe au VIIe siècle* (Paris 1985) 15–28; Ludwig Buisson, 'Die Entstehung des Kirchenrechts', ZRG Kan. Abt. 52 (1966) 1–175; O. Heggelbacher, *Geschichte des frühchristlichen Kirchenrechts bis zum Konzil von Nizäa 325* (Freiburg 1974); A. Faivre, 'La Documentation canonico-liturgique de l'Église ancienne', *Revue des sciences religieuses* 54 (1980) 204–15, 279–95; and the survey by Kenneth Pennington, 'Growth of Church Law', *The Cambridge History of Christianity: Constantine to c. 600*, ed. Augustine Casiday and Frederick W. Norris (Cambridge 2007) 386–402.

gression of ideas about the formation of institutions, practices, morality, dogma, and discipline. Finally, even fewer would deny that these principles eventually gained legitimacy and came to be accepted by the church as authoritative and, therefore, constitutive of its institutional identity.

The difficulty arises in attempting to understand precisely how this evolving corpus of ecclesiastical law acquired the legitimacy and authority that was the precondition for its later codification, for instance, in the collections of the canons of the ecumenical councils and of papal decretals. Long before their authority was accepted as fundamental, in other words, many of the institutional norms of organization, behavior, and discipline that these compilations of canon law expressed were the object of scrutiny and self-conscious reflection by the early communities that produced them, traces of which are contained in the church orders, letters, and conciliar legislation that remain. Because the formation of church law generally took place among nascent communities that could not assume that their legal pronouncements would be binding, nearly all of the early documents that we have are united by their emphatic determination to promote their own legitimacy.

Given these various assumptions and concerns, there are at least two methods by which the development of ecclesiastical law during this early period might be studied. Following the model of the early canonists and of those who collected papal decretals, the sources might be organized systematically according to the substantive legal topics that they treat. While this approach acknowledges what the later canonists surely believed to be true—that a coherent set of institutional and behavioral norms developed according to a kind of linear progression—it violates the integrity of the early sources by removing the legal material from the only context that might elucidate it. With the exception of two eastern councils, the early documents pertaining to ecclesiastical law were mainly contained in letters and tractates whose purpose was to shape the particular communities to which their principles of church organization and norms of moral conduct and behavior were addressed. Preserving this original context by examining each source individually, therefore, connects the legal material with the interests and concerns of the community that produced it. This method also illuminates the broader questions of legitimacy with which such texts and communities were actively engaged.

The idea that a body of Christian law existed, whose content could be identified and whose authority was binding, was already contemplated by the apostle Paul in his letters to the Romans and Galatians. As a hellenistic Jew he was, of course, well versed in the Jewish tradition, having received a thorough training in its laws and rituals, which he combined with his knowledge of Graeco-Roman culture to shape his reflections about life in a Christian community. Whether the Jewish law should be included in, and how it should be interpreted by, the incipient Christian communities were, however, points of persistent contention. Was it a law of ritual observances to be obeyed literally, as some in Galatia suggested? Or was it, as Paul maintained, a provisional set of legal guidelines to be reinterpreted spiritually as merely foreshadowing the law of Christ that was its abrogation and fulfillment? The content of this law, as Paul saw it, was not the ritual prescriptions of the Old Testament, but rather the summation of the single commandment to love.[2] While he defined this relationship between the Old Covenant and the New in his developing theology of the new community baptized in Christ, he, nonetheless, continued to grapple with more concrete matters of legal observance, including marriage, slavery, lawsuits, morality, and food offered to idols, to name only a few.[3] What is absent from his reflections upon a community whose structures he imagined would end shortly is any attempt to elaborate a model of church organization.

For that we turn rather to 1 Timothy and Titus, the so-called Pastoral Epistles of the late first century A.D. (which were written by the anonymous 'Pastors'), in which the faint outlines of a discernible hierarchy suggest that 'the Church was beginning to use the structures of the Greco-Roman household as a model for its own organizational structures'.[4] The *episkopos*, for example, whose personal qualities both letters described, was not the bishop of the later church hierarchy, but the Christian version of the Graeco-Roman overseer, God's steward who was responsible for managing His household. To perform that function admirably, he was expected not only to teach correct doctrine, but to embody such hellenistic virtues as hospitality, goodness, and temperance, and to refrain from arrogance, drunkenness, violence, and greed.[5] Deacons (or 'servers') were appointed to serve the community only if they too were found to be sober, honest, and free from greed, while women deacons were expected to be serious, temperate, faithful, and without slander.[6] (The slightly different catalogue of virtues and vices probably reflected the different responsibilities that women and men traditionally assumed in the household.) That church officials, such as bishops ('overseers'), deacons ('servers'), and presbyters ('elders'), were made to possess the same qualities as every other

---

2. See Gal 5:14; Rom 13:8–10; Lev 19:18.   3. See 1 Cor 5–8.
4. R. F. Collins, 'The Origins of Church Law', *The Jurist* 61 (2001) 134–56, especially p. 138.
5. See 1 Tim 3:2–8; Tit 1:7–8.   6. See 1 Tim 3:8–13.

upstanding member of the Graeco-Roman world suggests that the church intended to accommodate itself to the broader society. Its embrace of Graeco-Roman moral conventions, in other words, was the foundation not only for its condemnation of the overly rigorous asceticism practiced by the unnamed group of opponents whom the Pastor set out to defeat; it also suffused this developing hierarchy with legitimacy as it began to extend ever so slightly into the wider world.[7]

A similar interest in morality lay at the heart of the oldest church order that we have, the 'Lord's Teaching to the Gentiles through the Apostles', commonly known as the Didachè.[8] While it purports to be an apostolic document, the attribution is merely a fiction designed to lend its moral and regulatory pronouncements the weight of apostolic authority. The false attribution says something, in any event, about the church organization that this document reflects. Although bishops and deacons are mentioned and their personal qualifications for office described (men who are gentle, generous, faithful, and well-tried), the most celebrated leaders were the prophets and teachers that one might expect in a community that defined itself by its relationship to apostolic authority.[9] That bishops and deacons were to be given the same respect as these well-respected prophets and teachers suggests a community whose quasi-charismatic identity, with roots deep in the subapostolic period, sometimes conflicted with its growing need for a more elaborate church organization. This was a community on the verge of developing a hierarchy to which some of its members openly objected.[10]

---

7. See 1 Tim 4:1–4.

8. Originally composed in Greek, the Didachè, in whole or in part, was also apparently known in Syriac, Latin, Coptic, Arabic, Ethiopic, and Georgian translations. *Doctrina xii apostolorum (Didache)*. ClavisG 1735. Georg Schöllgen, *Didache: Zwölf-Apostel-Lehre: Lateinisch, griechisch, deutsch* (Fontes Christiani 1; Freiburg–New York 1991) 25–139; Willy Rordorf, André Tuillier, eds., *La doctrine des douze apôtres = Didachè: Introduction, texte, traduction, notes, appendice et index* (SC 248; Paris 1978). Basic bibliography: Clayton N. Jefford, ed. *The Didache in Context: Essays on Its Text, History and Transmission* (Supplements to Novum Testamentum 77; Leiden–New York 1995); see in particular the essay in the previous volume: K. J. Harder and C. N. Jefford, 'A Bibliography of the Literature on the Didache', 368–82 and the other essays cited in the following footnotes; Brian E. Ferme, *Introduzione alla storia delle fonti del diritto canonico* (Rome 1998) 47–49; Kurt Niederwimmer, *Die Didache* (Kommentar zu den Apostolischen Vätern 1; Göttingen 1989; translated by Linda M. Maloney and edited by Harold W. Attridge [Hermeneia: A critical and historical commentary on the Bible; Minneapolis 1998]); W. Rordorf, 'Un chapitre d'éthique judéo-chrétienne: les deux voies', *Revue des sciences religieuses* 49 (1972) 109–28: G. Schöllgen, 'Die Didache als Kirchenordnung', *Jahrbuch für Antike und Christentum* 29 (1986) 5–26; Arthur Vööbus, *Liturgical Traditions in the Didache* (Papers from the Estonian Theological Society in Exile, 16; Stockholm 1968); and the magisterial study by Aaron Milavec, *The Didache: Faith, Hope, & Life of the Earliest Christian Communities, 50–70 C.E.* (New York 2003).

9. The bishops and deacons mentioned in the Didachè are not the sort of bishops and deacons that one might expect in a more elaborated church hierarchy.

10. See J. A. Draper, 'Social Ambiguity and the Production of Text', *The Didache in Context*, 291–93.

The date and provenance of the church order cannot be identified precisely, although its allusions to, and quotations from, the Gospels of Matthew and Luke, and the common source it shared with the Epistle of Barnabas, suggest that it was redacted early in the second century.[11] Internal evidence indicates that the work is a compilation of earlier sources from Syria and Alexandria and that its setting was the rural countryside.[12] Two well-defined sections can be discerned in the text: the first (1–6.2) consists of catechetical instructions that the author has organized according to the 'Two Ways', the way of life, and the way of death ('an early Christian adaptation of a Jewish exemplar');[13] the second (6.3–15) consists of the church order proper, a series of regulations and disciplinary measures ordering life in a Christian community. Although scholars have posited a different provenance for each of the two sections (the Two Ways coming from Alexandria and the church order from rural Syria), the text as it has come down to us reflects the integrated design of its final redactor. The moral injunctions drawn from Scripture in the first section were the instructions to be imparted to catechumens during baptism as it was regulated in the second section. Regardless of its use of earlier sources, therefore, the current text has fully integrated a code of moral behavior with instructions about church life. Those instructions were first and foremost of a liturgical nature (7–10): catechumens were to be baptized in running water in the name of the Father, Son, and Holy Spirit; fasts were to take place on Wednesdays and Fridays to distinguish the community from 'the hypocrites' (who fast on Mondays and Thursdays); the Lord's Prayer (Matt 6:9-13) was to be recited in the prescribed manner; and the eucharist was to be understood as a meal of thanksgiving offered to the Lord (though surprisingly no mention is made of the body and blood of Christ). What is striking about these regulations is that they reveal how certain laws came to be recognized as normative for the life of the community. An abstract set of ecclesiastical laws was never imposed upon the incipient communities; rather, liturgical practices that were already recognized as traditional were gradually given the force of normative law.

Related to the Didachè with its self-conscious insistence upon its apostolic roots was a series of letters composed in the late first and early sec-

---

11. Though the precise date of the Didachè is unknown, scholars have suggested that the text reached its final form by no later than the middle of the second century. The Didachè and the Epistle of Barnabas both used a common source of the Two Ways. Cf. Didachè 1–6.2 and Epistle of Barnabas 18–20. J. S. Kloppenborg, 'The Transformation of Moral Exhortation in Did. 1–5', *The Didache in Context*, 89.

12. *Early Christian Fathers*, ed. C. C. Richardson (New York 1970) 163–66.

13. Kloppenborg, 'The Transformation of Moral Exhortation in Did. 1–5', *The Didache in Context*, 108.

ond centuries by church leaders who came to be known in the seventeenth century as the apostolic fathers. Because of their pastoral quality, however, these letters share more in common with the apostolic epistles of the New Testament than they do with the formal church order that the Didachè represents. The letters attest eloquently to the fact that norms of conduct and practice were developed in the context of individual communities that were wrestling each with a particular set of problems.[14] Clement of Rome in his Epistle to the Corinthians (c. A.D. 96/97), for instance, presented a model of church organization that responded directly to the challenges to the existing hierarchy that were raised by a faction within the community.[15] Identified by Irenaeus and Hegesippus as the third successor of St. Peter in Rome, Clement functioned as a kind of bishop-presbyter whose responsibilities extended to the outlying churches (63). That he was assisted in his duties by a representative, who was invested with authority to articulate his judgments, suggests that the claims of papal primacy, which were eventually to receive full expression by Leo the Great in the fifth century, were already being articulated in their most incipient form by Clement at the end of the first century (65). His intervention in the affairs at Corinth came about because a controversy had arisen there over the type of ecclesiastical leadership being exercised. Although the precise reasons for the conflict remain obscure, it seems that a faction of possibly charismatic leaders had removed from the community certain members of the regular church hierarchy (44.6; 47.6). In the time of Clement the hierarchy consisted of a laity that was distinct from the clergy, and a clergy that included among its ranks the bishops and deacons, and which was collectively known as the presbyters. Clement's contribution was to locate the authority for these hierarchical distinctions within the ministry of the apostles, who, having received their orders from Jesus himself, appointed the first converts to serve as bishops and deacons.

This model of church organization, which foreshadows the doctrine of apostolic succession that Irenaeus was to develop more fully at the end of the second century, was meant to ensure the smooth transition of leadership (42.4). In its current guise, however, the doctrine did not delineate precisely how that transition was to come about. It presupposed a loosely defined bishop-presbyter whose duties were mainly liturgical, and whose election to office was neither the result of a charismatic transfer of leader-

---

14. See generally, J. Duncan, M. Derrett, 'Scripture and Norms in the Apostolic Fathers', ANRW 2, 27, 649–99.
15. Clement of Rome, *Epistula ad Corinthios* (an. 95–96). ClavisG 1001. Gerhard Schneider, *Clemens von Rom: Epistola ad Corinthios, Brief an die Korinther* (Fontes Christiani 15; Freiburg-Vienna 1994).

ship that the apostles assumed, nor of the preferences voiced by the clergy and people, as Caelestine and Leo the Great later decreed. There is some indication, however, that bishops and deacons were chosen by a selected group of unspecified leaders and then approved by the whole church (44.3). Like the Didachè, therefore, this document portrays a community on the verge of developing a hierarchical leadership, the authority for which was articulated explicitly as being the direct heir to the charismatic leadership that the apostles exercised. Given this tension between charismatic and elected leadership, it is not surprising that several members of the community objected to the new model of church organization that was gradually unfolding.

A very different conception of ecclesiastical authority emerges from the letters of Ignatius, the bishop of Antioch who was martyred during the reign of Trajan (A.D. 98–117).[16] The doctrine of apostolic succession being nowhere in sight, Ignatius envisioned an elaborated hierarchy whose authority was grounded in the church's close resemblance to the celestial sphere: the bishop represented God, the presbyters the apostolic council, and the deacons the ministry of Jesus.[17] This well-articulated hierarchy was a departure from the more fluid conceptions of ecclesiastical office that the Pastoral Epistles, the Didachè, and Clement of Rome reflected. Here the bishop was responsible for contracting marriages, for celebrating the Eucharist, and for authorizing baptisms and *agape* feasts,[18] in all of which he was presumably assisted by his presbyters and deacons, whose obligations were defined according to the place that they mirrored in the cosmos. Perhaps what is most distinctive about this model is that the apostolic council is no longer understood as a part of living memory. Elevated to the status of a heavenly archetype, it has become the celestial paradigm to be imitated rather than the repository of a fluid tradition to be transmitted to future generations.

What this highly differentiated model of church organization may have

---

16. Ignatius of Antioch, *Epistulae vii genuinae*. ClavisG 1025. Franz X. Funk, *Die Apostolischen Väter*, revised by Karl Bihlmeyer (2nd ed. Sammlung ausgewählter kirchen- und dogmengeschichtlicher Quellenschriften, Reihe 2.1; Tubingen 1956) 82–113; *Die Apostolischen Väter, griechisch und deutsch*, ed. and trans. Joseph A. Fischer (Munich 1956) 142–224; Pierre-Thomas Camelot, ed. *Lettres: Martyre de Polycarpe: Texte grec, introduction, traduction et notes* (3rd ed. SC 10; Paris 1958). See generally W. R. Schoedel, *Ignatius of Antioch: A Commentary on the Letters of Ignatius of Antioch*, ed. Helmut Koester (Hermeneia: A critical and historical commentary on the Bible; Philadelphia 1985).

17. Ignatius, Epistle to the Magnesians, 6.1; Epistle to the Trallians, 3.1. A. Hensley, 'Submission to Bishop, Presbytery and Deacons in the Letters of St. Ignatius of Antioch', *Lutheran Theological Journal* 35, 2 (2001) 75–86; B. Allen, 'The Ignatian Epistles and the Threefold Ecclesiastical Order', *Journal of Religious History* 17 (1992) 18–32; W. R. Schoedel, 'Polycarp of Smyrna and Ignatius of Antioch', ANRW 2.27, 330–36; Charles Munier, 'La Question d'Ignace d'Antioche: 1870–1988', ANRW 2.27, 440–48.

18. Ignatius, Epistle to Polycarp, 5.2; Epistle to the Smyrnaeans, 8.1; ibid., 8.2.

sacrificed in the continuity of the apostolic tradition, however, it effectively gained in promoting the office of the bishop. This, the first clear statement of an episcopal monarchy, made obedience to the bishop not only the *sine qua non* of membership in the church, but implicitly of salvation itself.[19] Right conduct, a clear conscience, and freedom from heresy were thought to be possible only for those who submitted fully to the authority of the bishop and to those in his service, the presbyters (and deacons?) who were 'as closely tied to the bishop as the strings to the harp'.[20] Together the congregation and the clergy were to form a choir, singing of their harmonious love in hymns to Christ and God. The musical metaphor aptly expressed the vision of ecclesiastical and doctrinal unity that this celestial image of the church prescribed, by which each of its members participated in God through their proper relationship with respect to the hierarchy.[21] There was no more unambiguous expression than this of the benefits of a well-articulated and hierarchical model of church leadership.

The episcopal monarchy that Ignatius promoted was absent in the church organization that Polycarp of Smyrna described in his letter to the Philippians (which he appended to the several letters Ignatius had written while traveling to his martyrdom in Rome).[22] That Polycarp knew Ignatius makes it all the more surprising that he continued to subscribe to the more undifferentiated model of the hierarchy, in which a council of presbyters likely governed the church, and no mention was made of a bishop. This was the case even though Polycarp, in addressing the same problem of docetism (7.1) that Ignatius faced in his letter to the Trallians (9-10), might well have reached the similar conclusion, that obedience to the bishop was the equivalent of obedience to Christ. It was, so far as Ignatius was concerned, the only way to avoid heresy. The rather different conception of leadership to which Polycarp subscribed made compassion and righteousness, rather than innate correspondence to the celestial sphere, the defining characteristic for the presbyters and deacons. Presbyters were to care for the sick, widows, orphans, and poor, while avoiding anger, partiality, greed, and injustice (6.1). Deacons were to be blameless, temperate, and careful, while refraining from greed and slander (5.2). Although the orga-

---

19. Ignatius, Epistle to the Trallians, 6; Epistle to the Philadelphians, 3.3. Scholars are divided as to whether Ignatius in fact described a monarchical episcopate. For a discussion of the literature, see Schoedel, 'Polycarp of Smyrna', 331.
20. Ignatius, Epistle to the Trallians, 7.2; ibid., 6.
21. Ignatius, Epistle to the Ephesians, 4-5.
22. Polycarp of Smyrna, *Epistula ad Philippenses*. ClavisG 1040. Funk, *Die Apostolischen Väter* 114-20; Fischer, *Die Apostolischen Väter* 246-64; Camelot, *Ignace d'Antioch* 176-192; Schoedel, 'Polycarp of Smyrna' 272-358; idem, 'Polycarp's Witness to Ignatius of Antioch', *Vigiliae Christianae* 41 (1987) 1-10.

nization here is only partially developed, the move away from charismatic authority is complete. The presbyters and deacons were not the individual recipients of an apostolic tradition any more than their office alone entitled them to reflect a place in the cosmos. Their rigorous moralism was rather the visible expression of an eschatological world view in which the threat of the coming judgment was 'the motivation for pious living'.[23] As men who were chosen for service, they were also expected to embody all of the practical qualities and personal virtues needed to administer the churches.

The Epistle of Barnabas is an important source of ecclesiastical law for its self-conscious incorporation of Jewish ritual observances and moral commandments into the Christian context.[24] There is no sense here of a church organization, incipient or otherwise. Although its date and authorship are uncertain, the letter (which is not in fact a letter at all) was most likely written during the middle of the second century by an anonymous man from Alexandria whom later theologians (including Clement of Alexandria) identified improbably as the apostle Barnabas. With the Didachè, the text shares the common source of the Two Ways, understood here as the way of light and the way of darkness, into which are integrated a series of behavioral norms and moral pronouncements (18–21). Juxtaposed to this common source stands the main portion of the tractate, in which the author's purpose to communicate perfect gnosis is explored through his allegorical interpretation of the Hebrew Scriptures (1). In place of the old law practiced there stands the new law of Christ in which such ritual observances as sacrifice, fasting, circumcision, dietary restrictions, purity laws, Temple, and the sabbath are not, as the author claims, abolished, but rather reinterpreted allegorically as spiritual pronouncements that govern moral conduct. To follow these pronouncements, which are integrated thoroughly into an apocalyptic eschatology, is to acquiesce in the way of light and to partake in the kingdom.

Moral conduct and behavioral norms are similarly culled from the Jewish tradition and reinterpreted as part of a larger apocalyptic theology in the tractate known as the Shepherd of Hermas.[25] Composed no later than

---

23. Schoedel, 'Polycarp of Smyrna' 284, discussing A. Bovon-Thurneysen, 'Ethik und Eschatologie im Philipperbrief des Polycarp von Smyrna', *Theologische Zeitschrift* 29 (1973) 241–56.

24. Ps.-Barnabas, *Epistula Barnabae*, ClavisG 1050. Funk, *Die Apostolischen Väter* 10–34; Pierre Prigent and Robert A. Kraft, *Épître de Barnabé* (SC 172; Paris, 1971). See L. W. Barnard, *The 'Epistle of Barnabas' and its Contemporary Setting* (ANRW, 2.27; Berlin–New York, 1993) 159–207; J. Carleton Paget, *The Epistle of Barnabas: Outlook and Background* (Wissenschaftliche Untersuchungen zum Neuen Testament, 2. Reihe, 64; Tübingen, 1994).

25. Hermas, *Pastor Hermae*. ClavisG 1052. Molly Whittaker, *Der Hirt des Hermas* (2nd ed. *Die Apostolischen Väter*, 1, GCS 48; Berlin 1967); Robert Joly, *Le Pasteur* (2nd ed. SC 53 bis; Paris, 1986). See R. Joly, *Le milieu complexe du 'Pasteur d'Hermas'*, ANWR, 2.27, 524–51.

the middle of the second century,[26] the work presents itself in three sections, a series of visions, commandments, and similitudes which were the revelations that a man named Hermas (who is otherwise unknown) received in Rome and its environs from two heavenly figures. It was counted among the books of Scripture by Irenaeus, and by Clement and Origen as a work divinely inspired, and was read widely as a book of personal devotion in the East well into the fourth century. A controversy about the status of those who sinned after baptism is the larger ecclesiastical setting in which the work appeared, the purpose of which was to assure Christians that one more chance for repentance was possible for those who subscribed to the set of moral guidelines and behavioral practices delineated in the tractate.

Hermas received the twelve commandments from the angel of repentance who appeared in the form of a shepherd. The commandments were drawn mainly from hellenistic Jewish ethical teachings, which were also the norms the Christians were expected to follow. They included pronouncements on the unity of God, on lying, slander, almsgiving, care for the poor and the dispossessed, adultery, patience, gluttony, extravagance, and the necessity for continual prayer. Although a developed church organization consisting of apostles, bishops, teachers, and deacons is assumed, the legitimacy of these commandments, and the authority for their being carried out, resides not in the hierarchy but in the broader eschatological context that frames them (1.3.5). That the church tower under construction (according to the vision described in the third section) was delayed briefly in order to accommodate those who wished to repent illustrates not only that the view of repentance was universal, but that the moral pronouncements depended for their legitimacy upon the sense of urgency that an eschatological vision of the world inspired (3.9.14; 3:10.4). Because of this urgency, however, the sort of church imagined here is a community of individuals bound together primarily by a code of moral conduct and by a set of behavioral and devotional norms. Assenting to them sincerely was thought to secure each person his membership in an eschatological community that was imminent.[27]

The church order known in its Syriac version as 'The Didascalia, that is

---

26. The only internal evidence for the date is the claim made in the text (1.2.4) that Hermas was to make two copies of the revelation and give one to Clement (the same Clement who wrote the Epistle to the Corinthians in ca. A.D. 96–97) and the other to Grapte (presumably the deaconness). But that early date is contradicted by the Muratorian Fragment, which states: 'The Shepherd was written very recently in our times, in the city of Rome, by Hermas, while Bishop Pius, his brother, sat upon the chair of the city of Rome'. Pius I was pope in A.D. 140–50. Joly, *Le milieu complexe du 'Pasteur d'Hermas'* 527–29.

27. Joly, *Le milieu complexe du 'Pasteur d'Hermas'* 543–45.

catholic doctrine, of the Apostles and Holy Disciples of our Savior', was composed originally in Greek sometime in the middle of the third century, probably in Syria, by a sect of Jewish Christians.[28] Like the Didachè, the text, through its title and internal references, claimed that its authority derived from the apostles, with whom the anonymous author explicitly identified himself in order to address the divergent practices that had arisen in the community with respect to the Jewish law (24.6.12). Some of its members had been observing certain ritual practices of holiness, such as abstaining from wine and meats, maintaining the ritual laws of purity, and generally submitting themselves to the legal prescriptions of the Old Testament. Like the letter to the Galatians and the Letter of Barnabas, therefore, the Didascalia was deeply immersed in sorting out the relationship between the law that was no longer relevant because it had been fulfilled in Christ and the law that continued to shape the life of the community. How Paul and Barnabas resolved the tension has already been considered. The Didascalia resolved it by making explicit the distinction between moral and ritual law that merely simmered beneath the surface in the letters of Paul. Here the moral law, or the law that continued, was not only the command to love, but the entire Decalogue, the ten commandments that Moses revealed to the people before they reverted to idolatry, as well as the judgments that followed. This was identified as the simple law, the law of life that was free from the burdens imposed upon the people by the more detailed prescriptions of ritual observance, such as those pertaining to meats, incense, sacrifice and burnt offerings, and the laws of purity. It was to the second, provisional legislation that these complicated regulations belonged, the main function of which was to punish the people's apostasy. Only the legal prescriptions of this second legislation, to which some members of the community continued to subscribe, had been fulfilled and, therefore, abolished with the advent of Christ.

Because of its negative view of this second legislation, there is no interest here in the allegorizing of ritual found in Barnabas, for instance, where a special gnosis imparted to Christians the interpretive key to unlock the

---

28. *Didascalia apostolorum.* ClavisG 1738. Arthur Vööbus, *The Didascalia Apostolorum in Syriac* I–II (CSCO 401–402; Louvain 1979) 401. 407 (textus) 402. 408 (translatio); Erik Tidner, *Didascalia Apostolorum, Canonum ecclesiasticorum, Traditionis apostolicae Versiones latinae* (Texte und Untersuchungen zur Geschichte der altchristlichen Literatur, 75 [5. Reihe, 19]; Berlin 1963); R. H. Connolly, *Didascalia Apostolorum: The Syriac Version Translated and Accompanied by the Verona Latin Fragments* (Oxford 1929); basic bibliography: J. V. Bartlett, 'Fragments of the Didascalia Apostolorum', JTS 18 (1916–1917) 301–9; Péter Erd, *Periodica* 76 (1987) 381–412; P. Galtier, 'La date de la Didascalie des apôtres', RHE 42 (1947) 315–51; K. Rahner, 'Busslehre und Busspraxis der Didascalia Apostolorum', ZTK 72 (1950) 257–81; *Dizionario Patristico e di Antichità Cristiane* 948–49; Vööbus, *Didascalia Apostolorum*; Ferme, *Introduzione* 50–51.

spiritual meaning that had eluded the Jews. Through his use of allegory Barnabas did not wholly reject the law, but rather incorporated it, transformed though it was, into a Christian framework. For such authors, there was no question that the Old Testament law applied, but that its meaning was deciphered only by Christians, who were endowed with the special capacity to understand. While Barnabas integrated the allegorical interpretation of Scripture into his broader apocalyptic theology,[29] there is no sense in the Didascalia that the end was imminent and no attempt to incorporate its interpretation of the law into a moral eschatology. That men and women were never to regard each other as unclean, that no amount of ritual washing was ever to absolve a man who had committed adultery, were among the quasi-moral pronouncements that the Didascalia made, through its rejection of ritual law, in order to promote a well-ordered community life (26.62). Moral conduct, in other words, was prescribed in the context of relationships, the relationship between the hierarchy and the laity, between members of the community, between husband and wife, between the living and the dead.

The commitment to facilitating relationships, which infuses nearly every aspect of the text, accounts for its detailed pronouncements regulating the functions attributed to, as well as the conduct expected from, the various church officials. This was a well-defined hierarchy of bishops, deacons, deaconesses, presbyters, subdeacons, lectors, and widows (the functions of each of which cannot be elaborated here).[30] Of the many qualities that the bishop was expected to cultivate (to single out the office to which a large portion of the text is dedicated), including frugality, temperance, sobriety, purity, generosity, abstemiousness, patience, and diligence, as well as a studied indifference to the requests that were frequently made by the wealthy, perhaps the most important virtues he was to possess, under which nearly all of his other personal attributes could be subsumed, were the twin virtues of justice and mercy. Bishops were never to implement justice in a way that neglected the principle of compassion (6.12). Practically speaking, this meant that penitential discipline for the community was generally lax, for bishops were urged to emulate several Old Testament examples by readmitting to communion even those found guilty of idolatry, adultery,

---

29. See, for example, Barnabas's treatment of the Jewish sacrificial rite as a type for the death of Jesus. Epistle of Barnabas, 7.6–9; Helmut Koester, *History and Literature of Early Christianity*, 2: *Introduction to the New Testament* (2nd ed. New York–Berlin 1995) 278.

30. On the subordination of women and the laity to the bishops and deacons see Charles Methuen, 'For Pagans Laugh to Hear Women Teach: Gender Stereotypes in the Didascalia Apostolorum', *Gender and Christian Religion*, ed. R. N. Swanson (Studies in Church History 34; Woodbridge, England 1998) 23–35; idem, 'Widows, Bishops and the Struggle for Authority in the Didascalia Apostolorum', JEH 46 (1995) 197–213.

and murder.³¹ The deeper principles operating here were that form was never to dictate substance; that an overly rigorous observance of the rules was never to outweigh fairness; and that no one was ever so circumscribed by her place in society that she was beyond the reach of justice. A woman, for instance, who was not a widow was, nonetheless, qualified to receive financial assistance should the bishop determine that her need was greater than that of a widow whose status might otherwise have guaranteed her alms (4.10).

The function of the bishop in such instances (and the examples could be multiplied) was to act as the arbiter of justice according to the divine model that was God. In the manner of Ignatius (whose letters the author most certainly read) the ecclesiastical hierarchy was to be honored according to the place that each of its members mirrored in the celestial sphere, the bishop representing God, the deacons Christ, the deaconesses the Holy Spirit, the presbyters the apostles, and the orphans and widows the likeness of the holy altar (9.25). For the Didascalia, as it was for Ignatius, this relationship to the heavenly archetypes was the foundation for the authority of the church hierarchy, the basis for its demand of uncompromising obedience from the people. Unlike Ignatius, however, it also signaled to the bishop the gravity of the role he was expected to play. Modeled on the justice and mercy of God, the bishop was responsible for ferreting out and assessing every aspect of the complexity of human relationships that might have some bearing upon his implementing justice. This presumed, of course, that the bishop was alert to all of the nuances of human interaction that were the reality of community life. In court cases, for instance, he was to determine whether the accuser brought his charges out of envy or retaliation, whether the accused had in the past committed similar crimes, and generally to observe the behavior of each party as he existed in the world (11.28). Because the bishop was also charged with distinguishing the norms contained in the Decalogue from the second legislation, the same web of human relationships that were the object of his scrutiny shaped his understanding of the limits of the moral law (4.10). There is no better example of how behavioral norms and moral conduct were not imposed as an abstract set of legal principles, but rather developed in the context of human relationships and according to the vicissitudes of community life.

Although the Didascalia infused nearly every aspect of its church or-

---

31. Connolly, *Didascalia Apostolorum*. lv. See K. J. Torjesen, 'The Episcopacy—Sacerdotal or Monarchial? The Appeal to Old Testament Institutions by Cyprian and the Didascalia', *Studia Patristica* 36 (2001) 387–406, especially 401–5.

ganization with the divine model of justice and mercy, it contained virtually nothing of the rules for the election and ordination of church officials, nor any of the finer points of sacramental ritual.[32] The reverse was true for the Apostolic Tradition of Hippolytus, a church order composed sometime during the third to fourth centuries, that set out to record the 'traditions of the apostles' in order to oppose what its author perceived to be the incorrect practices endorsed by his opponents with a renewed commitment to tradition and rigorism.[33] Important both as a witness to the early traditions of the church and for its continuing influence in the East, where it served as a model for a number of later works,[34] the Apostolic Tradition was a studied attempt to respond to the 'lapse or error that was recently invented out of ignorance' by recording the orthodox rituals and practices that the author had received from the presbyters.[35] Because the author was vociferously opposed to innovation, the church order he produced is at once a reliable repository for the tradition that had been accepted into orthodox practice by the church and an argument for its continued observance. Legislation regulating the election and consecration of the hierarchy; the conversion, instruction, and baptism of the laity; and the

32. Connolly, *Didascalia Apostolorum*, xxxix.
33. *Traditio apostolica*, ClavisG 1737. Wilhelm Geerlings, *Traditio Apostolica: Apostolische Überlieferung. Lateinisch, griechisch, deutsch* (Fontes Christiani 1; Freiburg–New York 1991) 143–313; Bernard Botte, *Hippolyte de Rome: La tradition apostolique d'après les anciennes versions: Introduction, traduction et notes* (SC 11bis; 2nd ed. Paris 1984); basic bibliography: Gregory Dix and Henry Chadwick, *The Treatise on the Apostolic Tradition of St. Hippolytus of Rome* (2nd ed. London-Ridgefield 1992); Burton Scott Easton, *The Apostolic Tradition of Hippolytus* (Cambridge 1934; reprint Hamden 1962); Ferme, *Introduzione* 49–50; Jean Michel Hanssens, *La Liturgie d'Hippolyte: Ses documents, son titulaire, ses origines et son caractère* (OCA 155; Rome 1959); C. C. Richardson, 'Date and Setting of the Apostolic Tradition', *Anglican Theological Review* 30 (1948) 38–44; A. G. Martimort, 'Nouvel examen de la "Tradition apostolique" d'Hippolyte', *Bulletin de littérature ecclésiastique* 88 (1987) 5–25. See Alexandre Faivre, *Naissance d'une hiérarchie: Les premières étapes du cursus clérical* (Théologie historique 40; Paris 1977) 47–67 and Allen Brent, *Hippolytus and the Roman Church in the Third Century: Communities in Tension before the Emergence of a Monarch-Bishop* (Leiden-Cologne–New York 1995).
34. For example, the Apostolic Constitutions (Syria, c. 380) the Epitome or Constitutions Through Hippolytus, the so-called Testament of Our Lord, and the Canons of Hippolytus (Syria, c. 500). List from Johannes Quasten, *Patrology*, 2: *The Ante-Nicene Literature after Irenaeus* (Utrecht-Antwerp-Westminster, Maryland 1950–1986, reprint Allen, Texas 1995 and Notre Dame, Indiana 2005) 184–86. On the relationship between and among the various church orders see Arthur J. Maclean, *The Ancient Church Orders* (Cambridge 1910, reprint Piscataway, New Jersey 2004).
35. Easton, *Hippolytus* 25. The authorship and provenance have been called into question. See P. A. Bradshaw, 'Who Wrote the Apostolic Tradition? A Response to Alistair-Stewart-Sykes', *St. Vladimir's Theological Quarterly* 48 (2004) 195–206; J. F. Baldovin, S. J., 'Hippolytus and the Apostolic Tradition: Recent Research and Commentary', *Theological Studies* 64 (2003) 520–42; J. A. Cerrato, 'The Association of the Name Hippolytus with a Church Order Now Known as the Apostolic Tradition', *St. Vladimir's Theological Quarterly* 48 (2004) 179–94; C. Markschies, 'Wer schrieb die sogennante Traditio Apostolica? Neue Beobachtungen und Hypothesen zu einer kaum lösbaren Frage aus der altkirchen Literaturgeschichte', *Tauffragen und Bekenntnis*, ed. W. Kinzig, C. Markschies, and M. Vinzent (Arbeiten zur Kirchengeschichte 74; Berlin–New York 1999) 8–43.

various church rituals, including the eucharist, *agape*, and fast, constitute the major portion of the manual. In marked contrast to the Didascalia, there is no mention of the personal qualifications that were required of those who held church office. This might seem like a surprising omission for an ecclesiastical manual that was deeply committed to promoting rigorism, except that adherence to correct procedure has replaced moral purity as the basis for the legitimacy of the hierarchy. That is because the procedure by which the bishop was consecrated, the laying on of hands by the bishops which infused him with the Holy Spirit, made him a worthy successor to the apostles, who in turn were the successors of Christ and the 'righteous race of Abraham' (1.2.3; 1.3.1–2). His qualifications upon entering the ministry were not emphasized in the manual because it was the act of consecration itself that transformed him into that worthy successor.

The model of church organization adopted here is probably best understood in relation to the letters of Ignatius, where the celestial order consisting of God, the apostolic council, and the ministry of Jesus corresponded to each member of the ecclesiastical hierarchy. As a representative of that ministry, the bishop, according to the author, functioned as a high priest, whose authority to remit sins, to make consecrations, to preside over the sacraments, and to administer justice differentiated his powers from those exercised by his subordinates, the presbyters, deacons, confessors, widows, readers, virgins, subdeacons, and healers (1.3.4–5).[36] Their places in the hierarchy and their exercise of power was expressed and circumscribed by the ritual of initiation that was appropriate to their particular office. Unlike the bishops who were chosen by the people, for instance, the deacons were selected by the bishop alone to serve only him (1.9.1–2). To limit their function, they were not ordained into the priesthood, they did not receive the spirit (as the presbyters did), and only the bishop laid his hands upon them (1.9.2–4).[37] Lower in the hierarchy were the widows and readers, who were appointed rather than ordained, and after them the virgins and healers, who were merely recognized, but not appointed, according to their purpose and effectiveness respectively.

A rigorous examination of personal character was undertaken before admitting converts into the church. In the sections regulating the laity, for instance, the marital intentions and professions of hearers (or first-stage catechumens) were carefully prescribed. Many professions, such as mili-

---

36. See P. F. Bradshaw, 'The Participation of Other Bishops in the Ordination of a Bishop in the Apostolic Tradition of Hippolytus', *Studia Patristica* 18 (1989) 335–38.

37. Presbyters, in contrast, participated in the ordinations of new presbyters. For an excellent synthetic treatment of the rites of ordination, see Paul F. Bradshaw, *Ordination Rites of the Ancient Churches of East and West* (New York 1990) 59, 72, on the ordination of presbyters and deacons.

tary commanders or civic magistrates, were rejected altogether, while others, such as sculptors, were permitted to continue their profession if they agreed to abide by certain restrictions, such as refusing to make idols. The moral qualifications, which were omitted in the section pertaining to the clergy, were made the object of close scrutiny for catechumens in their second stage ('those set apart for baptism'): they were expected to live sober lives, to honor widows, visit the sick, and generally to perform good deeds (2.20.1–2). Once their moral purity was ensured, catechumens were invited to participate in the sacrament of baptism.

For its detailed description of the rituals prior to and during baptism, and for its preservation of the creed that the catechumens recited, this church order is an important witness to the early liturgy. From it we learn that catechumens were asked three questions pertaining to their belief in the Father, Son, and Holy Spirit, after each of which they responded in the affirmative, and then were submerged in the baptismal water by the presbyter, and attended by the deacons (2.21). Also noteworthy is its description of the baptismal eucharist, in which the bishop, through a prayer of thanksgiving, made the bread into an image of the body of Christ, and the wine into a likeness of his blood (2.23.1). New Christians were then given milk and honey, which functioned as a type of the nourishing flesh of Christ and as the fulfillment of the scriptural promise that those who entered the land of Israel would be similarly nourished (2.23.2).[38] The additional descriptions of church rites and practices, such as laws regulating burial, the offering of meals to widows, and the conduct appropriate at an *agape*, cannot be considered here. Together the regulations suggest, however, that adherence to the rites and forms of church worship that were the traditions inherited from the apostles, as well as reciting the appropriate creed, would prevent Christians from falling into heresy (3.38).

With its confidence in the effectiveness and legitimacy of the rituals and procedures that the author claimed to have inherited from the apostles, the Apostolic Tradition differs considerably from its precursor and closest model, the Didachè, for which the larger moral and eschatological implications of the Two Ways imposed the looming sense of obligation upon its community.[39] The authority for such rites and procedures was now made to reside not in the broader context of an implicit moral eschatology, but rather in the continuing commitment to the tradition of the apostles and to earlier

---

38. Tertullian (*Against Marcion* 1.14) and Clement of Alexandria (*Paedagogue* 1.6) also attest to this tradition. Easton, *Hippolytus* 94.

39. Vicky Balabanski, *Eschatology in the Making: Mark, Matthew and the Didache* (Society for New Testament Studies 97; Cambridge 1997).

church practice. This was an important step in recognizing the ongoing legislation of the church as legitimate. With the Apostolic Tradition, therefore, the eschatological threat of judgment for those who did not adhere to the rites of worship, forms of church organization, and norms of behavior contained in the Shepherd of Hermas, the Epistle of Barnabas, or implicitly in the Didachè, receded into the background as a more self-referential conception of the ecclesiastical law emerged.

The church councils of this early period were an extension of this way of understanding the formation and legitimacy of ecclesiastical law.[40] Unlike the pastoral epistles or the church orders, however, these early councils were not the expression of a particular community's internal regulation. They were rather the product of the collective deliberation of those who understood themselves to be a part of the church hierarchy and to be invested with the authority to speak on behalf of that hierarchy. When competing theologies emerged, such as gnosticism, Montanism, or the Sabellianism or subordinationism of Paul of Samosata, we know from the church historian Eusebius, for instance, that councils were held in the East as early as the second century to determine the boundaries of orthodoxy.[41] There is little doubt that these early councils were conceived on the model of the Jerusalem synod which the apostles held in ca. A.D. 50–52 in order to consider whether Christians were obligated to practice the ritual of circumcision as the Mosaic law required of the Jews (Acts 15; Gal 2:1–2). Although this association with the apostolic synod was never made explicit, the conviction that a council's decision-making power, like that of its model, had been infused with the Holy Spirit gave these deliberative bodies the legitimacy that the early church orders had struggled to obtain.

Although most of the eastern councils prior to Nicaea are known to us only secondhand, through the brief descriptions given them by the theologians and church historians of the period, the canons of two eastern councils, the Council of Ancyra in A.D. 314 and the Council of Neocaesarea in ca. A.D. 318, have been preserved in their entirety in a canon collection that was compiled prior to the Council of Chalcedon.[42] One of the

---

40. Mark Edwards has written a recent survey of early councils, 'Synods and Councils', *The Cambridge History of Christianity: Constantine to c. 600*, ed. Augustine Casiday and Frederick W. Norris (Cambridge 2007) 367–85.

41. See, for example, Eusebius, *Ecclesiastical History*, 5.16.10, which suggests that synods were held in Asia Minor to address the problem of Montanism. For a discussion of these early councils see Charles-Joseph von Hefele, *History of the Councils*, ed. William R. Clark and trans. William N. Oxenham and Edward H. Plumptre (Edinburgh 1883) 1.77–126, esp. 77–80, 118–26 and in Hefele, *Concilien* 1.83–133. For the texts of the eastern synods prior to Nicaea, see ClavisG 8500–8510.

42. The Paris edition of Balsamon states in a note to the canons of Ancyra that its canons, though placed after those of Nicaea, were in fact the more ancient. Henry R. Percival, ed. *The*

first, and certainly one of the most important, councils to be held after the persecution of the Christians ceased, once and for all, with the death of Maximinus in A.D. 313 was the Council of Ancyra.[43] According to the three lists of bishops that have come down to us, which differ considerably in the names of bishops recorded and in the provinces that they represented, somewhere between twelve and eighteen bishops were present from the various regions of Syria and Asia Minor.[44] Their purpose was to address the variety of disciplinary problems raised by those who faltered, either willingly or by force, during the persecutions, as well as to pass legislation pertaining to celibacy, marriage, adultery, and bestiality; sorcery and divinization; the sale of church property; the authority granted to the *chorepiscopi*; the kidnapping of virgins, and voluntary and involuntary homicide. Nearly all of these rules are united in their attempt to impose a set of punitive measures that were clearly defined and rigorous, without being exclusionary, and that applied broadly to the regions of Syria and Asia Minor that the members of the council represented. What separates this conciliar legislation from the earlier church orders is the way in which its disciplinary rules functioned not only to differentiate the degree of moral responsibility according to a set of legal principles that were easily identified and readily repeated, but also to establish in detail the conditions under which those who faltered were readmitted to community life.

The most uncompromising rules were, not surprisingly, those applied to the priests and deacons who had offered sacrifice during the persecutions: afterwards they were permitted to retain the dignity of their office, but not to perform the religious functions, no matter how sincerely they had repented (canons 1–2). Here was one of the few exceptions to a set of disciplinary measures that was, for the most part, determined to unearth the circumstances under which an ecclesiastical offense was committed in order to discern the state of mind of the penitent. The severity of the discipline was then made to correspond to the degree of moral culpabil-

---

Seven Ecumenical Councils of the Undivided Church: Their Canons and Dogmatic Decrees, together with the Canons of all the Local Synods which have Received Ecumenical Acceptance (NPNF) 14.59. See J. G. Herbst, 'Die Synoden von Ancyra und Neucaesarea', *Theologische Quartalschrift* 3 (1821) 399–447. See below, Ohme's section on the Council of Ancyra.

43. Ibid. 62. Canones xxv. Joannou, CSP 56–73. See S. Parvis, 'The Canons of Ancyra and Caesarea (314): Lebon's thesis revisited', JTS 52 (2001) 625–36, who, against Lebon, considers the last six canons of Ancyra (20–25) to be part of that council.

44. See Hefele, *History of the Councils* 200 (Hefele, *Concilien* 220–21), who states that the lists are unreliable because there is no Greek manuscript for them; most of the ancient Latin translations do not contain them; and the provinces named in them are inconsistent with the civil divisions at the time. See also H. Kaufhold, 'Griechisch-syrische Väterlisten der frühen griechischen Synoden', OrChr 77 (1993) 1–96; EOMIA 2.32, 50, 51; F. X. Funk, 'Der 17. Kanon der Synode von Ankyra', *Theologische Quartalschrift* (1879) 275–81.

ity. Canons 4 and 5, for instance, distinguished between those who were forced to sacrifice and then afterwards attended the meal offered to idols cheerfully, dressed in their best apparel, and those who attended while dressed in mourning attire, weeping, and generally miserable throughout the festivities. The former were to be admitted to full communion with the church only after serving for one year as a hearer (second class penitent), three years as a prostrator (third class penitent), and two years as a participant in the prayers (fourth class penitent). The latter, whose somber demeanor made their unwillingness to sacrifice apparent, were not subject to the second class of penitence, while those who did not eat at the meal were to be received in full communion in the fourth year, having served as prostrators for two years and been admitted to the service 'without oblation' in the third.[45] Repeat offenders, namely those who had sacrificed two or three times under force, were not admitted to full communion until the seventh year. The level of specificity contained in the rules reflects this council's commitment to understand acts of apostasy according to points along a continuum that differentiated precisely the degree of moral responsibility.

A somewhat different way of assessing mental state is apparent in the legislation pertaining to murder. Those found guilty of voluntary homicide were to be admitted to communion only at the end of life, while those who committed involuntary homicide were to be admitted, as might be expected, after serving the shorter penance of five years (canons 22–23). Prostitutes, however, who committed the crime of abortion were to remain penitents for ten years (canon 21), presumably because the death of the fetus was the result of an act of fornication that was, in and of itself, thought to be morally repugnant. (The disciplinary measures taken against married women who received abortions were not addressed by this council.) That the period of penance allotted to those found guilty of the crimes of involuntary homicide and abortion was shortened considerably with respect to earlier legislation—from seven years to five and from an eternity to ten years respectively—is a mark of the way in which this council saw its work: penitents were readmitted to full communion so far as the limits of mercy permitted.[46]

It is worth remarking that the only circumstances under which excom-

---

45. Note that canon 5 does not specify the duration of fourth-degree penitence required for those who actually ate at the sacrificial meal. Hefele suggests that they may have been treated according to the fourth canon, i.e., they were made to spend two years in the fourth degree of penitence. Hefele, *History of the Councils* 207 (Hefele, *Concilien* 227).

46. Canon 63 of the Council of Elvira prevented these women from receiving communion even on their death beds. Hefele, *History of the Councils* 220 (Hefele, *Concilien* 240).

munication was contemplated was the not infrequent case of the bishop who, having been rejected by the people and driven from his see, entered another diocese and raised a sedition against its bishop. Punishment, however, was not administered against such bishops who quietly rejoined the same congregation where they had once served as a priest, and in which they were permitted to retain the dignity of that former office (canon 18). This canon illustrates that the mere existence of a conciliar body invested with the authority to issue disciplinary measures presupposes a well-articulated ecclesiastical hierarchy, the smooth functioning of which was essential to the enforcement of its decrees. While the general ethos was to readmit penitent sinners, those bishops whose seditious actions implicitly undermined the very system that enabled such penitents to be forgiven were themselves to suffer the extreme punishment of permanent excommunication.

According to the Paris edition of the great Byzantine monk and scholiast John Zonaras, the Council of Neocaesarea in Cappadocia was held after the Council of Ancyra and before that of Nicaea. The absence of any canons pertaining to the lapsed further suggests that this council took place several years after Ancyra, when the lapsed had already received their sentence and the matter was no longer pertinent.[47] With nine of the fifteen canons bearing upon sexual behavior, at issue rather was the morality of the clergy and laity.[48] Priests, for instance, who married after ordination were to be deposed from the priesthood, while those found guilty of fornication or adultery were made to pass through all the stages of penitence before being readmitted to communion (canon 1). A layman whose wife committed adultery was prohibited from entering the priesthood, while a priest under the same circumstance was forced to leave his wife or be deprived of his sacerdotal functions (canon 8). Together these canons seem morally inconsistent because they allow for the possibility that an innocent priest of an adulteress wife might receive greater punishment than a priest who was himself found guilty of adultery or fornication. Their deeper purpose, however, was to evaluate the state of mind of the penitent, as it was explored by the Council of Ancyra several years earlier, whose commitment to the intimate bond of marriage presumed that the sinful actions of the wife brought dishonor upon the husband.[49] Because living with an adulterous wife was a continous and complacent transgression, the act suggested that the priest who was her husband implicitly condoned her iniquitous deed. His moral culpability was for that

---

47. Hefele, *History of the Councils* 223 (Hefele, *Concilien* 243).
48. Canones XV, Joannou, CSP 75–82. For the names of the bishops see EOMIA 2 32, 52, 53.
49. Hefele, *History of the Councils* 227 (Hefele, *Concilien* 247–48).

reason judged greater than that of the sinful priest who repented of his single act of adultery or fornication.

The remaining canons clarified the baptism of the sick and of married women; circumscribed the responsibilities of the country priests and *chorepiscopi*; established the age of ordination into the priesthood at thirty; and limited the number of deacons per local church to seven (canons 6, 11–15). The canons pertaining to the age of ordination (canon 11) and to the number of deacons (canon 15) derived their authority explicitly from Scripture: Jesus did not begin his ministry until the age of thirty, and the Acts of the Apostles specified only seven deacons. Even in the sophisticated ecclesiastical legislation that was the province of the councils, therefore, analogies to Scripture were the foundation for canon law. That is because council members were no less committed to the idea that the new canons and decrees that were the business of conciliar legislation were intrinsically connected to the apostolic past, even though they made that connection more subtly and less self-consciously than did the earlier church orders and letters.

Not until the time of Constantine was any attempt made to gather such conciliar legislation into canon collections. It is perhaps no coincidence that a similar effort emerged simultaneously in the secular sphere with the collections of Imperial Constitutions made by two lawyers, Gregorian and Hermogenes—the former contained the laws from Hadrian to Constantine and the latter produced the supplement.[50] The existence of such collections implied not merely an antiquarian interest in prior legislation, but a new interest in making that imperial past authoritative in the present. By this process, earlier imperial decrees steadily acquired the force of legitimate law. There is no reason to doubt that lawyers from the time of Constantine onward, equipped with this new repository of imperial legislation, used these collections, as they were meant to be used, as a source of binding legal precedent. The commitment to preserving the past was so deeply rooted in a Christian tradition that viewed innovation as equivalent to heresy that the emergence of canon law collections cannot be understood only according to this model. Because the New Testament itself was seen as an important source of the Christian law, with its reference to Graeco-Roman household codes, its allusions to an emerging church hierarchy, and its scattered references to the remnants of a Jewish law, the very idea that a binding set of legal norms existed was already implicit in the tradition. Paradoxically, that was the case in spite of the fact that the earliest letters of Paul were ambivalent about how the law, specifically the law that was inherited from the Jews, was to function.

50. Percival, *Seven Ecumenical Councils*, xxix.

The extant sources for the evolution of early canon law, including the church orders and letters discussed above, were an elaboration of the incipient processes of legal formation that were already apparent in the New Testament. Deeply interested in advancing their own legitimacy, these early texts, which were produced by individuals and by communities, established that legitimacy by drawing an explicit connection to the apostolic past, on the one hand, and by placing their legal pronouncements in the context of a moral eschatology, on the other. The prospect of securing a voluntary obedience to the norms of behavior and forms of church organization contained in these texts was grounded in one or the other assumption. To be effective, however, those assumptions required the community to acquiesce to the authority of whatever system of organization was being promoted, whether the highly developed episcopal monarchy of Ignatius, or the charismatic prophets and fledgling bishops of the Didachè.

With the early church councils, both sources of authority receded into the background in favor of a more democratic model of church organization, in which bishops from various regions came together in order to deliberate in common about the forms of church organization and the norms of behavior governing the clergy and laity. According to this way of generating law, no single bishop was authoritative in the way he might have been for the communities represented in the church orders and letters. The existence of councils attended by bishops also implied that the laws being enacted extended at the very least to the regions that were represented there. (By the fourth century, that principle was further reinforced as several local councils, including the two considered here, were recognized more widely because of their inclusion in canon collections.) No longer was morality defined in relationship to the implicit threat of an imminent end, as it was, for instance, in the Shepherd of Hermas or in the letter of Barnabas, but according to the broader social circumstances, as in the Pastoral Epistles. Members of the church hierarchy were expected to exhibit the appropriate personal qualities and norms of behavior in order to ensure their excellence according to the moral standards of the Graeco-Roman world, and to invest them with the moral authority needed to govern the Christian community. Laity were expected to conform to norms of behavior that were regulated by detailed rules of inclusion and exclusion from community life. In both cases the legitimacy of the laws that the clergy and laity were asked to obey rested upon a broader idea of the law itself, an idea that evolved from the notion of tradition as binding, which was deeply rooted in the Christian faith, and from the gradual development of the church organization into a well-elaborated hierarchy. Both developments were significant, because respect for tradition was accepted as fundamental, while the hierarchy gradually came to be seen as the continual embodiment of that tradition, the key, in other words, to its preservation. With the introduction of conciliar gatherings as early as the second century, the presumption of legitimacy no longer depended upon linking the present capacity to articulate moral conduct and forms of church organization to the distant authority of an apostolic past (which was sometimes further connected to a moral eschatology). It depended upon a nuanced conception of the law as normative that was largely self-contained.

2

Sources of the Greek Canon Law to the Quinisext Council (691/2)
Councils and Church Fathers

Heinz Ohme

Introduction: The Organization of the Material and the Most Important Editions

Organization of Materials. It is usual to organize the canonical material of Byzantine canon law into four groups: (1) Canons of the Apostles; (2) Canons of ecumenical synods; (3) Canons of local synods; (4) Canons of the Fathers. This organization is found in most of the editions available today.[1] It was first found in canon 1 of the Seventh Ecumenical Council (787), and it has been generally followed in the Orthodox Church in the second millennium. Its characteristic is a systematic organization of the material under dogmatic rubrics, which is demonstrated with the placing of the *Canons of the Apostles*, but particularly with the position of the synodal canons in the ecumenical synods as well as the local synods.

An exposition primarily interested in the history of the sources cannot adopt this organization without modification, since it is already rendered dubious by the pseudepigraphic character of the *Canons of the Apostles* as

---

1. Thus in Joannou, Pedalion, and Rhalles-Potles. See below for the editions.

well as by the historical problem of regarding the Constantinople synods of 381 and 692 as 'ecumenical councils'. The most problematic aspect of the systematic approach is the fact that it ignores the development and coming-into-being of the 'ecumenical council' as an institution with specific criteria, which were first generally recognized and accepted only in the eighth century.[2]

I have decided not to present the material in this essay in a strictly chronological order.[3] For example, the earliest tradition of treating the synods of Ancyra, Neocaesarea, Gangra, Antioch, and Laodicea as a block and in this sequence would fail, since Antioch would have to be placed before Gangra. It is more significant, however, that such a chronological order would lose the weighting of the canonical material in the early church as well as the process of formation that is clarified by the traditional order. The overwhelming significance of the synod of Nicaea (325), whose canons were also of central importance, would thus be obscured, and decisions that became significant only later, such as the canons of Carthage (258), Constantinople (394), and Carthage (419) would receive prior treatment. Such a chronological treatment would in fact produce an ahistoric ordering.

This portion of the *History of Medieval Canon Law* treats the sources of canonical material of Byzantine canon law down to the so-called Quinisext Council (*Trullanum*) (691/2). Although it is known that this council did not bring the development of canon law in the Byzantine East to a close,[4] this terminus is justified both historically and in terms of substance. Canon 2 of the *Trullanum* constitutes an apex and milestone for the canon law of the early church and its further development in the Greek East. It is this canon which first listed and authorized the canons of the apostles, the synods and the Fathers, hence the whole of the law applicable until then. One may speak here of the first synodical codification, and the canon is of basic importance for Orthodoxy.[5]

The model for c. 2 of the Quinisext was the canonical collection *Syntagma XIV titulorum*, which originated in Constantinople at the end of the sixth century.[6] The canon not only incorporates the canonical material developed there but also adopts the organization found in the second part of the *Syntagma*.[7] The canon established, so to speak, its synodal recognition.

---

2. Hermann Josef Sieben, *Die Konzilsidee in der alten Kirche* (Paderborn 1979) 319–21, 357–79.
3. This method is applied by Lauchert.
4. On its further development, see the chapters of Troianos, below.
5. Menevisoglou, Ἱστορική 73–83.
6. See Sp. Troianos, 'Byzantine Canon Law to 1100', 193–94.
7. Cf. Rhalles-Potles 1.10, 115, 149, 185; Menevisoglou, Ἱστορική 55–73. The edition of the *Syntagma* in its Old Slavonic translation by Beneševič does not advance an investigation of the original

Although the *Canons of the Apostles* are already placed at the very beginning, the further order is still entirely in keeping with the subsequent development of this *corpus canonum*. This is particularly the case with the synodal canons, which are not organized in the manner they would be later. Rather, the oldest corpus contained the synods of Nicaea, Ancyra, Neocaesarea, Gangra, Antioch, Laodicea, and Constantinople (381). These were followed by the synods of Ephesus, Chalcedon, and Serdica; finally the councils of Carthage (419) and Constantinople (394) are added, with the last text being the *Canons of the Fathers*.[8] This generic division appears to preserve the best ordering according to historical criteria, and for that reason it is the order that will be observed in the following exposition. It will not be possible to treat the *Canons of the Apostles* as a category in their own right. Rather, they will be treated as synodal canons, which in fact they are.

The Most Important Editions The edition by P.-P. Joannou published in 1962 in Grottaferrata by the 'Pontificia Commissione per la Redazione del Codice di Diritto Canonico Orientale' should be mentioned first.[9] It is the only one of the currently accessible textual editions that can be called a critical edition. The foundation of Joannou's text[10] is V. N. Beneševič's edition of the *Synogoga* of John Scholasticus.[11] Since the *Synogoga* comes to an end with Chalcedon and the *Canons of the Fathers* are represented only by Basil, and he only in an incomplete form, Joannou supplied the missing parts. For this he used the manuscript tradition of synodal acts and the Fathers of the Church, particularly exploiting many canonical collection manuscripts. He was committed to the systematic treatment of the material in sequence, though in places he supplemented the material in an often arbitrary manner.[12] In Joannou's introductions he always felt compelled to represent the Roman Catholic position, and, for that reason, he accepted the canons of the synod of Constantinople of 869, which are not preserved in any Byzantine collection, as 'canons of the Eighth Ecumenical Synod'.[13]

The most widely distributed edition among Orthodox canon lawyers is the *Syntagma*, edited by G. A. Rhalles and M. Potles from 1852 to 1859 in six volumes.[14] It may be described as the *textus receptus* or 'Vulgate' of Byzan-

---

organization of the material, since it had already altered the sequence of synods, placing the ecumenical synods before the local synods.

8. On their order, see the section 'Origin and Content of the Canons of the Fathers' below.
9. Joannou, CCO, CSP, and CPG.
10. On his procedure, see Joannou, CCO 1–11.
11. Beneševič, *Synagoga*.
12. Cf. his texts for Athanasius, Timothy, and Cyril.
13. Cf. Joannou, CCO 293–342.
14. Rhalles-Potles.

tine canon law. Volumes one to four consist of an edition of the *Syntagma XIV titulorum* in the form ca. 883,[15] the 'Nomokanon of Photius', with parallel printed commentaries of Byzantine canonists of the twelfth century: J. Zonaras, T. Balsamon, and A. Aristenos. The textual basis is the *editio princeps* of the Trebizond Codex of 1311, against which Rhalles-Potles collated all editions appearing until 1852.[16] Volume five contains synodal decisions and Διατάξεις of the patriarchs of Constantinople as well as a collection of *novellae* of Byzantine emperors, and volume six contains the *Syntagma* of Matthew Blastares.[17]

Together with the *Syntagma* of Rhalles-Potles, the so-called *Pedalion* of Saint Nikodemos the Hagiorite (1749–1809) enjoys the widest distribution among the Orthodox.[18] It consists of a collection for Orthodox clergy put together at the end of the eighteenth century out of *kanonika* and *nomika* hitherto available only in manuscript. Its selection of later canonical texts has been criticized up to the present day.[19] The Pedalion was edited with the approval of the Ecumenical Patriarch Neophytos VII (1789–94, 1798–1801), so that it has a certain official character. The first edition appeared in Leipzig in 1800. Since the third edition of 1864 appearing in Zante-Zakynthos, nine printings have appeared. Alongside the edition itself, the special contribution of Nikodemos is his translation of each canon into the vernacular ('Ερμηνείαι), as well as his cross-references to other decisions of similar content (Συμφωνίαι).

The textual edition of Friedrich Lauchert of 1896 is still being used for the synodal canons, although without the *Canons of the Fathers*.[20] He orders his material chronologically and mixes canons of the Latin West with those of the Greek East. As the texts are reprints of earlier editions, mostly from Mansi and Bruns,[21] the text offered by Lauchert thus has to be compared with more recent editions. The same applies to the even older edition of Cardinal J. B. Pitra, which was presented as a critical edition, though it has seldom been positively reviewed.[22]

15. Cf. the introduction in Rhalles-Potles I α'-ιθ'.
16. Cf. Rhalles-Potles ι'-ιε'.
17. On this work, see Sp. Troianos, 'Byzantine Canon Law from the Twelfth to the Fifteenth Century', 299–303 below. Both volumes are in a reprint of Leunclavius, JGR.
18. The edition is Pedalion. An English translation is *Rudder*. On Nikodemos the Hagiorite, cf. G. Podskalsky, *Griechische Theologie in der Zeit der Türkenherrschaft 1453–1821* (Munich 1988) 377–382.
19. Cf. P. Menevisoglou, Ἡ κανονικὴ συλλογὴ Πηδάλιον, in Χαριστεῖον Σεραφεὶμ Τίκα ἀχεπ. Ἀθηνῶν (Thessalonike 1984) 147–66.
20. Lauchert.
21. H. T. Bruns, *Canones apostolorum et conciliorum saeculorum IV, V, VI, VII, pars prior* (Bibliotheca ecclesiastica 1; Berlin 1839, reprint Torino 1959).
22. Pitra, *Juris*. Cf. Funk, *Didascalia* 1.XXIII; E. Schwartz, *Die Quellen über den melitianischen Streit (1905)* (Gesammelte Schriften 3; Berlin 1959) 89.

The Canons of the Apostles

Editions: Joannou, CSP 1–53; Funk, *Didascalia* 1.564–92; M. Metzger, *Les Constitutions Apostoliques* 3 (SC 336; Paris 1987) 275–309; Lauchert 1–13 (reprint Mansi); Rhalles-Potles 2.1–112; Pedalion 1–117; Pitra, *Juris* 1.13–36; *versio latina*: EOMIA 1.9–32; *Versiones*: see G. Bardy, DDC 2.1294.

Translations: English: *Rudder* 1–154; NPNF 14.591–601; German: Anargyros Anapoliotis, *Heilige Kanones der heiligen und hoch verehrten Apostel* (St. Ottilien 2009); French: Joannou, CSP 1–53; M. Metzger, *Les Constitutions Apostoliques* 3 (SC 336; Paris 1987) 275–309.

Literature: G. Bardy, 'Canons apostoliques', DDC 2.1288–95; P. F. Bradshaw, 'Kirchenordnungen I. Altkirchliche', TRE 18 (1990) 662–70; J. S. von Drey, *Neue Untersuchungen über die Constitutionen und Kanones der Apostel* (Tübingen 1832) 203–419; F. X. Funk, *Die apostolischen Konstitutionen* (Rottenburg 1891; reprint Frankfurt 1970) 180–206; M. Metzger, *Les Constitutions apostoliques* 1–3 (SC 320, 329, 336; Paris 1985–87) 3.9–13; M. Metzger, 'Konstitutionen (Pseudo-Apostolische)', TRE 19 (1991) 540–44; J. Mühlsteiger, 'Die sogenannten Canones Apostolorum', *Tradition—Wegweisung in die Zukunft: Festschrift Johannes Mühlsteiger SJ zum 75. Geburtstag*, ed. K. Breitsching and Wilhelm Rees (2 vols. Kanonistische Studien und Texte 46; Berlin 2001) 2.615–80; J. Mühlsteiger, *Kirchenordnungen: Anfänge kirchlicher Rechtsbildung* (Kanonistische Studien und Texte 50; Berlin 2006); J. G. Mueller, 'The Ancient Church Order Literature: Genre or Tradition?' *Journal of Early Christian Studies* 15 (2007) 337–80; P. Nautin, 'The 85 Apostolic Canons', EEC 62; Ohme, *Kanon* 485–97; B. Steimer, *Vertex Traditionis: Die Gattung der altchristlichen Kirchenordnungen* (Beiheft zur Zeitschrift für die neutestamentliche Wissenschaft 63; Berlin–New York 1992) 87–94, 114–33; C. H. Turner, 'Notes on the Apostolic Constitutions', JTS 16 (1914–15) 54–61, 523–38; JTS 31 (1930) 128–41; C. H. Turner, 'A Primitive Edition of the Apostolic Constitutions and Canons', JTS 15 (1914) 53–65; E. Schwartz, *Über die pseudoapostolischen Kirchenordnungen* (Strasbourg 1910); E. M. Synek, *Dieses Gesetz ist gut, heilig, es zwingt nicht . . . Zum Gesetzesbegriff der Apostolischen Konstitutionen* (Kirche und Recht 21; Vienna 1997); E. M. Synek, *ΟΙΚΟΣ: Zum Ehe- und Familienrecht der Apostolischen Konstitutionen* (Kirche und Recht 22; Vienna 1999).

The *Canons of the Apostles* is a collection of 85 canons.[23] The collection is included at the end of book 8 of the *Apostolic Constitutions* as Chapter 47. The short epilogue (8.48) describes them in the direct speech of the apostles as their 'canons' for the bishops. Hence the *Apostolic Constitutions* as a whole has the appearance of a conciliar document with canonical decrees passed by the apostolic council in Jerusalem (6.14.1). An historical evaluation of the *Canons of the Apostles* can take place only in the context of the *Apostolic Constitutions*. The work of J. S. von Drey, F. X. Funk, E. Schwartz and C. H. Turner has completely settled the older controversies that had arisen after the publication of the text in the sixteenth century and established a general scholarly consensus about the *Apostolic Constitutions* and the Canons of the Apostles. M. Metzger added a new edition to that of Funk in 1985–87 and essentially confirmed the main controverted questions.[24]

---

23. On the numbering, see below.
24. Von Drey, *Neue Untersuchungen*; Funk, *Didascalia*, and Funk, *Die apostolischen Konstitutionen*; Schwartz, *Über die pseudoapostolischen*; Metzger, *Constitutions*.

This research has established that the *Apostolic Constitutions* is a pseudepigraphic compilation consisting of the following elements: (1) A collection of the three older church ordinances, the *Didachè*, the *Didaskalia*, and the *Traditio apostolica* (Const. 7, 1–6, 8); (2) Insertion of liturgical prayer formulas and conciliar traditions; (3) Insertion of extracts and citations, particularly from the Holy Scriptures and the pseudo-Clementine literature; (4) Direct interpolations by the compiler himself. The unity of the entire *Apostolic Constitutions*, including the *Canons of the Apostles*, is no longer in doubt.[25] It is probably not the work of a single editor or compiler but rather the joint product of a 'workshop'. The land of origin is Syria, more precisely probably Antioch in the period around 380.[26]

The unity of the *Apostolic Constitutions* and the *Canons of the Apostles* is confirmed by the fact—as close inspection shows—that the *Canons of the Apostles* is also a compilation of older material, particularly from the synods of Antioch (328), Laodicea, and Nicaea (325), from which at least 28 canons have been taken.[27] The dependence of the Canons of the Apostles on the canons of Antioch in particular cannot any longer be doubted, since the corresponding canons are excerpts from those of Antioch, and they follow them in order, with corresponding gaps.

This is the case with the following canons (with the corresponding canons of Antioch in parentheses): canons 9, 10, 11, and 12 on the duty of clergy to take Holy Communion, the presence of the faithful at the *anaphora* and the ban on common prayer with excommunicates and those deposed from office (c. 2); c. 13 on the ban of receiving excommunicates into other congregations (c. 6); c. 14 on the ban against bishops changing dioceses (canons 18, 21); canons 15 and 16 on the rights of clerics who leave their congregations (c. 3); c. 29 on deposed clerics (c. 4); c. 32 on separating priests and deacons (c. 5); c. 33 on the reacceptance of excommunicated priests and deacons (c. 6); c. 34 on the reception of alien clerics (canons 7, 8); c. 35 on the rights of the metropolitan (c. 9); c. 36 on the ban on consecrating outside one's own diocese (canons 13, 22); c. 37 on the refusal of office by clerics and the rejection of a bishop by the congregation (canons 17, 18); c. 38 about the two eparchial synods every year (c. 20); canons 39 to 41 on church property and the private property of the bishop (canons 24 and 25); and c. 76 on the ban on designating one's successor (c. 23).

The synod of Laodicea was the source for the following canons: the

---

25. Metzger, *Constitutions* 1.31–2; Funk, *Die apostolischen Konstitutionen*; contra: Schwartz, *Über die pseudoapostolischen* 19.
26. Metzger, *Constitutions* 1.54–55ff.; Funk, *Die apostolischen Konstitutionen* 356–70.
27. Detailed narratives of derivations in von Drey, *Neue Untersuchungen* 403–14; Funk, *Die apostolischen Konstitutionen* 183–90.

ban by c. 45 on praying with heretics or conceding to their clerical functions has a parallel in canons 9, 33, and 34, and canons 70 and 71—banning sharing fasting, festivals or gifts with Jews, taking oil into their sanctuaries or lighting lamps—resonate with canons 37–39.

Besides Antioch and Laodicea, some individual canons of Nicaea (325) appear to be sources of the Canons of the Apostles: canons 21 to 24 concerning eunuchs in the clergy and on self-mutilation (Nicaea c. 1); c. 80 forbidding neophytes in episcopal office (Nicaea c. 2) and c. 44 banning the taking of usury by clerics (Nicaea c. 17).

The final piece of evidence indicating a direct connection to the *Apostolic Constitutions* is the fact that about twenty of the canons are taken directly from the *Apostolic Constitutions*. Here the passages of the *Apostolic Constitutions* in the Apostolic Canons are all interpolations of the compiler.[28] Canons 42 and 43 treating the private property of bishops, clerical gambling and drinking are taken from the *Didaskalia*.

Interpolations in the *Apostolic Constitutions* are sources of the following canons: canons 1 and 2 on the number of consecrators (3.20); c. 7 on the necessity for clerics to be free of worldly cares (2.6); c. 8 on the distinction of Easter and Passover (5.17); c. 17 on the second marriage after baptism as a hindrance to ordination (2.2, 6.17); c. 18 on particular marriages as hindrances to ordination (6.17); c. 20, that clerics should not guarantee loans (2.6); c. 27 on the ban on marriage after higher orders (6.17); c. 34 on the mode of receiving alien clerics (2.58, 7.28); c. 46 against heretical baptism (6.15); c. 47 on rebaptism (6.15); c. 49 on the formula of baptism (6.10, 11, 26); c. 51 on the ban on the asceticism of clerics out of disgust (6.8, 10, 11, 26); c. 52 on the reception of penitent sinners (2.10–20); c. 53 on deposing clerics who practice asceticism on festival days (5.20); c. 60 banning the books of the godless in the divine service (6.16); c. 64 banning praying in the synagogues of Jews and heretics (2.61); c. 66 on the ban on fasting on Saturdays and Sundays (5.20); c. 79, that one possessed cannot become a cleric before being healed (8.32), and many others.

The remaining canons deal with decisions on the following themes: forbidden offerings (canons 3–5); bans on divorce of married clergy under the pretext of piety (c. 6); forbidden degrees of relationship for the second marriage of clerics (c. 19); deposing clerics does not lead automatically to excommunication (canons 25, 26); use of force by clerics against sinners leads to deposing (c. 28); simony (canons 30, 31); gambling and drunkenness of clerics (canons 42, 43); ban on lay divorce with the intent of remarriage (c. 48); necessity of threefold submersion in baptism (c. 50); drunkenness

---

28. Cf. Funk, *Die apostolischen Konstitutionen* 188ff.

of clerics (c. 54); harrassment of clerics (canons 55, 56) and of the disabled (c. 57); neglect of official duties and cares (canons 58, 59); moral impediments for entering the clerical order (c. 61); apostacy of clerics (c. 62); ban on unbled meat (c. 63); clerics as killers (c. 65); abduction with intent to marry (c. 67); ban on second consecration (of clerics) (c. 68); non-observance of fasting times by clerics (c. 69); removal and misuse of the instruments of divine service (canons 72, 73); complaint proceedings against bishops (c. 74); requirements of the witnesses for such proceedings (c. 75); physical impediments for episcopal ordination (canons 77, 78); ban on political activities by bishops (c. 81); slaves in the episcopal office (c. 82); ban on war service for clerics (c. 83); lèse-majesté (c. 84); index of the canonical Holy Scriptures, including the *Apostolic Constitutions*.[29]

The content of the canons has little internal unity and barely any internal order. It is suprising, however, that out of the 85 canons, 76 deal with the clergy, and laymen are almost totally ignored. One can thus speak of the Canons of the Apostles as a selection and compilation of ecclesiastical discipline for clerics.[30]

The numeration of the canons in the manuscripts is diverse.[31] Since the oldest text, the *Fragmentum Veronense*, lacks all numeration, it is to be assumed this was also lacking in the Greek original.[32] The question remains open whether the compiler had a collection of older conciliar material before him, or whether he knew these decisions in isolation. The earliest canonical collections are believed to have arisen in the period of Constantinople I, about 381 (see below).

Hence, the Canons of the Apostles may be regarded as representing the literary type of pseudo-apostolic church orders of the early church; and together with the *Apostolic Constitutions* they may even be regarded as the apex of the genre. Their uniqueness appears to lie in the fact that actual canonical decisions of ecclesiastical synods are clothed with the claim of apostolic origin through literary fiction. The *Apostolic Constitutions* are, in fact, the last example of this genre within the imperial church, where they are soon to be definitively replaced by synodal canons. It is only in the separating churches in Syria and Egypt that they continued to be relevant.[33]

29. Cf. Zahn, *Geschichte* 2.184–93.
30. Thus von Drey, *Neue Untersuchungen* 436.
31. Cf. the concordance in Joannou, CCO 5–7, which is, however, not complete. In many manuscripts the material is distributed in 76 canons.
32. Cf. Metzger, *Constitutions* 1.72f.; 3.12. On the text, cf. Metzger, *Constitutions* 1.63–74; Funk, *Didascalia* 1.xlix–lii. On c. 50, Schwartz, *Über die pseudoapostolischen* 14–15 and Turner, 'A Primitive Edition' 524–30 have reconstructed a gloss in long as well as short form which is an index of later reworking (cf. Metzger, *Constitutions* 3.10–11).
33. Cf. Bardy, 'Canons apostoliques' 1294.

Hence the Canons of the Apostles, as a portion of the *Apostolic Constitutions*, like all church orders of the earliest period, filled a legislative vacuum in the formation of ecclesiastical institutions by collating, actualizing, and propagating the old normative texts and traditions.[34] The author of the *Apostolic Constitutions* wanted to unify ecclesiastical norms in order to fight the plethora of local traditions and particularism that had been characteristic of the fourth-century conciliar legislation. The compiler naturally made an evaluation in the course of his selection. Despite the unavoidable contradictions among various parts of the *Apostolic Constitutions*, the Canons of the Apostles are a good measure for what the compiler held to be absolutely binding and what he knew best from his own context.

The earliest indication of the use of the Canons of the Apostles appears in an extract from the acts of the synod of Constantinople of 29 September 394 (see below), where Nectarius of Constantinople refers to the 'apostolic canons' on the question of condemning a bishop.[35] According to these 'apostolic canons', a bishop could not be deposed by two or three other bishops, but only through the vote of a larger synod of the corresponding eparchy. This shows a knowledge of c. 74, which regulates in detail the deposition of a bishop after three summonses by a synod, and which is among the most-cited canons in the councils of the fifth century.[36] However, as J. S. von Drey and J. W. Bickell have already shown, we cannot assume that when the phrases κανὼν ἀποστολικός or ἐκκλησιαστικός or ἀρχαῖος are used in the sources that they are references to these collections of canons.[37] Rather references in texts before 394 that contain these phrases should be understood to mean that a canon rested on an ecclesiastical norm or practice dating from the time of the apostles.[38]

When Dionysius Exiguus (ca. 500 A.D.) translated a collection of canons from Greek into Latin for Bishop Stephanus of Salona, he placed the first 50 Canons of the Apostles at the head.[39] In his *praefatio*, he remarked that in his own time many had doubted the apostolic origin of the canons.

Incipiunt regule ecclesiastice sanctorum apostolorum, prolate per Clementem, Ecclesie romane pontificem, quae ex graecis exemplaribus in ordine primo ponun-

---

34. On this, Metzger, *Constitutions* 1.48–51.   35. Joannou, CSP 443.19–20.

36. Cf. Schwartz, *Über die pseudoapostolischen* 12. Bardy, 'Canons apostoliques' 1290, overlooks the reference to c. 74 and only considers a reminiscence of general practice in canons 14 and 15 on the abandonment of congregations and dioceses by clerics.

37. Extensive discussion of the dispute in von Drey, *Neue Untersuchungen* 378–403; J. W. Bikkell, *Geschichte des Kirchenrechts* 1 (Giessen 1843) 79–84. Until the most recent period, leaders of Orthodox canonical studies have used this method to prove the apostolic origins of the *Canons of the Apostles*. Cf. Menevisoglou, Ἱστορικὴ 109–14, 119–20.

38. Cf. Ohme, *Kanon* passim.

39. Cf. A. Strewe, *Die Canonessammlung des Dionysius Exiguus in der ersten Redaktion* (Arbeiten zur Kirchengeschichte 16; Berlin 1931).

tur, quibus quamplurimi quidem consensum non prebuere facile et tamen postea quaedam constituta pontificum ex ipsis canonibus adsumpta esse videntur.[40]

Doubts about the canons was possible in Greek as well as in Latin lands, since it appears that a Latin translation existed of the *Apostolic Constitutions*, including the Canons of the Apostles, even before Dionysius's translation.[41] What cannot be answered to this day is why Dionysius translated only the first 50 canons. It is unlikely that he broke off the translation because the subsequent canons contradicted Roman practice (such as c. 66), since that may also be said of some canons of the first part (such as canons 46 and 47). It is also not convincing to argue that he knew of only 50 canons, since the older Latin translation presents all 85 canons. E. Schwartz has declared that the gloss to c. 50 was the reason Dionysius broke off his translation, since, for him, the gloss was heretical.[42]

In 496 Pope Gelasius issued his decree *De libris non recipiendis* (see below), in which the formula *Liber qui appellatur Canones apostolorum, apocryphus* was inserted under Pope Hormisdas (514–23). In the second collection of canons that Dionysius compiled during Hormisdas's pontificate, he did not include the Canons of the Apostles. In his *praefatio* to Hormisdas, Dionysius declared that he had included canons in the volume that had been received by the entire church.[43] Since the first collection was granted more authority in later times, the Canons of the Apostles entered the pseudo-Isidorian Decretals and finally were excerpted in the *Decretum* of Gratian.[44]

In the East the use of the Canons of the Apostles can be traced in the councils of the fifth century.[45] John Scholasticus received all 85 canons in his *Synogoga* without any doubt about their authority. He pointed out that the canons had long been found in older collections.[46] The Canons of the Apostles were included in Justinian's Novellae 6 and 137. Consequently they had been confirmed by secular law, and their texts could be found in the *Corpus iuris civilis*. The council fathers of the Quinisext Council (692) underlined the great importance of the Canons of the Apostles in the East by placing them before Nicaea in the list of authorities, 'canonizing' their apostolic origin. The norms of the Canons of the Apostles were now declared βεβαίους and ἀσφαλεῖς. Even the *Apostolic Constitutions* were declared to be of apostolic origin because of being mentioned in c. 85, even though they had been partly falsified by the 'heterodox'.

40. EOMIA 1.8.
41. Cf. Spagnolo and Turner, 'A Fragment', and Turner, 'A Primitive Edition'.
42. Schwartz, *Über die pseudoapostolischen* 15.
43. Cf. Maassen, *Geschichte* 964.
44. Further testimony in Funk, *Didascalia* 2.40–50.
45. Schwartz, *Über die pseudoapostolischen* 12, n. 2.
46. Cf. Beneševič, *Synagoga*, Tit. I.

The Synod of Nicaea (325)

Editions: COGD 20–34; Joannou, CCO 23–41; Lauchert 37–43; Rhalles-Potles 2.113–64; Pitra, *Juris* 1.427–35; *Versiones:* ClavisG 8520–27.

Translations: English: L'Huillier, *Ancient Councils* 31–100; Tanner 6–19; NPNF 14.1–58; German: Wohlmuth 6–19; Ortiz de Urbina 288–93; French: Joannou, CCO 23–41; G. Fritz, 'Nicée (Ier Concile de)', DThC 11 (1931) 408–16.

Literature: COGD 3–15; H. C. Brennecke, 'Nicäa I', TRE 24 (1994) 429–41 (literature); Beck, *Kirche* 44 (literature); G. Cereti, 'The reconciliation of remarried divorces according to canon 8 of the Council of Nicaea', *Studies in Canon Law presented to P.J.M. Huizing*, ed. J. H. Provost (Leuven 1991) 193–207; H. Chadwick, 'Faith and Order at the Council of Nicaea', *Harvard Theological Review* 53 (1960) 171–95; H. Crouzel, 'Les digamoi visés par le Concile de Nicée dans son canon 8', *Augustinianum* 18 (1978) 533–46; B. E. Daley, 'Position and patronage in the early church. The original meaning of "primacy of honour",' JTS, N.S. 44 (1993) 529–53; T. G. Elliot, Constantine's preparations for the Council of Nicaea, JRH 17 (1992) 127–37; G. Fritz, 'Nicée (Ier Concile de)', DThC 11 (1931) 399–417; K. Girardet, 'Der Vorsitzende des Konzils von Nicaea (325). Kaiser Konstantin d. Gr.', *Klassisches Altertum, Spätantike und frühes Christentum. FS A. Lippold*, ed. K. Dietz (Würzburg 1993) 331–60; H. Hauben, 'Das Konzil von Nicaea (325) zur Wiederaufnahme der Melitianer: Versuch einer Text- und Strukturanalyse', *Timai Ioannu Triantaphyllopulu*, ed. Julie Vélissaropoulos-Karakosta (Athens-Komotene 2000) 357–78; Hefele-Leclercq *Histoire* 1.1.503–619, 1.2.1182–1202; W. Huber, *Passa und Ostern* (Supplement to ZNW 35; Berlin 1969); J. Janssens, 'Il Concilio di Nicea (325 d.C.) e la data della Pasqua', *'Haec sacrosancta synodus': Konzils- und kirchengeschichtliche Beiträge*, ed. R. Meßner and R. Pranzl (Regensburg 2006) 43–59; C. Kannengiesser, 'Nicaea', EEC 595; Kaufhold, 'Väterlisten'; G. Larentzakis, 'Das Osterfestdatum nach dem I. ökumenischen Konzil von Nikaia (325)', ZThK 101 (1979) 67–78; P. L'Huillier, 'Ecclesiology in the Canons of the First Nicene Council', *St. Vladimir's Theological Quarterly* 27 (1983) 119–31; L'Huillier, *Ancient Councils* 17–100; K. Lübeck, *Reichseinteilung und kirchliche Hierarchie des Orients bis zum Ausgange des vierten Jahrhunderts* (Münster 1901); R. Macina, 'Pour éclaire le terme *digamoi*', *Revue des sciences religieuses* 61 (1987) 54–73; Bernard Meunier, *Les premiers conciles de l'église: Un ministère d'unité* (Lyon 2003) 49–69; J. Meyendorff, 'One Bishop in One City (canon 8)', *St. Vladimir's Theological Quarterly* 5 (1961) 54–62; Ohme, *Kanon* 352–78; Ortiz de Urbina; V. Peri, 'Lo stato degli studi intorno alla origine della quaresima', *Aevum* 34 (1960) 525–55; S. Schima, 'Das Konzil von Nizäa, Rom und der Westen', *Österreichisches Archiv für Kirchenrecht* 44 (1995–97) 358–85; Schwartz, 'Kanonensammlungen' 203–20; J. v.d. Speeten, 'Le dossier de Nicée dans la Quesnelliana', *Sacris erudiri* 28 (1985) 383–450; J. Speigl, 'Das entstehende Papsttum, die Kanones von Nizäa und die Bischofseinsetzungen in Gallien', *Konzil und Papst: Historische Beiträge zur Frage der höchsten Gewalt in der Kirche: Festgabe für Hermann Tüchle*, ed. Georg Schwaiger (Munich 1975) 43–61; BISA.

The 20 canons of the First Ecumenical Council of Nicaea (325), together with its creed, a synodal letter to the Church of Alexandria, and the list of episcopal subscribers are the sole surviving direct sources for the decrees and negotiations of this council.[47] The council was accorded preeminent importance by the late fourth century. It became the foundation of the future development of ecclesiastical doctrine, as well as the exemplary expression of imperial power in an ecclesiastical synod.

---

47. Cf. ClavisG 8512–16.

The question of whether minutes of the proceedings of Nicaea once existed and were lost at an early date cannot be definitively answered.[48] In any case, it is not to be overlooked that there never was a single literary reference for the existence of such minutes, not even in the earliest accounts of the council.[49]

After Emperor Constantine had established sole rulership in 324, he called the council in accordance with the model of the council of Arles (314). The council opened on 20 May 325 or in June in the hall of the palace of Nicaea.[50] The reported number of participating bishops varies from 250 to more than 300.[51] Alongside the bishops of the East, who were most numerous, a few bishops from the West were also invited, for this was to be an imperial synod, an 'ecumenical' council.[52]

The tasks at hand did not consist solely of settling the Arian conflict but also of settling schismatic developments in the Church of Egypt, called the Melitian Schism.[53] The council also wanted to regulate questions about the norms for the entire church and to establish a common date for Easter.[54]

The synod of Arles had already called for a unified date for the Easter festival in its c. 1. The Nicene decision to celebrate Easter henceforth on the first Sunday after the first full moon of spring separated Easter from the Jewish calculation of Passover, which had been altered in the course of time to avoid the vernal equinox. This calculation of the Easter feast has been observed in principle to the present day. The decisions only survive in the writing of Emperor Constantine dedicated to this theme, 'To the churches',[55] as well as in the *epistula synodica* to the Church of Alexandria.[56] It is surprising that no formal canon touching upon the date of Easter has survived. The 'discovery' of such a 'canon' by J. B. Pitra and his edition of it, has to be viewed skeptically.[57] It is no more than another sum-

---

48. Opposed to this is Hefele-Leclercq *Histoire* 1.X 283–84; in favor, A. Wikenhauser, 'Zur Frage nach der Existenz von nizänischen Synodalprotokollen', *Constantin der Große und seine Zeit*, Supplement to *Römische Quartalschrift* 19, ed. F. Dölger (1913) 122–42; G. Loeschcke, 'Das Syntagma des Gelasius Cyzicenus', *Rheinisches Museum* 60 (1905) 594–613; 61 (1906) 34–77; Ortiz de Urbina 61.

49. Cf. Eusebius, *Vita Constantini* III; Athanasius, *De decretis Nicaenae Synodi* and the older historians: Socrates, Sozomen, Theodoret, Rufinus, Gelasius (see Ortiz de Urbina 328–29).

50. Socrates, *Historia ecclesiastica* 13, gives the May date for Nicaea; June according to T. D. Barnes, *The New Empire of Diocletian and Constantine* (Cambridge, MA 1982) 76.

51. See Brennecke, TRE 24, 431.

52. Besides Ossius of Cordoba and two Roman priests serving as legates, 4 more bishops are known.

53. On Arianism, cf. A. M. Ritter, 'Arianismus', TRE 3 (1978) 692–719; Hanson, *Search* 318–81. For the Melitian Schism, cf. M. Simonetti, 'Melitius of Lycopolis', EEC 551.

54. Cf. particularly, Huber, *Passa und Ostern* 61–75; A. Strobel, *Ursprung und Geschichte des frühchristlichen Osterkalenders* (Berlin 1977) 389–92; Ortiz de Urbina 106ff.

55. Eusebius, *Vita Constantini* 3.18 (= Opitz 3 document 26).

56. Opitz 3 document 23, 12.

57. Pitra, *Juris, Spicilegium* 4 (1858) 540–55 (541); and *Monumenta* 1.435–36, also called the 'C. de

mary of the decision made in Nicaea. This text was already found in the *Synagoge of Fifty Titles* by John Scholasticus,[58] but it cannot be described as a formal 'conciliar decree' either in form or style. At the same time it is clear that the Easter decision of the synod was not included among the 20 canons, where it would appear at first glance to belong.

In the same way, the conciliatory decision of the council on the Egyptian Melitians did not find a place in the canons. It has been preserved only in the synodal letter to the Church of Alexandria.[59] The thirty-three bishops, five priests, and three deacons consecrated by Melitius of Lycopolis were permitted to remain in their offices and churches after a laying-on of hands,[60] though they remained lower in rank than the 'Catholic' clerics. The bishops were to be without the right of electing or nominating clergy. They could, nonetheless, take the place of Catholic bishops on the death of incumbents. Melitius alone lost his right to consecrate. The synod made similar decisions about the 'Cathars' or Novatians in c. 8, even though there were several bishops of the synod who belonged to these groups.[61]

The mildness of these decisions becomes clear if one compares them with c. 19 on the reintegration of the 'Paulianists', in which the entire clergy, from bishops to deaconesses, who had adhered to the teachings of Paul of Samosata, had to be rebaptized and ordained again. The offer to the Melitians appears even milder than c. 8, in which Cathar bishops were given no hope of recovering their *cathedra* when the sees became free again. The will of the emperor to ensure peace in the Church in the East stood behind these decisions.

Theodoret of Cyrrhus († ca. 466)[62] reports that after the anathematization of the Arians, the bishops regathered and passed 20 'laws on the organization of ecclesiastical life' (περὶ τῆς ἐκκλησιαστικῆς πολιτείας νόμους ἔγραψαν εἴκοσι). Gelasius of Cyzicus after 475 also presents the text of all 20 canons (ἐκκλησιαστικοὺς κανόνας εἴκοσιν) without varying from the

---

Pascha' here. Skeptically with J. Schmid, *Die Osterfestfrage auf dem ersten Allgemeinen Konzil von Nicäa* (Vienna 1905) 66; and Huber, *Passa und Ostern* 65 n. 27. Ortiz de Urbina 106, 228, simply holds Pitra's 'decree' to be authentic without even discussing the question, and G. Larentzakis, 'Das Osterfestdatum nach dem I. ökumenischen Konzil von Nikaia (325)', ZKTh 101 (1979) 67–78, 68, follows him without further consideration.

58. Beneševič, *Synagoga* 156. The *lemmata* of the manuscripts used by Beneševič vary between 'Τῆς ἁγίας συνόδου τῆς ἐν Νικαίᾳ περὶ τοῦ ἁγίου πάσχα' and ''Εκ τῶν πρακτικῶν τῆς (ἐν Νικαίᾳ) πρώτης οἰκουμενικῆς συνόδου'.

59. Opitz 3 document 23, 6–11.

60. Cf. Athanasius, *Apologia Secunda* 71.

61. Specifically Akesios of Constantinople; cf. Sozomenus, *Historia ecclesiastica* 2.32 (GCS NF 4, 96–98; J. Bidez, G. C. Hansen); Socrates, *Historia ecclesiastica* 1.10 (GCS NF 1, 41 G. C. Hansen).

62. *Historia eccl.* 1.8 (GCS 19, 38 Parmentier-Schneidweiler).

content or sequence of what is found in Greek canonical collections.⁶³ Rufinus included the 20 canons in the Latin summaries in his *Ecclesiastical History* but divided canons 6 and 8 in two, hence producing 22 canons.⁶⁴ Hence the oldest historians of the church not only confirm the great significance attributed to the canons of Nicaea from the earliest times, but also their number.⁶⁵ In the Syrian, Arabic, and Ethiopian traditions, these 20 canons grew through the addition of a great number of other canonical norms.⁶⁶ This can be seen as a sign of the great authority attributed to the Council of Nicaea. Its canons enjoyed general acceptance and recognition from the end of the fourth century in all of Christendom. In the Roman tradition, doubtless for similar reasons, the canons of Serdica were passed on under the name of the *Nicaenum* (see below).

Of great historical importance were those canons which initiated a new organization of ecclesiastical leadership and administration in parallel with the secular reorganization of the empire carried out by Diocletian (284–305).⁶⁷ Under threat of excommunication, canons 15 and 16 intended to bind the entire clergy to the parish congregation, called the *paroikia* (c. 16), 'for which they were ordained', excluding any translation from one episcopal parish to another as well as any inducement to translate offered by another church, a practice which is incidentally described as virtually universal.⁶⁸ Both canons illustrate the ancient Christian bond of ordination to a certain local church, which is the *paroikia* of the bishop. The new ecclesiastical structures are formulated in canons four to seven. Episcopal congregations are formed into ecclesiastical provincial associations that corresponded geographically to secular imperial provinces (both of them use the same descriptive term, ἐπαρχία), headed by the bishop of the provincial capital or *metropolis*, as the 'metropolitan'. Hence c. 4 rules that episcopal elections must be attended by all the bishops of a province. Three bishops suffice for consecration, but those three must have the written approval of the others. The metropolitan must confirm the decision and the consecration (canons 4, 6). C. 5 established the provincial synod as the supreme ecclesiastical court of appeal which must be held twice a

---

63. *Historia eccl.* 2.32 (GCS 28, 112–13, G. Loeschcke–M. Heinemann).
64. *Historia eccl.* 10.6 (GCS 9, 2, 966–69, T. Mommsen).
65. Cf. on this Hefele-Leclercq *Histoire* 1.1 503–27; Ortiz de Urbina 109–10.
66. Cf. ClavisG 8521, 8523, 8524; Hefele-Leclercq *Histoire* 1.2 1139–76. On the Eastern churches, see the chapter by Kaufhold below.
67. Cf. A. Demandt, *Die Spätantike* (Munich 1989) 53ff.; and on the following, Konrad Lübeck, *Reichseinteilung und kirchliche Hierarchie des Orients bis zum Ausgange des vierten Jahrhunderts: Ein Beitrag zur Rechts- und Verfassungsgeschichte der Kirche* (Münster 1901) 52–98, 99–172.
68. On translation in the early church, cf. E. Heckrodt, *Die Kanones von Sardika aus der Kirchengeschichte erläutert* (Jenaer Historische Arbeiten 8; Bonn 1917) 4–42.

year.[69] C. 6 laid the foundation for the patriarchal system, which was further elaborated at Constantinople in 381 and became a generally accepted institution in the sixth century. In this canon, the Church of Alexandria's jurisdiction is compared to Rome's, and special regulations were also made for Antioch. In this way 'the old customs' and privileges (πρεσβεῖα) were confirmed, according to which these churches have jurisdiction and influence reaching across provincial boundaries. C. 7 confirmed to the bishop of Aelia (Jerusalem) a position of honor (ἀκολουθία τῆς τιμῆς), saving the rights of the metropolitan see of Caesarea.

It must not be overlooked that these canons for restructuring the church resulted from conditions prevalent in the Eastern Empire that did not necessarily prevail in the West, where, for example, the synods of the African provinces encompassed considerably larger units. It is in this light that we should understand the varied reception of the canons of Nicaea, as well as the variation in their Latin translations.[70]

The following canons dealt with the dignity, way of life, and hierarchical order of the clergy: c. 1 excludes from the clergy those who have willingly made themselves eunuchs, but not those who had been castrated against their will or for reasons of illness. C. 2 opposes any consecration of neophytes, and c. 3 forbids clerics to live together with a woman in sexual abstinence. C. 9 requires a prior examination of any consecration of a priest. If it is omitted and any impediment made itself known after the consecration, such candidates will not be allowed to function, despite their consecration. C. 10 confirms the ban on consecrating those who have denied the faith during persecutions (lapsi), and even a consecration which has taken place does not prejudice this. Clerics who practiced usury are to be deposed (c. 17). C. 18 regulated the hierarchical rank and sequence of the higher clergy: bishop, priest, deacon, weighted particularly to the disadvantage of the deacon.

Canons 11 to 14 deal with regulations of public penance: for those who lapsed under the persecution of Licinius (canons 11, 12); guaranteeing communion of penitents *in articulo mortis* (c. 13); for sinful catechumens (c. 14). In order not to erase the separation from the penitent 'kneelers', the synod finally ruled in c. 20 that the faithful should celebrate the divine service while standing.

---

69. Cf. on this K. M. Girardet, 'Appellatio. Ein Kapitel kirchlicher Rechtsgeschichte in den Kanones des 4. Jahrhunderts', *Historia* 23 (1974) 98–127; Ohme, *Kanon* 424–43.

70. Schwartz, 'Kanonensammlungen' 203–20, 203.

The Synod of Ancyra (314)

Editions: R. B. Rackham, 'The Text of the Canons of Ancyra', *Studia biblica et ecclesiastica* (Oxford 1891) 3.139–216; Joannou, CSP 56–73; Lauchert 29–34 (= Rackham); Mansi 2.515–34; Pitra, *Juris* 1.441–48; Rhalles-Potles 3.20–69; Pedalion 371–85; *Versiones:* ClavisG 8501.

Translations: English: *Rudder*, 489–503; NPNF 14.63–72; German: Hefele 1.219–42; French: Joannou, CSP 56–73.

Literature: Hefele-Leclercq *Histoire* 1.1.298–326; Kaufhold, 'Väterlisten'; X. LeBachelet, 'Ancyra (Concile de)', DThC 1 (1923) 1173–77; J. Lebon, 'Sur un concile de Césarée', *Le Muséon* 51 (1938) 89–132; Ohme, *Kanon* 329–34; S. Parvis, 'The Canons of Ancyra and Caesarea (314)', JTS N.S. 52 (2001) 625–36; BISA.

When Emperor Maximinus Daia took his own life following his defeat by Licinius in July 313, the last persecutor of the church since Diocletian in the eastern imperial district of the tetrarchy disappeared. Eusebius reported that in this period, after the Edict of Toleration issued by Licinius in Nicomedia on 13 June 313 many synods were held in the East once more.[71] Among these can be included the synod of Ancyra, the metropolis of Galatia.

Its dating can be determined by the presidency of Bishop Vitalis of Antioch (see below), who died in 319, but particularly from c. 6 on *sacrificati* who had fallen away as a result of the mere threat of punishment and who had asked to return to the church 'at the time of the synod'. They were to be received from now until next Easter into the penitential rank of 'hearers.' Then they had to spend five more years as penitential 'kneelers' and 'fellow-standers'. The earliest possible Pentecost, the usual date for a synod, would be 314. This earliest possible date has high probability, since the question of dealing with *lapsi* and the regulation of their potential recovery to the church was such a concern to the council (canons 1–9, 12).

Along with the 25 canons of the synod,[72] the Latin tradition preserves three lists of bishops who attended the council.[73] These vary between 12 and 18 participants. The Ballerinis showed long ago that one of the lists gave anachronistic provincial boundaries,[74] so that it must have been amended later. The lists given in the *Prisca* and the *Isidoriana* have no provincial titles attributed to bishops, but they were added later to the collection of Dionysius. Still, the lists are not necessarily inauthentic, since most participants can be dated to the period, and they were also present at Nicaea in 325. Just as is the case with the synod of Neocaesarea, Vitalis of Antioch held first place and should be seen as the president. The so-called

---

71. Eusebius, *Historia ecclesiastica* 10.3 (GCS E.2, 370 E. Schwartz).
72. There are 24 in Dionysius Exiguus, who unites canons 4 and 5.
73. Cf. EOMIA 2.32, 50, 51.
74. P. and J. Ballerini, 'De antiquis collectionibus et collectoribus canonum', *S. Leonis Magni Opera omnia* (Venice 1757) 3.xxii (= PL 56.31).

Libellus synodicus attributed the presidency to Marcellus of Ancyra, who was one of the participants, but it is unlikely that he presided.[75] It is striking, however, that the participants come from the sphere of influence of the Church of Antioch in Asia Minor, Syria, and Palestine. This was not, then, a local synod in the strictest sense, but rather a general synod of the churches in the imperial *dioecesis Oriens*.

The oldest preserved version of the Greek text with 25 canons dates to the ninth and tenth centuries.[76] For that reason the translations, particularly in the Latin tradition, are especially significant.[77]

Beyond the decisions concerning *lapsi* (canons 1–9, 12), no further system is to be discerned in the ordering of the material. These canons regulated the position of lapsed priests and deacons (canons 1 and 2), as well as the rules of return for those who had been compelled to participate in sacrifices or sacrificial banquets. Distinctions were made between those who participated in sacrifices with public confessions (c. 3), with forced but compliant participation (c. 4), and with participation accompanied by tears and mourning (c. 5). C. 6 dealt with those who took part in pagan sacrifices because of a threat of exile and confiscation of their property. Canon 7 discussed those who participated in sacrificial banquets but who did not eat the sacrificial meat; while c. 8 treated those who made repeated sacrifices, c. 9 dealt with those who fell into complete apostasy, and c. 12 those who sacrificed during their period as catechumens.

Questions treating the clergy are dealt with by the following canons: deacons were to declare at the time of their election whether they intended eventually to marry (c. 10); *chorepiscopi* were forbidden to ordain without a special license (c. 13); a principled rejection of the eating of meat led to deposition (c. 14). Further canons dealt with the sale of ecclesiastical property during a vacancy of the see (c. 15), the duties and status of bishops-elect who were not accepted in their parishes (c. 18), and the breaking of an oath of chastity (c. 19).

The other decisions dealt with the following themes: abducting betrothed girls (c. 11); sex with animals (canons 16 and 17); adultery (c. 20); abortion (c. 21); murder (c. 22); manslaughter (c. 23); magic (c. 24); and last-

---

75. Cf. Mansi 2.539; *The Synodicon Vetus. Text, Translation and Notes*, ed. J. Duffy and J. Parker (Corpus fontium historiae Byzantinae XV. series Washingtonensis; Washington, D.C. 1979) no. 31, p. 22. The *Synodicon vetus* developed only after 887 and works with a valuation of local and ecumenical synods as they were estimated then. According to this scheme, the presidency of the synod of Ancyra, understood as a local synod, was attributed to the bishop of the place. On the whole the *Synodicon* is not a reliable text; cf. Duffy and Parker, *Synodicon* p. xv.

76. Cf. Rackham, 'Canons of Ancyra'; now standard is Beneševič, *Syntagma* = Joannou, CSP 56–73.

77. Cf. ClavisG 8501 and EOMIA 2.3–11, 18–27, 36–43, 48–51, 54–115.

ly the special case of the seduction of a future sister-in-law by the bridegroom, resulting in the woman's death (c. 25).

The canons as a whole have great importance for the history of the institution of penance in the early church. They are among the earliest evidence for the three-step system of penance, which eventually even became a four-step system (canons 4–9, 16–17, 20–25).[78] The text and interpretation of c. 13 that treated the practical functions of *chorepiscopi* are in dispute.[79] This canon contained the first evidence for *chorepiscopi*.

J. Lebon has defended the thesis that canons 20 to 25 were originally passed by a synod in Caesarea of Cappadocia in the same year,[80] whose list of participants was later attributed to the synod of Neocaesarea.

The Synod of Neocaesarea (between 315 and 319)

Editions: Joannou, CSP 75–82; Mansi 2.539–43; Lauchert 35–36; Pitra, *Juris* 1.451–54; Pedalion 385–95; Rhalles-Potles 3.70–95; *Versiones*: ClavisG 8504.

Translations: English: *Rudder*, 507–19; NPNF 14.79–88; German: Hefele 1.242–51; French: Joannou, CSP 75–82.

Literature: G. Bardy, 'Néocésarée', DDC 6.995–97; Hefele-Leclercq *Histoire* 1.326–34; Kaufhold, 'Väterlisten'; BISA; C. Nardi, 'Neocaesarea', EEC 585.

In the Greek collections of canons, the decisions of the synod of Neocaesarea, the metropolis of Pontus Polemoniacus, always followed the synod of Ancyra. The fact that this indicated a chronological order is shown by the *lemma* of the Greek manuscripts of the canons, which dates the synod between that of Ancyra and Nicaea.[81] It also fits that the problem of *lapsi* obviously no longer played a role in the proceedings, in contrast to Ancyra. Consequently, it is likely that some time had passed since the Edict of Toleration (313).

Other than the 15 canons, there survives from this council in the Latin tradition a list of bishops with 17 to 20 names,[82] of which 6 are also found on the lists for Ancyra, and several are on the Nicene list as well. One can thus assume that the three synods were close together in time. As is the case with Ancyra, the first place on the list was held by Vitalis of Antioch, who died around 319. Here as well the participants come from churches of Antioch's

---

78. Cf. J. Grotz, *Die Entwicklung des Bußstufenwesens in der vornicaenischen Kirche* (Freiburg 1955) 428–29.

79. Cf., for example, the portrayal of the earlier discussion in LeBachelet, 'Ancyra' 1174ff. and in F. Gillmann, *Das Institut der Chorbischöfe im Orient* (Munich 1903) 74ff.

80. According to E. Honigmann, 'Two Alleged "Bishops of Great Armenia" as Members of the Synods of Ankyra (314 A.D.) and Caesarea in Cappadocia', *Patristic Studies* (Studi e Testi 173; Rome 1953) 1–5, the synod in question only took place in 315.

81. Cf. Joannou, CSP 75.

82. Cf. EOMIA 2.32, 52, 53.

sphere of influence in Asia Minor, Syria, and Palestine. J. Lebon attributed this list of bishops to a council in Caesarea in Cappadocia in 314.[83]

The decisions of the synod do not show any internal principles of organization; they were briefly formulated and dealt with the following themes: priests cannot marry after ordination (c. 1); marriage with a sister-in-law will lead to expulsion (c. 2); c. 3 dealt with penance for bigamy (i.e. second and further marriages); sins of thought were not subject to penance (c. 4); c. 5 formulated penance for catechumens; pregnant women were not to be excluded from baptism (c. 6); c. 7 ordered that priests cannot take part in weddings of bigamists; c. 8 dictated that a wife's adultery hindered the husband from becoming a cleric and if he were already a cleric he could not continue to exercise his office; priests who sinned physically before ordination should not perform the Eucharist, and deacons in such circumstances can only be servants of the church (canons 9, 10); the minimum age for priests was established as 30 years (c. 11); delaying baptism until an illness excluded a person from the priestly office (c. 12); canons 13 and 14 dealt with restricting the functions of a rural priest (ἐπιχώριοι πρεσβύτεροι) and *chorepiscopi*; c. 15 restricted the number of deacons in one town to seven.

The canons have particular importance for the development of the system of penance; the interpretation of c. 5 is in dispute.[84]

The Synod of Gangra (ca. 340–342)

Editions: Joannou, CSP 85–99; Lauchert 79–83; Pitra, *Juris* 1.487–92; Pedalion 398–405; Rhalles-Potles 3.96–121; Latin: EOMIA 2.145–214; *Versiones*: ClavisG 8553–54.

Translations: English: *Rudder* 523–31; NPNF 14.91–103; German: Hefele 1.780–88; French: Joannou, CSP 85–99.

Literature: G. Bardy, 'Gangres', DDC 5 (1953) 935–38; T. D. Barnes, 'The Date of the Council of Gangra', JTS 40 (1989) 121–24; J. de Churruca, 'L'anathème du concile de Gangres contre ceux qui sous prétexte de Christianisme incite les esclaves à quitter leurs maîtres', RHD 60 (1982) 261–78; J. Gribomont, 'Eustathe de Sébaste', DSDH 4.2 (1961) 1708–12; idem, 'Le monachisme au IVᵉ siècle en Asie Mineure: de Gangres au messalianisme', *Studia Patristica* 2 (TU 64; Berlin 1957) 400–415; W. D. Hauschild, 'Eustathius von Sebaste', TRE 10 (1982) 547–50; Hefele-Leclercq *Histoire* 1.2.1029–45; Kaufhold, 'Väterlisten'; A. Laniado, 'Note sur la datation conservée en Syriaque du concile de Gangrès', OCP 61 (1995) 195–99; F. Loofs, *Eustathius von Sebaste und die Chronologie der Basilius-Briefe* (Halle 1898) 79–90; BISA.

Greek collections of canons transmit the entire *epistula synodica* of the synod of Gangra, the metropolis of the province of Paphlagonia. Following the name of the addressee and of the sender, as well as a description

---

83. See Lebon, 'Sur un concile de Césarée'.
84. Cf. Grotz, *Die Entwicklung* 429–35.

of the motivation for the meeting of the synod, 20 so-called 'canons' are listed. The epilogue, often designated c. 21, closed the synodal communiqué. It was directed to the bishops 'in Armenia' and signed by 13 bishops. However, since their sees were not given, a certain identification of the bishops is possible only with difficulty.[85] The synod was convened because of practices contrary to the norms of the church taken 'by those around Eustathius' as well as 'by him personally' (ὑπὸ τούτων αὐτῶν τῶν περὶ Εὐστάθιον; ὑπ' αὐτοῦ). The offense described agreed with the content of the 20 decisions. These were all anathemas in form and content, all formulated according to the scheme, 'Εἴ τις . . . ἀνάθεμα ἔστω'. Errors and abuses of the anchorite-ascetic movement were condemned. This evidence demonstrated that Eustathius is the same person as Eustathius of Sebaste, an identification that had already been made by Socrates and Sozomenus. These canons reflect the background of the ascetic movement of 'Eustathians', particularly in the imperial diocese of Pontus.[86] The epilogue emphasized that the synod was not condemning asceticism, *enkrateia* or *parthenia*, which were extensively praised and approved, but only the arrogance of those who practiced them.

Socrates and Sozomenus had already differed in their dating of the synod. The former placed it after the synod of Constantinople in 360, the latter before 'the synod of Antioch'. The date of the synod is based on two letters of Basil the Great in the life of Eustathius (letters 244, 263) and their internal agreement. We can also identify 13 of the bishops with known bishops of the time of the synod of Serdica (342). This evidence leads us to the date of 'circa 340–342'. The definitive conclusions of F. Loofs on the date were thoroughly convincing.[87]

The council's anathemas were promulgated against the following beliefs: (1) that the marital union was an impediment to salvation; (2) that the eating of meat was an impediment to salvation; (3) that one should encourage slaves to leave their masters and become anchorites; (4) that one should avoid the religious services of married priests; (5) that one should have con-

---

85. Some different names are found in the Latin manuscript tradition (Mansi 2.1095, 6.1152; EOMIA 2.146), which has given rise to many speculations in the older historiography of councils, cf. Hefele 1.778.

86. Socrates, *Historia ecclesiastica* 2.43 (GCS NF 1,180 G. C. Hansen) and Sozomenus, *Historia ecclesiastica* 3.14.31, 4.24.9 (GCS NF 4, 123.180 J. Bidez, G.C. Hansen). In the attribution of the synod to 'circa 340', all 13 senders can be identified as Pontic bishops. The synod would then have been under the presidency of Eusebius of Nicomedia, and among the participants would be Gregory of Nazianzus and Basil of Ancyra.

87. *Eustathius von Sebaste und die Chronologie der Basilius-Briefe* (Halle 1898) 79–90. For an earlier effort of dating, see Hefele, *Concilien* 1.791–92. Dionysius Exiguus places Gangra before Antioch. Barnes, 'Council of Gangra', has argued for seeing the synod of Gangra as a Paphlagonian provincial council around the year 355.

tempt of the house of God and of congregational worship; (6) that one should hold private religious services without the consent of the bishop; (7) that a cleric should receive ecclesiastical income without the permission of the bishop; (8) that one might pay or receive such gifts without permission by the bishop; (9) that one should practice asceticism and condemn marriage; (10) that one should practice virginity and criticize the married; (11) that one should refuse to take part in and despise the *agape*; (12) that one should despise the clothing of ordinary people and value only the clothing of the ascetic class; (13) that a woman should wear men's clothing in order to practice asceticism; (14) that women should abandon their husbands in contempt of marriage; (15) and (16) that parents should abandon children and children abandon their parents for asceticism; (17) tonsure of women was anathematized; (18) fasting on Sundays was condemned; (19) that one should reject the norms of the general fasts of the church as insufficient; (20) that one should reject religious services held for the holy martyrs.

The influence of these canons was considerable. Seven translations have survived from the early church (see above, *versiones*); almost all of these canons passed into the *Decretum Gratiani*.[88]

The Synod of Antioch (ca. 330)

Editions: Joannou, CSP 104–26; Lauchert 43–50; Pitra, *Juris* 1.454–67; Pedalion 406–19; Rhalles-Potles 3.122–70. *Versiones:* ClavisG 8535–36.

Translations: English: *Rudder* 534–49; NPNF 14.104–22; German: Hefele 1.513ff.; French: Joannou, CSP 104–26.

Literature: G. Bardy, 'Antioche (Concile et canons d')', DDC 1.589–98; Hefele-Leclercq *Histoire* 1.702–33; Hamilton Hess, *The Canons of the Council of Sardica: A Landmark in the Early Development of Canon Law* (Oxford Theological Monographs 1; Oxford 1958) 2.145–50, revised edition Hamilton Hess, *The Early Development of Canon Law and the Council of Serdica* (Oxford Early Christian Studies; Oxford 2002) 182–84; Ohme, *Kanon* 391–399; E. Schwartz, 'Athanasius, VIII' 216–230; M. Simonetti, 'Antioch. II. Councils', EEC 48–49; BISA.

The 25 canons of the synod of Antioch are among the oldest canons in the Greek canonical collections, which normally form a solid traditional block in the sequence of Ancyra, Neocaesarea, Gangra, Antioch, and Laodicea. Even the oldest Syrian and Latin translations attributed these canons to the synod of dedication ('in encaeniis') held at Antioch in 341.[89] This dating already appeared as an accepted tradition in 403–404. At the time of the dispute in which the deposition of John Chrysostom was demanded, his enemies from the entourage around Theophilus of Alexandria cited

---

88. Gratian placed the canons in Distinction 30; he omitted canons 5, 7, 8.
89. Cf. Schwartz, 'Athanasius VIII' 216; on the synod *in encaeniis*: ClavisG 8556–59.

c. 4 of the Council of Antioch. Chrysostom's partisans attacked the validity of the canon, since it had been approved by an 'Arian synod' directed against Athanasius. It appears that this argument was not disputed by the other side.⁹⁰ Pope Innocent I (402–417) adopted this argument in his own defense of John Chrysostom,⁹¹ and when Palladius described the affair in his *Vita* of John composed in 408, he believed that this canon had been suspended by the synod of Serdica, since it had been directed against Athanasius and Marcellus.⁹² This situation only becomes understandable when one assumes that the canons of Antioch were already an established part of a Greek canonical collection by the end of the fourth century. In this collection the canons were attributed to the synod 'in encaeniis' and were cited from such a collection by Chrysostom's enemies. The historical argument made by adherents of the patriarch of Constantinople appears not to have had a chance in opposition to this factitious authority. To the present day there are those who attribute the canons to the synod of 341.⁹³

The Ballerinis were the first to take a decisive stand against this dating, which was later reinforced, particularly by E. Schwartz.⁹⁴ The following facts speak against the synod 'in encaeniis': 1. The surviving list of participants and subscribers shows that their roughly 30 participants were also members of the synod of Nicaea in 325, so that the two synods had to be seen as closely related in time; 2. 97 bishops took part in the synod of 341; 3. the synod was not presided over by the bishop of Antioch but was held under Eusebius of Caesarea. Eusebius, however, presided only over the synod of Antioch ca. 330, which gathered for the election of a new bishop after the fall of Eustathius.⁹⁵ The 'Antioch Schism' which arose as a result of this episode, with its troubles, formed the historical background reflected in the canonical decisions. The connection of these canons with the synod *in encaeniis* points to the period before 380, when this council was held in greater regard than the council of Nicaea in the homoiic imperial church.⁹⁶

---

90. Cf. Palladius, *Vita Ioan. Chrysost.* 9 (PG 47.30; ed. Coleman-Norton 53–54; ed. Malingrey and Leclercq [SC 341, 182.19ff., 186.60ff.]); Sozomenus, *Historia ecclesiastica* 8.20 (GCS NF 4, 376–77 J. Bidez, G. C. Hansen); Schwartz, 'Athanasius VIII' 217–18.

91. *Ep. 7 ad clerum et populum Constantinopolitanum* (PL 20.501; GCS NF 4, 386 J. Bidez, G. C. Hansen); Socrates, *Historia ecclesiastica* 6.18 (GCS NF 1, 342, 6–11 G. C. Hansen); Sozomenus, *Historia ecclesiastia* 8.26 (GCS NF 4, 376.25 J. Bidez, G. C. Hansen).

92. Palladius, *Vita Ioan. Chrysost.* 9 (ed. Coleman Norton, 53).

93. Cf. Hefele-Leclercq *Histoire* 1.X 706–14, 722–24; but also by Joannou, CSP 100–101; Menevisoglou, Ἱστορικὴ 351–66.

94. Ballerini, *S. Leonis Magni opera* 3.xxv–xxvii (= PL 56.35ff.). Schwartz, Gesammelte Schriften 3.216–26; cf. also EOMIA 2.2 VII; Bardy, DDC 1.591–94.

95. Cf. Schwartz, Gesammelte Schriften 3.224–26.

96. H. C. Brennecke, *Studien zur Geschichte der Homöer* (Tübingen 1988).

Canon 1 renewed the Nicene decision on the festival of Easter and threatened those with excommunication who kept the Easter festival according to Jewish usage. C. 2 excommunicated those who attended the service of God's Word but did not participate in the communal prayers and did not participate in the eucharist. They also must not share hospitality with excommunicated persons. Those excommunicated, according to c. 6, can only be received back by their own bishop or by a synod.

The majority of the canons rendered decisions concerning the relationship of priests to their bishops and of bishops to their metropolitans. Hence, priests should not abandon their congregations, on threat of being deposed (c. 3). Deposed clerics who continue to perform their duties squander by that act any chance of being restored (c. 4), and whoever established schismatic neighboring congregations was to be deposed; if he persisted, secular authority will enforce the sanction (c. 5). No stranger was to be received without a letter of peace (c. 7), but such letters were not to be issued by rural priests (c. 8).

Bishops who undertook to consecrate a cleric in another's district without permission are to be deposed (canons 13 and 22). If after consecration bishops did not take up their duties in the district designated for them, they are excommunicated (c. 17). C. 21 renewed the Nicene ban on the translation of bishops, and c. 23 forbade the designation of successors.

Several canons regulated the procedure for deposing bishops. If the provincial synod was unable to come to a unanimous conclusion in such a case, the metropolitan was supposed to summon additional bishops from a neighboring eparchy (c. 14). If the conclusion was then unanimous, all further possibility of appeal is excluded (c. 15). If anyone, after having been deposed, appealed to the emperor instead of to a larger synod, he lost all chances for restoration (c. 12). Any appeal to the emperor without the approval of the bishops or the metropolitan was forbidden (c. 11).

The authority of the metropolitan was remarkably strengthened. C. 9 insisted that all bishops restrict themselves to their dioceses, while the metropolitan was responsible for the entire province and enjoyed precedence over his fellow bishops. A vacant bishopric could be filled (c. 16) and the consecration of bishops could take place only in the presence of the metropolitan sitting in a synod (c. 19). He alone could summon a provincial synod, which should meet twice a year (c. 20). Since these canons renewed or made the decisions of Nicaea more precise, it can be assumed that the prerogatives of metropolitans established by Nicaea had not been fully accepted. C. 10 restricted the rights of *chorepiscopi*, and canons 24 and 25 regulated the administration of ecclesiastical properties.

It should be mentioned that the synod of Serdica (342) renewed some of the canons of Antioch, sharpening some of the penalties.[97]

At the Fourth Ecumenical Council of Chalcedon, at its twelfth session, canons 16 and 17 from Antioch were passed as canons 95 and 96, with the qualification that they were 'canons of the Holy Fathers', and at the fourth session the canons 4 and 5 from Antioch were read out as canons 83 and 84. This numbering is an important piece of evidence of the existence of an official canonical collection, in which the canons were arranged in numerical sequence.[98]

The Synod of Laodicea (before 380)

Editions: Joannou, CSP 130–55; Lauchert 72–79; Pitra, *Juris* 1.495–504; Pedalion 420–42; Rhalles-Potles 3.171–226; *Versiones*: ClavisG 8607.

Translations: English: NPNF 14. 123–34; *Rudder* 551–78; German: Hefele 1.746–77; French: Joannou, CSP 130–55.

Literature: G. Bardy, 'Laodicée (Concile et canons de)', DDC 6.338–43; Hefele-Leclercq *Histoire* 1.2, 989–1028; C. Nardi, 'Laodicea, Council of', EEC 472–73; Ohme, *Kanon* 402–6; Schneemelcher, 'Bibel III.' 22–48; Schwartz, 'Kanonensammlungen' 190–94; Zahn, *Geschichte* 193–202; BISA.

The synod of Laodicea in Phrygia, with its 59 or 60 canons,[99] was included in all old Greek canonical collections. It presents many almost insoluble puzzles concerning the dating and historical context.

A note was posted at the head of the text of the canons;[100] it informs us that the 'holy synod' which gathered in Laodicea in Phrygia Pacatiana, and whose participants were drawn from various provinces of the Asian (diocese) (ἐκ . . . τῆς Ἀσιανῆς), had issued the following decisions. There is no date on the note, and no synodal letter or any subscription list survived to explain why these canons appeared to be so important to the oldest collections.

The *lemma* found in Vienna, Österreichische Nationalbibliothek hist. gr. 7 (11th–12th century), 'Κανόνες νθ' τῆς ἐν Λαοδικείᾳ τῆς Φρυγίας συνελθόντων μακαρίων πατέρων συνόδου ἐπὶ τοῦ μεγάλου Θεοδοσίου', which Joannou adopted in his edition,[101] and the assertion in the *Decretum Gratiani* (D.16 c. 11) that the canons had been passed by 22 bishops under the presidency of one 'Theodosius', are chronologically not precise. Theodoret was the first to

---

97. Cf. c. 21 with c. Serdica 1+2; c. 11 with c. Serdica 8; c. 6 with c. Serdica 16; see Hess, *Sardica* 212–13, 216–17, 222–23.

98. Cf. ACO 2.1 pp. 407, 459–60; see also 2.5 p. 51, 20.

99. In John Scholasticus c. 59 and 60 form c. 59 together.

100. Only Latin text in Joannou (= Dionysius Exiguus, ed. Strewe, 52); on the Greek text, cf. Beneševič, *Syntagma* 267 and Lauchert. The note is found in all the Greek manuscripts.

101. Joannou, CSP 130.

mention the synod in his commentary on Colossians 2:18, written about 430. He referred to the ban on prayers to angels by the synod of Laodicea and used its c. 35 with its ban on the cult of angels.[102] Theodoret's assertion is the *terminus ad quem*, and the partition of Phrygia, which is admittedly not precisely dated, into Phrygia Salutaris and Phrygia Pacatiana about 325 is the *terminus non ante*.[103]

The decision of c. 7 concerning the return of heretics to the church, specifically of Novatians, Photinians, and Quartodecimans, without repetition of baptism, is surprising because of its mild treatment of the adherents of Photinus of Sirmium. He had often been condemned for his heretical doctrine of the Trinity, and he was deposed and banned in 351.[104] The mention of him provides a further piece of evidence for dating the synod, even though the Photinians are missing in the older Latin translations of the text.[105] A further temporal limit is drawn by the fact that the canons of Laodicea were already contained in the *corpus canonum* assembled under auspices of the homoians in Antioch before 379.[106] This dating is confirmed through internal evidence that takes into account the lack of decisions on 'lapsi', the extensive description of the forms of ecclesiastical organization, which indicates a time of peace, the mild treatment of sinners in c. 2, which contrasts with the strictness of the canons of Nicaea, and finally the liturgical references in canons 14 to 23 and 25 to 30.

The literary form of the 60 canons is surprising, since almost all consist of only a single brief sentence, giving the impression of a summary or a rubric. This practice also makes an impact on the style of the canons, since canons 1 to 19 begin with 'Περὶ τοῦ . . .' and canons 20 to 59 with 'Ὅτι οὐ δεῖ . . .'. Further, some canons are repeated in both of these stylistic forms, as is the case with the ban on marriage with heretics in canons 10 and 31, as well as the ban on visiting heretical cemeteries and places of martyrdom, in canons 9 and 34. Finally, canons 3, 4, 7, 8, and 20 are summaries of the Nicene canons 2, 17, 8, 19, and 18. Thus, it would be easy to assume that the canons of Laodicea are a comprehensive collection of the Phrygian canonical tradition, which possibly consisted of two successive synods in Laodicea.[107] E. Schwartz tried to explain the reception of the canons of Laodicea into the Greek *corpus canonum* through its stress

---

102. *Ad Coloss.* 2:18 (PG 82.614B, 620).
103. Cf. K. Belke and N. Mersich, *Phrygien und Pisidien, Tabula Imperii Byzantini* 7, ed. H. Hunger (Vienna 1990) 78.
104. Cf. G. Bardy, 'Photin de Sirmium', DThC 12.1532–36; B. Kotter, 'Photeinos', LThK² 8.483.
105. Cf. Hefele *Concilien*, 1.753–54; my opinion is that this speaks for the historicity of the attribution, contrary to Hefele.
106. Cf. Schwartz, 'Kanonensamlungen' 190–94.
107. Thus in Joannou, CSP 128.

on the ranking of the clergy and its origins in the equally anti-Nicene diocese of Asia. 'The epitomized form can be explained by the fact that it had been transcribed to order'.[108]

Alongside the canons on heresy mentioned above (7, 9, 10, 31), c. 8 prescribed rebaptism for Montanists. C. 6 forbade heretics to set foot in orthodox churches, and canons 32 and 33 forbade persons to accept *eulogiai* from heretics or to pray with them.

C. 1 allowed a second marriage with a small penance. C. 11 banned the installation of *presbytides*,[109] and c. 44 forbids women's access to the altar. No neophytes were to be received into the clergy (c. 3), and clerics were not to take usury (c. 4). Consecrations were not to be performed in the presence of the unbaptized (c. 5), the election of bishops pertained to the metropolitan and the bishops of the province (c. 12) and not to the people (c. 13).[110] Bishops were obligated to attend synods (c. 40). Canons 56 and 58 regulated further the rights and duties of bishops, and c. 56 ordered the establishment of *periodeutes* in the place of *chorepiscopi*. Canons 20, 21, 22, and 43 dealt with regulations for deacons and subdeacons, canons 15 and 23 for lectors and cantors. C. 24 forbade the entire clergy from visiting taverns, canons 41 and 42 forbade travel by clerics without permission and a letter of the bishop. Canons 25 to 28 regulated liturgical rights and bans. Canons 29, 30, 36, 39, and 53 to 55 forbade the use of pagan or Jewish practices. Regulations on dealings with the consecrated elements of the eucharist (c. 14) and the ordering the divine service (canons 16 to 19) were also passed. Questions of the practice of baptism were decided by canons 45 to 48, rules for fasts by canons 49 to 52. Finally, c. 59 forbade the liturgical usage of 'private psalms' and uncanonical books. C. 60 named the canonical books of the Old and New Testaments; in the former, the books of *Judith, Tobias, Wisdom of Solomon, Wisdom of Jesus of Sirach*, and *Maccabees* were missing, and in the latter, only *Revelation*.

The Synod of Constantinople (381)

Editions: COGD 64–70; Joannou, CCO 45–48; Lauchert 84–87; Pitra, *Juris* 1.508–9; Pedalion 155–65; Rhalles-Potles 2.165–91; *Versiones*: ClavisG 8600.

Translations: English: L'Huillier, *Ancient Councils* 111–42; NPNF 14.171–86; Cummings, *Rudder* 202–20 and Tanner, *Decrees* 31–35; German: Wohlmuth, *Dekrete* 31–35; Ortiz de Urbina, 313–14; French: Joannou, CCO 45–48.

---

108. Schwartz, 'Kanonensammlungen' 31–35, at 35.
109. Cf. Bardy, DDC 6.340–41; N. Afanasiev, 'Presbytides or Female Presidents', *Women and the Priesthood*, ed. T. Hopko (New York 1983) 61–74.
110. Cf. J. Gaudemet, 'Note sur la transmission des canons 12 et 13 du Concile de Laodicée relatifs à la désignation des évêques', *Liber amicorum Monseigneur Onclin* (Gembloux 1976) 87–98.

Literature: G. Bardy, 'Constantinople, concile de (381)', DDC 4.424–28; P. Chrestou, 'The Ecumenical Character of the First Synod of Constantinople 381: The Reception of the Synod', *The Greek Orthodox Theological Review* 27 (1982) 359–74; E. Chrysos, 'Die Akten des Konzils von Konstantinopel I (381)', *Romanitas-Christianitas: Festschrift J. Straub zum 70. Geburtstag*, ed. G. Wirth, et al. (Berlin–New York 1982) 426–35; D. J. Constantelos, 'Toward the Convocation of the Second Ecumenical Synod', *The Greek Orthodox Theological Review* 27 (1982) 395–405; B. E. Daley, 'Position and Patronage in the Early Church: The Original Meaning of "Primacy of Honour",' JTS N.S. 44 (1993) 529–53; Hefele-Leclercq *Histoire* 2.1.1–48; C. Kannengiesser, 'Constantinople II, Councils', EEC 195–96; L'Huillier, *Ancient Councils* 101–42; Bernard Meunier, *Les premiers conciles de l'église: Un ministère d'unité* (Lyon 2003) 93–108; Ohme, *Kanon* 510–42; Ortiz de Urbina, 133–289 [German version] 231–35; *Le IIe Concile Œcuménique* (Études théologiques 2; Chambésy 1982); Ritter, *Konzil*; A. M. Ritter, 'Das II. ökumenische Konzil und seine Rezeption: Stand der Forschung', *Le IIe Concile Œcuménique* 43–62; A. M. Ritter, 'Konstantinopel. Ökumenische Synoden. I. ökumenische Synode von 381', TRE 19 (1991) 518–24; COGD 37–54; BISA.

Ordinarily, the Greek canonical collections attribute seven canons to the Second Ecumenical Council of Constantinople in 381. Of these, general consensus identifies canons 1 to 4 as authentic. This is because the old Latin translations in the *Prisca*, Dionysius Exiguus, Isidore, and the Codex of Lucca contain only these first four canons, which are taken from independent sources, since they divide the text differently.[111] Further, the early historians speak only of the first four canons.[112] Hence, canons 5 and 6 probably belong to the Constantinople synod of 382;[113] c. 7, which is still missing in John Scholasticus and which contained a discussion of the practice of Constantinople for the return of heretics, appears to be an excerpt of a letter from the middle of the fifth century from the Patriarch Gennadius I of Constantinople to Martyrius of Antioch.[114] All three canons were only later joined to the council of 381 in the manuscript tradition.[115]

Canons 1 to 4 constitute the actual decisions of the council which were presented to the Emperor Theodosius I for his confirmation at the final session on 9 July 381 by the bishops through the *Logos Prosphonetikos*,[116] a

---

111. Cf. Hefele-Leclercq *Histoire* 2.1 18–19.

112. Socrates, *Historia ecclesiastica* 5.8 (ed. Hansen, GCS NF 1, 279–81); Sozomenus, *Historia ecclesiastica* 7.9 (ed. Bidez and Hansen, GCS NF 4, 311–13); Theodoret, *Historia ecclesiastica* 5.8 (ed. Parmentier and Scheidweiler, GCS 44, 287–89).

113. Cf. Joannou, *Die Ostkirchen* 272–81; S. Gerber, *Theodor von Mopsuestia und das Nicänum: Studien zu den katechetischen Homilien* (Supplement to Vigiliae Christianae 51; Leiden-Boston-Cologne 2000) 143–44.

114. See below, ooo.

115. This historical discovery has not yet been accepted in Orthodox theology. Cf. P. Rhodopoulos, 'Primacy of Honor and Jurisdiction (Canons Two and Three of the Second Ecumenical Synod)', *Le IIe Concile* 378. V. Pheidas, in 'Les critères des décisions administratives du IIe Concile oecuménique', *Le IIe Concile* 385–98, knows the historical problem, but he still deals with canons 5 to 7 as canons of 381; also see Menevisoglou, Ἱστορικὴ 192–93.

116. Mansi 3.557; Beneševič, *Syntagma* 94–95.

document which has survived. The emperor responded to this request for confirmation with his edict of 30 July 381.[117] The Nicene–Constantinopolitan Creed, which current research attributes to this council, but whose role at the council is still disputed, together with a doctrinal tome, which has not survived, and can only be reconstructed using the synodal letter of the Constantinople synod of 382, are (in agreement with A. M. Ritter) not to be regarded as decisions of the council in the narrower sense.[118]

Any statements about the course of the council can only be based on a historical reconstruction, though one of high probability, since minutes not only do not survive but were probably never even kept.[119] In keeping with Ritter's reconstruction, the composition of the four canons can be understood in the context of the council as follows.

The resolving of the question about the bishop of Constantinople after the opening of the council in May 381, with the election of Gregory of Nazianzus, ended the dispute involving the 'cynic' Maximus from Alexandria. He had been consecrated bishop of the imperial capital in 380 through a clandestine action supported by the Alexandrian bishop Peter. C. 4 declared that this election was invalid, as well as all of Maximus's consecrations and actions.[120] One must keep in mind this Alexandrian intervention into the affairs of the church of Constantinople to understand canons 2 and 3, which have the greatest historical importance among the canons of the council.[121]

Therefore, c. 2 forbade the bishops of an imperial diocese to intervene in the affairs of the bishops of another imperial diocese, to cross their boundaries without permission, or to undertake ordinations there. Specified were the five dioceses of the eastern half of the Empire: Aegyptus, Oriens, Asia, Pontus, and Thracia. This ruling would leave untouched the competence of provincial synods regulated in Nicaea (see above), as well as responsibilities for the missionary churches outside the boundaries of the empire. C. 3 directed that the bishop of Constantinople should have 'precedence in honor (πρεσβεῖα τῆς τιμῆς) (directly) behind the bishop of Rome', 'because this city is the new Rome'.

In this manner the reordering of the ecclesiastical structure continued, based on the foundation of the constitution of the Roman Empire. While the council of Nicaea (see above) had created ecclesiastical provinces (met-

---

117. *Codex Theodosianus* 16.1.3
118. Ritter, *Konzil* 132–209, 239–53; Ritter, 'Stand der Forschung' 48–52; COGD 64–70; for other positions, see these as well.
119. Chrysos, 'Die Akten'.   120. Cf. Ritter, *Konzil* 49–52.
121. Cf. Ritter, *Konzil* 85–96; Ritter, 'Stand der Forschung' 47–48; J. Meyendorff, 'The Council of 381 and the Primacy of Constantinople', *Le IIe Concile* 399–413;

ropolitan districts) beyond the episcopal 'parochia', which were geographically congruent with the civil provinces, the council at Constantinople established larger districts that conformed to the boundaries of the imperial dioceses and that encompassed a number of metropolitan districts. These districts were autonomous.

This was an important step toward the later Justinianic patriarchal order, although there is still no mention of patriarchs in this canon. The occasion for this reorganization was the experience that, since Nicaea, neither the emperor nor the various ecclesiastical parties had respected the rights and authority of provincial synods or metropolitans in the ecclesiastical disputes. Yet c. 2, and even more c. 3, could be interpreted as undermining the rights of the see of Alexandria, which traditionally had held second rank behind Rome and therefore the first rank in the East. Now, however, not only was the most important ally of the Roman Church in the East downgraded for the benefit of ecclesiastically traditionless Constantinople, but also the canons implied that even the precedence of Old Rome was only a 'precedence of honor' in analogy to the position of the imperial city and center of the *Imperium Romanum*. So, both canons were fateful steps toward the imperial church's conforming to the organization and administration of the empire.

In the final phase of the council the fathers must have turned to composing the doctrinal tome, which has been lost, as well as the dogmatic c. 1, which constituted a summary of the tome's doctrinal statements and anathemas.[122] The canon restricted itself to confirming the 'faith of the 318 Fathers' of Nicaea and anathematizing the 'Eunomians or Anhomoeans, the Arians or Eudoxians, the Semi-Arians or Pneumatomachians, the Sabellians, the Marcellians, the Photinians, and the Apollinarians'.[123] The formulation of these dogmatic decisions were in addition to the doctrinal tome, and its loss can be understood only if c. 1 is meant as the doctrinal decision of the council.[124] Through these decisions, the council put an end to all the trinitarian conflicts of the fourth century, which had created in the church great confusion and distress for more than five decades.

One may speak of a general recognition of the synod of Constantinople of 381 as the Second Ecumenical Council only after the Council of Chalcedon in 451 (see below). Its status as an ecumenical council was supported—at least in the West—by recognition of the Nicene-Constantinopolitan creed (and hence implicitly of c. 1). However, c. 2 and especially c. 3 were

---

122. Ritter, *Konzil* 116–27; Ortiz de Urbina 234–39.
123. For these groups, see Hanson, *Search*.
124. Cf. Ohme, *Kanon* 510–28.

not generally accepted in the Western Church. Pope Leo the Great lodged a vigorous protest against c. 3,[125] and the council was not declared one of the four ecumenical councils until the time of Pope Hormisdas (514–23).[126] Even the final Roman reception by Gregory the Great in his *epistula synodica* of February 591 did not include c. 3, which certainly led him at the same time to reject all the canons of 381.[127] The Roman Church was only ready to accept c. 3 at the Fourth Lateran Council in 1215; that is, at a time when a Latin patriarch occupied the throne of Constantinople.[128]

The Synod of Ephesus (431)

Editions: Joannou, CCO 57–65 (reprint Benešević, *Synogoga* see below); ACO 1.1–3, 27–28 (c. 1–6); 1.1–7, 105–6 (c. 7); 1.1–7, 122 (c. 8); Lauchert 87–88; Pitra, *Juris* 1.522–34; Rhalles-Potles 2.192–215; Pedalion 170–79; *Versiones:* ClavisG 8800; *Gesta:* ClavisG 8675–8802.

Translations: English: L'Huillier, *Ancient Councils* 154–79; *Rudder* 221–40; NPNF 14.225–42; German: P.-T. Camelot, *Ephesus und Chalkedon* (Mainz 1963) 207–11; French: Joannou, CCO 57–65; A.-J. Festugière, *Éphèse et Chalcédoine. Actes des conciles* (Paris 1982).

Literature: L. Abramowski, COGD 73–80; G. Bardy, 'Éphèse (Concile de 431)', DDC 5.362–64; P.-T. Camelot, *Éphèse et Chalcédoine* (Paris 1962); German translation *Ephesus und Chalkedon* (Mainz 1963); Franca de Marini Avonzo, 'Codice Teodosiano e concilio di Efeso', *Dall'impero crisitano al medioevo: Studi sul diritto tardoantico*, ed. Franca de Marini Avonzo (Bibliotheca eruditorum = Internationale Bibliothek der Wissenschaften 24; Goldbach 2001) 65–82; A. Grillmeier, *Jesus der Christus im Glauben der Kirche* 1 (Freiburg 1979) 642–91; Hefele-Leclercq *Histoire* 2.1.330–42; Kaufhold, 'Väterlisten'; L'Huillier, *Ancient Councils* 143–79; J. Liébaert, 'Éphèse (Concile d')', DHGE 15.561–74; J. Liébaert, 'Ephesus, ökumenische Synode (431)', TRE 9 (1982) 753–55; Bernard Meunier, *Les premiers conciles de l'église: Un ministère d'unité* (Lyon 2003) 113–38; L. I. Scipioni, *Nestorio e il concilio di Efeso* (Studia patristica Mediolanensia 1; Milan 1974); M. Simonetti, 'Ephesus. II. Councils', EEC 275; BISA.

As a rule, Greek canonical collections preserve eight canons of the Third Ecumenical Council of 431 in Ephesus. These are, for the most part, decisions which the partial synod of the Cyrillian majority made at various sessions on varying questions.

On 19 November 430, Emperor Theodosius II called the council to meet the following Pentecost, 7 June 431, to settle the Christological controversy which had raged between the patriarchs of Constantinople and Alexandria, Nestorius and Cyril, since 428. In his *sacra* to the council,[129] he informed it that no other question than the dogmatic one was to be discussed there. It

---

125. Epp. 105, 106: ACO 2.4, pp. 58, 61.
126. Ep. 76, 4 (*Epistulae Romanorum Pontificum*, ed. Thiel [1868] 873).
127. *Epistulae* I Letter 25 (PL 77.478 = Jaffé, 1092).
128. Fourth Lateran Council, c.5, Mansi 22.990, *Conciliorum oecumenicorum decreta*, ed. G. Albergo, et al. (Bologna 1973) 236. Tanner 236. Antonio García y García, ed. *Constitutiones Concilii quarti Lateranensis una cum Commentariis glossatorum* (Monumenta iuris canonici, Series A: Corpus Glossatorum 2; Città del Vaticano: Biblioteca Apostolica Vaticana, 1981) 52.
129. ClavisG 8668.

was the responsibility of the imperial '*comes domesticorum*', Candidianus, to oversee this and to see to it that the synod proceeded in good order. Imperial intentions were, however, subverted by a majority of 154 bishops under Cyril, Memnon of Ephesus, and Juvenal of Jerusalem, who opened the synod over the protests of Candidianus and 68 bishops on 22 June 431, even before the arrival of the bishops of the imperial diocese of Oriens led by John of Antioch. The synod was initiated as a trial against the absent Nestorius, and his deposition and excommunication were immediately ordered at the first session. This 'Ἀπόφασις' bears 197 signatures.[130] In the strictest sense the synod did not issue any dogmatic 'horos' nor a detailed description of the errors being condemned. One might see the confirmation of Cyril's so-called second letter to Nestorius[131] as a dogmatic statement, which was accepted by 125 votes, as well as the rejection of Nestorius's second letter to Cyril[132] by 35 votes.[133]

As soon as John of Antioch arrived on 26 June, he held a synod with a minority of the bishops, in which the deposition and excommunication of Cyril and Memnon were proclaimed in a 'ψῆφος', but it excluded all who held communion with them.[134] By this act the synod was split. Contrary to the emperor's mandate (*sacra*) of 29 June to reopen the council in the presence of all bishops,[135] Cyril's majority held second and third sessions on 10 and 11 July, after the arrival of the papal legates.[136] In keeping with the directions of Pope Celestine, his legates approved the decision of 22 June with their signatures. On 16 and 17 July, the 'Cyrillians' held two further sessions in the presence of the legates, in order to respond to the depositions and excommunications by the synod of the 'Orientals'. These *actiones* 4 and 5 were trial proceedings against John of Antioch, leading to the deposition and excommunication of John and 33 other bishops.[137] The letters to the emperor and to the pope as well as the *epistula universalis*[138] of the majority synod are certainly to be attributed to the time of this *actio 5*.[139] The reason for this assumption is because this 'συνοδικὸν γράμμα', as it was named in the surviving address to the bishops of *Epirus vetus*,[140] 'to the bishops, priests, deacons and the entire people in every eparchy', listed

---

130. ACO 1.1–2, pp. 54, 16–28.
131. ClavisG 5304.
132. ClavisG 5669.
133. ACO 1.1–2, 13–35.
134. ClavisG 8691.
135. ClavisG 8696.
136. ClavisG 8710.
137. ACO 1.1.3, pp. 15–26.
138. ClavisG 8718, 8719, 8717.

139. The writing is not dated. R. Schieffer in the 'Index Auctorum der ACO' (4.3.1.523) lists the *Epistula generalis de decretis* only after *actio* VI and after the *Gesta de episcopis Cypriis* and the *Gesta de episcopis Europae*, without attributing them to a specific session. Bardy, DDC 5.363 (without using the ACO) asserts the decree of 6 canons after the seventh session, as does Joannou, CCO 56. This temporal ordering is taken from Hefele *Concilien* 2.209 and Mansi 4.1469–73.

140. ACO 1.1.3, p. 70.

along with John the names of all 33 excommunicated and deposed bishops. In a second part, six specific rules were formulated on how to deal with adherents to Nestorius, and the synodal letter was concluded by a list of subscribers.

These six decisions, taken from the letter without alteration, constitute what is called canons 1 to 6 of the Council of Ephesus.[141] In the synodal letter itself or in other parts of the conciliar acts, they are not described as canons. The first canon proclaimed the deposition and excommunication of all metropolitans who either attended the minority synod or who had approved or approve the Pelagian, Caelestius (c. 1). Here for the first time the Eastern and Western Church condemn Pelagianism.[142] Bishops who maintained communion with 'apostasy' should be deposed (c. 2); clerics deposed by Nestorius were reinstated in their offices (c. 3). Clerics who were adherents of Nestorius or Caelestius were to be deposed (c. 4), and clerics uncanonically restored to office by Nestorius and his adherents were to remain deposed (c. 5). Finally, all efforts against the decisions of the synod would lead to deposition for clerics and excommunication for lay persons.

The acts of a further session are preserved in the *Collectio Atheniensis*, the so-called *actio* 6 of 22 July 431.[143] These acts are incomplete and were probably gathered after the fact by Cyril.[144] The emphasis in *actio* 6 is on the report of the priest and 'oikonomos' of the church of Philadelphia, Charisius, about a creed of Constantinopolitan origins circulating in Lydia. This creed was being presented to clerics for their signature, and it was also used when Quartodecimans and Novatians were received back. Charisius had resisted signing it and had been excommunicated. Yet the creed was, in his view, heretical and Nestorian but that the council should decide. The decision on this constitutes c. 7 in the canonical collections,[145] though it does not appear as a canon in the acts. It decrees the sole use of the *pistis* of the Nicene Fathers, the formula of 325, and directs that anyone using the *ekthesis* cited by Charisius would lie under the 'ἀπόφασις' of the synod, hence under the 6 decisions already described.

---

141. It is at least misleading to state, 'Après ce décret général viennent les six canons suivants' (Hefele-Leclercq *Histoire* 2.1, 337); but Hefele was already imprecise here, cf. 2.209.
142. Cf. J. Speigl, 'Der Pelagianismus auf dem Konzil zu Ephesus', AHC 1 (1969) 1–14; M. Lamberigts, 'Les évêques pélagiens déposés: Nestorius et Ephèse', *Augustiniana* 35 (1985) 264–280.
143. On the collection of the acts of the council, cf. Liebaért, DHGE 15.561ff. For the *actio*, cf. ClavisG 8721.
144. Cf. ACO 1.1.4, pp. xviii–xix; 1.1.8 p. 10.
145. Col. Athen. 77 = ACO 1.1-7, pp. 105–6; τούτων τοίνυν ἀναγνωσθέντων ὥρισεν ἡ ἁγία σύνοδος . . . On the decision, cf. M. Jugie, 'Le décret du concile d'Ephèse sur les formules de foi et la polémique anticatholiques en Orient', *Échos d'Orient* 30 (1931) 257–70; S. Gerber, *Theodor von Mopsuestia und das Nizänum: Studien zu den katechetischen Homilien* (Supplement to Vigiliae Christianae 51; Leiden-Boston-Cologne 2000) 273–75; COGD 76.

Collectio Atheniensis 81 preserves the protocol of *actio* 7 of the council, which constitutes the basis for the autocephaly of the Church of Cyprus.[146] The dating in *actio* 7, 31 August, was a scribal error for 31 July.[147] A petition (*libellos*) was read out from the Cypriot metropolitan Rheginus of Constantia, who was present with two other Cypriot bishops. The petition protested against the ban pronounced by the proconsul of Antioch, Dionysius, against the synod of Cyprus's filling the vacant metropolitan see of Constantia before the synod in Ephesus had decided whether this right pertained to the metropolitan of Antioch. Behind this lay a long history of efforts by the bishops of Antioch to assure themselves of superior metropolitan rights over the island of Cyprus. The Cypriots had ignored the proconsul's ban, and they elected Rheginus and asserted their traditional rights. The synod decided, on the basis of customary law established by the Nicene canons 4 and 6, that the synod of Cyprus might henceforth install their own bishops. This decision, which is entered in the canonical collections as c. 8, ends the minutes and is not even designated there as a canon.[148]

Between the *gesta* of *actio* 6 and the *gesta de episcopis Cypriis*, the *Collectio Atheniensis* preserves a resolution by the synod as well as two further decisions after the Cypriot affair that were not received into canonical collections, but which barely differ in form or content from the others. All three decisions are undated. The first is a *horos* against 'Messalians or Euchites'[149] and regulated their return to the church on the basis of a synodal decision of Constantinople for Pamphylia and Lykaonia as well as on Alexandrian practice. According to it, clerics might remain in office if they condemned their own errors. Laymen were also admitted to communion under the same conditions. In contrary cases, clerics were to be deposed and excommunicated, and lay persons excommunicated. No Messalian was permitted to enter a monastery, and one of their writings, entitled *Asketikon*, was condemned.

The second decision is also the *horos* to a petition (*libellos*) of two bishops of the province of Europa.[150] Euprepius of Bizye and Arkadiopolis and Cyril of Koila and Kallipolis expressed their anxiety that their metropolitan, Phritilas of Herakleia, the partisan of John of Antioch, was seeking to isolate them by trying to install new bishops for cities under them. The synod was to confirm the customary law of several *poleis* belonging to their sees, as was the general norm in Europe. The synod approved this request.

---

146. ClavisG 8744.
148. ACO 1.1.7, p. 122.1–22, Ἡ ἁγία σύνοδος . . .
149. ClavisG 8746.
147. Cf. Hefele-Leclercq 2.1 p. 334.
150. ClavisG 8745.

The third text was a letter to the eparchial synod of Pamphylia[151] on the matter of Bishop Eustathius, who had resigned his office but, with the agreement of his sucessor, asked to remain nominally as bishop. The synod ruled that he could retain the ὄνομα, τιμή, and κοινωνία of his episcopal position but could act as a bishop only with the approval of his successor.[152]

It is surprising that the 8 texts that later entered Greek canonical collections were never designated as 'canons' in the conciliar minutes. Even Socrates, whose report on the council of Ephesus is remarkably short for a contemporary, mentioned no canons.[153] The oldest known Greek canonical collections also appear not to have received the canons of Ephesus. So, for example, they do not appear in the Syrian translation of the Greek corpus of 500–501 in Hieropolis-Mabbug (= British Library addit. 14528), although six canons of Chalcedon are found there.[154] Dionysius Exiguus also knew nothing about them, so that he must have used a Greek model without these canons. The oldest Latin translation was taken from a translation of conciliar acts by the deacon Rusticus in the third quarter of the sixth century.[155] It is not a matter of a translation of canons but rather of the conciliar acts. These canons had obviously not yet entered Latin canonical collections.

The Ephesian decisions became valid as 'canons' only in the *Synogoge* of John Scholasticus in the middle of the sixth century. Yet their number and order was for a long time diverse, so that in the foreword to the *Synogoge*, 7, 6, and 8 canons are attributed to the synod of Ephesus in the manuscripts.[156] The canons themselves are distributed into *titloi* 37, 38, 1, and 47. The decision on Cyprus cited in title 1 was designated as c. 6, but many manuscripts also list it as c. 7 or 8.[157] In 545, when Emperor Justinian in his Novella 131.1 declared the canons of the ecumenical synods equal to laws, the canons of Ephesus were included.

The Synod of Chalcedon (451)

Sources: COGD (canons 1–28) 138–51; canons 1 to 27: ACO 2.1.2, 158–63 (354–59) (*actio 7*; c. 28: ACO 2.1.3, 88 (447) 28–94 (453), 32 (*actio 17*); c. 29: ACO 2.1.3, 108.11–21; 108.31–109.6; c. 30: ACO 2.1.2, 114.2–18; Joannou, CCO 69–97 (reprint Beneševič, *Synagoga* [canons 1 to 27]; Lauchert 89–97; Pitra, *Juris* 1.522–36; Rhalles-Potles 2.216–91; Pedalion 185–211; *Versiones*: ClavisG 9008, 9018, 9015.

---

151. ClavisG 8747. In some canonical collections it was placed after c. 8 (cf. Ralles-Potles 2.206ff.; Pedalion 178–79) and later even designated as 'c. 9' (cf. Menevisoglou, Ἱστορικὴ 224–25).
152. ACO 1.1.7, p. 124.20: ὡρίσαμεν . . .
153. *Historia ecclesiastica* 7.34 (ed. Hansen, GCS NF 1, 382–84).
154. Cf. Schwartz, 'Kanonensammlungen' 163–64.
155. Cf. ACO 1.1.4, pp. vii–xvi.   156. Cf. Beneševič, *Synagoga* 6.
157. Cf. Beneševič, *Synagoga* 33.

Translations: English: L'Huillier, *Ancient Councils* 206–328; NPNF 14.267–88; Tanner 87–103; *The Acts of the Council of Chalcedon*, translated with introduction and notes by Richard Price and Michael Gaddis (Translated Texts for Historians 45; Liverpool 2005). German: Wohlmuth 87–103; French: A.-J. Festugière, *Actes du Concile de Chalcédoine sessions III–VI*, Genf 1983; Joannou, CCO 69–97; Hefele-Leclercq *Histoire* 2.2.649–847, 767–828, 929–44.

Literature: G. Bardy, 'Chalcédoine (Concile de)', DDC 3.287–92; Camelot, *Éphèse et Chalcédoine*; E. Chrysos; 'Der sog. 28. Kanon von Chalcedon in der "Collectio Prisca"', AHC 7 (1975) 109–17; B. E. Daley, 'Position and patronage in the early church. The original meaning of "primacy of honour"', JTS N.S. 44 (1993) 529–53; R. Delmaire, 'Les dignitaires laïcs au concile de Chalcédoine', *Byzantion* 54 (1984) 141–75; *Das Konzil von Chalkedon: Geschichte und Gegenwart*, ed. Aloys Grillmeier and Heinrich Bacht (3 vols. Würzburg 1951–54; 5th ed. Würzburg 1979) 3.825–65; A. de Halleux, 'Le décret chalcédoine sur les prérogatives de la Nouvelle Rome', EThL 64 (1988) 288–323; André de Halleux, 'Le vingt-huitième canon de Chalcédoine', *Papers presented to the Tenth International Conference on Patristic Studies held in Oxford, 1987: Historica*, ed. Elizabeth A. Livingstone (5 vols. *Studia Patristica* 19–23; Leuven 1989) 1.28–36; André de Halleux, 'Les deux Rome dans la définition de Chalcédoine sur les prérogatives du siége de Constantinople', *Anaphora eis mnemen Metropolitu Sardeon Maximou* 2 (1989) 89–104; Hefele-Leclercq *Histoire* 2.2.649–847, 767–844; E. Herman, 'Chalkedon und die Ausgestaltung des konstantinopolitanischen Primates', *Das Konzil von Chalkedon* 2.459–90; St. O. Horn, *Petrou Kathedra* (Paderborn 1982); P. L'Huillier, 'Le décret du concile de Chalcédoine sur les prérogatives du siège de la très sainte église de Constantinople', *Messager de l'Exarchat du Patriarchat russe en Europe Occidentale* 27 (1979) 33–69; L'Huillier, *Ancient Councils* 181–328; P. L'Huillier, 'Un aspect estompé du 28e canon de Chalcédoine', *Revue de droit canonique* 29 (1979) 12–22; Kaufhold, 'Väterlisten'; Thomas O. Martin, 'The Twenty-Eighth Canon of Chalcedon: A Background Note', *Das Konzil von Chalkedon* 2.433–58; Bernard Meunier, *Les premiers conciles de l'église: Un ministère d'unité* (Lyon 2003) 151–82; E. Schwartz, *Der sechste nicaeanische Kanon auf der Synode von Chalkedon* (Sitzungsberichten der Preußischen Akademie der Wissenschaften, Phil.-hist. Klasse 27; Berlin 1930) 611–40; E. Schwartz, *Aus den Akten des Konzils von Chalkedon* (Abhandlungen der Bayerischen Akademie der Wissenschaften, Phil.-philolog.-hist. Klasse 32.2; Munich 1925); M. Simonetti, 'Chalcedon. II. Council', EEC 159; L. Ueding, 'Die Kanones von Chalkedon in ihrer Bedeutung für Mönchtum und Klerus', *Das Konzil von Chalkedon* 2.569–676; W. de Vries, 'Die Struktur der Kirche gemäß dem Konzil von Chalkedon', OCP 35 (1969) 63–122; L. R. Wickham, 'Chalkedon', TRE 7 (1981) 668–75; BISA.

With his *sacra* of May 451,[158] Emperor Marcian called a synod for 1 September 451 in Nicaea to bring ecclesiastical concord to the dogmatic question of the unification of the divine and human in Jesus Christ. The conflict, underway since the dispute over Nestorius and the synod of Ephesus in 431, had broken out into an open struggle during the proceedings against the Archimandrite Eutyches (from 8 to 22 November 448) and his rehabilitation at the Ephesian 'Robbers' Council' (8 to 22 August 449) by Dioscorus of Alexandria and Juvenal of Jerusalem. The Fourth Ecumenical Council was finally transferred from Nicaea to Chalcedon, in the immediate vicinity of the capital, and opened on 8 October 451. By its sixth session, on

---

158. ClavisG 8981, 8982.

25 October, it came to an agreement on the dogmatic question under the leadership of five legates of Pope Leo but especially under the leadership of 19 leading imperial officials.[159] The result of this agreement was the formulation of a doctrinal definition (*horos*),[160] which preceded the deposition of Dioscorus and the annulment of the decisions of Ephesus of 449.

At the sixth session,[161] the doctrinal formula was confirmed by the emperor and endorsed by 452 bishops[162] in his presence and in the presence of his wife, Pulcheria. At the end of the session Marcian asked the bishops not to leave Constantinople before all of the pending questions had been resolved.[163] These questions were exclusively of a canonical nature and would occupy the council for one more week. The emperor had already told the members of the synod that he expected the resolution of three questions, since their regulation had to proceed 'κανονικῶς' and not through secular laws.[164] For this purpose he had three pre-formulated *kephalaia* read out to the bishops at once.[165] They were adopted in modified form as canons 4, 3, and 20 among the Chalcedonian canons.

In the edition of the acts of Chalcedon by E. Schwartz,[166] the material of the Greek minutes have been distributed into 17 *actiones*.[167] This order goes back to the official first edition of the Greek acts prepared soon after 451, which is followed by the oldest of the three Latin translations, the so-called *Versio antiqua*. In this edition, it is clear that substantive topics took precedence over chronological order.[168] E. Chrysos has particularly questioned the order of the canonical *actiones* 7 to 17 with detailed arguments.[169] In keeping with the order of the Greek acts, the 27 canons of the council follow immediately on the order of the emperor already mentioned in what is called *actio* 7 on the same day (25 October).[170] It is in fact a surprise that this *actio* 7 consists only of the words of the 27 canons without any description of the proceedings.[171] In addition, with the close connection of

---

159. Among them was the *magister militum* (supreme commander of the military), the *praefectus praetorio Orientis* (supreme civil official in the eastern Imperial dioceses of Aegyptus, Oriens, Pontus, Asia, and Thracia) and the *praefectus urbis Constantinopolitanae*; cf. *actio* I.2.

160. *Actio* V.30–34; ClavisG 9005.   161. ClavisG 9007.

162. *Actio* VI.9; the Latin text has 449 signatures.

163. *Actio* VI.23.   164. *Actio* VI.16.

165. *Actio* VI.17–19.   166. ACO 2.1–6; cf. TRE 7.674–75.

167. ClavisG 9000–9020.

168. The principle of organization was clearly (1) the annulling of the Ephesian synod of 449 and the deposing of Dioscorus; (2) dogma and canons; (3) episcopal legal questions. For this reason E. Schwartz already reversed the order of *actio* II and III; cf. ACO II 1, 3, xxii.

169. E. Chrysos, 'Ἡ διάταξις τῶν συνεδρίων τῆς ἐν Χαλκηδόνι οἰκουμενικῆς συνόδου', *Kleronomia* 3 (1971) 259–84.

170. According to the Latin *Versio antiqua a Rustico correcta*, the canons only belong to *actio* XV of 31 October, standing after the session on the case of the bishop of Perre and before the acts on the jurisdiction of Constantinople. Cf. Hefele-Leclercq *Histoire* 2.2 767ff.

171. ClavisG 9008; ACO 2.1.2, pp. 158–63 (354–59).

the canons to the formal session of 25 October and the promulgation of the dogmatic *horos,* it is difficult to understand why the emperor presented the three *kephalaia* and did not pass immediately to the promulgation of the canons. Yet the synod did not adopt the three *kephalaia* moved by the emperor without modification, but rather added to them, altered them, and passed them on their own.[172] This took time, so that it was impossible to pass the canons immediately in keeping with the emperor's desire. Marcian had also referred to the synod a number of pending disputes in which the persons had appealed to the emperor. It would only be logical, once the synod had resolved the disputes and the 'negotia privata', to move to the presentation of general rules as can be seen in the unusual opening formula of canons 3, 12, 19, and 23, 'ἦλθεν εἰς τὴν ἁγίαν σύνοδον ὅτι . . .' and similar. It appears mandatory, then, to place the promulgation of the canons after *actio* 15, on 30 or 31 October. Then discussions took place about the so-called c. 28.[173]

The Greek acts of *actio* 8 of 26 October bring an end to the debates between Maximus of Antioch and Juvenal of Jerusalem on the region of jurisdiction between the two thrones.[174] The two of them presented to the synod an agreement they had negotiated on 23 October,[175] which was unanimously approved by the synod and which was entered into the acts by the imperial commissioners as synodal 'ἀπόφασις' and 'ψῆφος' with validity for all time.[176] Henceforth, only the provinces of Phoenicia I and II and Arabia would be subject to the see of Antioch, while the provinces of Palestina I to III were placed under the jurisdiction of the bishop of Jerusalem. There was no more talk about the rights of the metropolitan of Caesarea in Palestine, which had still been expressly defended in c. 7 of Nicaea. With that, Juvenal had achieved the goal of autonomy for Jerusalem that he had been pursuing since Ephesus in 431. The decision of *actio* 8 could be said to be the foundational charter of the patriarchate of Jerusalem.

In the course of *actio* 9 (also on 26 October), the case of Theodoret of Cyrrhus was given a legally clear decision.[177] Although his deposition by Dioscorus in 449 had been rendered null and void when the acts of the 'Robbers' Council' had been annulled, and he had taken a seat and had a

---

172. Ueding, 'Bedeutung' 602–9, offers a precise comparison of 'kephalaia' 1 and 2 with canons 4 and 3. On the content, see below, n. 197.

173. On that in detail, see p. 000 at n. 205.

174. ClavisG 9007; according to the *Versio antiqua a Rustico correcta: actio* VIII; on the following, cf. Schwartz, 'Aus den Akten' 4–7, 29–40, 43–46.

175. ClavisG 9006; Schwartz, 'Aus den Akten' 45–46.

176. *Actio* VIII 3.17.

177. ClavisG 9010.

vote as one of the synod participants at the first session, but his participation had been accompanied by loud protests of the Palestinians, Egyptians, and Illyrians.[178] The council proceeded to order his reinstatement as bishop of Cyrrhus after he anathematized Nestorius.[179]

The tenth and eleventh sessions on 26 and 27 October settled the case of Bishop Ibas of Edessa.[180] During these sessions the records of the proceedings held against him in Tyre and Berytus were read out, though the use of the proceedings of the *Latrocinium* was rejected. Ibas was rehabilitated, the orthodoxy of his letter to Maris was confirmed by the Roman legate,[181] and his reinstatement as bishop of Edessa was ordered after he had also explicitly anathematized Nestorius.[182]

In *actiones* 12 and 13 on 29 and 30 October, the legal dispute between the two bishops of Ephesus, Bassianus and Stephanus, was debated and both were ordered to be deposed.[183]

The dispute between the metropolitan of Bithynia, Eunomius of Nicomedia, and the bishop of Nicaea was recorded in *actio* 14 on 30 October.[184] The reason for this was the earlier elevation of Nicaea, which was ecclesiastically a suffragan of Nicomedia, to a (secular) metropolis by the emperors Valentinian and Valens, which led the bishop of Nicaea to make ecclesiastical claims on behalf of his see. The council restricted the ecclesiastical rights of Nicaea and confirmed the metropolitan rights of Nicomedia. This decision was recorded in general terms in c. 12 (see below).[185]

Actio 15 of 31 October dealt with the effort of Bishop Sabinianus of Perre,[186] deposed at Ephesus in 449, to obtain reinstatement. They did not come to a decision on this matter but referred it to Maximus of Antioch and asked that it be settled within 8 months.

The 27 canons of the council, under the title, Ὅροι ἐκκλησιαστικοὶ ἐκφωνηθέντες παρὰ τῆς ἁγίας καὶ οἰκουμενικῆς συνόδου τῆς ἐν Χαλκηδόνι συναχθείσης',[187] produced a plethora of new decisions on questions about discipline of the clergy and of monasticism, about the episcopal office, and about the structure of the church. At the head of the collection is a confirmation of all synodal canons enacted until then (c. 1).

The canons on monasticism have special importance, since monasti-

---

178. Actio I 25–46.
180. ClavisG 9011, 9013.
182. Actio XI 180.
183. ClavisG 9014, 9016; cf. on this Hefele-Leclercq 2.2 pp. 755–61.
184. ClavisG 9017; cf. Hefele-Leclercq 2.2 pp. 761ff.
185. These honorary metropolises would become the autocephalic archbishops of the next century. Cf. on this E. Chrysos, 'Zur Entstehung der Institution der autokephalen Erzbistümer', BZ 62 (1969) 263–86.
186. ClavisG 9019.

179. Actio IX 13.
181. Actio XI 161.

187. ACO 2.1.2, p. 354.

cism was given a legal standing as an institution and was integrated into the church.[188] C. 4 is fundamental; it placed monasteries under the control of bishops, without whose approval no monastery could even be founded. The monastery was to be the sole place where the monastic life was to be practiced, which was defined as *hesychia*, fasting, and prayer. Without the permission of the bishop, the monk was not allowed to leave the monastery. Monks were to intervene neither in ecclesiastical nor in public matters.[189] The demand for constancy and steadfastness is doubled, first by the ban on secularizing established houses and their property (c. 24), second by the threat to excommunicate virgins and monks who break their vows of voluntary celibacy (c. 16). An entire series of canons treated monks and clergy together. Hence c. 3 banned them from participating in any enterprise to make a profit,[190] and c. 7 banned them from accepting worldly office or exercising any military service. All clerics in charitable establishments, monasteries, or *martyria* were placed under bishops (c. 8), and any conspiracy against bishops was threatened with the penalty of deposition (c. 18). C. 23 sharpened the residency requirement once more for both clerical groups, particularly forbidding them to live in Constantinople without permission.

The following regulations dealt with the discipline and order of the clerical estate, including the bishops: c. 5 confirmed previous canons on the theme of translation, threatening the non-observant with excommunication (c. 20).[191] C. 6 forbade absolute ordination (ordination must be connected to a particular church), and c. 10 forbade the possibility of being ordained to two churches. Canons 11 and 13 regulated the necessity and distinction of letters of recommendation and peace. Lectors and cantors were forbidden to marry heterodox wives (c. 14). Consecration as deaconess was to be bestowed on women only after the age of 40 (c. 15), and the estates of deceased bishops was protected against clerical claimants (c. 22). Complaints against bishops and clerics demanded that the reputation of the plaintiff be investigated (c. 21).

The following canons dealt with the office of the bishop and his duties: any practice of simony is punished with deposition (c. 2). Lobbying at court to have a metropolitan district divided in order to create new *metropoleis* is also punished with deposition, and *metropoleis* already created this way are declared 'honorary *metropoleis*' (c. 12). Rural parishes should remain under the control of the bishop under whose jurisdiction they had been during the

---

188. On this particularly, cf. Ueding, 'Bedeutung'.
189. C.4 is taken extensively from the emperor's *Kephalaion* 1.
190. This decision as well goes back to a proposal of the emperor (*Kephalaion* 2) see above.
191. This decision is taken from the emperor's *Kephalaion* 3.

previous thirty years (c. 17). The duty of holding a provincial synod twice a year was reinforced (c. 19). Metropolitans had to complete the consecration of suffragans presented to them (c. 25) within three months, and every bishop had to transfer the financial administration to his *oikonomos* (c. 26).

It is clear that the immediate experiences and conflicts of the previous years are in the background of many of these canons: the disputes with Eutyches and his monks in Constantinople, the rabble-rousing of Syrian monks by Barsaumas and his intervention in the *Latrocinium*, the intrigue of clergy from Edessa against Ibas, as well as the struggles between Nicaea and Nicomedia, or between Tyre and Berytus.[192]

Two further canons that regulated appeals of ecclesiastical cases constituted the bishop of Constantinople as the highest court of appeal and brought him into competition with the 'exarchs' of the imperial dioceses. This led to the legal establishment of the primacy of the see of Constantinople before the battle erupted over the so-called c. 28 at Chalcedon. Thus, c. 9 specified that conflicts between clerics fall under the jurisdiction of the bishop, to the exclusion of all secular courts. In proceedings between clerics and bishops, the proper court is the provincial synod, but in proceedings against metropolitans it can be either the *exarchos* of the diocese or the bishop of the capital city. C. 17 already applied this canon to a conflict over the jurisdictional subjection of rural congregations (see above). Hence, the archbishop of Constantinople received the right to take the place of the 'exarchs' of the three dioceses surrounding the capital city, Pontus, Asia, and Thracia (the metropolitans of Caesarea in Cappadocia, Ephesus, and Heraclea), and to judge cases appealed from their courts, if the appellants turn to him.[193] This regulation offered, along with the so-called c. 28, a consistent general picture that the church had taken an essential step in the direction of a patriarchal constitution.

The Greek acts contain as *actio* 17 the minutes from a session on 30 October on the privileges of the archbishop of Constantinople.[194] The substance of these minutes consisted of the reading out of a resolution on this matter passed by a synodal session of the previous day, the so-called c. 28, with a subscription list of 185 bishops, who brought proxies for 23 more bishops.[195]

The resolution passed the following decisions: confirming c. 3 of the

---

192. Cf. Schwartz, 'Aus den Akten' 3–4.

193. A wider interpretation possible from the phrasing of the canon to include the exarchs of the dioceses of Oriens and Aegyptus, hence the archbishops of Antioch and Alexandria, can certainly be characterized as improbable. This position is, however, represented in the Roman Catholic literature, cf. Herman, 'Ausgestaltung' 474–77.

194. ClavisG 9018; on the rest, cf. Schwartz, 'Der sechste nicaenische Kanon' 611–40; Martin, 'Twenty-Eighth Canon'; Herman, 'Ausgestaltung'.

195. ClavisG 9015.

Council of Constantinople (381),[196] that the see of Constantinople–New Rome should receive the same privileges (τὰ ἴσα πρεσβεῖα) as those accruing to Old Rome and that Constantinople should hold the second rank after Rome. The justification for the precedence of both thrones is the fact that both cities are imperial residences and seats of the Senate. The ecclesiastical rank of both cities should correspond to their secular ranks. Further, in the future the metropolitans of the imperial dioceses of Pontus, Asia, and Thracia as well as bishops residing outside imperial territory should be consecrated by the patriarch of Constantinople. The suffragans in the named dioceses should henceforth only be consecrated by the metropolitans together with all eparchial bishops, after the archbishop of Constantinople had been informed of the election.

In this way the exarchs of the dioceses named were deprived of their traditional rights. In any case, it appears that this canon only confirmed what had long been the practice.[197] Yet the bishops of these dioceses resisted the implementation of the new law (see below). The patriarch of Constantinople obtained a jurisdictional district equal to that of old Rome, Alexandria, Antioch, and recently Jerusalem. Beyond that, Constantinople was to have a position of primacy in the East that was comparable to that of Rome in the West. This constitutional development in the church followed the structural logic of the secular state: with two emperors, two capitals, and two senates, the church would now have two heads.

It is surprising that the first reading of the resolution was not taken into the minutes,[198] and hence was not counted as a session. Further, the first reading appears not to have led to a final clarification, since a further session was needed on the following day for the same set of problems. E. Chrysos has convincingly shown that these minutes probably had been removed from the first edition of the Greek minutes because it included the votes of opponents and their arguments.[199] These are still discernible in the minutes of *actio* 17 with the protests of Eusebius of Ankara and Thalassus of Caesarea.[200] Further, there must have been other Pontic bishops, so that many more synodal participants were present than the 185 in the subscription list.[201]

The papal legates certainly refused cooperation from the outset, on the grounds that they had no instructions.[202] Beyond this there was the

---

196. See above, 51. There it still says τὰ πρεσβεῖα τῆς τιμῆς!
197. Cf. Herman, 'Ausgestaltung' 472.   198. ClavisG 9015.
199. Chrysos, 'Ἡ διάταξις' 275–82.   200. *Actio* XVII 35–42.
201. This number is often incorrectly cited as the number of participants; cf. for example, Herman, 'Ausgestaltung' 463.
202. ACO 2.1.3, p. 447.18–19.

legal necessity of carrying out a voting procedure (ψῆφος) that implied a discussion of substance. This is the only possible explanation for the fact that, together with the planned resolution, the minutes contained a subscription list as the result of a 'ψῆφος'. In keeping with that, this resolution was described by the bishops as a 'ψῆφος',[203] never as a 'canon'.

Chrysos had plausibly explained that *actio* 16 contained in the Greek minutes, with the reading of the letter of Pope Leo to the synod, is bogus.[204] The virtually unexplainable reading of this letter only at the end of the council and in a session held for it alone becomes comprehensible if one assumes that this letter stands in the place of the first reading of c. 28, with Leo's demand that the synod assure the canons and rights of the bishops after the restoration of ecclesiastical peace,[205] which was to witness the legitimacy of the proceedings that established the primacy of Constantinople, even against the position of the papal legates. Thus, the absence of *actio* 16 in the entire Latin tradition can be explained. According to this, the first reading of c. 28 was to be put in the place of *actio* 16, and *actio* 17 was to be dated on 1 November.

However, the papal legates now declared the entire resolution to be null and void, and they had their objections registered in the minutes.[206] The synod then turned to Pope Leo in its *epistula synodica* and asked him to approve this 'ψῆφος'.[207] The same was done by the emperor and Anatolius of Constantinople, who even described the decision as a restriction of his earlier rights.[208] Leo refused his approval in letters to Marcian, Pulcheria, and Anatolius,[209] as well as in his answer to the bishops.[210] Anything in opposition to the canons of Nicaea was not acceptable; c. 6 of Nicaea had established a definitive ranking: Rome, Alexandria, Antioch.[211] Anatolius appeared to be satisfied with that,[212] though his approval did not alter the

---

203. ACO 2.1.3, pp. 458.10ff.
204. Chrysos, ''Η διάταξις' 272–75. *Actio* 16: ClavisG 9020. Letter: ClavisG 8993.
205. ACO 2.4, pp. 51–53. 206. *Actio* XVII, 45.
207. ClavisG 9022; ACO 2.1.3, p. 477.7–8.
208. ClavisG 9026; ACO 2.1.2, p. 250.2–6; one may only understand this statement together with a comment of the archdeacon of Constantinople and first secretary of the synod, Aetius, at the fourteenth session (ACO 2.1, p. 421.17–25), to mean that Constantinople originally wished to claim the right to consecrate the entire episcopate of the dioceses in question, but that it had to retrench during discussions of the omitted first reading. Cf. Chrysos, ''Η διάταξις' 278–79.
209. ClavisG 9031–33; Jaffé 481–83.
210. ClavisG 9047; Jaffé 490.
211. This thesis is based solely on the Latin tradition of c. 6 falsified in Rome, which begins without any basis in the original: *Quod Ecclesia Romana semper habuit primatum*; cf. Schwartz, 'Der sechste nicänische Kanon' 627–640.
212. ClavisG (9065) = 5959, ACO 2.4, pp. 168–69 = PL 54.1082–83 (1084A). On the pope's attitude to the Council of Chalcedon, cf. F. Hofmann, 'Der Kampf der Päpste um Konzil und Dogma von Chalkedon von Leo dem Großen bis Hormisdas (451–519)', *Das Konzil von Chalkedon* 2.13–94.

de facto primacy of Constantinople in the East and did not change Constantinople's exercise of its rights.

In keeping with this result, only 27 canons were attributed to the council of Chalcedon even in the East until the second half of the sixth century. John Scholasticus in his *Synogoga L titulorum* around 550 documented only 27 canons.[213] Finally, canon 28 was included in the *Syntagma XIV titulorum*,[214] together with two further decisions. All three were admittedly not designated as 'canons'.[215] They consisted of excerpts from the minutes of the session on the affair of Photius of Tyre and Eustathius of Berytus,[216] as well as material from *actio* 4. One of the texts established the impossibility (sacrilege) of demoting a bishop to a priest and the other described the reluctance of Egyptian bishops to take a binding dogmatic position without the instruction of the archbishop of Alexandria, who still had to be elected. All 30 canons have been included in Byzantine ecclesiastical law ever since.

The Synod of Serdica (342)

Editions: EOMIA 1.2.442–560; Joannou, CSP 159–189; Lauchert 51–72; Pitra, *Juris* 1.468–483; Rhalles-Potles 3.227–85; Pedalion 443–61; *Versiones*: ClavisG 8570.

Translations: English: Hamilton Hess, *The Early Development of Canon Law and the Council of Serdica* (Oxford Early Christian Studies; Oxford 2002) 211–55; *Rudder* 583–99; German: Hefele 1.556–607; French: Joannou, CSP 159–89.

Literature: G. Bardy, 'Sardique (Concile de)', DThC 14 (1939) 1109–14; Leslie W. Barnard, 'The Council of Serdica: Some Problems Re-Assessed', AHC 12 (1980) 1–25; Leslie W. Barnard, *The Council of Serdica, 343 A.D.* (Sofia 1983); Hans Christof Brennecke, *Hilarius von Poitiers und die Bischofsopposition gegen Konstantius II* (PTS 26; Berlin 1984); Hans Christof Brennecke, 'Rom und der dritte Kanon von Serdika (342)', ZRG Kan. Abt. 69 (1983) 15–45; E. Caspar, *Geschichte des Papsttums* 1 (Tübingen 1930) 131–65; J. St. H. Gibaut, 'The Peregrinations of Canon 13 of the Council of Sardica', *Ritual, Text and Law Studies in Medieval Canon Law and Liturgy Presented to Roger E Reynolds*, ed. Kathleen G. Cushing and Richard F. Gyug (Aldershot 2004) 141–60; Girardet, 'Appellatio' 98–127; K. M. Girardet, *Kaisergericht und Bischofsgericht. Studien zu den Anfängen des Donatistenstreites (313–315) und zum Prozeß des Athanasius von Alexandrien (328–346)* (Antiquitas, ser. 1, vol. 21); E. Heckrodt, *Die Kanones von Sardika aus der Kirchengeschichte erläutert* (Jenaer Historische Arbeiten 8; Bonn 1917); Hefele-Leclercq *Histoire* 1.2, 737–823; Hamilton Hess, *The*

---

213. For the East, cf. for example, Theodorus Lector, *Historia ecclesiastica* 1.4 (PG 86.168B); the same is the case in the Syrian and Arabic translations, cf. ClavisG 9008. On John Scholasticus, cf. Beneševič, *Synagoga* 7.259 and Brian E. Ferme, *Introduction to the History of the Sources of Canon Law: The Ancient Law up to the Decretum of Gratian* (Gratianus; Montreal 2007) 86–87.

214. See Troianos.

215. The so-called 'canon 28' bears the title, 'Ψῆφος τῆς αὐτῆς ἁγίας συνόδου ἐκφωνηθεῖσα χάριν τῶν πρεσβείων τοῦ θρόνου τῆς ἁγιωτάτης ἐκκλησίας Κωνσταντινουπόλεως', cf. Beneševič, *Syntagma* 124–25. The so-called 'canons 29 and 30' are introduced without title as 'τῆς αὐτῆς συνόδου ἐκ τῆς πράξεως τῆς περὶ . . . and 'τῆς αὐτῆς . . . συνόδου ἐκ τῆς δ᾽ πράξεως . . .' Cf. Beneševič, *Syntagma* 126, 128.

216. Cf. on this Hefele-Leclercq *Histoire* 2.2 713ff.; Schwartz, 'Aus den Akten' 3ff.

Canons of the Council of Sardica: A Landmark in the Early Development of Canon Law (Oxford Theological Monographs 1; Oxford 1958), revised edition *The Early Development of Canon Law and the Council of Serdica* (Oxford Early Christian Studies; Oxford 2002); Kaufhold, 'Väterlisten'; Ohme, *Kanon* 408–49; E. Schwartz, *Zur Geschichte des Athanasius IX*, (NGWG; Göttingen 1911) 409–522 (reprint Gesammelte Schriften 3 [Berlin 1959] 265–334); E. Schwartz, *Der griechische Text der Kanones von Serdika* (ZNW 30; Berlin 1931) 265–334; Schwartz, 'Kanonensammlungen' 208–20; H. J. Sieben, 'Die sardicensischen Appellationskanones im Wandel der Geschichte', ders.: Die Partikularsynode, Frankfurt/M. 1990, 193–228; M. Simonetti, 'Serdica. II. Council', EEC 757; S. Troianos, 'Der Apostolische Stuhl im früh- und mittelbyzantinischen kanonischen Recht', *Il primato del vescovo di Roma nel primo millennio* (Vatican City 1991) 245–59; C. H. Turner, 'The Genuineness of the Sardican Canons', JTS 3 (1902) 370–97; J. Ulrich, *Die Anfänge der abendländischen Rezeption des Nizänums* (PTS 39; Berlin 1994); BISA.

The imperial synod in Serdica (modern Sofia, Bulgaria) in the autumn of 342 constituted the end of the first phase of the dispute begun by Arian conflict. Its failure was marked at the outset by the mutual anathemization of ecclesiastical leaders in the Eastern and Western Empire, and it would lead to the first schism between the Eastern and Western Church.[217]

Athanasius of Alexandria (295–373) had been deposed and excommunicated by the party of Eusebius of Nicomedia at the imperial synod of Tyre (335). After vain attempts to reverse this judgment, Athanasius had to flee from Egypt in 339. He turned to Pope Julius I (337–52), who summoned the Eastern bishops in early 340 to a Roman synod to review the judgment of Tyre. The bishops rejected the review and confirmed their decision at the so-called 'synod *in encaeniis*' in Antioch (341) and formulated their confession in the form of a new creed, colored by Origenism.[218] After an alliance of the two emperors, Constantius II and Constans, which was favorable to the West, the synod demanded by the Athanasian party was to be called for autumn 342. The place of meeting was Serdica, located near the border between the Eastern and Western Empires, where about 76 bishops from the East and 94 from the West gathered.[219] The Western party stood under the leadership of the aged Ossius of Cordoba.

The need for clarification had arisen in many matters: in the area of doctrine, since the Nicene formulation of the trinitarian faith was not interpreted uniformly. In other matters the anti-Arian spokesman of the Nicene

---

217. The discussion on the date of the synod has not yet been resolved. For a date of 342, see particularly Schwartz, 'Athanasius IX' 515ff.; cf. also Brennecke, *Hilarius* 25–29. For 343, see Hess, *Sardica* 140–44 (Appendix I). On the historical context, cf. Hess, *Sardica* 1–21; Hess, *Council of Serdica* 95–113; Caspar, *Geschichte* 1.142–65; Girardet, *Kaisergericht und Bischofsgericht* 106–20; Brennecke, *Hilarius* 17–64; and Barnard, 'Council of Serdica'.

218. Cf. J. N. D. Kelly, *Altchristliche Glaubensbekenntnisse* (2nd ed. Göttingen 1993) (translation of *Early Christian Creeds* [3rd ed. London 1972]) 260–72, 274–77.

219. On the spelling for Serdica (or Sardica; today Sofia), cf. ODB and EOMIA 1.2 p.533. On the number of synodal participants, cf. Hess, *Sardica* 3–4; Ulrich, *Die Anfänge* 91–96.

synod, Marcellus of Ancyra, had been excommunicated and deposed in the meantime by Eastern synods (Constantinople, 330–31 or 334–35), and Antioch, 341).[220] The fates of the leading representatives of the struggle against Arianism (Athanasius, Marcellus, Eustathius of Antioch, and others), who had been excommunicated and deposed in the East, raised the issue of the finality of synodal judgments. Could their cases could be heard again? Finally, the question arose whether the state could intervene in the proceedings, which would lead to the state carrying out judgments of banishment. The Eastern party had carried out the trial against the head of the Egyptian church and consisted primarily of representatives of the churches of Syria and Asia Minor, while, with the exception of the Melitians, the Egyptian church stood almost unanimously behind Athanasius.

Correspondingly, the synodal letter of Serdica to Pope Julius set the three following points on the agenda: *Tria fuerunt, quae tractanda erant. . . . ante omnia de sancta fide et de integritate ueritatis. . . . secunda de personis. . . . tertia uero quaestio, quae uere quaestio appellanda est. . . .*[221] H. C. Brennecke has presented a plausible case that interpreting the first point of the agenda in terms of Athanasius as a defense of the faith of Nicaea is not convincing, and that in the background of the planned discussion lay the doctrinal statements of Marcellus, which would have been a precondition for the Eastern bishops and their involvement in the question of a synod, as well as for their eventual appearance.[222] The agenda was, however, changed by the Western bishops, who appeared first and who preferred to deal at the outset with the second point, *de personis*, thus following the action of the Roman synod of the prior year and renewing communion with those who had been condemned. The Eastern bishops, who had arrived, demanded that the condemned had to be excluded, at least from these meetings. Their demand was rejected, so they departed the assembly and constituted their own synod in the city's imperial palace.[223] The position of the Westerners had provoked this step. Behind their decision stood a fundamental question of law within the church. Could synodal judgments henceforth be seen as irreversible or could their validity be judged by their reception? Could the West reverse Eastern judgments without the consent of the original synodal judges?[224]

Consequently, the council split even before the beginning of actual dis-

---

220. K. Seibt, *Die Theologie des Markell von Ankyra* (Arbeiten zur Kirchengeschichte 59; Berlin–New York 1994) 241–44.
221. Hilarius, *Collectanea Antiariana Parisina* B II.2.3 (ed. A. L. Feder) = CSEL 65.128.4–11.
222. Brennecke, *Hilarius* 30ff.
223. Not in Philippopolis: cf. Girardet, *Kaisergericht und Bischofsgericht* 113 n. 15.
224. This in Girardet, *Kaisergericht und Bischofsgericht* 116.

cussions. Both rump synods met separately and anathematized the leaders of the other side. After the departure of the Eastern bishops, the Western bishops continued to meet, promulgating canons as well as a theological declaration against eastern Origenism. Their declaration was not accepted. Both synods also made divergent decisions on the calculation of Easter that lasted for the next 50 or 30 years.[225]

The canons in ecclesiastical law passed by the Western bishops present problems in terms of numeration, form, and original language. The numbering of canons not only diverges between the Latin and Greek versions, but even for the Latin text there are various systems of numeration in the literature. The most widely distributed version is the numeration according to Dionysius Exiguus and the *Prisca*, according to which the text is divided into 21 canons with considerable variations. The Greek text brings 20 canons with great variations from the Latin version in the division of the material. Thus canons 10b, 12, and 18 are missing there, while in the Latin version the Greek canons 18 and 19 are missing. From this corpus and form of publication (see below), one can conclude 'that the canons were not originally numbered at all, but formed a continuous record of synodical acts'.[226] C. H. Turner, in his critical edition of what he regards as the original Latin text, introduced yet another system of division, which has the advantage of placing together in one canon material that belongs together.[227] Consequently, his edition has 13 canons. But his numbering has not been adopted in the literature.[228]

The original form in which the canons circulated reveals that this canonical material was shaped under Western influence.[229] The proof of this is that, though the canons of Eastern synods of the fourth century normally have the 'form of order' 'without preserving a trace of the discussion that produced the written product', the canons of Serdica appeared as proposals that the synod accepted, in the course of which extensive justifications, summaries, and proposals for amendments were given.[230] Such

---

225. On the many documents issued by the two synods, cf. ClavisG 8560–74. For the 'Symbolum Serdicense', see Ulrich, *Die Anfänge* 47–91, 96–111. On the calculations of Easter, cf. ClavisG 8574; Hefele-Leclercq, *Histoire* 1.2 p. 804.
226. Hess, *Sardica* 24; earlier reaching an identical conclusion, Turner, 'Genuineness' 374 n. 1.
227. EOMIA 1.2 p.442. The Greek text printed in Turner, EOMIA 1.490–531 does not have an adequate manuscript basis; cf. Schwartz, 'Der griechische Text' 9, 12–19. The model is the edition by Beneševič, *Syntagma* = Joannou.
228. Hess, *Sardica* 137 (Table A), Hess, *Council of Serdica* 210, presents a tabular overview of the numbering systems in use. In what follows, the numeration of Dionysius and the *Prisca* will be preserved. Also in keeping with Hess and for the purpose of simplicity, the Latin version will be designated with Arabic numerals and the Greek with Roman numerals.
229. Cf. in particular Hess, *Sardica* 24–41; Hess, *Council of Serdica* 60–84.
230. Schwartz, 'Kanonensammlungen' 209; similarly, Schwartz, 'Der griechische Text' 5.

a form of publication, presenting the canons as the result of discussion in which the connection with the minutes was preserved, is a distinguishing mark of African synods from the earliest times to the start of the fifth century.[231] The stylistic characteristics of this minute-style include the proposal by a named participant framed as a question (*N. N. episcopus dixit: . . . si omnibus [hoc] placet*) in discursive, informal diction, with the formula of approval added (*placet; placere sibi; omnes episcopi dixerunt*) with the acclamation of the whole synod. Hence the canons of Serdica are formed in groups (canons 1 to 2; 3, 4, and 7; 8 to 12; 14 and 15; 16 and 17) within the minutes of an occasionally interrupted discussion. Canons 12, XVIII, and XIX can hardly be described as canons but rather as concurrent contributions to discussions. If one takes the 23 Latin and Greek canons as a group, 'only thirteen may properly be classed as legislative acts; the other ten are dependent comments or resumés'.[232]

Accepting the theses of P. Batiffol, A. Steinwenter, and H. Gelzer on the parallels between the discussion methods of the Roman Senate and the synods (*relatio—sententia—acclamatio—senatus consultum*), one may see that the canons of Serdica emerge, according to Hess's analysis, as a reflection of this 'parliamentary method'.[233] In view of this discovery one might well conclude that there were never more complete minutes of this council than what is preserved in the canons.[234]

There exists no direct historical evidence for the question thoroughly discussed in the older literature concerning the priority of the Latin or Greek text.[235] Both of the forms of the text are well witnessed, yet each exhibits great differences not only in the order but in content. Each version contains material lacking in the other, with differences which are significant. All of the Latin versions of the text have a single common prototype, but the Greek manuscript versions also agree in their variations from the Latin text.

Due to the work of C. H. Turner and E. Schwartz, it is generally accepted today that the Latin text is closer to the original.[236] Schwartz saw the Greek version as a later translation.[237] Due to the presence of canons XVIII

---

231. Cf. Hess, *Sardica* 26ff; Ohme, *Kanon* 450–77.
232. Hess, *Sardica* 29.
233. P. Batiffol, 'Le règlement des premiers conciles africaines', *Bulletin d'ancienne littérature et d'archéologie chrétiennes* 3 (1913) 3–19; A. Steinwenter, 'Der antike kirchliche Rechtsgang und seine Quellen', ZRG Kan. Abt. 23 (1934) 1–116, 48–49; H. Gelzer, 'Die Konzilien als Reichsparlamente', *Ausgewählte kleine Schriften* (Leipzig 1907) 142–55; Hess, *Sardica* 31–35.
234. Hess, *Sardica* 40.
235. On this question, cf. Hess, *Sardica* 41–48 and Hess, *Council of Serdica* 117–34.
236. Turner, 'Genuineness' 370–97 and Schwartz, 'Der griechische Text'. Cf. Girardet, *Kaisergericht und Bischofsgericht* 111, n. 32; H. Brennecke, 'Rom und der dritte Kanon' 15–45, 19, n. 17.
237. Schwartz, 'Die griechische Text' 18ff., 31.

and XIX, which are found only here, and the special references to the church of Thessalonike, Schwartz concluded that the Greek version was prepared in Thessalonike about 360 or later. The attempt by G. R. von Hankiewicz to establish the priority of the Greek text must be seen as not convincing.[238]

Still, the detailed investigation undertaken by Hamilton Hess, renewing the thesis of the Ballerini assuming an originally double edition, does deserve respect.[239] It is in fact surprising that the Greek text often gives a truer image of the debates.[240] It must be added that among the synodal participants for whom we know their origins, there are about 38 Greek-speakers and 33 Latin-speakers, so that there was a distribution of languages which was truly unique for the synods of the fourth century.[241] While the language of proceedings under the presidency of Ossius was certainly Latin (all of the other synodal documents were composed in Latin), there still must have been a translation during the synod from Latin into Greek, which could be the cause of the unquestionable dependency of the Greek on the Latin text. Hence, according to Hess, the Greek version was a 'set of minutes taken from the Latin debate by a bilingual scribe or, as is more likely, a verbatim record of the proposals as they were repeated by the interpreter'.[242]

The canons of Serdica deal almost exclusively with questions of the office of the bishop.[243] In the course of this legislation, four major themes were addressed:

Translatio (Metathesis). One may hardly speak of an absolute ban on every translation of a bishop in the early church. Ecclesiastically ordered transfers appear to have been common. The canonical ban on translation dealt more with transfers made by oneself or in pursuit of one's own interests.[244] That is also the case with the decisions at Serdica, c. 1 even threatening excommunication for this practice. The background for this appears to be the efforts of Valens of Mursa to win the see of Aquileia, as well as the switch of Eusebius of Nicomedia to the throne at Constantinople. Correspondingly, c. 2 punishes with excommunication any influencing of the election of a bishop. C. 3a dealt with the same issue. It forbade any visit by

---

238. G. R. von Hankewicz, 'Die Kanones von Sardika. Ihre Echtheit und ursprüngliche Gestalt', ZRG Kan. Abt. 2 (1912) 44–99; following him, E. Caspar, 'Kleine Beiträge zur älteren Papstgeschichte, IV. Zur Interpretation der Kanones III–V von Sardika', ZKG 47 (1928) 162–77; I. Gelzer, 'Das Rundschreiben der Synode von Serdika', ZNW 40 (1941) 1–24.

239. Hess, *Sardica* 43–48, 57–61. P. and G. Ballerini, *De antiquis collectionibus et collectoribus canonum* I 5 = PL 56.41–44.

240. Cf. Hess, *Sardica* 43–44.   241. Cf. Ulrich, *Die Anfänge* 91–96.

242. Hess, *Sardica* 47.   243. Except for canons 16, 17, and 20.

244. Hence already Heckrodt, *Sardika* 4–42; Hess, *Sardica* 71–89, follows it; Hess, *Council of Serdica* 162–78.

a bishop to another province without an invitation. A bishop was not to spend more than three weeks in a city not his own (c. 14), and if he visited his own properties located in other provinces, he was to return after three weeks (c. 15). Bishops who receive excommunicated clerics were to report before a synod (c. 16). Canons 18 and 19 opposed the recruiting of clerical candidates in another diocesis. C. 20 regulated the time non-local clergy could stay in Thessalonike, in analogy to c. 14. C. 21 finally made a special rule for the length of residency of bishops who had been deposed over a matter of faith. The translation rules of Serdica relied upon canons 15 and 16 of Nicaea.[245]

Episcopal election.[246] C. 5 deals with the case when a bishop was unwilling to participate in an ordination. The context and terms addressed were entirely different in the Greek and Latin versions. The Greek version appeared to have been altered to fit later conditions.[247] C. 13 regulated the practice of episcopal elections of wealthy men and lawyers. If they were ordained, the preliminary clerical grades were to be bestowed on them in adherence to the rules that governed the proper time required between each grade. Both canons hearken back to canons 2 and 9 of Nicaea.

Appellatio.[248] Without any doubt the so-called 'appeal canons' have in all times attracted the greatest interest, and they play a central role in the question of the historical evidence that anchored Roman claims of primacy. Scholarly interest has been focused on canons 3 b+c, 4, 7, and less on c. 17, which foresaw a chance for appeal by priests and deacons to the bishops of the neighboring province, hence renewing c. 5 of Nicaea. In interpreting the canons first mentioned, what has been said of the form in which the canons circulated should be recalled. One should not look at these three canons as decisions made entirely independently of one another, that produced inevitable contradictions, but rather they must be seen as parts of a single resolution.[249] Consequently, Turner has brought all of these together in his edition into a single 'c. 3'.

In Serdica the following procedure for an appeal was established:[250] (1) In

---

245. See Sebastian Scholz, *Transmigration und Translation: Studien zum Bistumwechsel der Bischöfe von der Spätantike bis zum Hohen Mittelalter* (Kölner Historische Abhandlungen, 37. Cologne-Weimar-Vienna 1992) 31–36.
246. Cf. Heckrodt, *Sardika* 114–22; Hess, *Sardica* 90–108; Hess, *Council of Serdica* 146–61.
247. Hess, *Sardica* 90–100.
248. Cf. on this Girardet, *Kaisergericht und Bischofsgericht* 120–32; Girardet, 'Appelatio' 98–127; Heckrodt, *Sardika* 42–104; Hess, *Council of Serdica* 179–200; Troianos, 'Der Apostolische Stuhl' 243–59.
249. Cf. Hess, *Sardica* 109.
250. Relying on Girardet, 'Appellatio' 117.

a dispute between two bishops, no colleague from a neighboring province may be asked to judge. (2) A bishop who has been condemned by his colleagues within his own province may raise an objection against the judgment. (3) Those who carried out the proceedings (that is, his fellow provincials or the bishops of a neighboring province) may send a report of the objection to the bishop of Rome. (4) The see of the condemned person may not be occupied in the interim. (5) The bishop of Rome, after the review of the case, had two options: (a) if he thought the judgment correct, the judgment is final; (b) if he did not approve the judgment, he can order a *renovatio iudicii* and designate bishops as judges. The new trial would take place before bishops from a neighboring province. At the request of the defendant, the Roman bishop can send additional Roman priests.

With these canons the synod overturned previous legal practices, advocated by Eastern bishops, in which synodal judgments were in principle beyond appeal.[251] This corresponded to the understanding of synodal canons as immediately inspired by the Holy Spirit, so that they could not be reversed by the decisions of another synod. The canon of Serdica, however, created 'an instance for the entire church which made possible a *revocatio iudicii*, which had hitherto not been possible according to the synodal norms governing appeals; this canon also created a court which stood above the level of the province'.[252] The judgment of a synod over a bishop would, in the future, require the concurrence of the Roman bishop. The parallel to this procedure is not an appeal according to the norms of Roman imperial law. Rather the procedure demanded a *retractatio* of lawsuits whose judgments had been rendered by hitherto unappealable judgments. The judicial decisions could be confirmed or retried only through a *supplicatio* to the emperor. This process would not be described as an appeal but as a supplication.[253]

The notion that such rules were not based on the experience of the conflict over Athanasius, as E. Schwartz had argued in retrospect and that the purpose of the canons was only directed to the Western Empire, is generally rejected today.[254]

---

251. Cf., for example, Athanasius, *Apologia secunda* 22.6 (Opitz, 2.104, 18–19).
252. Girardet, *Kaisergericht und Bischofsgericht* 126.
253. First of all, E. Stein, review of Caspar's *Geschichte* 1, in *BZ* 32 (1932) 120; following him, A. Steinwenter, 'Der antike Rechtsgang' 85; L. Wenger, 'Appellation', RAC 1 (1950) 569; most recently, Girardet, *Kaisergericht und Bischofsgericht* 126ff. Troianos, 'Der Apostolische Stuhl' 252, has recently rejected an interpretation that recognized the model of *retractatio*.
254. Supporting this notion and purpose, cf. Schwartz, 'Der griechische Text' and H. Lietzmann, *Geschichte der alten Kirche* 3 (2d ed. Berlin 1953) 200. Rejecting it, cf. Girardet, *Kaisergericht und Bischofsgericht* 125, 129; Brennecke, 'Rom und der dritte Kanon' 20; and Caspar, 'Kleinere Beiträge IV' 165ff.

Episcopal relations with the imperial court. Episcopal petitions to the imperial court were regulated by canons 8 to 12, which hindered dubious and ambitious petitions, defined proper petitions, and clarified the rules of precedure.[255]

The history of the tradition of the canons of Serdica is rich in surprises.[256] It is remarkable that the canons were seen and cited by the Roman church until Dionysius Exiguus as decisions of the Council of Nicaea. The case of the priest Apiarius from Sicca in Numidia, who in 417–18 appealed to Pope Zosimus of Rome against his deposition, was much discussed. Zosimus's legates cited the Serdican canons at the synod of Carthage in 419 (see below) as canons of Nicaea. These 'canons of Nicaea' were, however, utterly unknown in Africa.[257]

The text of the canons appeared to have been unknown outside of the Roman Church before their circulation in the first canonical collections.[258] The practice of attributing canons to Nicaea was common and by no means restricted to the decisions of Serdica.[259] The Greek text was not contained in any Eastern canonical collection before the middle of the sixth century. It is first found in the *Synogoge L titulorum* of John Scholasticus and then in the *Syntagma XIV titulorum*.[260] All later Greek versions depended on these two collections. No direct literary witnesses of an older Greek text are known.

The Synod of Carthage (419)

Sources: C. Munier, *Concilia Africae A. 345–A. 525* (CCL 149; Turnhout 1974) 89–172: *Codex Apiarii causae* (canons 1–33 + *Gesta de nomine Apiarii*), 182–247: *Excerpta ex registro ecclesiae Carthaginensis* (canons 34–133); PL 67.181–230; Mansi 3.699–844; Joannou, CSP 197–436; Rhalles-Potles 3.286–624; Pedalion 462–542.

Translations: English: NPNF 14.441–511; French: Joannou, CSP 197–436.

Literature: G. Bardy, 'Afrique', DDC 1.288–307; F. L. Cross, 'History and Fiction in the African Canons', JTS 12 (1961) 227–47; Hefele-Leclercq *Histoire* 2.1, pp.196–211; Maassen, *Geschichte* 149–85; Jane E. Merdinger, *Rome and the African church in the time of Augustine* (New Haven 1997); Munier, *Concilia Africae* 79–87, 98ff., 173–81; C. Munier, 'Carthage. V. Councils', EEC 146–48; C. Munier, 'Vers une édition nouvelle des Conciles africains (345–525)', *Revue des Études Augustiniennes* 18 (1972) 249–59; Ohme, *Kanon* 460–69; Schwartz, 'Kanonensammlungen' 231–55.

---

255. Cf. Heckrodt, *Sardika* 105, 113; Hess, *Sardica* 128–36; Hess, *Council of Serdica* 201–9.
256. Cf. Hess, *Sardica* 49–67; also below 75 (Carthage, 419).
257. On this case, cf. Brennecke, 'Rom und der dritte Kanon' 15–19; Schwartz, 'Kanonensammlungen' 217ff.; Caspar, *Geschichte* 1.358–60, 365–72; W. Marschall, *Karthago und Rom* (Päpste und Papsttum 1; Stuttgart 1971) 161–204; M. Wojtowytsch, *Papsttum und Konzile von den Anfängen bis Leo I (440–461)* (Päpste und Papsttum 17; Stuttgart 1981) 254–61.
258. For a different interpretation: Brennecke, 'Rom und der dritte Kanon' 25–45.
259. Cf. Hess, *Sardica* 55.
260. See below, Troianos.

The Greek translation of the acts of the African general synod of 25 and 30 May 419 as well as the canons later attributed to it belong to the corpus of Greek canonical collections. The occasion for discussions by the 217 synodal participants under the presidency of Bishop Aurelius of Carthage was the conflict with Roman claims to hear an appeal in the case of the priest Apiarius of Sicca. The acts which are preserved (*Gesta de nomine Apiarii*),[261] including the 33 *Canones Apiarii causae*, also survive complete in the Greek version. Canons 34 to 133 appear to be a private selection of African canonical material from the end of the fifth century. These *Excerpta ex registro ecclesiae Carthaginiensis* were passed on into the Latin tradition separately and were widely distributed.[262] It was only with Dionysius Exiguus that they were ascribed to the acts of the synod of 419 in the second edition of his canonical collection as canons 34 to 133.[263]

In the Greek canonical collections, however, this identical body of acts with 133 canons is first found near the end of the sixth century in the *Syntagma XIV titulorum*.[264] The Quinisext Council (692) confirmed these 'canons of Carthage' in its c. 2. The basis of the Greek translation, whose author and precise date are unknown, was probably the *Dionysiana secunda*. This is vouched for particularly by the numeration, which is largely identical with Dionysius, as well as the ordering of the acts in the Greek tradition. There is also a close literary dependency. It would be the sole example for the use of the Dionysian collections in the Greek East. It is conceivable that there was an early translation by the imperial chancery for relations with the Latin Church in North Africa. Alongside that there appears to have been yet another translation,[265] for the verbatim citation of c. 81 in the *Epistula adversus Theodorum Mopsuestenum* by the Emperor Justinian, about 550. It offers a variant version.[266]

The Synod of Constantinople (394)

Sources: Joannou, CSP 438–44; Beneševič, *Syntagma* 456–59; *Pelagii diaconi ecclesiae Romanae, In defensione Trium Capitulorum*, ed. Robert Devreesse (Studi e Testi 57;

---

261. Munier, *Concilia Africae* 79–172.   262. Munier, *Concilia Africae* 173–247.
263. PL 67.139–230, 181–230; there under the title, *Synodus apud Carthaginem Africanorum, quae constituit canones CXXXVIII*; cf. Munier, *Concilia Africae* 178–81.
264. The statement by Munier, *Concilia Africae* 177, that the *Excerpta* (canons 34 to 133) were already contained in John Scholasticus, *Syntagma L titulorum*, is not true; cf. Beneševič, *Synagoga* 7.258–59.
265. PG 86.1091; E. Schwartz, 'Drei dogmatische Schriften Justinians' (Abh. Akad. 18; Munich 1939; reprinted *Legum Iustiniani imperatoris vocabularium Subsidia* 2, Milan 1973) pp. 68 and 124 respectively.
266. The editors of the Pedalion have made the traditional text unusable through the elimination of portions of acts which seemed to them not to be 'canonical', as well as through transposition, construction of novel 'canons', and a singular numeration. For their justification, see Pedalion 163, n. 4; there is a synopsis of the numeration in Joannou, CSP 193.

Rome 1932) 9–11; Pitra, *Juris* 2.162–65; Pedalion 461–62; Rhalles-Potles 3.625–28; ClavisG 8606.

Translations: English: *Rudder* 601ff.; NPNF 14.511–13; French: Joannou, CSP 438–44; Hefele-Leclercq *Histoire* (see below).

Literature: C. de Clercq, 'Les conciles de Constantinople de 326 à 715', *Apollinaris* 34 (1961) 345–68; L. Duchesne, 'Le pape Sirice et le siège de Bostra', *Annales de philosophie chrétienne* 111 (1885) 280–84; Hefele-Leclercq 2.1, pp. 97–100; E. Honigmann, *Trois mémoires posthumes d'histoire et de géographie de l'Orient Chrétien* (Subsidia hagiographica 35; Brussels 1961) 3–48; BISA.

It is only with the *Syntagma XIV titulorum* that Greek canonical collections transmitted an excerpt of the proceedings from the acts of the Constantinople synod of 394.[267] L. Duchesne (see above) discovered further fragments of these proceedings in Pope Pelagius I's (556–61) memorandum on the dispute over the Three Chapters in the Orléans, Bibliothèque muncipale (*Codex Aurelianensis*) 73 (70).[268] Even when joined in proper sequence,[269] the two parts appear to constitute only a fragment of a single session of the council.

We can learn from the Greek excerpt of the proceedings that the synod had assembled in the baptistry of the 'Church of Constantinople' on 29 September 394 under Arcadius and Honorius, hence still under Theodosius I. Pelagius added that this was done on the summons of the *praefectus praetorio* Rufinus on the occasion of the consecration of the Church of the Apostles which he had established. Hence this is a dedication synod similar to that of Antioch (341) and Tyre (335); in time it would be called the 'synod of Rufinus'. Emperor Theodosius had placed Rufinus at the side of his son Arcadius as regent for the Eastern Empire.

The proceedings cite 20 participants by name, in the first place Nectarius of Constantinople, Theophilus of Alexandria, and Flavian of Antioch, and among the others there are Gelasius of Caesarea in Palestine, Gregory of Nyssa, Amphilochius of Iconium and Theodore of Mopsuestia, all holders of metropolitan sees, as well as 'various other bishops'.[270] Pelagius knew of 37 bishops in all. Since almost all Eastern churches were represented, one might speak of a general council of the East. It had, however, not been called by the emperor.

The occasion for the gathering was the schism arising before 381 in the

267. Beneševič, *Syntagma* 456–59; Beneševič, *Sbornik* 86–87; cf. on that Honigmann, *Trois mémoires* 7–8; on the *Syntagma* see below, Troianos. Lemma: Ἐκ τῶν πραχθέντων ὑπομνημάτων ἐν Κωνσταντινουπόλει περὶ Ἀγαπίου καὶ Γαβαδίου, ἑκατέρου ἀντεχομένου τῆς ἐπισκοπῆς Βόστρης (Joannou, CSP 438).

268. Cf. Duchesne, 'Le pape Sirice'; cf. now the critical edition in Devreesse, *Pelagii*.

269. Cf. Honigmann, *Trois mémoires* 11–16.

270. Joannou, CSP 439–40; in detail, cf. E. Gerland and V. Laurent, *Les listes conciliaires* (Le Patriarcat byzantin II: Corpus Notitiarum Episcopatuum I; Kadiköy 1936) 1–8; Honigmann, *Trois mémoires* 12–13, 26–44.

Arabian ecclesiastical province. The former occupant of the metropolitan see of Bostra, Gabadius, disputed the legitimacy of the present metropolitan, Agapius.²⁷¹ The minutes mention that Gabadius had been deposed by two bishops, since deceased, and that Agapius had been raised in his place.²⁷² In Pelagius the names of Palladius and Cyril are found. Duchesne (see above) believed this latter name is Cyril of Jerusalem († 386).

Pelagius went on to report that both opponents appealed to Pope Siricius (384–99), who had referred them to Theophilus of Alexandria until the matter finally came before the synod of Constantinople. It is surprising that the case apparently was tried neither in Antioch nor in a synod of the diocese of Oriens. One can infer from that a greater independence, even insubordination, of the metropolitans there toward the see of Antioch. The long-enduring schism in Antioch in the fourth century makes this understandable. Duchesne had wanted to see in the appeal to Rome an application of the 'appeal canons' of Serdica (see above).²⁷³ Theophilus of Alexandria actually did play a leading role in the discussions.

The entire proceeding documented ten votes by Nectarius, Arabianus of Ancyra, Theophilus, and Flavian. The result was that the synod, citing the council of Nicaea, forbade that a bishop be deposed or be consecrated by two bishops. This was to be possible only through the act of a larger provincial synod, 'as the Apostolic Canons have ruled'. Apparently this is a citation of c. 74 of the Apostolic Canons. Nectarius passed the proposal of Theophilus in the form of a legal decision, to which the council gave its approval.

The Greek manuscripts transmitted their excerpt of the proceedings under the rubric of Κανών. Nikodemos Hagiorites (= Pedalion), who did not see this form of publication as proper for a 'canon', took two substantive sentences beginning with 'ὁρίζομεν' and called them Κανών Α' and Β' (= the proposal of Nectarius).

The Synod of Constantinople (691/2) (Quinisext Council)

Sources: COGD 219–93; Joannou, CCO 101–241 (Logos Prosphonetikos and canons); Ohme, *Quinisextum* 145–70 (subscription list); *Trullo Revisited* 41–186; Mansi 11.921–1006; Rhalles-Potles 2.295–554; Pitra, *Juris* 2.14–72; Lauchert 97–139; Pedalion 215–313.

Translations: English: *Trullo Revisited* 41–186; NPNF 14.359–65; *Rudder* 283–413; French: Joannou, CCO 101–241; German: Ohme, *Konzil* 169–293.

Literature: E. Brunet, 'Concilio Quinisesto (692): Recezione nelle fonti occidentali (VII–IX secc.),' Dissertation Turin 2008; Demetrios J. Constantelos, *Renewing the Church: The*

---

271. The lists of the Second Ecumenical Council already contain both names. Cf. Honigmann, *Trois mémoires* 9. The Latin tradition has 'Bagadius'. The original name was probably Badagios, cf. Honigmann, *Trois mémoires* 28ff.

272. Joannou, CSP 440.18ff.   273. Duchesne, 'Le pape Sirice' 281.

Significance of the Council in Trullo (Brookline, MA 2006); R. Flogaus, 'Das Concilium Quinisextum (691/2). Neue Erkenntnisse über ein umstrittenes Konzil und seine Teilnehmer', ByZ 102 (2009) 25–64; G. Fritz, 'Quinisexte (concile) ou in Trullo', DThC 13 (1937) 1581–97; Hefele-Leclercq *Histoire* 3.1 pp. 560–78; I. M. Konidaris, 'Das Mönchtum im Spiegel der Penthekte', AHC 24 (1992) 273–85; Peter Landau, 'Überlieferung und Bedeutung der Kanones des Trullanischen Konzils im westlichen kanonischen Recht', *Trullo Revisited* 215–27; V. Laurent, 'L'œuvre canonique du Concile de Trullo (691–692): Source primaire du droit de l'église orientale', REB 23 (1965) 7–41; George Nedungatt and S. Agrestini, COGD 205–215; *Trullo Revisited*; H. Ohme, *Konzil*; Ohme, *Quinisextum*; H. Ohme, 'Das Quinisextum auf dem VII. ökumenischen Konzil', AHC 20 (1988) 326–44; H. Ohme, 'Zum Konzilsbegriff des Concilium Quinisextum', AHC 24 (1992) 112–26; H. Ohme, 'Das Concilium Quinisextum—Neue Einsichten zu einem umstrittenden Konzil', OCP 58 (1992) 367–400; H. Ohme, 'In tempore. Weichenstellungen für die Edition des Concilium Quinisextum', AHC 41 (2009) 1–68; J.-M. Sansterre, 'Le Pape Constantin Ier (708–715) et la politique religieuse des Empereurs Justinien II et Philippikos', *Archivum historiae pontificiae* 22 (1984) 7–30; S. N. Troianos, 'Die Wirkungsgeschichte des Trullanum (Quinisextum) in der byzantinischen Gesetzgebung', AHC 24 (1992) 95–111; H.-J. Vogt, 'Zur Ekklesiologie des Trullanums', AHC 24 (1992) 127–44; BISA.

Emperor Justinian II (685–95, 705–11) called a synod in 691–92,[274] which met in the domed hall (Trullos) of the imperial palace in Constantinople to fill the canonical gaps left by the Fifth and Sixth Ecumenical Councils.[275] Other than the *Liber Pontificalis* (see below), the sole source of information about this council consists of the conciliar acts. Other Greek and Latin sources for this period either do not waste a word on the council or mention it only in passing.[276]

Besides the canons and the episcopal subscription list, the acts include the address of the council fathers to the emperor, the so-called *Logos Prosphonetikos*.[277] From this it can be learned that the emperor himself had taken the initiative for this synod;[278] the bishops had gathered at his command,[279] and the council had assembled as a 'holy and ecumenical' council.[280] The motivation for bringing the council into being was also declared.[281]

---

274. The date can be determined from the chronological information in c.3. It can only be limited to the period between 1 September 691 and 31 August 692. A session in early summer, 692, after Lent, Easter festivities, and the storms of the early part of the year is likely. On the dating question, cf. V. Peri, 'Introduction', *Trullo Revisited* 18–20. It is not compelling to date it between 1 September 691 and 31 December 691 (contrary to Menevisoglou, Ἱστορικὴ 281).

275. From these basic facts arise the usual nomenclature which is used here, which is Trullanum, the Council in the Trullos, Quinisextum, Pentheke.

276. Cf. Ohme, *Concilium Quinisextum* 8–25.

277. From this council we have only conciliar acts in the narrow sense and no proceedings. One may not argue that the actual proceedings have been lost. This has been shown by E. Chrysos in his distinction between the protocol of decisions by non-judicial synods and the procedural minutes of synods with court hearings.

278. Cf. Ohme, *Concilium Quinisextum* 28–35. 279. Joannou, CCO 110.19; 110.8; 110.10.

280. Joannou, CCO 109.11ff.; 101.17; cf. canons 3 and 51: CCO 125.18–19; 188.12–13.

281. The situation of the people of God had grown lamentable, had been torn into disorder and brought to a fall. The remnants of heathen and Jewish religions had been allowed to flourish like weeds: Joannou, CCO 109.17–18.

The critical edition of the subscription list and the forthcoming edition of the Acts for *Acta conciliorum oecumenicorum* permit us for the first time to make definitive statements on the number of participants.[282] Of the 226 or 227 participants, 190 bishops came from the provinces of the patriarchate of Constantinople, 10 came from Illyricum orientale; the Alexandrian patriarch, 24 Antiochenes, and 2 representatives of Jerusalem represented the three Eastern patriachates. Six places were left open for later signatures. Beyond that the list reveals significant alterations in the hierarchical sequence of subscribers, and it provides an answer to the question of Roman participation. Here we appear to have an early attempt to promote at the level of a conciliar proceeding the incorporation of East Illyricum into the jurisdiction of Constantinople.[283] The small Western participation in the Trullan Council is not unique among early councils. The reason why few Western clerics participated could have been the generally altered circumstances in the Balkans and Italy that had arisen from the migrations during the sixth and seventh centuries.[284]

The signature of the metropolitan of Crete, Basil of Gortyna,[285] has been seen in the Orthodox tradition since Balsamon as a sign of Roman participation at the Quinisext, even of its approval.[286] But Basil was no Roman *apocrisiarius*;[287] rather he had been co-opted into the Roman synodal delegation of 125 bishops in the course of the Sixth Ecumenical Council. He continued to use the style of signature he had given there. He was no papal legate and cannot have had a papal delegation of plenipotentiary powers. Therefore, the Roman see was not represented at the Trullan Council through papal legates.

The 102 canons constituted the actual work of the council and in some ways the final stage in the development of canon law of the early church. This was an attempt to reorder the spiritual and moral life of the church with ecclesiastical law, arising out of an emergency in which Christian life and communities were being subjected to severe stress. The disasters suf-

---

282. Cf. Ohme, *Concilium Quinisextum*, 77–176, 177–344; Flogaus, 'Das Concilium Quinisextum 25–48; Ohme, 'In tempore' 3–8.
283. This was a development whose conclusion is generally placed in the 730s, even though the time and process of final incorporation remains unclarified.
284. Cf. especially Georg Ostrogorsky, 'The Byzantine Empire in the World of the Seventh Century', (Dumbarton Oaks Papers 13; Washington 1959; reprinted in 'Zur Byzantinischen Geschichte', *Ausgewählte kleine Schriften* [Darmstadt 1973] 87); J. F. Haldon, *Byzantium in the Seventh Century* (Cambridge 1990) 21, 32, 43–45.
285. Βασίλειος ἐπίσκοπος τῆς Γορτυνέων μητροπόλεως τῆς φιλοχρίστου Κρήτης νήσου καὶ τὸν τόπον ἐπέχων πάσης τῆς συνόδου τῆς ἁγίας ἐκκλησίας Ῥώμης ὁρίσας ὑπέγραψα, cf. Ohme, *Concilium Quinisextum* 146, n. 15.
286. Cf. Ohme, *Concilium Quinisextum* 235–51.
287. *Contra* Laurent, 'L'Œuvre canonique' 14–15.

fered by the Byzantine Empire in the course of the seventh century constitute the historical background.[288]

Canons 62, 65, 71, and 94 actually enumerated a plethora of festivals, customs, and rites from the pre-Christian, Hellenistic cycle of festivities which continued to be practiced, besides occultism and mantic practices (canons 60 and 61).[289] Relations with Jews was the theme of c. 11. Public morality was also the object of bans on extensive pomp, on pornography, and on abortion, as well as the ban on sexual intercourse with nuns (canons 96, 100, 91, 4). Pimping was denounced (c. 86). Bathing of men and women together was banned (c. 77), as well as dice-playing (c. 50) and various forms of popular entertainment (c. 51). All public spectacles in the week following Easter were forbidden (c. 66).

In order to protect the sacred from profanation, holy places were not to be polluted by sexual intercourse (c. 97). No cattle were to be kept in churches (c. 88), and no inns were to be kept in their vicinity (c. 76). Even *agapes* were forbidden in the area of a church (c. 74). The cross was forbidden to be used as decoration on the floor (c. 73); similarly, the representation of Christ as a lamb (c. 82). The penalty for the destruction of holy books is excommunication (c. 68). The ban on laymen entering the area of the altar—with the exception of the emperor (c. 69)—and the renewal of the ban against secularizing religious houses (c. 49) were both designed to protect ecclesiastical areas.

Clerics were commanded to participate in Sunday services under the threat of deposition (c. 80). There was also a ban on clerics running taverns or loaning money (canons 9 and 10). They were enjoined not to participate in popular entertainments (c. 24). Further the synod regulated the ages of consecration (canons 14 and 15), the number of deacons in one city (c. 16), their rank behind the priests (c. 7), the tonsure (c. 21), and the wearing of special clothing (c. 27). C. 33 set conditions for ordination and condemned the Armenian practice of taking clergy only from clerical families. C. 17 ruled against translation; emigrated clerics should return to their congregations if conditions allowed (c. 18). Simony in ordination (c. 22) and in communion (c. 23) were threatened with deposition, as was conspiracy against the bishop (c. 34). A ban on living with women who are not above suspicion was renewed once more for priests in c. 5, as was any marriage after ordination (c. 6). Regulations in the case of a second mar-

---

288. Cf. John F. Haldon, *Byzantium in the Seventh Century: The Transformation of a Culture* (Cambridge 1990) 41–90.

289. For all canons of the Quinisext Council see now the commentary of H. Ohme, *Konzil* 35–157.

riage or impermissible marriage for clergy were establsihed by canons 3 and 26. A general imposition of celibacy was rejected, against the Roman practice (c. 13), but abstention is required when a priest said Mass. Priests living among the barbarians were permitted the oath of celibacy as an exception (c. 30). Yet bishops were held to celibacy, and they were forbidden to continue living with their wives (c. 12); the wives were to enter religious houses (c. 48). Bishops were not permitted to preach outside their own dioceses (c. 20), but within their dioceses they were required to do so daily, especially on Sundays. The definitions of synods and the doctrines of the Fathers are to be their standard (c. 19). Metropolitans were forbidden to seize the property of deceased bishops (c. 35).

For the reordering of the monastic life: monastic life was open to every Christian (c. 43). The age of entering a religious house may not be below ten years (c. 40). Further regulations dealt with cloistering (canons 46 and 47), tonsure (c. 45), breaking of the oath (c. 44), and with the eremitic life (canons 41 and 42).

On sacramental practice and care of souls: baptizing in private chapels was fundamentally forbidden (c. 59). The repetition of baptism in case of uncertainty was made possible by c. 84. Catechumens should learn everything about the Christian faith and display it to the bishop or priests (c. 78). C. 95 thoroughly renewed and supplemented rules for the rebaptism and the reception of heretics. Communion bestowed by hand was obligatory for all (c. 101). Self-communion for laymen was forbidden (c. 58), and dead persons must be given the eucharist under no circumstances (c. 83). C. 102 established a therapeutically understood practice of confession and guidance of souls.

Canons 53, 54, 87, 92, and 98 gave decisions concerning marital law.

For ordering the time of fasting: c. 56 opposed the Armenian usage, and c. 55 the Roman custom (see below); the church of the entire 'oikumene' should follow the same order.

For liturgical order: c. 52 regulated the liturgy of the presanctified. C. 32 condemned the Armenian practice of using wine for the Eucharist without mixing it with water. Canons 28 and 57 opposed the combination of grapes as well as honey and milk with the eucharist. C. 99 opposed the Armenian practice of bringing meat to the altar. There was a ban on laymen preaching and teaching in public (c. 64). Women were to remain totally silent during the divine liturgy (c. 70). Decisions on choir singers (c. 75), the Trisagion (c. 81), genuflection (c. 90), and the celebration of 'Mary's childbed' (c. 79) were also included in the conciliar decisions.

On the constitution of the church: the ecclesiastical rank of a city was determined by its civil status (c. 38); the established appropriation of a rural congregation to one eparchy should remain inviolate (c. 25). Provincial synods were to be held twice a year and at least once a year in difficult circumstances (c. 8). The rights of bishops who were unable to occupy the seat of their diocese due to barbarian conquests were regulated by c. 37. A special regulation for the exile of the archbishop of Cyprus along with his people in the eparchy of Hellespontus was the subject of c. 39.

It is clear that a large number of canons renewed or modified older decisions.[290] Particular canons have been seen as the reason for the rejection of the council by Rome. The listing of the canons in question takes up a large part of the scholarly literature.[291] It is certain that some of the canons were unacceptable to Rome, since they explicitly threatened clerics with deposition and excommunication if they followed the Roman practice of celibacy (c. 13)[292] and the Roman urban practice of the Saturday fast in Lent (c. 55). Similarly, in c. 2—the first listing of the sources of the canon law of the ancient church—Western local synods (with the exception of Serdica and Carthage) were ignored, and all 85 'Apostolic Canons' were accepted. In addition there was the condescending permission granting celibacy to priests in 'barbarian churches' (c. 30) and the ban on the consumption of blood (c. 67). C. 36 also 'touches a hot button' by renewing c. 3 of the Second Ecumenical Council and c. 28 of Chalcedon by ruling that the See of Constantinople should enjoy the same rights of honor as old Rome and rank in the second place behind it.[293]

The sole sources, other than acts of the councils, that are available to us on the conflict which arose between Rome and Constantinople over the Quinisext, are the entries in the *Liber Pontificalis*.[294] In the *vitae* of Popes Sergius I (687–701), John VII (705–7), Constantinus I (708–15), and Gregory II (715–31),[295] the *Liber Pontificalis* reports that Justinian II made three attempts to bring about a reception of the canons by the Roman see.[296] Pope Sergius I not only refused to receive the *tomoi* and to have them read publicly, but he even rejected them as invalid.[297] John VII did not accept Justinian's proposal 'to gather a council of the Apostolic Church and to confirm

---

290. Cf. Menevisoglou, Ἰστορικὴ 294–95.
291. Cf. H. Ohme, 'Die sogenannten "antirömischen" Kanones des Concilium Quinisextum', *Trullo Revisited* 307–22.
292. Cf. C. Pitsakis, 'Clergé marié et célibat dans la législation du concile à Trullo: Le point de vue orientale', *Trullo Revisited* 263–306.
293. Joannou, CCO 170.10ff.
294. *Liber Pontificalis*, ed. L. Duchesne (Paris 1886, 1955) 3 volumes.
295. *Liber Pontificalis* 371–76; 385–86; 389–93; 396.
296. Cf. Ohme, *Concilium Quinisextum* 55–76; Ohme, 'In tempore' 12–26; Sansterre, 'Jean VII' ; Sansterre, 'Le Pape Constantin Ier'.
297. *Liber Pontificalis* 1.373.6–7.

what he approved and to reject and declare invalid what he disapproved'. He sent the acts back to the emperor without alteration.²⁹⁸ It was only with Constantinus I, who himself traveled to Constantinople for this purpose, that an agreement over the Quinisext was reached in Nicomedia, satisfying both parties.²⁹⁹ Constantinus would accept only those canons that did not oppose Roman usage.³⁰⁰ It is likely that the Roman Church achieved a dispensation from the application of the canons in question. Yet Constantinus did recognize their validity.³⁰¹ The renewal of Roman privileges stressed by the *Liber Pontificalis* certainly makes this concession possible. C. 36 also conceded a certain primacy to Rome. Further 'privileges' might have been a confirmation of Roman jurisdiction over the see of Ravenna and a renewal of tax privileges for the papal patrimony.³⁰²

Yet the conflict over the Trullan Council is not primarily to be understood on the basis of its canonical material. This emerged into the foreground only later. Over the course of the seventh and eighth centuries, if not longer, there was a readiness to compromise.³⁰³ The Roman popes' refusal to sign appears to have been dominated by the following motives: (1) the ranking of the bishops of Illyricum orientale in the subscription list; and (2) the conciliar procedure and the idea of an ecumenical council embodied in the synod.³⁰⁴ According to this model, the criteria for an ecumenical council would appear to consist in the bishops of the entire territory of the Roman state being present or represented in response to an imperial command, and that matters of faith should be the subject of discussion. It was assumed that the Roman bishop would add his signature after the fact, after the canons had already been given force of law by the subscription of the emperor.

In 1054, the Quinisext Council served spokesmen for ecclesiastical polem-

298. *Liber Pontificalis* 1.386.1–3.
299. On this there is general consensus. Cf. H. Ohme, 'Die Beziehungen zwischen Rom und Konstantinopel am Ende des 7. Jahrhunderts', AHC 38 (2006) 55–72; Ohme, *Concilium Quinisextum* 73–74; Laurent, 'L'oeuvre canonique' 34–35; Sansterre, 'Le Pape Constantin Ier' 13–20; Peri, 'Introduction', *Trullo Revisited* 30–35.
300. There is no proof for the imputation that Justinian II suspended the canons offensive to Rome and effectively accepted their rejection by the pope. This thesis is found again in Laurent, 'L'œuvre canonique' 34–35; Sansterre ('Le pape Constantin Ier' 15–18) has made it clear in retrospect that this is not tenable.
301. Sansterre ('Le Pape Constantin Ier' 20–21) does not even wish to exclude c.36 from this. Earlier, Caspar speculated that 'not the least was changed' in the canons (*Geschichte* 2.640).
302. *Liber Pontificalis* 1.369; cf. C. Head, *Justinian II of Byzantium* (Madison 1972) 62; Sansterre, 'Le Pape Constantin Ier' 21 n. 87.
303. On the importance of the Quinisext for Rome in the struggle against iconoclasm, cf. Ohme, 'Das Quinisextum auf dem VII. Ökumenischen Konzil'.
304. Cf. on this, in detail, Ohme, *Concilium Quinisextum* 195–216, 345–88; H. Ohme, 'Zum Konzilbegriff des Concilium Quinisextum', AHC 20 (1992) 112–26; H.J. Sieben, *Die Konzilsidee in der Alten Kirche* (Paderborn 1979) 319ff., 357–79.

ics on both sides as a justification for schism. Niketas Stethatos attacked, using the Trullan canons against azyma, the Western practice of fasting, and celibacy, and demanded that they be observed.³⁰⁵ Cardinal Humbert rejected all of these canons on behalf of the Latin Church, since Rome had supposedly never accepted them and had never obeyed them, and because they were invalid and depraved.³⁰⁶

Theologians in the Byzantine Empire subsequently stressed the ecumenical status and the autonomy of this synod. As a result, the great canonists of the twelfth century, John Zonaras and Theodore Balsamon, stressed the ecumenical status of the Quinisext.³⁰⁷ It was, however, Matthew Blastares who drew the last consequence from its ecumenical status and gave it an extensive section in his *Syntagma* of 1335 with the title 'Holy and Ecumenical Council'.³⁰⁸ This has remained the usual evaluation of the Trullan Council in Orthodox theology to the present day.

The *Canons of the Fathers*

Origin and Content

Literature: G. Bardy, 'Épîtres canoniques des Pères', DDC 5.380–84; Joannou, CPG xiv–xxv (Introduction générale à l'édition t. II); C. Munier, *Les sources patristiques du droit du VIIIᵉ–XIIIᵉ siècle* (Mulhouse 1957); Schwartz, *Bußstufen* 274–362; Schwartz, 'Kanonensammlungen'.

Alongside the synodal canons, the canons of the fathers make up a significant portion of Greek canonical collections. C. 2 of the Quinisext Council (691/2) sealed (ἐπισφραγίζομεν) the 'canons established by our holy and blessed Fathers', and alongside the synodal canons gave the names of 13 Fathers with their episcopal titles.³⁰⁹ It is surprising that there is no additional information about which writings or canons of the various Fathers are referred to. From this, one might conclude that clarity about which fathers' writings were authoritative prevailed among the synodal participants in the Quinisext and in the Byzantine Church at the end of the seventh century.³¹⁰ However, a comparison of the list of Fathers

---

305. In his *Dialexis*. Cf. A. Michel, *Humbert und Kerullarios. Quellen und Studien zum Schisma des XI. Jahrhunderts* (Paderborn 1924, 1930) 2.333.15ff.; 335.14ff.; 337.1ff.; 339.20ff.

306. 'Capitula quae nobis sub ejus (scil. sextae synodis) auctoritate opponitis omnino refutamus, quia prima et apostolica sedes nec aliquando ea accepit nec observat hactenus; et quia aut sunt nulla, aut ut nobis libuit, depravata sunt' (PG 120.1030A). But cf. P. Landau, 'Überlieferung und Bedeutung der Kanones des Trullanischen Konzils im westlichen kanonischen Recht', *Trullo Revisited* 215–28; Brunet, 'Concilio Quinisesto'.

307. They deal with the theme, however, under the title, Περὶ τῆς λεγομένης ἕκτης συνόδου, cf. Rhalles-Potles 2.294, 300ff.

308. Περὶ τῆς ἁγίας καὶ οἰκουμενικῆς πενθέκτης Συνόδου, Rhalles-Potles 6.23–24.

309. Joannou, CCO 123.7–124.16.

310. P. Menevisoglou (Οἱ πατερικοὶ κανόνες καὶ ἕτερα 'κανονικὰ κείμενα' ἐν ταῖς κανονικαῖς

cap. 2 Quinisextum	Nomokanon	Pedalion	Rhalles-Potles
Dionysius of Alexandria	Dionysius of Alexandria	Dionysius of Alexandria	Dionysius of Alexandria
Peter of Alexandria	Peter of Alexandria	Gregory Thaumaturgus	Peter of Alexandria
Gregory Thaumaturgus	Gregory Thaumaturgus	Peter of Alexandria	Gregory Thaumaturgus
Athanasius		Athanasius	Athanasius
Basilius	Basilius	Basilius	Basilius
Gregory of Nyssa	Gregory of Nyssa	Gregory of Nyssa	Gregory of Nyssa
Gregory of Nazianzius		Gregory of Nazianzius	Gregory of Nazianzius
Amphilochius of Iconium		Amphilochius of Iconium	Theophilus of Alexandria
Timothy of Alexandria	Timothy of Alexandria	Timothy of Alexandria	Cyril of Alexandria
Theophilus of Alexandria	Theophilus of Alexandria	Theophilus of Alexandria	Gregory of Nazianzus
Cyril of Alexandria	Cyril of Alexandria	Cyril of Alexandria	Amphilochius of Iconium
Gennadius of Constantinople	Gennadius of Constantinople	Gennadius of Constantinople	Gennadius of Constantinople
Cyprian of Carthage		John the Faster and others	Tarasius of Constantinople

in c. 2 of the Quinisext with the Fathers listed in the so-called *Nomokanon* of Photius,[311] in the Pedalion, and in Rhalles-Potles still makes it clear that the content and sequence of the canons of the Fathers, even after the Quinisext, had not yet been settled and finally clarified.[312]

συλλογαῖς', *Kleronomia* 14 [1982] 125–61) has made the attempt, using the Patmos, Monastic Library (Codex Patmiacus) 172 (ninth century), which, according to Beneševič (*Sbornik* 230–42), represents the *recensio trullana* of the *Syntagma XIV titulorum*, to define the concrete corpus of canons of the Fathers described in c.2 of the Quinisext. Whether this can be done with a manuscript of the ninth century, in which text the canons of the Quinisext are already contained, has to be questioned. One would hardly end up with a corpus of the canon of the Fathers identical to the first version of the *Syntagma*.

311. According to Rhalles-Potles 1.10–11, it is an early version of the *Syntagma XIV titulorum*.

312. A restriction of the 'canons of the Fathers' to the corpus of the Quinisextum and an essential distinction between these and other 'canonical texts' ('κανονικὰ κείμενα') for which

Later additions found in the Pedalion and in Rhalles-Potles will be dealt with later in another place.[313] So far as the ordering of the Fathers is concerned, the surprising part is that Peter of Alexandria and Gregory Thaumaturgus exchange places, and Timothy of Alexandria, Theophilus of Alexandria, and Cyril form a solid traditional block which is, however, variously sequenced. The so-called *Nomokanon* of Photius lacked Athanasius, Gregory of Nazianzus, and Amphilochius.

P.-P. Joannou referred to the fact that most manuscripts of canonical collections prior to the twelfth century fail to confirm the content and sequence of Quinisext c. 2. In some manuscripts Gregory of Nazianzus is missing, and/or Amphilochius; however, others are added. Other manuscripts do not contain Gennadius. Sometimes, the sequence in general is altered, or the Fathers are included only in part.[314] Even as late as the eleventh century, Michael Psellus (1018–78) (who was a close friend of the learned jurist and later Patriarch John VIII Xiphilinus) knew only Dionysius, Gregory the Thaumaturgus, Timothy of Alexandria, Cyril, and Gennadius, as well as the 68 (!) canons of Basil the Great.[315] To be sure, he also did not mention the Quinisext Council. One may only agree with Joannou's conclusion that c. 2 Quinisext was only generally accepted in the twelfth century, and only after then may one speak of a relatively stable corpus and sequence of the Canons of the Fathers in the Eastern Church. This conclusion corresponds with what is known of the acceptance of the Quinisext Council itself, which was only completely contained in the collections of the twelfth-century canonists.[316]

Evaluating the opinions of significant theologians and Fathers of the Early Church as 'canons' and incorporating them into the collections of synodal canons must be understood as a long-developing process in which various local churches received this material differently, and their collections did not conform to a uniform pattern of acceptance. Hence the *Synagoga* of John Scholasticus (Patriarch of Constantinople, 565–77) contained, alongside the Canons of the Apostles and the synodal canons through c. 27 of Chalcedon, only material from the letters of Basil the Great.[317] What E. Schwartz

---

there is no synodal confirmation (such as in Menevisoglou, Ὁι πατερικοὶ κανόνες' 140–61) must be left to Orthodox dogmatics. This thesis cannot be supported by the corpus of Byzantine canonistic collection manuscripts (see below).

313. See below.

314. ClavisG, Introduction, xv–xvi; on the manuscripts individually, cf. ClavisG notes 16–20 and pages xix–xxi. In the incomplete manuscripts of his group 'C', Joannou sees represented the oldest canonistic corpus.

315. PG 122.921 BC (*Oblatio Nomocanonis ad Imp. Michaelem Ducam*).

316. Cf. Ohme, *Concilium Quinisextum* 332–44.

317. Beneševič, *Synagoga* 219, 249. The *Synagoga* contains 68 canons of Basil.

has called the 'Collection of Theodosius Diaconus' in Verona, Biblioteca Captiolare (Codex Veronensis) LX (seventh century), probably compiled about 367–68 in Alexandria,[318] contained no canons of the fathers whatsoever. This, however, is to be understood from their character as a dossier of acts from the archives of the Alexandrian See concerning the story of Athanasius. The principle purpose of the collection was not canonical or historical, but a dossier for a concrete issue of ecclesiastical politics.

Yet, the pre-Chalcedonian *corpus canonum* of the Greek imperial church, which was translated into Syriac about 500 in Hierapolis-Mabbug and preserved only in this form, and incorporated into later sixth-century collections, also contained no canons of the fathers.[319] From this Syriac tradition, as well as from the corresponding Latin tradition in what is called the 'Freising-Würzburg Version',[320] it has been concluded that it is 'a certainty that the oldest canonical collections contained no canons of the fathers, but only the canons of councils'.[321] It is only with the Paris, BNF syr. (Codex Parisinus syrus) 62 (ninth century) that we find a collection that adds the *Canons of the Fathers* to the canons of the councils. E. Schwartz thought that this collection is much older than the sixth century, and since Chalcedon follows the *Canons of the Fathers*, and he concluded that it predates Chalcedon.[322] The collection certainly provides the first evidence for a collection of the canons of the fathers. It consists of the following pieces:

1. Excerpts from the letters of Ignatius of Antioch.
2. Excerpts from the 'Logos' of Peter of Alexandria on *lapsi*, in a more complete version than what was received in Greek canonical collections.
3. The 15 'Erotapokriseis' of Timothy of Alexandria.
4. Letter of Athanasius to Ammun.
5. Basil: Letter 55 to Gregory the priest; Letter 53 to the bishops; Letter 160 to Diodorus; Letters 188, 199, 217 in this particular sequence.

On the one hand, this corpus can serve as evidence for how disparate such collections were at the beginning; Ignatius was not placed in the later collections. On the other hand, it is also an indication that the process of collecting and adding the canons of the fathers to synodal canons must have begun between 381 and 451.

Almost all the canons of the fathers consist of letters or occasional

---

318. Cf. Schwartz, 'Die Sammlung des Theodosius Diaconus (1904)', *Gesammelte Schriften* 3.30–72, 71 (= Cod. θ in EOMIA 1.xii).
319. Cf. Schwartz, 'Kanonensammlungen' 159–76.
320. Schwartz, 'Kanonensammlungen' 169–75.
321. Schwartz, *Bußstufen* 322.
322. Schwartz, *Bußstufen* 322ff.

writings directed to specific persons; they contain addressees and senders and often include proems and epilogues. One exception is the letter of Peter of Alexandria, which is only excerpted. Other exceptions include the metric index of the scriptural canon of Gregory of Nazianzus and Amphilochius, the 'Erotapokriseis' of Timothy of Alexandria, and the excerpts from the *De Spiritu Sancto* in canons 91 and 92 of Basil.

The titles of the canons into which the letters were later distributed were originally summaries of the entire canon, descriptions of its circumstance, or even a record of the penance imposed. These resumés were at first written in the margin of the text, often introduced by σημείωσον or τί φησί περί or τί τὸ. It was only later that these glosses were incorporated into the text, thus dividing it into paragraphs or 'canons'. Finally, numeration was added. Since numeration is virtually uniform in the manuscripts, it may be assumed that it was old and that the texts were taken into the collections at a point when they were already divided and being used in that manner.[323]

The degree to which the canonical letters were originally legally binding depended on whether these rescripts were directed to subordinates or to bishops of the same rank. In the prior case they had the authoritative character of an order, as when the metropolitan wrote to his suffragans (for example, Basil, c. 90; Theophilus of Alexandria and Cyril, canons 4 and 5; also Peter of Alexandria; Gregory the Wonder-Worker; and Athanasius, c. 3). In the latter case, they had more of an advisory function (for example, Dionysius of Alexandria, canons 1 to 4; Basil, canons 1 to 87).

'In the evolving law of the church', bishops exercised 'the function of *iureconsulti*, or as one said in Constantinople, of *prudentes*; they interpreted the applicable law, explained difficulties, developed important principles, but always only as advisors. . . . Whether the episcopal recipient of the letter would follow the counsel or not was up to him; this [genre] of canonical letter has in its own right no legal force. It is something quite different when a metropolitan issued directions to bishops placed under him; there he spoke with the authority of a "teacher"'.[324] [There are hence] 'essentially two forms in which bishops sought to create a unified disciplinary law, that of the rescript and that of the synodal decision'.[325] In terms of their prestige in the Byzantine East, one may compare the *Canons of the Fathers* with papal decretals, whose binding authority, however, remained restricted to the West.

---

323. Joannou, CPG Introduction, xxiii–xxiv.
324. E. Schwartz, 'Die Quellen über den melitianischen Streit (1905)', *Gesammelte Schriften* 3.87–116, 94.
325. Schwartz, 'Kanonensammlungen' 178.

The Quinisext Council (see above) sought to bestow the character of canon law binding for the entire church on the selection of episcopal rescripts gathered in its c. 2.[326]

Dionysius of Alexandria († 264–65)

Editions: C. L. Feltoe, *ΔΙΟΝΥΣΙΟΥ ΛΕΙΨΑΝΑ. The Letters and Other Remains of Dionysius of Alexandria* (Cambridge 1904) 94–105, 60–62; Joannou, CPG 1–16; Rhalles-Potles 4.1–13; Pedalion 544–51; PG 10.1272–90; Pitra, *Juris* 1.541–45.

Translations: English: C. L. Feltoe, *St. Dionysius of Alexandria: Letters and Treatises* (Translations of Christian Literature, series I; London 1908); *Rudder* 713–23; German: W. A. Bienert, *Dionysius von Alexandrien: Das erhaltene Werk* (Bibliothek der griechischen Literatur 2; Stuttgart 1972) 45–46, 54–58; French: Joannou, CPG 1–16.

Literature: W. A. Bienert, *Dionysius von Alexandrien: Zur Frage des Origenismus im dritten Jahrhundert* (PTS 21; Berlin 1978) 121–25, 180ff.; W. A. Bienert, 'Dionysius von Alexandrien', TRE 8 (1981) 767–71; U. Hamm, 'Dionysius of Alexandria', DECL 177–78; P. Nautin, 'Dionysius of Alexandria', EEC 238; Ohme, *Kanon* 296–304.

Dionysius was the most significant bishop of the Alexandrian church in the third century and the first to whom Eusebius of Caesarea gave the sobriquet 'the Great'.[327] Only fragments survive of his extensive writings.

The Letter to Basilides. Thanks to its solid anchoring in Greek canonical collections, this letter is one of the very few completely preserved letters of Dionysius. Eusebius reported that the addressee was 'bishop of the congregations in the Pentapolis', hence in the imperial province of Libya secunda which only became a province of the diocese of Oriens under Diocletian.[328] The sovereignty of the Alexandrian see over the Pentapolis was already recognized as 'old customary law' by c. 6 of Nicaea, but it cannot be assumed for this period. Eusebius said in the same place that Dionysius left 'various letters' to Basilides, but they do not survive.

The letter was a response to a written request by Basilides on the correct time to end the pre-Easter fast as well as three further requests for counsel in questions of sexual ethics. Two-thirds of the response dealt with the first theme. In the Pentapolis, according to this letter, there had arisen differences of opinion whether the fast, with a citation to Roman practice, was to continue until the first cock's crow of Easter morning or

---

326. An entirely different evaluation of the original canonical dignity of 'canonical letters' is taken by K. Bonis, Ἁἱ τρεῖς κανονικαὶ Ἐπιστολαὶ τοῦ Μεγάλου Βασιλείου πρὸς τὸν ἀμφιλόχιον', BZ 44 (1951) 62–78 (reprint Βιβλιοθήκη Ἑλλήνων Πατέρων καὶ Ἐκκλησιαστικῶν Συγγραφέων 51 [Athens 1975] 121–44; reprint *Theologia* 60 [Athens 1989] 201–20).

327. Eusebius, *Historia ecclesiastica* 7, praefatio (ed. Schwartz, GCS 9.2, 636). On the *vita*, cf. Bienert, *Werk* 1–17; Bienert, *Frage* 71, 106, 131. On his writings, cf. Bienert, *Frage* 51–70.

328. Eusebius, *Historia ecclesiastica* 7.26.3 (ed. Schwartz, GCS E.2, 700.22–25). Cf. K. Lübeck, *Rechtseinteilung und kirchliche Hierarchie des Orients bis zum Ausgang des vierten Jahrhunderts* (Münster 1901) 121ff.

only until Good Saturday evening or during the night between the two days. Basilides asked Dionysius whether he could issue a 'horos' on this point.[329] This, as well as the address to Basilides as 'συλλειτουργός', argues for the letter being not only a 'theological opinion on an ecclesiastical question in dispute' from Dionysius as leader of the catechetical school of Alexandria,[330] but also a response as bishop of Alexandria to the request to establish within the region under his influence a norm for a fasting practice that previously had not been uniform.

Dionysius replied that ending the fast before midnight is blameworthy; whoever waited long is to be praised, but uniformity is not to be sought. The end of the fast could be individually regulated depending on how long the fast had lasted, since it could be 2, 3, or 4 days, but for many was only one day.

The general exposition of his opinion constituted what is called c. 1, and the three remaining divisions of the letter were canons 2 to 4. They dealt with the ceremonial cleanness of menstruating women (c. 2), the frequency of marital relations (c. 3), and the burden on the conscience created by nocturnal emissions (c. 4). Yet even here, save for c. 2, Dionysius avoided detailed prescriptions.[331]

The Letter to Kolon. The Pedalion and Rhalles-Potles restrict themselves to these 4 canons. Pitra,[332] by contrast, has shown that some canonical collection manuscripts[333] also preserve a fragment of the letter to Konon (or Kolon),[334] which Joannou adds to his edition. Eusebius reported that Kolon was bishop of Hermopolis, hence under the bishop of Alexandria.[335] The fragment dealt with the question of how one was to deal with excommunicates who have been reconciled *in articulo mortis* and then recover. Dionysius expressly opposed banning them again and burdening them with their earlier sins.

Peter of Alexandria († 311)

Editions: Joannou, CPG 33–57 (reprint Beneševič, *Syntagma* 578–96); PG 18.468–508; Pitra, *Juris* 1.551–61; M. Routh, *Reliquiae sacrae* (Oxford 1846) 4.23–45; P. de Lagarde,

---

329. Joannou, CPG 5, 8.
330. Thus Bienert, *Frage* 121.
331. Cf. on this, Eva Maria Synek, 'Wer aber nicht völlig rein ist an Seele und Leib . . .': *Reinheitstabus im Orthodoxen Kirchenrecht* (Kanon Sonderheft 1; Egling an der Paar 2006).
332. Pitra, *Juris* 1.545–46.
333. Paris, BNF gr. (Codex Parisinus) 1324 and 1334; Oxford, Bodleian Library Bar. (Codex Bodleianus Bararoccus) 196.
334. Eusebius, *Historia ecclesiastica* 6.46.1–2 (ed. Schwartz, GCS E.2, 626.24–628.8); Feltoe, *Letters and Treatises* 60–62.
335. Eusebius, *Historia ecclesiastica* 6.46.1–2 (ed. Schwartz, GCS E.2, 626.24—628.8).

Reliquiae iuris ecclesiastici antiquissimae (Leipzig 1856) 63–73, 99–117; Pedalion 562–575; Rhalles-Potles 4.14–44; *Versiones:* ClavisG 1639.

Translations: English: *Rudder* 740–55; NPNF 14.601–2; French: Joannou, CPG 33–57.

Literature: Thomas Böhm, 'Peter I of Alexandria', DECL 479–80; *La concezione teologica della penitenza in Gregorio il Taumaturgo e in Pietro di Alessandria: Due epistole a confronto*, ed. Giovanni Ferrari (Pontificia Facoltà Teologica dell'Italia Meridionale, Sezione San Tommaso d'Aquino; Tesi di dottorato in Teologia, estratti, 25; Naples 2006); G. Fritz, 'Pierre d'Alexandrie', DThC 12 (1935) 1802ff.; C. W. Griggs, *Early Egyptian Christianity* (Leiden 1990) 117–20; Grotz, *Die Entwicklung* 409–13; F. H. Kettler, 'Der melitianische Streit in Ägypten', ZNW 35 (1936) 155–93; F. H. Kettler, 'Petros von Alexandrien', RE 19.2 (1938) 1281–88; Ohme, *Kanon* 307–11; Schwartz, 'Die Quellen' 87–116; M. Simonetti, 'Peter I of Alexandria', EEC 677–98; T. Vivian, *St. Peter of Alexandria. Bishop and Martyr* (Philadelphia 1988).

The so-called *Epistula canonica* of Peter of Alexandria, bishop from 300, belongs to the basic documents that recorded the outbreak of the 'Melitian Schism' at the start of the fourth century in the Egyptian Church.[336] Soon after the beginning of the Diocletian persecutions in Egypt, in 303, Peter had taken flight and was leading the church from exile. Bishop Melitius of Lykopolis in Upper Egypt, who believed that Peter had forfeited his office, now saw himself as the leader of the church, setting up clerics in foreign dioceses, even in Alexandria itself. On his return, when Peter ordered a mild treatment of *lapsi*, the conflict led to a schism in 306.

His directions for the norms of reconciliation of *lapsi* passed into Greek canonical collections, divided into 14 parts, constituting what is called the 'canons' of Peter. Although the Greek manuscripts speak in their *lemmata* of a *logos*,[337] it really is a letter, as demonstrated by the Syriac tradition, preserved in Paris, BNF syr. (Codex Parisinus syrus) 62, in the title placed at the end of the letter.[338] It is only in the Syriac tradition that the proemium as well as an extended concluding passage are preserved.[339] The address is missing, to be sure, but the proemium shows that the letter was 'not directed to an individual, but that it was a decree to all or a great number of Egyptian bishops. The language is one of authority'.[340] Since the *lapsi* themselves are addressed, however, it is certainly an encyclical 'to be read out in all Egyptian churches'.[341]

From the very first sentence of c. 1 it can be seen that the encyclical was written soon after the fourth Easter after the start of the persecutions, hence around Easter 306. The letter mentioned that the persecutions have

---

336. Central for their edition and the historical interpretation of the conflict are Kettler, 'Der melitianische Streit', and Schwartz, 'Die Quellen'.
337. Cf. Joannou, CPG 33.
338. Cf. Schwartz, 'Die Quellen' 93–94.
339. Schwartz, 'Die Quellen' 90–93, retranslated into Greek.
340. Schwartz, 'Die Quellen' 95.
341. Kettler, 'Der melitianische Streit' 35, 179.

abated in the meantime and that many *lapsi* have demanded reception back into the church, including particularly great masses of those who had sacrificed without compulsion and who had given no special sign of repentance (c. 3).[342] Others, on the other hand, who suffered torture at the very outset of the persecution, had been standing as 'weepers' before the church doors for three years (c. 1).[343] This made it mandatory to take a principled stance on the question of penance, as well as on other questions that Peter had received from the whole of Egypt.[344] Since Melitius is not mentioned in the encyclical, it can be assumed that this letter instigated the conflict over the treatment of the *lapsi*.

The decisions of Peter may be called a 'decree of pardon',[345] since the detailed resolutions, with their brief periods of penance, weighted according to the severity of the cases, assume in principle the admission of all *lapsi* to penance. Even those who simply performed sacrifices in keeping with the edict without scruple or risk were to receive penance after one year of probation (c. 3). In this way, those who had been entirely unready to do penance were kept under watch and thus were motivated to do penance (c. 4). The actual periods of penance are set for the following cases: 40 days for those who denied the faith only under torture, since they bore the wounds of Christ on their bodies (c. 1); 1 year for those who weakened immediately in prison (c. 2); only 6 months for those who officially participated in sacrifice but avoided performing sacrifice through tricks (c. 5); 3 years for masters who sent their Christian slaves (who received 1 year of penance) to sacrifice in their place (canons 6 and 7). Whoever fell away at the beginning but then recanted and even professed their faith under torture were received back without penance (c. 8). These norms were followed by a thorough treatment of those who had pressed for martyrdom and had reported themselves. Even if they professed their faith, they were to do penance (canons 9 and 11). Clergy from this group were to be deposed (c. 10). Avoidance of sacrifice through bribery was seen as model conduct (c. 12), flight was expressly approved (c. 13). Whoever was brought into contact with a sacrifice through force and with torture was to be numbered among the confessors (c. 14).

Thus generally binding norms were placed in opposition to the charismatic penitential power practiced by the confessors.[346] Epiphanius of Salamis reported that most confessors stood on the side of Melitius.[347]

---

342. Joannou, CPG 36.6–14.   343. Joannou, CPG 34.9–10.
344. Cf. Joannou, CPG 56.9ff. (c.14); 49.27–50.9 (c.11).
345. Thus Kettler, 'Der melitianische Streit'.   346. Cf. in c.5 (Joannou, CPG 38.23ff.).
347. Epiphanius of Salamis, *Panarion omnium haeresium*, ed. Karl Holl (3 vols. GCS 25, 31, 37 Berlin 1915–1933 [2nd ed. revised by Jürgen Dummer, 2 vols. Berlin 1980–85, 143, 6–9] 3.68.3–4.

The c. 15 on fasting on Wednesday and Friday, contained in most Greek canonical collections, was probably a passage from the work on Easter written to one Bishop Tricentius, which survives only in fragmentary form.³⁴⁸

Gregory Thaumaturgus (Wonderworker) ([210]–[270])

Editions: Joannou, CPG 19–30; PG 10.1019–48; Routh, *Reliquiae* 3.251–83; Pitra, *Juris* 1.562–66; Rhalles-Potles 4.44–66; Pedalion 553–61.

Translations: English: *St. Gregory Thaumaturgus: Life and Works*, trans. Michael Slusser (The Fathers of the Church 98; Washington, DC 1998); P. Heather and J. Matthews, *The Goths in the Fourth Century* (Translated Texts for Historians 11; Liverpool 1991) 5–11; Rudder 727–37; NPNF 14.602; German: P. H. Bourier, *Des heiligen Gregorius Thaumaturgus Ausgewählte Schriften* (2d ed. BKV; Kempten 1911); French: Joannou, CPG 19–30.

Literature: H. Crouzel, 'Grégoire le Thaumaturge', DSDH 6 (1967) 1014–20; H. Crouzel, 'Gregor der Wundertäter', RAC 12 (1983) 779–93; *Grégoire le Thaumaturge: Remerciement à Origène*, ed. H. Crouzel (SC 148; Paris 1969) 14–34; H. Crouzel, 'Gregory the Thaumaturge', EEC 368; P. Godet, 'Grégoire de Néocésarée', DThC 6 (1920) 1844–74; H. Grotz, *Die Entwicklung des Bußstufenwesens in der vornicänischen Kirche* (Freiburg 1955) 400–408; P. Heather and J. Matthews, *The Goths in the Fourth Century* (Liverpool 1991) 1–11; J. Modrzejewski, 'Grégoire le Thaumaturge et le droit romain', RHD 49 (1971) 313–42; K. Phouskas, Γρηγορίου Θαυματουργοῦ ἡ κανονικὴ ἐπιστολή. Εἰσαγωγὴ-κριτικὴ ἔκδοσις κειμένου-μετάφρασις-σχόλια (Athens 1978) (reprint Ἐκκλησιαστικὸς φάρος 60 [1978] 736–809); H. Schneider, 'Gregory the Wonderworker', DECL 269–70; Schwartz, *Bußstufen* 310ff.; M. Slusser, 'Gregor der Wundertäter', TRE 14 (1985) 188–91.

The so-called *Epistula canonica* of Gregory the Wonder-Worker belongs to the undisputed genuine works among the few surviving writings of the bishop of Neocaesarea in Pontus. The man venerated by posterity as the apostle of Cappadocia and Pontus had been the missionary of his homeland.³⁴⁹

About 254, 'Goths and Borads' had appeared, and they wasted and plundered Pontus.³⁵⁰ In the course of this invasion, many Christians apparently experienced hardships and were found guilty of crimes. The letter dealt with them. A bishop of Pontus, who remains nameless,³⁵¹ had possibly turned to Gregory for assistance in deciding how these sinners could be kept in the church. The 'canonical letter', probably written during 254, would have been a rescript in response to a question. However, it is more likely that the letter was an encyclical by Gregory to the bishops of his eparchy.³⁵² Since the letter survives without an address or a formal beginning or conclusion, its form is closer to an encyclical. Later, it was mostly di-

---

348. Cf. ClavisG 1640, *Sermo de Paschate ad Tricentium*.
349. Cf. Basil, *De spiritu sancto* 29; Gregory of Nyssa, *De vita Gregorii Thaumaturgi*, PG 46.893–958. On the *vita*, cf. Crouzel, *Grégoire: Remerciement* Introduction; Crouzel, 'Gregor der Wundertäter' 780ff.
350. On the historical background of the Gothic raids, cf. Heather-Matthews, *Goths*.
351. If the address, 'ἱερε πάπα' is to be understood in that way (Joannou, CPG 19.19).
352. Thus already in Routh, 2.447.

vided into 11 sections,³⁵³ which became the 'canons'. They were provided with a summary description of their contents.

Gregory declared that if Christians in captivity had been forced to eat sacrificial meat, this was ethically insignificant, and he referred to 1 Corinthians 6:13 and Matthew 15:11. In the same way, an innocent woman who had been raped was to have an unaltered status in the congregation, with reference to Deuteronomy 22:26. If such a woman were known as indecent before, however, they were not to hold common prayers with her (c. 1). Whoever became a robber during the invasion out of greed for possessions should be openly expelled from the church (canons 2 and 3). Whoever found the goods of another should not make any profit on them (c. 4), even to replace his own losses (c. 5). Collaborators were to be excluded from the 'hearers' (c. 7), as were accused robbers. If they confessed, however, and were willing to compensate, they should 'kneel' (c. 8). In the same way those who found the goods of others and did not return them: if they report themselves, they should participate in the prayers (c. 9). The commandment should be fulfilled without any thought of the desire for profit (c. 10).

This letter is a significant witness for the development of penance in the Early Church. It is in dispute whether there are more levels of penance behind the decisions of canons 7 to 9 than the levels of those excluded, those beseeching readmittance, and the penitent themselves.³⁵⁴ The so-called c. 11 describes a penitential system in four stages. It is not included in many manuscripts,³⁵⁵ and it is generally seen as a later addition.

Athanasius of Alexandria ([295]–373)

Editions: Joannou, CPG 63–84; Rhalles-Potles 4.67–81; Pedalion 576–85; Pitra, *Juris* 1.567–74; *Epistula ad Amunem*: ClavisG 2106, PG 26.1169–76; *Epistula festivalis* 39: ClavisG 2102 (2), PG 26.1436–40, 1176–80; *Epistula ad Rufinianum*: ClavisG 2107, PG 26.1180–81.

Translations: English: NPNF 14.602–3; *Rudder* 758–70; German: P. Merendino, *Osterfestbriefe des Apa Athanasios* (Düsseldorf 1965) 94–107; French: Joannou, CPG 63–84.

Literature: K. Metzler, 'Athanasius of Alexandria', DECL 54–59; S. Sakkos, ' Ἡ λθ' ἑορταστικὴ ἐπιστολὴ τοῦ Μ. Ἀθανασίου, in Τόμος ἑόρτιος χιλιοστῆς ἑξακοσιοστῆς ἐπετίου Μ. Ἀθανασίου 373–1973, ed. Geōrgios I. Mantzarides (Thessalonike 1974) 129–96; Schneemelcher, 'Bibel III.' 22–48; G. C. Stead, 'Athanasius', EEC 93–95; M. Tetz, 'Athanasius und die Einheit der Kirche', ZThK 81 (1984) 196–219; M. Tetz, 'Athanasius von Alexandrien', TRE 4 (1979) 333–49; M. Tetz, 'Zur Biographie von Athanasius von Alexandrien', ZKG 90 (1979) 304–38; M. Tetz, 'Über nikäische Orthodoxie: Der sog. Tomus ad Antiochenos des Athanasios von Alexandrien', ZNW 66 (1975) 194–222.

---

353. The codex of Trebizond used by Rhalles-Potles has achieved 13 canons by dividing c.1 into 3 parts (cf. Rhalles-Potles 4.43, n.); the Pedalion divides the same canon into 2 parts and thus comes to 12 canons.

354. Schwartz (*Bußstufen* 310ff.) doubts this; Grotz (*Die Entwicklung* 400–408) assumes a 4-step system of penance and holds c.11 to be authentic.

355. Cf. Joannou, CPG 18.

From the plethora of writings by the outstanding theologian and ecclesiastical politician of Nicene orthodoxy and bishop of Alexandria, three letters of different form and style entered Greek canonical collections.[356]

The *Epistula ad Amunem*, designated c. 1, answered a request from the monk Amun for an ethical evaluation of involuntary nightly pollutions.[357] Athanasius declared every natural emission to be sinless, and only what comes from a bad heart could be sinful. It is remarkable that the 'dual ways' of marriage and virginity are understood as being among the callings, although the higher nature of virginity is certainly clear, since it is promised a hundred-fold reward in a commentary on Matthew 13:8, while marriage only should receive a thirty-fold reward.[358] In an earlier interpretation, the hundred-fold reward was promised to martyrs.

The so-called 'c. 2' is an excerpt significant for the history of the canon of the Holy Scripture from the 39th Festival Letter of Athanasius from 367.[359] Due to its reception into canonical collections, this part of the letter has been well preserved in Greek, and other parts are preserved in Coptic.[360] In a polemical text directed against the use of 'apocryphal' scriptures by the Melitians,[361] Athanasius named the canonical books of the Old and New Testaments (τὰ κανονιζόμενα ... βίβλια) which were for him complete, untouchable, and unexceedable 'sources of salvation'. The Old Testament canon corresponded to the Hebrew canon with 22 books. For the New Testament, all 27 books including *Revelation* were enumerated. Further, Athanasius listed books which are certainly not canonical (οὐ κανονιζόμενα), but which can be read aloud for catechetical purposes: *Wisdom of Solomon*, *Wisdom of Jesus of Sirach*, *Esther*, *Judith*, *Tobit*, the 'so-called *Didache*', and *The Shepherd of Hermas*.

The *Epistula ad Rufinianum* appears to have been received into the Greek canonical collections as c. 3 only quite late; a large number of manuscripts preserve it only at the end of the canons of the fathers or not at all.[362] The letter was a response to the request to Athanasius of Bishop Rufinianus on the conditions 'decreed by the synods and elsewhere' for the return of someone who had fallen into error.[363] Athanasius responded by mentioning

---

356. On the *vita*, cf. Tetz, 'Athanasius von Alexandrien' 333–43; Tetz, 'Zur Biographie' 90.
357. Cf. on the same theme, c.4 of Dionysius of Alexandria and c.12 Timothy of Alexandria.
358. Joannou, CPG 69.7–8, 13.
359. On the complicated question of the preservation of the festival letters, cf. V. Peri, 'La cronologia delle lettere festivali di Sant'Atanasio e la quaresima', *Aevum* 35 (1961) 28–86; Tetz, 'Athanasius von Alexandrien' 344. On the *epistula festivalis* 39, cf. Zahn, *Geschichte* 2.203–12; Sakkos, 'Η λθ' ἑορταστικὴ ἐπιστολή'; Schneemelcher, 'Bibel III'.
360. Cf. L. T. Lefort, ed., CSCO 150 (1955) 1–72; CSCO 151 (1955) 1–54.
361. See above, 'Peter of Alexandria'.
362. Cf. Joannou, CPG Introduction générale pp. xx. Nikodemos Hagiorites uncovered this situation by going against tradition and ordering the *epistula ad Rufinianum* in the Pedalion as 'c.2'.
363. Joannou, CPG 77.19, 22ff.

that, immediately after the end of the persecutions, a synod including outside bishops had gathered in Alexandria; other synods took place in Hellas, Spain, and Gaul. All of them had made the same decision.[364] The request shows that due to the changes after the death of Constantius II on 3 November 361 and the coming to power of Julian the Apostate, norms were needed for the question of how to deal with clerics who had been hostile to the Nicenes and who now had come into the Nicene fold. Athanasius had returned to Alexandria on 21 February 362, and the Alexandrine synod mentioned probably took place as early as April 362.[365] Rufinus of Aquileia described this synod as 'the council of the confessors',[366] and it was motivated by the consolidation and unification of Nicene orthodoxy. The sole surviving written document is the so-called *Tomus ad Antiochenos*.[367] From this *Epistula synodalis* it can be learned that the question mentioned above was handled as the first item of business, while after the departure of most of the bishops a 'narrower synod' dealt specifically with the 'Antioch question'; the results were written down in the *Tomus* in order to send them to Antioch.[368] While the *Tomus* formulated the conditions of peace for reconciliation with old-Nicenes and Melitians in Antioch, the response to Rufinianus gave the principle decision of the synod of 362. According to this, even the leaders of the opponents should be offered forgiveness, insofar as they are penitent, though they are to be deposed from their offices. Whoever fell from the faith through force or compulsion would be forgiven and would remain a cleric, and whoever was deceived and suffered violence would also be forgiven.[369] The *Tomus ad Antiochenos* 3.1 preserves the general conditions: (1) the anathematization of the Arians, (2) the Nicene confession, and (3) the confession of the divinity of the Holy Spirit.[370]

The letter achieved special prominence in connection with the question of the return of iconoclastic clergy at the first session of Nicaea II (787), where it was read out.[371]

In his edition, P.-P. Joannou arbitrarily added *quaestio* 112 on communion with heretics from the *Quaestiones ad Antiochum ducem* here, although it is spurious and does not appear in the canonical collections.[372] Also found in

---

364. Joannou, CPG 78.6–7.
365. ClavisG 8593; C. B. Armstrong, 'The Synod of Alexandria and the Schism of Antioch in A.D. 362', JTS 22 (1921) 206–22, 347–55.
366. Rufinus of Aquileia, *Historia ecclesiastica* 10.29 (ed. Mommsen, GCS 9,2, 991.14).
367. ClavisG 2134; Tetz, 'Orthodoxie' 66.   368. Tetz, 'Orthodoxie' 196, 202.
369. Joannou, CPG 78.7–14; 79.14ff. Rufinus (*Historia ecclesiastica* 10.29, ed. Mommsen, GCS 9,2, 991) reports conflicts at the synod over this rule. The rigorists desired the treatment of the leaders to be applied to all.
370. Cf. Tetz, 'Orthodoxie' 200.
371. Cf. Mansi 12.1023E, 1027E–1030D, 1030E–1031D.
372. ClavisG 2257; PG 28.597–700; cf. Joannou, CPG 80–82.61.

some manuscripts and hence also accepted by Joannou is the fragment, *De non participando diuinis mysteriis sine discrimine*, on marital continence before receiving communion.[373]

The so-called *Canones Athanasii* were not received in the canonical collections. This is an 'ecclesiastical church order for the higher and lower clergy' from Egyptian sources from the second half of the fourth century, attributed to Athanasius and divided into 107 canons in the eleventh century.[374]

Basil the Great (330–79)

Editions: Joannou, CPG 85–199; Y. Courtonne, *Saint Basile, Lettres* I–III (Les belles lettres; Paris 1957–66); PG 32.219–1110; R. J. Deferrari, *St. Basil: The Letters, with an English Translation* I–IV (London 1926–34) (Greek text = PG 32.219–1110); Rhalles-Potles 4; Pedalion 586–651; Pitra, *Juris* 1.576–618; B. Pruche, *Basile de Césarée, Traité du S. Esprit* (2nd ed., SC 17; Paris 1968).

Translations: English: Deferrari, *St. Basil*; *Rudder* 771–864; NPNF 14.604–11; German: W.-D. Hauschild, *Basilius von Caesarea, Briefe*, 1–3 (Bibliothek der Griechischen Literatur 32 [Stuttgart 1990], 3 [1973], 37 [1993]).

Literature: K. Bonis, 'Αἱ τρεῖς κανονικαὶ Ἐπιστολαί' (reprint *Theologia* 201–20); P. J. Fedwick, ed., *Basil of Caesarea: Christian, Humanist, Ascetic: A Sixteenhundredth Anniversary Symposion* (Toronto 1981) 1–2; Paul J. Fedwick, *Bibliotheca Basiliana universalis*, 5: *Studies of Basil of Caesarea and his world: An Annotated Bio-Bibliography* (Corpus Christianorum; Turnhout 2004); P. J. Fedwick, *The Church and the Charisma of Leadership of Basil of Caesarea* (Toronto 1979); J. Gribomont, 'Basil of Caesarea in Cappadocia', EEC 114–15; W.-D. Hauschild, 'Basilius von Caesarea', TRE 5 (1979) 301–13; P. L'Huillier, 'Les sources canoniques de Saint Basile', *Messager de l'Exarchat du Patriarchat russe en Europe Occidentale* 44 (1963) 210–17; Ohme, *Kanon* 543–69; J. Pauli, 'Basil of Caesarea', DECL 94–100; F. van de Paverd, 'Die Quellen der kanonischen Briefe Basileios des Grossen', OCP 38 (1972) 5–63; R. E. Reynolds, 'Basil and the Early Medieval Latin Canonical Collections', in Fedwick, *Symposion* 513–32; Schwartz, *Bußstufen*; Schwartz, 'Kanonensammlungen'; Anna M. Silvas, *The Asketikon of St Basil the Great* (Oxford Early Christian Studies; Oxford 2005).

Basil the Great, the metropolitan of Caesarea in Cappadocia, was accorded a preeminent position in Eastern Christianity as a father of the church and a teacher in questions of dogma. He also gave instruction on the spiritual life and its organization. No other Greek father of the church has had so many of his letters included in Eastern canonical collections. For that reason, from fifth century the 'canons of Basil' occupy the most prominent place among the Canons of the Fathers in Greek canonical collections.[375] In most cases his letters, or excerpts from them, to various people were placed in the collections, but there are also two excerpts from his

---

373. ClavisG 2303 (*spuria*); Joannou, CPG 82–84.
374. G. Graf, *Geschichte der christlichen arabischen Literatur* I (Studi e Testi 118; Vatican 1944) 605ff.; ClavisG 2302.
375. Cf. above, Introduction section, 86.

De Spiritu Sancto. Portions of his ascetical writings or homilies, in contrast, were not received into the canonical literature.

The Maurists published 365 of Basil's letters.[376] All of his canonical letters were composed during his episcopacy (370–79). With one exception, they may all be viewed as authentic, and most of them can be fitted into the chronology of the life and works of Basil, which is relatively certain if not finally settled.[377] Eight letters as well as the excerpts from *De Spiritu Sancto*, divided into 92 canons, belong to the later 'normal corpus' of the Greek canonical collections. In addition there are three further letters or extracts there (canons 93 to 95) that are not found in all collections. These include c. 93, which is not authentic.

Before we examine the canons individually, the corpus should be explained schematically.

Canons 1 to 16 = Letter 188, *Amphilochio de canonibus* I a.374–75 (Joannou, CPG 92–116; Rhalles-Potles 4.88–137; PG 32.663–83; Courtonne 2.120–31).

Canons 17 to 50 = Letter 199, *Amphilochio de canonibus* II a.375/6 (Joannou, CPG 116–39; Rhalles-Potles 4.138–205; PG 32.715–32; Courtonne 2.154–64).

Canons 51 to 85 = Letter 217, *Amphilochio de canonibus* III a.376–77 (Joannou, CPG 140–519; Rhalles-Potles 4.206–56; PG 32.793–809; Courtonne 2.208–17).

Canon 86 = Letter 236, *Amphilochio Iconii episcopo* a.376 (Joannou, CPG 159–60; Rhalles-Potles 4.257–58; PG 32.875–85; Courtonne 3.47–55).

Canon 87 = Letter 160, *Diodoro* a.375–76 (Joannou, CPG 160–69; Rhalles-Potles 4.259–68; PG 32.621–28; Courtonne 2.88–92).

Canon 88 = Letter 55, *Gregorio presbytero* a.370–78 (Joannou, CPG 169–72; Rhalles-Potles 4.269–74; PG 32.401–4; Courtonne 1.141–42).

Canon 89 = Letter 54, *Chorepiscopis* a.370–78 (Joannou, CPG 172–75; Rhalles-Potles 4.275–57; PG 32.401–4; Courtonne 1.139–40).

Canon 90 = Letter 53, *Chorepiscopis* a.370–78 (Joannou, CPG 175–76; Rhalles-Potles 4.278–82; PG 32.396–99; Courtonne 1.137–39).

Canons 91–92 = *De Spiritu Sancto* 27.66–67; 29.71, a.375 (Joannou, CPG 179–87; Rhalles-Potles 4.283–91; PG 32.188–92, 200–201; Pruche, 478.15–482.34, 484.53–488.19, 500.1–502.23).

Canon 93 = *Sermo ob sacerdotum instructionem* (ClavisG 2933.1–2; Joannou, CPG 187–90; Rhalles-Potles 4.391–92; PG 31.1685–88).

---

376. PG 32.219–1110.

377. Cf. P. J. Fedwick, 'A Chronology of the Life and Works of Basil of Caesarea', Fedwick, *Symposion* 3–19. This chronology is the basis of the following temporal ordering of the canonical letters. On the life, J. Gribomont, 'Notes biographiques sur S. Basile le Grand', Fedwick, *Symposion* 21–48; Hauschild, *Briefe* 1. Introduction.

Canon 94 = Letter 93, *Ad Caesariam patriciam, de communione* a.372 (Joannou, CPG 191–93; Rhalles-Potles 4.389; PG 32.483–85; Courtonne 1.203–4).

Canon 95 = Letter 240, *Nicopolitanis presbyteris* a.376 (Joannou, CPG 193–98; Rhalles-Potles 4.386; PG 32.893–97; Courtonne 3.61–64).

Canons 1 to 85. The three extensive letters, called canonical letters (Letters 188, 199, 217), which were placed at the beginning of the collections, were directed to Amphilochius. He had sent a concrete and precise catalogue of questions to Basil at the outset of his episcopacy as metropolitan of the province of Lycaonia. In the proemium of Letter 188, Basil said that he was forced by this request to deal with problems he had never specifically considered. In response he wished to recall what he had 'heard' from earlier generations and draw the corresponding conclusions. The fact that this is not simply a conceit by a rhetorically trained letter writer is made clear by the fact that the letters are a collection of earlier church norms, to which were added his personal comments and solutions to questions.

From the proemium of Letter 199 we learn that Amphilochius had added a second letter to his first without having received an answer from Basil. The completed first reply had been lying for some time in Caesarea before Basil sent Letter 188 together with Letter 199 by the same courier. Hence it comes about that many of Basil's answers involve revisiting a question which had been raised again. There is no internal order to the material in the two letters whatsoever. Basil deals with complicated and difficult ethical questions, simply dealing with one question after another. Often it is clear that concrete individual cases lie behind the questions (for example, canons 2, 3, 8, 10). The fact that these were actual letters is well evidenced by the conclusion of Letter 188, in which two exegetical statements are given which, oddly enough, were later divided up as 'canons' (canons 15 and 16).

The following themes are dealt with (canons 1 to 16): norms for the return of Novatians (Cathars), Montanists (Pepuzenes), and Enkratites (c. 1); abortion was to be treated as murder (c. 2); deposition of a deacon due to indecency (c. 3); the duration of penance for polygamy (c. 4); reception of remorseful heretics *in articulo mortis* (c. 5); sexual intercourse between monks and nuns was not marriage (c. 6); homosexuality, sodomy, murder, poison, adultery, and apostacy deserved the same penalty (c. 7); considerations concerning premeditated and unpremeditated homicide (canons 8 and 11); unequal treatment of women and men in the practice of divorce according to customary law (c. 9); to what degree the oath of a cleric to remain in one place prevented his transfer (c. 10); no second marriage for clerics (c. 12); homicide in war (c. 13); the office of priest and the taking of usury are mutually exclusive (c. 14).

In the second letter as well (canons 17 to 50), Basil handled a great variety of themes. He began with his reply to the special inquiry of the priest Bianor as to whether he was hindered in carrying out his office because of an oath he had given in Antioch (c. 17). In the remaining material there are canons on permitted and forbidden marriage with questions of sexual misconduct predominating. Hence, there is a question on the breaking of an oath of chastity by virgins, widows, and men (canons 18 and 19); the immunity from the penalty for breaking an oath once given in heretical congregations (c. 20); sexually indecent husbands who cannot be punished for adultery according to customary law (c. 21); marriages compelled by abduction and rape (canons 22, 25, 30); marriages between two brothers and two sisters (c. 23); and the remarriage of widows and widowers (c. 24). Questions of marriage and sexual misconduct are also dealt with in canons 26, 31, 34–42, 46, and 48–50; sexual crimes of priests and deacons in canons 27, 32, 44. On other themes, he opposed an oath not to eat pork (c. 28), and said that an oath to do evil cannot be binding (c. 29); he regarded the exposure of an infant as the same as murder (c. 33) and determined that the reception of rigorous Enkratites (Saccophores and Apotactites) should be accomplished through rebaptism (c. 47).

The third letter (canons 51–85) began in much the same style. C. 51 once more dealt with the procedure for punishing clerics (cf. canons 3, 32); c. 52 once again dealt with the exposure of infants (cf. c. 33)—Amphilochius had certainly asked about this problem once more. The same appears to have been the case with c. 53 (cf. c. 30), and c. 54 (cf. c. 8). C. 55 dealt the special case of taking justice into one's own hands against robbers.

With c. 56 a clear change in the style of writing takes place. No more special questions of cases are discussed, but rather the capital sins are listed that required public penance. While Basil rarely spoke of different stages of penance in the earlier canons (only canons 4 and 22) and never explained the penalties because he assumed them to be well known, the penalties are now listed in detail and thoroughly discussed. There are four levels of penance, the (1) προσκλαίοντες = weepers, (2) ἀκροώμενοι = hearers, (3) ὑποπίπτοντες = kneelers, and (4) συνεστῶτες = standers. Due to this detailed description, these three letters of Basil form one of the most important sources for the stages of penance and for catechumen groups in the history of public confession.[378] To clarify Basil's thought, c. 56 is given here verbatim:

---

378. Cf. Schwartz, *Bußstufen*; E. Seeberg, *Die Synode von Antiochien im Jahre 324–325* (Berlin 1913) 32–56.

A man who has voluntarily slain anyone and has thereafter regretted the deed and has repented of it, shall be excluded from communion with the Holy for twenty years. The twenty years shall be allotted to him in the following manner, to wit: For four years he must weep outside of the portal, standing upright beside the oratory, and begging the faithful who enter to make a special prayer for him, while he confesses over and over again the same transgression. After four years he is to be stationed among the audients (or listeners), and for five years he shall be permitted to go out together with them. For seven years he shall be permitted to go out together with the kneelers, praying with them. Four years more shall he spend together with the faithful but shall not be permitted to participate in the offering. When these years have been duly fulfilled, he shall partake of the Holy Elements.

Unpremeditated murder (c. 57); adultery (c. 58); whoring (c. 59); breaking an oath of celibacy (c. 60); theft (c. 61); homosexuality (c. 62); sodomy (c. 63); perjury (c. 64); magic (c. 65); violating a corpse (c. 66); incest (c. 67); marriage within the forbidden degrees (c. 68); indecency by readers, deacons, and priests (canons 69 and 70); hiding debilities and their conviction (c. 71); soothsaying (c. 71); and denial of Christ (c. 73) are treated in a similar manner. An excursus on the possibility of shortening the periods of penance in cases of genuine repentance (c. 74) gives an impression of a break in the discussion.

In the remaining canons, the following sins are regulated once more with detailed presentations of the various levels of penance: incest with a sister or sister-in-law (canons 75 and 76); remarriage of a divorced man (c. 77); marriage with a sister-in-law (c. 78); incest with a stepmother (c. 79); polygamy (c. 80); apostasy during a barbarian raid (c. 81); perjury (c. 82); and soothsaying and heathen practices (c. 83). The conclusion constituted another long disquisition on the greater significance of the intensity and genuiness of penance over any mandatory length of penance (canons 84 and 85).

The stylistic oddity of canons 56 to 85 has led E. Schwartz in various studies on different topics to come to dramatic conclusions about the sources used by Basil in these letters.[379] He concluded that 'in the third letter from the 56th canon on, Basil copied earlier canons with small modifications, usually only stylistic'.[380] He wished to prove that the *corpora* of canons 56 to 74 and 75 to 85 are independent collections of older canons that Basil incorporated into his work.[381] Schwartz's evidence for his conjecture was his analysis of the Patmos, Monastic Library (Codex Patmia-

---

379. ' Zur Geschichte des Athanasius VI (1905)', *Gesammelte Schriften* 3.134–55; 'Zur Geschichte des Athanasius VII (1908)' *Gesammelte Schriften* 3.170–87; Schwartz, *Bußstufen*; Schwartz, 'Kanonensammlungen'.
380. Schwartz, *Bußstufen* 329.
381. Schwartz, *Bußstufen* 316–34.

cus) 172 and 173 (eighth to ninth centuries) and of the Paris, Bibliothèque nationale de France (Syriac Codex Parisinus) 62 (ninth century). F. van de Paverd has rejected Schwartz's conclusions.[382]

Canons 86 to 90. Letter 236 to Amphilochius dealt with different themes and topics in seven parts. The fourth part of the letter takes a position on the question of the Enkratites, forming the text for c. 86. The occasion for the inquiry by Amphilochius was certainly the argument raised by the Enkratites that even Catholics would not eat all foods, but that they drew the distinction between permitted and impermissible food. Basil answered that a distinction was to be made only between usefulness and injury, not sinfulness.

C. 87 contains parts 2 to 5 of Letter 160 to Diodorus of Tarsus, leaving out the proemium. There Basil expressly rejected the possibility of the marriage of a widower with a sister-in-law. A letter permitting this practice circulated under the name of Diodorus. This letter was used as a counter-argument, as was explained in the proemium. In c. 23 Basil had already mentioned his letter to Diodorus and also referred to a transcription that he had sent to Amphilochius.

Letter 55 to the seventy-year-old priest Gregorius or Paregorius[383] (c. 88) forbade him from continuing to live with his housekeeper, to whom he was not related. He cited c. 3 of Nicaea and added the threat of anathema for non-observance. In Letter 54 (c. 89), Basil turned to the *chorepiscopi* of his metropolitan district and complained about the undignified circumstances surrounding the appointment of lower clergy. Basil also asserted his own right to participate in their duties. The addressees of Letter 53 (c. 90) are also *chorepiscopi*.[384] He threatened deposition for every simoniac practice connected with ordination.

Further canons: Canons 91 to 92 are three excerpts from *De Spiritu Sancto*. In them he dealt with the significance of the *dogma* and *kerygma* of the church,[385] as well as the unwritten traditions of the church, which were just as binding as written doctrine. Basil described them concretely: crossing; praying facing east; the wording of the *epiklesis* (ἐπίκλησις); the bless-

---

382. van de Paverd, 'Die Quellen' 5–63. For the literature to the discussion encompassing the question at issue here of the authenticity of the synod of Antioch of 324, cf. van de Paverd, 'Die Quellen' 8ff.

383. Schwartz argued for this form of the name; cf. *Bußstufen* 323.

384. According to the *lemmata* of the canonical manuscripts, the letter was addressed to suffragans; cf. Joannou, CPG 175.

385. Cf. H. Dörries, 'De Spiritu Sancto', *Der Beitrag des Basilius zum Abschluß des trinitarischen Dogmas* (Abhandlungen der Akademie der Wissenschaften in Göttingen, Phil.-Hist. Klasse 39; Göttingen 1956) 73–75, 121–28.

ing of baptismal water and chrism; the chrism itself; the threefold immersion of the one being baptised; abrenuntiation; praying while standing; the inclusion of the Holy Spirit in the doxology with the formulation σὺν τῷ Πνεύματι; as well as 'most' sacraments.

The Pedalion closed the canons of Basil with the three excerpts from *De Spiritu Sancto*. Theodore Balsamon and Matthew Blastares considered Basil's 85 canons to be only those from the first three letters to Amphilochius, while they would not designate the remaining canonical decisions to be 'canons'. The Codex of Trebezond, the basis of Rhalles-Potles, also numbers only these 85 canons.[386] John Zonaras in his exposition of c. 54 Quinisext calls Letter 160 to Diodorus c. 86, which is today usually designated c. 87.

Some manuscripts add from one to three further decisions to those collections that contained 92 canons. In the Codex of Trebezond, for example, these canons are gathered together with other additions with the title 'Διάφορα'.[387] C. 93 bore the title 'Παράγγελμα πρὸς τὸν ἱερέα περὶ τῆς θείας χάριτος'. This is the pseudepigraphic *Sermo ob sacerdotum instructionem*,[388] certainly of Alexandrian provenance, which Joannou took into his collection in the longer variant reading.[389] C. 94 is an excerpt from Letter 93 to the Patrician Lady Kaisaria on the frequency of communion.[390] Basil approved of daily communion, but he also mentioned for Caesarea the practice of receiving communion on Sunday, Wednesday, Friday, and Saturday, besides holy days of the saints.

An excerpt from Letter 240 to the residents of Nikopolis is contained in c. 95.[391] Basil called upon the Nicene congregation there to continue to endure the discrimination of the party of 'homoiousians' since the state protected their errors. They should not, however, obey the bishops of the 'homoians'.

Gregory of Nyssa (331/340–[395])

Editions: Gregory of Nyssa, *Epistula canonica*, ed. Ekkehard Mühlenberg (*Gregorii Nysseni Opera*, vol. 3: Opera Dogmatica Minora, part 5; Leiden-Boston 2008) 1–14; Joannou, CPG 203–26; PG 45.221–326; Rhalles-Potles 4.295–330; Pedalion 651–62; Pitra, *Juris* 1.619–29; (ClavisG 3148).

Translations: English: *Rudder* 866–82; NPNF 14.611–12; *Gregory of Nyssa: The letters*, Introduction, translation and commentary by Anna M. Silvas (Supplements to Vigiliae Christianae, 83; Leiden 2007); French: Joannou, CPG 203–26.

---

386. Cf. Rhalles-Potles 4.255 n. 1.
388. ClavisG 2933.1–2.
387. Rhalles-Potles 4.386–92.
389. The shorter = PG 31.1685–88.
390. On Letter 93, cf. B. Gain, *L'église de Cappadoce au IVᵉ siècle d'après la correspondance de Basile de Césarée* (OCA 225; Rome 1985) 207–13.
391. Not 'To the priests' as the Maurists' edition formulates.

Literature: M. Altenburger and F. Mann, *Bibliographie zu Gregor von Nyssa* (Leiden 1988); D. L. Balás, 'Gregor von Nyssa', TRE 14 (1985) 173–81; M. Canévet, 'Grégoire de Nyssa', DSDH 6 (1967) 971–1011; H. Dörrie, 'Gregor III (Gregor von Nyssa)', RAC 12 (1983) 863–95; F. Dünzl, 'Gregory of Nyssa', DECL 263–68; J. Gribomont, 'Gregory of Nyssa', EEC 363–65; I. Kornarakes, ''Η πρὸς Λητόϊον κανονικὴ ἐπιστολὴ Γρηγορίου τοῦ Νύσσης ἐξ ἐπόψεως ποιμαντικῆς ψυχολογίας', *Gregorios o Palamas* 42 (Thessalonike 1959) 147–52, 219–31; *Lexicon Gregorianum: Wörterbuch zu den Schriften Gregors von Nyssa*, ed. Friedhelm Mann (7 vols. Leiden-Boston 1998–2008); F. van de Paverd, 'Disciplinarian Procedures in the Early Church', *Augustinianum* 21 (1981) 291–316; Schwartz, *Bußstufen* 314ff.

Only scanty information is available for a biography of the younger brother and pupil of Basil the Great.[392] His election in 372 as bishop of the small town of Nyssa,[393] lying between Caesarea and Ancyra, constituted a turning point; despite his own reluctance, he allowed himself to be persuaded by Basil to accept the position.

Among the 'three Cappadocians', Gregory is regarded as the 'philosophical head' and the systematic theological thinker. The fact that his gifts did not lie in the practical requirements of the episcopal office,[394] but rather in the systematic working out of theological questions, is shown by his letter to Bishop Letoius of Melitene, the metropolis of Armenia II, certainly written about 383. It is one of the few surviving letters of Gregory.

This letter, which was taken into the Greek canonical collections after being divided into 8 parts ('canons'), dealt with questions of public confession. In contrast to the so-called canonical letters of Basil, however, it dealt primarily with the systematic theological basis of the necessity for penance as well as its duration, so that his practical examples have an explanatory character.

The proemium (c. 1) offered a psychological foundation for therapeutic penance. The precondition for a healing is described as a correct recalling of the cause of an illness in one of the three parts of the soul, which is understood as threefold in keeping with the Platonic model. The capital sins are distributed in keeping with this division of the soul. C. 2 dealt with the sin attributed to the λογικόν part of the soul, apostasy; c. 3 dealt with soothsaying and conjuring. C. 4 analyzed the sins of adultery, indecency, and whoring, that pertained to the ἐπιθυμητικόν part of the soul. C. 5 treated sins of the third, θυμοειδές, part of the soul: homicide and murder; further, he described the penances that should be given to those 'in articulo mortis' and noted that if the person recovered, the penance had to be performed. In the same way he analyzed the greed for possessions

---

392. Cf. in particular Dörrie, 'Gregor III' 864–70 and Balás, 'Gregor von Nyssa' 173–75.
393. Cf. F. Hild and M. Restle, *Kappadokien* (Tabula Imperii Byzantini 2; Vienna 1981) 246ff.
394. This was notorious; cf. Basil Letter 58, 60, 100.

and their concrete manifestations, theft and robbery (c. 6), grave robbery (c. 7), and sacrilege (c. 8).

The periods of penance mentioned by Gregory[395] are different from those prescribed by Basil for the same case, so the question might be asked, whence came the tradition represented by Gregory?[396] What is surprising is a singular schematization of the periods of penance into three steps of equal length: murder (3 x 9 years); adultery, sodomy, pederasty (3 x 6 years); whoring (3 x 3 years).

Gregory of Nazianzus († 390)

Editions: Joannou, CPG 229–31; PG 37.472–74 (ClavisG 3034); Rhalles-Potles 4.363–64; Pedalion 662ff.; Pitra, *Juris* 1.654–55.

Translations: English: *Rudder* 883–84; NPNF 14.612; French: Joannou, CPG 229–31.

Literature: J. Gribomont, 'Gregory Nazianzen', EEC 361–62; C. Hartmann, 'Gregory of Nazianzus', DECL 259–63; John A. McGuckin, *St. Gregory of Nazianzus: An Intellectual Biography* (Crestwood, NY 2001); J. Mossay, 'Gregor von Nazianz', TRE 14 (1985) 164–73; Schneemelcher, 'Bibel III.', TRE 6 (1980) 22–48; B. Wyß, 'Gregor II (Gregor von Nazianz)', RAC 12 (1983) 793–863; Zahn, 2.212–19.

Gregory's year of birth in the Cappadocian town of Nazianzus cannot be established with certainty.[397] His father, Gregory the Elder, was bishop there from 329 to 374. About 372 Basil the Great consecrated him as bishop of the market town of Sasima, which belonged to Cappadocia II after the partition of Cappadocia. His consecration established the claim of Cappadocian Caesarea against the new (second) metropolis of Tyana and its metropolitan Anthimus. Anthimus, however, denied Gregory entry, so that he never entered his office.

From 379 onward, Gregory resided in Constantinople in order to care for the Nicene minority in the capital. Supported by the change in ecclesiastical politics under Theodosius I, he became bishop of Constantinople on 24 November 380, and after the death of Meletios of Antioch he also became president of the general council of the Eastern Empire, which had been meeting in the capital since May 381.[398]

Gregory must be seen as the most important Greek Christian poet. Through the roughly 17,000 verses composed by him, he sought to write Christian verses that would equal Hellenistic poetry, while observing all

---

395. Cf. Joannou, CPG 210.1ff., 23ff.; 211.20; 214.10ff.; 215.9ff.; 216.12–13; 218.13ff.; 219.5ff., 23ff.; etc.
396. Cf. F. van de Paverd, 'Die Quellen', 5–63, 41 n. 5.
397. On the place, cf. Hild and Restle, *Kappadokien* 244f. On the date, in discussion are 326 or 300; on this, and on the *vita* in general, cf. Mossey, 'Gregor von Nazianz' 164–67; Wyß, 'Gregor II' 794–98; and P. Gallay, *La vie de S. Grégoire de Nazianze* (Lyon-Paris 1943).
398. On Constantinople I, see above 49–53.

the formal rules.³⁹⁹ From the first part of the corpus of his poems, the so-called *Carmina dogmatica*, Carmen 1.1.12 entered the Greek canonical collections. There it was placed together with the iambics of Amphilochius (see below) on the same theme; yet both are missing in the *Synagoge* of John Scholasticus. These can be typified as mnemonic verses in which Gregory listed the books of the Old Testament and 26 books of the New Testament, omitting *Revelation*. Consequently, this listing proves that the canon of the 26 books had gained general acceptance by the end of the fourth century.⁴⁰⁰

Amphilochius of Iconium (340–45; 394–403)

Editions: Joannou, CPG 232–35; E. Oberg, *Amphilochii Iconiensis: Iambi ad Seleucum* (PTS 9; Berlin 1969) 36–39; PG 37.1593–98 (ClavisG 3230); Rhalles-Potles 4.365–67; Pedalion 664–65; Pitra, *Juris* 1.655ff.

Translations: English: *Rudder* 585–86; NPNF 14.612; German: E. Oberg, 'Das Lehrgedicht des Amphilochius', JAC 16 (1973) 67–97; French: Joannou, CPG 232–35.

Literature: K. Holl, *Amphilochius von Ikonium in seinem Verhältnis zu den großen Kappadokiern* (Tübingen 1904); G. Röwekamp, 'Amphilochius of Iconium', DECL 22–23; Schneemelcher, 'Bibel III', TRE 6 (1980) 22–48; S. J. Voicu, 'Amphilochius of Iconium', EEC 32; Zahn, 2.212–19.

After his education as a rhetor under Libanius in Antioch, Amphilochius practiced this profession in Constantinople from 363 to 370–71. He ended his practice in order to dedicate himself to the eremitic life.⁴⁰¹ Between 370 and 372, under Emperor Valens the province of Lykaonia was newly formed out of portions of the provinces of Galatia and Pisidia as well as from Isaurian lands.⁴⁰² The episcopal see of Iconium hence became both the civil and ecclesiastical metropolis. On the recommendation of Basil the Great, Amphilochius was elected metropolitan. Both of them were bound in close friendship. Amphilochius participated as executor of the heritage of Basil at the Council of Constantinople in 381, and along with Optimus of Antioch in Pisidia he was made a guarantor of orthodoxy in the imperial diocese of Asia.⁴⁰³ He died after the synod of Constantinople in 394 (see above), in which he participated, but before 403.⁴⁰⁴

The 333 iambic verses to Seleucus, placed among the works of Gregory of Nazianzus by the first editors as well as by Migne, are a guide to the pious life and for successful studies. He composed it for his ten-year-old

---

399. Cf. Wyß, 'Gregor II' 308–14.
400. W. Schneemelcher, *Neutestamentliche Apokryphen* 1 (5th ed. Tübingen 1987) 25.
401. On the biography, cf. Holl, *Amphilochius von Ikonium* 5–42.
402. Cf. K. Belke, *Galatien und Lykaonien* (Tabula Imperii Byzantini 4; Vienna 1984) 54–55.
403. *Codex Theodosianus* 16.1.3.
404. On his writings and theology, cf. Holl, *Amphilochius von Ikonium* 42–115, 235–63.

nephew about 396.⁴⁰⁵ Verses 251 to 319 contain an index of biblical books of the Old and New Testament, which is of significance for the history of the canon and is always combined with that of Gregory of Nazianzus (see above) in Greek canonical collections. Even at the end of the fourth century, Amphilochius documented the old doubts about the Epistle to the Hebrews, the four small 'Catholic Epistles', and Revelation.

Timothy of Alexandria († 385)

Editions: Joannou, CPG 240–58; PG 33.1296–1308; Pitra, *Juris* 1.630–45; Pedalion 666–76; Rhalles-Potles 4.331–41 (ClavisG 2520).

Translations: English: *Rudder* 889–901; NPNF 14.612; French: Joannou, CPG 240–58.

Literature: J. Faivre, 'Alexandrie', DHGE 2 (1914) 289–369, 317–19; A. V. Psarev, 'The 19th Canonical Answer of Timothy of Alexandria: On the History of Sacramental Oikonomia', *St. Vladimir's Theological Quarterly* 51 (2007) 297–320; B. Windau, 'Timothy of Alexandria', DECL 577.

Only a little is known of the biography of Timothy of Alexandria. Socrates reported that he succeeded his own brother,⁴⁰⁶ whom the Emperor Valens had exiled, to the see of Alexandria. At the Council of Constantinople of 381 he is found among those who sought the resignation of Gregory of Nazianzus after the deposition of the Alexandrian candidate, Maximus.⁴⁰⁷ Afterward the Emperor Theodosius named him one of the 'normal bishops' in the empire.⁴⁰⁸

Among the few surviving works of Timothy⁴⁰⁹ are those *responsa canonica* that are included in all Greek canonical collection manuscripts and are historically anchored in the *lemmata* there to an inquiry from the Fathers of the Council of 381.⁴¹⁰ It consists of brief 'questions and answers' (Ἐρωταποκρίσεις) of diverse content which are numbered as the 'canons' of Timothy.⁴¹¹ The number of responses varies in the tradition. The first 15 are found in all the canonical collection manuscripts and may be held as authentic;⁴¹² the rest are of dubious origin. The Pedalion and Rhalles-Potles offer 18 excerpts, and in Pitra there are further elements added in the

---

405. PG 37.1577–1600. Seleucus was the son of Olympias, who was the daughter of Amphilochius's sister Theodosia; cf. K. G. Bonis, Περὶ τῆς μητρὸς τῆς ἁγίας Ὀλυμπιάδος, *Studi bizantini e neoellenici* 8 (1953) 3–10.

406. Socrates, *Historia ecclesiastica* 4. 37 (ed. Hansen, GCS NF 1, 71–72). Cf. Faivre, 'Alexandrie' 317–19.

407. Cf. Ritter, *Konzil* 95ff., 115–16, etc.   408. *Codex Theodosianus* 16.1.3.

409. ClavisG 2520–30.

410. *Lemma*: Ἀποκρίσεις κανονικαὶ Τιμοθέου τοῦ ἁγιωτάτου ἀρχιεπισκόπου Ἀλεξανδρείας, ἑνὸς τῶν ρν' Πατέρων τῶν ἐν Κωνσταντινουπόλει συναθροισθέντων, πρὸς τὰς προσενεχθείσας αὐτῷ ἐπερωτήσεις παρά τινων ἐπισκόπων καὶ κληρικῶν (Joannou, CPG 240).

411. Thus the *lemma* in the Pedalion (666): Αἱ Ἐρωταποκρίσεις, ἤτοι οἱ ιη' Κανόνες Τιμοθέου . . .

412. Cf. Joannou, CPG 238.

tradition. Out of documentary interest, Joannou accepted 29 questions and answers in his own edition.

The following themes are dealt with: the *communion* of catechumens (c. 1), of the possessed (c. 2), of menstruating women (c. 7), after marital relations (c. 5), and after nocturnal emission (c. 12); the *baptism* of the possessed (c. 2), of catechumens in a coma (c. 4), and of menstruating women (c. 6); the *fasting practices* at Lent for childbearing women (c. 8) and the ill (c. 10); divine service in the presence of heretics (c. 9); conduct of clerics in cases of illicit marriage (c. 11); the days of the week on which married persons are to abstain from intercourse (c. 13); ecclesiastical prayer for suicides (c. 14); adultery on the grounds of illness of the wife (c. 15).

Theophilus of Alexandria ([345]–412)

Editions: Joannou, CPG 262–73; PG 65.33–45; Pitra, *Juris* 1.646–49; Rhalles-Potles 4.342–54; Pedalion 676–86 (ClavisG 2678).
Translations: English: *Rudder* 904–14; NPNF 14.613ff.; French: Joannou, CPG 262–73.
Literature: H. Crouzel, 'Théophile d'Alexandrie', DSDH 15 (1991) 524–30; R. Delobel and M. Richard, 'Théophile d'Alexandrie', DThC 15 (1946) 523–30; A. de Nicola, 'Theophilus', EEC 831; A. Favale, *Teofilo d'Alessandria (345–412)* (Turin 1958); G. Münch-Labacher, 'Theophilus of Alexandria', DECL 572–73; H. G. Opitz, 'Theophilus von Alexandrien', RECA 5A (1934) 2149–65. Norman Russell, *Theophilus of Alexandria* (Early Church Fathers; London 2007).

Information on the life of Theophilus before his elevation to the office of bishop of Alexandria in 385 rests only on the chronicle of John of Nikiu (about 700) and on the Alexandrian *Synaxarion* (fifteenth century), which have legendary elements.[413] He was already active as a cleric and deacon under his three predecessors, Athanasius, Peter, and Timothy. In the three decades of his office, he continued the struggle of the Alexandrine patriarchs against the capital see and its bishops for ecclesiastical precedence, which had been established by c. 3 of Constantinople I of 381 (see above). Under the leadership of Theophilus, the Alexandrian see achieved the leading position of ecclesiastical power in the Christian East. Theophilus played a decisive role in settling the schism in the ecclesiastical province of Arabia, as well as in the debates on this problem at the Constantinople synod of 394.[414] His reputation was tarnished after the fact by his ruthless struggle against Origen and his defenders among Egyptian monks in what is called 'the first Origenist controversy',[415] as well as by his intrigues

---

413. Cf. on this and on the biography, Crouzel, 'Théophile d' Alexandrie' 524–27; Favale, *Teofilo d'Alessandria*.
414. See above, 75–77.
415. K. Holl, 'Die Zeitfolge des ersten origenistischen Streits', *Gesammelte Aufsätze* 2 (Tübingen 1928) 310–50; Opitz, 'Theophilus von Alexandrien' 2152ff.

against Bishop John Chrysostom of Constantinople. Theophilus deposed him at the 'Synod of the Oak' (403).[416]

Among the extensive literary works of Theophilus, which have been preserved in fragments,[417] there are five letters which were divided into 14 canons and included in the Greek canonical collections. They are:

1. An excerpt entitled 'Προσφώνησις' in the manuscripts, dealing with the rules of fasting for the occasion when the vigil fast of the *Theophaneia* falls on a Sunday (c. 1). Joannou attributes this 'edict' to the fragment of the sixth Easter letter of Theophilus in 391.[418]

2. A 'memorandum' for (Bishop ?) Ammon, sent by Theophilus to Lycopolis,[419] with detailed directions for the problems which had emerged there, whose resolution had been requested by the local bishop, Apollon. The question of how to deal with clerics who had been in communion with 'Arians' (c. 2) dates the letter to the beginning of Theophilus's episcopate. Canons 3 to 6 and c. 9 decided specific cases of priests who are identified. C. 7 regulated ordination practice. C. 8 gave orders on what is to be done with the remnants of the eucharistic bread. Canons 10 to 11 established an *oikonomos* for the incomes of the church there, and the care prescribed for widows, the poor, and travelers.

3. A brief passage from a letter to a (Bishop?) Aphyngius on the process of receiving Cathars back into the church (c. 12). Here Theophilus regulated ordination by citing the synod of Nicaea (c. 8).

4. An excerpt from a letter to a Bishop Agathon on the concrete case of an illicitly contracted marriage (c. 13).

5. A letter to a Bishop Menas on the case of a woman excommunicated by priests, whose resolution was obviously disputed by Menas. Theophilus confirmed the decision as legal (c. 14).

Cyril of Alexandria ([380]–444)

Editions: Joannou, CPG 276–84; PG 77.361–65; Rhalles-Potles 4.916–22; Pedalion 687–92; Pitra, *Juris* 1.650–53 (ClavisG 5378–79).

Translations: English: *Rudder* 916–22; NPNF 14.615; Norman Russell, *Cyril of Alexandria* (Early Church Fathers; London–New York 2000) but not the canonical letters of Cyril; French: Joannou, CPG 276–84.

Literature: G. Bardy, 'Cyrille d'Alexandrie', DHGE 13 (1956) 1169–77; E. R. Hardy, 'Cyrillus von Alexandrien', TRE 8 (1981) 254–60; G. Jouassard, 'Cyrillus von Alexandrien', RAC 3 (1957) 499–515; H. du Manoir, 'Cyrille d'Alexandrie', DSDH 2 (1953) 2672–83;

---

416. ClavisG 8610; A. Wenger, 'Jean Chrysostome', DSDH 8 (1974) 331–55; J.-M. Leroux, 'Johannes Chrysostomus', TRE 17 (1988) 118–27.
417. ClavisG 2580–2684.
418. Cf. Joannou, CPG 260; ClavisG 2583.
419. Lemma: Ὑπομνηστικὸν ὅπερ ἔλαβεν Ἄμμων διὰ τὴν Λυκώ (Joannou, CPG 264).

G. Münch-Labacher, 'Cyril of Alexandria', DECL 153–57; M. Simonetti, 'Cyril of Alexandria', EEC 214–15.

As successor to his uncle Theophilus, Cyril mounted the episcopal throne of Alexandria on 17 October 412.[420] After the elevation of Nestorius to the see of Constantinople in 428, two problems occupied his duties as an ecclesiastical political leader: first, the struggle against Nestorius's questioning of title *Theotokos* for Mary in connection with the 'Antioch Theology', and second, the status and preeminence of the episcopal see of the imperial residence.[421] In April 433, Cyril agreed with the compromise formula of John of Antioch, so that ecclesiastical unity was restored in the East. In his later years, Cyril was particularly concerned with opposing extremists among his own adherents as well as among those of the Antiochene school.

Of the more than 100 surviving letters of Cyril,[422] two have entered the Greek canonical collections. They were divided into 5 'canons'.

1. The letter to Domnus II (441–49),[423] successor to John on the throne of Antioch, must have been written at the beginning of Domnus's tenure, about 442. Domnus had written to Cyril and Proclus of Constantinople in the matter of Bishop Peter, who was subject to him, and who had been forced to resign because of an accusation of mishandling church property. Peter continued to bear the title of bishop. Peter had sought the aid of Cyril, insisting on his innocence and complaining of the uncanonical procedure of his deposition. On the basis of his thirty years of exerpience Cyril responded and demanded that the novice (Domnus) carry out a just and proper trial. If Peter were guilty, then he would also have to lose his title (c. 1). Money taken improperly from Peter had to be given back so long as his guilt was not proved. Bishops must, under the judgment of God, be able to dispose of the property of their churches themselves (c. 2). Deposing a bishop could not proceed by means of a(n involuntary) resignation, but rather only through a demonstration of guilt based on the procedure of an ecclesiastical court (c. 3).

2. A letter to the bishops of Libya and the Pentapolis, which had been occasioned by complaints of monks from the Thebais over the ordination of unworthy persons by these bishops. Cyril admonished them once more to examine the way of life before every ordination (c. 4). Catechumens

---

420. On the biography, cf. Hardy, 'Cyrillus von Alexandrien' 254ff.; Jouassard, 'Cyrillus von Alexandrien' 499–509.
421. See above, Synod of Ephesus (431), 53–57.
422. ClavisG 5301–5411.
423. Cf. 'Domnus II', DHGE 14 (1960) 645; C. Karalevskij, 'Antioche', DHGE 3 (1913) 563–703, 575.

who were guilty of sins were capable of being baptized *in articulo mortis* (c. 5).

Joannou in his edition adds three additional pieces that are not contained in most canonical collections. In the *Syntagma XIV titulorum*, the excerpts from Theophilus and Cyril were entered from the beginning. The Syriac collection of Paris, BNF (Codex parisinus) syr. 62 (ninth century), which goes back to before the sixth century, still omits the two Alexandrian bishops, but this could have been in reaction to the Nestorian conflict.[424]

Gennadius of Constantinople ([400]–471)

Editions: Joannou, CPG 292–99; F. Diekamp, *Analecta Patristica* (OCA 117; Rome 1938) 79–82 (reprint Pitra, *Juris* 2.183–87); Mansi 7.912–16; PG 85.1613–21; Pedalion 692–97; Rhalles-Potles 4.368–74 (ClavisG 5977).

Translations: English: *Rudder* 923–28; NPNF 14.615; French: Joannou, CPG 292–99.

Literature: Diekamp, *Analecta Patristica* 54–108, 79–82, 96–98; Grumel, *Regestes* II N°. 143; J. Kirchmeyer, 'Gennade de Constantinople', DSDH 6 (1967) 204–5; DHGE 20 (1984) 497; C. Schmidt, 'Gennadius I of Constantinople', DECL 248; S. J. Voicu, 'Gennadius of Constantinople', EEC 342.

In 458 Gennadius was consecrated the successor to Anatolius as bishop of Constantinople.[425] He had been a priest in the imperial capital and had already participated in the conflict over Nestorius in 431–32 with a public and virulent rejection of the 12 anathemas of Cyril.[426] During his episcopate he expressly defended the christological definition of Chalcedon and was influentially involved in the deposition and exile of Timothy Ailurus from Alexandria in 460 and later of Peter the Fuller of Antioch.

Part of the literary work of Gennadius, which has survived in fragmentary form,[427] is an *'Epistula encyclica* of Patriarch Gennadius and the Holy Synod assembled by him, to all Metropolitans'.[428] Together with a subscription list of 81 bishops, including 20 metropolitans, it was included in Greek canonical collections.[429] From the preface it can be determined that the synod in question is the so-called Endemusa.

424. Cf. Schwartz, *Bußstufen* 324.
425. On his *vita*, Diekamp, *Analecta Patristica* 54–72.
426. ClavisG 5974.
427. ClavisG 5970–86.
428. Hence the *lemma*, Γενναδίου . . . καὶ τῆς σὺν αὐτῷ ἁγίας συνόδου . . . (cf. Joannou, CPG 292). The addition 'and to the Pope in Rome', preserved in some manuscripts and editions (cf. Joannou, CPG 292), is a later accretion lacking in the earliest manuscripts. Cf. also Grumel, *Les Regestes* 105; Diekamp, *Analecta Patristica* 98.
429. The subscriptions are preserved in most of the manuscripts (cf. Joannou, CPG 299); some transmit only the first subscription of Gennadius. Older editions are Mansi 7.916–20; Rhalles-Potles 4.371–74; critical edition, E. Schwartz, *Publizistische Sammlungen zum Acacianischen Schisma* (Abhandlung der Bayerischen Akademie der Wissenschaften, Phil-Hist. Abteilung 10; Munich 1934) 176.

The synodal decision sharply opposed the simoniacal ordination practices which had developed in Galatia and spread widely as a 'custom'. The sinfulness of simony was established with references to Matthew 10:9 and Acts 8:23 and was sharpened even more by recalling c. 2 of Chalcedon, which was cited verbatim. The threat of punishment was intensified by the threat of anathema.

A dating of the synod around 458–59 is probable, since several Egyptian bishops are included among the subscribers. They were driven from their sees in 457 by Timothy Ailurus and were residing in Constantinople. The inauguration and ordination of Gennadius would have been the primary purpose of this synod.

In his *Enkomion* to St. Gennadius,[430] which Neophytos Enkleistos wrote in Cyprus in the twelfth century, he included a shortened form of the encyclical letter.[431] In view of the uncomplicated tradition of the manuscripts before the thirteenth century,[432] this must have been a later epitome.

Among the *spuria* of Gennadius was a letter, addressed to Martyrius of Antioch according to the *lemma*, on the reception of heretics into the church.[433] A short version of this letter has been added to the later manuscripts of the canons of Constantinople I of 381 as 'c. 7' (see above).

Cyprian of Carthage († 258)

Sources: Caecilius Cyprianus. . ., *Opera omnia*, ed. G. Hartel (Vienna 1871; New York 1965) 2.766–70; Louis Bayard, *St. Cyprien: Correspondence* (2 vols. Collection des universités de France; 2 vols. Paris 1925; 2nd ed. 2 vols. Paris 1961–62; *Saint Cyprien: Lettres*, Selected by Denys Gorce [Namur 1961]) 2.252–56; Joannou, CPG 303–13; Rhalles-Potles 3.2–6; Pedalion 368–69.

Translations: English: R. B. Donna, *Saint Cyprian* (Letters 1–81, The Fathers of the Church 51; Washington 1964); NPNF 14.518–521; *Rudder* 483–88; German: BKV 2nd ed. 60.323–27 (J. Baer); French: Bayard, *St. Cyprien* II; Joannou, CPG 303–13.

Literature: G. Bardy, 'Cyprien', DSDH 2 (1953) 2661–96; G. Bardy, 'Cyprien de Carthage', DHGE 13 (1956) 1149–60; M. Bénevot, 'Cyprian von Karthago', TRE 8 (1981) 246–54; J. Patout Burns, *Cyprian the Bishop* (Routledge Early Church Monographs; London 2002); G. D. Dunn, 'Cyprian and Women in a Time of Persecution', JEH 57 (2006) 205–25; G. D. Dunn, 'Heresy and Schism according to Cyprian of Carthage', JTS 55 (2004) 551–74; G. D. Dunn, '"Sententiam nostram non novam promimus": Cyprian and the Episcopal Synod of 255', AHC 35 (2003) 211–21; J. A. Fischer, 'Das Konzil zu Karthago im Jahre 255', AHC 14 (1982) 227–40; J. A. Fischer, 'Das Konzil zu Karthago im Frühjahr 256', AHC 15 (1983) 1–14; J. A. Fischer, 'Das Konzil zu Karthago im Spätsommer 256', AHC 16 (1984) 1–39; Paolo Bernadini, *Un solo battesimo una sola chiesa: Il concilio di Cartagine del settembre 256* (Testi e ricerche di scienze religiose n.s. 43; Bologna

---

430. Cf. Beck, *Kirche* 633.
431. Diekamp, *Analecta Patristica* 81–82 = H. Delehaye, *Analecta Bollandiana* 26 (1907) 222–23.
432. Cf. Joannou, CPG 290.
433. ClavisG 5983; Grumel, *Les Regestes*; Diekamp, *Analecta Patristica* 83 = Pitra, *Juris* 2.187–88.

2009). A. Hoffmann, 'Cyprian of Carthage', DECL 148–53; Andreas Hoffmann, *Kirchliche Strukturen und römisches Recht bei Cyprian von Karthago* (Rechts- und staatswissenschaftliche Veröffentlichungen der Görres-Gesellschaft 92; Paderborn 2000); V. Saxer, 'Cyprian of Carthage', EEC 211–12; A. Stuiber, 'Cyprianus I', RAC 3 (1957) 463–66.

A Greek translation of the synodal letter of the Carthaginian synod of 255 on the validity of heretical baptisms found its way into the Greek canonical collections as a 'canon of Cyprian of Carthage.'[434] This synodal canon promulgated by 32 African bishops, preserved as number 70 among the letters of Cyprian, belongs (together with its confirmation by the Carthaginian synod of early 256 and the African general council attended by 87 bishops of 1 September 256) to the most important documents of the baptismal controversy between Cyprian and Bishop Stephan of Rome (254–56).[435] The decision of 255 opposed without distinction the validity of any baptism made by heretics and schismatics, since the Church was not there and since outside the Catholic Church no one may be baptized. A re-baptism was mandatory if they were seeking entry into the Catholic Church. The synodal proceedings of 1 September 256[436] were also occasionally received into the Greek canonical literature.[437]

The Greek translations were probably all written by the same person, whose translation was not precise. The author and time are unknown.[438] In the Greek collections, the 'canon of Cyprian' first appears in the *Syntagma XIV titulorum*,[439] even before the Quinisext Council. This already confirms its being a part of the canonical material of the Eastern Church. In any case, the statement in c. 2 of the Quinisext makes it clear that the decision represented only the African local tradition and had validity only there.[440] The Quinisext documented the regulation of the problem in question, which had been altered by c. 8 of Nicaea, c. 7 of Constantinople (381), canons 1 and 47 of Basil, and the Quinisext's own c. 95. In connection with this, we note that only a small number of Greek canonical *compendia* preserve the 'canon of Cyprian' at all.[441] At the same time, c. 2 of the Quinisext carried the canon as the last in a series of Canons of the

---

434. Cf. Fischer, 'Jahre 255'.
435. Cf. Fischer, 'Frühjahr 256' and 'Spätsommer 256'.
436. *Sententiae episcoporum numero LXXXVII de haereticis baptizandis*, Soden, ed. (NGWG; Berlin 1909) 247–307; CSEL 3.1.433–61.
437. Cf. Rhalles-Potles 3.7–9 (commentary of Zonoras); Paris, BNF (Codex Patmiacus) 172, fol. 38–49.
438. Cf. Bayard, *St. Cyprien* 2.252. In his edition, the translator's proemium to the synodal proceedings of 1 September 256 was placed by Joannou (CPG 303–4) before the decision of 255 without explanation.
439. Cf. below, Troianos.
440. Cf. Joannou, CCO 124.9–16.
441. Cf. Joannou, CCO 2 ('Introduction générale à l'édition'), CPG 303.

Fathers, thus documenting with historical correctness the late date of its addition to the Greek corpus.

When, in newer collections and editions, the concept of historicized organization and dogmatic weighting of canons grew dominant, 'The Synod of Carthage' (thus in the title) was placed among the local synods, even before the synod of Ancyra.[442]

442. Cf., for example, Pedalion 366–71; Rhalles-Potles 3.1–9.

3

Byzantine Canon Law to 1100

Spyros Troianos

The Collections of the Fourth and Fifth Centuries: The Creation of the *Corpus canonum*

During the fourth century, many councils, most of them local, convened and enacted provisions for the organization and the functioning the legal life of the Church. In connection with these provisions (the 'canons', as they were called), there soon appeared collections that came about solely through private initiative. These collections initially served local purposes and were not unrelated to dogmatic definitions that prevailed in the specific localities.

The basic collection, which passed through several phases of revision, is known as the *corpus canonum*. It has not survived in its original form, however, and the efforts to reconstruct its contents are based on other collections that were based on it or that were simply influenced by it. The first place among these indirect sources is held by the Syriac collection of 193 synodical canons that was put together in the year 500/501 in Hierapolis. This, as well as the Latin translations of the same period, provide significant help in the process of reconstruction.[1]

Based on the sources mentioned above, one can draw the following

---

1. See Schwartz, 'Kanonensammlungen' 1–114 (here 3ff.).

conclusions as to the origins and the original form of the *corpus canonum*. It was created in Antioch by circles of doubtful orthodoxy, and so it did not contain the creed and the canons of Nicaea. Determining the *terminus post quem* for its compilation is not easy because the exact time of the synod of Laodikeia, the canons of which are contained in the *corpus*, is not known. It is placed between 342 and 370. On the other hand, the *terminus ante quem* can be determined with greater accuracy. The organization of the *Apostolic Constitutions* (ca. 380)[2] presupposes the existence of the *corpus*. It contained the canons of the synods of Ankyra and Neokaisareia (possibly joined together), of Gangra, of Antioch (these having been attributed to a synod that convened in 341 for the consecration of the great church of the city, but in fact having originated from a much earlier—possibly around 330—synod of Arian composition), and finally the synod of Laodikeia. In this original form the canons were probably numbered only by synod.

During the reign of Theodosios I, the Arianism of the Church of Antioch was eliminated, and at that time the creed and canons of Nicaea were attached to the beginning of the *corpus canonum*. Thus, the chronological order of the canons, which apparently had been the basis of the collection's original order, was disturbed. In this way, however, the *corpus canonum* acquired an orthodox appearance and had no difficulty in preserving its authority. The fact that the origin of many of the canons was suspect from a dogmatic point of view was not an obstacle, because even these canons contained elements that dealt with the exercise of ecclesiastical administrative authority of a more general nature and thus were dogmatically completely neutral.

As already mentioned, the *corpus canonum* passed through more phases of revision. After the addition of the creed and the canons of Nicaea, the next two phases included the expansion of the collection with, first, the canons of the Council of Constantinople of 381 (Second Ecumenical Council) and, later, those of Chalcedon of 451 (Fourth Ecumenical Council). The 'canons' of the Council of Ephesus of 431 do not appear because they were shaped at a later time based on the minutes of the synod.

In its final form the *corpus canonum* certainly had a duplicate numbering of the canons, both according to synods and according to continuous sequence. It contained 193 canons (as many as the Syriac translation of Hierapolis) arranged as follows:[3]

---

2. M. Metzger, *Les Constitutions Apostoliques I.* (Sources chrétiennes 320; Paris 1985) 59.
3. See Honigmann, 'Le concile de Constantinople de 394 et les auteurs du "Syntagma des XIV titres",' *Trois mémoires* 50.

1–20	Nicaea	79–103 (1–25)	Antioch
21–44 (1–24)	Ankyra	104–162 (1–59)	Laodikeia
45–58 (1–14)	Neokaisareia	163–166 (1–4)	Constantinople
9–78 (1–20)	Gangra	167–193 (1–27)	Chalcedon

In spite of its unofficial origin, the *corpus canonum* enjoyed official recognition, as its use during the proceedings of the Fourth Ecumenical Council at Chalcedon shows.[4] This practice created a tradition in the Eastern Church: until the destruction of the Byzantine state, of the many canonical collections that were at times in use, not one was formed directly by the church authorities or even at their mandate.

After the completion of the four phases through which the *corpus canonum* passed before its final formulation, other canons also appeared, originating from either councils or other sources. Here belong the eighty-five so-called Apostolic canons, the canons of the Synod of Serdica in their Greek translation, the *materies Africana* or *corpus canonum Ecclesiae Africanae*, and also the canons of the fathers of the Eastern Church. This canonical material was never incorporated into the framework of the *corpus canonum* in a further, fifth phase of revision, but it was considered authoritative and was applied (especially the Apostolic canons) alongside the *corpus canonum*. The integration of the *corpus canonum* with the other canonical material (except for the canons of the fathers) took place in the Latin translations of the Greek canonical texts, especially in those translations that Dionysius Exiguus put together in three consecutive editions between the last years of the fifth century and 520.[5] Specifically regarding the Apostolic canons, it should be noted that they appear only in the work of Dionysius, and even then not all of them appear, but only the first fifty.

The Collection of the Sixty Titles

As mentioned in the preceding section, the *corpus canonum* was not systematic and arranged according to topics. In all of its versions, the canons were arranged according to councils, and these in turn had a chronological order, with the exception of the Council of Nicaea.

The first attempt at preparing a systematic collection (i.e., one organized according to the topics with corresponding canons) was made in the sixth century.[6] The need for a collection of this form was dictated by the increase in the number of canons (mostly due to the eighty-five Apostolic

---

4. E. Schwartz, *Acta conciliorum oecumenicorum* II.1.2 (1933) 79.11, 36; 118.8; II.1.3 (1935) 48.23.
5. See Schwartz, 'Kanonensammlungen' 61ff., 110ff.
6. See Zachariä von Lingenthal, 'Nomokanones', 2ff. (= 615ff.). Brian E. Ferme, *Introduction to the History of the Sources of Canon Law: The Ancient Law up to the Decretum of Gratian* (Gratianus; Montreal 2007) 86–87.

canons; for the *materies Africana* had not yet been translated into Greek), which made the general monitoring of this material as a whole extremely difficult. Perhaps this effort was also influenced by the codification of Justinian with regard to the provisions of civil law.

The product of this attempt has not survived. The only mention of its existence is contained in a prologue of a similar, later work that was based on that first collection. The later work is the *Synagoge of Ecclesiastical Canons Divided into 50 Titles* by John Scholastikos. From an analysis of the prologue of the *Synagoge*, one can come to the following conclusions about the first collection. The editor is not named. It was organized under sixty titles without subdivisions of chapters and without separation of the canons under each title. It also included the entire content of the *corpus canonum* in its final (most recent) form; the eighty-five Apostolic canons; the canons of the Synod of Ephesus, which had been compiled in the meantime; and the canons of the Synod of Serdica. This last conclusion, that the content of the collection was organized under sixty titles, is supported by the testimony of John Scholastikos, who clearly points out that, in the compilation of that collection, the canons of St. Basil were not considered, which implies that in the rest, the same canonical material as found in the *Synagoge* was used. It is conjectured that the collection with sixty titles was compiled in Antioch between 535 and 545. The *terminus ante quem* is established by dating the compilation of the *Synagoge*.

It is very probable that this collection was supplemented by a second one, in the form of an appendix, which contained imperial legislation of ecclesiastical interest. This opinion is based on the fact that John makes mention in his prologue not only of the great number of canons but also of the volume of laws that regulated ecclesiastical issues. This second collection, which was named *Collectio XXV capitulorum* by the historians of law in the nineteenth century, will be dealt with later.

The Collection of the 50 Titles

Critical edition: Beneševič, *Synagoga*.

Bibliography: Zachariä von Lingenthal, 'Nomokanones' 4ff. (= 617ff.); V. N. Beneševič, *Sinagoga v 50 titulov i drugie juridičeskie sborniki Joanna Scholastika* (St. Petersburg 1914; reprint Leipzig 1972); E. Schwartz, 'Die Kanonensammlung des Johannes Scholastikos', *Sitzungsberichte der Bayerische Akademie der Wissenschaften, Phil.-hist. Abt.* 6, 1933; reprint Leipzig 1972).

The preceding section mentioned the name of John Scholastikos and his contribution to the preservation of the only piece of information about the existence of that first collection of holy canons. John was a son of a cleric and was born in Seremi, near Antioch, at the beginning of the sixth century. He studied law and practiced the profession of attorney-at-law (scholastic) in Antioch until about 550, when he was ordained a presbyter by Domnos (or Domninos), the Patriarch of Antioch, and was sent to Constantinople as the *apokrisiarios* of the patriarchate. There he was distinguished not only for his abilities and his knowledge but also for his orthodox faith, and he was selected by Emperor Justinian I in January 565 as the successor to Patriarch Eutychius of Constantinople, who was removed from the throne for dogmatic reasons. John remained Patriarch until his death in August of 577. Good arguments suggest the identification of John Scholastikos with the historian John Malalas.[7]

While still in Antioch (i.e., before 550), John, considering that the first systematic collection of sixty titles did not, because of deficiencies in its organization, adequately cover the practical need of facilitating the speedy location of every topic being sought, put together a new collection. This collection, as we have already seen, was called *Synagoge of Ecclesiastical Canons Divided into 50 Titles* (Συναγωγὴ κανόνων ἐκκλησιαστικῶν εἰς ν′ τίτλους διῃρημένη). As this name reveals, the collection was organized under 50 titles (not 60, as in the previous one) according to criteria corresponding to the ecclesiastical hierarchy. The editor took into account the canons of all the ecumenical and local councils of the East as well as the Apostolic canons, the canons of the Synod of Serdica, and the sixty-eight canons of St. Basil derived from his second and third canonical epistles.

The canons under each title are referred to by their number according to synod or group (the canons of St. Basil have a consecutive numbering and are not by epistle) and have the following order: eighty-five Apostolic, twenty of Nicaea, twenty-five of Ankyra, fourteen of Neokaisareia, twenty-one of Serdica, twenty of Gangra, twenty-five of Antioch, fifty-nine of Laodikeia, six of Constantinople, seven of Ephesus, twenty-seven of Chalcedon, and sixty-eight of St. Basil. We see, that is, that the basic order of the *corpus canonum* has been followed, with the insertion of the canons of Serdica between those of Neokaisareia and Gangra.

The canons are presented whole and without division, even if they relate to more than one topic which may be classified under different titles. Deviation from this principle occurs with only six canons: canon 6 of Nicaea, canon 20 of Gangra, canon 2 of Antioch, canons 3 and 11 of Serdica, and canon 35 of St. Basil. Of these, three appear under two titles after hav-

---

7. See J. Haury, 'Johannes Malalas identisch mit dem Patriarchen Johannes Scholastikos?' BZ 9 (1900) 337–56. See also S. Troianos, Ἰωάννης Γ′ "ὁ ἀπὸ Σχολαστικῶν" καὶ Ἰωάννης Μαλάλας, "Ἀναφορὰ εἰς μνήμην Μητροπολίτου Σάρδεων Μαξίμου" V (Geneva 1989) 33–39. For a different opinion on this identification, see *The Chronicle of John Malalas*, trans. E. Jeffreys, M. Jeffreys, R. Scott, et al (Melbourne 1986) xxi–xxii.

ing been divided, while the other three have been inserted whole, or in part, twice under different titles. Therefore, with the exception of the above, every canon is contained in the *Synagoge* only once. References to thematically related canons under different titles do not exist.

Just as in the older collection of the sixty titles, the *Synagoge* was probably also accompanied by a collection of provisions of civil law, the *Collectio LXXXVII capitulorum,* which will be dealt with later.

Several centuries after its creation, approximately at the end of the ninth century, the *Synagoge* was translated into Slavic and became the basis for the compilation of the canon law of Methodios.[8]

The *Syntagma of Canons of 14 Titles*

During the last decades of the sixth century (probably ca. 580), a third systematic collection was formed. According to one unconfirmed hypothesis,[9] this collection was created by the patriarchs of Constantinople Eutychios and John IV Nesteutes (`Faster'). Although it does not survive complete, its text has been handed down to us in an indirect way through the *Nomokanon of 14 Titles,* which was based on it.[10]

The *Syntagma* differed substantially from the *Synagoge* of John Scholastikos. First, it was much richer in content because it included the *materies Africana* in a Greek translation (although not an especially good one) made ca. 550 that was divided into 137 canons, the canonical decisions of a synod of Constantinople in the year 394, and many canons of the fathers beyond those of St. Basil contained in the *Synagoge*. Second, the *Syntagma* was organized in a different way. It was divided into fourteen titles, and every title was subdivided into chapters. In every chapter, related canons are mentioned by their number according to synod, etc., without however the inclusion of their text there. The texts, listed according to their source (Apostolic canons, canons of synods, canons of the fathers), were gathered in a special collection. Constantinople must be regarded as the place where the *Syntagma* was edited.[11] The *Collectio tripartita* constituted a supplement in the form of an appendix.

The *Synopsis of Canons*

Editions: (a) 'Stephanos of Ephesus': M. Krasnožen, *Tolkovateli kanoničeskago kodeksa vostočnoj cerkvi: Aristin, Zonara i Valsamon* (Učenija Zapiski Imperat. Moskovskago Uni-

---

8. See H. Papastathis, Τὸ νομοθετικὸν ἔργον τῆς κυριλλομεθοδιανῆς ἱεραποστολῆς ἐν Μεγάλῃ Μοραβίᾳ (Ἑλλην. Ἑταιρεία Σλαβικῶν Μελετῶν 2; Thessalonika 1978) 49.

9. Honigmann, *Trois mémoires* 49–64.

10. Because of this relationship, the bibliography of the *Nomokanon of 14 Titles* also covers the *Syntagma*.

11. Zachariä von Lingenthal, 'Nomokanones' 7ff. (= 620ff.)

versiteta, Fasc. 8; Moscow 1894) Priloženija 207–21; M. Krasnožen, 'Acta et commendationes Imperat', *Universitatis Jurievensis* 19 (1911) N° 12 III–XVIII; M. Krasnožen, 'Sinopsis cerkovnich pravil i istorija ego obrazovanija', VV 17 (1910) 225–46. (b) Symeon: Voel-Justel II 710–748 (= PG 114.236–92). (c) Short form: Voel-Justel II 673–709 (= PG 133.64–113). (d) Aristenos: Beveregius 2.1, col. 188ff.; Rhalles-Potles II–IV *passim*; PG 137.35–1498 and 138.9–938.

Bibliography: A. Christophilopoulos, Ἡ 'κανονικὴ σύνοψις' καὶ ὁ Συμεὼν ὁ Μεταφράστης (EEBS 19; Athens 1949) 155–57; A. Christophilopoulos, Δίκαιον καὶ Ἱστορία (Athens, 1973) 138–40; Honigmann, *Trois mémoires* 8off.; van der Wal–Lokin 68ff.; K. E. Zachariä von Lingenthal, 'Die Synopsis canonum: Ein Beitrag zur Geschichte der Quellen des kanonischen Rechts der griechischen Kirche', *Sitzungsberichte der königlich-preussischen Akademie der Wissenschaften zu Berlin*, Jg. 1887, 1147–1163 (= *Kleine Schriften* 2.247–63).

Among the collections of canons that contain the canonical texts in their entirety, one also appears that includes these texts in epitome form. Perhaps the creation of these epitomes was influenced by the *summae*, which bear exactly the same relation to the texts of civil law. The date when this collection was created cannot be specified with accuracy. 'Stephanos the Ephesian' is named in some manuscripts as its author. A hypothesis has been put forward that this might be the bishop of Ephesus, Stephanos, who participated in the Council of Chalcedon (451). It has been pointed out, however, that bishops are never referred to with the name of their bishopric as a surname, and that in this case he would have been referred to as 'Stephanos of Ephesus.' It is also improbable that there was another bishop of Ephesus with the name Stephanos who participated in the proceedings of the Quinisext Synod.

The original text of the *Synopsis* does not seem to have survived. Of course, Krasnožen, from a codex from Vienna, Österreichische Nationalbibliothek theol. gr. 283, published a text that bore the heading 'Canonical Synopsis of Stephanos of Ephesus', proposing that this was the original form of this collection. This text contains epitomes of the canons (in order) of the Apostles, of Nicaea, of Ankyra, of Neokaisareia, of Gangra, and of Antioch. Unfortunately, because of missing pages in the codex, the text is interrupted toward the end of the canons of Antioch, and it is unknown what else the collection contained. This text, however, up to where it is interrupted, coincides with the one edited by Voel and Justel both in the content and in the order of the canons, with only minor differences in expression (not uncommon in the manuscript tradition of the Byzantine sources, even the legal ones, and often due to misreading by the copyists or, even, to 'improving' interventions by the scribes). This text, for which the manuscript tradition is not very broad, is also found in cod. Paris, BNF gr. 1302, fol. 8v–21r and is there attributed to Aristenos (Τοῦ Ἀριστηνοῦ). This finding and the many successive revisions that the *Synop*-

sis has undergone raise many doubts as to whether the text published by Krasnožen is the one that Stephanos wrote.

Aside from these reservations, however, it is possible to formulate some hypotheses about the content of the original form of the text. Specifically, the different position of certain groups of canons in later revisions of the text leads to the conclusion that these canons were not present in the original text. This holds true most especially for the canons of the Quinisext Synod. Since it does not seem that the *Synopsis* preceded the *Syntagma of 14 Titles*, it can be proposed with sufficient certainty that the *Synopsis* was put together between 580 (supposedly the time when the *Syntagma* was prepared) and 691/692 (the time when the Quinisext Synod convened).

A later revision of the *Synopsis* is attributed to a scholar of the tenth century, the magistrate and lawmaker Symeon.[12] In this form, the *Synopsis* contains epitomes of the following canons in the following order: of the Apostles, Nicaea, Constantinople (381), Ephesus, Chalcedon, Ankyra, Neokaisareia, Serdica, Gangra, Antioch, Laodikeia, Carthage, St. Basil, and the Quinisext Synod.[13] It is obvious that the above arrangement was based on criteria of importance: the canons of the Apostles come first, followed by those of the ecumenical councils, and then those of the local councils in chronological order. The reason that the canons of the Quinisext Synod are found at the end is that they were appended after the material had been already arranged.

The *Synopsis* was used much later, during the twelfth century, by Alexius Aristenos. This canonist based his commentary not on the authentic text of the canons but on the abridged version found in the *Synopsis*. There are differences, however, between the text of Symeon and the text that precedes the comments of Aristenos: (a) In many instances the text is different. (b) In the *Synopsis* of Symeon we note the omission of certain canons, especially those of Carthage. (c) Regarding synods, the *Synopsis* of Symeon stops at the Council of Trullo (Quinisext), and regarding the fathers, it contains only the canons of St. Basil the Great. By contrast, the *Synopsis* in the work of Aristenos also takes into account the canons of the synods of Constantinople (394), of the Seventh Ecumenical Coun-

---

12. It has been proposed that he is to be identified with Symeon the Metaphrastes; see Beck, *Kirche* 570ff., especially 572. See also Christophilopoulos, Ἡ κανονικὴ σύνοψις, as well as A. Marcopoulos, 'Sur les deux versions de la Chronographie de Syméon Logothete', BZ 76 (1983) 279–284.

13. The text of Symeon is contained in the codices Athon. Vatop. 543 fol. 5r–59v; Oxford, BodleianLibrary Baroc. 86 fol. 156v–172v; Marc. App. gr. III.2 (= Nan. 226) f. 205v–220v; Mosq. GIM Bibl. Synod. 397 (= 316 Vladimir) f. 162r–180r; and Paris, BNF gr. 1370 fol. 128v–140r (this is the manuscript used by Voel and Justel for their edition). Sometimes we find deviations from the order of canons. So in Firenze, Laurenziana Plut. V.22, fol. 119r–139r before all the canons (even those of the Apostles) we find the canons of Chalcedon.

cil, of Primasecunda, and of St. Sophia, just as it also does the canons of almost all the other fathers. d) The order in which the canons are presented differs. In Aristenos the following order pertains: Apostles, Nicaea, Ankyra, Neokaisareia, Gangra, Antioch, Laodikeia, Constantinople (381), Ephesus, Chalcedon, Serdica, Carthage, Constantinople (394), Quinisext, Seventh, Primasecunda, St. Sophia, St. Basil, and the rest of the fathers.

One might conjecture that all of these changes and additions were made by Aristenos, who may have revised the text of the *Synopsis* before he wrote his commentary. This hypothesis has to be rejected, however, because in one place Aristenos argues against the text of the *Synopsis*. Specifically, in his comments on canon 75 of the Apostles, he accuses its editor of error in rendering the content of the canon.[14] This means, first, that he is not the editor of the *Synopsis* and, second, that he did not attempt any interference with its text, because in that case he would have corrected the misunderstanding in the rendering of canon 75 of the Apostles.

These observations compel us to accept that the text, which Aristenos undertook to comment on in the twelfth century, was already in existence. This conclusion is verified by studying the manuscripts, because the text in question has been preserved in the codices Athon. Cutlum. 42 fol. IV–20v (eleventh century), Munich, Staatsbibliothek (Monacensis) gr. 122 fol. IV–22v (twelfth century), and Athon. Pantocr. 234 fol. 288r–300r (thirteenth century). In the first two, the whole text is not preserved (pages in the middle are lost), but this does not prevent its identification with the content of the third. Following the order of canons as described above (basically that of the codices containing the interpretation of Aristenos), this last manuscript also includes (after the canons of St. Basil) epitomes of the canons of Dionysius of Alexandria, of Peter of Alexandria, of Gregory the Theologian, of Athanasius of Alexandria, of Amphilochius, of Gregory of Nyssa, of Timothy of Alexandria, of Cyril, of Gennadius, and of certain other canonical texts coming from the 'Epitome of the eighth book of the injunctions of the holy apostles'. This order, as well as the rendering of the epitomes, is absolutely identical to that found in the manuscript tradition of Aristenos.

These three codices present a common characteristic: they contain the *Nomokanon of 14 Titles* in its third form (i.e., the revision of Theodore Bestes; the *Synopsis* is found within the manuscripts in close proximity to the text of the *Nomokanon*, and the *Synopsis* contains references to related chapters of the *Nomokanon*. At some time, furthermore, the person revis-

---

14. 'Ὁ τὸν παρόντα συνοψίσας κανόνα οὐ καλῶς τοῦτον ἐνόησεν· (. . .)' Rhalles-Potles 2.97, 25.

ing the *Synopsis*, instead of quoting an excerpt from it (e.g., the epitome of the canonical work of Amphilochius), simply referred to the chapter of the *Nomokanon* where this text had been recorded. All of this shows that we have before us a revision that has a direct relationship, in terms of both time and procedure, with the third edition of the *Nomokanon* by Theodore Bestes. Since this last edition took place in 1083 and since the oldest of our three manuscripts is from the eleventh century,[15] the revision of the *Synopsis* must be placed in this same period; i.e., toward the end of the eleventh century.

The purpose of this revision is obvious. It was evident that significant differences in content existed between the *Synopsis* in its last form (i.e., that of Symeon) and the *Nomokanon*. (The *Synopsis* of Symeon did not contain canons from any synods after the Quinisext or from the Synod of Constantinople (394) and, of the canons of the fathers, it contained only those of St. Basil.) Thus, it was thought necessary to bring the two texts to the same level from the point of view of the fullness of the content. It is quite certain that the completion of the *Synopsis* took place in stages. At least, this is the evidence of the source material, because, while the epitomes of the canons of the Seventh Ecumenical Council and those of the ninth century are fairly brief (yet not as brief as those of the older synods), the epitomes of the patristic texts are rather lengthy. In addition, there exist manuscripts with intermediate forms of the *Synopsis*, in which one can see the evolution of its form.[16] The first stage of the revision possibly had as an object not primarily to modify language and expression but to change the order of the canons and adapt them to follow those of the *Nomokanon of 14 Titles*.[17] It is from this stage that the somewhat abridged form (mainly with respect to the canons of Carthage, the Quinisext Synod, and St. Basil), as mentioned above, probably resulted.[18] In parallel, there appear sporadic and isolated collections with a smaller or greater number of excerpts.[19]

---

15. For the chronology of Cod. Athon. Cutlum. 42, see S. Lampros, Κατάλογος τῶν ἐν ταῖς βιβλιοθήκαις τοῦ Ἁγίου Ὄρους ἑλληνικῶν κωδίκων I (Cambridge 1895; reprinted Amsterdam 1966) 278; and J. Gouillard, 'Un Chrysobulle de Nicéphore Botaneiatès à souscription synodale', *Byzantion* 29–30 (1959–1960) 29–41 (here 29 n. 6). This manuscript was written in more than one stage, of which the older one belongs to the eleventh century. The text of the *Synopsis* is at 1v–20v, i.e., at the beginning of the codex.

16. To this belong Milan, Ambrosiana (Ambros). gr. 303 (E 94 sup.) fol. 200r–218r, which was, of course, written in the sixteenth century, but is apparently attributed to an older prototype. In this codex, while we find that the order of the codices of Aristenos is followed, the canons of Serdica are inserted between those of Neokaisareia and Gangra, just as in the *Synopsis* of Symeon.

17. This stage of reworking is represented in Oxford, Bodleian Library. 264 fol. 242r–253v.

18. See editions under (c) in Cod. Paris. gr. 1302 fol. 8v–21r, as well.

19. Cod. Scor. X. II. 10 fol. 399v–400v contains (in a mixed text of Symeon and the above

The Imperial Legislation of the Sixth to Eighth Centuries

Ecclesiastical Law in the Imperial Laws of the Sixth to Eighth Centuries: Justinian I and His Successors

Editions (only the most recent ones): (a) *Corpus iuris civilis*: Vol. 1: *Institutiones*, P. Krüger, ed., *Digesta*, T. Mommsen, ed., retract. P. Krüger (Berlin 1908; reprint Hildesheim 1993); Vol. 2: *Codex Iustinianus*, P. Krüger, ed. (Berlin 1954; reprint Hildesheim 1989); Vol. 3: *Novellae*, R. Schöll and W. Kroll, eds. (Berlin 1928; reprint Hildesheim 1993). (b) *Novellae of Herakleios*: J. Konidaris, 'Die Novellen des Kaisers Herakleios',' FM 5 33–106.

Translations: (a) *Corpus iuris civilis*: H. Hulot, J. F. Berthelot, P. A. Tissot, and A. Bérenger, *Corps de droit civil romain en latin et en français* (14 vols. Metz 1803–1811; reprint Aalen 1979; French); K. E. Otto, B. Schilling, and K. F. F. Sintenis, *Das Corpus iuris civilis* I–VII (Leipzig 1831–1839; reprint Aalen 1984–1985; German); O. Behrends, R. Knütel, B. Kubisch, and H. H. Seiler, *Corpus iuris civilis: Text und Übersetzung* 1 (Institutionen, Heidelberg 1990; German); *The Digest of Justinian*, Latin text edited by Theodor Mommsen and Paul Krueger; English translation edited by Alan Watson (4 volumes; Philadelphia 1985); P. Birks and G. McLeod, *Justinian's Institutes* (London 1987; English). (b) Konidaris, *Novellae of Herakleios* (German).

Bibliography: H. Alivisatos, *Die kirchliche Gesetzgebung des Kaisers Justinian 1* (Berlin 1913; reprint Aalen 1973); Beck, *Nomos*; B. Biondi, *Il diritto romano cristiano* I–III (Milan 1952–1954); C. de Clercq, 'Corpus iuris civilis', DDC IV (1949) 644–80; A.M. Demicheli, *La Μεγάλη Ἐκκλησία nel lessico e nel diritto di Giustiniano* (Milan 1990); A. Knecht, *System des Justinianischen Kirchenvermögensrechtes* (Stuttgart 1905; reprint Amsterdam 1963); R. Macrides, 'Nomos and Kanon on Paper and in Court', *Church and People in Byzantium*, R. Morris, ed. (London 1991) 61–85; R. Naz, 'Constitutions impériales', DDC IV (1949) 460–62; K. Pitsakis, '"Ius graeco-romanum" et normes canoniques dans les eglises de la tradition orthodoxe', *Incontro fra canoni d'Oriente e d'Occidente* 1 (Bari 1994) 99–132; S. Troianos, 'Nomos und Kanon in Byzanz', *Kanon* 10 (1991) 37–51.

Of the three parts of Justinian's codification—the *Pandects* (*Digest*), the *Codex*, and the *Institutes*—the *Codex* contains the greatest number of provisions dealing with the Church. The *Pandects* (*Digest*) and the *Institutes*, on the other hand, contain only a very small number of such provisions, and these occur specifically under the titles dedicated to the *ius sacrum*.

The *Codex Justinianus* was published in its first edition in 529 and in the second (*Codex Iustinianus repetitae praelectionis*) in 534. The first edition has not survived, so the structure and content of the second are all that are known to us. The work is divided into twelve books. The first thirteen titles of Book I refer to the Church, but this of course does not preclude the existence of provisions scattered throughout the remaining books, depending on their content and in accordance with the principles of the systematic arrangement followed by the editing committee of the Codex.

---

collection, according to the order of the *Nomokanon*) a few canons of the synods of Nicaea, Ankyra, Neokaisareia, Antioch, Laodikeia, Constantinople of 381, and Carthage. The codices Cod. Athon, Docheiar. 296 fol. 152v–155r and Vat. gr 828 fol. 346v–348r contain a selection of the canons of the Apostles (Athon) and of St. Basil the Great (Vatican).

Title 1 is labeled *De Summa Trinitate et de fide catholica* etc. and contains eight provisions beginning with two *constitutiones* of Theodosius I from the years 380 and 381. Then follow the provisions issued by Theodosius II (448), by Marcian (452), and finally by Justinian. In these *constitutiones* are repeated the dogmatic principles enacted by the ecumenical councils that had convened in the meantime, and in them are condemned the heretical teachings opposed to these principles. In place of a last provision is a letter from Pope John II to Justinian, which is a reply to a letter from the emperor.

Title 2 is labeled *De sacrosanctis ecclesiis*, with twenty-five *constitutiones*. The first one is by Constantine (321). Then follow others by Theodosius I, Theodosius II, Marcian, Leo, Zeno, and Anastasius. The last seven are by Justinian. They enact privileges (primarily with respect to public justice), but they also regulate issues relating to the management of ecclesiastical property.

Title 3 bears the heading *De episcopis et clericis,* with fifty-five *constitutiones*. It begins with laws by Constantine and ends with provisions by Justinian, which are the most numerous (fifteen) and the most extensive. These provisions regulate a multitude of issues that relate to clergy and the monks: Conditions for entering the ranks of the clergy, personal and property privileges of the clergy, the shaping of the monastic life, etc. Under this title also are enacted principles relating to the management of ecclesiastical property.

Title 4 has the title *De episcopali audentia,* with thirty-four provisions from Valentinian and Valens to Justinian (the last fifteen). These regulate the participation of bishops in the dispensation of justice—civil as well as penal.

Title 5 is labeled *De haereticis et Manichaeis et Samaritis* and contains twenty-two provisions from Constantine to Justinian. These designate the heresies along with the penalties, both penal and civil, which are meted out to their adherents.

Title 6, under the heading *Ne sanctum baptisma iteretur,* contains three *constitutiones* of emperors of the fourth and fifth centuries. These forbid the repetition of the sacrament of baptism.

Title 7 (*De apostatis*) includes seven *constitutiones,* again of emperors of the fourth and fifth centuries, by which they enact punishments against those who leave the Christian faith.

A provision of 427—the only content of title 8—prohibits carving the sign of the cross on the ground.

Title 9, inscribed *De Iudaeis et Caelicolis,* includes eighteen provisions (third-fifth centuries) regulating the legal status of the Jews. Similarly, title

10 contains two provisions that forbid heretics, pagans, and Jews to have Christians as slaves.

Title 11 (*De paganis sacrificiis et templis*) includes ten *constitutiones* of emperors of the fourth and fifth centuries and contains prohibitions and restrictions regarding the sacrifices and temples of the pagans.

Title 12 (*De his qui ad ecclesias confugiunt vel ibi exclamant*) includes eight *constitutiones* regarding the institution of asylum.

Finally, two provisions of Constantine were included in title 13, by which he regulated the emancipation of slaves in a church.

From the proportion of Justinian's laws in titles 2–5 (which are also the most extensive), it appears that the topics that attracted the attention of this emperor were the organization of the Church and the administration of its property, as well as the regulation of the personal status of clergy and monks.

The legislative activity of Justinian continued undiminished even after the publication of the *Codex*. The laws of general interest and content are known as 'novellae' ('νεαραί' ; *constitutiones* or provisions). No official collection of the novellae has survived; thus we draw our knowledge about them from unofficial collections or from didactic works. The best known of the private collections is the so-called *Collection of the 168 Novellae* (*Collectio CLXVIII novellarum*), which must have received its final form shortly after the death of Justinian (probably around 575). *Novellae* of Justinian comprise most of it, and it was completed with seven more from his successors; i.e., four from Justinian II and three from Tiberius II.

A great number of the novellae of this collection, approximately one-fourth, deal with ecclesiastical matters; specifically novellae 3, 5–7, 9, 11, 16, 37, 40–43, 45–46, 55–59, 65, 67, 76, 79, 81, 83, 86, 109, 111, 120, 123, 129, 131–133, 137, 144, and 146. These laws are primarily concerned with the operation of the ecclesiastical administration, the clergy, and the organization of the monastic life. Usually, every novella is dedicated to the regulation of one of the above topics. Two, however, stand apart: novellae 120 and 123; in the first of these are concentrated the property law of the Church and in the second the law relating to the people of the Church. These two novellae (along with 117 and 118, which deal with family and inheritance law), could be called 'codifying' because they repeat to a great extent previous law, introducing modifications only to a rather limited degree. This phenomenon may have its explanation in the following thought: It appears from the Constitution, *Cordi* (Nov. 16, 534) that Justinian aimed to proceed with a third edition of the *Codex* or, at least, to gather the subsequent legislative acts in an official collection. This intention was never realized, possibly because, in the summer of 542, the death of the *quastor sacri palatii* Tribonian intervened; he was the editor-in-chief of this work of codification. Therefore, it is possible that these novellae, which were all published after the death of Tribonian, constituted a portion of the preparation for the third edition of the *Codex,* which was not completed as originally planned.

The number of laws by Justinian that deal with the Church is astonishing. In essence, there is no sector of ecclesiastical organization and administration that remained unregulated. It would be unfair, however, to consider Justinian's concern to regulate every ecclesiastical subject as presumptuous, since in most cases it was imperative that this intense legislative activity be imposed because of the reality of the situation that had taken shape in the meantime.[20]

In comparison to the direct sources of the law of the Church (i.e., the holy scriptures, the canons of synods—especially the ecumenical ones—and tradition), the provisions of civil law (after the smoothing out of relations between church and state; i.e., since the fourth century) became sources, which were at least initially helpful. In this sense, it is natural that these same emperors decreed that their laws should not come into conflict with the holy canons.[21]

In 545, however, we have the following development. With novella 131 (chapter 1), it was decreed that the canons of the four ecumenical councils that had convened up to that time (Nicaea, Constantinople, Ephesus, and Chalcedon), should have the status of law (τάξις νόμων). In this way, all of the legislative content of the decisions of these synods was incorporated formally into the legal order of the state, and it brought about an equalization of laws and canons. This action had a double significance. From the ideological point of view, the emperor appeared in his function as 'general legislator' both to ratify in some way the text of the holy canons and to lend legislative force to them. From the legal point of view, since both laws and canons were more on the same level in terms of formal power, they had to be approached in the same way by those applying the law, whether they were officials of the state or of the church. Therefore, chance contradictions had to be removed by appealing to common methods of interpretation and primarily by applying the principle that the later law abolishes the earlier one when they regulate the same topic. This meant that in the future there was the possibility that holy canons might be abolished by imperial decrees or that their content might be modified

---

20. Beck, *Kirche* 12 n. 17a.
21. See Cod. 1.2.12 (a. 451), Cod. 1.3.44 (45).1 (a. 530), novella 6 pr. and chapt. 1 (a. 535).

by the same procedure, something that also was consistent ideally with imperial ideology.[22]

In spite of this action of Justinian, which was repeated up to a point by Leo VI, the problem of conflicting laws and canons was not dealt with throughout all the periods of Byzantine history in a uniform way, because factors often crept in that influenced the solution of the problem on a case by case basis. Nevertheless, even from later times there is evidence that the removal of contradictions was based on the assimilation of laws and canons and that the most recent decree prevailed, regardless of whether it originated from the church or from the state.

The policy of Justinian, to cover with imperial laws the issues of ecclesiastical administration as they arose, was also followed by his successors. The example of Herakleios is characteristic. All of his surviving legislative work deals with ecclesiastical topics and especially with the legal status of the clergy (primarily those of the Great Church of Constantinople).

The Legislation of the Isaurians and Their Successors

Editions: (a) *Ecloga*: L. Burgmann, *Ecloga: Das Gesetzbuch Leons III. und Konstantinos' V.* (Forschungen zur byzantinische Rechtsgeschichte 10; Frankfurt 1983) with an account of all the previous editions on 140ff. (b) appendix: L. Burgmann and S. Troianos, 'Appendix Eclogae', FM 3.24–125 (with an account of all the previous editions on 24ff.); L. Burgmann and S. Troianos, 'Nomos Mosaikos', FM 3.126–167. (c) Novellae of Eirene: L. Burgmann, 'Die Novellen der Kaiserin Eirene', FM 4.1–36. (d) Novella of Leo: D. Simon, 'Zur Ehegesetzgebung der Isaurier', FM 1.16–43.

Translations: (a) *Ecloga*: Burgmann, *Ecloga* 161ff. (German; on 145ff. reference is made to the English, French, Bulgarian, and Russian translations).

Bibliography: Burgmann, *Ecloga*; B. Sinogowitz, *Studien zum Strafrecht der Ekloge* (Πραγματεῖαι τῆς Ἀκαδημίας Ἀθηνῶν 21; Athens 1956); S. Troianos, Ὁ ʽΠοινάλιος' τοῦ Ἐκλογαδίου. Συμβολὴ εἰς τὴν ἱστορίαν τῆς ἐξελίξεως τοῦ ποινικοῦ δικαίου ἀπὸ τοῦ *Corpus iuris civilis* μέχρι τῶν βασιλικῶν (Forschungen zur byzantinische Rechtsgeschichte 6; Frankfurt 1980); J. Zhishman, *Das Eherecht der orientalischen Kirche* (Vienna 1864) 215ff.

The main legislative act of the Isaurian (or Syrian) emperors is the *Ecloga*. This was published by Leo III and his son Constantine V (the well-known iconoclast emperors), most probably in March of 741 (a 726 date is less likely). It constitutes an effort to gather together the legal rules that were basic to everyday life into concise phrases written in language that could be understood by the average person of that time. This was because, first, the legal texts of the Justinianic period were very difficult to find, and second, they were no longer comprehensible, since legal education was in great decline.[23]

---

22. See Troianos, 'Kirche und Staat' 291–96.
23. See also Pieler, 'Rechtsliteratur' 438ff.; Troianos, Πηγές 70ff.

The *Ecloga* is divided into 18 titles. The first eight contain the law of persons (marriage and inheritance law, guardianship [ἐπιτροπεία], and liberation). Titles 9-13 regulate some basic contractual relationship (purchase, loan, deposit, hire, and so forth). Titles 14 and 15 are about procedural matters (witnesses and agreement). Titles 16 and 18 contain special subjects, while title 17 is about the penal law.

The *Ecloga* was significantly influenced by the canons of the Quinisext Synod, which had taken place approximately half a century earlier.[24] This influence can be found primarily in two areas: in marriage law and in penal law. Canon 54 of the Quinisext Synod expanded the impediments to marriage that were provided by Justinian (*Institutes* 1.10.4 6–7) with regard to both blood relations and relations through marriage. The *Ecloga* adopted these impediments (chapter 2.2) and expanded them even further, providing for (besides the dissolution of illegal marriage) strict penal sanctions against the transgressors. These punishments were based on the degree of relation between the transgressors (chapter 17.33–34 and 37). In the same manner, the *Ecloga* repeated (here too with further expansion in chapter 2.2) the impediment due to a spiritual relationship (i.e., through baptism), which the Quinisext Synod introduced in canon 53, which is itself much stricter than the text in Justinian's Code (Cod. 5.4.26.2). In this case as well, the *Ecloga* provided penal sanctions for the transgressors (chapter 17.25–26).

While the canons of the first synods, up to the Council of Chalcedon, prohibited only certain types of mixed marriages, canon 72 of the Quinisext decreed a general prohibition of marriages between Orthodox and heretics.[25] As a result, the *Ecloga*, in chapters 1.1 and 2.1, provided the prerequisite that only *Christians* be joined in a betrothal or marriage.

One can see the influence of canon 87 of the Quinisext Synod on the issue of the dissolution of marriage. The Quinisext Synod considers as adultery the unreasonable abandonment of one spouse by the other and the co-habitation with a third person. Provisions 2.9.1–4 of the *Ecloga* enumerate the reasons for divorce in a restrictive way and thus exclude consensual divorce, which had been allowed by Justin II (novella 140).[26]

The influence of the same synod is also evident in the penal regulation of prostitution, of bigamy, and also of the abduction and seduction of

---

24. See also S. Troianos, 'Die Wirkungsgeschichte des Trullanum (Quinisextum) in der byzantinischen Gesetzgebung', AHC 24 (1992) 95–111.

25. See also S. Troianos, '*Der "Andere" in kanonischen Recht der Ostkirche: Die Mischehen <Identité et Droit de l'Autre>*', Studies in Comparative Legal History, ed. Laurent Mayali (Berkeley 1994) 89–102.

26. See also L. Burgmann, 'Eine Novelle zum Scheidungsrecht' (FM 4) 107–18; S. Troianos, 'Το συναινετικό διαζύγιο στο Βυζάντιο', Βυζαντιακά 3 (1983) 9–21.

nuns and other women dedicated to God (chapter 17.19–24 and 35). In the last instance, however, the *Ecloga* abolished property penalties that were collected by the monasteries to which the victimized women belonged. This action probably expresses an unfavorable attitude toward the monasteries, because they were the center of opposition to the ecclesiastical policies of the Isaurians.[27]

The following criminal provisions of the *Ecloga* make direct reference to the Church. These punish the violation of the asylum of churches (17.1), perjury (17.2), insult of a priest (17.4), apostasy during captivity (17.6), sacrilege (17.15), and the heresies of the Manichaeans and Montanists (17.52). For these last, the death penalty was decreed. It has been pointed out that this severe punishment for the followers of these heresies, which are 'Judaizing', may express an adaptation toward the intense anti-Semitic spirit of the Quinisext Synod.[28]

It is self-evident that all of the above provisions of the *Ecloga* were also included in its various derivatives.[29]

As mentioned above, the purpose of the editors of the *Ecloga* was to cover the needs of everyday life. It appears, however, that the practical needs surpassed the boundaries covered by the provisions of the *Ecloga*. Therefore, private initiative hurried to fill the gaps in the legislation, drawing primarily from the *Corpus iuris civilis*. In this way, a 'text' was created that was closely connected with the *Ecloga* and that, in recent years, has been called *appendix Eclogae*, since it usually appeared in the same manuscripts with the *Ecloga*.

The *appendix* constitutes a number of legal rules, divided into small, independent groups, which were not created as a unified work by one and the same collector in the context of the same synthetic process; rather, they were created in successive stages based on various sources that come (directly or indirectly) from Justinian's codification. The arrangement of these groups varies in the different manuscripts, but the basic phase of their formation must have been completed during the eighth century. In its larger part, the *appendix* contains material that concerns the Church, but with a clear orientation toward criminal law. Such texts are in groups III, V, VI, VII, and VIII (according to the last edition), which deal with heretics, pagans, Jews, and sorcerers. Another topic that appears frequently in the provisions of the *appendix* is that of marriage law (groups IV and IX).

In the wider framework of the *appendix* also belongs the so-called

---

27. See also S. Troianos, 'Bemerkungen zum Strafrecht der Ecloga', Ἀφιέρωμα στόν N. Σβορῶνο I (Rethymno, 1986) 97–112 (here 110).
28. See also G. Dagron, 'Juifs et chrétiens dans l'Orient du VII siecle', *Travaux et Mémoires* 11 (1991) 17–46 (here 44ff.).
29. See their enumeration in Burgmann, *Ecloga* 59ff.

the 'Pronouncement of Moses' (Μωσαϊκὸν παράγγελμα), a collection of about 70 excerpts from the Pentateuch (21 from Exodus, 29 from Leviticus, 3 from Numbers, and 18 from Deuteronomy). These Old Testament passages are usually quoted verbatim. The purpose for the composition of this collection (which has a rich manuscript tradition) was more educational and propagandistic. It served to underscore the historical continuity in the tradition of the rules of behavior from the lawgiver *par excellence*, Moses, to the legislation of the time. This should be seen in conjunction with the perception of the Byzantines that they had succeeded the Israelites as the 'chosen people'.

Very few novellae survive from the successors of Leo III and Constantine V: specifically, two from Empress Irene[30] and one from Leo V.[31] All three deal with topics of ecclesiastical interest. The first novella of Irene (780–790) regulates issues relating to preliminary proceedings (ἀποδεικτική διαδικασία), including the giving of an oath, among others; and the second (797–802) decrees the prohibition of a third marriage and of marriage between free men and slave women. The novella of Leo V (819/820) seeks to obstruct the unreasonable (i.e., without serious cause) dissolution of marriages (i.e., when the spouses used various ruses that they had previously agreed on). It appears that the legislative work of Nikephoros I (802–811) was directly related to the property laws of the Church (with the intention of limiting certain privileges). Unfortunately, however, these texts do not survive, and we have only indirect information about them.[32]

The Collections of Ecclesiastical Law of Civil Origins

The *Collectio XXV capitulorum*

Edition: Heimbach, *Anekdota* II 145-201.

Bibliography: Zachariä von Lingenthal, 'Nomokanones'; Pitra, *Iuris*; Beneševič, *Sinagoga* 290ff.

This collection was mentioned above in relation to the *Collection of the 60 Titles*, of which this is considered a supplement in the form of an appendix. Its name is due to the fact that, in the present format, it is made up of 25 chapters. Of these, the first 21 come from the first four titles of the first book of the *Codex* of Justinian and the last four from novellae of Justinian.

Except for the last chapter, which includes chapters 13–14 of novella 131

---

30. Dölger, *Regesten* N° 358–359.

31. Dölger, *Regesten* N° 338. The dating of the novella and its attribution to Leo V are due to O. Kresten, 'Datierungsprobleme "isaurischer" Eherechtsnovellen', I Coll. I 26, FM 4.37–106. For the issue of divorces by consent, see above note 25.

32. Dölger, *Regesten* N° 370ff.

under the heading 'Copy of a Divine Law' ('ἴσον θείου νόμου'), all the chapters contain entire provisions with complete *inscriptio* and *subscriptio*. Specifically, this collection contains the following: *Codex* 1.1.3, 1.2.25(26), 1.3.29, 1.3.41(42)–47(48), 1.3.52(53), 1.3.55(57), 1.4.14, 1.4.22–23, 1.4.25–26, 1.4.29–30, 1.4.33–34, and novellae 137, 133, 120, and 131.13–14. As to the provisions of the *Codex*, we find that they are *constitutiones* written in Greek by the emperors Theodosios II (one provision), Leo I (two provisions), and Justinian I (eighteen provisions).

The four final chapters, which contain novellae from the years 539 to 565, disturb the chronological order and thematic cohesion of the chapters of the collection that come from the *Codex*. In addition, the presence of these chapters in the collection overturns the hypothesis that this collection was meant to complete the *Collection of 60 Titles*, which is placed chronologically between 535 and 545. In order to remove this contradiction, it has been proposed that this collection was formed immediately after the publication of the second edition of the *Codex* in 534 and that the four final chapters were added later, not all at once but over a period of time.[33]

The heading of the collection also creates problems: 'Provisions of civil law from the novellae of Emperor Justinian advocating and ratifying the ecclesiastical canons of the holy fathers' (Διατάξεις νόμων πολιτικῶν ἐκ τῶν νεαρῶν Ἰουστινιανοῦ βασιλέως συνηγοροῦσαι καὶ ἐπικυροῦσαι τοὺς τῶν ἁγίων πατέρων ἐκκλησιαστικοὺς κανόνας). The mention of the novellae can be justified, if one were to accept that the heading was put in after the addition of the novellae. The question remains, however, as to why there is no mention of the *Codex*, from which the greatest part of the collection comes. In view of the fact that this heading does not appear in a uniform way throughout the manuscript tradition,[34] the existence of a gap in the heading (due to an omission during copying) has been proposed as a solution.[35] The following additions would complete the heading: 'civil law [from the *Codex* and] from the novellae' (πολιτικῶν [ἔκ τε τοῦ κώδικος] ἐκ [τε] τῶν νεαρῶν).

The *Collectio LXXXVII capitulorum*

Edition: Pitra, *Iuris* II 385–405.

Bibliography: Heimbach, *Anekdota* II, XLI–LXIII; Zachariä von Lingenthal, 'Nomokanones' 5 (= 618); Beneševič, *Sinagoga* 288ff.

---

33. See Zachariä von Lingenthal, 'Nomokanones' 3 (= 616ff.).
34. Some manuscripts add the words 'and of other emperors' after the word 'of the emperor'.
35. Heimbach, *Anekdota* II XXXI.

Also attributed to John Scholastikos, the editor of the *Synagoge of 50 Titles*, is a collection of ecclesiastical provisions of civil origin. This collection is made up of 87 chapters, which is why it was named *Collectio LXXXVII capitulorum* during the nineteenth century. It bears the heading 'Several provisions that especially harmonize with the divine and holy canons, which provisions came after the Codex of divine novellae that were ordered by the late, pious Justinian, and which bestow their own authority from abundance . . .' (Ἐκ τῶν μετὰ τὸν κώδικα θείων νεαρῶν . . .). This heading reflects the content of this collection (unlike that of the collection of the 25 chapters, because this one includes entire excerpts or, more commonly, abridgements of novellae from the years 535–546. These are, in the order in which they are presented: novellae 6 (chapters 1–5), 5 (chapters 6–11), 83 (chapter 12), 46 (chapter 13), 120 (chapters 14–17), 56 (chapter 18), 57 (chapter 19), 3 (chapter 20), 32 (chapter 21), 131 (chapters 22–26), 67 (chapter 27), and 123 (chapters 28–87). From this arrangement, it appears that no effort was made to organize the material in a systematic way during the creation of the collection. Its editor presented only a table of contents of each chapter and a brief introduction.

At first glance, the composition of the collection elicits the question as to why novellae of the same period (that is, novellae 16, 76, 79, 81, and 86, which likewise deal with the Church) were omitted. Perhaps the explanation lies in the fact that, first, novella 123 (which takes up more than two thirds of the chapters of the collection) and novella 120 cover, thanks to the codification of their content, the greatest part of the themes related to the organization and administration of the Church. Second, intervention in the text of novellae that were included in the collection broadened the field of their application in order to cover regulations contained in novellae that were omitted.[36]

From the heading and from the brief preamble to the collection, it appears that the time of its composition has to be placed after the death of Justinian. In the most recent investigation, however, the view prevails that only the heading and preamble are from a later time (perhaps from the period of John's patriarchate) and that in reality the collection was put together in Antioch shortly after 546; i.e., after the year in which novella 123, the chronologically last of the novellae included, was issued.[37]

---

36. E.g., in the summary of novella 3 (chapter 20) such a broad formulation has been given that the specific regulations of novella 16 are also covered. The same holds true also for novellae 76 and 79, which are covered by the newer regulations of novella 123 (chapters 54–56, 78–80).

37. See van der Wal–Lokin, 53. Opposed is A. Schminck, 'Collectio 87 capitulorum', ODB 1. 480.

The *Collectio tripartita*

Edition: Voel-Justel II 1223–1361 (= PG 138.1077–1336); Pitra, *Iuris* II 410–416 (variae lectiones); N. van der Wal–B. H. Stolte, *Collectio Tripartita: Justinian on Religious and Ecclesiastical Affairs* (Groningen 1994).

Bibliography: B. H. Stolte, 'The Digest Summa of the Anonymous and the Collectio Tripartita, or the Case of the Elusive Anonymi' *Subseciva Groningana* 2 (1985) 47–58; B. H. Stolte, 'The Collectio Tripartita and the Epitome Athanasii: Problems for an Editor', *Subseciva Groningana* 4 (1990) 221–31; van der Wal–Lokin, 61ff.; Zachariä von Lingenthal, 'Nomokanones' 7–8 (= 620–21).

The *Collectio tripartita* (or *Collectio constitutionum ecclesiasticarum*) was a supplement, in the form of an appendix, to the *Syntagma of Canons of 14 Titles*. It contains texts that were originally civil laws dealing with the Church. The name, *Collectio tripartita*, reflects the fact that it is made up of three parts. The first part includes provisions from Book I of the *Codex* of Justinian (titles 1–13), which came from an interpretive revision also containing subtitles (παράτιτλα).[38] It should be noted that in these subtitles other books of the *Codex* besides Book I, and also even novellae, were taken into consideration. Not only a summary but also part of the authentic text were inserted from some of the *constitutiones* written in Greek, which presented a particular interest. The second part, which is smaller, contained provisions relating to the *ius sacrum* from the *Pandects* (*Digest*) (based on the epitome of the old Anonymous) and the *Institutes*. These provisions of the *Pandects* (*Digest*), which derive from a pagan period, were the only ones that by analogy could be applied to the legal relations of the Church. Finally, the third part contains all the novellae of Justinian and of his immediate successor Justin II that had an ecclesiastical content. Here the editor of the *Collectio* used the epitome of the novellae of Athanasios of Emesa,[39] specifically the first three titles (of the 23 which constitute this work) along with their subtitles.

Athanasios probably composed his epitomes between May 572 and August 577.[40] Therefore, the *Collectio* was put together after this time, perhaps around 580. Stolte proposes the hypothesis that the author of the *Collectio* was the author of the *Nomokanon of 14 Titles*; i.e., the Anonymous Enantiophanes.

The *Collectio tripartita* differs in two ways from the other two related

---

38. According to Zachariä von Lingenthal, 'Nomokanones' 7 (= 620), the foundation of this was the work of the antecessor, Anatolios. According to van der Wal–Lokin, 44, however, the essence of the work comes from an unknown antecessor.

39. See the recent critical edition of D. Simon and S. Troianos, *Das Novellensyntagma des Athanasios von Emesa* (Forschungen zur byzantinischen Rechtsgeschichte, 16; Frankfurt 1989).

40. Simon-Troianos, *Das Novellensyntagma* VIII.

collections presented in the preceding sections (i.e., the *Collectio XXV capitulorum* and the *Collectio LXXXVII capitulorum*). First, with very few exceptions in regard to the *Codex*, it does not contain the authentic texts of the laws but only their epitomes. Second, its editor did not select the provisions he included in his collection from the available material but attempted to present a complete picture of the civil law that regulated ecclesiastical relations.

The *Collectio Ambrosiana*

The *Collectio Ambrosiana* owes its name to the fact that it survives in a unique manuscript, Milan, Ambrosiana L 49 sup. (484). It is included here because, in the form in which it has survived in this codex, its ecclesiastical nature predominates. It is a collection of Justinian's novellae presented partly in their authentic formulation and partly in epitome, which elicits many questions from every point of view (including the provisions and their differences in origin, the organization of the material, the process of its formation, etc.).

A satisfactory answer can be given to these questions if one accepts that the collection passed through many stages of revision. The *Collectio Ambrosiana* is subdivided into titles. In its final form it is probably made up of 14 titles. This number, however, has to be accepted with caution, because the *codex unicus* that preserves it is truncated, and therefore it is theoretically possible that the collection contained other titles (after the fourteenth) that have been lost. During the first phase of its formation (which, considering the novellae included, must be placed between March of 545 and March of 546), its editor divided his material (which, it must be noted, contained only complete novellae) into 11 titles. Of these titles, the first five were concerned with ecclesiastical law (novellae 131, 6, 3, 16, 86, 5, 133, 79, and 7); the next three with marriage law (novellae 19, 2, and 12); the following two with inheritance law (novellae 115 and 1); and the last one with agricultural loans (novella 32). The selection of the novellae does not reveal the special interest of the editor, who most probably was concerned with concealing his own personal needs. The collection of the 168 novellae, or some precursor of it, could not have been used as the basis for the composition of this collection. Rather, the editor of the *authenticum* must have used the same model or something similar to it.[41]

All the subsequent novellae were added in the second phase of revision. These novellae, which regulated ecclesiastical subjects, were not giv-

---

41. For general information on the collection of the 168 novellae and the *authenticum*, see van der Wal–Lokin, 45ff. and 58ff.

en in their entirety, however, but in the epitome of Athanasios of Emesa (including also his titles).[42] The new texts either were inserted under the already existing titles or were added as new titles at the end of the collection, and so the present form of the work resulted. This form is truly curious, as much in the organization of its material as in the lack of uniformity of its content. The date of this stage of revision cannot be determined with accuracy, but it cannot be earlier than the formation of the epitomes of Athanasios (between 572 and 575).

Either during this second stage, or even at a subsequent time, which I consider more likely (a third stage of revision), but certainly not before the reign of Herakleios, certain 'insertions' crept into the text of the novellae (specifically in nov. 3.1.1 and 131.14.3). At the same time, a complete replacement of the Latin terms with the corresponding Greek ones was completed.[43]

The Nomokanons

The *Nomokanon of 50 Titles*

Edition: Voel-Justel 2.603–660. Pitra, *Iuris* 2.416–420 (variae lectiones).

Bibliography: Beneševič, *Sinagoga* 292–321; J. Gaudemet, *Nomokanon* (RE Suppl. 10; 1965) 417–19; van der Wal–Lokin, 67ff.; Zachariä von Lingenthal, 'Nomokanones'.

Collections of ecclesiastical law were initially one-sided. As we have seen, the first collections contained provisions either of ecclesiastical origin alone (κανόνες; 'canons') or of civil origin alone (νόμοι; 'laws'). From the combination of these two forms of collections resulted a third type that contained both 'laws' and 'canons'. Because of their contents, these collections were named 'nomokanons' (νομοκάνονες). However, this name (sometimes also occurring as 'nomokanonon'; νομοκάνονον) does not appear before the eleventh century. Later, however, the etymology of the word was forgotten, and this term was used even for collections with provisions of exclusively ecclesiastical origin.

The most important Byzantine nomokanons are the *Nomokanon of 50 Titles* and the *Nomokanon of 14 Titles*. The first is the earlier of the two. It was put together by an unknown compiler probably in Antioch, during the reign of Justin II (565–578) according to some, or of Maurice (582–602) according to others.

In terms of structure, the *Synagoge of 50 Titles* of John Scholastikos constituted a basis for this work. To this (after every title under the heading τὰ

---

42. See Simon-Troianos, *Das Novellensyntagma*.
43. On this collection, see S. Troianos, *Die Collectio Ambrosiana* (FM 2, 3, 1977) 30–44, with a partial edition and bibliography.

συνᾴδοντα νόμιμα, 'The legal precepts') were added Justinianic provisions coming primarily from the *Collectio LXXXVII capitulorum*, as well as from other revisions of the texts. Specifically, the excerpts from the *Pandects (Digest)* perhaps come from the work of the antecessor Dorotheos, the excerpts from the *Codex* belong to the antecessor Isidore, and the novellae have as their source the epitomae of the novellae of the scholastic Athanasios of Emesa.

Beneševič distinguishes three phases in the development of this nomokanon. In the first one, the initial text resulted from the joining together of the *Synagoge* and the *Collectio*. In the second, the remaining texts were added; i.e., the excerpts from the *Pandects (Digest)* and the *Codex*, and the epitome of Athanasios. Finally, in the third phase, which was not (according to the same opinion) earlier than the end of the ninth century, the canons of the newer synods were added and the original extent of the text was limited. I have many reservations about the correctness of this opinion, especially with regard to the second and third phases, because the systematic organization of the material of the novellae indicates that the editor drew simultaneously from two different sources; i.e., the *Collectio LXXXVII capitulorum* and the *Epitome novellorum* of Athanasios.

This *Nomokanon* is inferior to the *Nomokanon of 14 Titles* in terms of both structure and the completeness of the civil sources. In spite of that, it was widely circulated, as indicated by the rather large manuscript tradition—much smaller, however, than that of the other nomokanons. At any rate, it continued to be used, in spite of its imperfections, even during the twelfth century.[44]

The Nomokanon of 14 Titles

Edition: C. Justel(lus), *Nomocanon Photii Patriarchae Constantinopolitani cum commentariis Theodori Balsamonis Patriarchae Antiocheni* (Paris 1615) 1–162; Voel-Justel II 785–1140; Rhalles-Potles I 5–535; Pitra, *Iuris* II 433–640.

Bibliography: V. N. Beneševič, *Kanonizeskij Sbornik XIV. Titolov So Vtoroij Cetverti VII. Veka Do 883 G.* (St. Petersburg 1905); V. N. Beneševič, *Drevneslavjanskaja Kormcaja XIV titulov bez tolkovanij* (St. Petersburg 1906; reprint. Leipzig 1974); Gaudemet, *Nomokanon* 420–27; Milasch 180–83; Mortreuil I (1843) 222–30; III (1846) 416–21; M. Petrovic, Ὁ Νομοκάνων εἰς ΙΔ´ Τίτλους καί οἱ βυζαντινοί σχολιασταί (Athens 1970); van der Wal–Lokin 66ff.; Zachariä von Lingenthal, 'Nomokanones'; Zachariä von Lingenthal, *Über den Verfasser und die Quellen des (Pseudo-Photianischen) Nomokanon in XIV Titeln* (Mémoires de l'Académie impériale des sciences de St. Pétersbourg, VIIe sér. vol. 32 N° 16; St. Petersburg 1885) (= *Kleine Schriften* 2.145–185).

---

44. That this nomokanon continued to be in use is pointed out with much indignation by Theodore Balsamon (twelfth century) in his commentary on canon 2 of the Synod of Trullo (Rhalles-Potles II 311).

The original form of this work, which is among the most important sources of the law of the Eastern Church, was the result of the incorporation into the *Syntagma of Canons of 14 Titles* the provisions from the legislation of Justinian that dealt with the Church. These provisions were drawn basically from the *Collectio tripartita*. Concerning the novellae, however, although it has been proposed that another epitome of Justinian's novellae (besides the epitome of Athanasios contained in the *Collectio*) had been used,[45] I believe that the editor of the *Nomokanon* was also aware of the authentic text of the novellae (regardless of whether this text was the collection of the 168 novellae or some other one), because he cites phrases that by their nature do not come from any epitomae. At any rate, it generally appears that material was drawn from several earlier works.

Thanks to two references to novellae of Emperor Herakleios, it is possible to determine the time frame for the origin of the *Nomokanon*. The two novellae are from the years 612 and 629. No doubt at all has been expressed about whether the reference to the novella of 612 belongs to the authentic text. However, it has been proposed that the novella of 629 constitutes a later addition. Based on this idea, the composition of the *Nomokanon* is placed between the years 612 and 629, perhaps (with van der Wal–Lokin) even before 619. At any rate, even if the above reservations were to be rejected, the work was certainly completed before the death of Herakleios in 641.

Constantinople is thought to be the place where this work was composed. Various opinions have been expressed about the identity of the editor, and the problem can be considered only partially solved. For centuries it was believed that this nomokanon was the work of Patriarch Photios, who died in 893. When it was realized, however, that its original composition belongs to the seventh century, this opinion collapsed. This is why the characterization 'Nomokanon of Pseudo-Photios' is used sometimes in the bibliography.

A note in the text of the *Nomokanon* helps to determine the identity of the editor—but only up to a point. In chapter 4.10 of the *Nomokanon*, its compiler refers to a monograph, 'περὶ ἐναντιοφανειῶν' (i.e., 'Concerning apparent contradictions'), as his own legal work. Because he is the author of this monograph, he is called 'Anonymous-Enantiophanes'. This note,

---

45. Zachariä von Lingenthal, *Über den Verfasser* 5ff. (= II 149ff.). It is possible that the second epitome was that of Julian. See related arguments in D. Simon, S. Troianos, and G. Weiss, *Zum griechischen Novellenindex des Antecessor Iulian* (FM II) 1–29 (here 4ff.). For an opposing position, see N. van der Wal, 'Wer war der "enantiophanes"?' *Tijdschrift. voor Rechtsgeschiedenis* 48 (1980) 125–36 (here 134ff.).

however, does not solve the problem of the authorship of the *Nomokanon*, because it is unknown who this lawyer was. For many decades, he was identified with the antecessor Stephanos, but the last edition of the *Basilika* and its commentary overturned this hypothesis. Another, parallel theory claimed that this Anonymous is to be identified with the Anonymous who wrote the *summae* in the *Pandects* (*Digest*). But this hypothesis was also abandoned, because the works of each of the two anonymous men are so separated in time that they cannot be spanned by the lifetime of one person. So, finally, it became accepted that there are two Anonymoi and that the younger of them is the editor of the *Nomokanon of 14 Titles*. However, the problem of determining who he is still remains open.[46]

Photios, however, is not completely unrelated to the text of the *Nomokanon*. At the time he was patriarch, about 882/883, the text was expanded by an addition of the canons that had been issued in the interim. It is not certain whether the revision was done by Photios, but convincing arguments have been put forward that the prologue of this second edition was written by him.

Approximately two centuries later, in 1089/1090, Theodore Bestes issued a third edition of the work (which can be inferred from the third prologue). Passages from the *Basilika* were included in this, along with other texts of civil law dealing with the Church, texts which until then had not been sufficiently taken into account. With the text of this third edition as a basis, Theodore Balsamon was commissioned to ascertain whether all the texts of civil law contained in the *Nomokanon* were also included in the *Basilika* and consequently retained their authority. Thus, a fourth prologue was also added, which Balsamon placed before his interpretive notes to the *Nomokanon*.

The *Nomokanon* is divided into 14 titles (as indicated by its name), and every title is divided into chapters. Every chapter is introduced by an enumeration of the holy canons (without their text, although in the manuscript tradition there is a version with the entire text of the canons), followed by the civil provisions. Besides the prologue, there is also at the beginning a table of contents with titles and chapters. In its original edition, the *Nomokanon* took into consideration all of the existing holy canons (i.e., those of the ecumenical councils—up to the fourth—and the local synods, as well as of the apostles and fathers), and consequently, from this point of view, it is more complete than the *Nomokanon of 50 Titles*. In

---

46. For a bibliography on the problem of the 'Anonymous', see Wenger, *Quellen* 673 n. 261; P. J. Zepos, 'Die byzantinische Jurisprudenz zwischen Justinian und den Basiliken', *Berichte zum XI. Intern. Byzantinistenkongreß* (Munich 1958; num. V.1) 11ff.; van der Wal, 'Enantiophanes' 125–36.

addition, in terms of the civil legislation, it is supported by a much broader base than the previous nomokanon. For this reason the second edition was translated into Slavic quite early—in the time of Photios. The manuscript tradition of the *Nomokanon* (in its second edition more than its third) is very large, which is a significant factor standing in the way of a new—and needed—critical edition.

Other Collections of Nomokanons: Nikon of the Black Mountain

Editions: (a) *Pandects*: Index: A. M. Bandini, *Catalogus codicum manuscriptorum Bibliothecae Mediceae Laurentianae varia continens opera graecorum Patrum* I (Florence 1764) 93–98 (= PG 106.1360–1381); D. Sophianos, Τὰ χειρόγραφα τῶν Μετεώρων (Athens 1986) 3.213–224, 234–249; Excerpts: Cotelerius 3.420–423, 439–444 (= PG 86.69–73 and 127.528–32); Rhalles-Potles 4.589–91; Pitra, *Spicilegium* 445–55; C. de Clercq, *Les Pandectes de Nicon de la Montagne Noire* (Archives d'histoire du droit oriental 4; 1949) 187–203 (191–203); A. Longo, 'Il testo integrale della "Narrazione degli Abati Giovanni e Sofronio" attraverso le "Ἑρμηνεῖαι" di Nicone', *Rivista di studi bizantini e neoellenici* 1.2 (1965–66) 223–67; T. Giagkou, Ἀποσπάσματα ἀγνώστου ἁγιορειτικοῦ τυπικοῦ στό ἀνθολόγιο "Ἑρμηνεῖαι τῶν ἐντολῶν τοῦ Κυρίου", Ἐπισ. Ἐπετ. Θεολ. Σχολῆς Πανεπιστημίου Θεσσαλονίκης, Τμῆμα Ποιμαντικῆς Ι (1990) 327–57 (343–49). (b) Taktikon (Excerpts): Cotelerius 3.432–39 (= PG 127.520–25); Rhalles-Potles IV 585–88; V. N. Beneševič, *Catalogus codicum manuscriptorum graecorum qui in monasterio Sanctae Catharinae in Monte Sina aservantur* (St. Petersburg 1911; reprint. Hildesheim 1965) 1.561–601; V. N. Beneševič, *Taktikon Nikona Cernogora Greceskij tekst po rukopisi No 441 Sinajskago monastyrja sv. Jekateriny, Zapiski Ist.* (Filol. Fakulteta Petrogradskago Universiteta 139; St. Petersburg 1917) 4–6, 13–119.

Bibliography: C. de Clercq, *Les textes juridiques dans les Pandectes de Nicon de la Montagne Noire* (Venezia 1942); T. Giagkou, Νίκων ὁ Μαυρορείτης (Thessalonika 1991), on pages 13–27 is a complete bibliography.

The collections presented in this section do not constitute 'nomokanons' in the strict sense of the word, but they share with them a common characteristic: they combine ecclesiastical sources with sources of secular law. An author of such collections was Nikon, a monk originally in the monastery of the Theotokos of Roidion in the Black Mountain of Syria and later in the monastery of Symeon the Younger in the Marvellous Mountain close to Antioch. He lived during the eleventh century (approximately between 1025 and 1100).

The main work of Nikon is the 'Interpretations of the divine injunctions of the Lord' (Ἑρμηνεῖαι τῶν θείων ἐντολῶν τοῦ Κυρίου) or, as they are usually referred to in the bibliographies, the *Pandects* (Πανδέκται). Nikon himself uses other names as well, such as the 'Great Book', etc. This work was in the making for a long time and must have been completed during the reign of Constantine I Doukas (1059–1067), perhaps around the year 1060. It is a lengthy anthology divided into 63 sections, with passages from the Bible and texts from the works of the church fathers, in which the scriptural passages are interpreted. Next, Nikon cites related material, again from the patristic literature but also from secular authors. Finally, he inserts holy canons and civil laws (mainly from the legislation of Justinian) that relate to the topic of each subdivision.

The book, after the introduction (Section 1), is divided into two parts. The first is theoretical and deals with the interpretation of the divine commandments (Sections 2–50), while the second is practical and deals with repentance, confession, holy eucharist, fasting, etc. (Sections 51–62). Section 63, in the form of an appendix, contains holy canons and other canonical texts that relate to the clergy but that do not appear in the previous 62 sections. The influence of the *Nomokanon of 14 Titles* is obvious in the references to sources of secular law, although the same format is not always used. With regard to the novellae, Nikon must have had available the collection of the 168 novellae.

These collections made by Nikon serve pastoral rather than interpretive purposes. From the methodological point of view, however, the value of the *Pandects* must not be underestimated, because the hermeneutical approach to the legal texts is based on the principle that the canons have a theological content and therefore their interpretation must be theological.

The *Pandects* of Nikon have a very rich manuscript tradition. Sixty codices have been located up to now, and perhaps there are even others, still unknown, since sometimes the work is passed on anonymously or pseudepigraphically and so it is not easy to locate in the manuscript catalogues. Unfortunately, this work is still unedited. Only the tables of contents, which contain epitomae of the 63 sections, have been published and, in addition to these a few isolated fragments. From the evidence furnished by those who study Nikon, it appears that the *Pandects* (which, we must note, were translated very early into Arabic, Ethiopian, and Slavic) do not contain new, unknown texts. Nevertheless, they are very useful for the history of the texts (both civil and ecclesiastical) because of the excerpts that they contain.

From the *Pandects*, Nikon put together an epitome with the title Κανόνες καὶ ὅροι καὶ μερικὰ διηγήματα προσήκοντα μοναχοῖς ('Canons and rules and particular stories for monks'). In this way, the dissemination of the work was ensured, even to those who were unable to acquire the authentic text because of its great size.

Another work of Nikon (besides the *Pandects* and its epitomes) was the *Taktikon* (Τακτικόν). Under this general title are found several smaller works: the 'Diatheke' (Διαθήκη); the 'Kanonarion' (Κανονάριον); the 'Typikon' (Τυπικόν) of the monastery of the Theotokos of Roidion; the 'Nomokanonon' (Νομοκάνονον); comments on the supposed works of

Patriarch John IV Nesteutes ('Faster'); and many letters. In the *Taktikon* he frequently appeals to the holy canons, but he does not appear to use the provisions of secular law. Most of this work also remains unpublished.

The Canonical Work of the Seventh Ecumenical Council and the Synods of the Time of Photios

The Second Council of Nicaea (787)

Editions: J. Tilius, *Apostolorum et sanctorum conciliorum decreta* (Paris 1540) 110–15; Beveregius col. 284–330; Harduinus 4 col. 485–501; Melias 2.884–89; Mansi 13.417–39; Agapius (Leonardos), Συλλογὴ πάντων ἱερῶν καὶ θείων κανόνων (Venice 1787) 314–32; Pedalion 322–41; Rhalles-Potles 2.555–646; PG 137.876–1002; Pitra, *Iuris* 2.103–21; Lauchert 139–51; DThC 11.1 426–40; Hefele-Leclercq *Histoire* 3.2 776–93; Beneševič, *Syntagma* 205–28; Alivisatos 120–133; Joannou CCO 245–85.

Translations: G. Fritz, DThC 11.1 426–40 and Joannou CCO 245–85 (French); *Rudder* 413–52 and NPNF 14.555–71 (English); G. Dumeige, *Nizäa* (Mainz 1985) 2.297–309 (German); Beneševič, *Syntagma* 205–28 (Old Slavonic).

Bibliography: The bibliography has been collected by B. Staurides, Ἡ Z' Οἰκουμενικὴ Σύνοδος, Νίκαια (B'), 787 (Thessalonika 1987) 37–46. To this, add: H. G. Beck in *Handbuch der Kirchengeschichte* (Freiburg-Basel-Vienna 1966; reprint 1985) 3.1.31ff.; P. Speck, *Kaiser Konstantin VI.* (Munich 1978) 1.131–79, II 534–94; P. Schreiner, *Der byzantinische Bilderstreit, Setimane di studio del Centro italiano di studi sull'alto medioevo* (Spoleto 1988) 319–407 (plus 409–27, discussion); Menevisoglou, Ἱστορική 392–23; see also the entire AHC 20 (1988).

The abdication of Patriarch Paul on August 31, 784 and external conditions (a prevailing calm along all the borders of the empire) created favorable internal conditions for the final resolution of the problems caused by the iconoclastic controversy.

The iconoclastic controversy was a multifaceted and complex problem. That is why there is no consensus among researchers regarding either its causes or the order of importance of those causes. This is a result of examining the facts from different perspectives, which have been skewed by the ideological prejudices of the authors who have been busy with this topic. At any rate, it is absolutely certain that the causes were neither only religious nor only political-economic. This also must be emphasized: although the eastern origin of Emperor Leo III (and the Jewish and Islamic influences that this carried with it) certainly played a significant role in the emergence of iconoclasm, the place within which the hostility against the icons developed (as a reform effort) must be sought primarily within ecclesiastical circles. At any rate, in the subsequent development of the dispute, it becomes intensely obvious that the state, as an element in the more general relations between church and state, exercised a policy of intervention even in dogmatic matters.

Independent of other, chronologically uncertain actions, the issuing of an edict against icons on January 17, 730 must be considered as an official starting point of the iconoclastic controversy. Following that, the iconoclastic disputes shook the Church as well as the whole empire. From the point of view of intensity, these disputes can best be compared to the turmoil caused by the Arians after the first council of Nicaea or by the Monophysites in the fifth and sixth centuries. They differ from those, however, in that they ended without leaving behind a dogmatic separation, as did Arianism and Monophysitism. But they differ also in something else: while, in the earlier dogmatic conflicts, the topic in dispute could be understood only by those with theological training, here, in the iconoclastic controversy, the topic had a material substance and in consequence was reasonably accessible to everyone. Thus, the struggles for dominance spread to the broader secular strata of society.

When, in December 784, the lay officer (*a secretis*) Tarasios was appointed as the new patriarch, the required documents were sent to Rome and the eastern patriarchates for the purpose of convening a great synod. In August 786 the synod assembled in the Church of the Holy Apostles in Constantinople. But the supporters of iconoclasm (mainly bishops trying to avoid condemnation), assisted by military divisions holding the same opinions, intervened and dissolved the synod.

The synod finally assembled in Nicaea in September 787, after systematic preliminary work had been done by Irene and Tarasios: the first, using various ruses, took care of removing from the capital those soldiers faithful to iconoclasm; the second ensured that the opposing bishops would not lose their positions. The business of the synod lasted for one month, from September 24 to October 23. The sessions were not held every day, however. There is evidence of seven sessions in Nicaea (September 24, 26, and 28; October 1, 4, 6, and 13) in the Church of Hagia Sophia, and one (the concluding session) in the palace of Magnaura in Constantinople on October 23.

The seven sessions in Nicaea were dedicated to purely dogmatic issues; i.e., the fate of the iconoclastic bishops (condemnation for the unrepentant and restoration for the rest), the theological foundation for the Church's teaching about the veneration (τιμητικὴ προσκύνησις) of icons, the refutation of the horos (ὅρος; 'provision') of the iconoclastic synod of Hiereia of 754, and the approval of the horos of this synod. During the session in Constantinople the emperors signed the minutes, including the horos; first Irene and then her son, Constantine.

The Seventh Ecumenical Council brought together a large number of participants. Although (as we can see from the lists included in the minutes) not all the fathers took part in every single session, the total number of bishops (or of clergy representing bishops) who took part in the synod seems to have been as high as 367. To these must be added a large number of abbots and monks (132) who participated in the discussions and who signed the minutes of the fourth session.

The legislative work of the synod is very significant and includes 22 canons, which appear in the minutes of the last session without any indication that any discussion of their content had preceded their approval. Most likely, they were formulated under the supervision of Patriarch Tarasios (perhaps even by the patriarch himself) and later were submitted to the synod's fathers for approval as a whole.

By contrast with the previous synods, the canons of which mostly dealt either with dogmatic issues or with the exercise of the liturgical authority of the clergy, the Seventh Ecumenical Council regulated administrative issues almost exclusively with its decisions. Specifically, canon 1 requires the exact observance of all the holy canons (of the Apostles, of the synods, and of the fathers). Canon 2 specifies the educational qualifications of episcopal candidates. Canon 3 forbids any meddling whatsoever by secular noblemen in an election of a bishop, presbyter, or deacon. Canons 4 and 5 exclude any gift-giving by clerics to the bishops who are administratively superior to them, either for entrance into the clergy or for any other reason whatsoever. Canon 6 repeats the obligation for an annual meeting of the provincial synods (see also canon 8 of the Quinisext Synod). Canon 9 requires the surrender of all heretical writings to the patriarchate. Canon 10 forbids the transfer of clergy without approval from the local bishops (both of the place of origin and of the place of new installation). Canons 11 and 12 deal with issues of management of ecclesiastical property. Canon 13 forbids the secularization of bishoprics, monasteries, and ecclesiastical institutions. Canon 14 specifies the details about the ordination (χειροθεσία) of readers. Canon 15 forbids clergy (as a matter of principle) to hold positions in two churches, and canon 16 forbids them to wear extravagant clothing. Canon 17 requires bishops to make sure that, before the erection of a chapel begins, the founders have sufficient means for its completion. Canon 18 forbids women from living in episcopacies or male monasteries, and canons 19, 20, 21, and 22 deal with the organization of the monastic life and the obligations of the monks. Dogmatic and liturgical issues are dealt with only in canons 7 and 8 (the consecration of churches through the deposition of holy relics and the reception of Jews into the Orthodox Church).

With the enactment of these canons, the synod aimed at restoring and stabilizing ecclesiastical discipline, which had been greatly disturbed in the period of the iconoclastic controversy. It also aimed at eliminating all those phenomena that the previous decades had caused and that hindered the functioning of the Church's administration. However, an analysis of the synod's legislative work shows that there are no impressive innovations. The canons contain a rather limited amount of new legislation; in most cases they repeat regulations that had been introduced by previous synods[47] or, more frequently, by imperial legislation.[48]

The repetition of provisions of the civil legislation probably is an expression of a tendency of the Church to formulate its law on its own, fully independent from the legislative process of the state. This was certainly influenced by the fact that by this time the Eastern Roman Empire had ceased to contain the entire Christian world within its boundaries. So, since the eastern patriarchates had come under the domination of the Arabs, the enforcement of the Byzantine emperors' laws would certainly have presented many problems. These problems were minimized when the same provisions were enacted by a church synod, especially an ecumenical one.

The Synod of Constantinople (Church of the Holy Apostles) of 861 (Protodeutera)

Editions: *Canones SS. Apostolorum et SS. Conciliorum cum commentariis John Zonarae . . . studio et labore John Quintini Haedui* (Paris 1618) 238–59; Beveregius 331–59; Harduinus 5 col. 1197–1208; Melias 920–24; Mansi 16.535–50; Pedalion 345–60; PG 137.1005–1082; Rhalles-Potles 2.648–704; Pitra, *Iuris* 127–41; Alivisatos 307–18; Joannou CSP 447–79.

Translations: *Rudder* 455–74 (English); Joannou CSP 447–79 (French).

Bibliography: Hefele-Leclercq *Histoire* 4.1 275–80; J. Hergenröther, *Photios Patriarch von Konstantinopel* I (Regensburg 1867; reprint Darmstadt 1966) 419–38; F. Dvornik, *The Photian Schism* (Cambridge 1948) 70–90; F. Dvornik, *The Patriarch Photios in the Light of Recent Research* (Berichte zum XI. Intern. Byzantinistenkongreß; München 1958) Heft 3.2; Beck, *Kirche* 198ff.; D. Stiernon, *Constantinople IV* (Paris 1967) 35–44 (= *Konstantinopel IV*; Mainz 1975; 41–48); Menevisoglou 478–92; G. Dragas, *Towards a Complete Bibliographia Photiana in Chronological Progression with an Index to Authors* (Ἐκκλησία καὶ θεολογία 10; 1989–91) 531–669.

The synods that follow were convened because of the disputes associated with the successive patriarchates of Ignatios and Photios. Although they are not counted among the ecumenical synods (since these had a more general character), their canonical work has been included in the collections of canons of the Eastern Church.

---

47. See also H. Ohme, 'Das Quinisextum auf dem VII. Ökumenischen Konzil', AHC 20 (1988) 325–44.

48. See also S. Troianos, 'Die Kanones des VII. Ökumenischen Konzils und die Kaisergesetzgebung', AHC 20 (1988) 289–306.

After the abdication of Patriarch Ignatios, Photios (until then a high government official) ascended to the patriarchal throne. Since he was a layman, all of his ordinations up to the episcopal rank (Christmas 858) were completed within a few days. The defrocking of Ignatios was followed by a synod that convened during March 859 in the Church of the Holy Apostles in the capital. The reason given for his defrocking was that his election was uncanonical because of the intervention of the secular authority in the process.

During the year 860, letters were exchanged between Patriarch Photios and Emperor Michael III on the one side and Pope Nicholas I on the other. These asked the pope to send legates to Constantinople for the convening of a synod against the iconoclasts (it seems that some remnants of this heresy still continued to exist). The synod convened during the next year in the Church of the Holy Apostles. Many details about the proceedings of this synod are not known, because its minutes have not been preserved except for a very few excerpts in a Latin translation. In fact, the minutes were destroyed at the direction of the synod against Photios in 869–870.

The following information comes from various sources. It seems that the sessions of the synod began before Easter (April 6) 861, contrary to the prevailing opinion, which places the beginning of the proceedings in May 861. The number of participants was approximately 318 (the same as the First Ecumenical Council). The proceedings lasted until September 861, and there were probably seven sessions divided into two cycles. The first cycle dealt with the condemnation of Patriarch Ignatios, a matter that was discussed at the insistence of the papal legates. The second dealt with the actual topic for which the synod was convened; i.e., iconoclasm. There is evidence that separate minutes were kept for each cycle.[49]

The synod of 861 appears in the sources under the name 'synod "first and second"' or 'protodeutera' (*Primasecunda*). There is uncertainty as to the origin of this name, and several theories have been proposed: that two meetings were held (meaning the two cycles);[50] that it was considered to be a second 'First' Ecumenical Council (among other things because of the same number of participants; i.e., 318);[51] or that it was the continuation of the synod of 859, which condemned Ignatios (given also that both of them were held in the Church of the Holy Apostles).[52]

The decisions of the synod included the ratification of the condem-

---

49. Menevisoglou, Ἱστορική 482 nn. 8 and 9.
50. Milasch 98; Joannou CSP 446.
51. B. Stephanides, 'Νέα ἑρμηνεία τοῦ ὀνόματος τῆς Πρωτοδευτέρας συνόδου', Ἐκκλησία (1947) 132–34.
52. Menevisoglou, Ἱστορική 488.

nation of Ignatios and the recognition of Photios as the canonical Archbishop of Constantinople, the repetition of the decisions of the Seventh Ecumenical Council with respect to the veneration of the holy icons, and finally, the issuance of 17 canons. These canons can be divided into three groups: those dealing with the organization of the monastic life (canons 1–7), those dealing with liturgical and worship issues (canons 10 and 12), and those dealing with the observance of the canonical order (canons 8, 9, 11, and 13–17).

Regarding the first seven canons, canon 1 places the founding of monasteries under the complete control of the local bishop. Canons 2 and 5 require that the monastic tonsure be performed in the presence of the abbot and after the candidate has undergone a trial period. Canons 3 and 4 decree that abbots who neglect their duties or accept and keep monks belonging to other monasteries be punished. Canon 6 imposes absolute monastic poverty. Canon 7 forbids bishops to found monasteries to the detriment of their dioceses. These regulations sought to prevent abuses in the area of organization of monasteries and the monastic life, something that potentially could have led to a relapse into the iconoclastic controversy.

Canons 10 and 12 touch upon topics known from older canons, specifically the prohibition of the appropriation of consecrated liturgical vessels (canon 10 = canon 73 of the Apostles). They also prohibit the celebration of worship services in privately owned chapels without permission from the local bishop (canon 12 = canons 31 and 59 of the Quinisext Synod).[53]

The canons that deal with ecclesiastical order in part reiterate previous prohibitions; specifically, they prohibit castration except for reasons of health (canon 8), a priest taking the law into his own hands (canon 9), and the assumption of secular offices (canon 11). In part, the canons also formulate new provisions, such as canons 13–15, which prohibit the clergy from breaking off ecclesiastical relations with their presiding bishop, metropolitan, or patriarch for any reason whatsoever, unless he had been previously condemned by synodal decision. These canons were probably directed against Patriarch Ignatios's supporters, who had broken off relations with Photios. Likewise, canons 16 and 17 aim at the resolution of specific problems. The first forbids the ordination of a bishop while his predecessor is still alive (unless he has resigned or is canonically removed from his position). The second precludes the repetition of Photios's case; i.e., the elevation of a layman or monk to bishop with successive ordinations within a very short period of time (an 'all-at-once'—'ἀθρόα'—ordination).

53. For the connection among these canons, see Menevisoglou, Ἱστορική 292f.

The Synod of Constantinople (Church of Hagia Sophia) of 879–880

Editions: Haeduus, *Canones* 260–263; Beveregius I 360–364; Harduinus VI/1 col. 213–344; Melias 924–25; Mansi 16.549–50; Agapius 452–54; Pedalion 363–65; PG 137.1083–1096; Rhalles-Potles II 705–12; Pitra, *Iuris* 142–43; Alivisatos 320–21; Joannou CSP 482–86.

Translations: *Rudder* 477–81 (English); Joannou CSP 482–86 (French).

Bibliography: Beck, *Kirche* 209ff.; Hefele-Leclercq *Histoire* 4.1 585–606; Hergenröther II 379–578; P. Stéphanou, *Deux concils, deux ecclésiologies? Les concils de Constantinople en 869 et en 879* (OCP 39; 1973) 363–407; Menevisoglou, Ἱστορική 493–511.

In September 867 Emperor Michael III was murdered. Basil I, co-emperor since 866 but also organizer of the murder, seized the throne. The new emperor removed Photios and reinstated Ignatios to the patriarchal throne (November 23, 867). He did this for reasons of domestic policy (that is, to attract to himself the numerous supporters of Ignatios) and also for reasons of external policy (to appease Pope Nicholas I who, in August or September 867, had been defrocked and anathematized by Photios in a synod in Constantinople).

While—at the initiative of Ignatios—a new great synod was being prepared in Constantinople, Photios was condemned by a synod convened by Pope Hadrian II in the Church of St. Peter in Rome during the summer of 869. Finally, the synod that had been prepared in Constantinople convened in the Church of Hagia Sophia on October 5, 869. In spite of the emperor's desire to maintain a calm environment, in a very tense atmosphere the decisions of the Roman synod were accepted in principle, and Photios was condemned. The synod finished its proceedings on February 28, 870 after having held ten sessions with a varying number of participants (12 in the first session, 103 in the last). The official minutes of this synod, which the Western Church considers to be the Eighth Ecumenical Council, have been lost. Only a Latin translation and a Greek summary survive. The synod also issued canons: 27 according to the Latin translation, 14 according to the Greek summary.[54] These canons, however, are not included in the sources of Orthodox canon law, because the decisions of this synod were overturned ten years later.

Having secured himself from both external and internal dangers, Basil I did not hesitate, when Patriarch Ignatios died on October 23, 877, to restore Photios to the patriarchal throne and thus attain the complete pacification of the Church. However, since the decision that condemned him at the synod in 869–870 was still in effect, Photios's return could not be legitimate until this condemnation was lifted. So, after letters from the

---

54. See Joannou CCO 293–342 (including a French translation).

emperor and the patriarch, Pope John VIII appointed representatives for the formation of a new synod. This synod convened in November 879 and ended on March 13, 880. It held seven sessions: six in the Church of Hagia Sophia, and one (the sixth) in the palace of the Chrysotriklinos. Three hundred eighty-three bishops of the patriarchate of Constantinople and seven representatives of the pope and of the eastern patriarchates took part in the proceedings.

The synod decided to do away with the decisions of the synod of 869–870 and of the Roman synod of 869 against Photios, and it recognized him as the canonical archbishop of Constantinople. Once more the decisions of the second synod of Nicaea (787) against the iconoclasts were ratified and that synod was officially recognized as the Seventh Ecumenical Council. During the sixth session (in the palace), at which Emperor Basil and the co-emperors (his sons Leo and Alexander) were also present, a horos was issued that declared the immutability of the creed of Nicaea-Constantinople. The minutes of the synod, which were written in Greek, have been preserved in their entirety.

This synod also issued three canons in its fifth session. The first canon ordered that all of the sentences declared by bishops John of Rome and Photios of Constantinople had general force and must be mutually respected. This canon, broadly interpreted, precludes any legal action against the decisions of the pope and the ecumenical patriarch. According to canon 2, monastic tonsure that is received after ordination to the episcopacy carries with it the rejection of the bishop's administrative authority as bishop, because the episcopal position is incompatible with the monastic declaration of submission and obedience. Finally, the third canon establishes that the person of a bishop is inviolable, and it threatens with anathema any layman who would attempt a violent act against a bishop without a legal reason (that is, the bishop having been found guilty of having committed a crime).

Ecclesiastical Law in the Legislation of the Macedonian Dynasty, the Dynasty of the Dukas, and the Comneni

The *Eisagoge*

Edition: K. E. Zachariä von Lingenthal, *Collectio librorum iuris Graeco-Romani ineditorum* (Leipzig 1852) 53–217 (= Zepoi, JGR 2.229–368).

The legislative program of the Macedonian emperors (Basil I was the founder of the dynasty) included the 'cleansing of the laws', meaning the restoration of the old law by the elimination of all the 'modernizing' elements that had, in the meantime, crept in.[55] The first legislative text that pursued this goal was the *Eisagoge*.[56] We do not know if isolated laws (novellae) issued by Basil I existed. Of course, in later texts we encounter hints about various regulations with laws of this emperor, but careful study usually leads to the conclusion that these are about provisions of the *Eisagoge* and not about independent novellae.

The *Eisagoge* was published most probably in the last year of the reign of Basil I; i.e., between 885 and 886. Today, it is generally accepted that Patriarch Photios participated in the composition of the *Eisagoge*. The exact extent of his participation is not known, but certain sections of the work were surely written by him.[57] This is probably the main reason why the *Eisagoge* included significant provisions (in number and content) relating to the Church. These provisions are found mainly in the first titles (of the 40 comprising the work) and are dedicated to the organization of the state and to public law.

It is characteristic of the *Eisagoge* that its provisions introduced a system regulating the relations between church and state that was completely different from the one that had been in effect before then. That is, according to the understanding which had prevailed since the time of Constantine the Great, church and state were not two separate institutions but rather two forms of the one and indivisible concept of Christendom, forms which, in the political and theological thought of the Byzantines, could not be thought of separately. A result of this conception was the existence of two legal systems but of only one authority.[58] The *Eisagoge*, on the other hand, attempted to sanction the theory of the 'two authorities'. This theory was expressed indirectly by the definition of specific rights and duties of the emperor and of the patriarch as equally powerful bearers of the two highest authorities within the state.

This regulation was included in titles 2 and 3 of the legislation, the first of which has the heading 'about the king' and the second 'about the patriarch'. The dividing lines of the authority of these two bearers are defined more specifically in chapter 8 of title 3. According to this provision, the state is made up of members and parts, as is the human body. Among the members of the state, the biggest and most important are the emperor

---

55. See the analysis by P. E. Pieler, Ἀνακάθαρσις τῶν παλαιῶν νόμων und makedonische Renaissance', *Subseciva Groningana* 3 (1989) 61–77, who gives ideological dimensions to the term.

56. This work was known as *Epanagoge*, but more recent research has shown that the correct name is *Eisagoge*. See A. Schminck, *Studien zu mittelbyzantinischen Rechtsbüchern* (Forschungen zur byzantinischen Rechtsgeschichte 12; Frankfurt 1986) 12ff.

57. See J. Scharf, 'Photios und die Epanagoge', BZ 49 (1956) 385–400; J. Scharf, 'Quellenstudien zum Prooimion der Epanagoge', BZ 51 (1959) 68–81.

58. See Troianos, 'Kirche und Staat' 291–96.

and patriarch. Therefore, concord and unanimity between emperor and patriarch are preconditions for the spiritual peace and material prosperity of their subjects. From this formulation it appears that the work of the emperor was concern for the material well-being of the subjects, while that of the patriarch was care for their souls and spiritual interests. Similar thoughts had been expressed 350 years earlier in the preamble of novella 6 of Justinian, but there the functional separation between emperor and patriarch does not appear; consequently they are not presented there as bearers of two different authorities. Besides, this would not have been possible then, because in the sixth century the eastern empire had within its territorial boundaries four patriarchal sees. At the end of the ninth century, however, the empire encompassed only the patriarchate of Constantinople, so it was then possible in theory and in practice to speak of two equally powerful bearers of authority.

In order to attain and preserve the 'concord and unanimity' of the provision, the person who inspired the regulation thought it expedient to anticipate in chapter 4 of title 2 several principles which the emperor had to observe during the enactment of new canons of law. These principles were to respect the holy scriptures, the decisions of the seven ecumenical councils, and the 'approved Roman laws' (a provision that may imply the judicial system as it had been shaped in the Roman tradition *after* the 'cleansing of the old laws' which Basil I had attempted). At the same time, chapters 5 and 6 of title 3 sanctioned the exclusive right of the patriarch to interpret both the decisions of the synods and the practice followed by the Church. These regulations introduced an essential limitation on the legislative authority of the emperor. Of course, they did not seek to exclude his legislative activities in ecclesiastical matters (something impossible given the situation), but they tried to legislate his respect for the existing canonical order so as to prevent him from issuing laws having content contrary to the holy canons.

Furthermore, chapters 9 and 10 of the same title 3 introduced significant changes in inter-church relations; they established through law that it was within the jurisdiction of the ecumenical patriarchate to resolve differences between patriarchates or to ratify the judicial opinions of the other three patriarchates of the East.

Since the composer of the *Eisagoge* wanted to present in its first titles the general principles of structure and function for the united church-state organization, he could not limit himself to the political organization of the empire and omit the ecclesiastical one. So, after dedicating titles 4–7 to the secular authorities (political and military), in titles 8–10 he included the organization of the church, mainly using provisions from the novellae of Justinian. Finally, title 11, in which court organization is explained in general terms, discusses both the secular and the ecclesiastical courts.

The influence of Photios is felt even in the criminal law of the *Eisagoge* (title 40), which includes many more provisions relating to the Church (apostasy, heresies, etc.) than the *Ecloga*, which was earlier by 150 years.

In spite of the peculiarity of the contents of the *Eisagoge* (especially in the first titles), legal historians have been cautious about this collection, because it has been disputed whether it was ratified as law. Earlier, the prevailing opinion was that the *Eisagoge* had remained an unapproved draft of law even though it was accepted by many that, in spite of its lack of ratification, it was generally applied. However, the findings of recent research converge without reservation toward the opposite opinion; that is, that the *Eisagoge* was 'law'.[59]

Its preamble is very informative about the procedure that was followed during the formation of the *Eisagoge*. According to this information, first the legislative material was collected, then the elements considered useless were discarded, and finally the remaining material was distributed in 40 units. All of these units together comprised one codified work in 40 books. By selecting from the content of these 40 books, an equal number of thematically corresponding titles resulted, titles which comprised the content of the *Eisagoge*. This enormous codifying work, which certainly contained a significant number of provisions regarding the Church and its officials (as can be inferred primarily from the proportion of such provisions in the *Eisagoge*),[60] has not been preserved except in a very few fragments.

The Legislative Work of Leo VI the Wise

Among the emperors of the Eastern Roman Empire, Leo VI holds second place after Justinian regarding volume of legislative output. The greatest part of Leo's laws is found in one collection that contains 113 novellae. The latest editors of this collection have proposed that the novellae were published not individually but all together in one corpus.[61] This opinion was based on the observation that it is not rare to find references from one novella to another, something that presupposes their simultaneous publication. However, this position has been seriously shaken by a discovery of N. Van der Wal, who recently located a tenth-century manu-

---

59. See Schminck, *Studien* 72ff.
60. See A. Schminck, '"Frömmigkeit ziere das Werk". Zur Datierung der 60 Bücher Leons VI.', *Subseciva Groningana* 3 (1989) 79–114 (here 90).
61. Latest edition: P. Noailles and A. Dain, *Les Novelles de Léon VI le Sage* (Paris 1944). The theory that the work was published in one book is found on VIIIff.

script with excerpts from 12 of Leo's novellae. The numbering of these novellae is entirely different from that of the collection of the 113 novellae.[62] In spite of this, the theory of the *corpus* still continues to have supporters, even among more recent scholars. I consider it more likely that the novellae were published separately but within a short period of time, so that changes or additions could be made either to the provisions of Justinian's legislation that were still in effect or to the regulations that the *Eisagoge* had recently included. Certainly, the possibility that the novellae were codified into one unified text during the lifetime of Leo cannot be ruled out altogether. This opinion finds strong support not only in the existence of a preamble to the whole collection but also in this heading in it: 'The corrective cleansing of the laws by Leo, in immortal Christ Ruler of All, the pious emperor of the Romans'.[63]

In terms of the content of the regulations, about one-third of the collection's 113 novellae refer to ecclesiastical matters. Specifically, these 35 novellae are 2–17, 54, 55, 58, 65, 68, 73–76, 79, 86–91, 96, 97, and 109. An analysis of the content of these laws indicates that they either modify the provisions of the civil legislation (usually that of Justinian) regarding the Church in order to adapt them to the requirements of the holy canons or other canons of ecclesiastical origin, or they adapt secular law in general to canonical law.[64] This adaptation was pursued both by changing old provisions and by introducing completely new regulations. However, the holy canons that were the cause of this particular legislative activity presented one common characteristic: Either they were decrees from the Quinisext Synod or the Seventh Ecumenical Council; or they pertained to the canons ratified by the Quinisext Synod (that is, the canons of the local synods), to the Apostolic canons, or to the canons of the fathers. In other words, these were the canons that did not fall under the regulation of Justinian's novella 131, because this novella limited its application to the canons of the first four ecumenical councils, which it also explicitly named.

It certainly cannot be coincidence that the holy canons that were the source for the novellae of Leo had this common characteristic. This allows the following inference. Issuing the novellae may have come at the emperor's initiative, but it more likely came at the request of the ecclesiastical leadership, if not in all cases then at least in most of them. In my

---

62. N. van der Wal, 'La tradition des Novelles de Léon le Sage dans le manuscrit palimpseste Ambrosianus F 106 sup.', TRG 43 (1975) 257–69.

63. Λέοντος ἐν Χριστῷ ἀθανάτῳ πάντων βασιλεῖ εὐσεβοῦς βασιλέως Ῥωμαίων αἱ τῶν νόμων ἐπανορθωτικαὶ ἀνακαθάρσεις.

64. See S. Troianos, 'Die kirchenrechtlichen Novellen Leons VI. und ihre Quellen', *Subseciva Groningana* 4 (1990) 233–47.

opinion, the motive for this move must be sought in the perception that the canons issued by the later ecumenical synods (after Chalcedon), along with all the canons ratified later, did not have the formal power of law and so did not have the power to overrule provisions of civil law, even if the canons had been issued or ratified at a later time. For the regulation of the canons to prevail, it apparently was necessary to repeat their content with a legislative act of the emperor.

Therefore, issuing the novellae was a way to strengthen the formal power of the holy canons. With their modification, Leo proved himself to be, from the point of view of substance, very parsimonious. His stance on this matter leads to the inference that he did not share—except perhaps on a very limited scale—Justinian's perception that the governmental legislative machine is in the position to replace the synods in the exercise of their legislative work. Leo believed, rather, that the regulations decreed by the proper organs of the Church are by inference more correct than those issued by laity. And so his novellae usually do not have as a goal the introduction of new canons of law into the ecclesiastical arena. Therefore, the equation of laws and canons, which was sanctioned by Justinian, preserved its power base and even expanded farther. Because the provision of Justinian's novella 131, in which only the first four ecumenical councils were mentioned, was no longer complete after the synods of the sixth, seventh, and eighth centuries, its text was revised in the *Basilika* (5.2) by adding the fifth, sixth (which also includes the Quinisext Synod), and seventh councils.

As to the time frame within which the novellae were published, their content compels us to accept that the time of their composition is directly connected with Leo's attempt to revise the codifying work of Basil I. After some changes had been made to the content of its provisions and to their organization (we do not know the exact extent of the changes, however), the codified work of the forty books of Basil was republished as a new codification of sixty books. This new codification later took the name *Basilika*. We observe that *interpolationes* were introduced during the transfer of many of the provisions of the *Corpus iuris civilis* to the *Basilika*. These *interpolationes* had no other purpose than to adapt Justinianic provisions to the content of the novellae of Leo.[65] From this it appears that the publication of the novellae must have taken place before the *Basilika* was issued (a position supported by various internal and external criteria); that is, they were published between August 888 and August 889.[66]

65. M. T. Fögen, 'Legislation und Kodifikation des Kaisers Leons VI.', *Subseciva Groningana* 3 (1989) 23–35. See also Schminck, 'Frömmigkeit' 91.
66. Schminck, 'Frömmigkeit' 92.

Moreover, it is very possible that the novellae were issued within the above time period but originally contained only their basic regulations because of the need to complete the codification that was being prepared at the same time (the *Eisagoge*), and that the novellae were only later completed with their preambles. This may explain, in my opinion, the curious phenomenon that the collection of 113 novellae includes two pairs of laws (novellae 16 and 75 and novellae 74 and 109), which have either absolutely the same content (the first pair) or nearly the same content (the second pair). In this case, one text constituted the provisional wording (perhaps the outline) and the other the final formulation of the legislation. However, possibly due to an oversight or to some other reason unknown to us, both were included in the collection.

In Leo's codification, it appears that the number of ecclesiastical provisions was considerably limited when compared to the corresponding work of Basil I. This reduction is reflected also in the *Procheiros Nomos*, a collection of laws that was formed a few years later, in 907, and that replaced the *Eisagoge*. One of the substantial differences between these two texts is that the editor of the *Procheiros Nomos* omitted all the original titles of the *Eisagoge* that had provisions about the unique foundation of the ecclesiastical-political organization, possibly with the purpose of striking out Photios's theory of the 'two authorities'. The result was that only three titles deal with ecclesiastical topics: title 15, 'περὶ ἐμφυτεύσεως' ('about *emphyteusis*'; ecclesiastical long term leases); title 24, 'περὶ διαθήκης ἐπισκόπων καὶ μοναχῶν' ('about wills of bishops and monks'); and title 28, 'περὶ χειροτονίας ἐπισκόπων καὶ πρεσβυτέρων' ('about ordination of bishops and presbyters'). In terms of the number of chapters, this means that the provisions of the *Eisagoge* that dealt directly with the Church and its organization were four times as many as those in the *Procheiros Nomos*. However, there was no reduction in the number of provisions that dealt only indirectly with topics of ecclesiastical interest, such as the requirements for marriage or issues of a criminal nature.[67]

Besides the 113 novellae, which were mentioned above, four more novellae are attributed to Leo.[68] Many basic reservations have been expressed about the genuineness of two of these four.[69] Independent of the problems of their authenticity, however, these texts will not be dealt with here because they do not relate to ecclesiastical issues.

---

67. Edition of the *Procheiros Nomos*: K. E. Zachariä von Lingenthal, 'Ὁ Πρόχειρος Νόμος', *Imperatorum Basilii, Constantini et Leonis Prochiron* (Heidelberg 1837) 1–258 (= Zepoi, JGR II 107–228).
68. Edition: Noailles-Dain 376–78.
69. See A. Schminck, '"Novellae extravagantes" Leons VI', *Subseciva Groningana* 4 (1990) 195–209.

The Imperial Legislation of the Successors of Leo until the Comneni (1081)

Editions: The various editions of the laws are cited in detail by Dölger, *Regesten*. For the laws cited in the following section, the last edition is noted in a footnote.

Although the legislative output of the successors of Leo VI did not match the volume of his work, it is not entirely insignificant. Many of the general laws (novellae) of this period deal with the Church, either directly or indirectly. Worth mentioning are two laws that were issued by Constantine VII Porphyrogennetos between 944 and 959 and that deal with murderers.[70] The first novella provides asylum even to those who commit premeditated murder, if they come for confession before their crime is discovered. The second novella then compels these same murderers to become monks. Two other novellae by the same emperor regulate issues of intestate inheritance and provide that one third of the property left behind be turned over to the Church for the salvation of the soul(s) of the deceased.[71]

A series of novellae by various emperors relate directly to ecclesiastical property, specifically to monastic property, and make an effort to limit them. This was part of a general effort to protect small–land ownership from the pressures of the powerful landowners, among which were the large monasteries.[72] These laws were issued by the emperors Romanos I Lakapenos,[73] Constantine VII,[74] Nikephoros II Phokas,[75] Basil II the Bulgarslayer,[76] and Isaac I Comnenos.[77]

Some novellae issued in the second half of the eleventh century by emperors Isaac I, Constantine I Doukas, and Nikephoros III Botaneiatis present greater thematic variety. Some of these deal with issues of marriage law, and especially the observance of marriage prohibitions.[78] Others regulate internal matters of the Church, primarily of an administrative nature, such as the hierarchical order of episcopal sees and contributions to the ecclesiastical authorities for ordination or the *kanonikon*.[79]

---

70. Zepoi, JGR 1.230–235 (Dölger, *Regesten* N° 676, 677).
71. Zepoi, JGR 1.235–239 (Dölger, *Regesten* N° 678, 681).
72. See the analytic account of I. Konidaris, Τὸ δίκαιον τῆς μοναστηριακῆς περιουσίας ἀπὸ τοῦ 9ου μέχρι καὶ τοῦ 12ου αἰῶνος (Athens 1979) 133.
73. Zepoi, JGR 1 205–14 (Dölger, *Regesten* N° 628).
74. Ibid. 214–17 (Dölger, *Regesten* N° 656).   75. Ibid. 249–55 (Dölger, *Regesten* N° 699, 712).
76. Ibid. 262–72 (Dölger, *Regesten* N° 783).
77. The content of this novella, the text of which has not survived, is known only from literary sources.
78. Zepoi, JGR 1 288–90 (Dölger, *Regesten* N° 1048).
79. Ibid. 275–78 (Dölger, *Regesten* N° 943–44, 961).

The Penitential Literature

Bibliography (on repentance and penance in general): J. Grotz, *Die Entstehung des Bußstufenwesens in der vornicänischen Kirche* (Freiburg im Breisgau 1955); K. Holl, *Enthusiasmus und Bußgewalt beim griechischen Mönchtum* (Leipzig 1898); H. Koch, 'Zur Geschichte der Bußdisziplin und Bußgewalt in der orientalischen Kirche', *Historisches Jahrbuch* 21 (1900) 58–78; G. Rauschen, *Eucharistie und Bußsakrament in den ersten sechs Jahrhunderten der Kirche* (2nd ed. Freiburg im Breisgau 1910); E. Schwartz, *Bußstufen und Katechumenatsklassen* (Schriften der gelehrten Gesellschaft zu Straßburg 7; 1911; reprint *Gesammelte Schriften* 5; Berlin 1963); G. Wagner, 'Bußdisziplin in der Tradition des Ostens', *Liturgie et rémission des péchés* (Bibliotheca Ephemerides liturgicae. Subsidia, 3; Rome 1975) 251–64.

Works Attributed to John IV Nesteutes ('Faster')

Editions: (a) 'Kanonarion' (Κανονάριον): J. Morinus (Morin), *Commentarius historicus de disciplina in administratione Sacramenti Poenitentiae tredecim primis seculis in Ecclesia occidentali, et huc usque in orientali observata* (Paris 1651) appendix 101–17; M. Arranz, *I penitenziali bizantini: Il Protokanonarion; Kanonarion Primitivo di Giovanni Monaco e Diacono e il Deuterokanonarion; "Secondo Kanonarion" di Basilio Monaco* (Rome 1993) 30–128. (b) 'The Service and Order of Confession' (Ἀκολουθία καὶ τάξις ἐπὶ ἐξομολογουμένων): Morinus, 1. c. 77–90 (= PG 88.1889–1918). (c) 'Homily to One About to Confess' (Λόγος πρὸς τὸν μέλλοντα ἐξαγορεῦσαι): Morinus, 1. c. 91–97 (= PG 88.1920–1932). (d) 'Teaching of the Fathers' (Διδασκαλία πατέρων): N. Suvorov, 'Verojatnyj sostav drevnejsago ispovednago i pokajannago ustava v vostocnoj cerkvi', VV 8 (1901) 398–401; Arranz, 152–206. (e) 'Instruction for Nuns' (Διδασκαλία μοναζουσῶν): Pitra, *Spicilegium* 4.416–28. (f) 'Kanonikon' (Κανονικόν) (according to M. Blastares): Rhalles-Potles 4.432–46.

Bibliography: A. I. Almazov, *Tajnaja ispoved v pranoslavnoj Vostocnoj Cerkvi* (Zapiski imperatorskago Novorossijskago Universiteta 63–65; 1894–1896); J. H. Erickson, 'Penitential Discipline in the Orthodox Canonical Tradition', *St. Vladimir's Theological Quarterly* 21 (1977) 191–206; Grumel-Darrouzès, *Regestes* N° 270; E. Herman, 'Il piu antico penitenziale greco', OCP 19 (1953) 71–127; N. Suvorov, *Vopros o nomokanone Ioanna Postnika v novoj postanovke* (Jaroslavl 1898); Suvorov, 'Verojatnyj', VV 8 (1901) 357–434; 9 (1902) 378–417; M. A. Zaozerskij and A. S. Chachanov, *Nomokanon Ioanna Postnika v ego redakcijach: gruzinskoj greceskoj i slavjanskoj* (Moscow 1902).

Fairly early on, the canons of the first synods, of the apostles, and of the fathers defined particular behaviors of the faithful as an offense which carried an ecclesiastical penalty (a penance, ἐπιτίμιον).[80] In this way an ecclesiastical penal system developed parallel to the civil. These two systems did not coincide exactly, because while the civil offenses usually were also ecclesiastical offenses, the reverse was not always true. Many ecclesiastical offenses (especially in the area of sexual behavior) were not also civil offenses.

At some point in time, the related provisions began to be codified; in this way the category of legal sources known as confession literature was created. This literature served a specific purpose: to make the work of the

---

80. See also G. Bardy, 'Canons pénitentiaux', DDC 2 (1937) 1295–1301.

spiritual fathers (confessors) easier. The largest part of these collections of *epitimia* (ἐπιτίμια) is attributed to the patriarch of Constantinople, John IV Nesteutes ('Faster'; 582–595). It should be noted, however, that the specific references in the sources to John as author of these collections (whose legal value is disputed there)[81] are not older than the eleventh century.

These texts were transmitted in different forms. However, none of these texts was put together by John IV Nesteutes ('Faster'), a conclusion based on their content. Specifically, they presuppose marriage impediments introduced by the Quinisext Synod (691–692), and they cite a distinction between monks in major and minor clerical orders, a distinction that was sanctioned by Theodore the Studite in the eighth century. This pseudepigraphic attribution was due either to a misunderstanding or to an effort to give more authority to these compilations.

The most ancient of these works is called the 'Kanonarion'. It bears the inscription: 'By John, monk and deacon, student of Basil the Great, whose surname was "child of obedience", most compassionate; a kanonarion which discusses in detail all the passions and the proper *epitimia* for them, and about the holy communion, eating and drinking, and prayers'.[82] According to Herman's opinion, which is based on the extensive works of Russian researchers, this text must have been put together between the end of the eighth and the middle of the tenth centuries (most likely in the middle of the ninth century) and is a unified work and not, as Suvorov believes, a compilation.[83] Nothing is known, however, about its author, the monk and deacon John.

The work contains a prologue and three parts. The prologue discusses, with much verbosity and repetition, divine philanthropy and concern for the salvation of sinners. The author tries to justify his attempt to unify the related provisions by citing the confusion that reigned in practice because of the length of the *epitimia* required by the canons of the fathers, particularly those of Basil the Great. In the first part he describes the content of the seven or eight grave carnal sins; i.e., masturbation, fornication, adultery, homosexuality, defilement of a virgin (i.e., defilement of a virgin younger than 12 years old), bestiality, and incest, to which he also adds

---

81. See canon 24 and the reply of the Patriarch of Constantinople, Nicholas III, in Pitra, *Spicilegium* 4.474 and 480, and Rhalles-Potles 4.425. The archivist Nikephoros (eleventh century) takes an opposite position, however. See P. Gautier, 'Le chartophylax Nicéphore; oeuvre canonique et notice biographique', REB 27 (1969) 159–95 (here 176, 186).

82. Ἰωάννου μοναχοῦ καὶ διακόνου, μαθητοῦ τοῦ μεγάλου Βασιλείου, οὕτινος ἡ ἐπωνυμία, τέκνον ὑπακοῆς, κανονάριον διαγορεῦον περὶ πάντων λεπτομερῶς τῶν παθῶν, καὶ τῶν τούτοις προσφόρων ἐπιτιμίων, περί τε τῆς ἁγίας κοινωνίας, βρωμάτων τε καὶ πομάτων καὶ εὐχῶν λίαν συμπαθέστατον.

83. Suvorov, 'Verojatnyj', VV 9 (1902) 383ff.

manslaughter and premeditated murder. In the second part he specifies the length of the *epitimia* for each sin, which, except for very minor cases, varies from seven years (e.g., for fornication) to thirty years (e.g., for incest with a spiritual child) or even until the end of one's life. He especially emphasizes the need for individualizing the penance; i.e., for the spiritual father to take into account the special circumstances of each penitent. At any rate, those who are younger than 30 years old are treated with more leniency than those who are older than 30. The third part is devoted to the penitents' specific obligations in terms of fasting and prayer. Regarding fasting, the author proposes to the confessor three different provisions (ὅροι) adapted to the different personalities of the penitents. Finally, there are brief directions for the special treatment of eunuchs, βαρβάτα (teenage boys), and women.

Three more works appear during the evolution of this literary *genre*: the 'Service and Order of Confession', the 'Homily to One About to Confess to His Spiritual Father', and the 'Teaching of the Fathers Concerning Those Who Ought to Confess Their Sins'. These works deal more with the ritual of confession and less with the *epitimia*. These texts, however, sometimes appear in the manuscript tradition mixed up with excerpts from the earlier 'Kanonarion', something which causes confusion when trying to distinguish them.

Thereafter, in the tenth century, the so-called 'Nomokanon' of the Faster was formed, the new part of which was the 'Instruction for Nuns' (canons with *epitimia* for nuns). Various excerpts circulated under the name 'Kanonikon' and basically contained miscellaneous sins and the corresponding *epitimia*, with a clear tendency to shorten the duration of the latter.[84] Much later, in the fourteenth century, Matthew Blastares composed an epitome of such a collection. Because of their great practical importance (which is nevertheless smaller in the East than the importance analogous texts had in the West), all of the above texts had a large distribution even in areas beyond Byzantium, as the Georgian and Old Slavonic translations bear witness.[85]

The Canons of 'Nikephoros'

Editions: Bonefidius 2.19-21; Leunclavius JRG 1.195–197; Mansi 14.119–124 (= PG 100.852–853); Pedalion 738 5–9; Pitra, *Spicilegium* 4.381–411; Pitra, *Iuris* 2.320–348; Rhalles-Potles 4.427–431.
Bibliography: Grumel-Darrouzès, *Regestes* N° 403, 405–407.

---

84. That is why the value of their content is doubted (see above, n. 80). See also M. V. Strazzeri, *Drei Formulare aus dem Handbuch eines Provinzbistums* (FM 3) 323–51 (here 334ff.).
85. See Suvorov, 'Verojatnyj' and the bibliography of Zaozerskij-Chachanov, *Nomokanon Ioanna Postnika*.

Canons attributed to the patriarch of Constantinople, Nikephoros I (806–815), appear divided into many groups under different names: 'Typikon', 'Syntaxeis' or 'Diataxeis', and 'Chapters on Various Subjects'. A large part of these deal with the sacrament of confession, the various moral sins, and the corresponding *epitimia*. The oldest of the related manuscripts are placed in the twelfth century, but Codex Coisl. 363 (fol. 64ff.) seems to represent the most ancient form of the tradition of these canons.

The nucleus of collections with such content was probably created around the end of the tenth or the beginning of the eleventh century. In time, these collections expanded and changed in terms of the composition as well as the content of the canons. So the variety of titles under which the texts containing the canons of Nikephoros appear, as well as their many forms, completely darken the general picture of the manuscript tradition. Some of these canons are mentioned in the sources as early as the end of the eleventh century. Otherwise, however, the authenticity of these canons is extremely doubtful for two reasons. First, canons do not appear under the name of Nikephoros in any of the manuscripts that have canonical contents and existed before the twelfth century. Second, these canons are ignored by the contemporary and later sources, especially the interpretive ones, and most especially by the canonists of the twelfth century (Aristenos, Zonaras, and Balsamon).

It cannot be ruled out that a few isolated canons came from Patriarch Nikephoros, to which were gradually added an unknown number of other provisions (dealing with ecclesiastical discipline in general), with the purpose of giving the canons greater authority and thus insuring their observance. This hypothesis is strengthened by the fact that in some manuscripts the canons of Nikephoros are mixed up with texts of the (pseudo-)Faster,[86] and also by the fact that other works that are attributed to Nikephoros have been proven to have been written by another author.[87] Furthermore, the tendency to expand the canons of 'Nikephoros' with additions and paraphrases is seen also in subsequent compilations, such as the nomokanon of Manuel Malaxos (sixteenth century).[88]

Other Works Dealing with Ecclesiastical Discipline

Editions: (a) Studite: A. Mai, *Nova patrum bibliotheca* 5.4 (Rome 1849) 78–90, 130–138, 138–145 (= PG 99.1721–1729, 1733–1757). (b) Various *Epitimia*: Pitra, *Spicilegium* IV 456–465; Rhalles-Potles 4.404–405; Suvorov, 'Verojatnyj', 8 VV (1901) 366–369.

---

86. Suvorov, 'Verojatnyj', VV 8 (1901) 363.
87. See Rhalles-Potles 4.431c–431i, which reads 'Epistle of (. . .) Nikephoros, Patriarch of Constantinople, the Confessor'. In reality, this epistle belongs to Theodore the Studite. See G. Fatouros, *Theodori Studitae epistolae* 2 (Corpus Fontium Hist. Byzantinae, 31; Berlin 1992) 831–46.
88. A selection of such canons from Malaxos's work was published by Pitra, *Spicilegium* 412–15.

Translations: (a) Studite: *Tvorenija Svjatago Otca Našego Feodora Studita* . . . 2 (St. Petersburg 1908) 830–836, 838–853 (Russian); I. Gošev, *Pravilata na Studijskija monastir* (Godišnik na Sofijskija universitet, Bogoslavski facultet, 17.69; Sofia 1939–1940) (Bulgarian).

Bibliography: S. Schiwietz, *De s. Theodoro Studita reformatore monachorum Basilianorum* (Dissertation; Breslau 1896).

A collection of canons comes from Theodore the Studite (759–826), a well-known ecclesiastical personality of the two iconoclastic periods and successively abbot of the monasteries of Sakkoudion and Studion. These canons make reference to confession in connection with certain weaknesses of the human character and the appropriate spiritual means (*epitimia*) of dealing with them. Two other large groups of *epitimia*, dealing exclusively with monks, have also been passed on to us under the name of Theodore. The first one contains 110 chapters and the second 65.

Theodore was concerned with the organization of the monastic life (his works contain the original form of the *typikon* of the monastery of Studion, whence comes his nickname) and for insuring discipline among the monks. Thus, it is natural to assume that he composed a collection of *epitimia* and, consequently, its authenticity is not initially problematic. However, from the perspective of content, the second group (with the 65 chapters) raises many doubts about its authorship.[89] Circulating in Arabic are many texts which, although apparently translations of Theodore the Studite's canons of *epitimia*, in reality are all pseudepigraphical.[90]

Besides the collections of *epitimia* referred to above, many other groups with similar contents appear in the manuscripts. These are in part or totally pseudepigraphic, either because they are a collection of injunctions or prohibitions, accompanied by *epitimia*, which come from a revision (*epitome*) of one or more works of the author to whom they are attributed, or because they have a completely different origin.

Pitra has published a series of such texts from various codices. There we find canons of 'the blessed Athanasios' (this is Athanasios the Athonite of the tenth century, as inferred from his *typikon*), *epitimia* of Saints Athanasios (archbishop of Alexandria, fourth century) and John Chrysostom, of St. Ephraim, of Basil the Great, of Epiphanios of Cyprus (according to other codices: of the fathers of the Synod of Nicaea), again of John Chrysostom, of the fathers of the Synod of Chalcedon, and of Patriarch Sisinnios (996–998).

Some of the texts of this form are still unedited, such as the *epitimia* of

---

89. Schiwietz, *Theodoro Studita* 26; see also Beck, *Kirche* 494.
90. See also G. Graf, *Geschichte der christlichen arabischen Literatur, I: Die Übersetzungen* (Studi e testi 118; Vatican City 1944) 610ff.

the fathers of the Synod of Ankyra (e.g., in the codices Athon, Docheiar. 296 fol. 152r–v; Paris, Coisl. 211 fol. 281r; Sinait., 1117 fol. 301v; Vat. gr. 828 fol. 346v). There also exists the possibility that such small collections have been put among appendices that accompany larger works, just as, for example, the *epitimia* of St. Basil the Great are found in the so-called 'Synopsis of Aristenos', which has been published by Rhalles and Potles.

Patriarchal and Synodical Acts of the Tenth and Eleventh Centuries

The Administrative Power of the Patriarchal Synod: The 'Endemousa' Synod

Bibliography: Beck, *Kirche* 42–44; J. Hajjar, *Le Synode permanent dans l'église byzantine des origines au XIe siècle* (Orientalia christiana analecta, 164; Rome 1962); B. Pheidas, Σύνοδος ἐνδημοῦσα (Athens 1971); B. Stephanides, *Die geschichtliche Entwicklung der Synoden des Patriarchats von Konstantinopel* ZKG 55 (1936) 127–57; S. Troianos, Ἡ ἐκκλησιαστικὴ δικονομία μέχρι τοῦ θανάτου τοῦ Ἰουστινιανοῦ (Athens 1964) 28ff.; S. Vailhé, 'Constantinople (Eglise de)', DTC 3.2 (1923) 1307–1519 (here 1326–1329).

The ecumenical councils were the ultimate bearers of general ecclesiastical administrative authority; i.e., as this authority is usually perceived in the narrow sense: legislative, judicial, and administrative. The synods of the time of Photios were not recognized by the Eastern Church as ecumenical and, consequently, the second synod of Nicaea of 787 is considered to be the last ecumenical council. Since, according to the understanding of the Eastern Orthodox Church, a synod is considered ecumenical only if all of the administratively independent (autocephalous) churches are represented at it, and given the alienation, in many aspects, of the Eastern from the Western Church that led to the great schism of 1054, convening an ecumenical council became both theoretically and practically impossible.

The void in the exercise of the highest administrative authority within the Church was filled by the patriarchal synod of Constantinople. The evolutionary path followed by this synod, from its first appearance until its final formation, has the following main phases.

In its typical form, the synod included initially the administrative exarchs and later the patriarchs. Because of this it was called an administrative synod or sometimes even 'the greater synod of bishops' (canon 12 of Antioch and canon 6 of the Second Ecumenical Council).

Another of its forms was the gathering of the metropolitans who had been ordained by the patriarch but who did not have the right to ordain other bishops and therefore lacked the possibility of holding their own provincial synod. These were called together by the patriarch in conformity with novellae 137.4 of Justinian, which imposed the obligation not only on the metropolitans but also on the patriarchs to convene a provincial synod once a year. However, because the patriarch of Constantinople, who was originally a bishop of the metropolitan see of Herakleia, did not have his own province, this annual synod dealt with topics that belonged to the jurisdiction of the patriarchal synod; this synod evolved into a special form of the patriarchal synod.[91]

In addition, the participants of the patriarchal synod were chosen early on—apparently since the fourth century—in another way. The bishops who participated in the synod were those who 'by chance' found themselves in Constantinople and who met under the presidency of the patriarch when a serious question arose. Because these bishops were characterized as 'resident' (ἐνδημοῦντες), this synod was called *Endemousa* (Ἐνδημοῦσα), a name preserved for many centuries. This gathering of bishops, which originally occurred on an occasional basis, soon took on a permanent character. At times, it may have met on a daily basis.

In this form, the synod quickly acquired great importance and replaced the other forms. Gradually, it expanded its jurisdiction even into the affairs of the other patriarchates, beyond those of the patriarchate of Constantinople.[92] So, in addition to the metropolitans, archbishops, and (starting with the ninth century) high-ranking patriarchal officers, others not infrequently also participated in the synod: metropolitans of the other patriarchates and even patriarchs, if they found themselves in the capital. Another factor that contributed to this expansion was that, after the appearance of the Arabs, many bishops of areas of the eastern patriarchates that were occupied by foreigners were unable to take up their positions in their sees and so resided in Constantinople. Canon 18 of the Quinisext Synod, addressing this situation, permits the 'temporary' absence of these bishops from their Church. Of course, in certain cases, when a large number of bishops from other patriarchates participated in a synod, it is not easy to distinguish whether it was an ordinary *Endemousa* synod or if it bore more of the character of an extraordinary synod. At any rate, under these circumstances it is not difficult to explain why the *Endemousa* synod took the place of the ecumenical councils as the highest organ of the Church.

Included among the functions that the synod exercised was ecclesias-

---

91. By a misunderstanding, Milasch 321 claimed that this was originally the exclusive form of the patriarchal synod of Constantinople.

92. See also the *Eisagoge* 3.9–10.

tical legislative power. As the bearer of this authority, the synod issued many legislative measures which were often called *tomoi* (τόμοι; 'volumes') and which dealt mainly with two sections: marriage law and the organization and administration of the Church. These measures appear as synodal decisions, but most of the time they were really decisions of the patriarchs, which had only been ratified formally by the synod. That is why some of these acts are even connected by name with the patriarch who issued them (e.g., the *tome* of Patriarch Sisinnius).

The most important of these acts, through which new laws were put into place, are presented in the following section. At the same time, however, it should be noted that the synod too contributed to the shaping of these laws through the exercise of jurisdictional functions; that is, by resolving differences and issuing judicial decisions, since often an essentially new legislative measure appeared as an interpretation of older canons of law.

The Most Important Patriarchal and Synodal Acts of the Tenth and Eleventh Centuries

Editions: The various editions of the numerous partial acts are given in detail by Grumel-Darrouzès, *Regestes*. For the acts referred to in this section, only the latest edition is listed in the footnotes.

First in the series of marriage laws is the famous 'tome of union' (τόμος τῆς ἑνώσεως) of July 9, 920, published under Patriarch Nicholas I. This brought to a close the subject of the fourth marriage of Emperor Leo the Wise, which for many years disturbed the relations between state and church. This decision completely forbade the contracting of a fourth marriage, and it permitted a third marriage only under certain conditions; i.e., it was dependent on the existence of children from a previous marriage and on the age of those concerned, and it was accompanied by the imposition of strict ecclesiastical *epitimia*. At any rate, a third marriage was forbidden to those who were more than 40 years of age and who already had children.[93]

The tome of Patriarch Sisinnios of February 21, 997 acquired even greater significance than the 'tome of union' for marriage law in Byzantium. At first glance, this act simply introduces an impediment to a marriage that reaches the sixth degree of relationship through marriage (e.g., two brothers with two cousins), thus modifying the holy canons (canon 54 of the Quinisext Synod) and the imperial laws (*Ecloga* 2.2). In reality,

---

93. Grumel-Darrouzès, *Regestes* N° 715 [669]. Edition: L. G. Westerink, *Nicholas I Patriarch of Constantinople Miscellaneous Writings* (Corpus Fontium Historiae Byzantinae 20; Washington 1981) 58–68 (with English translation).

however, this tome established a new way of thinking about marriage impediments by adopting the principle that every marriage that causes confusion in the names of kinship is impeded. This principle supposedly has its origin in canon 87 of Basil the Great; there, however, it is used without specific legal content. From the tome of Sisinnius, however, the distance was not very great to the extreme impediments which characterize the marriage law of the later Byzantine years.[94]

Also from Patriarch Sisinnios comes another act, of unknown date. This decrees that only during the service of the first marriage is there to be the crowning of the newlyweds,[95] and only if there had been no sexual intercourse between them. An exception was to be made in this last case—in spite of the unworthiness of the persons—if the fornication had not become publicly known.[96]

Several decades later, under Patriarch John VIII Xiphilinos, a distinguished lawyer of his time, the synod twice dealt with topics of marriage law. Both on April 26, 1066 and on March 19, 1067 (in some ways the second decision ratifies the first) it was decided, by invoking canon 98 of the Quinisext Synod, that an engagement (μνηστεία) that does not lead to marriage (because of death or dissolution) creates the same impediments as marriage itself.[97]

A tome published in 1081 under Patriarch Kosmas I also refers to aspects of marriage law. It does not appear, however, to introduce new regulations—at least in the part that survives—but rather repeats provisions of the canonical and civil law, mainly with regard to concubinage (παλλακεία) and abduction (ἁρπαγή).[98]

Greater in number are the acts dealing with administrative issues of the Church. During the second term of Patriarch Nicholas I (912–925), an act was issued requiring that copies of patriarchal documents, which were kept in the archives, be made available at no cost to those asking for them.[99]

Patriarch Antonios III issued an act in the last quarter of the tenth century specifying the fees which ought to be paid to their fellow clergy by

---

94. Grumel-Darrouzès, *Regestes* N⁰ 804. Edition: Rhalles-Potles 5.11–19. Bibliography: K. Pitsakes, '"Παίζοντες εἰς ἀλλοτρίους βίους". Δίκαιο καὶ πρακτικὴ τῶν γαμικῶν κωλυμάτων στὸ βυζάντιο', in Ἡ καθημερινὴ ζωὴ στὸ Βυζάντιο (Athens 1989) 217–36 (here 221ff.).

95. Crowning (τὸ στεφάνωμα) of the couple is one part of an Eastern Orthodox wedding ceremony.

96. Grumel-Darrouzès, *Regestes* N⁰ 807. Edition: A. Pavlov, 'Sinodalnoe Postanovlenie Patriarcha Sisinnija o nevencaniej vtorobrancnych', VV 2 (1895) 152–59 (the text 156–59).

97. Grumel-Darrouzès, *Regestes* N⁰ 896–97. Edition: Rhalles-Potles 5.51–52, 53–54. Bibliography: S. Papadatos, Περὶ τῆς Μνηστείας εἰς τὸ Βυζαντινὸν δίκαιον (Πραγματεῖαι τῆς Ἀκαδημίας Ἀθηνῶν 50; Athens 1984) 102ff.

98. Grumel-Darrouzès, *Regestes* N⁰ 919. Edition: A. Papadopoulos-Kerameus, *Varia graeca sacra* (St. Petersburg 1909; reprinted Leipzig 1975) XXXIV–XXXVI.

99. Grumel-Darrouzès, *Regestes* N⁰ 783 [733]. Edition: Westerink, 84–87.

the 'weeklies' (ἑβδομαδάριοι); i.e., the clergy who took part in the weekly service teams. The regulation aimed at the restriction of the excesses and of the exploitation of the younger clergy by the older ones within these groups.[100]

Toward the end of the same period, Patriarch Sisinnios II (mentioned above) issued another act that likewise dealt with the income of the clergy, but this time with that of bishops. This act contains a series of prohibited exactions (e.g., the collection of the so-called 'kanonikon', or any other contribution whatsoever for the appointment of abbots or for the investiture of clergy in the diocese) so that the work of the bishop should not be changed into a source of financial exchange and making money.[101]

Three important acts were issued during the third decade of the eleventh century under Patriarch Alexios I the Studite (1025–1043). The first act (July 1026), which also bears the signature of Emperor Constantine VIII and so is considered an imperial act as well, provides the penalty of anathema for use against rebels and anyone who in general plots against the imperial authority.[102] The second act (November 1027) establishes certain limits regarding donations to monasteries (e.g., prohibition of further transfers; prohibition against a monastery of men belonging to a woman and vice versa) and requires that permission be received from the patriarchate for the leasing of real estate belonging to monasteries.[103] Finally, the third act (January 1028) regulated many issues relating to the good management of ecclesiastical property and the restoration and maintenance of ecclesiastical discipline through the strict observance of the holy canons.[104]

Two acts issued under Patriarch John VIII Xiphilinos also refer to the exact observance of the canons with regard to the proper selection of episcopal candidates and generally with the procedure for episcopal election and ordination. The first was issued on November 9, 1071[105] and the second on March 14, 1072.[106] The second one in particular permitted the elections and ordinations of bishops to be made at the capital and not at

---

100. Grumel-Darrouzès, *Regestes* N° 798. Edition: S. Troianos, Περὶ τὰ οἰκονομικὰ τοῦ κλήρου τῆς Μ. Ἐκκλησίας κατὰ τὸν Ι΄ αἰῶνα (Δίπτυχα 1; 1979) 37–52; and A. Stauridou-Zaphraka, Ἀνέκδοτο ὑπόμνημα τοῦ πατριάρχη Ἀντωνίου Γ΄ Στουδίτη (974–79) (*Byzantina* 10; 1980) 179–91.

101. Grumel-Darrouzès, *Regestes* N° 808. Edition: S. Troianos, 'Ein Synodalakt des Sisinios zu den bischöflichen Einkünften' FM 3 (1979) 211–20.

102. Grumel-Darrouzès, *Regestes* N° 830; also Dölger, *Regesten* N° 823. Edition: Rhalles-Potles III 103.14–20; Zepoi, JGR I 273–274. Bibliography: K. Mpourdara, Καθοσίωσις καὶ τυραννὶς κατὰ τοὺς μέσους Βυζαντινοὺς χρόνους Μακεδονικὴ δυναστεία (Athens 1981) 181ff.

103. Grumel-Darrouzès, *Regestes* N° 833. Edition: Rhalles-Potles V 20–24; PG 119.837–44.

104. Grumel-Darrouzès, *Regestes* N° 835. Edition: Rhalles-Potles V 25–32; PG 119.828–37.

105. Grumel-Darrouzès, *Regestes* N° 900. Edition: S. Kougeas, Γράμμα τοῦ αὐτοκράτορος τοῦ Βυζαντίου Ῥωμανοῦ Διογένους, «Εἰς μνήμην Σπ. Λάμπρου» (Athens 1935) 574–75.

106. Grumel-Darrouzès, *Regestes* N° 900a. Edition: N. Oikonomidès, 'Un décret synodal inédit du patriarche Jean Xiphilin', REB 18 (1960) 52–78 (57–58).

the metropolitan see, because otherwise there was a delay in filling the vacant bishopric, something harmful for the church from every perspective.

Canonical *responsa* and Canonical Treatises

Canonical *responsa* (ἀποκρίσεις)

Editions: The various editions of the *responsa* attributed to Patriarch Photios are mentioned in detail by Grumel-Darrouzès, *Regestes* numbers 562 [531], 569 [539], 570 [540], 572 [542], and 575 [545].
Bibliography: Grumel-Darrouzès, *Regestes*; Herman, Introductio 7ff.; Milasch 55ff.

During the middle Byzantine period it became the custom (which continued into the later period) to direct questions about various topics of ecclesiastical law either to (ecclesiastical) authorities or to individuals who had special knowledge of the law because of their official position or because of their legal knowledge. The answers to these questions are referred to by the term 'canonical *responsa*' (κανονικαὶ ἀποκρίσεις).

According to Milasch, this practice had its beginnings in the official opinions (γνωμοδοτήσεις; *responsa*) of the Roman jurists, to whom the rulers had given the right to give an opinion (*ius publice respondendi*). These opinions are clearly mentioned in the *Institutes* (1.2.8) as a source of law (*responsa prudentium*). If the works of the fathers (canonical epistles, etc.), from which the canons of the fathers resulted (see Ohme above), are regarded as an intermediate stage between the opinion-giving activities of the Roman law-teachers and the *responsa* (given that the practice followed by the Church had been modeled, to a certain extent, on the practice of civil law), then there is an indirect connection between the *responsa* and the earlier Roman practice, and Milasch's opinion is not groundless.

The difference between the early canonical works of the fathers, which bear a decision-making character, and the *responsa* of the middle and late period lies in the fact that the first sought to fill the significant gaps left by the legislative activity, which was restricted in scope, of the synods of the fourth and fifth centuries. On the other hand, the *responsa* tried to interpret the wealth of material that had accumulated in the meantime and to adapt it to the continuously evolving social conditions. The same principle, however, is valid regarding the extent of the authority of both of these categories of *responsa*. If the questions came from someone hierarchically lower than the one giving the opinion (e.g., questions from a bishop to a metropolitan or from a metropolitan to a patriarch), then the answer had an absolutely binding power. If, on the other hand, the cleric asking the questions was of the same hierarchical rank as the respondent, then the answers were regarded as simply opinions which had the character of advice or suggestion.

The only canonical *responsa* from before 1081 that have survived from the Eastern Church are those by Patriarch Photios (first term 858–867, second term 877–886). These *responsa*—some of which solve several problems at the same time while others deal with isolated issues—cover a very broad spectrum. More specifically, the canonical conditions for the celebration of sacraments (e.g., baptism, ordination) and the reception of the holy eucharist, marriage issues, and issues of misconduct in the area of sexual morality are dealt with there. Many of the *responsa* of Photios have a richer manuscript tradition than other works of the same patriarch because they also survive in codices that have mixed canonical content.

Canonical Treatises

Editions: (a) Arethas: J. Compernass, 'Zwei Schriften des Arethas von Kaisareia gegen die Vertauschung der Bischofssitze' *Studi bizantini e neoellenici* 4 (1935) 87–125 (92–97). (b) Demetrius: Leunclavius, JRG 1.397–405 (= Rhalles-Potles 5.354–366 and = PG 119.1097–1116). (c) Nicholas: A. Schminck, 'Kritik am Tomos des Sisinnios' FM 2.215–261 (223–230). (d) Euthymios: Darrouzès, *Documents* 108–115, with translation in French.

Bibliography: Beck, *Kirche* 532, 591ff.; Compernass, 'Zwei Schriften' 87–125; Herman, *Introductio*; Schminck, 'Kritik' 215–61; Darrouzès, *Documents* 8–20.

The studies on subjects of ecclesiastical law have a more theoretical character than the *responsa*, which aim at the treatment of specific practical needs. These studies were monographic in content and were produced by various ecclesiastical writers during the middle and late Byzantine period.

Among the first of these works must be mentioned the study on the transfer of bishops written by Arethas, the well-known scholar of the ninth and tenth centuries, metropolitan of Caesarea (ca. 850–944), and student of Patriarch Photios.

To the same category also belong the study by the metropolitan of Kyzikos and 'synkellos'[107] Demetrios (first half of the eleventh century) on the degrees of relationship with regard to the impediments to marriage and the 'Logos Antirrhitikos' by Nicholas Skrivas, which also deals with marriage impediments. This Nicholas is not known from any other work, and it is most probable that the 'Skrivas' does not denote a surname but rather his type of service. The hypothesis has been proposed that the 'Logos' was composed between 1030 and 1040. Both works (i.e., of Demetrios and of Nicholas) are directed against the expansion of the marriage impediments which had been established by Patriarch Sisinnios (996–998).

---

107. σύγκελλος is an associate of a patriarch.

4

Byzantine Canon Law from the Twelfth to the Fifteenth Centuries

Spyros Troianos

Patriarchal and Synodal Acts of the Twelfth to Fifteenth Centuries

Editions: The various editions of the numerous particular acts are given in detail in Grumel, Laurent, and Darrouzès, *Regestes*. With regard to the acts presented in this section, only the most recent editions are cited.

From the twelfth to the fifteenth century, the activity of the patriarchal synod of Constantinople, as the highest organ of the Eastern Church, continued, mainly in the form of the 'Endemousa Synod' (see the previous chapter for details). This gathering, however, gradually shed its character as an 'accidental' meeting of bishops and became rather a formal and legal entity.[1] Just as during the previous period, the synod in its legislative capacity mainly addressed two areas: legislation with regard to marriage and the organization and administration of the Church. During the period in question, legislation with regard to marriage developed on the basis of the tome of Patriarch Sisinnios of 997, the 'interpretation' of which led the synod to establish even the seventh degree of relation-

---

1. Beck, *Nomos* 11.

ship as an impediment to marriage.² The synod reached this decision on April 11, 1166, at the time of Patriarch Loukas Chrysoberges.³ This extension of marriage impediments encountered some opposition. Thus the synod, meeting at the time of Patriarch Michael III, ca. June 1175, judged that the tome of Sisinnios was not binding.⁴ In spite of this, the tendency to extend impediments continued. This was done through decisions of the synod that were of a judicial character. It should be noted that, from a novella of Emperor Alexios I of the year 1083, it is evident that the ecclesiastical courts had absolute authority with regard to the handling of problems of family justice, especially marital differences.

Even greater was the number of synodal and patriarchal decisions through which either new legal measures were adopted or old regulations (which had been relaxed in practice) were repeated. Of such content were the decisions of a synod that convened around 1107, at the time of Patriarch Nicholas III Grammatikos, which formulated 29 canons. These were not of a purely administrative nature, however, because they regulated liturgical issues as well.⁵

One problem that never ceased to preoccupy the Orthodox Church was the assumption of political posts by members of the clergy or, in general, their involvement in secular affairs. A decision with regard to this problem was made by the synod on February 16, 1115, at the time of Patriarch John IX Agapetos. By this decision, clerics and monks were forbidden to act as advocates in both civil and ecclesiastical courts, except when this was in connection with an ecclesiastical case and when patriarchal permission had been granted to them.⁶ It seems, however, that this prohibition was lifted during the same century by another patriarch, Loukas Chrysoberges, who was mentioned above.⁷ Nevertheless, this patriarch also strongly disapproved of the common practice of clergy taking up positions in the hierarchy of the government. A decision on this subject was made by the synod on December 8, 1157.⁸ A short time later the question was raised whether the above prohibitions applied also to readers, who did not exercise liturgical responsibilities in the holy sanctuary. The answer to this was given by the synod on January 13, 1171, at the time of Mi-

---

2. See Pitsakis, Τὸ κώλυμα γάμου and Schminck, 'Zur Entwicklung' 555–87.
3. Grumel-Darrouzès, *Regestes* N° 1068. Edition: Rhalles-Potles 5.95–98.
4. Grumel-Darrouzès, *Regestes* N° 1130. Edition: A. Schminck, 'Kritik am Tomos des Sisinnios', FM 2.215–54 (237–40). See this in general for the reactions against the tome and the critical observations of the editor.
5. Grumel-Darrouzès, *Regestes* N° 980 (985). Edition: Pitra, *Spicilegium* 4.67–476.
6. Grumel-Darrouzès, *Regestes* N° 999. Edition: Rhalles-Potles 3.349, 1–17.
7. See also S. Troianos, Ἡ θέση τοῦ νομικοῦ/δικαστῆ στῆ βυζαντινὴ κοινωνία (Athens 1993) 43.
8. Grumel-Darrouzès, *Regestes* N° 1048. Edition: Rhalles-Potles 3.345–48.

chael III, and it was affirmative; i.e., even readers belonged to the clergy and were bound by the same obligations.⁹

Donations of monasteries were always regarded with suspicion because of the abuses to which they usually led. Because of this, by a synodal decision of May 1094, at the time of Patriarch Nicholas III, it was forbidden for a donation to be registered before completion of the drawing up of a record of transfer, containing an inventory of the properties of the monastery. If the drawing up of the record of transfer was not completed within three months, the donation was invalid.¹⁰

The amount of the *kanonikon* (the mandatory donation to the local bishop) was the subject of a synodal decision of November 15, 1101, during the time of the same patriarch.¹¹ Another controversial subject, which always generated conflict, was the assignment of new clergy to the patriarchal administration. Thus, at the time of Patriarch Michael II, by a decision of November 19, 1145, the method of filling the positions of the *Mega Skeuophylakion* was regulated.¹² Conflict was also created by the activities of metropolitans whose sees were adjacent to Constantinople or who temporarily resided in the capital, because they often ordained for their dioceses clergy who belonged under the patriarchate, thus transgressing the limits of their territorial and personal jurisdiction. The limits of the liturgico-sacramental and administrative jurisdiction of these hierarchs and the consequences for transgressing these limits were defined at the time of Patriarch Michael III, with a decision made in November 1170.¹³ The transfer of bishops within the limits of the same eparchy with the metropolitan's approval, as well as the entrusting of the administration of a second diocese to a bishop 'as a supplement' to his income, was approved by the synod on July 10, 1250, at the time of Manuel II.¹⁴ Selection and ordination based on gifts (simony) of whatever type were forbidden from the early centuries of the life of the Church. In spite of this, they were never completely eliminated in practice. The prohibition of these practices was repeated in October 1310, at the time of Patriarch Niphon I.¹⁵ It seems that

---

9. Grumel-Darrouzès, *Regestes* N° 1119. Edition: V. Laurent, 'Rèsponses canoniques inédites du patriarcat byzantin', *Échos d'Orient* 33 (1934) 288–315 (310–311).

10. Darrouzès, *Regestes* N° 3416 (962a). Edition: Darrouzès, 'Dossier' 150–65 (157–58, with French translation).

11. Grumel-Darrouzès, *Regestes* N° 970 [942]. Edition: Rhalles-Potles 5.60–62. See also K. Pitsakis, ' Ἀνύπαρκτο συνοδικό ψήφισμα τοῦ Μιχαήλ Κηρουλαρίου', EKEID 22 (1975, circ. 1977) 38–58 (50f.) and Papagianni, Οἰκονομικά.

12. Grumel-Darrouzès, *Regestes* N° 1019. Edition: E. Papagianni–S. Troianos, *Die Besetzung der Ämter im Großskeuophylakeion der Großen Kirche im 12. Jahrhundert* (FM 6; 1984) 87–97 (88–90, with German translation).

13. Grumel-Darrouzès, *Regestes* N° 1118. Edition: Rhalles-Potles 3.440–44.

14. Laurent, *Regestes* N° 1316. Edition: Rhalles-Potles 5.116–18.

15. Darrouzès, *Regestes* N° 2005. Vat. grec. 847 f. 260v–271v (unedited).

customs contrary to the holy canons developed not only with regard to ordination but also with regard to the administration of church property. Thus in June 1370, under the presidency of Patriarch Philotheos Kokkinos, the synod reminded the Church of provisions prohibiting the appropriation of ecclesiastical goods.[16]

A very serious area of continuous conflict between the patriarchate and the metropolitans and bishops of the eparchies was the patriarchal 'stauropegia', i.e., monasteries that were directly under the patriarch. The problem seems to have taken a serious turn at the end of the twelfth century and in the first decades of the thirteenth century. During this period, a series of patriarchal and synodal acts was issued: under George II Xiphilinos, on November 27, 1191[17] and February 24, 1197;[18] under Germanos II in June 1232;[19] and another one a few months later.[20] Through these acts, it was specified that clergy from the patriarchate should serve in monasteries established by the placement of a patriarchal cross in their foundations and that they should commemorate the patriarch in the liturgy and pay to him the *kanonikon*. Conversely, in churches and monasteries which belonged to stauropegial monasteries but which themselves were not stauropegial, the clergy belonged to the jurisdiction of the local bishop and were obligated fully to him as required by the holy canons.

In addition to the patriarchal monasteries, there were also some bearing the title '*basilikes*' (royal), because they had a privileged status and enjoyed the protection of the emperor or of some other independent potentate (e.g., the state of Epiros in the thirteenth century). In these cases, however, the rights of the local hierarch were not diminished. This was decided by the synod in June 1233, also during the time of Patriarch Germanos II, which decreed that there could be no monastery that was not under the authority of some bishop.[21]

The place of the Byzantine emperor within the Church has been a topic that has always provoked controversy among specialized researchers. Byzantine canon lawyers approached the problem very carefully, but only on one occasion, during the ninth century, did they make an effort to specify the rights and responsibilities of the emperor, with a clear tendency to limit rights in the ecclesiastical area. Nevertheless, the intervention of em-

---

16. Darrouzès, *Regestes* N° 2576. Edition: PG 152.1418–1420.
17. Grumel-Darrouzès, *Regestes* N° 1179. Edition: A. Papadopoulos-Kerameus, BZ 11 (1902) 74–78.
18. Grumel-Darrouzès, *Regestes* N° 1185. Edition: Rhalles-Potles 5.101–2.
19. Laurent, *Regestes* N° 1259. Edition: Rhalles-Potles 5.110–112.
20. Laurent, *Regestes* N° 1260. Edition: Rhalles-Potles 5.112–13.
21. Laurent, *Regestes* N° 1265. Edition: E. Kurtz, 'Christophoros von Ankyra als Exarch des Patriarchen Germanos II.', BZ 16 (1907) 120–47 (137–39).

perors in the internal affairs of the Church was something established in practice—however much the relations of church and state might depend on the personal rapport between emperor and patriarch. The substance of this practical reality was, at a certain point in time, the subject of a synodal decision. A synodal decision survives from 1380, the time of Patriarch Neilos, in which the privileged rights of the emperor with regard to issues of ecclesiastical administration are specified in nine chapters.[22]

The last patriarchal act worth mentioning is the 'formulation' (ὑποτύπωσις) of Patriarch Matthew I, issued just before the end of the fourteenth century (ca. June 1398), by which the patriarch attempted to reorganize the patriarchal administration, specifying the responsibilities of the various patriarchal officials.[23] Especially detailed are provisions concerning the operation of the patriarchal court. There is also another earlier act, from the time of Patriarch Michael III (September 2, 1177), which is related to the juridical life of the Church.[24] It is a decision concerning the granting of pardon, in which, however, it is specified that the measure does not apply if the person being punished is a heretic.

In addition to the acts mentioned above which clearly had canonical content, the canonical and ecclesiastical law was of course influenced also by acts that had a purely administrative character (e.g., changes in the ranking of metropolitan and diocesan sees, elections and transfers of hierarchs, approval of monastic typika, and so forth). The same thing also applies to the juridical decisions of the synod. It would be impossible, however, to list all of these acts and decisions because of their great number.

Ecclesiastical Law in Imperial Legislation from the Twelfth to the Fifteenth Centuries

Editions: The various editions of specific laws are listed in detail in Dölger, *Regesten*. With regard to the laws referred to in this section, the most recent edition is given in the footnote.

During the first one hundred years of the period examined in this volume (1081–1185), emperors of the Comnenan dynasty were ruling, who issued many laws concerning ecclesiastical issues. Most of these laws came from Alexios I (1081–1118) and Manuel I (1143–1180). The legislative produc-

---

22. Darrouzès, *Regestes* N° 2699. Edition: V. Laurent, 'Les droits de l'empereur en matière ecclésiastique', REB 13 (1955) 5–20 (14–16, with French translation).
23. Darrouzès, *Regestes* N° 3066. Edition: Oudot, *Patriarchatus* I 134–63 (with French translation).
24. Grumel-Darrouzès, *Regestes* N° 1134. Edition: S. Troianos, 'Ein Synodalakt Michaels III. zum Begnadigungsrecht', FM 6.(1984) 205–18 (205–6, with German translation).

tion of their successors, especially the Palaeologoi, was much more limited with regard to these issues.

Some laws, such as those of Alexios, dealt with issues of an administrative nature, such as the right of hierarchs to collect contributions for ordinations, the blessing of marriages and the judging of certain disputes,[25] and the way positions were to be filled in the Great Church.[26] The laws and canons of Manuel prohibited hierarchs to remain in the capital longer than necessary.[27] The laws of Isaac II Angelos (1185–95), the first successor of the Comnenoi, regulated the formation of the synod for election of hierarchs[28] and the future of the wives of clergymen who were consecrated as bishops.[29] The laws of Andronikos II (1282–1328) defined the procedure for election of bishops and the fees paid to those performing the ordination.[30] From this last emperor comes also the 'novella of Patriarch Athanasios' (so called because it was issued after the intervention of this patriarch), by which many internal issues of the Church were settled as well as issues relating to inheritance (the inheritance of the property of couples without children) and penal law (the prosecution of serious crimes).[31]

Manuel Comnenos regulated a matter of legal procedure of interest also to the Church with the specification of law court holidays.[32] The same emperor, through a novella 'Regarding murderers', entered into issues of asylum and the monastic tonsure for those convicted of murder.[33] Many laws of the Comnenoi dealt with marriage issues—specifically, two novellae issued by Alexios, one dealing with the contracting and dissolution of betrothals (impediments, ecclesiastical blessing, reasons for dissolution), the other with the blessing of the marriage of slaves, and finally a novella by Manuel dealing with the impediment to marriage due to the seventh degree of relationship.[34]

A great number of imperial acts dealt with financial issues. Worthy of mention are a novella by Alexios forbidding the expropriation of ecclesiastical items, especially sacred vessels,[35] and one by Manuel, to whom the

---

25. Zepoi, JGR I 311–12 (Dölger, *Regesten* 1127).
26. P. Gautier, 'L'édit d'Alexis Ier Comnène sur la réforme du clergé', REB 31 (1973) 165–201 (179–201) (Dölger, *Regesten* 1236).
27. J. Darrouzès, 'Décret inédit de Manuel Comnène', REB 31 (1973) 307–15 (Dölger, *Regesten* 1333a).
28. Zepoi, JGR I 430–34 (Dölger, *Regesten* 1572). 29. Zepoi, JGR I 435–36 (Dölger, *Regesten* 1573).
30. Zepoi, JGR I 522 (Dölger, *Regesten* 2159). 31. Zepoi, JGR I 533–36 (Dölger, *Regesten* 2295).
32. R. Macrides, 'Justice under Manuel I Komnenos: Four Novels on Court Business and Murder', FM 6 (1984) 99–204 (104–55, with English translation) (Dölger, *Regesten* 1466).
33. Macrides, 'Justice' 156–67 (with English translation) (Dölger, *Regesten* 1467).
34. Zepoi, JGR I 305–9, 321–25, 341–44, 408–10 (Dölger, *Regesten* 1116, 1167, 1177, 1468). See also Pitsakis, Τὸ κώλυμα γάμου and Schminck, 'Zur Entwicklung'.
35. Zepoi, JGR I 302–4 (Dölger, *Regesten* 1085).

nickname 'healer' was given, for covering deficiencies in the churches' titles of ownership with regard to their real estate acquisitions.[36] Beyond these laws there were a multitude of legislative acts under various forms through which financial benefits were granted to churches and monasteries or the clergy.[37] Of a somewhat general character was the *chrysoboullos logos* (the most solemn kind of imperial document) issued between 1267 and 1271 by Michael VIII Palaeologos for the recognition and confirmation of the real properties of the Great Church after the recapture of Constantinople,[38] as also was the *chrysoboullos logos* of Andronikos II of 1319 concerning the see of Ioannina.[39]

It should not be deduced from the content of the acts mentioned above that the emperors avoided issues relating to the dogmatic teaching of the Church in their legislative activity. The contrary is evident from quite a few examples, e.g., the novella of Alexios ratifying the condemnation of John Italos[40] and the novella of Manuel through which the synodal decision concerning the interpretation of the words of Jesus Christ, 'my Father is greater than I', was made known to the imperial subjects.[41]

The Great Canon Lawyers of the Twelfth Century

Bibliography: Oikonomides, *Byzantium* (concerns all of the canon lawyers of the twelfth century; in the paragraphs that follow only the studies concerning each one of them will be referenced); E. Papagianni–S. Troianos, 'Διατάξεις τῆς πολιτειακῆς νομοθεσίας εἰς τὸ ἑρμηνευτικὸν ἔργον τῶν Ἀριστινοῦ, Ζωναρᾶ καὶ Βαλσαμῶνος (Provisions of the civil legislation regarding the hermeneutical work of Aristenos, Zonaras, and Balsamon), EEBS 45.201–38.

In the area of hermeneutical legal philology—as well as in the whole of ecclesiastical law—three names stand out: John Zonaras, Alexios Aristenos, and Theodore Balsamon. All three of these canon lawyers lived primarily during the twelfth century. The first two were almost contemporaries. With regard to age, Zonaras is earlier, but Aristenos began his literary activity before him; thus, his work is earlier.

John Zonaras

Editions: Beveregius 1.1–680, 2.1–188 (= PG 137.35–1498, 138.9–938); Rhalles-Potles 2–4 *passim.*

---

36. Zepoi, JGR I 376–78 (Dölger, *Regesten* 1372).
37. In general about the tax privileges of clergy, see Papagianni, Οἰκονομικά 265–82.
38. Zepoi, JGR I 659–66 (Dölger, *Regesten* 1941a).
39. M-M, Acta 5.77–84 (Dölger, *Regesten* 2412).
40. J. Gouillard, 'Le procès officiel de Jean l'Italien: Les actes et leurs sous-entendus', *Travaux et Mémoires* 9 (1985) 133–74 (141–57) (Dölger, *Regesten* 1078).
41. Zepoi, JGR 1.410–16 (Dölger, *Regesten* 1469).

Bibliography: Beck, *Kirche* 656; Beck, *Nomos*; Herman, Introductio 23–24; H. Hunger, *Die hochsprachliche profane Literatur der Byzantiner* 1 (Munich 1978) 416–19; Mortreuil 423–432; A. Pavlov, 'К вопросу о хронологическом отношении между Аристином и Зонарой, как писателями толкований на церковные правила' ('On the question of the chronological relationship between Aristenos and Zonaras, as authors of commentaries on church regulations') Журнал Министерства Народного Просвещения 303 (January 1896) 172–99; P. E. Pieler, 'Johannes Zonaras als Kanonist', Oikonomides, *Byzantium* 601–20; Troianos, Πηγές 146–48; van der Wal–Lokin 108ff; K. Ziegler, 'Zonaras', RE 718–32.

John Zonaras, whose life began at the end of the eleventh century and ended after the middle of the twelfth, occupied high positions in the hierarchy of the government. As the 'great *droungarios* of the guard,' he was commander of the imperial bodyguard and president of one of the highest courts, the court of the hippodrome. As the *protasekretis*, he was the head of the imperial secretariat. Toward the end of his life he became a monk in the monastery of St. Glykeria on an island of the Propontis (close to Constantinople) and dedicated himself to his literary activity, which was not limited exclusively to legal works but also included the *Epitome of Histories* (which covered political history up to the year 1118) as well as theological works. These, primarily hagiographical, homiletical, and liturgical in nature, remain in part unedited.

Of the fruits of Zonaras's literary activity, of special interest to legal science is his great hermeneutical work on the holy canons, that is to say, the canons of the apostles, the synods (ecumenical and local), and the fathers. As can be concluded from his scholion on canon 7 of Neokaisareia,[42] this work was probably completed after 1159, i.e., the year of the second marriage of Emperor Manuel I Comnenos.

According to information given by Zonaras himself in the introduction to his scholia on the apostolic canons, the initiative for the composition of this work did not belong to him but was rather the result of requests by others to whom he apparently owed obedience.[43] Beyond the suspicion that this may just be a topos without any special historical value, this information does not allow us to draw any conclusions as to the conditions under which Zonaras decided to undertake the task of creating a commentary on the canons.

This hermeneutical work—far more extensive than the slightly earlier similar work of Aristenos (which was probably known to Zonaras)[44] but

---

42. '... ἡμῖν δὲ καὶ πατριάρχης ὤφθη, καὶ μητροπολῖται διάφοροι, συνεστιώμενοι δευτερογαμήσαντι βασιλεῖ' (Rhalles-Potles 3.80, 29–31).

43. Rhalles-Potles 2.1ff.

44. See the similarities in the interpretations of Zonaras and Aristenos with regard to canons 4 and 5 of Neokaisareia (Rhalles-Potles 3.75–78).

shorter than the corresponding work of Balsamon—is analytical, with wide reference to other ecclesiastical sources (both legal and non-legal). The use of sources from secular law, on the other hand, is quite limited, especially when compared to the hermeneutical work of Balsamon. The difference is not only quantitative but also qualitative, because Zonaras set down only texts from the *Basilika*, to which specific citations are very rare. In addition, he usually used the terms 'civil law' or 'civil laws' in a vague manner, and his quotes were only infrequently verbatim. It is quite possible, therefore, that his quoting of texts was from memory and that the actual text of the *Basilika* was not available to him.[45] In spite of the fact that ecclesiastical sources took precedence over secular ones in his work—something which Balsamon did not fail to notice[46]—it is certain that Zonaras had legal training, a fact that becomes apparent from the hermeneutical methodology he followed.

Zonaras's work has a rich manuscript tradition. At times it is found together with the corresponding work of Balsamon and at other times by itself. In the codices of the first category, we occasionally encounter some confusion as to the origin of certain scholia, i.e., whether they belong to Zonaras or Balsamon. This confusion is due to the fact that sometimes Balsamon adopted and repeated Zonaras's scholia, even long passages from them, which he expanded with his own comments of a more specialized legal nature or with material from more recent sources.[47] The work of Zonaras, which included brief legal treatises in addition to his commentary on the canons, had a decisive impact on subsequent interpreters of the canons, especially Theodore Balsamon, and on the literature of canon law in general. His interpretation of the canons has also been translated into Old Slavonic.

Alexios Aristenos

Editions: Beveregius 1.1–680, 2.1–188 (= PG 137.35–1498, 138.9–808); Rhalles-Potles 2–4 *passim*.

Bibliography: Beck, *Kirche* 657; Herman, Introductio 21–23; M. Krasnožen, 'Комментарий Алексея Аристина на канонический Синопсис = (The Commentary of

---

45. Pieler, 'Johannes Zonaras' 618 and n .69.
46. Although he praises the depth of the interpretation of Zonaras in his scholion on the canonical letter of Athanasios to Ammoun (ὁ ὑπερφυέστατος ἐκεῖνος Ζωναρᾶς σοφῶς καὶ ὑπερδεξίως, καὶ ὡς οὐκ ἄν τις εἴποι κρειττόνως ἡρμήνευσε; Rhalles-Potles 4.76, 12–13), Balsamon points out that the focus of Zonaras's interpretation is on biblical texts while his is on legal analysis: Ἡμῖν δε οὐκ ἐμέλησεν ὅλως ἐν τῇ παρούσῃ ἐξηγήσει συνθήκης ῥητορικῆς, ἢ εὐεπείας λέξεων, ἢ ῥημάτων γραφικῶν ἑρμηνείας, ἀλλὰ κανονικῆς καὶ νομικῆς διδασκαλίας, καὶ ἑρμηνείας τῶν δοκούντων ἐναντιοφανῶν νόμων τε καὶ κανόνων … (Rhalles-Potles 4.77, 12–16). See also Beck, *Nomos* 7 n. 8.
47. That is why many manuscripts give only the parts of Balsamon' s scholia that differ from those of Zonaras. An example of such a manuscript is the Vat. grec. 1661.

Alexios Aristenos on the canonical Synopsis), VV 20 (1913) 189–297; Mortreuil 3.412–416; Menevisoglou, 'Συνόψεις' 77–95 (83–85); A. Pavlov, 'К вопросу о хронологическом' 172–99; S. Petrides, DHGE 2 (1914) 394–95; Troianos, Πηγές 148; van der Wal–Lokin 108; K.E. Zachariä von Lingenthal, 'Die Synopsis canonum: Ein Beitrag zur Geschichte der Quellen des kanonischen Rechts der griechischen Kirche' (Sitzungsberichte der Königlich-preussischen Akademie der Wissenschaften zu Berlin, Jg. 1887) 1147–67 (= *Kleine Schriften* 247–63).

Alexios Aristenos had a notable career in the Church. Having acquired the rank of deacon, he ascended in the Great Church (Hagia Sophia) to the honorable positions of *hieromnemon, nomophylax, protekdikos, orphanotrophos* and finally of *megas oikonomos*, but he also received the position of *dikaiodotes* (which was a lay position).[48] He must have died after 1166, because there is a record of his presence in a synod of that year. His fame has been due to his scholia on the canons. Although he was younger than Zonaras, Aristenos wrote his hermeneutical work before Zonaras. As mentioned in the full title of the work, its composition began at the request of Emperor John Comnenos (1118–1143),[49] around the middle of his reign, ca. 1130.

Consequently, the interpretation of Aristenos is the oldest of those written in the twelfth century. At the same time, it is the shortest when compared to the works of Zonaras and Balsamon. As the basis for his work, Aristenos used the text of the canons not in their complete form (as found in the *Syntagma of Canons*) but rather in the abbreviated version of the *Synopsis of Canons*, and specifically in a version that was the product of a reworking at the end of the eleventh century. Aristenos wrote scholia on the canons of the apostles, the ecumenical synods and the local synods, and on the canons of St. Basil the Great that are found in his three canonical epistles to Amphilochios. But supplementary material on the canons, chiefly those of the fathers, or other canonical texts that in the manuscript tradition or the editions are attributed to Aristenos, do not come from him but are part of the *Synopsis of Canons* in its last evolutionary stage. The manuscript tradition of the hermeneutical work of Aristenos is significant in size but not uniform. At any rate, in the manuscripts (with the exception of excerpts in codices of miscellaneous canonical content) his scholia never appear together with those of Zonaras and Balsamon—a principle that was not adhered to by modern editors, who mingled both

48. See the scholia of Balsamon on canon 6 of the apostles (Rhalles-Potles 2.9) and on canon 37 of the Synod in Trullo (Penthekti) (Rhalles-Potles 2.389). See also what Theodore Prodromos mentions in his praise of Aristenos (PG 133.1031–1047), as well as W. Hörandner, *Theodoros Prodromos: Historische Gedichte* (Vienna 1974) 466ff.

49. Νομοκάνονον σὺν θεῷ περιέχον συνοπτικῶς ὅλους τοὺς κανόνας τῶν ἁγίων καὶ οἰκουμενικῶν ἑπτὰ συνόδων, καὶ τῶν ἁγίων ἀποστόλων, καὶ τοῦ μεγάλου βασιλείου, καὶ ἑτέρων θεοφόρων πατέρων ἑρμηνευθὲν προτροπῇ τοῦ εὐσεβεστάτου βασιλέως κῦρ Ἰωάννου τοῦ Κομνηνοῦ παρὰ τοῦ λογιωτάτου διακόνου τῆς τοῦ θεοῦ μεγάλης ἐκκλησίας καὶ νομοφύλακος κυροῦ Ἀλεξίου τοῦ Ἀριστηνοῦ.

the authentic text of the canons and the *Synopsis* with scholia from all three commentators. The work of Aristenos has been translated into Old Slavonic and Romanian.

Theodore Balsamon

Editions: 1. Commentary on the *Nomokanon*: C. Justel (Justellus), *Nomokanon Photii Patriarchae Constantinopolitani cum commentariis Theodori Balsamonis Patriarchae Antiocheni* (Paris 1615) 1–162; Rhalles-Potles 1.5–335. 2. Commentary on the canons: Beveregius 1.1–680, 2.1–188 (= PG 137.35–1498, 138.9–938); Rhalles-Potles 2–4 *passim*. 3. Commentary on the *responsa* of Nicholas III: Beveregius, between II.1 and II.2 (unnumbered pages) (= PG 138.937–950); Rhalles-Potles 4.417–26.

Bibliography: Beck, *Kirche* 657ff.; Beck, *Nomos* 17ff. and *passim*; Herman, Introductio 24–26; H. Hunger, 'Kanonistenrhetorik im Bereich des Patriarchats am Beispiel des Theodoros Balsamon', in Oikonomides, *Byzantium* 37–59; J. Meyendorff, 'Balsamon, the Empire and the Barbarians', in Oikonomides, *Byzantium* 533–42; Mortreuil 3.432–46; V. Narbekov, Номоканон константинопольского патриарха Фотия с толкованием Вальсамона; (I) Историко-каноническое исследование; (II) Русский перевод с предисловием и примечаниями (The Nomocanon of the Patriarch of Constantinople Photius with the commentary of Balsamon: (I) Historical-canonical research; (II) Russian translation with introduction and annotations) (Kazan 1899); K. Pitsakis, 'Η έκταση της εξουσίας ενος υπερόριου πατριάρχη: Ο πατριάρχης Αντιοχείας στην Κωνσταντινούπολη του 12ου αιώνα' ('The Extent of the Power of a Patriarch outside His See: The Patriarch of Antioch in Constantinople in the twelfth century'), in Oikonomides, *Byzantium* 91–139; D. Simon, 'Balsamon zum Gewohnheitsrecht', *Σχόλια: Studia ad criticam interpretationemque textuum Graecorum et ad historiam iuris Graeco-Romani pertinentia viro doctissimo D. Holwerda oblata* ed. W. J. Aerts et al. (Groningen 1985) 119–33; G. P. Stevens, *De Theodoro Balsamone. Analysis operum ac mentis iuridicae* (Rome 1969); Tiftixoglu, 'Zur Genese' 483–532; Troianos, Πηγές 148–51; van der Wal–Lokin, 109–11.

Theodore Balsamon was one of the most significant ecclesiastical personalities of the twelfth century. He was born in Constantinople toward the end of the decade 1130–40. He joined the ranks of the clergy quite early. As deacon of the Great Church, he assumed the positions of *nomophylax* and *chartophylax* as well as that of *protos* of the Blachernai church. Shortly after the death of Isaac I Comnenos (September 1180)—possibly at the beginning of the reign of Isaac II Angelos (1185–95), who showed great respect for Balsamon's scholarly formation and abilities—he occupied the patriarchal throne of Antioch,[50] without, however, ever being able to be installed in his see because of its occupation by the Latins. He spent the last years of his life in the monastery of Zipoi (the exact location of which

---

50. According to Tiftixoglou ('Zur Genese' 489), Balsamon's appointment as patriarch of Antioch took place earlier, during the reign of Patriarch Theodosios Boradiotes of Constantinople (1179–1183), who did not have a good relationship with him and who thought that this appointment would be an ideal way to distance Balsamon from the business of the Great Church. See the various opinions regarding the dating of Balsamon's patriarchate in Pitsakis, Το κώλυμα γάμου 346 n. 84.

is not known; it was probably on the outskirts of Constantinople). Precisely when Balsamon died has not been established. This must have been after 1195. It is even possible that he was still alive in 1198.

The literary work of Balsamon is very extensive and consists mainly of legal texts. The chief place in his work is held by his hermeneutical annotations on the *Nomokanon of Fourteen Titles* and the canons. The hermeneutical work on the *Nomokanon* was written at the request of Emperor Manuel I Kommenos and Patriarch Michael III Anchialos under the following circumstances. Because the metropolitan of Amaseia was negligent in filling the empty see of Amisos, the patriarch intervened and appointed a bishop based on a provision in the novellae of Justinian. The metropolitan of Amaseia appealed to the emperor, who declared the patriarchal decision invalid, using the argument that the patriarch was basing his position on a provision of Justinian not included in the *Basilika* and hence no longer in effect. At this point Balsamon (in his capacity as *chartophylax*) was charged with the responsibility of studying the civil laws contained in the *Nomokanon of Fourteen Titles* in order to find out whether they continued to be in effect or whether they had been abolished.

Balsamon undertook the investigation based on the edition of the *Nomokanon* made by Theodore Bestes, and he completed it very quickly. It is possible that the entire commentary on the *Nomokanon* began and ended within the year 1177.[51] Then followed the hermeneutical work on the canons (of the apostles, synods, and fathers), in which, it seems, the larger groups of canons (such as those of Trullo and Chalcedon) came first. This is at least what one can conclude from the internal references found in the work. It seems that this stage of the work reached its first completed form shortly before the death of Manuel (September 1180).[52]

Even after this point, and possibly even until his death, Balsamon did not stop adding to his work. That is how one can explain the phenomenon that in his commentary he took into account later imperial novellae as well as patriarchal acts. The last novella of certain chronology which he mentioned was one by Isaac II issued after April 1193; the last patriarchal act mentioned was that of Niketas II, dated November 17, 1186. These additions, through which Balsamon not infrequently modified his original opinion[53] or improved on his argumentation,[54] were entered by the author in the margin next to his text, which was made up of two volumes, the sec-

---

51. Schminck, 'Zur Entwicklung' 584 n. 171.
52. Tiftixoglu, 'Zur Genese' 494. According to Schminck, 'Zur Entwicklung,' after the death of Patriarch Michael (March 1178) the project proceeded with some difficulty.
53. For example, see the scholia on Apostolic Canon 17 (Rhalles-Potles 2.23ff.).
54. For example, see the scholia on Apostolic Canon 31 (Rhalles-Potles 2.41ff.).

ond one starting with the canons of Ankyra. He himself referred to these notes and scholia as 'the outside' in order to distinguish them from the 'the inside' (i.e., of the text), which comprised the original version of his commentary.[55] During the copying of the manuscripts, these notes were often transferred to the text by the copyists as 'another interpretation' but were not always placed in the correct position. Hence, in the manuscript tradition (which appears quite confusing because of this) there are three basic types of codices, which represent the three evolutionary stages of the text: the original text, a text with additions to the margin (the number of which varies from manuscript to manuscript), and a text with the additions in the body of the text.[56]

Balsamon used a great number of sources for the completion of his commentary. With regard to the novellae of Justinian, he also used the shortened form found in the *Collectio tripartita*, as becomes obvious from the dual method of reference used in the scholia on the *Nomokanon*. He also had at his disposal the entire text of the *Basilika*, at least during his service as *chartophylax*. His quotations from the *Basilika* are usually accompanied by reference according to book, title and chapter, and they are basically correct.

The contribution of Balsamon was especially valuable with regard to the development and shaping of the manuscript tradition of the novellae and patriarchal acts of the period after Justinian. In his hermeneutical work he has a multitude of references to these texts either in the form of a simple mention or a summary or even by quoting the text itself in part or in its entirety. A great number of these documents have survived only because Balsamon included them in his commentary, since in his function as *chartophylax* he had free access to the archives. Specifically, of the 93 post-Justinianic novellae he mentions, the texts of 27 of them are known only through him. A similar situation—but to a smaller extent—is also seen with regard to the patriarchal acts.

The method followed by Balsamon in his interpretation of the canons is primarily exegetical (in continuity with the tradition of the law teachers of the Justinianic period): He set down a paraphrase of the text, interpreted the difficult concepts, made reference to the reason that led to the enactment of the decree and also to the historical framework in which it appeared, compared similar canons, and pointed out conflicts with later canonical or civil provisions—usually based on the practice followed in his time. During the composition of his commentary, Balsamon also made

---

55. For example, see the scholia on Serdica canon 17 (Rhalles-Potles 3.277, 21).
56. On this, see Tiftixoglu, 'Zur Genese' 483ff.

use of the corresponding work of Zonaras, as mentioned earlier, but he kept his distance from it.[57] One cannot speak of plagiarizing or even of dependence on the work of Zonaras, because these two lawyers' approach to the text is completely different. The work of Balsamon—which also includes scholia on answers given to questions from monks at the time of Patriarch Nicholas III,[58] *responsa*, small treatises on ecclesiastical law and various other theological and philological texts—has influenced later lawyers considerably, especially those who dealt with ecclesiastical law. During both the late Byzantine and the post-Byzantine periods, excerpts from his hermeneutical work were used by later compilers in their collections. His influence can also be observed in Slavic canonical literature, which Balsamon entered through translations either of his own works or of those who were influenced by him, especially those of Matthew Blastares. The influence of his work was based on his general recognition as an expert on both the secular as well as the ecclesiastical law of his time. One should also mention, however, that some criticism was also leveled against him, because at times the solutions he gave to the legal questions set before him were dictated by reasons of expediency.[59]

The 'Anonymous' of Codex Sinaiticus 1117 (482)

Editions: V. Tiftixoglu and S. Troianos, 'Unbekannte Kaiserurkunden und Basilikentestimonia aus dem Sinaiticus 1117', FM 9 (1993) 137–79.
Bibliography: Tiftixoglu, 'Zur Genese'.

Soon after its original form was completed, the hermeneutical work of Balsamon became the object of further reworking, as well as of criticism, by a canon lawyer contemporary with, but younger than, Balsamon. The product of the work of this canon lawyer is preserved in pages 2–210 of Codex Sinaiticus 1117 (482), which is the only manuscript of the work known today (*codex unicus*). The identification of this work (which, due to its title, was long considered to be part of the manuscript tradition of Balsamon) is one of the most significant discoveries of recent years in the area of the general history of Byzantine law.

No information can be drawn from the work with regard to the person of the author, except that he must have been a member of the clergy, as is evident from the positions he took on controversial issues, which were always favorable toward the Church, the synod, and the clergy in general.

---

57. See n. 46 above.
58. Grumel-Darrouzès, *Regestes* N° 977 (982).
59. See also A. Failler, 'Une refutation de Balsamon par Nil Kabasilas', REB 32 (1974) 211–223; Tiftixoglu, 'Zur Genese' 505ff.; Troianos, Δημήτριος ο Χωματιανός 345–53.

It is possible that he served in an office that provided him with easy access to the material he needed for the completion of his work (perhaps in the imperial secretariat of the orphanage,[60] which was manned primarily by clergy). An attempt has been made to identify this 'Anonymous' with the metropolitan of Chalcedon John Kastamonites, a well-known canon lawyer of the same period, because other works by him are found in the same manuscript.[61] However, differences in style between the two works under consideration dictate that this attempt should be looked upon with a certain degree of reserve.[62]

The work of 'Anonymous' contains an interpretation both of the *Nomokanon of Fourteen Titles* (2r–67r) and of the canons (67r–203v). As a basis for his commentary on the *Nomokanon*, 'Anonymous' used the work of Balsamon, which he broke up by adding a multitude of excerpts from legal sources, mainly the *Basilika*, and accompanying scholia. Indicative of the extent of the expansion is the fact that, to the approximately 200 excerpts contained in Balsamon's work were added 1100 more, in part unknown until now. As mentioned before, 'Anonymous' not only supplements the interpretation of Balsamon in that it provides further sources but also subjects it to criticism, often intense, on matters on which he believed that Balsamon interpreted the sources arbitrarily. From historical elements contained in the commentary of the 'Anonymous,' it can be concluded that he worked on both the *Nomokanon* and the canons during the reign of Alexios II (September 1180–September 1183), and consequently he was aware of Balsamon's commentary in its original form. At the end of his scholia on the canons, however (204r–210v), he cites some of Balsamon's additions.

In his work on the canons, 'Anonymous' acted more as someone providing a supplement. He did not set down the text of the canons as a whole but broke it up by explanatory words or phrases coming from the commentaries of Zonaras and Balsamon. At the end of each canon he composed a unified text with the most important points drawn from the corresponding scholia of these two interpreters.

The work of 'Anonymous' reveals an excellent knowledge of the sources, extensive legal training, and a great ability in composition. If the fact that this work did not circulate more widely (as the work of Balsamon did) is not due to personal reasons, it means that it was probably intended to

---

60. This assumption is based on the fact that he mentions certain imperial acts concerning the orphanage which are unknown from other sources.

61. See also J. Darrouzès, 'Fragments d'un commentaire canonique anonyme', REB 24 (1966) 25–39 (here 26); Darrouzès, 'Dossier' 150–165 (here 150); Katsaros, Ἰωάννης Καστομονίτης 300ff.

62. Tiftixoglu, 'Zur Genese' 514.

cover specific needs, possibly academic—as one may conclude from the author's obvious effort to analyze the ideas found in the text of the canons.

Collections of Canonical and Ecclesiastical Law

The *Syntagma* of Matthew Blastares

Editions: (1) *Syntagma*: Beveregius 2.1–272 (= PG 144.960–1400, 145.9–212); Rhalles-Potles 6.1–518. (2) *Synopses*: Rhalles-Potles 4.432–45 and 427–43. (3) *Offikia*: J. Verpeaux, *Pseudo-Kodinos. Traité des Offices* (Paris 1966) 318–25. (4) Lexikon: E. Kalužniacki, Λέξεις λατινικαί *in einer älteren bulgarisch-slovenischen Übersetzung* (Archiv für slavische Philologie 14; 1892) 84–88; L. Burgmann, 'Das Lexikon auseth', FM 8 (1990) 249–357 (335–37).

Bibliography: Beck, *Kirche* 786ff.; T. Florinskij, Памятники законодательной деятельности Душана, царя Сербов и Греков (Monuments of the legislative activity of Dushan, tsar of the Serbs and Greeks) (Kiev 1888); E. Herman, DDC 2 (1937) 920–25; N. Il'inskij, 'Синтагма Матфея Властаря' (The Syntagma of Matthew Blastares), Чтения в обществе любителей духовного просвещения (1891) 328–45, 409–28, 437–50, 742–72; (1892) 698–723, 800–834; (1893) 44–94, 155–201; N. Il'inskij, Собрание по алфавитному порядку...или Алфавитная Синтагма М. Властаря (The collection in alphabetical order ... or the Alphabetical Syntagma of M. Blastares) (Simferopol ²1901); N. Matsis, 'Περί την παράφρασιν του Συγτάγματος του Ματθαίου Βλάσταρη υπό του Κουνάλη Κριτόπουλου' ('Concerning the paraphrase of the *Syntagma* of Matthew Blastares by Kounales Kritopoulos'), EEBS 34 (1965) 175–201; N. Matsis, Περί την κριτικήν του Συγτάγματος του Ματθαίου Βλάσταρη (*Concerning the paraphrase of the Syntagma of Matthew Blastares*) 1–2 (Athens 1979–1980); V. Mošin, 'Властарева синтагма и Душанов Законик у Студеничком "Отечнику"' (The Syntagma of Blastares and the Codex of Tsar Dushan in the Studenitsa "Otechnik"), Поводом шестогодишњице Душанова законика Старине 42 (1949) 7–93; S. Novaković, Матије Властара Синтагмат (The Syntagma of Matthew Blastares) (Beograd 1907); P. B. Paschos, Ο Ματθαίος Βλάσταρης και το υμνογραφικόν έργο του (*Matthew Blastares and his hymnographical work*; Thessaloniki 1978); A. Soloviev, 'L'oeuvre juridique de Matthieu Blastarès', *Studi bizantini e neoellenici* 5 (1939) 698–707; S. Troianos, 'Περί τας νομικάς πηγές του Ματθαίου Βλάσταρη' ('Concerning the Legal Sources of Matthew Blastares'), EEBS 44 (1979–80) 305–29; S.V. Troicki, Допунски чланци Властареве Синтагме (Supplementary articles on the Syntagma of Blastares) (Beograd 1956); van der Wal–Lokin 117.

The most important of the collections of ecclesiastical origin from the late Byzantine period is the *Syntagma kata stoicheion*, or *Alphabetical Syntagma*, of Matthew Blastares (ca. 1280–ca. 1350). Blastares was a priest-monk. He lived for most his life in the monastery of Kyr Isaac (the monastery of the Peribleptos) in Thessalonike, where he died. He had an extensive education and left behind a great literary legacy, which is not confined to the area of law. The *Syntagma* is an alphabetically arranged encyclopedia consisting primarily of ecclesiastical law but including other fields to the extent that these were of practical use to the members of the clergy. During the last centuries of Byzantium, the clergy became more involved in the judicial process, and it seems that Blastares's purpose was to help them. The *Syntagma* is divided into 24 sections according to the letters of the Greek alphabet, and every section is subdivided into chapters. In the beginning is found the preface, or *protheoria* (which includes the history of the sources of canon law in chronological order, followed by that of the civil law), a table of the chapters, and a concise forward 'Concerning the Orthodox faith'.

The collection of Blastares was created in 1335 and was based on several sources.[63] From the ecclesiastical side, he used the *Nomokanon of Fourteen Titles* and the commentaries of John Zonaras and Theodore Balsamon. From the civil side, he used the legislative and codifying works of the Isaurians (*Ecloga*) and those of the Macedonian dynasty (the *Epanagoge* or *Eisagoge*, the *Procheiron* or *Procheiros Nomos*, the novellae of Leo, and the *Basilika*). Blastares also used many private collections and compilations created between the ninth and fourteenth centuries.

In its manuscript tradition, the *Syntagma* is usually accompanied by an appendix containing texts of nomokanonic content. Some of these are works of Blastares himself (such as certain synopses; see below), while some others probably had undergone only some reworking by him (such as the *responsa* of Niketas of Heraclea and a part of the *responsa* of John of Kitros). It is not certain, however, whether these texts were selected—at least as a whole—by Blastares or whether they were a later addition to the appendix.

Thanks to its rich content as well as to the practical, useful arrangement of its material (and perhaps also thanks to the support it received from certain theological circles, the hesychasts),[64] the *Syntagma* had great circulation, as its rich manuscript tradition indicates. It was also the object of further reworking (in the paraphrase of Kounales Kritopoulos)[65] as well as the direct source of later works of compilation in the post-Byzantine period. It also circulated widely in the Slavic countries and in Romania. Shortly after its composition it was translated into Serbian. It was also translated into Bulgarian in the sixteenth century and into Russian in the seventeenth century. In those countries it became an integral part of the basic sources of their canonical law.

Of the other works of Blastares, the following also are of legal interest: a synopsis of the *Kanonikon* attributed to John Nesteutes; another synopsis

---

63. For the problem of dating, see C. G. Pitsakis, 'De nouveau sur la date du "Syntagma" de Matthieu Blastarès', *Byzantion* 51 (1981) 638–639, who rejects the date of 1355 proposed by G. I. Theocharidis in 'Ο Ματθαίος Βλάσταρης και η μονή του κυρ-Ισαάκ εν Θεσσαλονίκη', *Byzantion* 40 (1970) 437–459 (here 442) and by I. P. Medvedev in 'La date du Syntagma de Mathieu Blastares', *Byzantion* 50 (1980) 338–339.

64. See Theocharides,'Ο Ματθαίος Βλάσταρης' 439.

65. This paraphrase constitutes a combined reworking of the *Syntagma* and the *Hexabiblos* of Constantine Harmenopoulos.

of the canons of Pseudo-Nikephoros; a listing in verse form of the offices of the Great Church and the palace of Constantinople; and a dictionary of Latin legal terms, known as the *Adnoumion Lexikon*.[66]

The *Syntagma* of Makarios

Bibliography: Beck, *Kirche* 787; L. Petit, DThC 9.2 (1927) 1455–56.

After Matthew Blastares, a priest-monk by the name of Makarios—who has been held by some to be the same person as the metropolitan of Philadelphia Makarios Chrysokephalos (fourteenth century)[67] and by others to be Makarios, the metropolitan of Ankyra (end of the fourteenth, beginning of the fifteenth centuries)[68]—edited and reshaped the work of Blastares into a new nomokanonic collection to which he also gave the name *Syntagma*. The difference between this new work and the *Syntagma* of Blastares is that here the material is arranged thematically rather than alphabetically. Our knowledge of this collection is based on the description found in a codex of the fifteenth century bearing the number I.136, which earlier belonged to the library of the then-Austrian city of Nikolsburg.[69] According to this codex, the work contains 236 chapters and bears the title '*Syntagma* in summary containing all of the topics of the divine and holy canons prepared and compiled by Makarios, the least among priest-monks. *Syntagma* of Makarios, the pitiful of monks'. A preface is found before the text along with a table of the contents of the chapters. The first chapter is entitled 'Concerning the Orthodox faith', and the last one deals with the feast of Pascha. The text is followed by the following note which specifies its relationship with the *Syntagma* of Blastares: 'Those laws which Matthew presented briefly in the past, Makarios has now laid down in detail'.

The *Syntagma* of Makarios has not yet been edited, and it seems that its publication will not be possible for a while, because the manuscript tradition appears to be rather confused. Collections of nomokanons appear in various manuscripts,[70] the editor of which is held to be a certain

---

66. In spite of certain doubts (see Troicki, Допунски чланци 49), the arguments proposed by Burgmann, 'Das Lexikon' 332–34, show that it is more than probable that the lexicon comes from the hands of Blastares.

67. Beck, *Kirche* 787. For an opposing view, see Petit, DThC 9.2 (1927) 1455–56.

68. V. Laurent, 'Le Trisépiscopat du patriarche Matthieu 1er (1397–1410)', REB 30 (1972) 5–166 (here 31).

69. See E. Gollob, *Verzeichnis der griechischen Handschriften in Österreich auberhalb Wiens* (SB der Kaiserlichen Akademie der Wissenschaften, 1902–3, 146.7; Vienna 1903) 75ff. It is not known where this manuscript is to be found today.

70. Such a codex is, for example, the Vat. Borg. grec. 13 (olim L. VI. 14), fol. 1r–121v. Also see V. Beneševič, 'Сведения о греческих рукописях канонического содержания в библиотеках

priest-monk Makarios. Closer examination, however, shows that these are later nomokanons related to confession, which from the point of view of content have no relationship whatsoever with the *Syntagma* of Makarios, at least as that is found in the old codex of Nikolsburg. This manuscript, therefore, according to the information currently available, appears to be a *codex unicus*.

The *Synopsis of Canons* by Arsenios

Edition: Voel-Justel 2.749–784 (= PG 133.9–61).
Bibliography: Beck, *Kirche* 711; E. Lousse, DHGE 4 (1930) 749; Menevisoglou, 'Συνόψεις' 89–90; L. Petit, DThC I.2 (1931) 1994; Troianos, Πηγές 168; van der Wal–Lokin 118ff.

A monk from the monastery of Philotheou on the Holy Mountain (Mount Athos) called Arsenios, who lived during the twelfth or possibly the thirteenth century, compiled a *Synopsis of the Divine Canons* made up of 141 chapters. In these the editor included all the injunctions of the holy canons, also taking into account the laws of civil origin based on the *Collectio LXXXVII Capitulorum* of John Scholastikos, which he listed under the title 'legal chapter'. With regard to the canons, he followed (with occasional minor deviations) the order of the *Nomokanon of Fourteen Titles*, i.e., canons of the apostles, Nicaea, Ankyra, Neokaisareia, Gangra, Antioch, Laodikeia, Constantinople (381), Ephesus, Chalcedon, Serdica, Carthage, Penthekte (Trullo), II Nicaea, Protodeutera or 'First-and-Second,' Hagia Sophia, and Basil and the other fathers.

This Arsenios has been identified in the *editio princeps* of the work with the patriarch of Constantinople Arsenios Autorianos (1254–60 and 1261–64). This is inaccurate, however, because this patriarch never belonged to the monastery of Philotheou as a monk.[71]

The *Epitome of Canons* of Constantine Harmenopoulos

Editions: Leunclavius, JGR 1.1–71 (= PG 150.45–168); S. Perentidis, 'Edition critique et commentaire de l'Epitome des saints canons de Constantin Harmenopoulos' (Paris 1980–1981; typed manuscript).

монастырей Ватопеда и Лавры св. Афанасия на Афоне' ('Notes on Greek manuscripts of canonical content in the libraries of the monasteries of Vatopedi and the Lavra of St Athanasius on Athos'), VV 11 (1904). Приложение 2.65–67 (see also 98–99) describes the codex from Lavra K 14 (according to the numbering of that time), which contains a work corresponding to that of the codex Vaticanus, and also points out the codex 293 from Docheiariou (which in S. Lamprou, Κατάλογος των εν ταις βιβλιοθήκαις του Αγίου Όρους ελληνικών κωδικών [Cambridge 1895; reprint Amsterdam 1966; 267] bears the number 2967) as having the same contents. The codex Leidensis Vossianus graecus Q. 54, pages 35–49, contains an interpretation of the apostolic canons attributed strictly to Makarios Chrysokephalos that has absolutely no relation to the *Syntagma* of Makarios. All of these codices are from the sixteenth century.

71. L. Petit, DThC 1.2 (1923) 1993.

Bibliography: Menevisoglou, 'Συνόψεις' 91–95; K. Pitsakis, Πρόχειρον Νόμων ἡ Ἑξάβιβλος (Athens 1971); K. Pitsakis, 'Γύρω από τις πηγές της Ἐπιτομῆς κανόνων' του Κωνσταντίνου Ἁρμενοπούλου: Τα σχόλια' ('Concerning the Sources of the "Epitome of Canons" of Constantine Harmenopoulos: The Scholia') EKEID 23 (1976 [ca. 1978]) 85–122.

Between September 1344 and August 1345, a high judge in Thessalonike, Constantine Harmenopoulos, about whom not much is known, compiled the most important legal collection of the late Byzantine period. This collection was named *Hexabiblos* because it was made up of six books. In it the author organized in a systematic way material related to civil (both substantive and procedural) and penal law, which he gathered from older as well as more recent collections, both formal and informal.[72]

At the end of the work there is an appendix consisting of four titles which, because of their content, could not be included in any of the six books. The last one of these titles reads 'Concerning the ordination of bishops and presbyters'. Under this title, Harmenopoulos gathered together provisions of imperial legislation relating to the clergy and the administration of ecclesiastical property. It is understood, however, that spread throughout the rest of the work are provisions of ecclesiastical law that are related to the topics of each book and title, such as the institution of asylum, the laws of marriage, the penal protection of the Orthodox faith, etc.

Harmenopoulos, however, to whom other works are also attributed (some of which are of purely theological content) did not neglect canon law. Thus, alongside the *Hexabiblos*, which contained only civil law, he created slightly later (1346) a second collection, the *Epitome of the Holy and Divine Canons*. The *Epitome* is divided into six sections (corresponding to the six books of the *Hexabiblos*), which are further defined by inscriptions instead of titles. The six sections are inscribed: 1. Concerning bishops; 2. Concerning presbyters, deacons, and subdeacons; 3. Concerning the clergy; 4. Concerning monks and monasteries; 5. Concerning the laity; and 6. Concerning women. At the beginning of the *Epitome* (as also in the *Hexabiblos*), Harmenopoulos placed a preface in which he listed the sources he used. It is worth noting that although he took into account the so-called canons of pseudo-Nikephoros and Nicholas III, he did not take into account the synod of Constantinople of 394 and a number of fathers (canons of Athanasios the

---

72. The bibliography concerning the *Hexabiblos* is very large. Everything up to 1971 has been gathered together by Pitsakis, Πρόχειρον Νόμων. See also Pieler, 'Rechtsliteratur' 474ff. and M.T. Fögen, 'Die Scholien zur Hexabiblos im Codex vetustissimus Vaticanus Ottobonianus gr. 440', FM 4 (1981) 256–345; Troianos, Πηγές, 160ff. Regarding Harmenopoulos in general, see also the volume Κωνσταντίνου Ἁρμενοπούλου ἐπί τη ἐξακοσιετηρίδι της Ἑξαβίβλου αυτού, 1345–1945 (Thessaloniki 1952). There have been many editions of the *Hexabiblos*. The last one is by G. E. Heimbach, *Const. Harmenopuli Manuale Legum sive Hexabiblos* (Leipzig 1851; reprint Aalen 1969), which has been reissued by Pitsakis, Πρόχειρον Νόμων, with minor improvements.

Great, Gregory the Theologian, Amphilochios bishop of Ikonion, Theophilos of Alexandria, and Gennadios).

The work is accompanied by scholia, which were most probably compiled—if not in their entirety at least in greater part—by Harmenopoulos himself. From the point of view of content, these scholia for the most part had their origin in the works of the commentators of the twelfth century and the *Syntagma* of Blastares, as well as in the canonical *responsa*.

Other Collections

One of the characteristics of the law of the middle and later Byzantine period was the plethora of works—plain collections and compilations—that appeared in a great variety of forms, from a simple rearrangement of the basic work with shortening or expansion of the text, to a fusion of several works, either keeping the arrangement of the material of one of them or with a new arrangement (*mutatio, compositio*). This phenomenon occurred in the areas of both civil and ecclesiastical law. There was a series of works composed of the same primary material with respect to topics but differentiated by the number of elements of which they were composed and by the method of composition. Very few of these works were a product of the theoretical interest of their composers. The overwhelming majority of them were created in order to meet certain practical needs, either of a specific group of people or of the author himself. This is why their content is at times very peculiar or very specifically technical. The golden era of this activity fell within the second half of the middle Byzantine period (tenth to twelfth centuries). It continued during the later period (thirteenth to fifteenth centuries), during which it did not stop completely, although it diminished considerably.

The collections from the area of civil law worth mentioning here are the following: *Ecloga privata aucta* (ninth–tenth century); *Epitome legum* (original form ca. 913); *Synopsis Basilicorum maior* (tenth century); *Eisagoge/Epanagoge aucta* (tenth–eleventh centuries); *Ecloga Basilicorum librorum* 1–10 (eleventh century); *Synopsis minor* (end of thirteenth century); and *Prochiron auctum* (fourteenth century). To these collections (whose editors are not known) we also have to add the *Ponema Nomikon* of the judge Michael Attaleiates (1073–74) and the *Hexabiblos* of Harmenopoulos mentioned above. What was noted regarding this last collection also applies to the ones just mentioned; i.e., they all contain provisions (always of civil origin) that deal with the Church and the clergy.

The collections in which the laws of ecclesiastical origin were gathered (i.e., canon law) have been described in the previous sections. In addition to these, however, there exist also some others of lesser importance.

There is a table of holy canons rendered in verse form (in 78 verses), with the title 'Concerning the *Nomokanon*', which was put together by the well-known intellectual and politician of the eleventh century Michael Psellos (1018–78). To the rich literary activity of Psellos belongs also the *Synopsis of Laws*, which was also written in verse form. This was, in essence, a teaching manual created for the young emperor Michael VII Doukas.[73] The fact that both works are in verse form leads one to believe that 'Concerning the *Nomokanon*' was written by Psellos as a complement to the *Synopis of Laws*, although it consists only of a simple enumeration of the canons without any mention of their content. As has already been noted,[74] it can be concluded from the composition of this synopsis of canons that Psellos here relied on the *Nomokanon of Fifty Titles* of John Scholastikos and not on the later and more complete *Nomokanon of Fourteen Titles*.[75]

An epitome of the *Nomokanon of Fourteen Titles* has been attributed to Gregory Doxopatres or Doxapatres (first half of the twlefth century).[76] However, in spite of the doubts that emerged with regard to the identity of the supposed editor (i.e., whether he can be identified with any of the other people with the name Doxopatres or Doxapatres—Nicholas or Neilos), the point remains that such a work does not exist. The Codex Vaticanus graecus 2019 may be the only manuscript,[77] and, from a direct comparison of the epitome and the scholia contained in pages 9vff. with the *Synopsis of Canons* and the hermeneutical work of Alexios Aristenos, it has been discovered that these two epitomes and their scholia are absolutely identical.[78] It is possible that, during the copying of this codex, the name of Aristenos was replaced by that of Doxapatres with no other change.

Around the middle of the twelfth century, the archbishop of Ohrid, John Comnenos, also seems to have done some work on the *Syntagma of Canons*. This archbishop bore the name of Adrianos (Hadrian) before his ordination and was possibly identified with some other archbishop also known by the same last name. This work is found in the Codex Vaticanus graecus 2198 and is still unedited.[79]

---

73. See Pieler, 'Rechtsliteratur' 464ff. See also M.T. Fögen, 'Zum Rechtsunterricht des Michael Psellos', JÖB 32.2 (1982) 281–302.

74. Menevisoglou, 'Συνόψεις' 88. With regard to the work of Psellos, see also Mortreuil 3.446–48.

75. Edition: L. G. Westerink, *Michael Psellus Poemata* (Stuttgart-Leipzig 1992) 7–80. On page xv of this last critical edition are also mentioned the five previous ones.

76. See Mortreuil 3.411–12.

77. See Turyn, *Codices graeci vaticani* 28–34 (28).

78. See also K. E. Zachariä von Lingenthal, 'Die Synopsis canonum. Ein Beitrag zur Geschichte der Quellen des kanonischen Rechts der griechischen Kirche' (SB. der königlich-preussischen Akademie der Wissenschaften Berlin, 1887, 1147–1163; = *Kleine Schriften* 2.247–263; here 1160ff. and 260ff.) and Menevisoglou, 'Συνόψεις' 85–86.

79. See S. Vailhé, DHGE 1 (1912) 613–614; Beneševič, VV 22 (1915–1916) 41–61; Beck, *Kirche* 659.

Alongside these collections that bear the names of their authors, there also appear other anonymous ones.[80] In these the absence of some obvious, systematic criterion with regard to their compilation indicates that they were created with the purpose of meeting certain personal needs of their authors. Such collections will continue to come to light as the study of the contents of manuscripts, which often appear in the catalogues of various libraries as νομοκάνων or νομοκάνονον without any further specification, continues.

The Jurisprudence of the Ecclesiastical Courts

Bibliography: A. Christophilopoulos, Ἡ δικαιοδοσία των εκκλησιαστικών δικαστηρίων επί ιδιωτικών διαφορών κατά την βυζαντινή περίοδον' ('The jurisdiction of the ecclesiastical courts with regard to private disputes during the Byzantine period') EEBS 18 (1948) 192–201 (= Christophilopoulos, Δίκαιον 244–54); Papagianni, Νομολογία; D. Simon, 'Byzantinische Provinzialjustiz', BZ 79 (1986) 310–43; S. Troianos, 'Ἡ εκκλησιαστική διαδικασία μεταξύ 565 και 1204' ('Ecclesiastical procedure between 565 and 1204'), EKEID 13 (1966, ca. 1969) 3–148.

Of special interest to observe in every legal system is the way in which law is enforced, especially where one suspects that there may be a gap between the adopted law and that which is applied in reality. Not infrequently such a gap is observed in Byzantine law, much more so in the area of civil law and less so in the area of canon law. This last element should not be surprising, since the holy canons were subjected to a hermeneutical reworking so that they could continue to be applicable for centuries after their adoption.

The best witness to the method of enforcement of the canons of law are the decisions of the courts. Unfortunately, the samples of jurisprudence of the Byzantine civil courts that have survived are very few. On the other hand, the decisions of ecclesiastical courts fortunately have enjoyed better luck. Many decisions of agencies of the Church with judicial responsibilities have survived, especially from the later period. However, as has already been mentioned in connection with the various collections, during this period the participation of the clergy in the administration of justice had increased and overstepped by a wide margin the *stricto sensu* boundaries of ecclesiastical and canonical law.

In the area of ecclesiastical justice during the later Byzantine period, two names stand out: John Apokaukos and Demetrios Chomatianos (or Chomatenos). Both of them lived and worked in the territory of one of

---

80. Such a collection is described by S. Troianos, 'Ἡ νομονοκανονική συλλογή του Cod. Cryptof. Zy VII', Χαριστείον Σεραφείμ Τίκα (Thessalonike 1984) 453–73.

the Greek states created after the capture of Constantinople by the Latin crusaders in 1204, the state (the so-called 'despotate') of Epiros. It is possible that the reason for the survival of these decisions lies both in the reputation of these two hierarchs and in the high quality of their decisions from the legal point of view. Also preserved are decisions of the patriarchal synodal court of Constantinople from the fourteenth century. To this judicial material must be added the decisions—quite numerous—of the agencies of justice of the Holy Mountain, which survive in the archives of the monasteries of Mount Athos.

The Court Decisions of John Apokaukos

Editions: A. Vasilievskij, 'Epirotica saeculi XIII', VV 3 (1896) 233–99; A. Papadopoulos-Kerameus, Ἀνάλεκτα Ιεροσολυμιτικῆς σταχυολογίας, 2 and 4 (St. Petersburg 1894–98; reprint Brussels 1963) 2.361–62, 4.119–25; A. Papadopoulos-Kerameus, 'Κερκυραϊκά', VV 13 (1907) 334–51; A. Papadopoulos-Kerameus, 'Συνοδικὰ γράμματα Ιωάννου του Ἀποκαύκου μητροπολίτου Ναυπάκτου' ('The Synodal Letters of John Apokaukos, Metropolitan of Naupaktos'), Βυζαντίς 1 (1909) 3–30; A. Papadopoulos-Kerameus, Ιωάννης Ἀποκαύκος και Νικήτας Χωνιάτης "Τεσσαρακονταετηρὶς τῆς καθηγεσίας Κ. Σ. Κόντου' ('John Apokaukos and Niketas Choniates', Fourtieth Anniversary Celebration of the Professorship of K. S. Kontos; Athens 1909) 373–82; A. Papadopoulos-Kerameus, 'Κανονικαὶ πράξεις Γεωργίου Βαρδάνη και Ιωάννου Ἀποκαύκου περὶ κληρονομικῆς ὑποθέσεως Θεοδώρου Διαβατηνοῦ' ('Canonical Acts of Georgios Bardanes and John Apokaukos with regard to the issue of inheritance of Theodoros Diabatenos'), Ἐκκλησιαστικὸς Φάρος 4 (1909) 62–67; A. Papadopoulos-Kerameus, Noctes Petropolitanae (St. Petersburg 1913; repr. Leipzig 1976) 246–94; S. Petrides, 'Jean Apokavkos, Lettres et autres documents inédits', Известия русского археологического института в Константинополе 14 (1909) 69–100; N. Tomadakis, 'Οἱ λόγοι του δεσποτάτου τῆς Ἠπείρου ('The intellectuals of the Despotate of Epiros'), EEBS 27 (1957) 3–62; H. Bei-Seferli, 'Unedierte Schriftstücke aus der Kanzlei des Johannes Apokaukos des Metropoliten von Naupaktos (in Aetolien)', Byzantinisch-neugriechische Jahrbücher 21 (1971–76) Part 2.55–243.

Bibliography: (1) General: R. J. Macrides, ODB I (1991) 135; G. Prinzing, LMA 1 (1980) 758 and footnotes; K. Lampropoulos, 'Ιωάννης Ἀπόκαυκος' (Ιστορικές μονογραφίες 6; Athens 1988). (2) Regarding the decisions: M. T. Fögen, 'Rechtsprechung mit Aristophanes', Rechtshistorisches Journal 1 (1982) 74–82; M. T. Fögen, 'Ein heißes Eisen', Rechtshistorisches Journal 2 (1983) 85–96; M. T. Fögen, 'Ein ganz gewöhnlicher Mord', Rechtshistorisches Journal 3 (1984) 71–81; M. T. Fögen, Horor iuris, 'Cupido legum' (Frankfurt am Main 1985) 47–71; Katerelos, Die Auflösung; Kiousopoulou, Θεσμός; Laiou, 'Contribution'; T. Maniati-Kokkini, 'Μαρτυρία Ιωάννου Ναυπάκτου του Ἀποκαύκου για την κοινωνία του ΙΓ' αιώνα. Δύο υποθέσεις φόνου', Πρακτικὰ Α' Ἀρχαιολ. και Ιστορικοῦ συνεδρίου Αιτωλοακαρνανίας ('The witness of John Apokaukos of Naupaktos with regard to the society of the thirteenth century: Two cases of murder'; Proceedings of the First Archaeological and Historical Conference of Aetoloakarnania) (Agrinion 1991) 297–306; E. Papagianni, 'Μία απόφαση του Ἀποκαύκου και ο εκκλησιαστικός βίος στο 13ο αιώνα'. Πρακτικὰ Α' Ἀρχαιολ. και Ιστορικοῦ συνεδρίου Αιτωλοακαρνανίας ('A decision of Apokaukos and the ecclesiastical life of the thirteenth century'; Proceedings of the First Archaeological and Historical Conference of Aetoloakarnania) (Agrinion 1991) 291–96; K. Pitsakis, 'Ζητήματα κωλυμάτων γάμου από την νομολογία και την πρακτική του «δεσποτάτου» της Ηπείρου', Πρακτικὰ Διεθνοῦς Συμποσίου για το

Δεσποτάτο της Ηπείρου ('Issues of impediments to marriage from the jurisprudence and practice of the "despotate" of Epiros', Proceedings of the International Symposium on the Despotate of Epiros; Arta, 1992) 355–374; S. Troianos, 'Οι λόγοι διαζυγίου στο νομολογιακό έργο του Ιωάννου Αποκαύκου ('Reasons for divorce in the juridical work of John Apokaukos'), Βυζαντινά 16 (1991) 43–63.

John Apokaukos was probably born in the capital between 1153 and 1160 and died around 1233/34. He was the nephew of the metropolitan of Naupaktos and well-known chronicler of that time, Constantine Manasses. He received a good education in Constantinople, where he worked for a number of years as a deacon in the patriarchal secretariat (in 1193 he is witnessed as the patriarchal *notarios*). Around 1200 he became metropolitan of Naupaktos. In that position he became actively involved in the political issues of his time and played a significant role in the antagonism between the empire of Nicaea and the state of Epiros, fomenting the political ambitions of the rulers of the latter with the ultimate goal of gaining jurisdiction over the area of Epiros, which was under the patriarchate at the time. His actions led to sharp conflict between the ecumenical patriarchate and the church of Epiros. Shortly before his death he resigned his position as metropolitan and withdrew to the monastery of Kozyle outside of Ioannina.

More than thirty decisions survive from the activity of Apokaukos in the area of administering of justice. In these decisions, a great part of which deal with marriage issues (mainly divorce and annulments of marriages), one witnesses leniency but also good judgment, at times showing an amazing agility in evaluating the real evidence without restricting the essence of the case to legal formalities. In his decisions, Apokaukos only rarely sets down quotations from the sources—and then only from memory—because he must not have had a library rich in the sources of laws available to him.

The Court Decisions of Demetrios Chomatianos

Editions: Pitra, *Analecta* 6 (*Juris ecclesiastici Graecorum selecta paralipomena*; reprint Farnborough 1967); Zepoi, JGR 7.499–548.

Bibliography: (1) General: R.J. Macrides, ODB I (1991) 426; G. Prinzig, LMA II (1983) 1874–75. (2) Regarding the decisions: A. Christophilopoulos, 'Δημητρίος Χωματιανός', Θεολογία 20 (1949) 741–49 (= Christophilopoulos, Δίκαιον 155–63); A. D'Emilia, 'Tre αποφάνσεις di Demetrios Chomatianos in materia di αλληλοκληρονομία', *Riv. di studi bizantini e neoellenici* NS 1 (1964) 103–19; Katerelos, *Die Auflösung*; Kiousopoulou, Θεσμός; Laiou, 'Contribution'; A. Laiou, *Mariage, amour et parenté à Byzance au XIe–XIIIe siècles* (Paris 1992) passim; A. Laiou–D. Simon, 'Eine Geschichte von Mühlen und Mönchen. Der Fall der Mühlen von Chantax', *Bullentino dell'Istituto di diritto Romano* 91 (1988, ca. 1992) 619–76; N. Matsis, Νομικά ζητήματα εκ των έργων του Δημητρίου ('*Legal issues from the works of Demetrios Chomatianos*'; Athens 1961); D. Simon, 'Witwe Sachlikina gegen Witwe Horaia', FM 6 (1984) 325–75; D. Simon, 'Princeps legibus solutus', *Gedächtnisschrift W. Kunkel* (Frankfurt am Main 1984) 449–92; D. Simon, 'Gewissensbisse eines Kaisers', *Festschrift für H. Hübner* (Berlin–NewYork 1984) 263–71; D. Simon, 'Νομοτριβούμενοι', *Satura Roberto Feenstra: Sexagesimum quintum annum aetatis complenti ab alumnis collegis amicis oblata*, ed. J. A. Ankum, J. E. Spruit, F. B. J. Wubbe (Fribourg 1985) 273–83; Troianos, Δημήτριος ο Χωματιανός.

Whatever evidence we have about the life of Chomatianos (or Chomatenos) comes mainly from the writings of his older friend and fellow-student in Constantinople, John Apokaukos. He initially served as *apokrisiarios* of the archdiocese of Ohrid in Constantinople around the end of the twelfth century and later became *chartophylax* of the same archdiocese. Finally, with the help of Apokaukos, he became the archbishop around 1217. The election was carried out by the civil authorities, and his ordination was performed without the participation of the patriarchate. This was based on the thinking that the church of Epiros was administratively independent, something which brought about sharp reaction and protests on the part of the patriarchate. Chomatianos, in turn, engaged in ecclesio-political activities similar to those of Apokaukos. With his participation especially in the crowning of the ruler of Epiros, Theodore I Doukas, as emperor in Thessalonike (possibly in 1227), Chomatianos had an even greater part than Apokaukos did in the antagonism, and consequently in the conflict, between Nicaea and Epiros.

The juridical material from the archdiocesan court of the Justiniana Prima (as they used to call the archdiocese of Ohrid in order to strengthen its historical status, identifying it—wrongly, of course—with the Justiniana Prima of Justinian)[81] is much more voluminous and impressive than the corresponding material from Naupaktos. It contains more than 150 texts, both decisions as well as opinions of the court. Based on this material, Chomatianos appears to have been one of the greatest lawyers of his time, with regard not only to the interpretation of the holy canons but also to other areas of law, for his decisions cover more or less all branches of law, private and public. His excellent knowledge of the sources was combined with his acute legal judgment. Based on the observation that Chomatianos (unlike Apokaukos) often provides texts from the sources that he used for substantiating his decisions, it must be assumed that he had a substantial legal library.

The edition of the legal works of Chomatianos is old, but a new critical edition is now underway (G. Prinzing). Besides the decisions and judicial opinions of Chomatianos, several *responsa* also survive.

---

81. See 'Prima Justiniana im Titel des bulgarischen Erzbischofs von Achrida', BZ 36 (1929–30) 484–89 and G. Prinzing, 'Entstehung und Rezeption der Justiniana Prima-Theorie im Mittelalter', *Byzantinobulganica* 5 (1978) 269–75.

The Decisions of the Patriarchal Court

Editions: M-M, Acta 1–2; H. Hunger–O. Kresten, *Das Register des Patriarchats von Konstantinopel* (Vienna 1981; indices developed by C. Cupane, Vienna 1981); H. Hunger, 'Zu den restlichen inedita des Konstantinopler Patriarchatsregisters im Cod. Vindob. hist. gr. 48', REB 24 (1966) 58–66.

Bibliography: P. Lemerle, 'Recherches sur les institutions judiciaires à l'époque des Paléologues, 2: Le tribunal du Patriarcat ou tribunal synodal', *Analecta Bollandiana* 58 (1950) 318–33; N. Matsis, Το οικογενειακόν δίκαιον κατά την νομολογίαν του Πατριαρχείου Κωνσταντινουπόλεως των ετών 1315–1401 (*Family law according to the jurisprudence of the patriarchate of Constantinople for the years 1315–1401*'; Athens 1962); N. Matsis, Κριτικαί παρατηρήσεις εις τα Acta Patriarchatus Constantinopolitani, Ι'–ΙΕ' ('*Critical observations on the Acta Patriarchatus Constantinopolitani, X–XV*'; Athens 1983–1984); N. Matsis, 'Ο τόκος εν τη νομολογία του πατριαρχείου Κωνσταντινουπόλεως κατά τους ΙΔ' και ΙΕ' αιώνας' ('Interest according to the jurisprudence of the patriarchate of Constantinople during the fourteenth and fifteenth centuries'), EEBS 38 (1971) 71–83; P. E. Pieler, 'Die Entscheidungen des Patriarchalgerichts von Konstantinopel in zivilrechtlichen Streitfällen und das System der Quellen des byzantinischen Rechts', *Österreichische Landesreferate zum VIII. Internationalen Kongreß für Rechtsvergleichung in Pescara 1970* (Vienna 1970) 7–16.

A significant number of court decisions, issued not by the provincial, or eparchial, courts (such as the ones examined in the previous sections) but by the patriarchal court itself, are contained in the 'codex' of the patriarchate of Constantinople, along with acts from the years 1315–1402. This 'codex' has survived and is found in the National Library of Austria under the designation *Codices Vindobonenses historici graeci* 47 and 48. It contains acts of the patriarchs John XIII Glykes, Gerasimos I, Isaiah, John XIV Kalekas, Isidore, Kallistos I, Philotheos Kokkinos, Makarios, Neilos, Antony IV, Kallistos II Xanthopoulos, and Matthew.

Not all of the acts contained in the 'codex' are of a judicial character. Only a part of them consists of court decisions, and these are disproportionately divided with regard to time. It has been observed that from the period 1315 to 1330 there are approximately 30 decisions; from the period 1330 to 1394 there are only 10; and then there is a sudden increase in the numbers: For just the two years 1399 and 1400 there are a total of 60 decisions. These changes certainly are not accidental and most probably are due to internal political reasons. It has been proposed by way of explanation that up until 1330 the observed frequent appeal to the ecclesiastical courts was due to the corruption that was plaguing the civil courts.[82] This corruption led to an effort to remedy the situation by the introduction of the institution of the 'universal judges of the Romans'.[83] Later, in view of

---

82. Lemerle, 'Recherches' 319ff.
83. This effort for bringing about renewal was undertaken by Emperor Andronikos III; see Troianos, Πηγές 156ff. See related bibliography in Pieler, 'Rechtsliteratur' 473.

the better operation of the civil courts, appeals to the ecclesiastical ones decreased in number. According to the same opinion, the sudden increase of such appeals at the end of the fourteenth century was again due to the non-functioning of the government because of civil strife. It also has been pointed out,[84] however, that the great increase in the activity of the synodal court, especially during the reign of Patriarch Matthew, must be attributed to the personal influence of this patriarch—and possibly of other members of the synod of this period—which won the trust of the disputants, since, it must be noted, most of these decisions were not related to ecclesiastical issues but usually concerned property disputes.

Decisions of the Judicial Agencies of Monasteries

Editions: (1) Athos: F. Ternovskij, Акты русского на святом Афоне монастыря св. (...) Пантелеймона (Acts of the Russian monastery on holy Athos ... of Panteleimon) (Kiev 1873); 'Actes de l'Athos', VV 10, 12, 13, 17, 19, and 20 (1903–13); Приложение, *Archives de l'Athos I–XVII* (Paris 1937–1991). (2) Other monasteries: T. Ouspensky–V. Beneševič, *Actes du Vazélon* (Leningrad 1927); F. Dölger, *Die Urkunden des Johannes-Prodromos-Klosters bei Serrai* (Munich 1935); A. Guillou, *Les archives de Saint-Jean-Prodrome sur le mont Ménécée* (Paris 1955).

In the archives of several monasteries is a rich treasure of material in the form of records. The greatest part of these are records (i.e., legal documents) constituting a given monastery's titles of ownership for its real estate holdings. Also among these records are found court decisions that served the same purpose, since they were issued on account of disagreements regarding the ownership or the boundaries of land, in disputes either between monasteries or between monasteries and individuals. Some of these decisions came from civil courts, but many were issued by ecclesiastical judicial agencies. This holds true primarily for the documents from the monasteries of Mount Athos, since the administrative authorities of the Holy Mountain, especially the *protos,* also had judicial authority. Because of this, these records are of interest as a source of law, more so of property law than of ecclesiastical law, since, as has already been pointed out, these decisions concerned disputes about real estate. From the point of view of ecclesiastical law, their value is concentrated mainly in the judicial procedures employed.

A large part of the archives of the monasteries of Athos has already been published. The first effort at a systematic publication of the documents of Athos took place in Russia at the beginning of the twentieth century in the series 'Actes de l'Athos,' in which documents from the archives of the monasteries of Xenophontos, Pantokrator, Esphigmenou, Zographou, Hilandar and Philotheou were published consecutively. The

---

84. Papagianni, Νομολογία 7ff.

effort was continued several decades later in Paris with the establishment of the series 'Archives de l'Athos'. In this series, documents from the Protaton and from the monasteries of St. Panteleemon, Dionysiou, Docheiariou, Esphigmenou, Iveron, Kastamonitou, Koutloumousiou, Lavra, Pantokrator, Xenophontos, and Xeropotamou have already been published.

Canonical *Responsa* and Canonical Treatises

Editions: All of the editions of the *responsa* or treatises coming from patriarchs of Constantinople are listed in detail in the *Regestes* of Grumel-Darrouzès or Laurent. In these cases their number in the *Regestes*, along with the latest (or most accessible) edition, is listed in the footnotes. In cases where the *responsa* come from other people, all of their editions are mentioned.

Bibliography: Beck, *Kirche*, *passim*; Herman, Introductio, *passim*.

Canonical *Responsa*

The expansion of the exclusive jurisdiction of ecclesiastical agencies, both administrative as well as judicial, to a wider range of cases resulted in an increase in the practical problems that these agencies encountered on a daily basis. Thus, the custom that had appeared in previous centuries, for inquiries on various issues of ecclesiastical law to be directed either to the ecclesiastical authorities or to special canon lawyers, spread even further from the eleventh century onward. As a result of the great increase of the *responsa*, we not infrequently find in the manuscript tradition that the same *responsa* is attributed each time to different people, thus making the establishment of the authorship of these texts more difficult. In other cases, the *responsa* of the same canonists survive in several versions, which differ with regard either to their format (long or brief) or to their number. In the section that follows an effort is made to present as complete a picture as possible of this category among the sources of canon law.

Known authors of *responsa* from the end of the eleventh century and the beginning of the twelfth are the *chartophylakes* Peter and Nikephoros; Patriarch Nicholas III Grammatikos of Constantinople; and the metropolitans Niketas of Herakleia, Elias of Crete, and possibly Niketas of Thessalonike.

The name of the *chartophylax* Peter appears three times at the end of the eleventh and the beginning of the twelfth centuries. It is not known whether in all three cases we are dealing with the same person. There survive, however, 24 *responsa* in two series, written during the last decade of the eleventh century (1092 or 1095–96), of which 16 coincide.[85]

---

85. Editions: Series I: Leunclavius, JGR 1.395–97 (= PG 119.1093–1097); Rhalles-Potles 5.369–73. Series II: V. Beneševič, Ответы Петра Хартофилакса (Responses of Peter the Chartophylax) (Записки императорской академии наук, 8th series, vol. VIII, N° 14; St. Petersburg 1909).

The *chartophylax* Nikephoros seems also to have been active at the end of the eleventh century. The effort to identify him with Patriarch Nikephoros II (1260–61) is totally unfounded. Three of his letters survive, containing responses to questions of the monk and recluse of Corinth, Theodosios, as well as other *responsa* to the monk Maximos.[86]

Patriarch Nicholas III Grammatikos (1084–1111) of Constantinople lived at the turn of the eleventh to the twelfth centuries. He was born in Pisidia, where he lived for many years. After the raids of the Seljuk Turks, he sought refuge in Constantinople, where he established the monastery of John the Forerunner (*Prodromos*) called *tou Lophou*. Because of his monastic background, he turned his attention to issues of faith, liturgics, and spiritual discipline. His *responsa* to the monks of Athos survive in various forms, along with *responsa* to questions from the bishop of Zetounion.[87]

Metropolitan Niketas of Herakleia also lived during the eleventh to twelfth centuries. He was born around 1060 and ascended to the throne of Herakleia in 1117. Among his works belong 13 *responsa* to Bishop Constantine of Pamphilia.[88]

Problems arise with regard to the chronological placement of a certain Niketas, metropolitan of Thessalonike, to whom are attributed *responsa* dealing primarily with issues of marriage law. Under this name we find both a certain metropolitan of Thessalonike from the eleventh century with a rich theological output as well as someone else from the twelfth century who had previously served in the capacity of *chartophylax* of the Great Church.[89] The problem is further complicated because the text of his *responsa* occasionally appears attributed to a certain 'Niketas of Serres',[90] who can

---

86. Editions: (1) Bonefidius 3.197–202; Leunclavius, JGR1.341–344 (= PG 100.1061–1065); Rhalles-Potles 5.399–402. (2) V. Beneševič, VV 12 (1906) 518–24. (3) Gedeon, EKA 36 (1916) 1ff. All the other *responsa* were published in a critical edition by P. Gautier, 'Le chartophylax Nicéphore, Oeuvre canonique et notice biographique', REB 27 (1969) 159–95 (175–95, with French translation).

87. Grumel-Darrouzès, *Regestes* N° 972 [977], 977 [982], 978 [983], and 990 [972]. Editions: (1) to the monks of Athos: Rhalles-Potles 4.417–26; Pitra, *Spicilegium* 476–80; Oudot 1.12–27 (with French translation). (2) to the bishop of Zetounion: J. Darrouzès, 'Les réponses de Nicolas III à l'évêque de Zètounion', ΚΑΘΗΓΗΤΡΙΑ: *Essays presented to Joan Hussey*, ed. J. Chrysostomides (Camberley, Surrey 1988) 327–343; E. Papagianni and S. Troianos, 'Die kanonischen Antworten des Nicolaos III.: Grammatikos an den Bischof von Zetunion', BZ 82 (1989) 234–50 (with German translation). Bibliography: A. Kazhdan and A. Cutler, ODB 2.1467; P. Plank, LMA 6.1166–67.

88. Editions: Bonefidius 3.133–35; Leunclavius, JGR 1.310–11 (= PG 119.936–37); Rhalles-Potles 5.441–42; A. Pavlov, 'Канонические ответы Никиты, митрополита Ираклийского (XI–XII века)' ('Canonical responses of Nikita, Metropolitan of Heracleia'), VV 2 (1895) 160–176; Sophronios Leontopoleos, Ἐκκλησιαστικὸς Φάρος 6 (1916) 93–95; Dyobouniotis, Νομοκανονικαί μελέται (Athens 1917) 181ff.; Gedeon, EKA 36 (1916) 17–18. Bibliography: G. Podskalsky, LMA 6.1160.

89. Editions: Bonefidius 3.203–16; Leunclavius, JGR 1.344–51 (= PG 119.997–1009); Rhalles-Potles 5.443–45 and 382–88; Pavlov, 'Канонические' 378–87; Gedeon, EKA 36 (1916) 2–3. Bibliography: Beck, *Kirche* 580, 621; G. Prinzing, LMA 6.1160–61.

90. Gedeon, EKA 14 (1894) 17–18.

be none other than the aforementioned metropolitan of Heracleia Niketas, nephew of the metropolitan of Serres.[91]

Metropolitan Elias of Crete belongs more to the twelfth century, although he was born at the end of the eleventh. He is mainly known for his interpretation of patristic texts. However, a series of 8 *responsa* on various themes to a certain monk Dionysios also survives.[92]

The same problems with regard to chronology that we encounter with Niketas also apply to Michael Choumnos, well known for his treatises on marriage issues and fasting, who was originally *chartophylax* of the Great Church and later metropolitan of Thessalonike. Certain manuscripts (e.g., Vaticanus graecus 2019ff. 135v–137r, Berolinensis Philips. fol. 299v–301v) contain a response (dated 1122) to a certain monk Neophytos.[93] To another metropolitan of Thessalonike, Euphemianos by name, are attributed *responsa* addressed to a certain monk Gerasimos of the Holy Mountain. It is not known when this metropolitan lived. He could not, however, have lived after the end of the twelfth or, at the latest, the beginning of the thirteenth century.[94]

Entirely to the twelfth century belong the patriarchs of Constantinople Kosmas II Attikos (1146–47), Nicholas IV Mouzalon (1147–51) and Loukas Chrysoberges (1157–70); Archbishop Basil Achridenos of Thessalonike; Metropolitan John Kastamonites of Chalcedon; the *chartophylax* John Pantechnes; Neilos Doxopatres; and Theodore Balsamon, with whom we have already dealt above.

The names of the *chartophylax* John Pantechnes (who was probably the same as the *megas skeuophylax* bearing the same name) and of Patriarch Kosmas are connected in the area of the *responsa* because the latter published a response dealing with issues of fasting in order to rebut a previous opinion on the same topic by this *chartophylax*.[95]

Under the name of Patriarch Nicholas IV has been transmitted (in a

---

91. J. Darrouzès, 'Nicétas d'Héraclée ὁ τοῦ Σερρῶν', REB 18 (1960) 179–84.

92. Editions: Bonefidius 2.185–97; Leunclavius, JGR 1.335–41 (= PG 119.985–97); Rhalles-Potles 5.374–81; Gedeon, EKA 18 (1894). Bibliography: S. Salaville, DThC 4.2 (1939) 2331–33.

93. Contrary to what Beck, *Kirche* 659, assumed, this response cannot be identified with a small treatise by Choumnos published by V. Beneševič, 'Monumenta Vaticana' 121–86 (184), in spite of the fact that their contents are related.

94. L. Petit, 'Les évêques de Thessalonique', *Échos d'Orient* 5 (1901–2) 90, places him at the beginning of the fourteenth century, something impossible because his *responsa* appear also in a codex which was written before 1234 (Vat. grec. 2019; see also Turyn, *Codices graeci vaticani* 28). These *responsa* of Euphemianos cannot be identified with those attributed to Loukas Chrysoberges (see below, n. 97), which are thought to have been initiated through questions of the abbot of the monastery of the Christ the Savior Philanthropos. It is not impossible, however, that this abbot later became metropolitan of Thessalonike and is the author of these *responsa*.

95. Grumel-Darrouzès, *Regestes* N° 1024. Edition: A. Papadopoulos–Kerameus, *Varia graeca sacra* (St. Petersburg 1909; reprint Leipzig 1975) 273–84.

very complex manuscript tradition which creates problems of authenticity) a series of *responsa* on various issues. This was probably compiled by the then *chartophylax* Constantine at the request of the patriarch.[96]

Similar problems exist with regard to *responsa* attributed to Patriarch Loukas, which appear in various codices.[97] Such problems are more frequently encountered in connection with texts that are reputed to emanate from patriarchs—first, because it is always possible that these were simply repetitions and ratifications of older opinions that were known in ecclesiastical practice, and second, because the manuscript tradition was not infrequently modified by subsequent additions, with the obvious purpose of strengthening their content with respect to authority.

Neilos Doxapatres, deacon of the Great Church and patriarchal *notarios* and *nomophylax*, lived and worked during the years of Emperor John II Comnenos (1118–43). His literary activity seems to have been significant, but in the area of canon law only one response survives. It deals with the interpretation of canon 31 of Laodikeia.[98]

During the same period, a certain Basil lived in Constantinople as *protonotarios* of Patriarch Michael II (1143–46). He received the nickname Achridenos because he came from Ohrid. Later he became metropolitan of Thessalonike, developed many relations with the West, and must have died in 1169 at the latest. From his work in canon law only one response survives; it concerns marriages in the seventh degree of relationship.[99]

A series of *responsa* (63 or 66, depending on the edition), answering questions that Patriarch Mark of Alexandria directed to the synod during the reign of Patriarch George II Xiphilinos, has been transmitted in many manuscripts. The synodal reply is dated February 1195, and Theodore Balsamon, patriarch of Antioch, is held to be the author of the *responsa*. However, we also find in other manuscripts some of Mark's questions with answers more or less different from those of Balsamon. The investigation of this problem during the last few years has led to the conclusion that the mandate for drawing up the *responsa* was originally given to Metropolitan John Kastamonites of Chalcedon. The responsibility for their final formulation, however, was delegated to Balsamon.[100]

---

96. Grumel-Darrouzès, *Regestes* N° 1034, includes a discussion of the problems of authenticity. The text is still unedited.

97. Grumel-Darrouzès, *Regestes* N° 1087. A. I. Almazov. Неизданные канонические ответы Константинопольского Патриарха Луки Хрисоверга и митрополита Родосского Нила. (Unpublished canonical responses of Patriarch Loukas Chrysovergis of Constantinople and Metropolitan Neilos of Rhodes) Odessa 1903. See also Schminck, 'Zur Entwicklung' 580.

98. Gedeon, EKA 2 (1881).

99. Editions: Bonefidius 3.131–32; Leunclavius, JGR 1.309–10 and 408–9 (= PG 119.933–36 and 1119–20); Rhalles-Potles 5.389–90.

100. Grumel-Darrouzès, *Regestes* N° 1184. Editions: (1) Kastamonites: M. Gedeon, Νέα

Beyond his *responsa* to the questions of Mark of Alexandria, John Kastamonites seems also to have been the author of other *responsa*, which appear anonymously in certain manuscripts side by side with the *responsa* to Mark[101]—something which indicates that this metropolitan of Chalcedon had engaged specifically in the study of canon law.

Names from the thirteenth century connected with *responsa* are those of the patriarchs of Constantinople Manuel II and John XI Bekkos; of Metropolitan John Apokaukos of Naupaktos; and of Archbishop Demetrios Chomatianos of Ohrid; as well as the name of Metropolitan John of Kitros.

During the patriarchate of Manuel II (1243–54), a synodal act, dated July 1250, was issued containing *responsa* to questions from Metropolitan Romanos of Dyrrachion on various topics.[102] A few decades later, on August 12, 1276, during the patriarchate of John XI (1275–82), another synodal act was issued in which answers were given to questions of canonical content from the bishop of Sarai in the Crimea.[103]

The nomokanonical work of John Apokaukos was, as we have already seen, very rich, but it contains mainly judicial decisions. Certain *responsa* that he gave to Metropolitan George Bardanes of Kerkyra also survive, however.[104]

On the other hand, the *responsa* attributed to the other significant canon lawyer of the same period, Demetrios Chomatianos, are greater in number.[105] Some of these were issued in response to questions from Metropolitan Constantine Kabasilas of Dyrrachion. *Responsa* to the same metropolitan with the same content also appear, however, in other manuscripts where they are attributed to a certain Bishop John of Kitros,[106] about whom not much is known but who is placed chronologically in the first half of the thirteenth century. In view of this situation in the manuscript tradition, the opinion which prevailed in earlier years was that the authorship of the *responsa* appearing under the name of the bishop of Kitros actually belonged

---

βιβλιοθήκη εκκλησιαστικών συνγραφέων I (Constantinople 1901) 135–60 (= EKA 35 [1915] 169–73, 177–82, 185–89). (2) Balsamon: Bonefidius 3.237–300; Leunclavius, JGR 1.362–94 (= PG 119.1032–93 and 138.951–1012); Rhalles-Potles 4.448–96. Bibliography: V. Grumel, 'Les résponses canoniques à Marc d'Alexandrie: Leur caractère officiel, leur double rédaction', *Échos d'Orient* 38 (1939) 321–33; Katsaros, Ιωάννης Κασταμονίτης (for the topic of the *responsa*, see especially 305–36).

101. See also Katsaros, Ιωάννης Κασταμονίτης 336ff.
102. Laurent, *Regestes* Nº 1315. Editions: PG 119.808–12; Rhalles-Potles 5.114–16.
103. Laurent, *Regestes* Nº 1427. Edition: Oudot 1.90–97 (with French translation).
104. Edition: A. Papadopoulos-Kerameus, VV 13 (1906) 334–51.
105. Editions: Bonefidius 3.145–59; Leunclavius, JGR 1.316–23 (= PG 119.947–60); Rhalles-Potles 5.427–36; Pitra, *Analecta* 617–20, 727–30; Gedeon, Νέα βιβλιοθήκη III 1–26. Bibliography: A. G. Jameson, *The Responsa and Letters of Demetrios Chomatianos, Archbishop of Achrida and Bulgaria: A Study in Byzantine Legal and Economic History of the Thirteenth Century* (Cambridge, MA 1957).
106. Editions: Bonefidius 3.159–84; Leunclavius, JGR 1.323–34 (= PG 119.960–85); Rhalles-Potles 5.403–20; Gedeon, EKA 36 (1916) 1.

to Chomatianos. The systematic research conducted by J. Darrouzès has proven that a certain number of the *responsa* attributed to John are authentic, while the rest are indeed from the hands of Chomatianos.[107] Recently the opinion has been advanced that possibly both of these authors used for their *responsa* to Kabasilas some already-existing nomokanonical work.[108]

During the last hundred years of the life of the empire, authors of *responsa* were the metropolitans Neilos Diasorenos of Rhodes, Symeon of Thessalonike, Prochoros of Stauroupolis, and Ioasaph of Ephesus.

Neilos, a native of Chios and supporter of Gregory Palamas, was elected metropolitan of Rhodes in 1357 during the patriarchate of Kallistos I. He held that throne for approximately two decades before being defrocked during the patriarchate of Makarios (1376–79). Responding to questions from a certain monk Jonah, he issued 21 *responsa* on issues of law concerning the divine liturgy.[109]

Symeon, known for his extensive theological work, ascended to the throne of Thessalonike after the second decade of the fifteenth century. He died in 1429. Eighty-three of his *responsa* to questions from Bishop Gabriel of Pentapolis survive.[110] At the turn of the fourteenth to the fifteenth centuries lived also Metropolitan Prochoros of Stauroupolis, who also bore the title of administrator (*proedros*) of Crete. He authored a response to a certain priest-monk on issues of marriage law.[111]

Ioasaph, who as a layman seems to have developed a career as diplomat, was later ordained and in 1431 is witnessed as being the *megas protosynkellos,* or chancellor. In the beginning of 1437 he occupied the metropolitan throne of Ephesus, but he died a few months later before he was able to participate in the Council of Florence as representative of the patriarch of Antioch. While he was still *protosynkellos*, he drew up 58 *responsa* to questions from a priest named George Drazinos, which dealt with liturgico-canonical issues.[112]

---

107. J. Darrouzès, 'Les réponses canoniques de Jean de Kitros', REB 31 (1973) 319–34. See also A. Schminck, LMA 5 (1991) 584 and (especially for the *responsa*) D. Simon, 'Fragen an Johannes von Kitros', Αφιέρωμα στον Ν. Σβορώνο 1 (Rethymnon 1986) 258–279.

108. V. Katsaros, 'Ανέκδοτο «σημείωμα διαζυγίου» (...) και το πρόβλημα του συντάκτη επισκόπου Κίτρους Ιωάννου', Μνήμη Λίνου Πολίτη 21.12.1982 (Thessaloniki 1983) 53–63 (62).

109. Edition: Almazov, Неизданные канонические 50–84.

110. Edition: Dositheos, Patr. of Jerusalem, Jassy 1683 (= PG 155.829–952). Bibliography: M. Jugie, DThC 14.2 (1941) 2976–84.

111. Edition: Gedeon, ΕΚΑ 36 (1916) 18–19.

112. Editions: A. Almazov, Канонические ответы Иоасафа митрополита Ефесского (Canonical Responses of Joasaph, Metropolitan of Ephesus) (Записки императорского новороссийского университета; Odessa 1903) 153–214; V. Beneševič, VV 11 (1904) 86–88 and 12 (1906) 525; A. Korakidis, Ιωάσαφ Εφέσου (Athens 1992) 213–248.

Canonical Treatises

Most of the people mentioned in the previous section as authors of *responsa* also composed treatises (usually small ones) concerning issues in canon law. When a response concerning a specific topic is attributed to a certain author, it is not always easy to differentiate it from a treatise. The criterion used for the classification of texts as *responsa* and not as treatises is whether they were in direct answer to a previously asked question.

A certain text, entitled 'Concerning the fasts' and written in verse for the purpose of easy memorization, comes from the hands of Patriarch Nicholas III Grammatikos (1084–1111). The certainty of its authorship has been established by its latest editor, Koder. This poem, which cannot be considered to be a typikon despite the fact that such a title appears in many manuscripts, is directed to the *protos* of Mt. Athos, who is referred to by different names in the manuscript tradition. It is most probable that this *protos* was John Tarchaneiotes. The time of composition of this poetic work is possibly the year 1107–1108.[113] A second work, titled 'Concerning fasting,' was also attributed to the same patriarch by its editor, Pitra. According to most of the manuscripts in which it survives, however, it was probably the work of Patriarch John III of Antioch.[114]

A certain metropolitan of Ankyra, Niketas, was the author of five treatises about the right of the patriarch to ordain bishops, the annual synods, the election of bishops, the right of bishops to resign, and marriages with impediments. (His authorship of this last one is accepted with many reservations.) Metropolitans of Ankyra bearing this name appear in the patriarchal archives for the year 1038 and for the period of 1082–1084. The great span of time between these two dates, however, excludes almost every possibility that we are dealing here with the same person.[115]

Another study connected in some way with the name of the aforementioned metropolitan of Ankyra (since he knew of its existence, although he himself had not composed it) has been transmitted anonymously. It concerns the election of metropolitans, archbishops, and bishops and their general legal status. Judging from its content, this treatise must have been written at the beginning of the eleventh century or rather at the end of the tenth.[116] Yet another Metropolitan Niketas of Amasea, whose small

---

113. Grumel-Darrouzès, *Regestes* N° 982 [975]. Edition: J. Koder, 'Das Fastengedicht des Patriarchen Nikolaos III, Grammatikos', JÖB 11 (1970) 203–41 (208–35, with German translation).

114. Pitra, *Spicilegium* 481–87. Bibliography: Beck, *Kirche* 660.

115. Edition: Darrouzès, *Documents* 176–265 (268–75, with French translation). Bibliography: Darrouzès, *Documents* 37–53; A. Kazhdan, VV 30 (1966) 281–84; A. Kazhdan, ODB 3.1481; B. Plank, LMA 6.1160.

116. Edition: Darrouzès, *Documents* 116–59 (with French translation); see also 21–29.

treatise concerning the election of metropolitans and the vote of the patriarch survives,[117] must also be placed at about the same time.

A treatise entitled 'Concerning the transfer of bishops' must have been formed gradually, taking its final form during the second decade of the twelfth century. It appears, however, in many variations in the manuscript tradition.[118]

Michael Choumnos was recorded in 1121 to be the *chartophylax* of the Great Church. Soon after (1122), he became metropolitan of Thessalonike, and he died in 1133. He dealt mainly with the law of marriage, especially with the degrees of relationship[119] and the marriage of those related through the sixth degree, which he considered admissible.[120] He also wrote another small work about the fast of Wednesdays and Fridays.[121]

Both of the important canon lawyers of the twelfth century, Zonaras and Balsamon, wrote small as well as large treatises. We have two small works from Zonaras: 'Concerning that two second-cousins should not be married'[122] and 'Homily to those who believe that natural human excretion is unclean.'[123] Balsamon was even more productive in the area of monographs. Eight treatises by him survive that deal with issues of ecclesiastical law, such as 'Concerning novices (*rasophoroi*)', 'That one should not be reading books on mathematics', 'Concerning the offering of incense', 'A study concerning the two offices of *chartophylax* and *protekdikos*', and 'A study concerning the patriarchal privileges'.[124]

The Codex Sinaiticus 1117 (482) fol. 241r–248v contains an anonymous work, only a part of which has been edited, dealing with issues of canon law regarding the judicial process of appeal against the decisions of the patriarch.[125] This is the same manuscript in which the anonymous rework-

---

117. Edition: Darrouzès, *Documents* 160–75 (with French translation); see also 30–36.

118. Edition: J. Darrouzès, 'Le traité des transferts', REB 42 (1984) 147–214 (171–89, with French translation).

119. Editions: Leunclavius, JGR 1.519–520 (= PG 119.1297–1300); Rhalles-Potles 5.397–98. These editions are only partial; the complete text of the work still remains unpublished.

120. Edition: S. Lampros, 'Σταχυολογία εκ κωδίκων του βαταβικού Λουγδούνου', Νέος Ελληνομνήμων 12 (1915) 385–420 (393–395). There is also an unedited σκέψις, which contains a decision of Eustathios Romaios. See A. Schminck, 'Vier eherechtliche Abhandlungen aus dem 11. Jahrhundert', FM 3 (1979) 221–79 (234).

121. Edition: Beneševič, 'Monumenta Vaticana' 184–85. It is possible that this is the same as a small treatise concerning the fasts which survives in Berlin, Staatsbibliothek, Phil. 1477 and is still unedited.

122. Edition: Cotelerius 2.483–92; Rhalles-Potles 4.592–97.

123. Editions: Bonefidius 2.216–37; Leunclavius, JGR 1.351–61 (= PG 119.1011–32); Rhalles-Potles 4.598–611.

124. Editions: Leunclavius, JGR 1.442–78; Cotelerius 2.492–514, 3.473–94; PG 119.1162–1224, 138.1013–76, and 138.1335–82; Rhalles-Potles 4.497–579.

125. Edition: Darrouzès, *Documents* 332–39 (with French translation); see also 75–85. See also Darrouzès, 'Fragments d'un commentaire canonique anonyme (fin XIIe – début XIIIe siècle)', REB 24 (1966) 25–39.

ing of the hermeneutical work of Balsamon also survives, the identification of whose writer presents many difficulties. The particular work mentioned above, however, is believed (with reasonable certainty) to be from the hands of Metropolitan John Kastamonites of Chalcedon.[126]

Several small treatises of canonical content are believed to be the work of the Archbishop Demetrios Chomatianos of Ohrid. They all deal with issues of marriage law: 'Concerning the degrees of marriages with impediment and without', 'Concerning the degrees of relationship from marriage and from blood', 'Concerning illegal (αθεμίτων) and forbidden (κεκωλυμένων) marriages', 'Concerning degrees of relationship', and so forth.[127] Studies regarding other issues—such as the use of unleavened bread, fasting, and the marriage of the clergy—have also been attributed to Chomatianos.[128] In reality, however, these belong to Archbishop Leo of Ohrid and to the monk Niketas Stethatos, two outstanding personalities of the eleventh century.[129]

During the last centuries of the later Byzantine period, legal studies in the form of monographs became rarer. An important work of this type, however, coming from around the end of the thirteenth century and bearing the title 'Concerning marriages' was written by John Pediasimos, who was a deacon and *chartophylax* of the archdiocese of Ohrid and *hypatos ton philosophon* ('the chief of the philosophers') (last quarter of the thirteenth and first decades of the fourteenth century). This work, containing the impediments to marriage, survives in two versions, which differ with regard to length. The shorter was most probably a later epitome of the original edition. The treatise by Pediasimos was used by the editors of collections of the fourteenth century, specifically by Matthew Blastares and Constantine Harmenopoulos, as well as by the author of *Prochiron Auctum*. The wide circulation of this treatise is also indicated by its rich manuscript tradition.[130]

In addition to the works mentioned so far, there are also other unedited works, even some as yet unknown, whose main subject is the degrees of relationship and their effect on whether a marriage is permissible or not.[131]

Besides the collections mentioned above, Constantine Harmenopoulos

---

126. See Katsaros, Ιωάννης Κασταμονίτης 300–303.

127. Editions: Bonefidius 2.135–45; Leunclavius, JGR1.311–16, 411–14 (= PG 119.937–45 and 1125–29); Rhalles-Potles 5.421–27, 437–40; Pitra, *Analecta* 1–12, 33–38, 49–52, 719–28.

128. Edition: Pitra, *Analecta* 745–84.

129. See also Beck, *Kirche* 534–36, 709.

130. Edition: A. Schminck, 'Der Traktat Περὶ γάμων des Johannes Pediasimos', FM 1 (1976) 126–74.

131. Such a small study, 'περὶ βαθμῶν συγγενείας' by an unknown author, survives in Venice, Biblioteca nazionale Marciana grec. 174, fol. 305r–306v. It is still unedited.

also wrote other works. Those relating to canon law are 'Concerning heresies' and 'Concerning the orthodox faith.'[132] A small work with the title 'Concerning the fasts' is also attributed to him.[133]

A work by Metropolitan Neilos of Rhodes (see the previous section) survives bearing the title 'A synoptic account of the holy and ecumenical councils'.[134] It is noteworthy that the author considered the synod of Hagia Sophia of 879–880 as the eighth ecumenical council and another synod, which also convened in Hagia Sophia in 1341 on the occasion of the hesychastic disputes (Gregory Palamas and Barlaam), as the ninth ecumenical council.

Monastic Typika

Bibliography: C. Galatariotou, 'Byzantine Ktetorika Typika: A Comparative Study', REB 45 (1987) 77–138; E. Herman, 'Ricerche sulle istituzioni monastiche bizantine. Typika ktetorika, caristicari e monasteri "liberi"', OCP 6 (1940) 293–375; I. Konidaris, Νομική θεώρηση των μοναστηριακών τυπικών (A legal examination of the monastic typica) (Athens 1984); K. Manaphis, Μοναστηριακά τυπικά-Διαθήκαι (Monastic typika-wills; Athens 1970); P. de Meester, 'De monachico statu iuxta disciplinam byzantinam' (Codificazione canonica orientale, Fonti, Series 2, fasc. 10; Vatican City 1942); P. de Meester, 'Les typiques de fondation (Τυπικά κτητορικά)', Atti del V Congresso Internazionale di Studi Bizantini II (Studi bizantini e neoellenici 6; 1940) 487–506; A. M. Talbot, 'Typikon, monastic', ODB 3.2132; A. A. Thiermeyer, 'Das Typikon—Ktetorikon und sein literarhistorischer Kontext', OCP 58 (1992) 475–513.

Every type of record—ecclesiastical or civil, official or private, whatever its origin—constitutes a significant source of church law. Among these records, a special position has been held by the monastic typika. Many opinions have been expressed as to how to categorize these typika. A basic distinction used is whether they were liturgical (i.e., concerning worship life in the monastery) or were of canonical content (i.e., establishing rules with respect to the organization of the monastery and the life of the brotherhood in it).

Another distinction made refers to the author of the typikon; i.e., whether the typikon originated from an ecclesiastical or civil authority or some other person of generally recognized repute, or whether it was composed by the founder or renovator of a particular monastery. In this last case we speak of 'founding typika' (τυπικά κτητορικά). These could come into existence either through an act during the life of the author or through a will

---

132. Editions: J. Leunclavius (Löwenklau), Legatio imp. Caesaris Manuelis Comneni aug. ad Armenios (Basel 1578) 557–83 (= Leunclavius, JGR 1.547–54 [= PG 150.20–32]); Rhalles-Potles 5.446–54.

133. Edition: K. Pitsakis, 'Κωνσταντίνου Αρμενοπούλου: Ανέκδοτη "πραγματεία" περί νηστειών ('Unedited treatise concerning the fasts') EKEID 18 (1971 [ca. 1973]) 223–28.

134. Edition: Voel-Justel 2.1155–1160; Rhalles-Potles 1.389–95.

after his death. In these, provision usually was also made for the financial well-being of the monastery by supplying the material necessities for its operation. These two major distinctions usually intersect.

The liturgical typika have very limited importance as a source of law. Therefore, in the following paragraphs the focus is placed on the typika with canonical content, regardless of whether or not they were 'founding typika'.

In spite of the fact that the laws governing monasteries and monks—both in the holy canons as well as in the imperial legislation (most especially here)—were obligatory (*ius cogens*), deviations not infrequently were introduced through the typika, which reveal a gap between the official laws and the ones enforced in practice.

In the typika, especially the 'founding' ones, the author often dealt with the legal status of the monastery and its future after his death. In this context, the typika shaped the institution of 'self-rule and self-government' of the monastery, with the purpose of protecting it from intervention on the part of the various officials of the civil or ecclesiastical authorities. To the latter category belonged the local bishop as well, whose recognized rights differed widely in extent in the various typika. These typika always show a clear tendency to try to make things as painless as possible for the monastery. At the same time, the position of the *epitropos* or *ephoros* (overseer) was fashioned. This was usually either a person closely related to the circle of the founder and author of the typikon or a distinguished official (at times, the emperor himself), whose function was to oversee the operation of the monastery according to the typikon and the observance of its right to self-government. The office of the *epitropos*, whose responsibilities differ in the various typika, was not in the beginning a paid one. Some typika, nevertheless, provided for an income for this official from the monastery's properties, something that led at times to excesses, in spite of all of the measures taken by the authors of the typika to prevent abuse.

The abbot, or *hegoumenos*, was the absolute ruler in the monastery, and to his office the typika dedicated many provisions, especially concerning his selection (for which there were various methods—from assignment by the founder or the last abbot to election by the brotherhood) and concerning the causes that could lead to his deposition from office, including also the required procedure. Deposition was provided for very serious offenses from which the abbot would not refrain even after repeated censure by the notables of the monastery (e.g., violation of the typikon or embezzlement or other abuses at the expense of monastic property, the inalienability of which was very rigorously enjoined).

Within the framework of the organizational structure of the monastery, the typika usually contain provisions for other administrative agencies as well: first, with regard to the office of steward, or *oikonomos* (the administrator of the property of the monastery), and second, with regard to the hierarchy under the abbot. However, both the selection and the appointment of the *oikonomos* and other officials of the monastery as well as the supervision and censure of their actions—including their removal from office if they were found deficient in the execution of their duties—were the prerogative and responsibility of the abbot.

Very few provisions in the typika dealt with the personal prerequisites for entrance into the monastery (age, family status, etc.), perhaps because these issues were regulated in sufficient detail by the canons and civil legislation and the authors of the typika had no interest in modifying these regulations. On the other hand, we often encounter provisions dealing with the financial prerequisites for entrance into the monastery, which are rather uniform in the various typika. It was forbidden to require a compulsory contribution by new monks (something that to all intents and purposes prevailed in practice), but it was not forbidden for new monks to offer material properties on a free-will basis. In practice, of course, this exception could easily be transformed into a rule.

In the typika, a division of the monks into categories is also evident. The distinction between monks of the 'great habit' (*megaloschemoi*) and those of the 'little habit' (*microschemoi*) appeared in the ninth century, and it was treated with disapproval in some typika. This, however, was of no legal significance, because the obligations of the monastic life were brought about through the tonsure and were uniform for all. It seems, however, that there was real distinction between 'church' monks, mainly those having spiritual and liturgical responsibilities, and the 'servants' (*diakonetai*), whose duties were to attend to the physical needs of the brotherhood.

The basic requirement of the monastic tonsure was observance of the three monastic vows of poverty, obedience, and chastity. Many provisions of the typika were devoted to putting these vows into practice and ensuring their observance. We thus find many provisions regarding 'inaccessibility,' i.e., the prohibition of the presence of persons of the opposite sex in the monasteries—as well as of female animals in the male monasteries. The prohibition of going outside the monastery was very strongly emphasized, with exceptions foreseen only in limited situations—usually for the execution of an assignment outside the monastery and always with the prior permission of the abbot. There were also similar prohibitions regarding the establishment of factitious relationships (adoptive brotherhood [ἀδελφοποία] or godparenthood [συντεκνία]) in order to prevent the association of monks with lay people.

With respect to the life of the monks, the typika required the cenobitic system (the idiorrythmic system appeared during the last centuries of Byzantium), and an effort was made to limit every form of deviation. However, while some typika absolutely prohibited deviations, others regulated them with such detail that the rule was nearly overturned.

The lifelong residence (*stabilitas loci*) of the monks in the monastery was of special interest to the authors of the typika, who attempted to ensure this even through economic measures, i.e., through the provision that all material belongings that the monk brought with him to the monastery upon entering monastic life would remain with the monastery if he were ever to leave in order to enroll in another monastery. Notwithstanding the existence of detailed provisions in civil legislation, the typika ceaselessly reiterate the monks' obligation of poverty. Some do so with unbending strictness, while others allow for exceptions—all this revealing that the obligation of poverty was sometimes violated.

Particular Monastic Typika

Editions: The editions are listed in detail by Konidaris, Νομική 45–67 and Galatariotou, 'Typika' 137–38.

Sixty typika survive from the entire Byzantine period. Twelve of these fall within the period covered by the previous chapter. It seemed preferable, however, that they all be presented together here, since most of them belong anyway to the period discussed in this chapter, so that the material would not be broken up.

The earliest information we find about a text of this type concerns the typikon that was composed in the sixth century by St. Sabas, the founder of the lavra in Palestine bearing his name. It is possible that other earlier typika existed, but about these we have no information. The typikon of St. Sabas in its original form does not survive, but we have a later reworking of it from the eleventh century.[135]

Something similar also happened to the typikon of the famous monastery of Stoudios in Constantinople. It was composed by its abbot, the well-known opponent of iconoclasm Theodore the Studite (759–826), but it survives only in a later formulation. However, the will of Theodore, through which he completed the typikon, survives intact.[136] These two

---

135. Edition: E. Kurtz, BZ 3 (1894) 168–70.
136. Editions: (1) of the typikon: A. A. Dmitrievskij. Описание литургических рукописей,

texts became the prototype for many subsequent monastic typika. From the middle of the tenth century comes the typikon of St. Paul, which has to do with an equally famous monastery on Mount Latros (later Latmos), located close to Miletos.[137]

From 970 to 1045, a series of typika were composed for Mount Athos, some of which came from the founder of the Great Lavra, Athanasios the Athonite.[138] Others, however, bear the form of imperial acts and concern all the monasteries of the Holy Mountain.[139]

The one hundred years from the middle of the eleventh century to the middle of the twelfth were characterized by a wave of new monasteries, both in the capital as well as in the countryside. The founding of these monasteries was accompanied in most cases by the composition of a corresponding typikon. From the area of Constantinople survive the typika of the monastery of the Theotokos Euergetis (the Benefactress), a prototype for many subsequent typika (1065);[140] the monastery of Christ Panoiktirmon (the All-merciful), founded by the patrician and proconsul (ἀνθύπατος), Michael Attaleiates, a member of the high court (1077);[141] the monastery of the Theotokos Kecharitomene (Full of Grace), which was renovated by the Empress Irene, wife of Alexios I (ca. 1118);[142] the monastery of the Pantokrator (the Almighty), which was established by Emperor John II Comnenos (1136);[143] and the monastery of St. Mamas, which was renovated by the brothers George and Theocharistos Kappadokes and whose typikon was put together by Abbot Athanasios Philanthropenos (1158) at their request.[144]

Some very well known typika from monasteries of the countryside are those of the Great *Domestikos* of the West, Gregory Pakourianos, for the monastery of the Theotokos at Petritzos, near the present city of Backovo

---

хранящихся в библиотеках Православного Востока. (Description of liturgical manuscripts in the libraries of the Orthodox East) Vol. 1–3. Kiev. 1895–1917. (2) of the will: PG 99.1813–24.

137. Edition: S. Lampros, ʽΔιαθήκη Παύλου τοῦ Λατρινοῦ' ('The will of Paul Latrinos'), Ν. Ἑλληνομνήμων 12 (1915) 198–203.

138. Edition: P. Meyer, *Die Haupturkunden für die Geschichte der Athosklöster* (Leipzig 1894; reprint Amsterdam 1965) 102–40.

139. Edition: D. Papachryssanthou, *Actes du Protaton* (Paris 1975) 209–15, 224–32.

140. Edition: P. Gautier, 'Le typikon de la Théotokos Évergetis', REB 40 (1982) 5–101 (14–95, with French translation).

141. Edition: P. Gautier, 'La Diataxis de Michel Attaliate', REB 39 (1981) 5–143 (16–130, with French translation).

142. Edition: P. Gautier, 'Le typikon de la Théotokos Kécharitôménè', REB 43 (1985) 5–165 (19–155, with French translation).

143. Edition: P. Gautier, 'Le typikon du Christ Sauveur Pantocrator', REB 32 (1974) 1–145 (26–131, with French translation).

144. Edition: S. Eustratiadis, ʽΤυπικόν τῆς ἐν Κωνσταντινουπόλει μονῆς τοῦ ἁγίου μεγαλομάρτυρος Μάμαντος' ('Typikon of the Monastery of the Holy and Great Martyr Mamas in Constantinople'), Ἑλληνικά 1 (1928) 245–314 (256–311).

in Bulgaria (1083);[145] of the monastery of Theotokos Eleousa (the Merciful) in Strumica, built by the monk and later bishop of the area, Manuel (between 1085 and 1106);[146] of the monastery of St. John the Theologian, founded by St. Christodoulos on the island of Patmos (*hypotyposis* and will with a codicil in 1091 and 1093);[147] of the monasteries established on the island of Crete by the monk John, nicknamed 'the foreigner';[148] of the monastery of the Theotokos of Roidiou (Pomegranate) of Nikon of the Black Mountain;[149] of the monastery of St. John Prodromos (the Forerunner), surnamed the Fearful, at Monacheion on the Black Sea, which was renovated by a certain monk John, who also wrote the typikon shortly after 1112, having as a prototype the typikon of the Euergetis;[150] of the monastery of Christ the Savior in Messina, composed by the abbot Loukas shortly after 1130;[151] of the monastery of the Theotokos of Areia in Nauplia, composed by the local bishop, Leontios, founder of the monastery; of the monastery of Kosmosoteira (Savior of the World), established in 1152 near Aenos in Thrace by the pious Emperor Isaac Comnenos, brother of John II;[152] of the monastery of St. Nicholas in Casale near Otranto, the typikon of which was composed in 1160 by Abbot Nicholas;[153] and the monastery of the Theotokos Heliou Bomon (Altars of the Sun) or Elegmoi in Bithynia, whose typikon was written on the basis of that of the Euergetis by a certain Nicholas Mystikos (1162).[154] It is possible that the typikon of the monastery of St. John in modern Pantelleria belongs to the same period as well.[155]

The opening of new monasteries and renovation of old ones occurred also from the end of the twelfth to the fifteenth century. The most significant of the typika of this period were those of St. Sava, archbishop of Ser-

---

145. Edition: P. Gautier, 'Le typikon du sébaste Grégoire Pakourianos', REB 42 (1984) 5–145 (18–133, with French translation).

146. Edition: L. Petit, 'Le monastère de Notre Dame de Pitié en Macédoine', *Izvestija Russk. Arkeol. Inst. v Konstantinopole* 6 (1900) 1–153 (69–93).

147. Edition: M-M, Acta 6.59–90.

148. Edition: N. Tomadakis, 'Ὁ ἅγιος Ἰωάννης Ξένος και η διαθήκη αυτού' ('St. John the Foreigner and his will'), Κρητικά Χρονικά 2 (1948) 47–72 (57–61).

149. Edition: V. Beneševič, 'Тактикон Никона Черногорца' (The Taktikon of Nikon of the Black Mountain), Записки Инст.-Филол. Факультета Петроградского Университета 139 (1917) 1–120 (22–80).

150. Edition: A. Papadopoulos-Kerameus, *Noctes Petropolitanae* (St. Petersburg 1913; reprint Leipzig 1976) 1–87.

151. Edition: J. Cozza-Luzi, *De typico sacro messanensis monasterii archimandritalis* (Nova Patrum Bibliotheca 10.2; Rome 1905) 117–37 (121–30).

152. Edition: L. Petit, 'Typikon du monastère de la Kosmosotira près d'Aenos (1152)', *Izvestija* 13 (1908) 17–77 (19–75).

153. Edition: J. Cozza-Luzi, *De excerptis liturgicis e Typico monasterii Casulani* (Nova Patrum Bibliotheca 10.2; Rome 1905) 149–66 (155–66).

154. Edition: Dmitrievskij, Описание литургических рукописей 715–769.

155. Edition: I. Dujčev, 'Il tipico del monastero di S. Giovanni nell' isola di Pantelleria', *Bolletino della Badia Graeca di Grottaferrata* N.S. 25 (1971) 3–17.

bia and son of Kral Stephan Nemanja, for the cell he established in Karyes on the Holy Mountain around 1197;[156] of Bishop Neilos of Tamasia, founder of the monastery of the Theotokos of Machairas in Cyprus (1210);[157] of the monk and recluse Neophytos, for the monastery named 'the new Zion' in Paphos of Cyprus (the final form of his 'typikon-will' [τυπικόν διαθήκη] comes from 1214);[158] of the monk Maximos, founder of the monastery of the Theotokos Skoteine (1247);[159] and of Nikephoros Blemmydes for the monastery he established in the area of Ephesus (1248).[160]

There is a series of important typika connected with Emperor Michael VIII Palaeologos (1259–82) and his family circle. Around the end of his reign, he composed a typikon for the monastery of the Archangel Michael, also called the monastery of Auxentios, which his father had founded.[161] Another typikon of Michael, dated in 1282, contains many autobiographical elements and was written for the monasteries of St. Demetrios in Constantinople and of the Theotokos in Kellibara on Mount Latros.[162] From Empress Theodora, wife of Michael, have come the typika of the monastery of Lips in Constantinople, which was probably established in the tenth century and renovated by her;[163] and of the monastery of the Holy Unmercenaries Cosmas and Damian, also located in the capital.[164] Michael's niece, Theodora (Theodoule as a nun), wife of the great court official John Synadenos, was the author of the typikon of the monastery of the Theotokos Bebaias Elpidos (Sure Hope), which she established in Constantinople. This typikon was completed after her death by her daughter, Euphrosyne Palaeologina.[165]

To the family of the Palaeologoi also belonged Irene Choumnaena (Eulogia as a nun), wife of the Despot John Palaeologos, son of Andronikos II, who renovated the monastery of Christ the Savior Philanthropos in 1312 and composed its typikon.[166]

156. Edition: V. Ćorović, 'Списи Св. Саве' (Writings of St. Sava), Српска Краљевска Академија, Зборник за Историју 18.1 (1928) 5–13.
157. Edition: I. Tsiknopoulos, Κυπριακά τυπικά (Cypriot typika) (Nikosia 1969) 1–68.
158. Edition: Tsiknopoulos, Κυπριακά τυπικά 71–104.
159. Edition: M. Gedeon, 'Διαθήκη Μαξίμου μοναχού, κτήτορος της εν Λυδία μονής Κοτινής (1247)' ('The will of Maximos the monk, founder of the monastery of Skoteine in Lydia (1247)'), Μικρασιατικά Χρονικά 2 (1939) 263–91 (271–90).
160. Edition: M. A. Heisenberg, *Nicephori Blemmydae curriculum vitae et carmina* (Leipzig 1896) 93–99; J. Munitz, 'A Missing Chapter from the Typikon of Nikephoros Blemmydes', REB 44 (1986) 199–207 (204ff., with English translation).
161. Edition: Dmitrievskij, Описание литургических рукописей 769–794.
162. Edition: H. Grégoire, 'Imperatoris Michaelis Palaiologi de vita sua', Byzantion 29–30 (1959–60) 447–74 (with French translation).
163. Edition: H. Delehaye, *Deux typica byzantines de l'époque des Paléologues* (Brussels 1921) 106–36.
164. Edition: Delehaye, *Deux typica byzantines* 136–40.
165. Edition: Delehaye, *Deux typica byzantines* 18–105.
166. Edition: P. Meyer, 'Bruchstücke zweier τυπικά κτητορικά', BZ 4 (1895) 48–49.

From the same period we also have certain typika of monasteries of the Holy Mountain and Meteora. Finally, we must mention the typika of Constantine Akropolites for the monastery of the Anastasis (Resurrection) in Constantinople;[167] of Metropolitan Ioakeim of Zichnai for the monastery of the Prodromos (Forerunner) on Mount Menoikeion near Serres (1324–1332);[168] of Makarios Choumnos for the 'New Monastery' in Thessalonike (between 1360–1370);[169] of the monk Neilos Damilas for the monastery of the Theotokos in Baionaia on Crete (1400);[170] and of Patriarch Matthew I for the Charsianeites monastery in Constantinople (1407).[171]

167. Edition: H. Delehaye, 'Constantini Acropolitae, hagiographi byzantini, Epistularum manipulus', *Analecta Bollandiana* 51 (1933) 263–84 (279–84).
168. Edition: A. Guillou, *Les archives de Saint-Jean-Prodrome sur le mont Ménécée* (Paris 1955) 163–76.
169. Edition: V. Laurent, 'Écrits spirituels inédits de Macaire Choumnos (...)', Ελληνικά 14 (1955) 40–86 (60–71, 76–85).
170. Edition: S. Pétridès, 'Le typicon de Nil Damilas pour le monastère de femmes de Baconia en Crète (1400)', *Isvestija* 15 (1911) 92–111 (95–109).
171. Edition: I. Konidaris–K. Manaphis, 'Ἐπιτελεύτιος Βούλησις (...) Ματθαίου', EEBS 45 (1981–82 [ca. 1984]) 462–515 (472–510).

5

Sources of Canon Law in the Eastern Churches

Hubert Kaufhold

The Common Heritage of Canon Law in the Eastern Churches

In the Christian East the ecclesiastical landscape was patterned after geographical units that followed the territorial lines of the Roman Empire, namely the boundaries of the patriarchates of Alexandria, Antioch, Constantinople, and Jerusalem. Christian communities also extended outside the boundaries of the empire into Persia, Armenia, Georgia, and Ethiopia. The Christian East and its communities were also defined by dogmatic considerations. The Christological conflicts of the fifth and sixth centuries created several churches that still exist and that coexisted historically within the same political territories. The first group of these churches included the adherents to the Council of Chalcedon (A.D. 451), called the Orthodox churches, among which are the Melkites and (from the seventh century on) the Georgians. The second large group consists of the Monophysites, now sometimes called Miaphysites, who did not agree with the decisions of Chalcedon. These churches included the Western Syrians (Jacobites), the Copts, the Ethiopians, and the Armenians, as well as the Georgians, who became a part of the Orthodox Church in the seventh century. The third group included the Nestorians, who settled in the Persian Empire and who went their own way from the fifth century onward. The last group consists of the Maronites, who originally adhered to a Monothelite doctrine but who have been united with the Latin Church since the Crusades.

Sources from the Period before the Division of the Churches

Most of these churches possessed and still possess a common tradition of canon law sources, particularly from the period before the schism. The canons of Greek synods, particularly the ecumenical councils of Nicaea (A.D. 325) and Constantinople (A.D. 381), as well as the local synods of Ancyra, Neocaesarea, Gangra, Antioch, and Laodiceia (all fourth century) were the primary and most important sources of law. Historians have assumed on good grounds that the earlier canons were collected in Greek at Antioch shortly before the Council of Constantinople and that the canons of Constantinople were added to them soon after.

This collection, the *Corpus canonum*, is not preserved in Greek but was soon translated into various Oriental languages. The various versions of this text will be treated below with the individual churches.

These translations of old conciliar canons did not constitute a 'reception'. The authority of the canons had already been recognized by all the churches. The members of these churches had sometimes participated in the councils and helped to approve them. The translations only made them more accessible.

Alongside the conciliar canons, legal texts circulated that were traced back to the apostles or their followers. Most prominent in this group was what was called the 'Apostolic canons'. In the Greek version they usually numbered 85, but their number varied in the Eastern churches. For the most part they derived from fourth-century synods. The fact that the 'Apostolic canons' appear in almost all collections indicates that they commonly circulated before the schism. Beyond these, canonical collections of Eastern churches have various pseudo-apostolic texts, often in widely varying versions.

The history of the tradition of these Greek sources must be further studied in detail in order to answer some important questions: do the Oriental translations rest directly on the Greek texts and do the collections of the various churches differ from one another in content despite their common origin?

This basic reservoir of canonical decisions was later enlarged within the individual churches in various ways. The Western and Eastern Syrian churches, as well as the Armenian Church, held their own synods, whose canons survived and were passed on in the canonical collections along with the earlier texts. In contrast to Syria and Armenia, decisions of that type do not exist for the Melkite, Maronite, Georgian, or Ethiopian churches.

Further Translations from Greek

Even after doctrinal differences had led to schism, there was still a certain permeability so far as the reception of Greek legal texts was concerned. That applied in the first instance to writings of Greek Fathers of the Church who were recognized by all. Most important of these were the fifteen canonical responses of Timotheos of Alexandria, the oldest portion of this group of writings. Works of Athanasius of Alexandria, Basil of Caesarea, Gregory of Nazianzus, and Gregory of Nyssa appear in later collections, though not in all the churches and not with the same frequency. Not all works of lesser-known authors have survived in Greek and, consequently, they have not yet been exploited for the history of Greek canon law.

Later Byzantine conciliar canons and works on canon law continue to be found among the Melkites and Georgians, communities still in communion with Constantinople.

Civil law was also part of the common heritage of some Eastern churches. Remarkably, some of this material does not survive in Greek. The reason that civil law was included in canonical collections was that, under Islamic rule, Eastern churches had jurisdiction over some secular matters in which their members were involved. The first example of such a collection is the *Syro-Roman Lawbook*, which was translated by Western Syrians from Greek into Syriac at an unknown time, but no later than the eighth century, and which reached the Eastern Syrians probably at the start of the ninth century. It was later translated from Syriac to Arabic and received by the Melkites and Copts in this linguistic garb. Toward the end of the twelfth century it was translated into Armenian, and in the eighteenth century from Armenian to Georgian. A second Roman law source not as widely distributed, the so-called *Sententiae Syriacae*, was known to the Western Syrians and the Armenians. In addition, we also find later works of civil law among the Melkites and Copts, specifically the *Procheiros Nomos* and the *Ekloge* as well as the ecclesiastical legislation of Byzantine emperors.

The Melkites and Copts also circulated a text with the title, 'Statutes from the Old Testament'. It consists of excerpts from the Pentateuch that do not appear to be translated from Greek. They are not to be identified with the Greek *Nomos Mosaikos*. The relationships among the collections of excerpts from the Old Testament surviving in various languages, whether in Latin (*Collatio legum Mosaicarum et Romanarum*), Greek, Arabic, Armenian, or Georgian, should be more closely investigated.

Receptions in the Arab Period

In the course of the Arabic conquest of the Near East, Greek and also the other native languages, particularly Syriac and Coptic, were gradually repressed. The result of this linguistic repression was that those churches living under Islamic rule translated their canonical texts into Arabic in the course of time. The possible exception to this development is the Western Syrian Church, where such Arabic translations appear only much later in the fourteenth century. Among the Western Syrians, Syriac is never completely replaced by Arabic as a literary language.

But Arabic did not replace Syriac completely or at once in the Eastern Syrian Church, either. The Eastern Syrian Bishop Elias al-Ǧauharī translated the synodal rulings of his church into Arabic as early as circa A.D. 900. In the first half of the eleventh century Ibn aṭ-Ṭaiyib produced an Arabic translation of the canons of earlier Greek synods as well as of the most important Nestorian canonical texts. However, the two most important systematic canonical collections of the Eastern Syrians were composed in Syriac circa 1300.

Such Arabic translations of canonical sources had great importance not only for a particular church, but also for Oriental Christians of other confessions. Once a text existed in Arabic, the barriers between the various churches were relatively permeable, and so no further translation was needed. This conclusion applies only to those churches that used Arabic alone or to a great extent, not to the Armenians, Georgians and Ethiopians.

Roughly after the year 1000, the mutual exchange of Arabic canonical texts appears to have become much more frequent. Or, to formulate it more carefully, similar Arabic texts were known in the Eastern churches. We do not know whether they were used. In particular, we find many canonical sources in the Coptic Church. We know from Coptic-Arabic collections of the twelfth through the fourteenth centuries that the Copts were not only relatively well informed about the canon law of the other churches, particularly the Melkites, but that they also preserved these texts in part or at least cited them. A Coptic author of the fourteenth century, for example, knew the Eastern Syrian collection of Ibn aṭ-Ṭaiyib, despite the deep dogmatic differences between the two churches. Conversely, the Eastern Syrian ʿAbdīšōʿ bar Brīkā at the start of the fourteenth century copied long passages from the Coptic *Nomokanon* of Ibn al-ʿAssāl in one of his two canonical works, the *Ordo iudiciorum*, though he did so surreptiously and without any citation of his source. The Maronites also made use of various Coptic legal sources.

As previously mentioned, this exchange of texts did not occur with the same frequency in those churches in which Arabic played no role, such as the Armenians. Yet they took over foreign canonical sources, too. The translation of the *Syro-Roman Lawbook* and of the *Sententiae Syriacae* at the end of the twelfth century has already been mentioned. In this case the exchange was serendipitous. A notation in one manuscript reported how the translation came about: at the time of the Armenian Katholikos Gregory, the Armenian Church did not possess copies of any civil law. Only ecclesiastical canons were to be found in the palace library. Then the text continued: 'Quite disturbed about this, the Patriarch made inquiries among the other nations [= confessions]. A learned Syrian priest by the name of Theodosios, who happened to be there, revealed to my lord that he had this "abbreviated civil code"'. This text, certainly the *Sententiae Syriacae*, was then translated.

Outside of the Eastern sources, in the thirteenth century the Armenian leader Smbat had the Old French *Assizes of Antioch* translated into Armenian. This happened because of the close ties of Armenian Cilicia to the West in the age of the crusaders. There is no a trace of the *Assizes* in the other churches.

It appears that the Georgian Church adopted only Greek legal sources. Besides these works only indigenous legal books survive. It was only at the beginning of the eighteenth century that King Vaḫtang VI added translations from Armenian and Greek to his extensive legal collection.

Shared Legal Perceptions

Until now the discussion has been about the reception of common canonical sources. It is a much more difficult to ask the extent to which there were shared legal perceptions, where there were borrowings and where there was parallel development. To answer these questions, there would first have to be reliable descriptions of the law of the individual churches. In most churches we are still far from that stage.

Conclusion

No clear response can be given to the question of the shared juristic heritage of Oriental Christians. The old Greek canons from the era of an undivided Christianity were considered authentic and were obviously unproblematic. Their translation into native languages was to be expected.

Naturally, dogmatic harmony played a great role in the evolution of common sources. This may be seen in the reception of Greek sources by their fellow Chalcedonian Georgians and Melkites. But the reception of canonical texts did not cease at the confessional frontier. There are many examples of this. On the other hand, the legal sources of a church were not received by another without further ado. For example, many Greek texts were never translated and thus not received.

One also has the impression that external factors played a role in the translation of such sources. We should consider that they always circulated in a very limited number of manuscripts. It was by no means the case that they were easily accessible to those of other confessions and were always available to be translated.

In addition, a translation demanded a considerable investment and a suitable translator. Texts received their greatest circulation if they were composed in a common language, such as Arabic in later times.

It also appears to have been decisive that a particular person was interested in a juridical text and its translation. It does not appear that churches formally adopted canonical texts of other confessions and declared them binding through synodal resolutions. As a rule, translations were private efforts. This poses the question of their validity and authority as law, which has not been a concern of this investigation.

Literature: [Various authors:] *Studi storici sulle fonti del diritto canonico orientale* (Fonti, fasc. 7; Vatican City 1932); J. Deslandes, 'Les sources canonique du droit oriental', *Échos d'Orient* 37 (1933) 476–87; 38 (1934) 443–64; J. Dauvillier, C. de Clercq, *Le mariage en droit canonique oriental* (Paris 1936); C. de Clercq, 'Introduction à l'histoire du droit canonique oriental', *Archive d'histoire du droit canonique* 3 (1947) 309–48; A. Coussa, *Epitome praelectionum de iure ecclesiastico orientali* (Grottaferrata 1948) vol. 1, 103–201 ('De fontibus cognoscendi iuris'); C. de Clercq, 'Oriental (Droit canonique)', DDC 7 (1957) 1172–76; idem, *Fontes iuridici ecclesiarum orientalium. Studium historicum* (Rome 1967); Saïd Elias Saïd, *Les églises orientales et leurs droits, hier, aujourd'hui . . . demain* (Paris 1989) 83-137 ('Sources particulières du Droit Canonique Oriental', 83–98: 'Sources communes et byzantines', 99–137: 'Des sources des Orientaux Catholiques').

Melkites

History of the Church

Melkites (also Melchites) are Christians of the patriarchates of Antioch, Jerusalem, and Alexandria. The Christological conflicts of the fourth and fifth centuries had the result that the churches of Antioch and Alexandria split in two. The final schism arose from two rival hierarchies, each with a patriarch at its head, one imperial and in communion with the Byzantine emperor in Constantinople, and one Monophysite: in Egypt from the middle of the fifth century and in Antioch from the middle of the sixth century. The object of this section is the canon law of the Melkite Church (from the Syriac 'malkā', 'king' or 'emperor'). The law of the Antiochene Monophysite (Jacobite) Church is the subject of the next section, and the section on the Copts will deal with the Alexandrian Monophysites. The patriarchate of Jerusalem remained loyal to the imperial church.

The conquest of Palestine, Syria, and Egypt by Islamic armies marks a sharp break in the history of the Melkite Church. The Melkites no longer lived as adherents of the state church under the Byzantine Emperor but rather under non-Christian rule. Consequently, under Arabic rule, patriarchs could be installed on a regular basis only from the middle of the eighth century.

After Antioch returned to Byzantine rule in the tenth century, it fell under the strong influence of Constantinople. Many of the patriarchs came from the capital.

Another epoch-making event was the crusades as well as the establishment of the Latin states in the Middle East during the twelfth and thirteenth centuries. During this period the patriarchs of Antioch and Jerusalem still resided at these places,[1] but in part they also resided in Constantinople, and many never visited their sees.

The efforts of Rome to unite the Christian churches lie beyond the limits of this study, but they led eventually in the eighteenth century to a uniate Melkite Church, with a distinct hierarchy of its own. Today scholars apply the term 'Melkites' only to uniate Christians. Non-uniate Christians are referred to as 'rūm-orthodox' (= ῥωμαίος 'Byzantine') in Arabic.

The larger part of the Melkite population was certainly not Greek at all, but Aramaic (Antioch and Jerusalem) or Egyptian (Alexandria). Besides the Greek language, Syriac, a branch of Aramaic, was used in the patriarchate of Antioch. In the Patriarchate of Jerusalem, the Christian Palestinian language (also Aramaic) was used as the vernacular and in Alexandria the Coptic language. Syriac, later Coptic, and to a much lesser degree Christian Palestinian, continued to be used as the language of the liturgy, literature, and theology in these regions.

Literature: C. Charon (Karalevskij), *Histoire des Patriarcats Melkites (Alexandrie, Antiochie, Jérusalem)*, 2: *La periode moderne (1833–1902)* (Rome-Paris-Leipzig 1910); 3: *Les institutions: Liturgie, hiérarchie, statistique, organisation, listes épiscopales (Rome* 1911), English translation by J. Collorafi (Fairfax, Virginia 1999-2001); Graf, *Geschichte* 1.59–65; 3.23–41; S. Descy, *Introduction à l'histoire et l'ecclésiologie de l'église Melkite* (Beirut-Jounieh 1986); J. Chammas, *Die Melkitische Kirche* (Cologne 1990); I. Dick, *Les Melkites: Grecs-orthodoxes et Grecs-catholiques des Patriarchats d'Antioche, d'Alexandrie et de Jérusalem* (Turnhout 1994); G. Troupeau, 'Les Églises melkites', *Histoire du Christianisme des origines à nos jours* (Paris 1993) 4.383–407 (German edition: 399–422); J. Richard, 'L'Èglise melkite',

---

1. See J. Pahlitzsch, *Graeci und Suriani im Palästina der Kreuzfahrerzeit* (Berliner Historische Studien, 33; Berlin 2001) 101–34.

Histoire du Christianisme des origines à nos jours: Un temps d'épreuves (Paris 1990) 6.221–5 (*Die Geschichte des Christentums: Religion-Politik-Kultur: Die Zeit der Zerreissproben (1274–1449)* (Freiburg im Breigau-Basel-Wien 1991) 6.217–22).

Melkite Literature

The fact that the Melkite churches continued in communion with the patriarchate of Constantinople and the Byzantine emperor certainly had the result that Greek continued to play a larger role than was the case in the other churches. Further, the proportion of the faithful who were of Greek origin was higher in these churches. Despite that, the Syriac and Christian-Palestinian languages were not without literary significance. On the contrary, they continued to serve for many centuries as a language of liturgy,[2] as many manuscripts of liturgical books through the seventeenth century demonstrate.[3] Canon law literature in the Christian-Palestinian language, however, is not known.

Following the Muslim conquest, the use of Arabic spread among the Melkites as well. From the eighth century onward, it gradually became a literary language as well. In the course of time there arose a considerable amount of writing in Christian-Arabic. Alongside many translations, particularly from Greek, Syriac, and Coptic, many original works, particularly theological literature and history, exist today in Christian-Arabic.

Literature: Baumstark, *Syrische Literatur* 336–39 (literary life among the Melkites); Graf *Geschichte* 1 (= literature in translation), passim; 2 (literature through the middle of the fifteenth century), 3–93; 3 (middle of the fifteenth to the end of the nineteenth century), 79–298; Nasrallah, *Histoire* 2.2 (750 to tenth century); 3.1 (969–1516); 4.1 (1516–1724); 4.2 (1724–1800).

Sources of Melkite Canon Law

Earlier Historical Work

So far as the early period is concerned, Melkite canon law is in the first instance a part of Greek-Byzantine canon law. Its investigation is only beginning. Cyril Charon (Karalevsky) dedicated only a few pages in his *Histoire des Patriarcats Melkites* to older canon law.[4] Among the historical studies published in 1932 in the course of the codification of the law of the Catholic Eastern churches, there were two contributions on the canon law of the Melkites. The first, by Charles Abéla, contains fewer than three pages on 'droit ancien', contributing virtually nothing in terms of con-

---

2. Cf., for example, Charon, *Histoire des Patriarcats Melkites* 3.23ff.; Ch. Cannuyer, 'Langues usuelles et liturgiques de Melkites au XIIIe siècle', OrChr 70 (1986) 110–17.

3. Charon, *Histoire des Patriarcats Melkites* 3.30–41.

4. Charon, *Histoire des Patriarcats Melkites* 3.361–65. See also idem, 'Les sources du droit canonique melkite catholique', *Échos d'Orient* 11 (1908) 295–302.

tent. The second, by Acace Coussa, deals more thoroughly with the 'Les sources de l'ancienne discipline' and lists the old Greek authorities, but then deals only with the question of the extent to which these authorities have been recognized by the Latin Church and have validity for the Uniate Melkite Church. The presentation by Coussa in the *Dictionnaire du Droit Canonique* (1937) is also very concise. The first significant progress was made by Jean Baptiste Darblade with his work on the Melkite canonical collections, in which he critically examined and commented on the Arabic manuscripts. In his fundamental *Geschichte der christlichen arabischen Literatur* (1944–53), Georg Graf went into great detail on many points of the literature of canon law. The most recent monograph by Elias Jarawan compares Arabic texts with the Greek originals, and he restricts himself to the canons of the first four ecumenical councils. In his not completed, multi-volume history of Melkite literature (1979–96), Joseph Nasrallah devoted several entries to the sources of canon law. There is as yet no general history of Melkite canon law.

Literature: Graf, *Geschichte* passim; Nasrallah, *Histoire* passim; C. Abéla, 'Melkiti: Primo studio', *Studi storici* 282–373 (Droit ancien: 282–84); A. Coussa, 'Melkiti: Secundo studio: Indication des sources du droit canon chez les Melchites', *Studi storici* 375–468 (Les sources de l'ancienne discipline: 383–99); idem, 'Byzantin (Droit canonique)', DDC 2 (1937) 1170–76; ('Droit ancien') 1182–83 (Uniate, since the seventeenth century); Darblade, *Collection arabe*; P. Nabaa, 'Les sources de l'ancien droit matrimonial des Melkites', POC 2 (1952) 302–18; Jarawan, *Collection canonique arabe*.

Early Period

Sources of canon law in Syriac, Christian-Palestinian, or Coptic cannot be linked to one of the Melkite churches with certainty. The presumption is that canonical literature was read primarily by the Greek-speaking hierarchy. One must assume that the synodal canons, writings of the Church Fathers, and canonical collections that had legal force in the Byzantine imperial church had the same authority among the Melkites.

Only brief accounts of the three synods of Constantinople in 536, 553, and 571 survive in Syriac. These are not, however, canonical literature in the proper sense, but rather parts of a Syrian Melkite chronicle.[5] Such reports on synods survive in many versions and languages in the Christian East.

It is, however, not true that the Melkite Church simply drew its canonical sources from Constantinople. In any case, the patriarchate of Antioch stood out for its concern with canon law. Several synods took place in An-

---

5. A. de Halleux, 'Trois synodes impériaux du VIe s. dans une chronique syriaque inédite', *A Tribute to Arthur Vööbus: Studies in Early Christian Literature and its Environment, Primarily in the Syrian East*, ed. R. H. Fischer (Chicago 1977) 295–307; complete text of the chronicle with translation: A. de Halleux, 'La chronique melkite abrégée du ms. Sinaï syr. 10', *Museon* 91 (1978), 5–44.

tioch which were significant for the entire imperial church, particularly the purported synod of dedication (*in encaeniis*) of the church (which actually concerns a synod which took place in the period around 330) that was included in all the canon law collections. It is likely that the first large collection of canons of the earlier Greek synods, the so-called *Corpus canonum*, was compiled in Antioch. It was also in Antioch that John III Scholastikos, a jurist there and later patriarch of Constantinople (565–77), composed a systematic canonical collection.[6]

The most extensive collection of pseudo-apostolic texts, containing numerous rules, the *Apostolic Constitutions* in eight books, was compiled at the end of the fourth century in Syria, perhaps in Antioch itself. The sources upon which this work rested, the *Didascalia* (books 1–6) and the *Didache* (book 7), also were written in Syria.[7] The *Apostolic Constitutions* played a role in the East only as model for the Coptic-Arabic *Didascalia*.

From the letters of the Monophysite Patriarch Severus of Antioch (512–18) we learn that he had a canonical collection at hand for which there is no Greek example extant. It contained continuously numbered canons of the imperial councils (Nicaea to Laodicea and perhaps beyond, that is the *Corpus canonum*), *Canons of the Apostles*, the Synod of Carthage (A.D. 256), the *responsa* of Timothy of Alexandria, the Testament of Our Lord Jesus Christ, and perhaps the letters of Ignatius. The Syrian collections are based on this material.[8]

Similar works from the patriarchates of Jerusalem and Alexandria are unknown, although a portion of the Coptic legal sources to be dealt with below might have derived from the period before the schism, from Greek originals spread by the Melkites of Egypt.[9]

Alongside the shared sources there were certainly also local usages. We learn about them only from occasional remarks in the writings of the Fathers.[10]

Following the Muslim Conquest

Legal works in Greek continued to be written among the Melkites even after the Muslim conquest and the gradual spread of Arabic.

---

6. These sources have been treated by Heinz Ohme in this volume.

7. See the chapter by Heinz Ohme.

8. See. H. Kaufhold, 'Welche Kirchenrechtsquellen kannte Patriarch Severos von Antiocheia (512–518)', *Ius Canonicum in Oriente et Occidente: Festschrift für Carl Gerold Fürst*, ed. H. Zapp, A. Weiß, and S. Korta, (Adnotationes in Ius Canonicum; Frankfurt am Main 2003) 259–74.

9. See H. Kaufhold, 'Unbeachtete Quellen byzantinischen Kirchenrechts aus dem 6. Jh.', *Kirchenrecht und Ökumene: Festgabe für Panteleimon Rodopoulos* (Kanon: Jahrbuch der Gesellschaft für das Recht der Ostkirchen 15; Eichenau 1999) 113–30.

10. Cf. Charon, *Histoire des Patriarcats Melkites* 362–63.

1. At the end of the eleventh century the monk Nikon of the Black Mountain near Antioch composed two Greek works of primarily canonical content, the *Pandects* and the *Taktikon* (also *Kanonarion, Typikon*).[11] We shall return to him when we treat the Arabic legal literature of the Melkites.

2. John IV (V) Oxeites, patriarch of Antioch from 1089, also wrote a canonical work, 'On Monastic Teaching', in which he argued against giving monasteries to laymen (Charistikion).[12]

3. Patriarch John III Polites of Antioch (996–1021) was also known as a canonist. He came from Constantinople, however, and his canonistic responses on baptism originated there. He thus cannot be claimed by the Melkites.[13]

4. The same also applies to the famous canonist Theodorus Balsamon, who was nominally patriarch of Antioch at the end of the twelfth century, but who never resided there. We have reached the period of Crusader rule, when Latins ruled in both Antioch and Jerusalem.[14]

5. From the patriarchate of Jerusalem we have only the metropolitan Anastasios of Caesarea in Palestine, a contemporary of John Oxeites, who composed a tract on fasting at the time of the Koimesis festival, which was of a liturgical and canonical nature.[15]

There were connections between the East and Constantinople. While the Melkite Patriarch Markos of Alexandria visited Constantinople in 1195 he sent about sixty canonical questions to the Byzantine synod. Theodore Balsamon wrote the answers to his questions, and they were probably of significance for the Melkites of the Alexandrian patriarchate.[16]

Anonymous Arabic Canonical Collections

Origin and Scope

From the eighth century onward, as Arabic became the dominant language, the Melkites began to translate legal texts into Arabic, along with

---

11. Beck, *Kirche* 600, 613; I. Croce, *Textus selecti ex operibus commentatorum byzantinorum iuris ecclesiastici* (Fonti, serie 2, fasc. 5; Vatican City 1939) 12, 16; C. de Clercq, 'Les Pandectes de Nicon de la Montaigne noire', *Archive d'histoire du droit orental* 4 (1949) 187–203; idem, *Les textes juridiques dans les pandectes de Nicon de la Montaigne Noire* (Fonti, serie 2, fasc. 30; Venice 1942).

12. Edition and translation: P. Gautier, 'Réquisitoire du patriarche Jean d'Antioche contre le charisticariat', *Échos d'Orient* 33 (1975) 77–132. Literature: Beck, *Kirche* 136, 613; Croce, *Textus selecti* 10; E. Herman, 'Charisticaires', DDC 3.611–17; P. Gautier, 'Jean V l'Oxite, patriarche d'Antioche. Notice biographique', *Revue des études byzantines* 22 (1964) 128–57, 352–62; Nasrallah, *Histoire* 3.1, 86–89.

13. Beck, *Kirche* 599.

14. Beck, *Kirche* 657–58; Nasrallah, *Histoire* 3.1, 340.

15. Beck, *Kirche* 659; Croce, *Textus selecti* 17; Nasrallah, *Histoire* 3.1, 126. On the works mentioned, see the contribution of Spyros Trojanos on Byzantine law until 1100.

16. Edition: Rhalles-Potles IV 447–96. Literature: Beck, *Kirche* 658; V. Grumel, 'Les réponses canoniques à Marc d'Alexandrie', *Échos d'Orient* 38 (1939) 231–33.

many other works. The canons of the Greek synods were among the first to be translated. They had long been gathered into collections, and such collections were the models for the Arabic collections.

The number of surviving manuscripts is formidable.[17] They vary considerably in size and in some cases the sequence of texts included in them varies as well. Some of the differences may be attributed to the scribes. More detailed analysis of the Arabic collections is difficult, since there is as yet no critical edition of the sources.

The manuscripts are best divided into five groups according to the Greek synods they include.

1. The first group includes versions that contain only the following Greek synods: Nicaea, Ancyra, Neocaesarea, Gangra, Antioch, Laodiceia, Constantinople I, Ephesus, and Chalcedon, along with two pseudo-apostolic texts (81 Apostolic Canons; and 'Canons on the Priesthood'). This is the corpus of the expanded Antiochene *Corpus canonum*. Typical of this group is the fact that, in contrast with all other versions, Nicaea is placed before the local synods. Only the 20 authentic canons of Nicaea are present. The synod of Sardica is missing.

Since the translation could not have made before the eighth or the ninth centuries, it is astonishing that the later Byzantine synods that had been held up to that time (Constantinople II and III, the Trullan Synod, Nicaea II) do not appear. The question arises whether the translator used an older Greek collection or perhaps even the collection of another Eastern church whose collections did not contain these later synods: perhaps a Western Syrian collection? It is less likely that the translator (or a later copyist) simply left out the texts of his predecessor.

A representative of this group is the oldest Arabic manuscript of a canonical collection, British Library, Or. 5008 from A.D. 917. In addition to the synods mentioned, it contains only the ten canons of pseudo-Epiphanios, the precise contents of which nothing has yet been said.[18]

The second manuscript of the same type is Dair aš-Šīr 1;[19] it contains

---

17. Riedel, *Kirchenrechtsquellen* 138–46; Darblade, *Collection arabe* 1–39, 168–77; Graf, *Geschichte* 1.562; Jarawan, *Collection canonique arabe* 13–15; Nasrallah, *Histoire* 2.2, 188–96; 3.1, 345–47, 408–11; 3.2, 172–74.

18. Very brief description by A. G. Ellis and E. Edwards, *Descriptive List of the Arabic Manuscripts Acquired by the Trustees of the British Museum since 1894* (London 1912) 70; cf. also Graf, *Geschichte* 1.575, more precisely Nasrallah, *Histoire* 2.2, 189. Manuscript catalogues are only mentioned in what follows if the manuscript is not listed by Darblade.

19. Signature according to Darblade, *Collection arabe* 37. (A.D. 1300). The manuscript number is now 767 and is in the monastery St. Sauveur (*Dair al-muḥalliṣ*) in Sarba (Kaslik, Lebanon). The collection has only a typescript catalogue. From the Islamic date the manuscript was written in the year 1301 A.D.

both Constantinople I and II as well as the Trullan Synod, but the copyist could have supplemented his material from another more extensive model. The canons of Epiphanios are lacking, and in their place the *Syro-Roman Lawbook* and the *Spiritual Canons* are added. The third manuscript of this group is represented by Yabrūd 1, which strongly resembles Dair aš-Šīr because of its added texts.[20]

Jerusalem, St. Saveur 307 appears to belong to the same group,[21] which on the one hand has more texts (including the *Syro-Roman Lawbook* and the *Spiritual Canons*, etc.), but on the other hand, according to Jarawan offers only a resumé of the canons and completely omits the synods from Laodiceia to Chalcedon.[22]

2. A second group is formed by manuscripts that contain canons only up to Ephesus, hence excluding the Council of Chalcedon, which was theologically unacceptable for Monophysites.[23] This evidence inclines one to conclude that this version rests on a non-Byzantine model, Western Syrian or Coptic. At the beginning, as in subsequent versions, there are three sequences of pseudo-apostolic canons; Nicaea follows Ancyra and Neocaesarea, and Sardica is added after Laodiceia. In this group we also find the pseudo-Nicene ('Arabic') canons and the pseudo-Nicene canons for monks (see below). All of the manuscripts contain other texts from various sources (*Spiritual Canons*, the letter of Peter to Clement, Basil, Epiphanios, and others), which the copyist appears to have taken from other collections and inserted where it suited him.

3. The third group is represented by manuscripts that contain canons up to the third synod of Constantinople (A.D. 680–81).[24] This corpus could derive from a Greek collection that originated before the Trullan Synod; only the canons of Carthage and the texts of the Church Fathers are missing from the list of approved canonical texts in canon 2 of Trullo. On the other hand, the manuscripts of this group contain a large number of uniform texts in the same sequence. This group may be organized in two subgroups. One subgroup of manuscripts places all the local synods before Nicaea and the remaining ecumenical synods,[25] and the other subgroup places Sardica between Gangra and Antioch.

---

20. J. Nasrallah, 'Manuscrits melkites de Yabroud dans le Qalamoun', OCP 6 (1940) 89–92.
21. Darblade, *Collection arabe* 35 (A.D. 1300).   22. Jarawan, *Collection canonique arabe* 34.
23. Paris ar. 235, first part (fourteenth century); Paris ar. 242 (sixteenth century) (Troupeau, *Catalogue* 1.198–99, 203–4); Borg. ar. 148 (1592); Makarios Monastery 270 (fifteenth century?) (U. Zanetti, *Les manuscrits de Dair Abû Maqâr* (Cahiers d'Orientalisme 11; Geneva 1986) 39.
24. Paris ar. 234 and 235 (second part) (Troupeau, *Catalogue* 1.197–99) Beirut 514, Mardin, Orth. 312, Damascus Syr.-orthodox Patr. 8/3 (all about thirteenth century), Vat. ar. 409, Scharfeh ar. 4 (fourteenth century).
25. Mardin Orth. 312, Vat. ar. 409 and Scharfeh ar. 4.

4. The fourth group consists of manuscripts that contain the next synod, the Trullan Synod (Quinisext, Penthekte).[26]

5. The last group marks the final stage of the Melkites' recensions. These manuscripts contain an additional 27 authentic canons of Nicaea II (787) and a further 88 purported canons of this synod that are actually taken from the *Collectio LXXXVII titulorum* (excerpts from the *Novels* of Justinian with ecclesiastical contents).[27] The additional material (following the synods) resembles that of the previous group. In this version as well, there are two subgroups. The first contains no significant differences from group five,[28] while the second subgroup includes the 137 canons of Epiphanios between the synods of Constantinople II and III.[29]

The list of manuscripts is not complete for these texts. In particular the manuscripts from the twelfth and thirteenth centuries of the Holy Monastery of St. Catherine in Sinai must be studied. To date they have been described so summarily that no further conclusions can be drawn from them.[30]

The contents of the various collections are presented in the table, showing where some manuscripts transpose, omit, or add particular texts. The numbers indicate the sequence of texts. The irregularities in one group are indicated in bold type.

The Genesis, Translator or Editor of the Collection of Synods

Because the text is in Arabic, the translation could not have been made before the eighth or ninth centuries. In the case of British Library Oriental 5008 we have only a *terminus ante quem* (A.D. 917) for the text of the first group. We do not know who was the translator. The same applies to the miscellaneous manuscripts that have been augmented by additional texts. Since all the synods had already taken place by the eighth and ninth centuries, the augmentations cannot be established chronologically. We also

---

26. Beirut ar. 515 (thirteenth century), Barb. or. 111 (1308) and perhaps the supplement at the end of the aforementioned Dair aš-Šīr 1 and Yabrūd 1 (with only a brief notice on the Trullanum).

27. Darblade, *Collection arabe* 113–17. Cf. Beck, *Kirche* 144 on the *Collectio*.

28. Damascus 1561 (1234; see Nasrallah, *Histoire* 3.1, 308–9 A) Jerusalem, St. Saveur 309 (thirteenth century), Paris ar. 236 (fifteenth century), Damascus 1565 (before 1574), and Dair aš-Šuwair 19 (1586). A description of the Mardin and Damascus manuscripts is in preparation by H. Kaufhold and W. Selb. Jerusalem, Holy Sepulchre 10, supplement (seventeenth century), Tyre 31 (?). Also Vat. ar. 154 (thirteenth century) might belong to this group, but according to Jarawan, *Collection canonique arabe* 232–33, it differs from the others in wording.

29. Jerusalem, Holy Sepulchre 20 (thirteenth century), Oxford ar. 36 (fourteenth century), Aleppo 61 (1687).

30. Cf. M. D. Gibson, *Catalogue of the Arabic Manuscripts in the Convent of S. Catharina on Mount Sinai* (London 1894) nos. 390–93, 590, 598, 600; M. Kamil, *Catalogue of all manuscripts in the Monastery of St. Catharine on Mount Sinai* (Wiesbaden 1979) 51 (nos. 582–590); I. E. Meimaris, Κατάλογος τῶν νεῶν ἀπαβικῶν χειρογράφων τῆς ἱερᾶς Μονῆς Ἁγίας Αἰκατερίνης τοῦ ὄρους Σινᾶ (Athens 1985) 98 (no. 54); 37 (no. 3).

Group	a	b	c¹	c²	d	e¹	e²
List of Synods			1	1	1	1	1	1
List of Heresies					2	2	2
Acts of the Apostles		2	2	2	3	3	3
Apostolic Canons	1	3	3	3	4	4	4
Canons of the apostles about priesthood	2	4	4	4	5	5	5
Ancyra	4	5	5	5	6	6	6
Neocaesarea	5	6	6	6	7	7	7
Report about Constantin and Helena		7	7	11	8	8	8
Nicaea: 20 authentic Canons	3	8	8	12	9	9	9
Nicaea: 84 Arabic Canons		9	9	13	10	10	10
Nicaea: 33 Canons for monks		10	10	14	11	11	11
Gangra	6	11	11	7	12	12	12
Antioch	7	12	12	9	13	13	13
Laodiceia	8	13	13	10	14	14	14
Sardica		14	14	8	15	15	15
Constantinople I	9	15	15	15	16	16	16
Ephesus	10	16	16	16	17	17	17
Chalcedon	11		17	17	18	18	18
Constantinople II			18	18	19	19	19
Constantinople III			19	19	20	20	21
Trullan Synod					21	21	22
Nicaea II: 22 Kanones						22	23
Nicaea II: 88 Kanones						23	24
Ephiphanios			20	20	22	24	20
List of 20 heresies			21	21	23	25	
Good Friday Mystagogy			22		24	26	
List of the 72 Disciples					25		
Spiritual Canons			23	22	26	27	
Statutes of the Old Testament			24	23	27	28	
Letter of Peter to Clement			25	24			27
Syro-Roman Lawbook			26	25	28	29	
Epiphanius (45 canons)			27	26	29	30	25
Basil (14 canons)			28	27	30	31	26
Confession of Hierotheos			29	28			
Procheiros Nomos			30 (?)		31	32	

do not know who the editors were. The names proposed until now in the scholarly literature cannot be accepted.

Nasrallah proposes the name of the Ayyubid official Hibatallāh ibn Yūnus ibn abi 'l-Fatḥ (flourished at the beginning of the thirteenth century), who is named in the colophons of two manuscripts (including Damascus 1561).[31] The text of the colophon, however, is more likely to mean that he ordered the copying of the manuscript, not that he had anything to do with the compiling of the collection of canons.

The same argument applies to Joseph 'of Egypt', who was consecrated a priest for a church in Alexandria in 1378, and who copied Oxford Arabic 36.[32] The manuscript is typical of miscellaneous collections (group 5, second subgroup). Insofar as this subgroup shows any peculiarities, such as the listing of the names of the Fathers at Nicaea, Father Joseph could have been responsible for them. There is, however, no reasonable basis for considering him the translator of the entire collection or for thinking that he substantially edited it. Graf has already demonstrated adequately that Joseph was not the compiler.[33]

The Arabic manuscript British Library, Or. 4950 contains a theological tract in 25 chapters that Melkite Bishop Theodore abū Qurra from Harran (ca. 800) had perhaps composed. In any case the manuscript was written in 877 in the monastery of Holy Chariton in Palestine. The last chapter was formed from a selection of canons and has the rubric: 'Words of apostles and fathers over those things that Christians are forbidden to do: dietary regulations, rules for marriage, and their relationships with non-Christians'. Nicaea was counted as the first synod, and then he numbered the following: Ankyra (2), Neokaisareia (3), Gangra (5), Laodikeia (7) and Chalkedon (10 or 6?). He received above all the 'Apostolic Canons' as well as the canons from Gangra and Laodicea. He accepted the other synods and the canons of Basil in only limited numbers.[34] There is very little discernable organization in the work. The rubric fits the contents only in a general way. The translation of the canons is literal, and the numbering of them departs sometimes from his Greek source. There is not, as far as we know, a source in Greek or Ara-

---

31. Nasrallah, *Histoire* 3.1, 343–44.

32. Riedel, *Kirchenrechtsquellen* 138–40; Darblade, *Collection arabe* 27–29; Nasrallah, *Histoire* 3.2, 174–83.

33. Nasrallah, *Histoire* 1.559–60. He holds the corresponding passage to be a later marginal note. Nasrallah, on the other hand, is correct in naming Joseph as the copyist of the manuscript.

34. Graf, Geschichte der christlichen arabischen Literatur 2.16–19; Sidney H. Griffith, 'A Ninth Century Summa Theologiae Arabica', *Actes du deuxième congrès international d'études arabes chrétiennes*, ed. Khalil Samir (Orientalia Christiana Analecta 226; Rome 1986) 123–41; reprinted in Sidney H. Griffith, *Arabic Christianity in the Monasteries of Ninth-Century Palestine* (Variorum CSS 380; Aldershot 1992) IX. The text of the *Summa* is not yet published. A German translation can be found in the papers of Georg Graf (1875–1955).

bic that might have been the model for his work. We cannot know whether he used a Greek or Arabic canonical collection.

Of the thirteenth- or fourteenth-century Melkite emir Wahbatallh Ǧamāl ad-Dīn, who in one manuscript is called the compiler of the canons of councils and Fathers, nothing further is known.[35]

With all due caution, the following may be said in summation: the Arabic canonical collections of the Melkites began with a limited number of texts. The oldest collection included synods only up to Chalcedon, and a later recension extended only to Ephesus. At the time of the translation, these collections were no longer current for the Byzantine Orthodox churches. It is clear that the translators did not exploit contemporary collections of the Greek church. They must have used older Greek manuscripts. It is at least conceivable that there were older Melkite collections in Syriac or Coptic, which have not survived, and that these were then translated into Arabic. The possibility is also worth considering that exemplars from other, non-Chalcedonian churches, were used. This hypothesis is particularly appealing with the type that included canons up to the Council of Ephesus. Solutions of these problems will be possible only through further study of these texts.

According to Jarawan, the texts of the first four ecumenical councils, to which he restricted his analysis, agreed in almost all the manuscripts he used. Jarawan studied only one of the manuscripts of the first group, St. Sauveur 307; it contained a 'brief review of the the canons of the council'.[36] Whether that is also true for other manuscripts of this group, especially the oldest from A.D. 917, must remain an open question. The question of whether the translation agrees with the texts of the other manuscript groups must also remain unanswered.

The texts of the other versions appear, so far as the texts of the synods are concerned, to be identical. Jarawan used some manuscripts of the groups 2 through 5 without being able to establish differences: 'All of them present the same identical text, the same words, the same turns of phrase, virtually the same errors of form, with a few minor omissions or additions of words or small phrases. One may say that the text is substantially the same'.[37]

The conclusion one must draw from this evidence is that the original collection was simply supplemented by new texts. The old translation continued to be used. It appears that no new translations were made.

---

35. Graf, *Geschichte* 2.82 with reference to P. Sbath, *Al-Fihris (Catalogue de Manuscrits Arabes)* (Cairo 1938) 66 (no. 178 = 540).
36. Jarawan, *Collection canonique arabe* 34.
37. Jarawan, *Collection canonique arabe* 33.

Insofar as the later groups were supplemented by later Greek synods, the texts naturally could be translated only from Greek, since they were not received by the other Eastern churches. Hence, in a certain way they reflect the contemporary development of Greek canonical collections.

It is surprising that the writings of the Fathers contained in Greek canonical collections are completely lacking in the Melkite collections. We also look in vain for other synods that chronologically could have been included, such as the Prima-Secunda (Proto-Deutera) of 861, as well as the synods of Constantinople in 869 and 879. The manuscripts have other texts in their place, to which we shall now turn.

The Individual Parts of the Collection

Describing the individual texts in more detail would exceed the limits of this treatment. The reader is referred to the thorough descriptions by Darblade and to the rest of the scholarly literature. We shall confine ourselves to a few remarks that follow the order of the contents of the table (above). Most of the texts are printed in the collection of the Patriarch Silvester (see below).

1. The 'List of Synods' is not a table of contents for the collection but rather a work in its own right that briefly describes the individual synods (place, number of participants, occasion, chief representatives); it belongs to the genre of 'conciliar synopses', which circulated widely in the Greek-speaking regions, as well as in other Eastern churches.[38] Its organization varies in the manuscripts. Most of them begin the text with the 'small' (local) synods, then follow the 'big' (ecumenical) synods. In this case as in others, only a critical edition, which does not yet exist, could lead to further information.

2. The 'List of Heresies' (or a similar text?) appears once again later. More cannot be said at this time.[39]

3. The first text of the 'Pseudo-Apostolic Canons', the 'Acts (aḫbār) of the Apostles Following the Ascension of Christ', is also preserved in the Syrian collections as the 'Teaching of the Apostles' ('Teaching of the Apostle Addai'), and also in Coptic. The second text consists of the 'Apostolic Canons', which are numbered differently in the various versions. The third text is a parallel text to the eighth book of the *Apostolic Constitutions*. The last two are also preserved in Greek and in the other oriental languages.[40]

---

38. Particularly H. J. Sieben, *Die Konzilsidee in der Alten Kirche* (Paderborn 1979) 344–80.
39. Darblade, *Collection arabe* 49–50.
40. ClavisG 1740, 1741 (and Supplement); Darblade, *Collection arabe* 51–59; Graf, *Geschichte* 2.572–80; Nasrallah, *Histoire* 2.2, 197–99.

4. The second of the local synods, Neocaesarea, is called the synod of 'Carthage' in some of the manuscripts. The canons of the genuine synod of Carthage of 419, which form a part of Greek collections, appear only exceptionally in the Melkite collections.[41]

5. Along with a report on the synod of Nicaea I and the 20 authentic canons, the Melkite collections also included 84 Arabic 'Canons of the 318 Fathers' and 33 canons for monks, monasteries and clerics, whose origin is not yet convincingly understood. The 84 canons also appear in the Maronite *Kitāb al-Hudā* as well as among the Coptic collections. They correspond in part to the 73 (at most) canons ascribed by the Eastern Syrians to Bishop Mārūtā of Maipherkat: the first 32 canons have no parallels in Syriac, the Canons of the 318 Fathers are identical with the Syrian canons 1–47, and the canons for the monks with the Syrian canons 48–73.[42]

The list of bishops at Nicaea appears only in one Oxford and one Jerusalem manuscript. It is missing in all the other manuscripts, as are the lists of participants for all other synods.[43]

6. There were four canons from the First Council of Constantinople (381) that correspond to the first six Greek conciliar canons. The seventh canon is missing. It is identical with the letter of the church of Constantinople to Martyrios that is contained in the West Syrian collections. There is only one canon from the Council of Ephesos, which is the same as the seventh Greek canon.[44]

7. Of the later ecumenical synods, Constantinople II and III (A.D. 553 and 680) left no canons and do not appear in the Greek canonical collections. In the Melkite collections they are represented by brief notices and other fragments.

Nicaea II (787) appears with its authentic canons. Darblade has shown that the purported 88 canons of this synod are actually the *Collectio LXXXVII capitulorum* of John III Scholastikos, a compendium of the canonical *Novels* of Justinian from 535 to 546.[45]

---

41. Darblade, *Collection arabe* 60–68; Graf, *Geschichte* 1.593–97; Nasrallah, *Histoire* 2.2, 204–6.

42. The Jesuit F. Torres (Turrianus 1509–84) and the Maronite A. Eccellensis (1605–64) printed Latin translations of several texts, and they were reprinted by J. Hardouin, *Acta conciliorum et epistolae decretales . . . ab anno 34 ad 1714* (Paris 1715) 1.335–44, 463–528, and Mansi 2.705–20, 947–1064. ClavisG 8511–27, Darblade, *Collection arabe* 69–89; Graf, *Geschichte* 1.586–93; Nasrallah, *Histoire* 2.2, 200–204; R.-G. Coquin, 'Nicaea, Arabic Canons of', CE 6.1789–90.

43. Edition of the list of bishops according to an Oxford manuscript: H. Gelzer, H. Hilgenfeld, O. Cuntz, *Patrum Nicaenorum nomina* (Leipzig 1898) 143–81, reprinted with an afterword by C. Markschies (Leipzig 1995).

44. Graf, *Geschichte* 1.597–600; Nasrallah, *Histoire* 2.2, 206–7; Darblade, *Collection arabe* 100–102; Jarawan, *Collection canonique arabe* 16, 46–47.

45. Darblade, *Collection arabe* 99–117; Graf, *Geschichte* 1.597–601; Nasrallah, *Histoire* 2.2, 206–9; Beck, *Kirche* 423; N. van der Wal and J.H.A. Lokin, *Historiae iuris graeco-romani delineatio: Les sources du droit byzantin de 300 à 1453* (Groningen 1985) 53.

8. The title for the canons of Epiphanios usually reads, 'Canons and Rulings (aḥkām) which St. Epiphanius, Patriarch of Constantinople, established for the believing and exalted-in-faith Emperor Justinian'. The canons exist in three forms. The shortest version in British Library 5008 has only ten canons. It has not been printed, so nothing may be said of its contents. The second version contains between 136 and 138 canons, the first 13 deriving from Justinian's Novel 6, and the others from the older canonical literature (Apostolic Canons, synods of Nicaea, Neocaesarea, Gangra, Laodiceia and Chalcedon, as well as the canons of Basil). On the whole it consists of laws governing the morals of clerics and laymen. The third version is excerpted from the second version and contains between 42 and 47 canons. The Coptic translation has between 35 and 45 canons.[46]

9. Good Friday Mystagogy.[47]

10. List of the 72 disciples.[48]

11. The complete title of the 'Spiritual Canons' is 'Volume of Spiritual Canons, which are an explanation of the orders (ḥuqūq) of God, and it derives from the books of the emperors, the four writings that were composed in the presence of the synod of 318 [the Fathers of Nicaea] and in the presence of Constantine the Great'. Darblade believed that the reference to the four books meant the 20 authentic canons, the 'Arabic' canons, the canons for monks, and this text. Yet the 'Spiritual Canons' do not stand together with the three other texts mentioned. It is preferable to conclude with Graf that the collector is referring to the four 'Books of the Canons of the Kings' known to the Copts, which were ascribed to the synod of Nicaea but were not received by the Melkites in this form (they also lack the 'Ekloge'). It is easy to assume that this is borrowed from a Coptic collection. We find the 'Spiritual Canons', if in a variant version, in Coptic collections. It remains to be seen how much the Spiritual Canons resemble the first thirteen chapters of the Maronite *Kitāb al-Hudā*, as Darblade has asserted.[49] In terms of content, it is a compendium of ecclesiastical discipline (duties, marriage, religious persons, fasts, prayer, burial, etc.).[50]

12. The 'Statutes of the Old Testament' consists of excerpts from Exodus 21–23, Leviticus 12–15, 18–22, 25, 27, Numbers 5, 6, 35, and Deuteron-

---

46. Darblade, *Collection arabe* 118–24; Graf, *Geschichte* 1.620–21; Nasrallah, *Histoire* 2.2, 209, 3.1, 348; R.-G. Coquin, 'Canons of Epiphanius', CE 2.456–57.

47. Graf, *Geschichte* 1.571?   48. Ibid., 1.267.

49. Darblade, *Collection arabe* 94f.

50. Latin translation: A. Ecchellensis, 'Sanctiones et decreta', J. Hardouin, *Acta conciliorum et epistolae decretales ab anno 34 ad 1714* (Paris 1714) 1.508–18, and Mansi 2.1029–54. See Darblade, *Collection arabe* 90–98; Graf, *Geschichte* 1.619–20; Nasrallah, *Histoire* 3.1, 347–48.

omy 11, 20–26, in 51 chapters. It is also found in Coptic collections. Such excerpts from the Pentateuch are to be found in other languages, in Greek as the *Nomos Mosaikos*, which was also translated into Armenian. Similar collections are also found among the Western Syrians and the Georgians. Further research would be necessary to establish any relationship among these excerpts, as well as to the Old Testament parts of the Latin *Collatio legum Mosaicarum et Romanarum*.[51]

13. The 'Letter of Peter to Clement' is among the few pseudo-apostolic texts of the Melkite canonical collections. It also appears among the collections of the Maronites and the Copts. It consists of moral teachings and directions concerning worship that were supposedly written down by Jesus and given to Peter before his Ascension on the Mount of Olives, and Peter passed them on to Clement.[52]

14. The *Syro-Roman Lawbook* contains primarily civil law, and hardly any ecclesiastical law. The Arabic translation cannot have come from the Greek but rather derives from a Syriac exemplar. Among the Copts it is a part of the four 'Books of the Canons of the Kings'.[53]

15. The undoubtedly spurious 14 'Canons of Basil' contain penal rulings against priests and deacons as well as a ban on burning the reliquaries of martyrs. Among the Copts the text consists of 13 canons. Beyond that, the Copts also knew another series of 106 pseudo-Basilian canons (see below). The genuine letters of Basil preserved in the Greek collections and in excerpts in the Western Syriac collections do not appear in Melkite or Coptic manuscripts.[54]

---

51. Edition of the Greek text: L. Burgmann and S. Troianos, *Nomos Mosaikos* (Fontes minores III; Frankfurt am Main 1979) 126–67, ed. D. Simon. Literature on the Latin 'collatio': F. Schulz, *Geschichte der römischen Rechtswissenschaft* (Weimar 1961) 394–98; D. Liebs, *Die Jurisprudenz im spätantiken Italien* (Berlin 1987) 162–74. P. E. Pieler, 'Lex Christiana', *Akten des 26. Deutschen Rechtshistorikertages Frankfurt am Main 1986*, ed. D. Simon (Frankfurt am Main 1987) 485–503, especially 494–503.

Editions of the Arabic text (with translation): B. Sanguinetti, 'Aḥkām al-'atīqa ou les préceptes de l'Ancien Testament', *Journal asiatique* 5th series, 14 (1959) 449–500, 15 (1960) 5–66; G. Galbiati and S. Noja, *Precetti e canoni giuridico morali per arabi cristiani*, 1: *Il manuscritto Ambrosiano e la versione Italiana* (Milan 1964) (no further appeared). See Darblade, *Collection arabe* 115–28; Graf, *Geschichte* 1.584–85; Nasrallah, *Histoire* 3.1, 348–49.

52. Darblade, *Collection arabe* 129–31, Graf, *Geschichte* 1.580–81; Nasrallah, *Histoire* 3.1, 349–50; J. Hofmann, *Unser heiliger Vater Klemens* (Trier 1992) 36–38.

53. Edition and translation of the Arabic version: K. G. Bruns and E. Sachau, *Syrisch-römisches Rechtsbuch aus dem 5. Jahrhundert* (Leipzig 1880) 1.68–94, 2.75–114 (based on only a few manuscripts). A critical edition of the Syriac text with a thorough introduction and commentary by Selb-Kaufhold, *Rechtsbuch*.

On the Arabic version: Nallino, 'Libri giuridici' 101–65 (= *Raccolta* 324–82); Darblade, *Collection arabe* 141–45; Graf, *Geschichte* 1.616; Nasrallah, *Histoire* 3.1, 352; H. Trofimoff, 'Les arrhes en droit syro-romain arabe', *Revue internationale des droits de l'Antiquité* 3rd series, 39 (Brussels 1992) 259–326. Selb-Kaufhold, *Rechtsbuch* 1.65–67, 162–72.

54. Darblade, *Collection arabe* 150–53; Graf, *Geschichte* 1.606–8; Nasrallah, *Histoire* 3.1, 350–52.

16. 'Confession of Hierotheos'.⁵⁵

17. The 'Procheiros Nomos', a well-known Byzantine authority, is part of the four 'Books of the Canons of the Kings' among the Copts, but it circulated as a separate work among the Melkites. It contains civil law without canonical content.⁵⁶

The Origins of the non-Synodal Portion of the Canon Collections

Groups 1 and 2 of the canonical collections originally contained only synodal texts.⁵⁷ Where individual manuscripts contain additional texts that are completely different, this is obviously a supplement by individual scribes. The non-synodal 'appendices' of groups 3 through 5 agree with one another in essence, so that within certain limits they represent a unified corpus that was commonly transmitted, though with occasional modification. Who the translators were and when these texts were compiled cannot be determined. They were not taken as a whole from the Greek, for the Greek collections look entirely different and consist in the main of patristic writings. So far as I can see, not a single one of the added texts comes from such Greek collections. Both Western and Eastern Syrian canonical collections also have to be excluded as a possible source. We find only similar texts in Coptic-Arabic manuscripts, but on the whole they have a quite different contents. There may be, however, no doubt that there were connections between the Melkite and the Coptic-Arabic collections, but this requires further study.⁵⁸

Legal Works Surviving Outside the Canon Collections

The commodious canonical collections described in their various stages of development are certainly the most important source for Melkite ecclesiastical law. Still, there are other texts with canonical contents that have come to us either independently or in miscellaneous manuscripts.

1. The more than 120 canons of the Synod of Carthage (419) form a part of Coptic-Arabic collections.⁵⁹ When they appear in a Melkite manuscript (Dair aš-Šuwair 19), it is due to a borrowing from a foreign exemplar.

2. The same holds true for the 107 canons of 'Pseudo-Athanasius'.⁶⁰

---

55. Riedel, *Kirchenrechtsquellen* 184–86. Graf, *Geschichte* 1.371.
56. An edition of the Arabic version is in preparation by J. Pahlitzsch under the auspices of the Frankfurt research group for Byzantine Law. See Nallino, 'Libri giuridici' 101–65. Darblade, *Collection arabe* 146–49; Graf, *Geschichte* 1.616–18; Nasrallah, *Histoire* 3.1, 354–55.
57. See the table above p. 229 for a description of these groupings.
58. On the editions and translations of texts in Arabic according to the Maronite and Coptic traditions, cf. the sections on the ecclesiastical law of the Maronites and Copts. Literature on the canonical collection as a whole: Darblade, *Collection arabe*; Graf, *Geschichte* 1.556–620; Jarawan, *Collection canonique arabe*; Nasrallah, *Histoire* 2.2, 188–210, 3.1, 340–57, 3.2, 172–74.
59. Graf, *Geschichte* 1.597
60. Graf, *Geschichte* 1.605–6.

They were adopted by Mardin, Orth. 312, which has both Melkite and Coptic material.

3. The canons ascribed to John the Faster (Nesteutes)[61] are found only occasionally in conjunction with Melkite manuscripts (for example, Vat. Barb. Or. 111, Jerusalem Holy Sepulchre 10, Jerusalem St. Saveur 307). Nothing more precise may be said about these texts for now.[62]

4. In the same way the penitential canons of Theodore of Studios, which are more widely represented among the Copts, can be found only in a few Melkite manuscripts.[63]

5. The works of Nikon of the Black Mountain (end of the eleventh century) gained greater acclaim and have already been discussed above. His 'Pandects', as Graf has noted, 'a compendium of Christian doctrine, but even more of moral teachings in the form of a "florilegium" from the Holy Scriptures, the works of the Fathers and ecclesiastical canons' bears the title al-Hāwī al-kabīr, 'The Great Collector', and survive in whole or in excerpts in many Melkite and Coptic manuscripts. It was further translated into Ethiopian in 1582. The Arabic version of his 'Taktikon' (Typikon), a collection of ethical and canonical or liturgical content aimed at monks, must have been prepared by another translator in Syria (al-Hāwī as-saġīr, 'The Little Collector'). Only a few manuscripts of that work are known. It was obviously less important to the Melkites. A third work,[64] of whose Greek exemplar little may be said, was translated into Arabic. It is also a work of moral and canonical materials aimed primarily at monks.[65]

6. As may be seen from its many manuscripts, the Melkites had great affection for a sort of penitential handbook, the 'Book of Spiritual Medicine' (Kitāb aṭ-Ṭibb ar-Ruḥānī), which was systematically divided into 47 sections. It certainly derived from the Copt Michael of Aṭrīb and Malīǧ, who also used sources of obviously Melkite origin. An appendix found only in Melkite manuscripts contains, to an extent varying from manuscript to manuscript, many further canonical authorities, some of which we have already encountered: the 'Letter of Peter to Clement', the 'Canons of Epiphanius', 'Canons of Theodore of Studios', 'Canons of Basil', 'Canons of John the Faster', 'Canons of John the Deacon' (a pupil of Basil the Great)[66] and many others.[67]

---

61. ClavisG 7555. Beck, Kirche 423–24.
62. Graf, Geschichte 1.610–11. Nasrallah, Histoire 3.1, 356–57; 3.2, 184, 188–89, 195.
63. Beck, Kirche 494; Graf, Geschichte 1.611. Nasrallah, Histoire 3.2, 184–85, 195.
64. Beck, Kirche 600.
65. Graf, Geschichte 2.64–69; Nasrallah, Histoire 3.1, 110–22, 341–42.
66. Beck, Kirche 424, 598.
67. On the Melkite version of Spiritual Medicine and on the appendix, see Nasrallah, Histoire 3.2, 183–92. Another manuscript of the text in the appendix is Balamand 192, see R. Hadad and F. Freijate, Manuscrits du couvent de Belmont (Balamand) (Beyrouth 1970) 128–29 (in Arabic).

7. Another Melkite collection also aimed at fathers confessor joined the previous item and similar pieces in chronological order.[68]

8. We do not possess any decisions of Melkite synods before the sixteenth century. We know only of a synod of 1363 that transferred the patriarchal see of Antioch to Damascus.[69] Further, we do not have any decisions of the patriarchs for our period.[70]

9. Patriarch Silvester of Antioch (1724–66) lies outside our chronological limits. Still he should be mentioned here because he collected the canons of the ecumenical and provincial councils,[71] as well as the canons of the Fathers and other canonical texts contained in the usual Greek collections translated from Greek into Arabic by the deacon Elias ibn Faḫr († 1758) and gathered into the most comprehensive of collections. He himself provided only a foreword to the collection.[72]

Works Not Received

In view of the close ties between the church of Constantinople and the Melkite churches of the patriarchates of Antioch, Jerusalem and Alexandria, it is astounding that basic works of Byzantine canon law were not translated into Arabic. Thus the canonical collection of John Scholastikos, particularly the *Nomokanon* in fourteen titles was not translated, even though it was widely distributed in Greek, gained general authority, and was translated into the Slavic languages, even into Georgian. Since there is not a trace of it, we cannot assume that it was translated but did not survive. The standard works of later Byzantine canon law, such as the canonical commentaries of John Zonaras, Alexios Aristenos and Theodore Balsamon (all twelfth century) were not translated into Arabic. The canon law handbook of Matthew Blastares (composed 1335) only entered Arabic literature in the eighteenth century as a result of the activities of the Patriarch Silvester.

Western Syrians (Jacobites)

History of the Church

As was already mentioned in the treatment of the Melkite Church, the Western Syrian Church (Jacobite or Syrian Orthodox) is the church of the

---

68. Nasrallah, *Histoire* 3.2, 194–97.   69. Nasrallah, *Histoire* 3.2, 198.

70. Nasrallah, *Histoire* 3.2, 198; on later synods and decisions of Melkite patriarchs, cf. Nasrallah, *Histoire* 4.1, 276–79, 279–80, 4.2, 369–79 respectively.

71. In contrast to the Melkite-Arab tradition, but in accord with the normal tradition in the Greek collections, Silvester included seven canons from Constantinople and eight canons from Ephesos.

72. Edition: Ǧāmiʿ at al-Balamand, Markaz ad-dirāsāt al-urṭūduksī al-Antākī, (ed.) *Kitāb an-Nāmūs aš-šarīf* (Beirut 1992).

Literature: Graf, *Geschichte* 1.561, 563–64 (with reference to an older partial edition of the ecumenical and local councils, Cairo 1894), 3.125–26; Nasrallah, *Histoire* 4.2 86, 212–14.

patriarchate of Antioch that adhered to the 'Monophysite' party during the Christological controversies. Although the conflict was not resolved at once, and for a while the patriarchs and bishops of the patriarchate were of various persuasions, the Chalcedonian party prevailed with the assistance of the Byzantine emperor. An autonomous ecclesiastical hierarchy of Monophysites arose only as a result of the unrelenting activities of Bishop Jacob Baradaios († 578) over decades, who consecrated several patriarchs and many bishops. His name is the source of 'Jacobite'.

The Church also arose in Persian Mesopotamia. The ecclesiastical head there, subordinated to the patriarchs of Antioch, bore the title of 'Maphrian'. For a time there were also bishoprics in the border regions of Arabia and in the interior of Asia.

The Arab conquest in the seventh century liberated the Western Syrian Church from a largely hostile Byzantine rule, but in the course of centuries it led to great losses of faithful to Islam. As was the case with the other churches of Western Asia, there was massive decimation as a result of the harrowing conquests of the Mongols (twelfth through fourteenth centuries). Further weakening came from the sixteenth century on as a result of efforts at union by the Latin Church, which led to a Syrian-Catholic Church in communion with Rome.[73]

Western Syrian Literature

It is obvious that the Monophysite residents of the patriarchate of Antioch at first used Greek, even though their native Syriac, an eastern Aramaic language resting on the dialect of Edessa, was also of great importance. After the emergence of an autonomous ecclesiastical organization, however, Syriac becomes the exclusive liturgical and literary language in the Syrian Church. Arabic gradually won ground after the Muslim conquest, but the use of Syriac remained entrenched through the fourteenth century and even beyond, surviving as a liturgical language and occasionally as a literary language to the present day. An attempt was even made to revive it as a spoken language. Beyond that, large numbers of the Syrian-Orthodox faithful still speak a Syriac dialect to the present day. The oldest literary works in Arabic, however, appear as early as the first quarter of the ninth century.

Literature in Syriac is extraordinarily rich, and alongside translations, especially from Greek, there are numerous original works in theology,

---

73. Spuler, *Die morgenländischen Kirchen* 170–216; Heiler, *Ostkirchen* 336–44; Atiya, *Eastern Christianity* 167–235; Müller, *Nationalkirchen* 274–94. G. Troupeau, 'L'église jacobite d'Antioch', *Histoire du Christianisme* 4.411–22 *Geschichte des Christentums* 4.425–35); J. Richard, 'L'Église syrienne', *Histoire du Christianisme* 6.219–21 (*Geschichte des Christentums* 6.214–17).

liturgy and liturgical poetry, hagiography, monastic literature, and much more. Arabic ecclesiastical literature in this period consists, apart from translations, almost exclusively of apologetic and dogmatic works.[74]

Western Syrian Sources of Canon Law

The history of Western Syrian law, together with that of the Eastern Syrians, is one of the best-researched Eastern Christian laws. Editions and translations exist of the most important sources. There are also many individual studies and a synthesis. Although the Spanish canonist Francisco Peña († 1612) had already been concerned with Syrian legal sources, the true beginning was made by the Maronite Joseph Simonius Assemani (1687–1768), who worked in Rome, dedicating the second volume of his still-fundamental *Bibliotheca orientalis* (Rome 1721) to Syrian Monophysite authors. He not only dealt thoroughly with the authors and their juridical works using the manuscripts of the Bibliotheca Vaticana, but he also prefaced his *Bibliotheca* with a penetrating narrative of history, of theology, and of ecclesiastical organization. Further, among other things he was responsible for a catalogue of the Syriac manuscripts of the Vaticana, including those with juristic contents. Angelo Mai presented a Latin translation of the most important legal compendium, the *Nomokanon* of Bar Hebraeus, in volume 10 of his *Scriptorum veterum nova collectio* (Rome 1838). Syriac studies in the Occident burgeoned considerably after the middle of the nineteenth century. Catalogues were compiled for all significant European manuscript collections, and there were editions of many texts, including those on canon and civil law. Among those who should be mentioned are Paul de Lagarde (*Reliquiae iuris ecclesiastici antiquissimae syriace*), Paul Bedjan (*Nomokanon* of Bar Hebraeus), the Syrian Catholic patriarch Ignatius Ephrem Rahmani (*Testamentum Domini*), François Nau (editions and translations of many legal texts), and Friedrich Schulthess (Greek synods). Further stimulation came from the preparation of a Code for the Uniate Eastern churches (*Codificazione Canonica Orientale*) starting in the 1930s (Hindo). Fundamental works on the law of Syrians were also written by the Italian orientalist Carlo Alfonso Nallino (1872–1938). After the Second World War, Arthur Vööbus (1909–88) in particular distinguished himself by finding manuscripts in the East and through important works on the history of Western Syrian canon law. Walter Selb (1929–1994) produced the first thorough treatment of Western Syrian canon law (1989).

---

74. W. Wright, *A Short History of Syriac Literature* (London 1894); C. Brockelmann, 'Die syrischen und christlich-arabischen Litteraturen', *Christliche Litteraturen* 1-64; Baumstark, *Syrische Literatur*; A. Baumstark and A. Rücker, 'Die syrische Literatur', HbOr 3.1 pp. 168–204; I. Ortiz de Urbina, *Patrologia syriaca* (2nd ed. Rome 1965); M. Albert, ' Langue et littérature syriaque', *Christianismes orientaux* (Paris 1993) 297–372. On the literature in Arabic, Graf, *Geschichte* 2.220–93.

Literature: A. Baumstark, 'Frances Peña und die kirchenrechtliche Literatur der Syrer', OrChr 3 (1903) 211–14; G. Riciotti, 'Disciplina Antiochena: II. Siri', *Studi storici* 117–38; Hindo, *Persones*, idem, *Sacrements*, idem, *Lieux* (each with extensive citations from Western Syrian legal sources, cf. lists of sources and indices); W. de Vries, *Sakramenttheologie bei den syrischen Monophysiten* (Orientalia Christiana Analecta 125; Rome 1940) (also cites many canon-law sources); Vööbus, *Kanonensammlungen*; Selb, *Orientalisches Kirchenrecht* 2; H. Kaufhold, 'Römisch-byzantinisches Recht in den Kirchen syrischer Tradition', *Atti del congresso internazionale 'Incontro fra canoni d'oriente e d'occidente'*, ed. R. Coppolla (Bari 1994) 1.132–64 ; idem, 'Die syrische Rechtsliteratur', *Nos Sources: Arts et Littérature Syriaques* (Antelias, Libanon 2005) 261–72; idem, 'La littérature pseudo-canonique syriaque', *Les Apocryphes syriaques*, ed. A. Desreumaux et al. (Études syriaques 2; Paris 2005) 147–67; idem, 'Carlo Alfonso Nallinos Arbeiten zum Recht der orientalischen Christen', Studi Maġrebini, Nuova Serie, vol. 7 (Naples 2010) 133–47.

Pseudo-Apostolic Texts

Didascalia

This work that regulated the life of the Church probably arose in Syria at the beginning of the third century. Only a few fragments survive of what was certainly originally a Greek text, and it survives in part in a Latin translation, and in a complete Syriac translation. It appears in several canonical collections in the Western Syrian Church, only after the seventh and eighth centuries. It seems not to have had significant influence on later legal sources, though it is cited a few times in the *Nomokanon* of Bar Hebraeus.

Newest edition and translation: A. Vööbus, *The Didascalia Apostolorum in Syriac* (2 vols. in 4; CSCO 401–2; 407–8; Louvain 1979)

Translations: H. Achelis and J. Flemming, *Die ältesten Quellen des orientalischen Kirchenrechts*, 2: *Die syrische Didaskalia* (TU 25.2; Leipzig 1904); F. Nau, *La Didascalie des douze apôtres* (2nd ed. Littérature canonique 1; Paris 1912); R. H. Conolly, *Didascalia Apostolorum: The Syriac Version Translated* (Oxford 1929, reprint Norwich 1969).

Literature: ClavisG 1738; Baumstark, *Syrische Literatur* 263; G. Bardy, 'Didascalie d'Apôtres', DDC 4 (1942) 1218–24; Altaner, *Patrologie* 84–85 (earlier translations and literature); J. C. J. Sanders, 'Autour de la Didascalie', *A Tribute to Arthur Vööbus: Studies in Early Christian Literature and Its Environment, Primarily in the Syrian East*, ed. R. H. Fischer (Chicago 1977) 47–54; Steimer, *Vertex Traditionis* 49–59; LACL 167–68 (Steimer); Johannes Mühlsteiger, *Kirchenordnungen: Anfänge kirchlicher Rechtsbildung* (Kanonistische Studien und Texte, 50; Berlin 2006) 95–107.

Apostolic Church Order

This work, which probably originated in Egypt at the start of the fourth century, appears among the Western Syrians only as a part (book 3) of the *Octateuchus Clementinus* (see below) and as an insertion in chapter 3 of the Syriac *Didascalia* (only in some manuscripts).

Edition and English translation: A. Stewart Sykes, *The Apostolic Church Order*; J. P. Arentzen, 'An Entire Syriac Text of the "Apostolic Church Order",' JTS 3 (1902) 59–80. More editions and translations, see below with the *Octateuchus Clementinus*.

Literature: Altaner, *Patrologie* 80, 254–55; Hanssens, *Hippolyte* 62–65; A. Vööbus, 'Die Entdeckung der ältesten Urkunde für die syrische Übersetzung der Apostolischen Kirchenordnung', OrChr 63 (1979) 37–40. Steimer, *Vertex Traditionis* 60–71; Mühlsteiger, *Kirchenordnungen* 105–117; A. Stewart-Sykes, *The Apostolic Church Order. The Greek Text with Introduction and Annotation*, Strathfield, NSW (Australia) (= Early Christian Studies, vol. 10).

Testament of Our Lord Jesus Christ *(Testamentum Domini Nostri Jesu Christi)*

This extensive work consists of an edition of the 'Church Order' of Hippolytus. It forms the first two books of the *Octateuchus Clementinus*, and it appears mainly in this form (among others) in those Western Syrian canonical collections that also contain the *Didascalia*; these texts were placed at the beginning of the work only later. As may be noted from a remark at the conclusion of the manuscripts, the 'Testament' was first translated from Greek into Syriac in 686–87 by Jacob (of Edessa, see below). The Copts knew of a similar text.

Edition: I. E. Rahmani, *Testamentum Domini Nostri Jesu Christi nunc primum edidit, latine reddidit et illustravit* (Mainz 1899, reprint, Hildesheim 1968). For other editions, see *Octateuchus Clementinus*.

Translations: Rahmani, *Testamentum Domini*; J. Cooper and A. J. MacLean, *The Testament of Our Lord: Translated into English from the Syriac with Introduction and Notes* (Edinburgh 1902); G. Sperry-White, *The Testamentum Domini: A Text for Students* (Bramcote, Nottingham 1991). For more, see *Octateuchus Clementinus*.

Literature: ClavisG 1743. Baumstark, 'Ueberlieferung und Bezeugung der Διαθήκη τοῦ Κυρίου', *Römische Quartalschrift* 14 (1900) 1–45; Baumstark, *Syrische Literatur* 252; Altaner, *Patrologie* 257; S. Janin, 'Testamentum domini nostri Jesu Christi', DDC 7 (1965) 1206–7; Hanssens, *Hippolyte* 70–73; R.-G. Coquin, 'Le Testamentum Domini: Problèmes de tradition textuelle', ParOr 5 (1974) 165–88; Selb, *Orientalisches Kirchenrecht* 2.93–95; Steimer, *Vertex Traditionis* 95–105; M. Kohlbacher, 'Wessen Kirche ordnete das Testamentum Domini Nostri Jesu Christi?' *Zu Geschichte, Theologie, Liturgie und Gegenwartslage der syrischen Kirchen*, ed. M. Tamcke, A. Heinz (Studien zur Orientalischen Kirchengeschichte 9; Hamburg 2000) 55–137; Mühlsteiger, *Kirchenordnungen* 245–55. See also under Copts (p. 270).

Octateuchus Clementinus

This collection of pseudo-apostolic canons perhaps goes back to the Western Syrian Bishop Jacob of Edessa, who was the first to translate a part of the texts received from the Greek. It is divided into eight books, probably having been modeled after the Apostolic Constitutions, but purports to be the work of the disciple of the apostles, Clement of Rome; it consists of the 'Testament of Our Lord Jesus Christ' (books 1 and 2), the Apostolic Church Order (book 3), a parallel text to the eighth book of the 'Apostolic Constitutions', also surviving in Greek (books 4–7), as well as the 'Apostolic Canons' (book 8). The *Octateuchus Clementinus* stands after the Didascalia at the beginning of the comprehensive Syrian canonical collection, which probably was compiled by Jacob of Edessa. The Copts knew of a similar collection in Arabic. Books 6 and 8 of the *Octateuch* are also found among the Eastern Syrians.

Editions (only excerpts): Lagarde, *Reliquiae syriace* 2–32 (books 1–3, 6) 44–61 (book 8); Vööbus, *Synodicon* X.1–49 (books 1–2) 58–84 (8, 6). I am preparing an edition of the Syriac *Octateuchus Clementinus*.

Translations: F. Nau, *La version syriaque de l'Octateuque de Clément* (Littérature canonique 4; Paris 1913; reprint by P. Ciprotti, Milan 1967). Excerpts (see above): Vööbus, *Synodicon* (translation) X.27–64, 72–94.

Literature: Baumstark, *Syrische Literatur* 252; G. Bardy, 'Octateuque de Clément', DDC 6 (1967) 1065–66; A. Vööbus, 'Nouvelles sources de l'Octateuque Clémentin syriaque', *Muséon* 86 (1973) 105–9. H. Kaufhold, 'Octateuchus Clementinus', KLCO 393–943; Steimer, *Vertex Traditionis* 141–47; Mühlsteiger, *Kirchenordnungen* 257–60.

Teachings of the Apostles (Teachings of the Apostle Addai)

The text begins with an account of the Ascension of Christ and the assembly of the apostles for Pentecost, where 'ordinances and laws' were decreed. Then the 27 canons are given. There follows a narrative of the preaching activities of the apostles and an enumeration of their areas of mission. The proper title is 'Teachings of the Apostles'. Where it appears in Western Syrian manuscripts as the 'Teachings of the Apostle Addai', the title derives from a scribal error. The text actually has nothing to do with the famous legend of the Christianization of Edessa by the apostle Addai at the time of King Abgar, which circulated under the same title. It is to be found as 'The Teachings of the Apostle Addai' in several canonical collections of the Western Syrians, and the text is cited under that title by Bar Hebraeus in his *Nomokanon*. The Syriac text possibly is derived from a Greek model of the fourth century that does not survive. The canons deal with prayer, liturgy, festivals, ecclesiastical offices, and misconduct. Canon 24 permits orthodox kings to enter the altar area. These canons were also known to the Eastern Syrians.

Editions and translations: Lagarde, *Reliquiae syriace* 32–44; W. Cureton, *Ancient Syriac Documents* (London 1884) 24–35 (translation: 166–73); M. D. Gibson, *The Didascalia Apostolorum in Syriac* (Horae Semiticae 1; London 1903) 27–31; eadem, *The Didascalia Apostolorum in English* (Horae Semiticae 2; London 1903) 18–21; F. Nau, *La Didascalie des douze apôtres* (2nd ed. Littérature canonique 1; Paris 1912), Appendice 1: La Didascalie d'Addaï (pp. 223–24); Vööbus, *Synodicon* X.200–11 (translation: 187–97); a fragment: J.-M. Sauget, 'Le fragment de papyrus syriaque conservé à Florence', *Annali del Istituto Universitario Orientale* 45 (Naples 1985) 1–16; continuation, S. P. Brock, 'Two Syriac Papyrus Fragments from the Schøyen Collection', OrChr 79 (1995) 9–14.

Literature: Baumstark, *Syrische Literatur* 82–83; H. Kaufhold, 'Die "Lehre des Apostels Addai" (Lehre der Apostel),' *Paul de Lagarde und die syrische Kirchengeschichte* (Göttinger Arbeitskreis für syrische Kirchengeschichte; Göttingen 1968) 102–28; A. Vööbus, 'New

Light on the Text of the Canons in the Doctrine of Addai', *Journal of the Syriac Academy* 1 (Baghdad 1975) 3–21; W. Witakowski, 'The Origin of the "Teaching of the Apostles"', IV Symposium Syriacum 1984 (OCA 229; Rome 1987) 161–71; A. Desreumaux, 'Les titres des œuvres apocryphes chrétinees et leurs corpus: Le cas de la 'Doctrine d'Addai' syriac', *La formation des canons scripturaires*, ed. M. Tardieu (Paris 1993) 203–17 (at 214–15).

Synodal Canons

Greek Synods

The Syriac canons of the Greek synods are preserved in two versions. We are well informed about one of these translations. From a note in British Library Add. 14528 we know that the translation into Syriac was made in the year 812 of the Seleucid era (501–502 A.D.) in Mabbug (Hierapolis).[75] It contains the Antiochean *Corpus canonum* that was already enlarged and included the Synod of Chalcedon.[76] The canons are not only numbered within the individual synods, but each canon in the text is also consecutively numbered from 1 to 193. The other Syriac translation comprises almost the same texts.[77] In both translations there are four canons from Constantinople I. Canon two corresponds to the Greek canons two and three; canon three to the Greek canons four and five. The Greek canon seven is missing in the Syriac and the Melikite collections (see above). The relationship of the two translations to each other must be studied further. The second translation is probably just an adaptation of the first. It is closer to the original Greek text.

The second translation was probably made at the end of the seventh century by Jacob of Edessa. He adapted the first translation with the help of a Greek version.[78] While both of the translations knew only one Ephesian canon which corresponded to the seventh Greek canon, Jacob's revision contains two canons from Ephesos, which are identical with the eighth and seventh Greek canons. Furthermore several other documents are added: e.g. a letter of the fathers of Nicaea to the church of Alexandria and a letter from Antioch to Alexander of 'New Rome'.[79] Only in the later collections were Cyprian's synod in Carthage from the year 256 added (also translated by Jacob of Edessa from the Greek in 686–87), as

---

75. W. Wright, *Catalogue of Syriac Manuscripts in the British Museum* (London 1871) 2.1032.

76. E.g. British Library, Add. 14,528 (6. Jh.), British Library Add. 14,529 (7./8. Jh.), Harvard Syr. 93 (8./9. Jh.), Damaskus Orth. 8/11 (1204).

77. E.g. Hss. British Library Add. 14,526 (7. Jh.), British Library Add. 12,155 (8. Jh.), Vat. Syr. 127 (9. Jh.).

78. Zur griechischen Vorlage: H. Kaufhold, Welche Kirchenrechtsquellen kannte Patriarch Severos von Antiocheia.

79. E.g. Mardin Orth. 309 (8th/9th cent.) and 310 (9th/10th cent.), Paris Syr. 62 (9th cent.), Borg. Syr. 148 (1576).

well as 20 canons from the council of Sardica and a part of the acts of the council of Ephesos.

In contrast to collections of most of the other Eastern churches, the (73 Syrian) pseudo-Nicaean 'Canons of the 318 Fathers of Nicaea' are not found in the chronological collections of the Western Syrians. Bar Hebraeus cited them only twice in his *Nomokanon* (7.1 and 10); in the second citation, he asserted, 'This derives from the second book of the Synod of Nicaea, whose canons number 84 among the Greeks and Syrians'. The mention of this number implies the use of the Arabic version. Probably Bar Hebraeus acquired both citations from an Arabic version of either Melkites or Maronites (= Syrians?). According to the Copt Abū 'l-Barakāt, the text also had authority among the Jacobites.[80]

Editions: F. Schulthess, *Die syrischen Kanones der Synoden von Nicaea bis Chalcedon nebst einigen zugehörigen Dokumenten* (Abh. Göttingen, 2nd series, 10. 2; Berlin 1908); Lagarde, *Reliquiae syriace* 62–98 (synod of Cyprian of Carthage); Nau, 'Littérature canonique', 3.12–24 = ROC 14 (1909) 12–24 (letter from Antioch to Alexander; with translation), 3.62–4 = ROC 14 (1909) 125–27 (Ephesus); Vööbus, *Synodicon* 1.95–138 (English translation 85–139); H. Kaufhold, 'Die syrische Übersetzung des Briefes der Synode von Nikaia an die Kirche von Alexandreia', *Garten des Lebens: Festschrift für W. Cramer* (Münsteraner Theologische Abhandlungen 60; Altenberge 1999) 119–37.

Literature: ClavisG 8521; Selb, *Orientalisches Kirchenrecht* 2.98–102; idem, 'Die Kanonessammlungen der orientalischen Kirchen und das griechische Corpus canonum der Reichskirche', *Festschrift für W. M. Plöchl* (Vienna 1967) 371–83; B. Botte, 'Les plus anciens collections canoniques', OrSyr 5 (1960) 331–50; A. Vööbus, 'Discovery of Important Syriac Manuscripts on the Canons of the Ecumenical Councils', *Abr-Nahrain* 12 (Leiden 1972) 94–98; H. Kaufhold, 'Griechisch-syrische Väterlisten der frühen griechischen Synoden', OrChr 77 (1993) 1–96; V. Ruggieri, 'The IV Century Greek Episcopal List in the Mardin, Syriac 7 (olim Mardin Orth. 309/9)', OCP 59 (1993) 315–56.

Western Syrian Synods

The canons of the Western Syrian Church encompass highly varied themes of ecclesiology, discipline, liturgy, etc., so that what follows will make no more detailed reference to substantive content. Vööbus, *Kanonessammlungen* 5–127, offers a review of content. There also are many references to penal regulations.

The series of Western Syrian ecclesiastical councils of which canons have been preserved begins with the 22 canons of the synod that was held in 785 under the authority of Patriarch George in the vicinity of Sarug. The next was assembled in 794 under the Patriarch Kyriakos in the area of Harran and issued 46 canons. A further synod was held in Harran in 812–813 under the same patriarch (26 canons). His successor, Dionyius of

---

80. Samir Khalil, *Misbāh* 135; Riedel, *Kirchenrechtsquellen* 39.

Tel-Maḥrē, called the next ecclesiastical assembly in 817–818 in Kallinikos, with 12 canons. The synod that met during the reign of Patriarch John in 846 at a monastery near Sarug issued 26 canons. All that survives of a synod held under the same patriarch in Kefartūtā is a citation in the *Nomokanon* of Bar Hebraeus (chapter 7, item 1, at the end); it deals with the relationship between the patriarch and the second-ranking bishop, residing in present-day Iraq, the 'Maphrian'. The first two of the 12 canons of Patriarch Ignatios, issued at a synod in a monastery near Kallinikos, do not survive. The entire collection of canons of Western Syrian synods is completed with the 15 canons of the synod of Patriarch Dionysius held in a monastery near Sarug in 896, preceded by an introductory text of the synodal Fathers. It is not known who compiled the collection. It is preserved only in manuscript 8/11 of the Syrian Orthodox Patriarchate in Damascus. Other than citations in systematic miscellaneous collections (see below), there are only scattered textual witnesses for this conciliar collection; thus, for example, the canons of Kyriakos are also found in British Library Add. 14,493.[81]

Naturally there are other synods whose decisions are not preserved, or are known only from citations, or which issued no canons. For example, the synod held in 1064 under Patriarch John as well as those held in 1166, 1169, and 1174 under Patriarch Michael the Syrian are such synods. Further, we posses the canons of a few local synods, such as those of the monastery of Mar Mattai (629) and of the Metropolitan John of Mardin (about 1153).

Edition: Vööbus, *Synodicon* 2.1–68, 190–97, 233–56 (translation, 1–64, 197–208, 247–69).

Literature: J. Mounayer, *Les synodes syriens jacobites* (Beirut 1963); Vööbus, *Kanonessammlungen* 5–127; Selb, *Kirchenrecht* 2.119–29; H. Teule, 'Le lettre synodale de Cyriaque, patriarche monophysite d'Antioche (793–817)', *Orientalia Lovaniensia periodica* 9 (1978) 121–40.

Translations of Greek Canon Law Writings

Earliest Corpus

The 'Fifteen Questions' of Timothy of Alexandria belongs to the oldest tradition of Western Syrian chronological collections, and, alone of all the writings of the Fathers in Greek canonical collections, it seems to have been translated into Syriac at a very early date. In the older collections it immediately follows the Council of Chalcedon.

Edition and translation: Vööbus, *Syndicon* 1.140–43 (translation, 138–41).
Translation: Nau, 'Littérature canonique', 3.35–37 = ROC 14 (1909) 35–37.
Literature: ClavisG 2520; Selb, *Orientalisches Kirchenrecht* 2.110–11.

---

81. French translation, Mounayer, *Les synodes syriens jacobites* 45–54 (see below).

First Stage of Augmentation of Canonical Collections

It is obvious that some further canonical texts of Greek origins were later received into Syrian canon law collections. They are useful for the history of Byzantine canon law because they no longer survive in Greek, even though they mostly came from Monophysite authors. They are preserved as additions in London, British Library Add. 12,155 (eighth century) and 14,527 (eleventh century). There we find the following texts, all of them from the first half of the sixth century: (1) 42 'Chapters written out of the Orient'; (2) 7 'Ecclesiastical canons issued by the Holy Fathers in the time of persecution'; (3) 'From a letter which the Holy Fathers wrote to the priests and abbots Paulos and Paulos and the village of Lisos in the region of Cilicia'; (4) 'From the letter of the Holy Konstantinos, Metropolitan of Laodiceia, to Abbot Markos from Isauria'; (5) 'From a letter which one of the holy bishops wrote to his friend'; (6) 5 'Canons of Theodosios of Alexandria'.

Editions: (1) I. E. Rahmani, *Studia Syriaca* (Sharfeh 1908) 3.5–23 of the Syriac pagination; Vööbus, *Synodicon* X.163–76; (2)Vööbus, *Synodicon* I.159–163; (3) Vööbus, *Synodicon* I.176–79; (4) Vööbus, *Synodicon* I.178–79; (5) Vööbus, *Synodicon* I.180–82; (6) I. B. Chabot, *Documenta ad origines monophysitarum illustrandas* (CSCO 17; Louvain 1933) 79–84; A. van Roey —P. Allen, *Monophysite Texts of the Sixth Century* (Orientalia Lovaniensia Analecta 56; Leuven 1994) 255–59.

Translations: (1) Rahmani, *Studia Syriaca*; Vööbus, *Synodicon* 1.157–68; Nau, 'Littérature canonique' 3.39-48 = ROC 14 (1909) 39–48; (2) Nau, 'Littérature canonique' 3.50-52 = ROC 14 (1909) 113-115; Vööbus, *Synodicon* 1.154-157; (3) Nau, 'Littérature canonique' 3.52–53 = ROC 14 (1909) 116f.; Vööbus, *Synodicon* 1.168–70; (4) Nau, 'Littérature canonique' 3.53 = ROC 14 (1909) 117–19; Vööbus, *Synodicon* 1.170–71; (5) Nau, 'Littérature canonique' 3.53–55 = ROC 14 (1909) 117–19; Vööbus, *Synodicon* 1.171–73; (6) Nau, 'Littérature canonique' 3.57–60 = ROC 14 (1909) 120–23. Chabot, *Documenta* 55–58; van Roey–Allen, *Monophysite Texts* 260–63.

Literature: H. Kaufhold, 'Unbeachtete Quellen byzantinischen Kirchenrechts aus dem 6. Jh.', *Kirchenrecht und Ökumene: Festgabe für P. Rodopoulos* (Kanon XV. Jahrbuch der Gesellschaft für das Recht der Ostkirchen; Eichenau 1999) 113–30 (general).

(1) ClavisG 7109; Vööbus, *Kanonessammlungen* 167–75 (giving the substantive content of the canons); Selb, *Orientalisches Kirchenrecht* 2.113–14; (2) ClavisG 7108; Vööbus, *Kanonessammlungen*, 269–73; Selb, *Orientalisches Kirchenrecht* 2.114; (3) Vööbus, *Kanonessammlungen* 164–67; Selb, *Orientalisches Kirchenrecht* 2.114; (4) ClavisG 7107; Selb, *Orientalisches Kirchenrech* 2.114–15; (5) ClavisG 7110; Vööbus, *Kanonessammlungen* 182–83; Selb, *Orientalisches Kirchenrecht* 2.115; (6) ClavisG 7138; Vööbus, *Kanonessammlungen* 223–27; Selb, *Orientalisches Kirchenrecht* 2.115.

The Second Stage of Augmentation of the Canonical Collections

In a second stage, for which Jacob of Edessa (end of the seventh century) appears to be responsible, a canonical collection arose that survives in several manuscripts (Mardin, Orth. 309, 310; Vat. Syr. 520; Paris, Syr. 62;

Vat. Borg. Syr. 148) containing much more Greek material, including texts that have been lost in Greek. These texts are: (1) a letter from Italy to the bishops of the East (in actuality it is an excerpt of the third letter of Basil to Amphilochios), (2) excerpts from the letters of Ignatios of Antioch, (3) the text of Peter of Alexandria on 'lapsi', (4) letters of Athanasius of Alexandria, (5) of Gregory of Nyssa (to Litoios), (6) of John of Cyprus to Egypt, (7) from Constantinople to Martyrios of Antioch,[82] (8) of Severos of Antioch to various persons, (9) of Anthimos of Constantinople to Jacob of Edessa, (10) 12 canons of Basil for monks, (11) canons of one Sergios Amphiator, and others. It is possible that at the same time secular texts were included in the collection namely, the *Sententiae Syriacae* and the *Syro-Roman Lawbook*.

Editions of several or individual texts: Lagarde, *Reliquiae syriace* 99–117 (Peter of Alexandria); Nau, 'Littérature canonique', 3.27–31 = ROC 14 (1909) 27–31 (*Letter from Italy*); Vööbus, *Synodicon*, 1, passim; W. Selb, *Sententiae Syriacae* (Vienna 1990); Selb-Kaufhold, *Rechtsbuch*, vol. 2.

Translations: Nau, 'Littérature canonique' 3.25–27 (Letter from Italy); 3.48–49 = ROC 14 (1909) 48–49 (John of Cyprus); 3.56–57 = ROC 14 (1909) 119–20 (Martyrios); 3.57 = ROC 14 (1909) 120 (Severos); 3.60–61 = ROC 14 (1909) 123–24 (Anthimos); 3.64–65 = ROC 14 (1909) 127–28 (Sergios Amphiator and others); Vööbus, *Synodicon* 1, passim; W. Selb, *Sententiae Syriacae* (Vienna 1990); Selb-Kaufhold, *Rechtsbuch*, vol. 2.

Literature: Vööbus, *Kanonessammlungen*, passim; Selb, *Orientalisches Kirchenrecht* 2.110–19.

Canons of Western Syrian Fathers

Alongside translations from Greek there are numerous canonical texts that were originally composed in Syriac. Only the most important will be mentioned in what follows.[83]

1. Rabbula, noted Syrian author and bishop of Edessa († 435), composed monastic canons and 59 rules for clerics and 'Sons of the Covenant', a particular group of ascetics.

Edition and translation: Vööbus, *Documents* 24–50.

Translation: Nau, 'Littérature canonique' 2.83–91 = CC 28 (1905) 645–53.

Literature: ClavisG 6490–92; Baumstark, *Syrische Literatur* 71–73; L. Köhler, 'Zu den Kanones des Rabbula, Bischofs von Edessa', *Schweizerische Theologische Zeitschrift* 30 (Zürich

---

82. The largest part of the text in the Greek collections is canon seven of the First Council of Constantinople (ClavisG 5983) and canon 95 of the Council in Trullo. In the West Syrian collection contained in London, British Library 14528 (beginning of the sixth century) the text follows the Council of Chalcedon; the name of Martyrios does not appear, see Friedrich Schulthess, *Die syrische Kanones der Synoden von Nicaea bis Chalkedon nebst einigen zugehörigen Dokumenten* (Abh. Göttingen, 2nd series, 10.2; Berlin 1908) ix, 145 (text).

83. Further details can be found particularly in Vööbus, *Kanonessammlungen* 128–306, passim; numerous citations in Hindo, *Personnes, Sacrements* and *Lieux*. Some other texts are contained in the *Nomokanon* of Bar Hebraeus (see below); translation of these texts in Nau, 'Littérature canonique' 2.92–97, 101–2 = CC (1905–6).

1908) 210–13; idem, 'Nochmals die Kanones des Rabbula, Bischofs von Edessa', ibid., 31 (1909), 133–34; Vööbus, *Kanonessammlungen* 128–38; Selb, *Orientalisches Kirchenrecht* 2.113.

2. The rules of Symeon Stylites, the respected ascetic and spiritual advisor († 459) tend more to regulate social life in general, but they also deal with canonical matters in the narrower sense.

Translation: H. Hilgenfeld in H. Lietzmann, *Das Leben des heiligen Simeon Stylites* (Leipzig 1908) 180ff.

Literature: ClavisG 6642; Baumstark, *Syrische Literatur* 60–61; Vööbus, *Kanonessammlungen* 138–46; Selb, *Orientalisches Kirchenrecht* 2.159.

3. Johannes bar Qursos, bishop of Tella († 538), composed two series of canons. The first (27 canons) regulated various canonical questions and had been already included in older collections (before Jacob of Edessa). His 48 'Answers to the Questions of Sergios the Priest' deal with the liturgy.

Editions and translations: T. J. Lamy, *Dissertatio de Syrorum fide* (Louvain 1859) 62–97; C. Kuberczyk, *Canones Johannis bar Cursus, Tellae Mauzlatae episcopi, e codicibus syriacis Parisino et quattuor Londiniensibus editi* (Diss. phil. Breslau; Leipzig 1901); Vööbus, *Synodicon* 1.145–56, 211–21 (translation, 142–51, 197–205).

Translation: Nau, 'Littérature canonique' 2.8–30 = CC 26 (1903) 408–19, 532–42.

Literature: Baumstark, *Syrische Literatur* 174; Vööbus, *Kanonessammlungen* 56–164, 263–69. Selb, *Orientalisches Kirchenrecht* 2.163.

4. Athanasios of Balad, Western Syrian patriarch from 683/84 to 686, hence already under Muslim rule, regulates the relationship to Muslims and heretics, among others, in four canons.

Edition and translation: F. Nau, 'Littérature canonique' 3.65–67 = ROC 14 (1909) 128–30.

Literature: Baumstark, *Syrische Literatur* 256–57; Vööbus, *Kanonessammlungen* 200–202.

5. The metropolitan Jacob of Edessa († 708), a very productive theological author and translator who has already been frequently mentioned, is of special importance for Western Syrian canon law. He is probably responsible for combining the *Octateuchus Clementinus* and the new edition of the chronological canonical collection already described. This collection contained many new texts. He also composed several series of canons that survive in various versions and that need further study. These consist particularly of the 24 canons, of letters to Thomas the Hermit, answers to Addai the Priest (two tracts), of John the Stylite (27 and 17 questions) as well as of Abraham the Hermit (3 questions). He is also the author of a work that survives only in part and that deals with those who violate the canons, among other things. Michael the Syrian reports in his chronicle (2. 472) that Jacob, when he was not able to gain approval from the patriarch and bishops for his demands of stricter obedience to the canons, ordered a collection of canons burned before the gates of the patriarchate monastery while shout-

ing, 'I am burning the canons you are treating as superfluous and worthless, treading underfoot and do not respect'.

Editions and translations: C. Kayser, *Die Canones Jacob's von Edessa, übersetzt und erläutert* (Leipzig 1886); Lagarde, *Reliquiae syriace* 117–44; Vööbus, *Synodicon* X.221–72 (translation: 206–47); K.-E. Rignell, *A Letter from Jacob of Edessa to John the Stylite. Syriac Text with Introduction, Translation and Commentary* (Malmö 1979); Vööbus, *Synodicon* 1.221–72 (translation: 206–47).

Translation: Nau, 'Littérature canonique', 2.38–75 = CC 27 (1904) 269–76, 366–76, 468–77, 562–72.

Literature: Baumstark, *Syrische Literatur* 248–56; R. Naz, 'Jacques d'Edesse', DDC 6 (1957) 82; A. Vööbus, 'The Discovery of New Cycles of Canons and Resolutions composed by Jaʿqōb of Edessa', OCP 34 (1968) 412–19; idem, *Kanonessammlungen* 202–16, 273–98; Selb, *Orientalisches Kirchenrecht* 2.117.

6. The 10 responses to questions of a deacon Yešūʿ concerning the liturgy by the Patriarch Kyriakos (793–817).

Edition and translation: Vööbus, *Synodicon* 2.180–84 (translation, 185–88).

Literature: Vööbus, *Kanonessammlungen* 298–99; Selb, *Orientalisches Kirchenrecht* 131, 170.

7. A brief listing of forbidden marriages written by Patriarch John (846–73).

Edition and translation: Vööbus, *Synodicon* 2.46–50 (translation, 49–53). French translations of a similar text in Nau, *La Didascalie des douze apôtres* (Littéraire canonique 1; Paris 1912) 1.235–37.

8. One of the most important authors of the twelfth century was Dionysius bar Salībī, who died as metropolitan of Amida in 1171. He wrote canons on fasting. He also composed canons on donations to churches and monasteries. Dionysius is also the author of an extensive tract that included penitential canons. It usually contains nine chapters, of which the last two include canons on diverse sins and their punishment. The others deal with sins and penance in a more general form, including the rite of penance.

Translation of the penitential canons: H. Denzinger, *Ritus Orientalium* (vol. 1; Würzburg 1863) 493–500 (other penitential canons, 474–93).

Literature: Baumstark, *Syrische Literatur* 295–98; J. Dauvillier, 'Denys bar Salibhi', DDC 4 (1949) 1128–31; Vööbus, *Kanonessammlungen* 240–53, 405–39; Selb, *Orientalisches Kirchenrecht* 2.158, 164.

9. Canons on the election and duties of office for patriarchs are thought to derive from Dionysius bar Salībī and the Patriarch Michael the Syrian (1166–99). A tract ascribed to Michael on ecclesiastical *Oikonomia* (a dispensation from the strict rules of the canons)[84] was written not by him but by an unknown author of the ninth century.

---

84. P. L'Huillier, 'L'economie dans la tradition de l'Église Orthodoxe', *Kanon: Jahrbuch für das Recht der Ostkirchen* 6 (1993) 19–38; P. Rhodopoulos, 'Oikonomia nach orthodoxem Kirchenrecht', *Österreichisches Archiv für Kirchenrecht* 36 (1986) 223–31.

Literature: Baumstark, *Syrische Literatur* 298–300; A. Vööbus, *Kanonessammlungen* 254–56; idem, 'Discovery of a Treatise about the Ecclesiastical Administration Ascribed to Michael the Syrian', *Church History* 47 (1978) 23–26; H. Kaufhold, 'Ein syrischer Brief über die kirchenrechtliche Oikonomia', OrChr 73 (1989) 44–67.

10. Two anonymous texts that circulated in Arabic were written at a later, not yet determined time. They dealt with feasts, fasting, and the marriage of clerics.

Editions: F. Cöln, 'Eines Anonymus' Abhandlung über Feste und Fasten, Autorität und Gehorsam in der syrischen Kirche', OrChr 8 (1908) 230–77; F. Cöln, 'Über Priesterehe und degradation in der syrisch-jakobitischen Kirche', OrChr 8 (1908) 458–65.

11. The West-Syriac manuscript Cambridge Add. 2023, which could be dated to the thirteenth century, contains numerous texts of legal and other materials that are partially either not or only little known. They are of various origins and are put together without any discernable organizational principles. Among other things, it contains a long pseudo-apostolic text with the rubric: 'Discourse ascribed to St. John the Evangelist delivered at Constantinople'. It begins with a prolix, moral admonition addressed primarily to priests and deacons. In this section the author treats for the most part questions about the Eucharist. After this work the manuscript contains numerous canonical texts dealing with many different subjects, in particular some that treat ecclesiastical offices. Marriage law is also handled. The rules are partially known from other sources, but here reasons for the rules are given in much more detail. The work is not yet edited and needs a thorough study.

Monastic Canons

A widely distributed genre of canonical literature was canons for monks and monasteries. The authors of these texts, in some cases already named, are Ephrem the Syrian (spurious), Rabbūlā, Philoxenos of Hieropolis (Mabbug), Johannes bar Qursus, Jacob of Edessa, George the Bishop of Arabs, Patriarch Kyriakos, and John of Mardin; there are also some anonymous writings.

Editions and translations of several sources: Vööbus, *Documents*; only translations: idem, *History of Asceticism in the Syrian Orient* (CSCO 500; Louvain 1988) 3.170–93, 279–96, 350–60, 411–27 (in each case under the title 'Monasticism in the light of the legislative sources').

Individual editions and translations: Nau, 'Littérature canonique', 3.37–38 (Philoxenos); J. Mounayer, 'Les canons relatifs aux moines, attribué à Rabboula', OCP 20 (1954) 406–15; A. Vööbus, 'Ein Zyklus der Verordnungen für die Ausbildung der Novizen im syrischen Mönchtum', OrChr 59 (1975) 36–46; Vööbus, *Synodicon* 2.211–32 (translation, 223–45) (canons for the monasteries of Mar Hananyā and Mar Abai).

Literature: Vööbus, *Kanonessammlungen* 307–404; Selb, *Orientalisches Kirchenrecht* 2.131–32, 166–71. On individual sources: A. de Halleux, *Philoxène de Mabbog* (Louvain 1963)

197–98; A. Vööbus, 'Eine wichtige Urkunde über die Geschichte des Mār Hananjā Klosters: Die von Jōhannān von Mardē gegebene(n) Klosterregel', OrChr 53 (1969) 246–52; idem, 'Entdeckung einer neuen Klosterregel über die Zusammenwirkung der klösterlichen Gemeinschaften, verfasst von Johannan von Marde', ZKG 88 (1977) 330–32; idem, 'Syrische Verordnungen für die Novizen und ihre handschriftliche Überlieferung', OrChr 54 (1970) 106–12.

Eastern Syrian Legal Sources

We also find some Eastern Syrian legal sources among the Western Syrians. They consist of the synod of the Katholikos Isaac in 410 (Synod of Persian Bishops in Seleucia-Ctesiphon, cf. section on the canon law of the Eastern Syrians, see below). The synod owes its reception to Jacob of Edessa, since it first appears in the chronological collection that he compiled. In manuscripts from the twelfth and thirteenth century (Cambridge University, Add. 2023; Holy Monastery of St. Catherine, Sinai Syr. 82) we find further excerpts from the law codes of the Eastern Syrian Katholikos Timotheus I and Īšōʿbarnūn (eighth–ninth centuries). All three of these sources are cited in the *Nomokanon* of Bar Hebraeus.

Edition of the synod of Seleucia-Ctesiphon: J. T. Lamy, *Concilium Seleuciae et Ctesiphonti habitum anno 410* (Louvain 1868) 21–86; excerpt, Vööbus, *Synodicon* I.198–99.

Translation: Lamy, *Concilium Seleuciae*; Nau, 'Littéraire canonique', 2.98–101 = CC 29 (1906) 5–8; (only quotations from the *Nomokanon* of Bar Hebraeus); Vööbus, *Synodicon* X.186–87.

Literature: Kaufhold, *Gabriel von Basra* 51–56; Vööbus, *Kanonessammlungen* 303.

Bar Hebraeus

With the Maphrian Gregorios Abu ʾl-farağ Bar ʿEbrōyō ('Bar Hebraeus'), an extraordinarily multifaceted but not always original writer († 1286), Western Syrian literature reaches its last peak before beginning its decline in the fourteenth century.[85]

Bar Hebraeus composed the first and only comprehensive systematic legal collection of the Western Syrians, the 'Book of Direction' (Ktōbō d-Hudōyō), which is better known in the literature under the title of *Nomokanon*. The work contains 40 chapters of ecclesiastical and civil law. Bar Hebraeus cites the sources already known from the chronological collections, specifically pseudo-apostolic texts, Greek synods, canons and writings of Greek and Syrian Fathers, Eastern Syrian texts, the *Syro-Roman Lawbook*, and (without attribution) Islamic law. In most cases he exploits his sources freely, abbreviating and altering them, but he also adds something of himself to them. The first eight chapters deal with ecclesiastical law and bear

---

[85]. Baumstark, *Syrische Literatur* 312–20; C. de Clercq, DDC 2 (1937) 204–6; J. M. Fiey, 'Esquisse d'une bibliographie de Bar Hébraeus', ParOr 13 (1986) 279–312.

the following titles: (1) On the Church and its leadership; (2) On Baptism; (3) About the divine Myron; (4) About the Eucharist; (5) About fasting, festivals and prayer; (6) About the burial of the dead; (7) About the ranks of priests; (8) About marriage. The *Nomokanon* still enjoys great respect and today is regarded as authoritative by the Syrian Orthodox Church. The *Nomokanon* also exists in an excerpted Syriac version, in two Arabic translations, and in an Arabic epitome in seventeen chapters (probably by Daniel ibn al-Ḥattāb, fourteenth century) and also in a Malayalam (South Indian) translation.

In his presentation of moral doctrine, the *Ethicon* (Kṯōḇō d-Ēṯīqōn), Bar Hebraeus also deals with questions of ecclesiastical law, frequently citing canonistic literature.

Nomokanon: Editions: P. Bedjan, *Nomocanon Gregorii Barhebraei* (Paris-Leipzig 1898); [J. Çiçek,] *Nomocanon of Bar Hebraeus* (Glane-Losser 1986).

Translations: I. A. Assemanni, 'Ecclesiae Antiochenae Syrorum Nomocanon a Gregorio Abulpharagio Bar-Hebraeo syriace compositus', printed in A. Mai, SVNC 10 (1838) 1–268; excerpts: G. Ricciotti, *Disciplina antiochena* [Siri] 1: *Nomocanone di Bar-Hebraeo* (Fonti, Serie 1, fasc. 3; Vatican City 1931).

Literature: Vööbus, *Kanonessammlungen* 499–561; Selb, *Orientalisches Kirchenrecht* 2.154–57; Fiey, 'Esquisse' 293–95 (droit canon); C. A. Nallino, 'Il diritto musulmano nel Nomocanone siriaco cristiano di Barhebreo', *Rivisti degli studi orientali* 9 (1921/23) 512–80 (= *Raccolta* 214–90); Kaufhold, *Gabriel von Basra* 51–55; C. Gallagher, *Church Law and Church Order in Rome and Byzantium. A Comparative Study* (Aldershot 2002) (= Birmingham Byzantine and Ottoman Monographs, vol. 8) 191–203; H. Takahashi, *Barhebraeus: A Bio-Bibliography* (Piscataway 2005) 227–43.

On the Arabic translation: Graf, *Geschichte* 2.278; S. Khalil, 'Barhebraus, le <Daf' al-Hamm> et les <Contes Amusants>', OrChr 64 (1980) 153–54; Arabic epitome, Graf, *Geschichte* 2.283.

Ethicon: Editions: P. Bedjan, *Ethicon, seu Moralia Gregorii Barhebraei* (Paris-Leipzig 1898); [J. Çiçek] *Ethicon: Christian Ethics (Morals)* (Glane-Losser 1985); H. G. B. Teule, *Gregory Barhebraeus: Ethicon (Memra I)* (CSCO 534; Louvain 1993).

Translation: Teule, loc. cit. (= CSCO, 535).

Literature: Fiey, 'Esquisse' 291–92; H. G. B. Teule, 'Judicial Texts in the Ethicon of Bar Hebraeus', OrChr 79 (1995).

Other Sources

1. A law code containing mostly the Islamic law of inheritance is preserved in a (fragmentary) Arabic version as an appendix to the 'Law of Christianity' by the Eastern Syrian Ibn aṭ-Ṭaiyib, where it is attributed to the Eastern Syrian Katholikos Johannes bar Aḇgārē. Syriac versions, on the other hand, are preserved only in the Western Syrian tradition and are there attributed to 'Mār Ignatios and Mār Johannes', who were probably Western Syrian patriarchs. The question of the authorship of the work is open.

Editions: G. Furlani, 'Sulle divisione delle eredità di Giovanni V Abgare', *Accademia Nazionale dei Lincei, Rendiconti della Classe di Scienze morali, storiche e filologiche* (series 8, vol. 5, Rome 1950) 143–56; H. Kaufhold, *Syrische Texte zum islamischen Recht: Das dem nestorianischen Katholikos Johannes V. bar Aḇgārē zugeschriebene Rechtsbuch* (Abh. Munich 2nd series, 74; Munich 1971); idem, 'Islamisches Erbrecht in christlich-syrischer Überlieferung', OrChr 59 (1975) 19–35 (supplements); Vööbus, *Synodicon* 2.64–91.

Translations: Kaufhold, *Syrische Texte*; idem, 'Islamisches Erbrecht'; A. Vööbus, *Important New Manuscript Sources for the Islamic Law in Syriac* (Papers of the Estonian Theological Society in Exile 27; Stockholm 1975); idem, *Synodicon* 2.68–97.

Literature: H. Kaufhold, 'Über die Entstehung der syrischen Texte zum islamischen Recht', OrChr 69 (1985) 54–72; Selb, *Orientalisches Kirchenrecht* 1.78, 179; 2.137.

2. The fragmentary manuscript, Cambridge, Harvard University, Syr. 105 (olim Harris 99) preserves a remarkable canonical collection. In the seven surviving leaves there are excerpts of texts that are known from chronological collections (John bar Qurson, letter of a bishop to a friend, canons of Patriarchs Dionysius, Kyriakos, George, Ignatios, 'The Synod of Persian Bishops', letter of Basil to Parogorios). There is no recognizable systematic order.

Literature: Vööbus, *Kanonessammlungen* 487; Selb, *Orientalisches Kirchenrecht* 2.151.

3. The Arabic 'Book of the Guide' (Kitāb al-Muršid) of Abū Naṣr Yaḥyā ibn Ǧarīr (eleventh century) should be mentioned, which is a compendium of theology that is also of interest for ecclesiastical law.

(Editions and) translations: W. Cureton, *The Lamp that Guides to Salvation* (London 1865) (chapter 31: Priesthood); G. Khoury, 'Le Livre du Guide de Yahya ibn Jarīr', OrSyr 12 (1967) 303–54, 421–80 (chapter 29: 'De la Construction de l'église'; chapter 30: 'De la resurrection'; chapter 31: 'Du sacerdoce'); E. Aydin, *Die Entwicklung des Eherechts der syrisch-orthodoxen Kirche seit dem 11. Jahrhundert bis heute* (Vienna 1994) appendix (chapter 47: marital law).

Excerpts in Latin translation in Hindo, *Personnes;* idem, *Sacrements;* idem, *Lieux,* passim in each case (see the indices).

Literature: Graf, *Geschichte* 2.259–62; S. Jargy, ''Ibn Djarir 'at-Takriti', DDC 5 (1953) 1244–54; Selb, *Orientalisches Kirchenrecht* 2.165.

India

The Western Syrian Church took root in southern India (Kerala) only in the seventeenth century. After that date, their legal sources were authoritative. Many Syrian manuscripts, including some with juridical contents, reached indigenous Christians, whose Catholic branch is called the 'Syro-Malankaya Church'.

Systematically organized excerpts from various sources, including modern sources, translated into Latin: Placidus a S. Joseph [Podipara], *Fontes iuris canonici Syro-Malankarensium* (Fontes, serie 2, fasc. 9; Vatican City 1937).

Literature: N. J. Thomas, *Die Syrisch-Orthodoxe Kirche der Südindischen Thomas-Christen: Geschichte, Kirchenverfassung, Lehre* (Würzburg 1967); C. Malancharuvil, *The Syro Malankara Church* (Ernakulam 1974); Placidus a S. Joseph [Podipara], *Fontes iuris ecclesiastici Syro-Malankarensium: Commentarius historico-canonicus* (Fontes, serie 2, fasc. 8; Vatican City 1937); Kaufhold, *Syrische Handschriften*.

Maronites

History of the Church

Little is known of the history of the Maronite Church before the twelfth and thirteenth centuries. It had its origins in the patriarchate of Antioch. Its theological origin was the attempt made by the Byzantine emperors in the first half of the seventh century to resolve the christological dispute between the imperial church and the Monophysites through the compromise that Christ had only one will (Monothelitism). This doctrine did win many adherents, but in the end it did not win general acceptance. Its believers remained faithful only in the area of Lebanon and Syria. Its spiritual center was the monastery of St. Maron on the Orontes, after which the community was named. A Maronite ecclesiastical organization and hierarchy was established from the seventh and eighth centuries onward. Their use of the title 'patriarch of Antioch' for their leader is documented only in the twelfth century. During the era of crusades, the Maronites came into contact with the Latin Church and subjected themselves to the pope. The Maronite Church is the sole entire Eastern church to have remained in union with Rome.

Literature: Graf, *Geschichte* 1.65–68; 3.4–56; P. Dib, *L'Église maronite*, 1: *L'Église maronite jusqu'à la fin du Moyen-Age* (Paris 1930); 2: *Les Maronites sous les Ottomans du XVIe siècle à nos jours* (Beirut 1962); 3: (Beirut 1973); idem, *Histoire de l'église maronite* (Beirut 1962); Spuler, *Die morgenländischen Kirchen* 217–25; Atiya, *Eastern Christianity* 389–423; B. Dau, *Religious, Cultural and Political History of the Maronites* o. p. (Lebanon 1984); Breydy, *Syro-Arabische Literatur* 26–69; L. Wehbé, *L'église maronite* (Jerusalem 1985). G. Troupeau, 'L'église Maronite d'Antioche', *Histoire du Christianisme* 4.407–11 (*Geschichte des Christentums* 4.422–25); J. Richard, 'L'Église maronite', *Histoire du Christianisme* 6.226–27 (*Geschichte des Christentums* 6.222–23); H. Suermann, *Die Gründungsgeschichte der Maronitischen Kirche* (Wiesbaden 1998) (= Orienalia Biblica et Christiana, vol. 10).

Maronite Literature

The Maronites used Syriac as their language of conversation, liturgy, and literature. Very few written Syriac materials have survived, however. The first Arabic writings of the Maronites of which we know, but which does not survive, comes from the beginning of the tenth century. Later, particularly since the seventeenth century, Arabic-Maronite literature achieved considerable importance. Maronite scholars residing in Rome or elsewhere in

Europe have contributed considerably to the rise of Middle-Eastern Studies from the seventeenth century on.[86]

Maronite Canonical Sources

Since Maronite scholars worked in Europe on the history and literature of their Church and brought manuscripts with them, the canon law of the Maronites could have been well researched. Maronite scholarship had been primarily concerned with the more modern synodal canons that arose under Latin influence and with the papal legislation for the Uniate Eastern churches. The earliest sources are sparse, and therefore knowledge of early canon law is slight. Today this situation has not changed. Dib's narrative in the context of the codification of the law of the Eastern churches devotes only eight pages to 'ancient law', essentially restricted to listing the content of the sources. In 1935, to be sure, an important Arabic source was edited, the Kitāb al-Hudā, but it was not translated into a European language. Consequently this source has not been explored in the West, and research remains in the beginning stages. We can thank Georg Graf and Michael Breydy for more detailed information. Also Ibrahim Aouad treats some canonical doctrines in his book despite its title, though only for the later period. Charles de Clercq gave the first historical survey in his article in the *Dictionnaire du Droit Canonique*. The *Histoire du droit de l'église maronite* by Joseph Feghali, appearing in 1962, ignored the earlier period, as is shown the subtitle of the first volume: *Les conciles des XVIᵉ et XVIIᵉ siècles*.[87]

Kitāb al-Hudā

The best known of the Maronite legal collections, but not the most important in practice, is the Kitāb al-Hudā ('Book of Correct Guidance'). It is obviously not a single work but consists of several parts, probably from two completely distinct works.

The first part (chapters 1–13 of the Fahed edition) is a self-contained 'Book of Doctrine and Morals' (Graf) without juristic content. Two letters at the beginning inform us that a monastic priest named Joseph petitioned a Metropolitan David in A.D. 1058–59 to ask him to 'explain the

---

86. Baumstark, *Syrische Literatur* 339–43 (Literary life among the Maronites); Graf, *Geschichte* 2.94–102; 3.299–512; Breydy, *Syro-Arabische Literatur*.

87. Dib, 'Maroniti', 89–116; *Disciplina Antiochena: Maroniti. I. Ius particulare Maronitarum, A) Textus iuris approbati* [compiled by P. Sfair] (Fonti, fasc. 12; Vatican City 1933); I. Aouad, *Le droit privé des maronites au temps des Emirs Chihab (1697–1841) d'après des documents inédits. Essai historique et critique* (Paris 1933); C. de Clercq, 'Maronite (droit canonique)', DDC 6 (1957) 811–29; J. Feghali, Histoire du droit de l'église Maronite, 1: *Les conciles des XVIe et XVIIe siècles* (Paris 1962) [none further appeared]; H. Kaufhold, 'Die syrische Rechtsliteratur', *Nos Sources: Arts et Littérature Syriaques* (Antelias, Lebanon 2005) 272–74.

book that is attributed to the holy father and to translate it from Syriac to Arabic'. These two persons are otherwise not known to us, and it is also not said who the 'holy father' might be. In the response with which he sends the book, the bishop describes it as Kitāb al-Kamāl ('Book of Perfection'). Following a theological treatment of the necessity of faith ('Canon of Faith'), there follows, as the 'first canon', a 'broad-ranging treatise on the basic truths of Christian doctrine, the Trinity and the Incarnation'.[88] Following this are canons about prayer (3), purification from menstruation (4), the reason for purification and the times of prayer (5), mass and communion (6–8), baptism (9), fasts (10), and alms (11–13). A thorough listing of contents is found in Graf.[89] The work is marked by 'a casuistry elevated almost to an unbearable degree', by a 'certain lack of direction and breadth of narrative'.[90] The author does not cite ecclesiastical canons but rather refers generally to the commandments of the Apostles and the Fathers. In the second part, the work rests partially on the writings of the Eastern Syrian Elias of Nisibis, who worked in the first half of the eleventh century. Further, the author calls on the Eastern Syrian Ibn aṭ-Ṭaiyib, who died in 1043. The 'Book of Perfection' hence cannot have come into being long before its translation into Syriac; perhaps the Metropolitan David compiled it and then translated it into Arabic himself. The Monothelite confession of the author becomes evident in the theological treatise.[91] Since the seventeenth century, Maronite authors have stressed the 'perpetual orthodoxy' of their church. Consequently, they have held that Monothelite passages are later interpolations. The Maronite Patriarch Stephan ad-Duwaihi (1630–1704) mentioned the Kitāb al-Hudā in a report on the books of the Maronites reviewed by the papal legate Giambattista Eliano in 1578, and he writes:[92]

The eighth <book> is the Kitāb al-Hudā; it is old and recognized (maqbūl). It was composed in Syriac; then in the year of the Greeks 1370 [A.D. 1058–59] Metropolitan David translated it into Arabic. Then it fell into the hands of Thomas of Kefartāb; he inserted his confession concerning the one will <of Christ> on his own.

The second part of the Kitāb al-Hudā contains a series of legal sources and consists of many, originally scattered parts. Samir Khalil gave it the name of Kitāb an-Namūs ('Book of the Law'),[93] a name that is also used along with others (Kitāb al-Muhdī ['Book of the Leader']) Kitāb al-Qawānīn ('Book of Canons') for the entire work.[94]

88. Graf, 'Nomokanon' 215.
89. Graf, 'Nomokanon' 214–20.
90. Graf, 'Nomokanon' 216, 220.
91. Graf, 'Nomokanon' 215–16.
92. S. Kuri, Monumenta Proximi-Orientis I: Palestine-Liban-Syrie-Mésopotamie (1523–1583) (Rome 1989) 386 (text), 390 (not entirely correct translation).
93. Khalil, 'L'exposé' 258–59.
94. M. Breydy, Études maronites (Orientalia Biblica et Christiana 2; Glückstadt 1991) 86–94.

A series of pseudo-Nicene texts appears as chapters 14 to 22.[95] Chapters 23 to 29 are highly varied and in some cases from unknown sources. In these chapters are found canons 7, 8, and 10–20 from a 'synod of Constantinople', which has not been further identified. Breydy believes these canons are excerpts from the 73 pseudo-Nicene canons (of Mārūtā),[96] but the extent of textual agreement is not very convincing. A reputed canon of Kyrillos of Jerusalem on baptism and marriage also appears, as do two 'canons' of John the Evangelist,[97] theological tracts, and an explanation of the Lord's Prayer.[98]

The last part consists of a canonical collection with the standard set of texts, beginning with the 'Canons of Clement, which he [received, held and] wrote down', the 81 Apostolic canons and a parallel text to the eighth book of the *Apostolic Constitutions*. In addition, there follows a free editing of the canons of Nicaea, Ancyra, Neocaesarea, Gangra, Antioch, Laodiceia, Constantinople,[99] Chalcedon, and—at the end—Ephesus.[100] The next part is of unknown origin: 'canons of the synod gathering in Nicaea, canons of Basil and Gregory' on the *Apocrypha* of the Holy Scriptures.[101] At the end of the collection is the Arabic version of the *Syro-Roman Lawbook*. It is as yet unclear from which language this collection was translated.

The usual title for the entire work, *Kitāb al-Hudā*, appears to be of late date. Despite the statement by Stephan ad-Duwaihī, cited above, that the *Kitāb al-Hudā* was 'recognized', it is to be doubted that it played a large role among the Maronites in practice. Graf justly writes:[102]

> Due to the lack of an extensive literature from the earlier period, it cannot be said to what degree the canons assembled in the *Kitāb al-Hudā* had any genuine authority in the Maronite Church. On internal grounds one may hardly accept that the mass of the more theological 'decisions' of the first and original part ever had any practical application as a whole.

Consequently, few manuscripts have become known.[103] Further evidence that the Maronites made use of Coptic juristic works (see immediately be-

---

95. For more detail, see Graf, 'Nomokanon' 220–22.
96. Breydy, *Syro-Arabische Literatur*, 159–60
97. These are extracts from a 'Disourse ascribed to S. John the Evangelist delivered at Constantinople', which is transmitted in the ms. Cambridge Add. 2033, s. above (=p. 251 no. 11).
98. For more detail, see Graf, 'Nomokanon' 222–23.
99. The first six Greek canons are divided into four canons, as in the West Syrian collections.
100. There is only one canon from the Council of Ephesos, as in the West Syrian collections. It is the seventh canon from Ephesos; see Graf, 'Nomokanon' 223–25, for all these synods.
101. Ibid. 225–26.
102. Graf, *Geschichte* 2.97.
103. Vat. Syr. 133 (1402); Paris, Bibl. nat. syr. 223 (sixteenth century); Rome, Bibl. Ang. or. 64 (sixteenth century); P. Sbath, *Al-Fihris (Catalogue des manuscrits arabes)* (1st part; Cairo 1938) 338. Otherwise, there are manuscripts with excerpts, see Graf, *Geschichte* 2.98. On the primary manuscripts see also Breydy, *Études maronites* 108–35.

low) militates against a greater use of the *Kitāb al-Hudā*. More investigation will be required to resolve all the conundrums that arise from this source.

Edition: Pierre Fahed, *Kitāb al-Hudā, ou Livre de la Direction: Code maronite du Haut Moyen Age* (Aleppo 1935). Edition of the section on the Trinity: S. Khalil, 'L'exposé sur la Trinité du Kitāb al-Kamāl: Edition critique', ParOr 6–7 (1975–76) 257–79. Reprint of Kitāb al-kamāl: B. Fahed, *Kitāb al-Hudā. Dustūr aṭ-ṭā'ifat al-mārūnīya* (Beirut 1985).

Literature: On the entire work: Riedel, *Kirchenrechtsquellen* 146–48; P. Dib, 'Maroniti', 92–99; Graf, 'Nomokanon' 212–32; Graf, *Geschichte* 2.94–98; C. de Clercq, 'Maronite (droit canonique)', DDC 6 (1957) 812–13; Breydy, *Syro-arabische Literatur* 151–70; A. Joubeir, 'Les divers titres de Kitāb al-Hudā', OCP 38 (1972) 408–29; idem, *Kitab al-Huda: Essai* (Jounieh, Lebanon 1974); S. Khalil, 'Kitāb al-Hudā, Kitāb al-Kamāl et Kitāb an-Namūs', OCP 42 (1976) 207–16; M. Breydy, 'Abraham Ecchellensis et al collection dite (Kitab) al Huda', OrChr 67 (1983) 123–43; idem, 'Les Problèmes de la Littérature compilée en Proche-Orient chrétien: Rectifications autour de Kitāb al-Hudā', *Études Maronites* (Orientalia Biblica et Christiana 2; Glückstadt 1991) 81–140.

On individual areas: E. Khoury, 'Les canons sur l'eucharistie dans "Kitāb al-Huda",' *Melto* 2 (1966) 251–71; idem, 'Les sacrements de l'initiation chrétienne dans Kitāb al-Hudā', *Melto* 3 (1967) 309–22; idem, 'Canons sur la prière dans Kitāb al-Huda', *Melto* 4 (1968) 45–57; M. Breydy, 'Abraham Ecchellensis et les canons arabes de Nicée', ParOr 10 (1981–83) 223–55. Selb-Kaufhold, *Rechtsbuch* 1.67, 162–66.

Mūsā al-ʿAkkarī, Petros II al-Ḥadaṯī

An Oxford manuscript, Bodleian Library Syr. 170, containing an extensive legal collection in fifty-one chapters, was copied in 1559 by the Maronite Patriarch Petros (= Mūsā al-ʿAkkarī, 1524–67). Because of Payne-Smith's error in the catalogue of the Oxford manuscript—he interpreted the date 1870 of the Seleucid Era (= A.D. 1558–59) as A.D. 1509—Graf assumed that it must concern Petros II al-Ḥadaṯī (1458–92), who could not figure as copyist but only as the author. However, the question of which patriarch wrote the text is moot. The work is, as Breydy demonstrated, unequivocally the *Nomokanon* of the Copt Ibn al-ʿAssāl (see below). It was in fact used by the Maronites; not only are several more Maronite manuscripts of the work preserved,[104] but we know that it was examined and rejected by the papal legate sent to the Maronites, Giambattisto Eliano. ('This book contains a certain number of errors and deserves to be burned'.[105]) Patriarch Stephan ad-Duwaihī later expressed something closer to neutrality:[106]

---

104. Cf. the list of manuscripts in P. Dib, 'Maroniti', *Studi storici* 89–116 at 96–97, and Graf, *Geschichte* 3.399–400, 401–2. In the first instance, consideration must be given to the Karshuni manuscripts (Arabic in Syriac script): Vat. Barb. or. 41 (thirteenth century), Paris Bibl. nat. syr. 225 (1475), Kuraim 31a (1550), Oxford Bodleian Library Syr. 89 (1558); Cambridge University add. 3283 (1678).

105. S. Kuri, *Monumenta* 238, n. 5. Cf. also S. Kuri, Monumenta 113* and the report of Stephan ad-Duwaihī on the third of the reviewed books: 385 (Arabic text), 389 (French translation). The exemplar used by Eliano is Paris, Bibl. nat. syr. 225, which contains a corresponding Italian notation from his hand (see H. Zotenberg, *Catalogue des manuscrits syriaques et sabéens [mandaïtes] de la bibliothèque nationale* [Paris 1874] 173).

106. Ibid., 185 (text), 389 (translation). Dib, 'Maroniti' 95 writes, 'The Maronites adopted it to fill the gaps of their own *Nomokanon*'.

The third [of the books reviewed] is the book of Ibn al-ʿAssāl; it embraces the knowledge of human (ǧusdānī) and spiritual law; it belongs to the Coptic people and holds firmly that people should be circumcised and baptized.

Literature: Graf, *Geschichte* 3.333; Breydy, *Syro-Arabische Literatur* 212–17; idem, *Études maronites* 130–35.

Ǧirǧis of Ehden

In the third part of his Apology,[107] Patriarch Stephan ad-Duwaihī cites the manuscript of a legal collection that was either compiled in 1471–72 by the Periodeut Ǧirǧis (George) from Ehden in Lebanon or, more likely, was simply copied by him. The title he gives is simply the 'Book of Canons' (*Kitāb al-qawānīn*). The manuscript has since disappeared. On the basis of citations and page references in ad-Duwaihī, Breydy reports the following contents:[108]

1. Ritual for anointing the sick, with citations from the (pseudo-Apostolic) canons of Clement (fol. 1–30 of the manuscript of Ǧirǧis),
2. Apostolic canons (fol. 31–130),
3. Canons of Rabbūlā (fol. 130–143),
4. Canons of the Fathers and others (fol. 143–207),
5. Sermon (maimar) on fasting (fol. 207ff.),
6. Synods (Gangra) (fol. 246),
7. Sermons of John Chrysostom on penance (fol. 287),
8. Rules of Christianity (fol. 291),
9. Dialogue between the teacher and the pupil (fol. 311),
11. Canons of the (Eastern Syrian) Katholikos Timotheos and Īšōʿbarnūn (only one page citation, fol. 185, hence placed among the 'Canons of the Fathers'?).

The description of the manuscript cannot be entirely correct. Stephan ad-Duwaihī wrote in more detail about the work in the third part of his 'Apology', when the Maronite books were reviewed by the papal legate Eliano:[109]

The twentieth <book> is the 'Dialogue between Pupil and Teacher', against which Ibn al-Qulāʿī has written. The twenty-first is the 'Book of Canons', which Ǧirǧis, the periodeut of Ehden, superior of the monastery of Mar Antonios in Quzḥaiyā copied (nasaḫahū) in the Greek year 1783 [= A.D. 1471–72]; it contains many canons from the sayings (qaul) of the apostles, from the instruction (taʿlīm) of Clement, from the decisions (sunan) of the synods, the ordinances (qaḍāya) of the kings, the rulings (farāʾid) of the Fathers, as well as the sayings (qaul) of

---

107. Cf. Graf, *Geschichte* 3.368–69.
108. Breydy, *Syro-Arabische Literatur* 210–11.
109. Kuri, *Monumenta* 386 (Arabic text); a somewhat different French translation, 391.

Rabbūlā, the bishop of Edessa, and of Timotheus the Easterner, patriarch of Alexandria. [Footnote 144: 'As the citations of ad-Duwaihī demonstrate, this patriarch is actually the Eastern Syrian Katholikos Timotheos I'.] At the beginning is The Book of the Lamp (Kitāb al-qandil) in Syriac, on the blessing (takrīs) of anointing the sick.

The 'Dialogue between Pupil and Teacher', the Coptic penitential handbook of Kyrillos ibn Laqlaq[110] thus has nothing to do with the collection of Ğirğis, but is a work in its own right. The collection is not identical with the *Kitāb al-Hudā*, which also appears in the list of reviewed books. Its content may be more precisely established from the citations. Since Rabbūlā of Edessa appears, and since Stephan ad-Duwaihī gives the citations from Timotheos and Īšō'barnūn in Syriac language and script, it is to be supposed that Ğirğis's collection is based on a Western Syrian collection (in some Western Syrian manuscripts the Eastern Syrian Katholikoi actually appear). A manuscript-model corresponding in all particulars is not known. The collection has some originality, even though the description given in the citation of ad-Duwaihī (nasaḥahū) infers that Ğirğis was only a copyist.

Literature: Dib, 'Maroniti' 99–100; Graf, *Geschichte* 3.333; Breydy, *Syro-Arabische Literatur* 210–12; idem, 'La IIIe apologie de Duwayihi et la tradition des canons de Timothée I, d'Īšō'barnūn et autres', *Actes du premier congrès international d'études arabes chrétiennes, Goslar, 1980* (Orientalia Christiana Analecta 218; Rome 1982) 241–50.

Spiritual Medicine

Stephan ad-Duwaihī mentions one further work with canonical contents that was reviewed by Gianbattista Eliano. It is the 'Book of Spiritual Medicine', already mentioned in the context of Melkite canon law sources, a sort of penitential handbook that was probably composed by the Copt Michael of Aṭrīb and Malīğ (middle of the thirteenth century). The patriarch wrote:[111]

The second <of the books> is 'The Spiritual Medicine' (aṭ-Ṭibb ar-rūḥānī); this book is old and recognized among most of Eastern Christians; it contains descriptions of sins and canons dealing with penitents. Gianbattista read it in two copies, specifically nos. 2 and 14. In the second case the 'Childhood Gospel' was added, which is recognized among the Jacobites.

In fact, manuscripts of the 'Book of Spiritual Medicine' came from the Maronites.[112] The work will be examined in more detail below in the context of the canon-law sources of the Coptic Church.

110. Graf, *Geschichte* 2.365–66.
111. Kuri, *Monumenta* 385–89.
112. For example, Vat. Syr. 134 [A.D. 1537].

Anonymous Syrian Treatise on the Priesthood

More specialized in content is a theological-canonical work in 40 chapters on the priesthood that was composed in Syriac, perhaps written by John of Dārā (ninth century). It might be an excerpt from a larger work on the sacraments. It survives in several versions and is also attributed to Moses bar Kepha and, among the Maronites, to Johannes Maron. Chapters 31 and following in particular, which appear only in Maronite manuscripts, contain rules for the selection and conduct of the clergy, although these rules have more the form of moral exhortation.

Edition: M. Breydy, *La doctrine Syro-Antiochienne sur le Sacerdoce dans sa version Maronite* (Jounieh, Lebanon 1977).

Literature: Baumstark, *Syrische Literatur* 277; Graf, *Geschichte* 2.102; M. Breydy, 'Les compilations syriaques sur la sacerdoce au IXe siècle', *Symposium Syriacum 1976* (Orientalia Christiana Analecta 205; Rome 1978) 267–93.

Gabriel ibn al-Qulāʿī

At the end of the fifteenth century Gabriel ibn al-Qulāʿī († 1515), who was the bishop of Cyprus at the end of his life, wrote a 'Nomos of the Holy Church of Antioch. It is not a legal work, but a 'detailed pastoral handbook that dealt with the sacraments, questions of faith, morals, and canon law in a rich stew' (Graf). He followed strictly the doctrine and the practice of the Latin Church.

Literature: Graf, *Geschichte* 3.309–33, especially 313–17; Breydy, *Syro-Arabische Literatur* 179–99, at 187–88; F. El-Hage, *Kitāb an-Nāmūs d'ibn al-Qilāʿī dans l'histoire juridique du mariage chez les Maronites* (Bibliothèque de l'Univerité Saint-Esprit de Kaslik 34; Kaslik, Lebanon 2001).

Maronite Synods

We know nothing about Maronite synods until the end of the sixteenth century. The first known synod took place in 1580 under the papal legate Gianbattista Eliano in the monastery of Qannūbīn. Its canons, and the canons of the later synods of Mount Lebanon (1596), Daiʿa Mūsā (1598) and Harrāš (1644), all of which show Latin influence, were of fundamental importance for the law of the Maronite Church, but they stand outside the period of this study.

Translation: C. de Clercq, 'Les Conciles des orientaux catholiques', *Histoire des Conciles* (vol. 11, Paris 1949) 3–32.

Literature: Graf, *Geschichte* 3.501–4; P. Dib, *Les conciles de l'Église maronite de 1557–1644* (Le Puy 1926); C. de Clercq, 'Conciles des orientaux catholiques', *Histoire des Conciles* (vol. 11.1, Paris 1949) 3–22; B. Feghaly, *L'application du Concile Libanais au sujet du patriarche: Étude historico-canonique* (Rome, Universitas Gregoriana 1950); G. Khadige, *La situation originale du Patriarche dans l'Église maronite et sa modification par la Concile du Mont-Liban: Mémoire présenté à l'Université de Lyon* (Lyon 1963).

Also outside the scope of this study is the collection by Bishop Michael ʿUbaid ibn Saʿāda composed in the middle of the seventeenth century on inheritance and marriage law, with excerpts from synodal canons as well as writings of earlier patriarchs or bishops. Also of a later date is the canonical collection of Yūḥannā ibn Zindah from Aleppo, completed in 1690. They are still mentioned, however, since they contain the seven ecumenical synods, the old provincial synods, the *Syro-Roman Lawbook* and the *Procheiros Nomos*, though all of it from the Melkite tradition, with texts on the Council of Florence as the 'eighth council'.

Literature: Graf, *Geschichte* 3.351 (Michael ʿUbaid), 381; Breydy, *Syro-Arabische Literatur* 247 (Yūḥannā ibn Zindah).

Copts

History of the Church

Just as was the case in the patriarchate of Antioch, there soon arose in Egypt, which traces its Christian heritage back to the Apostle Mark, two ecclesiastical institutions, each with its own hierarchy and a patriarch of Alexandria: the Melkite Church (see above) and the 'Monophysite' Coptic Church, which shall be the subject of this chapter. The Coptic Church suffered greatly under Byzantine rule. The conquest of Egypt by Muslim Arabs (639–41) ended this oppression but replaced it with a new yoke, even though the relationship between the Coptic Church and the new rulers was a good one over the short term. The number of Christians dwindled through more or less voluntary conversions to Islam, and Coptic gradually declined as a colloquial language. It survived only as an ecclesiastical language. Still, one is not justified in portraying the history of the Coptic Church in terms of continual decline. In the thirteenth and fourteenth centuries there was a cultural flowering, and even in our own time a strong growth of Coptic ecclesiastical activity may be seen.

Until its collapse in the fourteenth century, Nubian Christianity was dependent upon Alexandria. The Ethiopian Church also stood in close contact with the Coptic Church until a few decades ago. It will be discussed below.

Literature: Spuler, *Die morgenländischen Kirchen* 269–308; Atiya, *Eastern Christianity* 11–145; C. D. G. Müller, *Grundzüge des christlich-islamischen Ägypten* (Darmstadt 1969); idem, *Orientalische Nationalkirchen* 320–43; O. F. A. Meinardus, *Christian Egypt: Faith and Life* (Cairo 1970); idem, *Christian Egypt, Ancient and Modern* (Cairo 197); Heiler, *Ostkirchen* 344–60; M. P. Roncaglia, *Histoire de l'église copte* 1 (2nd ed. Beirut 1987); P. du Bourget, *Les Coptes* (Paris 1988); C. W. Griggs, *Early Egyptian Christianity: From Its Origins to 451 C.E.* (Coptic Studies 2; Leiden 1993). G. Troupeau, 'L'Église jacobite d'Alexandrie' (including Nubia and Ethiopia), *Histoire du Christianisme* 4.422–38 (*Geschichte des Christentums* 4.435–52); J. Richard, 'L'Église copte', *Histoire du Christianisme* 6.237–39 (*Geschichte des Christentums* 6.233–36).

Coptic Literature

The early literature of the Copts is in their own language, which is the last stage of Egyptian. Coptic falls into a series of dialects (particularly Sahidic and Bohairic) written in Greek script with some additional letters. Alongside translations from Greek (the Bible, Apocrypha, Acts of Apostles, writings of Church Fathers) there is an indigenous Coptic literature of limited scope, including a literature of aphorisms from monastic circles, monastic rules, ecclesiastical law, preaching in the wider sense, epistolary literature, legends, medical works, and magic literature. The translations of many Gnostic and Manichee writings should also be noted, since they are of immeasurable value in studies of those communities. At about the turn of the millennium, Arabic replaced Coptic as the language of literature, much more comprehensively than among the Syrians. There the Syriac language continued to be of importance. The Christian-Arabic literature of the Copts thus has greater importance simply in terms of its breadth. In time there arose a literature of translations from Coptic and Greek, but also from Syriac, although original works were also composed in the areas of biblical studies, ascetics, liturgy, homiletics, law, history, hagiography, and philology.

On literature in the Coptic language: A. Baumstark, 'Die koptische Literatur', *Die christlichen Literaturen des Orients* 1 (Leipzig 1911) 106–29; J. Leipoldt, 'Geschichte der koptischen Literatur', *Christliche Litteraturen* 131–83; S. Morenz, 'Die koptische Literatur', HbOr 1.207–19; T. Orlandi, *Elementi di lingua e letteratura copta* (Milan 1970); idem, 'Literature, Coptic', CE 5.1450–60; M. Krause, 'Koptische Literatur', *Lexikon der Ägyptologie*, 3 (Wiesbaden 1980) 694–728; R.-G. Coquin, 'Langue et littérature copte', *Christianismes orientaux* 167–217.

On literature in Arabic: Graf, *Geschichte* 2.294–475. A. S. Atiya, 'Literature, Copto-Arabic', CE 5.1460–67.

Coptic Sources of Ecclesiastical Law

The first investigation of Coptic church law was the work of Johann Michael Wansleben, who traveled to Egypt, brought back Coptic manuscripts, and particularly described canon law sources in his *Histoire de l'église d'Alexandrie*.[113] Information on this subject is also found in the *Historia Patriarcharum Alexandrinorum Jacobitorum* by Eusebius Renaudot.[114] Editions of Coptic pseudo-apostolic texts derive from Henry Tattam (1848), Paul de Lagarde (1883), and George William Horner (1904); Daniel Bonifatius Haneberg edited a Coptic-Arabic text in 1869. Fundamental work on Coptic canon law begins only with the work of Wilhelm Riedel, which appeared

---

113. (Paris 1677).
114. (Paris 1713).

in 1900, providing a comprehensive survey of the *Kirchenrechtsquellen des Patriarchats Alexandriens*, although needing some improvement in detail. We may thank the labors of Franz Joseph Cöln for providing further insight in his plan for a *Corpus fontium Juris Canonici et Civilis christiani Arabicum* using primarily Coptic legal sources,[115] which he was unfortunately unable to carry out. The already-mentioned contribution of Francis Gozman in the course of the *Codificazione canonico orientale* and by Charles de Clercq in the *Dictionnaire de droit canonique* provided only a short survey of the sources. As was the case with the entire field of Christian-Arabic literature, it was only with the literary history of Georg Graf (1944ff.) that further progress was made. Since then, works on Coptic canon law have kept appearing. In this context it is not possible to ignore the *Coptic Encyclopedia*, edited by Aziz S. Atiya, including specialized articles.[116]

For the study of Coptic canon law, Coptic and Arabic legal documents should also be studied; these were usually written on papyrus, but also on pottery sherds. Many editions and translations have been made of these texts. They are of much more significance for the secular law of the Copts. After W. E. Crum and Georg Steindorff, it was particularly Artur Steinwenter, Arthur Schiller and Walter Till who dedicated themselves to the study of Coptic documents. Adolf Grohmann and Werner Diem studied Arabic papyri, including those of Christian origin.

Literature: Riedel, *Kirchenrechtsquellen*; F. J. Cöln, 'Legal Literature among the Arabic-speaking Churches', *The Catholic University of America Bulletin* 20 (Washington 1914) 443–56; idem, 'Nomocanonical Literature'; F. Gozman, 'Disciplina Alexandrina: Copti', *Studi storici* 33–71; C. Kopp, *Glaube und Sakramente der koptischen Kirche* (Orientalia Christiana 25.1; Rome 1932); C. de Clercq, 'Copte (Droit canonique)', DDC 4 (1949) 594–601; O. F. A. Meinardus, 'A Study of the Canon Law of the Coptic Church', *Bulletin de la Société d'Archéologie Copte* 16 (Cairo 1962) 231–42; idem, *Christian Egypt: Faith and Life* (Cairo 1970) 76–89 and passim; Brogi, *Patriarcha*; Masson, *Divorce*.

On Law in Coptic and Coptic-Arabic Documents (Selection): A. Steinwenter, *Das Recht der koptischen Urkunden* (Handbuch der Altertumswissenschaft, Division 10, Part 4, Vol. 2; Munich 1955); L. S. B. MacCoull, 'Law, Coptic', CE 5.1428–32; A. A. Schiller, 'Coptic Documents', *Zeitschrift für vergleichende Rechtswissenschaft* 60 (1957) 190–211; idem, 'A Checklist of Coptic Documents and Letters', *The Bulletin of the American Society of Papyrologists* 13 (1976) 99–123; B. Menu, 'Une esquisse des relations juridiques privées en droit copte', *Le Monde Copte* 20 (Limoges 1992) 71–78; H.-A. Rupprecht, *Kleine Einführung in die Papyruskunde* (Darmstadt 1994) 12 (with further literature).

K. Reinhardt, 'Eine arabisch-koptische Kirchenbannurkunde', *Aegyptiaca: Festschrift für Georg Ebers* (Leipzig 1897) 89–91; A. Steinwenter, 'Kinderschenkungen an koptische Klöster', ZRG Kan. Abt. 11 (1921) 175–208; 12 (1922) 385–86; idem, 'Die Rechtsstellung der Kirchen und Klöster nach den Papyri', ZRG Kan. Abt. 19 (1922) 1–50; idem, 'Die Ordinationsbitten koptischer Kleriker', *Aegyptus* 11 (Milan 1931) 29–34; N. Abbot, 'Ara-

---

115. Cöln, *Legal literature* 454–55.
116. (New York 1991).

bic Marriage Contracts among Copts', ZDMG 95 (1941) 59–81; W. Till, 'Die koptische Eheverträge', *Festschrift für Josef Bick* (Vienna 1948) 627–38; E. Balogh and P. E. Kahle, 'Two Coptic Documents Relating to Marriage', *Aegyptus* 33 (1953) 331–40; A. Steinwenter, 'Aus dem kirchlichen Vermögensrecht der Papyri', ZRG Kan. Abt. 44 (1958) 1–34; H. J. Thissen, 'Koptische Kinderschenkungsurkunden: Zur Herodulie im christlichen Ägypten', *Enchoria* 14 (1986) 117–28; M. Krause, 'Ein Vorschlagschreiben für einen Priester', *Lingua Restituta Orientalis: Festgabe für Julius Assfalg*, ed. R. Schulz and M. Görg (Wiesbaden 1990) 195–202; idem, 'Die Kirchenvisitationsurkunden', *Meroitica* 12 (Berlin 1990) 225–36; idem, 'Carl Schmidts Beiträge zum ägyptischen Mönchtum auf Grund koptischer Urkunden', *Carl Schmidt Kolloquium Halle-Wittenberg 1988*, ed. P. Nagel (Halle an der Saale 1990) 119–27; W Diem, *Arabische Briefe auf Papyrus und Papier aus der Heidelberger Papyrus-Sammlung* (Wiesbaden 1991); Khoury, Raif Georges, *Chrestomathie de papyrologie arabe. Documents relatifs à la vie privée, sociale et administraive dans les premiers siècles islamiques* (Leiden a. o. 1993); S. Schaten, 'Koptische Kinderschenkungsurkunden', BSAC 35 (1996) 129–42; G. Schmelz, *Kirchliche Amtsträger im spätantiken Ägypten nach den Aussagen der griechischen und koptischen Papyri und Ostraka* (Munich–Leipzig 2002) (= Archiv für Papyrusforschung und verwandte Gebiete, Beiheft 13).

Pseudo-Apostolic Sources

The *Didache* was undoubtedly known in Egypt, as two Greek fragments found in Oxyrrynchos papyri demonstrate. The Coptic fragment (preserved certainly from the fifth century) obviously did not belong to a canonical collection, but rather was only a writing exercise. It is not possible to establish any influence of the *Didache* on later legal sources of the Coptic Church. If the Ethiopian translation of the *Didache* did go back to a Coptic original (see below), it must be assumed that there was once a complete Coptic version.

Editions: G. W. Horner, 'A New Papyrus Fragment of the Didaché in Coptic', JTS 25 (1923–24) 225–31; C. Schmidt, 'Das koptische Didache-Fragment des British Museum', *Zeitschrift für die Neutestamentliche Wissenschaft* 24 (1925) 81–99; A. Neppi-Modona, 'Nuovo contributo de papiri per la conoscenza di antichi testi Cristiani', *Bilychnis* 27 (1926) 161–74 [*Didache*]; L. T. Lefort, *Les Pères apostoliques en copte* (CSCO 135–36; Louvain 1952) 32–34 (text), 35–38 (translation).

Literature: ClavisG 1735; G. Bardy, 'Didache', DDC 4 (1949) 1210–18; Audet, *Didaché* 28–34; Niederwimmer, *Didache* 39–43; Schöllgen, *Didache* 88–89; K. H. Kuhn, 'Didache', CE 3.898–99.

There is no Coptic or Arabic translation of the '*Didascalia* of the Apostles', in the form in which it has survived in Syriac and Latin versions. These versions provided the foundation of the first six books of the 'Apostolic Constitutions'. In contrast, the Arabic work of the same name was taken from books 1 to 7 of the 'Apostolic Constitutions'. One of the two surviving versions, in 44 chapters, with the title *Didascalia* (ad-dasqalīya or ad-dusqūlīya) or 'Teachings of the Apostles' (ta'alīm ar-rusul) was translated in A.D. 1295 by the priest Abu Isḥāq ibn Faḍlallāh on the basis of a Coptic Sahidic model. An older (at the latest from the eleventh century) and freer reworking in 39 chapters, relying on a Bohairic text, was more widely distributed; it was taken into the collection of Makarios and cited in later systematic collections. A fragment of a Coptic version of the text may survive.

Edition of the earlier translation: Ḥāfiẓ Dā'ud, *ad-Dasqūlīya au ta'ālīm ar-rusul* (Cairo 1924) (reprint, Cairo, n.d.). Another version: W. S. Qilāda, *Kitāb ta'ālīm ar-rusul ad-Dusqūlīya* (Cairo 1979) (reviewed by Samir Khalil, OCP 48 [1982] 207–9); M. Kohlbacher, *Zum liturgischen Gebrauch der Apostolischen Konstitutionen in Ägypten, Paramone*, ed. J. M. S. Cowey and B. Kramer (Archiv für Papyrusforschung, Beiheft 16; Leipzig 2004) 305–6.

Translation of the preface and of chapters 35–39: A. Socin, in F. X. Funk, *Die Apostolischen Konstitutionen* (Rottenburg 1891) 215–42.

Literature: ClavisG 1730; Riedel, *Kirchenrechtsquellen* 28–32, 164–65; A. Baumstark, 'Die Urgestalt der "arabischen Didaskalie der Apostel",' OrChr 3 (1903) 201–8; Graf, *Geschichte* 1.564–69; C. W. Griggs, 'Didascalia', CE 3.899–900; A. Camplani, 'A Coptic Fragment from the Didascalia Apostolorum (M579 F.1)', *Augustinianum* 36 (1996) 47–51 (without enough comparisons of all the texts); M. Kohlbacher, *Zum liturgischen Gebrauch der Apostolischen Konstitutionen in Ägypten* 306–10.

Among the Copts can be found an extensive corpus of other pseudo-apostolic texts which are gathered in their own miscellaneous manuscripts and hence not preserved together with synodal canons. They consist of the following:

1. The *Apostolic Church Order*, which has already been encountered in the context of the Western Syrian Church.
2. The so-called 'Egyptian Church Order' or the 'Church Order of Hippolytus', which rests on the apostolic tradition of Hippolytus.
3. The parallel text to the eighth book of the *Apostolic Constitution* (= *Epitome*), which has already been mentioned, and
4. The well-known *Apostolic Canons*, circulating in all churches.

These sources are gathered into two books in the Coptic-Sahidic tradition, of which the first is divided into 71 canons and entitled 'Canons of the Church'; it consists of a continual sequential numbering through the Apostolic Church Order (canons 1–30), the 'Egyptian Church Order' (without liturgical texts, canons 31–62), as well as the parallel text (canons 63–78). The second book consists of 56 canons, bearing the title 'Canons of Our Holy Fathers the Apostles', and contains the 'Apostolic Canons' in an order different from that found in the other churches.

Edition of London, British Library Orient. 1320 (cf. W. E. Crum, *Catalogue of the Coptic Manuscripts in the British Museum* [London 1905] 52–53 [no. 162]): P. de Lagarde, *Aegyptiaca* (Göttingen 1883) (pp. 239–48 = Apostolic Church Order; pp. 248–66 = Egyptian Church Order; pp. 266–91 = parallel text; pp. 209–38 = Apostolic Canons). Edition of a manuscript of the Coptic patriarchate: U. Bouriant, 'Les canons apostoliques de

Clément de Rome', *Recueil des travaux relatifs à la philologie et à l'archéologie égyptiennes et assyriennes* 5 (1884) 199–216; 6 (1885) 97–115.

Edition and translation of a fragment with the beginning of the Apostolic Church Order: A. I. Elenskaya, *The Literary Coptic Manuscripts in the A. S. Pushkin State Fine Arts Museum in Moscow* (Supplements to Vigiliae Christiana; Leiden. 1994) 207–11.

Translation of the 71 canons according to the edition of the Sahidic text of Lagarde: G. Steindorff, in H. Achelis, *Die ältesten Quellen des orientalischen Kirchenrechts*: Erstes Buch, (Leipzig 1891) (= TU 4.4) 35, 39–136; G. Horner, *The Statutes of the Apostles or Canones Ecclesiastici* (London 1904) 295–363.

Edition and German translation of the 'Egyptian Church Order' alone: W. Till and J. Leipoldt, *Der koptische Text der Kirchenordnung Hippolyts* (Berlin 1954) (= TU 58).

Literature: ClavisG 1732; F. X. Funk, 'Das achte Buch der Apostolischen Konstitutionen in der koptischen Überlieferung', *Theologische Quartalschrift* 86 (1904) 429–42 (= Kirchengeschichtliche Abhandlungen und Untersuchungen, 3; Paderborn 1907) 362–81; J. Leipoldt, *Saïdische Auszüge aus dem 8. Buch der Apostolischen Konstitutionen* (Leipzig 1904) (= TU, 2d series, 11.1b); L. T. Lefort, 'Note sur le texte copte des Constitutions apostoliques', *Muséon* 12 (1911) 23–24; Till and Leipoldt, *Der koptische Text*, introduction; Hanssens, *Hippolyte* 31–35; idem, *La liturgie d'Hippolyte. Documents et études* (Rome 1970); R.-G. Coquin, 'Canons, Apostolic', CE 2.451–53; idem, 'Canons, Ecclesiastical', CE 2.453–56; M. Kohlbacher, *Zum liturgischen Gebrauch der Apostolischen Konstitutionen in Ägypten* 306–10.

In chapter 5 of the Arabic theological encyclopedia of Abū 'l-Barakāt ibn Kabar († 1325) there is a review of canonical sources of Coptic law and of the 'Canons of the Apostles'. As is shown from the list of contents, these consist of the two books just dealt with. Alongside the enumeration of canons there is also a division into books 2 to 8 'of Clement' (the first book corresponds to the second of Clement, then comes the third book of Clement, and so on). We are obviously dealing here with the division of the Syriac *Octateuchus Clementinus*, which also contains the 'Apostolic Canons', the parallel text and the 'Apostolic Canons'. It appears that someone had added the division to a manuscript of the Coptic-Sahidic collection already described. This secondary division was adopted by the Copt Makarios (fourteenth century). Makarios placed a version of the 'Testament of Our Lord Jesus Christ' at the beginning of his Arabic chronological collection of canons, as was the case in Syriac, creating an Octateuch similar to that of the Western Syrians.

Edition of the passage in the encyclopedia of Abū 'l-Barakāt: Samir Khalil, *Misbāh*. German translation: Riedel, *Kirchenrechtsquellen* 69–74.

On Makarios, who will be treated below, see Riedel, *Kirchenrechtsquellen* 126.

A Coptic-Bohairic translation obviously resting on a Sahidic manuscript with a secondary division into seven books (without the 'Testament of Our Lord') was created at the beginning of the nineteenth century. Just as was the case with the second book of the original Sahidic collection, it bore the title, 'Canons of the Apostles', and it is divided as follows:

Book 1 (chapters 1–30): Apostolic Church Order.

Book 2 (chapter 31–62): 'Egyptian Church Order'.

Books 3–6 (chapters 63–79): parallel text to the eighth book of the 'Apostolic Constitutions'.

Book 7 (new numeration, 85 canons): 'Apostolic Canons'.

Edition and translation: H. Tattam, *The Apostolic Constitutions or Canons of the Apostles in Coptic with an English Translation* (London 1848) 1–30, 31–92, 93–173, 174–212.

Literature: ClavisG 1733; Riedel, *Kirchenrechtsquellen* 157–58; Graf, *Geschichte* 1.581–84; Till and Leipoldt, *Der koptische Text*, introduction, pp. xi–xix; Kaufhold, 'Octateuchus Clementinus', KLCO 303–4; R.-G. Coquin, 'Octateuch of Clement', CE 6.1824.

The Sahidic collection in two books also exists in an Arabic translation. It is also divided into 71 and 56 canons respectively, and it bears the title 'Qawānīn ar-rusul' ('Canons of the Apostles').

Edition and translation of the first book (71 canons): G. Horner, *The Statutes of the Apostles* 89–125 (text) and 233–93 (translation).

Edition and translation of both books: J. Périer and A. Périer, *Les '127 Canons des Apôtres': Texte arabe* (PatrOr 8; Paris 1912; Part 4.553–710; reprint Turnhout 1971) pp. 23–40 (= can. 1–20): Apostolic Church Order; pp. 41–72 (= can. 21–47): Egyptian Church Order; pp. 72–113 (= can. 48–71): parallel text; pp. 114–43 (= can. 1–56): Apostolic Canons.

On the Arabic translation on the margin of the Bohairic version: G. Goeseke, in Till and Leipoldt, *Der koptische Text* 47–63.

Literature: Graf, *Geschichte* 1.573–77; Hanssens, *Hippolyte* 35–40.

In some later Arabic collections there are also three texts at the beginning that were originally known to the Melkites (as well as to Eastern and Western Syrians): (1) the (30) 'Traditions of the Apostles' (sunan ar-rusul), a text corresponding to the Syriac 'Doctrine of the Apostles' ('The Doctrine of Addai the Apostle'); (2) a version of the 'Apostolic Canons' in 82 canons; and (3) a part of the parallel texts to book 8 of the 'Apostolic Constitutions'. The work is probably an adoption from Arabic Melkite manuscripts.

Literature: Riedel, *Kirchenrechtsquellen* 18–21, 123–24; Graf, *Geschichte* 1.578–79.

The 'Canons of Hippolytus'

The 38 'Canons of Hippolytus' also represent a reworking of the 'Apostolic Tradition of Hippolytus'; they arose about A.D. 500 in Egypt. The Greek original, and the putative Coptic translation lying in between, have not survived. The text is found in the chronological collection of Makarios and similar anonymous miscellaneous manuscripts. It was used for the systematic canonical collections of the twelfth and thirteenth centuries.

Editions: D. B. de Haneberg, *Canones S. Hippolyti Arabice e codicibus Romanis* (Munich 1870); R.-G. Coquin, *Les Canons d'Hippolyte* (Patrologia Orientalis 31.2 = no. 149; Paris 1966).

Translations: H. Achelis, *Die ältesten Quellen des orientalischen Kirchenrechts. 1. Buch: Die Canones Hippolyti* (TU 6.4; Leipzig 1891); Coquin, *Les Canons d'Hippolyte*; P. F. Bradshaw, *The Canons of Hippolytus* (Grove Liturgical Study 50; Bramcote, Nottingham 1987).

Literature: ClavisG 1742; Graf, *Geschichte* 1.602–5; G. Bardy, 'Hippolyte, Écrits canoniques', DDC 5 (1953) 1154–59; Hanssens, *Hippolyte* 73–74; idem, 'L'édition critique des Canons d'Hippolyte', OCP (1966) 536–44; H. Brakmann, 'Alexandreia und die Kanones des Hippolyt', *Jahrbuch für Antike und Christentum* 22 (1979) 139–49; R. G. Coquin, 'Canons of Hippolytus', CE 2.458; Steimer, *Vertex Traditionis* 72–79; Mühlsteiger, *Kirchenordnungen*, 147–56.

'Testament of Our Lord Jesus Christ' *(Testamentum Domini)*

The apocryphal revelation of Jesus to his Apostles, already known to us from Western Syrian literature, also contains canon law and liturgical guides that go back to the apostolic tradition of Hippolytus. A text similar to the Syrian must have existed in Coptic-Sahidic. It was translated into Arabic using a Bohairic intermediary, and as is the case with the Syrian, it was placed in front of the pseudo-apostolic texts, grouped in seven books, making an octateuch. Abū Isḥāq ibn Faḍlallāh, to whom we also owe an Arabic translation of the *Didascalia*, translated another Sahidic version at the end of the thirteenth century. A third Arabic version (in a St. Petersburg manuscript) has still to be examined. The *Testamentum Domini* was also translated from Arabic into Ethiopian.

Literature: A. Baumstark, 'Ueberlieferung und Bezeugung der Διαθήκη τοῦ Κυρίου . . .', *Römische Quartalschrift* 14 (1900) 1–45; idem, 'Die arabischen Texte der Διαθήκη τοῦ Κυρίου', ibid. 291–300; Riedel, *Kirchenrechtsquellen* 66–69; S. D. Dib, 'Les versions arabes du "Testamentum Domini Nostri Jesu Christi",' ROC 10 (1905) 418–23; Graf, *Geschichte* 1.569–72; R.-G. Coquin, 'Le "Testamentum Domini": Problèmes de tradition textuelle', ParOr 5 (1974) 165–88, (especially 169–84); Steimer, *Vertex Traditionis* 97–98, and see the West Syrian 'Testamentum' above.

'The Epistle of Peter to Clement'

This apocryphon, already familiar from the sources of canon law of the Melkites and Maronites, and which still deserves further study, also appears in the Coptic-Arabic tradition. There was probably never a Coptic version.

Translation: Riedel, *Kirchenrechtsquellen* 166–75.

Literature: Graf, *Geschichte* 1.580–81; J. Hofmann, *Unser heiliger Vater Klemens* (Trier 1992) 36–38; R.-G. Coquin, 'Canons of Clement', CE 2.456; Steimer, *Vertex Traditionis* 97–98.

Early Greek Synods

Canon Collections in Greek

In the patriarchate of Alexandria, the *Corpus canonum* of Antioch was first used in Greek. However, a Greek collection with a connection to Egypt does not appear to have survived. We know, however, from the Arabic encyclopedia of Abū 'l-Barakāt that the Copts made use of Greek manuscripts. In the 'Apostolic Canons', which the Copts divided into 56 parts (see above), the author refers to a note of Patriarch Markos ibn Zurʻa (1166–89) in his copy of the collection. He states that these canons were called 'titloi' (at-titlūsāt), and that their number was 81.[117] The author also knows that the canons of Antioch and Laodiceia, which are usually ascribed in Coptic only to the synod of Antioch, are preserved separately in Greek.[118]

Canonical Collections in Coptic

Although several entire Coptic libraries have been found, so far only a single manuscript has been discovered with the early Greek synods in Coptic. It is a parchment fragment which was written, according to its colophon, in the year A.D. 1003. Only 48 of the original 101 leaves are preserved. These leaves are located in various places today: in the Biblioteca Vaticana (pp. 19–26, four pages without numeration, pp. 47–48 and 69–72), in the Biblioteca Nazionale in Naples (pp. 49–64, 73–84, 187–94), in the Bibliothèque Nationale in Paris (pp. 101–2, 151–68, 185–86, 199–202) as well as in the Institut Français d'Archéologie Orientale in Cairo (pp. 135–50).

Despite its fragmentary state of preservation, the contents of the collection can be almost completely reconstructed. At the beginning are texts belonging to the tradition of the Council of Nicaea (confession of faith, list of bishops, 20 authentic canons, the Syntagma Doctrinae,[119] letter of Epiphanius of Salamis to Rufinus, Gnomai of Nicaea). Following a gap of about fifteen pages there follows the synod of Ancyra. The synods of Neocaesarea and Gangra must have occupied the following 16 leaves. There follow canons 20–24 of Antioch, the 59 canons of Laodiceia, as well as the confession of faith of the synod of Constantinople. The text continues with the decree of the Council of Ephesus and various pieces with dogmatic content. The conclusion consists of the canon-law responses of Timothy of Alexandria. As the added texts demonstrate, it is not a pure collection of canons.

Partial editions and translations: G. Zoëga, *Catalogus codicum coptorum manuscriptorum qui in Museo Borgiano Velitris adservatur* (Rome 1810; Leipzig 1903, Repr. Hildesheim 1973) no. CLIX; C. Lenormant, 'Fragmenta versionis copticae libri synodici de primo concilio oecumenico Niceno a Zoëga Georgio primum edita', *Spicilegium Solesmensa*, ed. J. B. Pitra (Paris 1852) 513–36; H. Leclercq, 'Les fragments coptes relatifs au Concile

---

117. For the text, see Samir, *Misbāḥ* 120; for a translation: Riedel, *Kirchenrechtsquellen* 28.
118. Samir, *Misbāḥ* 163. Riedel, *Kirchenrechtsquellen* 34.
119. This text is the *Didascalia CCCXVIII patrum Nicaenorum*, see ClavisG 2298 (and 2264); Riedel, *Kirchenrechtsquellen* 179. It was originally written in Greek and—attributed to various authors—circulated widely in many Greek and Eastern versions (but not Syrian), and in the form of citations. It contains a doctrinal part as well as rules for monks and priests.

de Nicée', K. J. Hefele and H. Leclercq, *Histoire des Conciles* (2nd edition, Paris 1907) 1.1125–38; W. E. Crum, *Der Papyruscodex saec. VI–VII der Philippsbibliothek in Cheltenham: Koptische theologische Schriften. Mit einem Beitrag von A. Eberhard* (Schriften der Wissenschaftlichen Gesellschaft in Strassburg 18; Strasbourg 1915); F. Haase, *Die koptischen Quellen zum Konzil von Nizäa übersetzt und untersucht* (Paderborn 1920); R.-G. Coquin, 'Le Corpus canonum copte: Un nouveau complément: Le ms. I. F. A. O.', Copte 6', *Orientalia* 50 (Rome 1981) 40–86 (synodal canons). Lists of bishops from Nicaea: H. Gelzer, H. Hilgenfeld, and O. Cuntz, *Patrum Nicaenorum Nomina* (Stuttgart-Leipzig 1898; repr. with an Afterword by C. Markschies [Stuttgart-Leipzig 1995]) 77–93.

Literature: ClavisG 8522; C. Lenormant, *Études sur les fragments coptes des conciles de Nicée et d'Ephèse* (Paris 1852); G. I. Dosetti, *Il simbolo di Nicea e di Constantinopoli* 123ff. (Il Corpus Canonum in copto); T. Orlandi, 'Les papyrus coptes du Musée égyptien de Turin', *Muséon* 87 (1974) 115–27 (Cod. VIII, IX: *Sententiae Synodi Nicaeni*); Coquin, 'Le Corpus canonum copte'; H. Kaufhold, 'Griechisch-syrische Väterlisten der frühen griechischen Synoden', OrChr 77 (1993) 1–96; at 8–10.

Syntagma Doctrinae: ClavisG 2298 and 2264; M. Kohlbacher, *Minor texts for a History of Asceticism: Editions in Progress*, St. Emmel a. o. (ed.) *Ägypten und Nubien in spätantiker und christlicher Zeit* (Wiesbaden 1999), vol. 2, 145–54 (part 3: A Neglected Monastic Rule of the Mid-fourth Century; with extensive literature).

A Paris manuscript with the acts of the Council of Ephesus has less canon law.

Editions and translations: U. Bouriant, 'Actes du Concile d'Ephèse: Texte copte traduit et publié', *Memoires de la Mission française d'archéologie orientale du Caire* 8 (1892); W. Kraatz, *Koptische Akten zum Ephesinischen Konzil vom Jahre 431* (Texte und Untersuchungen, 2d series, 11.2; Leipzig 1904).

References to Other Texts in Arabic Sources

It is obvious that there were once other Coptic versions of the canons of Greek synods. In a remark on the canons of Antioch and Laodiceia in his Encyclopedia, Abū 'l-Barakāt stated that they are 'ascribed to the synod of Laodicea' in the 'large manuscript translated from Coptic'.[120] We learn from the Arabic collections of Abū 'l-Barakāt and of Makarios and from other sources that there was a particular Coptic version of the 20 authentic canons of Nicaea which was translated into Arabic.[121]

Origin of the Coptic Translation

The surviving Coptic translation of the Greek synods, which can only derive from a Greek original, was composed in Sahidic, the dominant dialect until the eleventh century. The translator is unknown. The only known manuscript is dated A.D. 1003. Since canon law sources were needed primarily by bishops and higher clergy of whom the knowledge of Greek might be assumed even after the division of the churches, the need for a

---

120. Samir Khalil, *Misbāh* 163; Riedel, *Kirchenrechtsquellen* 34.
121. Riedel, *Kirchenrechtsquellen* 36–37, 125.

translation into Coptic was not particularly pressing. According to Orlandi the translation of the canons of the council took place only in the second 'classic' period of translation (fifth-sixth centuries).[122] It is possible that they date to an even later time.

Literature: T. Orlandi, 'Le traduzioni dal greco e lo sviluppo della letteratura copta', *Graeco-Coptica: Griechen und Kopten im byzantinischen Ägypten* ed. P. Nagel (Halle an der Saale 1984) 181–203. Also in general on translation from Greek, T. Orlandi, 'Traduzioni dal greco al copto: Quali e perché', *Autori classici in lingue del vicino e medio oriente,* ed. G. Fiaccadori (Rome 1990) 93–104.

Collections of Canons in Arabic

Information on the corpus of Greek synodal canons is given on the one hand by the chronological collections, such as Paris, Bibl. nat. arab. 238, 239, 240, 241 (fourteenth and fifteenth centuries) and the comprehensive work of Abū ʾl-Barakāt and of Makarios.[123] On the other hand, there are also the systematic collections of Michael of Damietta († after 1208) or of Ibn al-ʿAssāl (thirteenth century), which not only give citations but also have a chronological index of their sources.[124] These collections are anything but unified, and they have the synods in what is partially a peculiar sequence. More than the others Michael of Damietta had preserved the order of the older councils: Ancyra, Neocaesarea, Gangra, Antioch, Laodiceia, Sardica, Constantinople, and Ephesus. This agrees completely with manuscript group 2 of the Melkites (see the table on page 229 above). Ibn al-ʿAssāl and Makarios place Gangra and Antioch before Nicaea, and Makarios also places Laodiceia and Sardica only after Ephesus. In some manuscripts (for example Paris, Bibl. nat. arab. 238, 239, 241) the 'great synods' (Nicaea, Constantinople, and Ephesus) are first; the following 'little' (local) synods begin with Ancyra; the sequencing of the others appears to be entirely arbitrary.

As we have seen, the Arabic versions rest at least in part on Coptic originals. It is, however, also possible that some were translated directly from the Greek or adopted from the Arabic collections of other churches. There are no indications that conciliar canons were translated from Syriac. We know, nevertheless, from several remarks in the *Encyclopedia* of Abū ʾl-Barakāt that Syriac collections were known.[125] Further, Abū ʾl-Barakāt also had available the Arabic canonical collection of the Eastern Syrian ʿAbdallāh ibn aṭ-Ṭaiyib (eleventh century).[126]

122. Orlandi, 'Traduzioni' 99.
123. Troupeau, *Catalogue* 200–203; Riedel, *Kirchenrechtsquellen* 32–45 and 124–25 respectively.
124. Riedel, *Catalogue* 93–97; Ğirğis, *Kitab al-Qawānīn* 6–10; Tzadua, *Fetha Nagast* 6–8.
125. Samir, *Misbāh* 109, 120, 135; Riedel, *Kirchenrechtsquellen* 19, 20, 28, 39.
126. Samir, *Misbāh* 111, 127, 158, 162; Riedel, *Kirchenrechtsquellen* 19, 33–36.

Literature: Riedel, *Kirchenrechtsquellen* 135–38; Graf, *Geschichte* 1.586–600; Troupeau, *Catalogue* 1.200–205. For literature on later collected works, see below.

Remarks on Individual Synods

In the collections, the synod of Nicaea includes, besides a historical introduction and the 20 authentic canons, the following pieces more or less complete: the 84 'Arabic' canons and the 'canons for monks'—both known from Melkite sources, the authentic canons according to a Coptic original, the 'Syntagma Doctrinae' (see above) and the confession of faith.

Literature: ClavisG 8522; Riedel, *Kirchenrechtsquellen* 178–80; Graf, *Geschichte* 1.586–93; A. Camps, 'Two Spurious Arabic Canons of the Council of Nicea Found by the Franciscan Missionaries of Upper Egypt', SOCC 5 (1960) 171–81; R.-G. Coquin, 'Nicaea, Arabic Canons of', CE 6.1789–90.

The synod of Constantinople is represented with four canons (canons 1–6 of the Greek version), also known in other Eastern churches (ClavisG 8600), along with 23 spurious 'canons', which are really anathemas from a letter of Pope Damasus and which also appear in the Eastern Syrian collections of Elias al-Ǧauharī and, in a shortened form, the collection of Ibn aṭ-Ṭaiyib. In the Synod of Ephesos there is a relationship with the other Eastern versions; we have only one canon, and it corresponds to the seventh Greek canon.

Translation of the 23 canons: Riedel, *Kirchenrechtsquellen* 94–97.
Literature: Riedel, *Kirchenrechtsquellen* 180–83; Graf, *Geschichte* 1.597–98.

The synod of Neocaesarea is also called the synod of Carthage. This is also what it is usually called in the Melkite collections. The 123 canons of the synod of 419 appears as the second synod of Carthage in Abū ʾl-Barakāt and in Paris, Bibl. nat. arab. 239, and in other places; it is also found in Melkite manuscripts.

Literature: Riedel, *Kirchenrechtsquellen* 33, 126, 136–37, 178.

It is a peculiarity of some of the collections that the two synods of Antioch and Laodiceia are united and then number 83 canons, corresponding to a Coptic original (expressly so in Paris, Bibl. nat. syr. 239).

Literature: Riedel, *Kirchenrechtsquellen* 33–34, 126, 136–37, 178; Troupeau, *Cataloque* 1.202.

Canons of Greek Church Fathers

Among the Copts the canonical responses of Timothy of Alexandria obviously belong to the oldest group of canonical collections. Alone among the patristic texts known from the Greek collections, they were taken into the Coptic manuscript described above, along with the Greek synods, though under the name of Peter of Alexandria. The Western Syrians had the same set of texts, but the Melkites did not. Whether the Western Syrians and Copts used a shared Greek original or whether there was influence of one church on the other must remain an open question.

The text is rare among Coptic-Arabic collections. Michael of Aṯrīb and Maliǧ cited canon 3 at one point. Ibn al-ʿAssāl named Timothy in his index of sources, but he does not appear to cite him.[127]

Literature: cf. Graf, *Geschichte* 1.309, 316, 2.401.

Peculiar to the Coptic Church are 107 spurious canons of Athanasius of Alexandria, with rules of all sorts for the clergy, divine service, the administration of ecclesiastical property, and the like, as well as instructions of duties for laymen, monks, and nuns. A Coptic Sahidic text survives only in fragments. The Arabic translation rests on an unknown Coptic Bohairic version. The division into 107 canons was arranged by Bishop Michael of Tinnīs (probably eleventh century). Michael of Damietta and Ibn al-ʿAssāl do not use the canons in their legal works.

Edition and translation of the Coptic and Arabic text: W. Riedel and W. E. Crum, *The Canons of Athanasius, Patriarch of Alexandria, ca. 293–373* (London 1904, Repr. Amsterdam 1973).

Literature: ClavisG 2302; Riedel, *Kirchenrechtsquellen* 5–8 (table of contents), 230–31; F. H. Hallock, 'The Canons of Athanasios', *Anglican Theological Review* 9 (1926–27) 378–86; Graf, *Geschichte* 1.605–6; R.-G. Coquin, 'Canons of Pseudo-Athanasius', CE 2.458–59.

Two series of canons with respectively 13 and 105 (or 106) canons are ascribed to (Pseudo-) Basil of Caesarea. Their origin has not yet been clarified. The shorter series, with rules for punishments for priests and deacons, is also found in Arabic among the Melkites (14 canons). No Coptic version of this text is known. The Arabic version appears only in the collection of Makarios and the similar manuscript Paris, Bibl. nat. arab. 238. The longer series (dealing, among other things, with marital law, prayer, fasting, ban on magic, qualifications for the various levels of clergy, and the liturgy) can be found only among the Copts. Only fragments of the Coptic Sahidic text (from the sixth and seventh centuries) survive, but the somewhat different Arabic versions may be encountered in almost all collections.

Editions of the Coptic fragments: F. Rossi, *I Papiri Copti del Museo Egizio di Torino* (Turin 1893) vol. 2.4, 18, 81–92; J. Drescher, 'A Coptic Lectionary Fragment', *Annales du Service des Antiquités d'Égypte* 51 (1951) 247–56 (here: excerpts from canon 1); P. E. Kahle, *Balaʾizah* (London 1954) 1.412–16.

---

127. Ǧirǧis, *Kitab al-Qawānīn* 10; Tzadua, *Fetha Nagast*, 9.

Translations of the Coptic fragments: W. E. Crum, 'The Coptic Version of the "Canons of S. Basil"', *Proceedings of the Society of Biblical Archeology* 24 (1904), 57–62; Kahle, *Bala'izah* 1.415–16.

Translation of the 106 Arabic canons: Riedel, *Kirchenrechtsquellen* 233–83.

Literature: Clavis G 2977; Riedel, *Kirchenrechtsquellen* 231–33; Graf, *Geschichte* 1.606–8; F. Cayré, 'Le divorce au IVe siècle dans la loi civile et les canons de St. Basile', *Echos d'Orient* 19 (1920) 295–321; L. T. Lefort, 'Les constitutions ascetiques de [S. Basile]', *Muséon* 69 (1956) 5–10; T. Orlandi, 'Les papyrus coptes du Musée égyptien de Turin', *Muséon* 87 (1974) 115ff. (p. 125: Cod. XIII: Canones Basilii); R.-G. Coquin, 'Canons of Saint Basil', CE 2.459.

The five canons containing moral admonitions are attributed to (pseudo-) Gregory of Nyssa. A second text under his name, cited in the *Nomokanon* of Michael of Damietta, contains rules for the altar and altar utensils.

Translation of the 5 canons: Riedel, *Kirchenrechtsquellen* 283–84.

Literature: Graf, *Geschichte* 1.608–9; R.-G. Coquin, 'Canons of Gregory of Nyssa', CE 2.457.

The 12 canons of John Chrysostom consist of excerpts from his works on the priesthood.

Translation: Riedel, *Kirchenrechtsquellen* 285–87.

Literature: Graf, *Geschichte* 1.609; R.-G. Coquin, 'Canons of Saint John Chrysostom', CE 2.459–60.

Two series of canons circulated among the Melkites under the name of Epiphanius of Constantinople. One contains 137 and the other 45 canons of mostly moral admonitions. Epiphanius was supposed to have composed them for the Emperor Justinian. Both series contain excerpts from the Sixth Novel of Justinian and older canon law literature. The shorter series was received by the Copts in Arabic; a Coptic text is not known. One manuscript attributes them to one Athanasius of Constantinople.

Translation of the short series (35 canons): Riedel, *Kirchenrechtsquellen* 289–94.

Literature: ClavisG 6842; Riedel, *Kirchenrechtsquellen* 288–89; Graf, *Geschichte* 1.620–21; R.-G. Coquin, 'Canons of Epiphanius', CE 2.456–57.

Coptic miscellaneous works attribute to the Fathers of the synod of Nicaea the four books of 'Canons of the Kings'. The first and second books are the 'Procheiros Nomos' and the *Syro-Roman Lawbook*, which also survive among the Melkites in Arabic. The third book is the *Ekloge* in Abū ʾl-Barakāt and Ibn al-ʿAssāl, which is a law book of Roman-Byzantine origins like the first two books. In Makarios it is placed fourth. The fourth book of Abū ʾl-Barakāt and the third of Makarios is a text with the title 'Rulings of the Nicene Fathers'. Ibn al-ʿAssāl uses as his fourth book the 35 chapters of the 'Statutes of the Old Testament'.

Edition and translation: S. Leder, *Die arabische Ekloga: Das vierte Buch der Kanones der Könige aus der Sammlung des Makarios* (Forschungen zur byzantinischen Rechtsgeschichte 12; Frankfurt am Main 1985).

Literature: Riedel, *Kirchenrechtsquellen* 296–98; Nallino, 'Libri giuridici' (= *Raccolta* 4.324–82); Graf, *Geschichte* 1.618–20; Selb-Kaufhold, *Rechtsbuch* 1.65–66, 162–66; see also above in the section on Melkites.

Coptic Synods

Historical sources inform us of an entire series of synods of the Coptic Church. There are, however, no known canons in Coptic. Arabic synodal canons will be dealt with in the following section under the name of the presiding patriarch.

Native Sources of Canon Law

The 'Order of Priesthood' (Tartīb al-kahanūt) of Severos ibn al Muqaffaʾ, the first important Coptic author to use Arabic (second half of the tenth century), does not belong to canon law in the strict sense. This handbook deals among other things with the church and its equipping as well as with the various ranks of the clergy, their consecration and obligations.

Edition: J. Assfalg, *Die Ordnung des Priestertums* (Publications du Centre d'Études Orientales de la Custodie Franciscaine de Terre Sainte, Coptica 1; Cairo 1955).
Literature: Graf, *Geschichte* 2.300–317 ('Order of Priesthood': 313–15).

The Patriarch Christodulos (1047–77) issued 31 (32) canons on comportment in the church, on fasting, the Holy Week and Pentecost, on marriage with Melkite women, and on conduct between clergy. In his biography in the Arabic *History of the Patriarchs* the text is extensively discussed. It was also included in later collections.

Edition and translation: O. H. E. Burmester, 'The Canons of Christodulos, Patriarch of Alexandria (A.D. 1047–77)', *Muséon* 45 (1932) 71–83. Thorough description of contents: *History of the Patriarchs of the Egyptian Church*, ed. A. S. Atiya et al. 2.3 (Cairo 1959) 166–68 (text), 250–55 (translation).
Literature: Riedel, *Kirchenrechtsquellen* 299; Graf, *Geschichte* 2.321; de Clercq, 'Copte (Droit canonique)', DDC 4 (1949) 595; Brogi, *Patriarca* 37–47; S. Y. Labib, 'Christodoulos', CE 2.544–47 (with contents).

A synod under Cyril II (1078–92) in 1086 promulgated 34 canons the patriarch had composed at the urging of the Muslim vezir Badr al-Ǧamālī (a former Armenian slave). They are addressed to bishops and deal particularly with simony, the visitation duties of bishops, the keeping of Sunday, ecclesiastical jurisdiction, fasts, and marital law, as well as the way of life of clerics and laymen. These also were included into miscellaneous works.

Edition and translation: O. H. E. Burmester, 'The Canons of Cyrill II, LXVII Patriarch of Alexandria', Muséon 49 (1936) 245–88 (260–88: canons; 246–57: report from the *History of the Patriarchs*, the latter is also in *History of the Patriarchs* 215–16 (text), 237–340 (translation).

Literature: Riedel, *Kirchenrechtsquellen* 299; Georg Graf, *Ein Reformversuch innerhalb der koptischen Kirche im zwölften Jahrhundert* (Paderborn 1923) (with excerpts: pp. 95, 103, 117); Graf, *Geschichte* 2.323–24; Brogi, *Patriarca* 47–60; Masson, *Divorce* 125–27; S. Y. Labib, 'Cyril II', CE 3.675–77.

Patriarch Gabriel II ibn Turaik (Tarīk) (1131–45), composed 32 canons directed to bishops and priests concerning their conduct and aimed at eliminating abuses during ecclesiastical celebrations and controlling the conduct of laymen. A further eight canons for priests regulate their training and conduct in office, the eucharistic liturgy and ecclesiastical festivals. Further, Gabriel wrote a compendium on marital law. His *Nomokanon* will be dealt with below.

Editions and translations: O. H. E. Burmester, 'The Canons of Gabriel ibn Turaik, LXX Patriarch of Alexandria (First Series)', OCP 1 (1935) 5–45; idem, 'The Canons of Gabriel ibn Turaik, LXX Patriarch of Alexandria', Muséon 46 (1933) 43–54; idem, 'The Laws of Inheritance of Gabriel ibn Turaik, LXX Patriarch of Alexandria', OCP 1 (1935) 315–27.

Literature: Riedel, *Kirchenrechtsquellen* 61–64, 300; Graf *Geschichte* 2.324–27; de Clercq, 'Copte (Droit canonique)', DDC 4 (1949) 595–96; Brogi, *Patriarca* 60–78; Masson, *Divorce* 128–31; Samir Khalil, 'Gabriel II, Patriarche copte d'Alexandrie (1131–45)', DHGE 19 (1980) 528–39; idem, 'Ibn Tarīk ou Ibn Turayk?' Muséon 101 (1988) 171–78; idem, Arabic introduction to the *Nomokanon* treated below, 71–118; S. Y. Labib, 'Gabriel II', CE 4.1127–29.

An extract from a treatise of Michael of Damietta (Dimyāṭ) († after 1208) organized into 10 canons, concerning the special customs of the Copts (crossing with one finger, removal of shoes in church, circumcision, customs in connection with communion, etc.) had some circulation but was only received into the collection of Makarios.

Translation: Graf, *Reformversuch* 147–80 (treatise), 192–97 (canons).

Literature: Riedel, *Kirchenrechtsquellen* 90, 301; Graf, *Reformversuch* 22–23; Graf, *Geschichte* 2.333–34; de Clercq, 'Copte (Droit canonique)', DDC 4 (1949) 595.

In response to the demand of a synod held in 1238 or 1239, the controversial Patriarch Cyril III ibn Laqlaq (1235–43) confirmed various rules for the election of bishops, the creation of an authoritative collection of law, annual synods, circumcision before baptism, hindrances to consecration, consent to consecration, excommunication, episcopal jurisdiction, matters of property, and so on (in 12 chapters).

Editions: M. Ğirğis, *Kitāb al-Qawānīn* (Cairo 1927) [= *Nomokanon* of Ibn al-'Assāl], appendix pp. 9–16; O. H. E. Burmester, 'The Canons of Cyril III ibn Laklak, 75th Patriarch of Alexandria, A.D. 1235–50. I', BSAC 12 (1946–47) 81–136 (with translation). Report on the synod and a thorough review of the contents of the canons: *History of the Patriarchs of the Egyptian Church,* ed. A. Khater et al., 4.2 (Cairo 1974) 85–87 (text), 175–80 (translation).

Literature: Masson, *Divorce* 181–92.

Together with the bishops, Patriarch Cyril III issued the compendium mentioned, in 5 chapters and 19 articles concerning baptism, marital law (based on a writing by a Coptic Patriarch Cosmas), inheritance, priests, and deacons.

Editions: Ǧirǧis, *Kitāb al-Qawānīn* appendix, pp. 16–27 (= chapters 1–3), 1–9 (= chapter 4), 27–30 (= chapter 5); Burmester, 'Canons of Cyril III.': II, BSAC, 14 (1950–57), 113–50 with translation. Translation of the chapter on marital law, Tzadua, *Fetha Nagast* 313–18. Brief mention of the compendium, Khater, *History,* loc. cit. 87 (text), 180 (translation).

There were several agreements between Cyril and the bishops, an order about foundations, on liturgical service, and so on, ten answers to questions posed by Metropolitan Christodulos of Damietta, and a protocol on the rank order of Egyptian bishops.

Edition: Ǧirǧis, *Kitāb al-Qawānīn* appendix, pp. 31–36 (agreement of 1240), 36–39 (foundations), 39–45 (responses); G. Graf, 'Die Rangordnung der Bischöfe Ägyptens nach einem protokollarischen Bericht des Patriarchen Kyrillos ibn Laklak', OrChr 24 (1927) 299–337 (translation).

Also of importance is Cyril's 'Penance Book' (Kitāb al-I'tirāf), which is also called the 'Book of the Teacher and the Pupil' (Kitāb al-Mu'allim wa-t-tilmīd). Closely associated with this is an anonymous 'Book of [33] Chapters' (Kitāb ar-Ru'ūs).

Literature on all of them: Riedel, *Kirchenrechtsquellen* 301–2; Graf, *Geschichte* 2.360–69; Brogi, *Patriarca* 78–98; S. Y. Labib, 'Cyril III ibn Laqlaq', CE 3.677.

A similar book with the same title comes from Markus ibn al-Qanbar (twelfth century); it was discovered only a few years ago.

Literature: Graf, *Geschichte* 2.327–32 (here 329, no. 1); U. Zanetti, 'Le livre de Marc Ibn Qanbar sur la confession retrouvé', OCP 49 (1983) 426–33.

Besides the confessors' manuals already mentioned, Coptic-Arabic manuscripts contain further, anonymous books for confession and penance that are connected with the work of John the Faster (see the section on the Melkites above) or even circulate under his name.

Translation: G. Graf, 'Ein arabisches Poenitentiale bei den Kopten', OrChr 32 (1935) 100–123.

Literature: Graf, *Geschichte* 2.367–69 ('Book of Chapters') 1.612 (other texts).

Patriarch Gabriel V (1409–28) wrote a liturgical handbook (Kitāb Tartīb) mostly in Arabic that is partially a source of canon law.

Literature: Graf, *Geschichte* 1.642, 647–48; 2.456; A. 'Abdallah, *L'ordinamento liturgico di Gabriele V—88° Patriarca Copto 1409–1427*, 2 (Cairo 1962); K. Samir, CE 4.1130–33 (with description of contents).

Monastic Rules

Monastic literature is very extensive in the Coptic Church. Regulations for novices and monks are treated in different writings. The canonical-legal content of such 'rules' is sometimes small (cf. the 'rule' of Moses of Abydos).

Systematically ordered excerpts in translation: F. Kozman (Gozman), 'Textes législatifs touchant le cénobitisme égyptien' (Fonti, serie 2, fasc. 1, Vatican City 1935); R.-G. Coquin, 'La "règle" de Moïse d'Abydos', *Mélanges Antoine Guillaumont* (Geneva 1988) 103–9.

There exists a fragmentary monastic rule in Coptic by the founder of cenobitic monasticism, Pachomius († 346–48). It was translated into Arabic, but not taken into the major miscellaneous works. It circulated in Greek, Latin, and Ethiopian.

Edition and translation of the Coptic rule: L.-T. Lefort, *Oeuvres de s. Pachôme et de ses disciples* (CSCO 159–60; Louvain 1956) 30–36 (text), 30–37 (translation).

Translation of one Arabic version: By P. Karge in Johann Georg Herzog zu Sachsen, *Streifzüge durch die Kirchen und Klöster Ägyptens* (Leipzig-Berlin, 1914) 19–26.

Literature: ClavisG 2353; Graf, *Geschichte* 1.459–61; Lefort, *Oeuvres de s. Pachôme* IX–XII; H. Bacht, 'Ein verkanntes Fragment der koptischen Pachomiusregel', *Muséon* 75 (1962) 5–18; A. Veilleux, *Pachomian Koinonia, 2: Pachomian Chronicles and Rules* (Cistercian Studies Series 46; Kalamazoo, Michigan 1982); idem, 'Pachomius, Saint', CE 6.1859–64; T. Baumeister, 'Der aktuelle Forschungsstand zu den Pachomiusregeln', *Münchener Theologische Zeitschrift* 40 (1989) 313–21.

Pachomius's pupil and successor, Horsiesios († around 380) also wrote rules in Coptic that may survive in Arabic.

Edition and translation: Lefort, *Oeuvres de s. Pachôme* 82–99 (text), 81–99 (translation).
Literature: Graf, *Geschichte* 1.461; Lefort, *Oeuvres de s. Pachôme* XXII–XXX; A. Veilleux, *Pachomian Koinonia, 3: Instructions, Letters and Other Writings of Saint Pachomius and His Disciples* (Cistercian Studies Series 47; Kalamazoo 1982) idem, 'Horsiesios, Saint', CE 4.1257–58.

The most important Coptic writer and energetic 'monk's father', Shenoute 'the Great', composed nine (books) 'Canons' ca. A.D. 348–466 for his monks and nuns. Only a part of this work survives.

A critical edition is in preparation (see Layton, below): D. W. Young, 'An Unplaced Fragment from Shenute's *Fourth Canon*', *Journal of Coptic Studies* 3 (2001) 133–47, pls. 16–17.

Literature: J. Leipoldt, *Schenute von Atripe* (TU NF. X/1; Leipzig 1903) 99–106; K. H. Kuhn, 'Shenute, Saint', CE 7.2131–3; B. Layton, 'Social Structure and Food Consumption in an Early Christian Monastery: The Evidence of Shenoute's Canons and the White Monastery Federation A.D. 385–465', *Muséon* 115 (2002) 25–55.

From an anchorite Isaias, who lived in Skete and died around 488, there are instructions for the ascetic life which gained wide circulation, even in the West.

Edition and translation: J.-M. Sauget, 'La double recension arabe des Préceptes aux novices de l'abbé Isaïe de Scète', *Mélanges Eugène Tisserant* (Studi e testi 233; Vatican City 1964) 3.299—356.

Literature: Graf, *Geschichte* 1.402–3.

The 'Rules and Commands' of St Antonios for the monks of Naqlūn, have a similar character. They are mostly moral admoninitions.

French translation: M. Breydy, in: E. Wipszycka, *Études sur le christianisme dans l'Égypte de l'Antiquité tardive* (Rome 1966) 395–403.

Literature: Graf, *Geschichte* 1.457–58.

In the *History of the Patriarchs* there is a report of a dream of Patriarch Benjamin I (622–61) in connection with the consecration of the church of the Makarios monastery in Skete in which an angel gives him seven canons for the monastery that are to secure the sanctity of the place and to obligate the clergy to wear liturgical clothing and admonish them to behave properly. It was believed that Benjamin received them in Arabic, but they also exist in a Coptic manuscript of the tenth century. Their genuineness is in dispute.

Editions: H. G. Evelyn White, *The Monasteries of the Wâdi'n Natrûn* (New York 1926) 1.127–31 (Coptic); B. Evetts, *History of the Patriarchs of the Coptic Church of Alexandria* 2 (Paris 1904) (= Patrologia orientalis, 1.4), 513–14 (Arabic).

Literature: Graf, *Geschichte* 1.470; C. D. G. Müller, *Die Homilie über die Hochzeit zu Kana und weitere Schriften des Patriachen Benjamin I. von Alexandrien* (Abh. Heidelberg 1968, 1) 26 n. 2; idem, 'Benjamin I', CE 2.375–77.

Later Chronological Collections of Canon Law

It is very difficult to have an overview of the development and scope of later Arabic collections. The primary sources of our knowledge are the manuscripts in which the canons are arranged in chronological order. Among these are Paris, Bibl. nat. arab. 238–241, 243, and 244[128]; Oxford, Bodleian Library Ar. christ. Nicoll 40[129]; Berlin, Staatsbibl. Diez Or. quart. 107[130];

---

128. Troupeau, *Catalogue* 1.200–205.
129. Riedel, *Kirchenrechtsquellen* 135–36.
130. Riedel, *Kirchenrechtsquellen* 129–35.

Birmingham, Mingana ar. christ. 40;[131] Cairo 440 and 578;[132] Makarios Monastery in Egypt, 263 and 264,[133] and not least of all the collection of Makarios.[134] But the systematic collections that offer a chronologically ordered index of sources are also worth looking at, particularly the works of Michael of Damietta[135] and of Ibn al-ʿAssāl (see below).

The core of the Arabic collections is doubtless established by the two pseudo-apostolic texts consisting of 71 and 56 canons respectively (see above), as well as the Greek synods. In some collections there are also the three pseudo-apostolic writings known already from the Melkites (see above), either placed first (Makarios, Oxford 40) or afterward (Cairo 578, Makarios Monastery, 264). Usually the first two are placed at beginning (Abū ʾl-Barakāt, Ibn al-ʿAssāl, Paris, Bibl. nat. arab. 243 [in that case the third text stands after the *Didascalia*]). Michael of Damietta has only the 81 Apostolic Constitutions at the beginning. For chronological reasons the *Didascalia*, the letter of Peter to Clement and—with Makarios—even the 'Statutes of the Old Testament' usually are placed before the Greek synods. The various sequences of the Greek synods have already been mentioned. They are usually followed by the 38 canons of Hippolytus and the 106 canons of Basil. John Chrysostom is also often included. The older systematic collections rest upon this corpus.

In this context the theological encyclopedia of Abū ʾl-Barakāt ibn Kabar, frequently mentioned above, is also useful. It bears the title 'Lamp of Darkness for Performing (ecclesiastical) Services' (Miṣbāḥ aẓ-ẓulma fī-īdāḥ al-ḫidma). Its fifth chapter enumerates the canon law texts known to the author and gives an extensive account of their content. Since the manuscripts that served for editions or translations (or their models) often have misbound leaves, the sequence of texts often cannot be followed on the basis of the published works as they now exist. Abū ʾl-Barakāt made use of a collection of canons that was not inferior to that of Makarios.

Partial edition: Samir, *Misbâh* (chapters 1–42).

Partial translation: Riedel, *Kirchenrechtsquellen* 15–80 (parts of the text in variant sequence).

Literature: Graf, *Geschichte* 2.438–45; A. S. Atiya, 'Ibn Kabar', CE 4.1267.

The chronological collection of the monastic priest Makarios (first half of the fourteenth century), surviving in a number of manuscripts, 'is among

---

131. A. Mingana, *Catalogue of the Mingana Collection of Manuscripts* (Cambridge 1936) 2.42–44.

132. G. Graf, *Catalogue de manuscrits arabes chrétiens conservés au Caire* (ST 63; Vatican City 1934) 162–63, 215.

133. U. Zanetti, *Les manuscrits de Dair Abû Maqâr* (Cahiers d'Orientalisme 9; Geneva 1986) 38.

134. Riedel, *Kirchenrechtsquellen* 123–29.

135. Riedel, *Kirchenrechtsquellen* 92–97.

the richest of its sort, and it remains a quarry of knowledge of legal literature applicable to the Coptic Church and beyond'.[136]

There are similarities to the collection in Paris, Bibl. nat. arab. 238, Berlin, Staatsbibl. Diez Or. quart. 107 as well as to Cairo, Coptic Patriarchate 440 and 635. It still has not been established whether these represent a version Makarios used as a model or whether they are excerpts of his collection. The degree of originality of the work cannot be determined definitively, since one must assume continual additions or omissions by copyists.

Literature: Riedel, *Kirchenrechtsquellen* 121–29 (description of contents); Graf, *Geschichte* 1.560–63; 2.437; R.-G. Coquin, 'Macarius the Canonist', CE 5.1490–91.

Systematic Collections of Canon Law

The Coptic Church distinguished itself through the fact that after the turn of the millennium it produced several Arabic legal collections (called *nomokanones* by modern authors) in which excerpts from the older legal sources were gathered together according to their contents.[137]

Abū Ṣulḥ (Ṣāliḥ) Yūnus (Yūwannīs?) ibn ʿAbdallāh, an otherwise unknown author who must have lived in the tenth and eleventh centuries, compiled what is believed to be the oldest *nomokanon*. As he himself explained, he translated the canons (from Greek or Coptic?) into Arabic. In the introduction he stressed the significance of the canons, which had replaced the old law of Moses, and he stressed their authority. He exploited the pseudo-apostolic and synodal legal literature. The brief work consists of 48 chapters. It dealt with election, consecration, and conduct in office of bishops, religious service, fasting, baptism, the relationship to Jews and heretics, marital law, slaves, commemoration of the dead, apostasy, departure from the monastic community, robbery, and the like. The sources are not cited verbatim but are referred to at the beginning of each chapter, and their contents were freely summarized.

Translation of the introduction: Riedel, *Kirchenrechtsquellen* 80–89.

Literature: Cöln, 'Nomocanonical Literature' 116–19 (description of contents); Graf, *Geschichte* 2.320–21; Brogi, *Patriarca* 99–104; Masson, *Divorce* 105–7.

Patriarch Gabriel ibn Turaik (Tarīk?) (1131–45) composed not only canons and a compendium of inheritance law but also a *Nomokanon*. The work is known from the *Encyclopedia* of Abū ʾl-Barakāt, who gives the contents of 74 chapters[138] and from a mention in the *Nomokanon* of Ibn

---

136. Graf, *Geschichte* 2.437.
137. Cöln, *Nomocanonical Literature* 113–41; R.-G. Coquin, 'Nomocanons. Copto-Arabic', CE 6.1799.
138. Samir, *Misbāḥ* 203–4; Riedel, *Kirchenrechtsquellen* 61–64.

al-ʿAssāl.[139] It had been believed to be lost. In the 1960s René-Georges Coquin discovered it in manuscript Canon 13 of the Coptic patriarchate of Cairo.[140] The manuscript ends in chapter 57. The chapters are not very systematically ordered, and they touch all possible subjects, so that the index of contents in Abū ʾl-Barakāt must be used. Sources include the *Didascalia,* which is often cited, pseudo-apostolic and synodal canons, the 'Canons of the Kings' (see immediately below), the canons of Basil, Hippolytus, John Chrysostom, and Athanasius. The author obviously had a collection of canons at hand that had not yet approached the breadth of later collections, such as Makarios.

In an appendix Gabriel offers a selection from the 'Canons of the Kings' in 11 parts: marital law (1, 7, 8), slaves (2–4), purchase and sale (5), inheritance (6, 11), superannuation (9), and the ban on priests washing the dead (10).[141] A citation from this collection is to be found in the *Nomokanon* of Michael of Damietta, who also places the entire appendix at the close of his own work.[142] According to this evidence, there were supposed to be 12 chapters. The individual sources were given; Gabriel used the 'Canons of Basil' and the 'Statutes of the Old Testament' (once each), as well as Cyriacus of Antioch (twice), but otherwise he used only the *Syro-Roman Lawbook* out of the four books of the 'Canons of the Kings'. The citations from Cyriacus cannot be located in the canons of that Western Syrian patriarch.

Edition: *Le Nomocanon du patriarche copte Gabriel II ibn Turayk (1131–1145): Introduction par Kh. Samir: Étude et Édition critique* by A. A. Mina, 1re partie, (Patrimoine arabe chrétien 12; Beirut 1993) [chapters 1–12]; 2ème partie (Patrimoine arabe chrétien 13; Beirut 1999) [chapters 13–60];Antonius Aziz Mina, *Le nomocanon de Gabriel Ibn Turayk* (El-Minia 1980).
Literature: Riedel, *Kirchenrechtsquellen* 61–64, 300; Graf, *Geschichte* 2.324–27; Coquin, *Hippolyte* 280–81; Samir Khalil, introduction to the edition, 25–164 (on the *Nomocanon* 119–64); idem, 'Remariage des prêtres veufs? L'attitude du patriarche copte Gabriel II ibn Turayk', POC 44 (1994) 277–84; Selb-Kaufhold, *Rechtsbuch* 1.168.

Michael of Damietta (Dimyāṭ) († after 1208) has also already been treated as an author of canons. It was probably in 1188 when he composed a *nomokanon* that has been preserved in two versions. It contained 72 chapters in more or less systematic order and dealt, among other things, with the rank order of the patriarchs, the construction and equipping of churches, elections, consecration, and conduct of bishops and other clergy, monks and nuns, deaconesses, the conduct of laymen, baptism, Eucharist, fast-

---

139. 'Introduction to the Canons of Hippolytus', see Ğirğis, *Kitāb al-Qawānīn* 9; Tzadua, *Fetha Nagast* 8.
140. Very brief description in Graf, *Catalogue* 163–64, no. 442.
141. Riedel, *Kirchenrechtsquellen* 64.
142. Ibid. 102 (34), 114f (72).

ing, festivals of martyrs, the care of the sick and the poor, eunuchs, oaths, donations, conduct toward Jews and heretics, magical and idolatrous practices, usury, marital and penal canons. As mentioned above, the conclusion is the appendix from the *Nomokanon* of Gabriel ibn Turaik. His sources are the Bible and the usual works on canon law: the pseudo-apostolic texts,[143] *Didascalia*, Greek synods, as well as canons of Hippolytus, Basil, and John Chrysostom. Beyond the works given in the index of sources,[144] he also cited the second book of the 'Canons of the Kings' (the *Syro-Roman Lawbook*), Gregory of Nyssa, and Epiphanius (of Constantinople).[145]

Translation of the introduction: Riedel, *Kirchenrechtsquellen* 92–97; O. H. E. Burmester, 'The Sayings of Michael, Metropolitan of Damietta', OCP 2 (1936) 101–28.

Literature: Riedel, *Kirchenrechtsquellen* 89–115 (thorough description of contents); Cöln, 'Nomocanonical Literature' 119–26; Graf, *Geschichte* 2.333–35; Coquin, *Hippolyte* 281–82; Brogi, *Patriarca* 104–12; Masson, *Divorce* 131–43; R.-G. Coquin, 'Mikha'il', CE 1624–25; Selb-Kaufhold, *Rechtsbuch* 1.168–69.

The most significant systematic collection is by aṣ-Ṣafī abu ʾl-Faḍāʾil ibn al-ʿAssāl, one of the most important Coptic-Arabic authors. He belonged to an influential family and lived around the middle of the thirteenth century. His work can truly be called a *nomokanon*, since it also included a considerable amount of civil law. Of the 51 chapters, the first 22 dealt with canon law, and the following with secular law (including marital and criminal law). The collection is organized in a strictly systematic order. The sequence of canon law chapters resembles that of Michael of Damietta: church buildings, canon of the Holy Scripture, baptism, patriarchs, bishops, priests, deacons, lower clergy and deaconesses, again priests, monks, and nuns, directions for laymen, the mass and Eucharist, prayer, fasting, charitable gifts and donations, holidays, martyrs, confessors and apostates, the sick, and the dead. His sources, to which he gave sigla, are presented in an index at the start of the work. In addition to the sources used by Michael of Damietta he included the 30 'Traditions of the Apostles', the 'Epistle of Peter to Clement', all four books of the 'Canons of the Kings', and he also knew the Coptic patriarchs Christodulos, Timothy (of Alexandria), and Dionysius (of Alexandria). The civil law portion rests extensively on Islamic law.

His *Nomokanon* survives in two quite different versions, of which the longer is probably the original. It was translated into Ethiopian under the title *Fetha Nagašt* ('Laws of the Kings'). There is also a translation among the Western Syrians (at least of the chapter on the patriarchs). Excerpts

---

143. Including unidentifiable canons; see Riedel, *Kirchenrechtsquellen* 175–77.
144. Riedel, *Kirchenrechtsquellen* 92–97.
145. See the index of sigla, Riedel, *Kirchenrechtsquellen* 97 n. 1.

from the *Nomokanon* are to be found in the Arabic collections of the Maronite ʿAbdallah al-Qarāʾali (first half of the eighteenth century) and in Syriac translation in the *Ordo iudiciorum* of the Eastern Syrian ʿAbdīšōʿ bar Brīkā (see below).

Editions: G. F. Auwad, *al-Maǧmūʿ aṣ-Ṣafawī* (Cairo 1908); Ǧirǧis, *Kitāb al-Qawānīn*.

Translation of the Ethiopian version: I. Guidi, *Il 'Fetha Nagast' o la 'Legislazone dei Re': Codice ecclesiastico e civile di Abessinia* (2 vols. Rome 1897–99, repr. of vol. 1: Naples 1936); P. Tzadua, *The Fetha Nagast: The Laws of the Kings* (Addis Ababa 1968).

Literature: Riedel, *Kirchenrechtsquellen* 115–19; Cöln, 'Nomocanonical Literature' 136–41; Nallino, 'Libri giuridici' 144–56 (= *Raccolta* 4.362–73); A. d'Emilia, 'Influssi di diritto musulmano nel capitolo XVIII, 2 [= pious foundations] nel nomocanone arabo cristiano di Ibn al-ʿAssāl', RSO 19 (1941/42) 1–15; Graf, *Geschichte* 2.387–403 (on the *Nomocanon* 398–403); S. Jargy, DDC 5 (1953) 127–1242; Coquin, *Hippolyte* 282–83; Brogi, *Patriarca* 112–19; Masson, *Divorce* 147–81; H. Kaufhold, 'Der Richter in den syrischen Rechtsquellen: Zum Einfluß islamischen Rechts auf die christlich-orientalische Rechtsliteratur', OrChr 68 (1984) 91–113 (adoption by ʿAbdīšōʿ bar Brīkā and ʿAbdallah Qarāʿalī); idem, *Syrische Handschriften* 19–20 (Western Syrian translation); Wadi Abullif, 'Bibliografia commentata sugli Aulād al-ʿAssāl, tre fratelli scrittori del sec. XIII', SOCC 18 (1985) 31–79; Samir Khalil, *Patrologia Orientalis* 192 (1985) 678–80 (bibliography); idem, 'L'utilisation des sources dans le Nomocanon d'Ibn al-ʿAssāl, OCP 55 (1989) 101–24; idem, CE 7.2075–79. Selb-Kaufhold, *Rechtsbuch* 1.169–71.

An Arabic work that is partly transmitted anonymously, but partly attributed to Bishop Michael of Aṭrīb and Malīǧ, an important author of the thirteenth century, is less a *nomokanon* than a handbook for confessors in 47 chapters. In the literature (Cöln, for instance), Markos ibn al-Qanbar (mentioned above) is also identified as the author of this work. The title is 'Book of Spiritual Medicine' (Kitāb aṭ-Ṭibb ar-rūḥānī). Following two introductory chapters are moral-theological treatments of various sins and a compilation of penalties from the Bible, synodal canons, Fathers of the Church, and the 'Canons of the Kings' (chapters 3–26). Chapters 27–37 deal with Baptism and the various classes of believers. Chapters 38–47 deal with fasting, Holy Week, holidays, prayer, alms, oaths, and the celebration of the liturgy. The book is also known among the Melkites and the Western Syrians. In the seventeenth century it was translated into Ethiopian (Faus manfasāwi, 'Spiritual Medicine').

Edition and translation: F. J. Cöln, 'Der Nomokanon Mîhâ'îls von Malîg', OrChr 6 (1906) 70–237; 7 (1907) 1–135; 8 (1908) 110–229. Arabic text: al-Anbā Samūʾīl, *aṭ-Ṭibb ar-rūḥānī* (Cairo 1999).

Literature: Riedel, *Kirchenrechtsquellen* 119–21 (without having identified the work); Cöln, 'Nomocanonical Literature' 124–29; Graf, *Geschichte* 2.414–27 ('Spiritual Medicine' 420–26); R.-G. Coquin, 'Mikhaʾil', CE 5.1625–27; Selb-Kaufhold, *Rechtsbuch* 1.171.

The *Nomokanon* of Faraǧallāh al-Aḥmīmī from the thirteenth or fourteenth centuries, which 'almost can be regarded as an act of plagiarism'

(Graf), relies on the 'Book of Spiritual Medicine' and the *Nomokanon* of Ibn al-ʿAssāl. As additional sources he used writings of the Eastern Syrian Ibn aṭ-Ṭaiyib and Elias of Nisibis (bar Šīnāyā).

Literature: Riedel, *Kirchenrechtsquellen* 121; Cöln, 'Nomocanonical Literature' 129–36 (description of contents); Graf, *Geschichte* 2.427–28; W. Frederic, 'Faragallah al-Akhmīmī', CE 4.1089 (reproducing Graf).

Recently Ugo Zanetti discovered a new anonymous *nomokanon* in manuscript 267 (canon 6) of the Makarios Monastery in Egypt. The text begins in the third chapter and breaks off in chapter 88, though it could not have been much longer. It is as comprehensive as, but less systematic than, the *Nomokanon* of Ibn al-ʿAssāl, including all possible subjects of ecclesiastical and civil law. As is the case with almost all *nomokanones*, the complete text follows each attribution of source (with the sigla). The sources are the usual, but secular sources are completely omitted. In the case of chapters on civil law, there are only titles, and the text is either completely missing or represented only by citations from ecclesiastical literature, particularly the *Didascalia*. It is possible that it is an unfinished work.

Literature: U. Zanetti, 'Le Nomocanon du Ms. St.-Macaire 267 (can. 6)', ParOr 16 (1990–91) 189–206.

Nubia

Sources of ecclesiastical law in Nubia were probably written in Greek and Coptic.[146] Few legal texts have been found among the scarce remains of Nubian literature, but one surviving text contains the Pseudo-Nicaean canons that deal with the reception of the Eucharist. Papyrus documents are also important for Nubian law.

Literature: G. M. Browne, 'Griffith's "Nicene Canons",' *Bulletin of the American Society of Papyrologists* 20 (1983) 97–112.

Legal documents: F. Ll. Griffith, 'The Nubian Texts of the Christian Period', *Abhandlungen der Königlichen Preußischen Akademie der Wissenschaften. Jahrgang 1913*, Phil.-hist. Classe, 8 (Berlin 1913) 53–55: 'IV. Berlin Museum P. 11277. (Sale.)'; idem, 'Christian Documents from Nubia', *Proceedings of the British Academy* 14 (London 1928) (pp. 12–18: A Legal Document on Leather); E. Zyhlarz, 'Neue Sprachdenkmäler des Altnubischen', *Studies Presented to F. Ll. Griffith* (London 1932) 187–95 (187–90: 'Ein altnubischer Bauern-Kontrakt'); C. D. G. Müller, 'Deutsche Textfunde in Nubien', *Kunst und Geschichte Nubiens in christlicher Zeit,* ed. E. Dinkler (Recklinghausen 1970) 245–58 (here: 245–50, 257); idem, 'Ergänzende Bemerkungen zu den deutschen Textfunden in Nubien', OrChr 62 (1978) 135–43 (here: 136); M. Khalil, 'Der Berliner Kaufvertrag P. 11277', *Nubica* 1–2 (Cologne 1990) 267–71; G. M. Browne, 'Griffith's Old Nubian Sale', *Orientalia* N.S. 61 (1992)

---

146. P. O. Scholz and D. Müller, 'Nubien' and 'Nubische Sprache', KLCO 375–79, 387–88; W. Y. Adams, various articles on Nubia in CE 6 1800–1819; J. Richard, 'L'Église de Nubie', *Histoire du Christianisme* 6.240–41 (*Geschichte des Christentums* 6.236–37).

454–58; M. M. Khalil and C. D. G. Müller, 'Das unternubische Rechtswesen im Mittelalter', *Nubica et Aethiopica* 4–5 (Warsaw 1999) 5–23.

Ethiopians

History of the Church

The beginnings of Christianity in Ethiopia reach back at least to the fourth century when King 'Ezana, ruler of the northern realm of Aksum, converted to Christianity. The conversion probably occurred through the work of Monophysites expelled from Byzantine territory in the course of the Christological disputes, which marked the theological development of the Ethiopian Church. The spread of Islam led to increased isolation and finally to the collapse of the Kingdom of Aksum in the tenth century. In the twelfth century the center of political power moved south. Little is known of the history of the church in Ethiopia in the Middle Ages. In the course of time the ties between the Ethiopian and Coptic Churches grew very close.

Literature: Spuler, *Die morgenländischen Kirchen* 309–18; E. Ullendorff, *The Ethiopians: An Introduction to Country and People* (2nd ed., London 1965); E. Hammerschmidt, *Äthiopien: Christliches Reich zwischen Gestern und Morgen* (Wiesbaden 1967); Atiya, *Eastern Christianity* 146–66; E. Heyer, *Die Kirche Äthiopiens: Eine Bestandsaufnahme* (Berlin–New York 1971); Heiler, *Die Ostkirchen* 361–75; Müller, *Nationalkirchen* 344–53; J. Richard, 'L'Église d'Ethiopie', *Histoire du Christianisme* 6.241–46 (*Geschichte des Christentums* 6. 238–43); H. G. Marcus, *A History of Ethiopia* (Berkeley 1994); *Encyclopaedia Aethiopica* 2 (2005) 414–26.

Ethiopian Literature

The older literature of Ethiopia is written in Old Ethiopian (Ge'ez), a language belonging to the southern Semitic group. During the Aksumite period, between the fourth and fifth centuries and the end of the seventh century, the Bible and other theological works were translated directly from the Greek. During the second major period of Ethiopian literature, from the thirteenth to the eighteenth centuries, these were supplemented by translations of Coptic-Arabic works. It is only in this period that the known canon law sources were translated into Ethiopian. There is no certain knowledge of earlier sources.

Literature: E. Littmann, 'Geschichte der äthiopischen Literatur', *Christliche Litteraturen* 185–270; J. M. Harden, *An Introduction to Ethiopic Christian Literature* (London 1926); Guidi, *Letteratura*; E. Cerulli, *La letteratura etiopica* (3rd ed., Milan 1968); L. Ricci, 'Ethiopian Christian Literature', *CE* 3.975–79.

Sources of Ethiopian Canon Law

Hiob Ludolf (1624–1704) is regarded as the founder of Ethiopian studies, and he gave the first reliable account of the Ethiopia of his day. He also explored canon law. Further information also was provided by the

Histoire de l'église d'Alexandrie by J. M. Vansleb (Wansleben), which appeared in Paris in 1677. Various legal sources have been published since the beginning of the last century and have been made accessible to scholars through translations. Some studies on particular questions have appeared, but there is still no comprehensive analysis of Ethiopian canon law. It is still impossible to say anything about the extent to which particular sources were applied in practice. Due to the dependence on Coptic-Arabic originals, we can usually trace a Ethiopian work's contents to corresponding sources in the Coptic Church.

Translation of sources in selection: Mauro de Leonissa, *Disciplina alessandrina (Etiopi): Testi di diritto antichi e moderni riguardanti gli Etiopi* (= Fonti, Serie 1, fasc. 5; Vatican City 1931) [particularly drawing from the *Fetha Nagašt*]; *Disciplina alessandrina (Etiopi): Testi di diritto antichi riguardanti gli Etiopi* (= Fonti, Serie 1, fasc. 6; Vatican City 1931) [particularly drawing on the *Senodos*].

Literature: S. Grébaut, 'Disciplina alessandrina: II. Etiopi', *Studi storichi* 73–85; N. V. Dură, 'Receptarca canoanelor în biserica etiopanaă', *Studi Teologice* 37 (1975) 96–108; R. W. Cowley, 'The Identification of the Ethiopian Octateuch of Clement', *Ostkirchliche Studien* 27 (1978) 37–45 (on many pseudo-Clementine writings); A. Bausi, 'New Egyptian Texts in Ethiopia', *Adamantius: Rivista del Gruppo Italiano di Ricerca su 'Origine e la tradizione alessandrina'* 8 (2002) 146–51; idem, 'San Clemente e le tradizioni Clementine nella letteratura etiopica canonico-liturgica', *Studi sul Clemente Romano*, ed. Philippe Luisier (Orientalia Christiana Analecta 268; Rome 2003) 13–55; idem, 'La Collezione Aksumita canonico-liturgica', *Adamantius: Rivista del Gruppo Italiano di Ricerca su 'Origine e la tradizione alessandrina'* 12 (2006, published 2010) 43–70.

The *Synodos (Senodos)*

Only in the fourteenth century was the most important source of Ethiopian canon law translated from Arabic, the *Senodos* (Synodos). It was even received into the biblical canon. It was a miscellaneous work that contained pseudo-apostolic canons in various versions, canons of early Greek synods, and some Greek Fathers. In view of the connections between the Ethiopian Church and the Coptic Church, it must have been compiled from a Coptic-Arabic original. Indeed, there are many possible sources. Guidi and Hammerschmidt, who follows him, assume that the translation comes from a Melkite original because the canons of Ancyra have a preface that is characteristic of Melkite collections.[147] This conclusion is not persuasive, because Melkite influence may occasionally be detected in Coptic-Arabic collections as well. Such a Melkite-influenced manuscript could have been the original for the anonymous Ethiopian translator. The work survives in several manuscripts that do not completely agree with one another.[148] Since some texts

---

147. I. Guidi, 'Der äthiopische "Sēnodos"'; E. Hammerschmidt, 'Pseudo-apostolisches Schrifttum' 116.
148. Cf. Hanssens, *Hippolyte* 40–44; Bausi, *Il Sēnodos etiopico* (see below) preface to the edition.

have various versions, different collections could have been used. More research and a careful comparison of the texts with the Arabic versions must be made before we will understand the transmission of these texts.

Literature: I. Guidi, 'Der äthiopische "Sēnedos",' ZDMG 55 (1901) 495–502; Riedel, *Kirchenrechtsquellen* 154–55; A. Baumstark, 'Der äthiopische Bibelkanon', OrChr 5 (1905) 162–73 (165–70); Guidi, *Letteratura* 37–38; C. Conti Rossini, 'Il "Senodos" etiopico', *Atti della Reale Accademia d'Italia: Rendiconti della classe di scienze morali e storiche*, ser. 7, vol. 3 (1941) 41–48; Hammerschmidt, 'Pseudo-apostolisches Schrifttum' 116–18; idem, *Äthiopien* 55, 57, 107; K. Wendt, 'Der Kampf um den Kanon der hl. Schriften in der äthiopischen Kirche der Reformen des XV. Jahrhunderts', JSSt 107–13; R. W. Cowley, 'The Biblical Canon of the Ethiopian Orthodox Church Today', *Ostkirchliche Studien* 23 (1974) 318–23; Hanssen, *Hippolyte* 40–44; A. Bausi, 'Alcune considerazioni sul Sēnodos etiopico', *Rassegna di Studi Etiopici* 34 (1990) 5–73; idem, 'San Clemente 27–41; idem, 'Senodos', *Encyclopaedia Aethiopica* 4 (2010) 623–25.

The *Synodos* contains the following ten parts.

1. 71 'Canons of the Apostles', which, as in Coptic collections, consist of the 'Apostolic Church Order', the 'Egyptian Church Order' and the parallel text to the eighth book of the 'Apostolic Constitutions'. Duensing established that the Ethiopian text of the 'Egyptian Church Order' is partly supplemented by the addition of liturgical pieces but it otherwise agrees largely with the known Arabic text. The model of the Ethiopian translator must have been riddled with errors, or perhaps he occasionally read it wrongly or understood it incorrectly.

Editions: H. Ludolf, *Ad suam historiam Aethiopicam ... Commentarius* (Frankfurt am Main 1691) 305–10, 314–28 (excerpts); G. Horner, *The Statutes of the Apostles or Canones Ecclesiastici* (London 1904) 1–87 (text), 127–232 (English translation); H. Duensing, *Der äthiopische Text der Kirchenordnung des Hippolyt: Nach 8 Handschriften herausgegeben und übersetzt* (Abh. Göttingen, 3d series, no. 32; Göttingen 1946).

Literature: E. von der Goltz, 'Unbekannte Fragmente altchristlicher Gemeindeordnungen nach G. Horners englischer Ausgabe der äthiopischen Kirchenrechtsbücher', *Königlich Preußische Akademie der Wissenschaften* (Berlin 1906) 141–57.

2. 56 'Canons of the Apostles', the well-known apostolic canons.

Editions: Winand Fell, Canones apostolorum aethiopice (Leipzig 1871) (57 Canons); Alessandro Bausi, *Il Sēnodos etiopico: Canoni pseudoapostolici, Canoni dopo l'Ascensione, Canoni di Simone Cananeo, Canoni apostolici, Lettera di Pietro* (2 vol. CSC" 552–553; Leuven 1995) 116–47 (text), 51–61 (translation).

Translation: Fell, *Canones apostolici*; G. H. Schodde, 'The Apostolic Canons translated from the Ethiopic', *Journal of Biblical Literature and Exegesis* 5 (Boston 1885) 61–72; Bausi (CSCO 553) 51–61.

3. 81 Abṭelisāt (= titloi) of the Apostle (Bausi: 1st recension), another version of the 'Canons of the Apostles'.

Edition and translation: Bausi, *Canones apostolici* 180–233 (text), 73–90 (translation).

4. Canons of Simon the Canaanite (Bausi: 2nd recension), a part of the parallel texts to the eighth book of the 'Apostolic Constitutions'. It corresponds to the sixth book of the Syrian 'Octateuchus Clementinus'.

Edition and translation: Bausi, *Canones apostolici* 72–115 (text), 36–50 (translation).

5. 'Canons of the Apostles' after the Resurrection. These are also included in the Melkite and later Coptic-Arabic collections ('30 Traditions of the Apostles') and correspond to the 'Canons of the Apostles' (or 'of the Apostle Addai') of the Syrian collections.

Edition and translation: Bausi, op. cit. 9–40 (text), 4–18 (translation).

6. 80 Abṭelisāt (= titloi), other (Bausi: the second) recension of the 'Apostolic Canons'.

Edition and translation: Bausi, 234–83 (text), 91–108 (translation).

7. Other (Bausi: the first) recension of the 'Canons of Simon the Canaanite' (see 4 above).

Edition and translation: Bausi, op. cit. 41–71 (text), 19–35 (translation).

8. Other versions of the 'Apostolic Canons' (81 canons), that are not called Abṭelisāt.

Edition and translation: Bausi, op. cit. 148–79 (text), 62–72 (translation).

9. 'Epistle of Peter to Clement', also known from Coptic collections.

Edition and translation: Bausi, op. cit. 284–305 (text), 109–18 (translation).

10. Greek canons of the synods of Ancyra, Neocaesarea, Nicaea: 20 and 84 canons and the 'Sermo de Trinitate' (= the dogmatic part of the 'Syntagma doctrinae', see above), Gangra, Sardica, Antioch, Laodiceia, Canons of John Chrysostom, Responses of Timothy of Alexandria, Penitential Canons, and so on.

In Alessandro Bausi's newly discovered and described manuscript (see 1 above) there are, among other items, the following texts: a letter of Constantine the Great to the Church of Alexandria, a letter of Constantine over the condemnation of Arius, and the canons of Constantinople, Ephesus, and Chalcedon.

Editions and translations of parts: Mauro a Leonissa, 'La versione etiopica dei canoni apocrifi del Concilio di Nicea', *Rassegna di Studi Etiopici* 2 (1941) 29–89; L. Guerrier and S. Grébaut, 'Les canons du concile de Gangres', ROC 23 (1922–23) 303–13; L. Guerrier, 'Canons pénitentiels', ROC 21 (1918–19) 5–24, 345–55; A. Bausi, 'La versione etiopica della *Didascalia dei 318 Niceni* sulla retta fede e la vita monastica', *Ægyptus Christiana. Mélanges d'hagiographie égyptienne et orientale dédiés à la mémoire du P. Paul Devos*, ed. U. Zanetti and E. Lucchesi (Geneva 2004) 225–48 (Syntagma Doctrinae).

Two short pieces of the *Didache* (11, 3–13; 7 and 8, 1–2) are to be found in the Ethiopian version of the '71 Canons of the Apostles'. Since they are not present in the Coptic and Arabic versions of this work, it must be assumed that they come from an Ethiopian translation of the whole of the *Didache* which has not survived and to which there are no other references. The variations from the Greek text are insignificant.

Edition: G. Horner, *The Statutes of the Apostles or Canones Apostolici* (London 1904) 54–55, 193–94.

Literature: Audet, *Didaché* 34–45; Niederwimmer, *Didache* 43–44; Schöllgen, *Didache* 89.

The *Didascalia*

This Ethiopian translation of the *Didascalia*, which also originated at the end of the fourteenth century, rests on the later Coptic-Arabic version in 44 chapters which Abū Isḥāq ibn Faḍlallāh translated from Coptic in 1295, and which was taken from books 1 to 7 of the 'Apostolic Constitutions'. It consists of 43 chapters and was, as was the case with the *Synodos* and the 'Testament of Our Lord Jesus Christ' to be treated below, included in the New Testament canon.

Editions and translations: P. T. Platt, *The Ethiopic Didascalia; or the Ethiopic Version of the Apostolical Constitutions, Received in the Church of Ethiopia* (London 1934) (based on an incomplete manuscript, through chapter 22); J. Françon, 'La Didascalie éthiopienne: Traduit en français', ROC 16 (1911) 161–66, 266–70; 17 (1912), 199–203, 286–93; 19 (1914), 183–87 (incomplete); J. M. Harden, *The Ethiopic Didascalia* (Translation of Christian Literature; Oriental Texts 1; London, New York 1920) (complete translation).

Literature: Guidi, *Letteratura* 37–39; Hammerschmidt, 'Pseudo-apostolisches Schrifttum' 115; idem, *Äthiopien* 55, 107; N. V. Dură, '"Didascalia" versiunea etiopiana', *Studi Teologice* 37 (1975) 436–51.

The 'Testament of Our Lord Jesus Christ'

The Ethiopian translation was taken from an Arabic original and must also have been written at the end of the fourteenth century. There is as yet no close examination of this text. This reworking of the Church Order of Hippolytus is not to be confused with an Ethiopian 'Testament of Our Lord Jesus Christ in Galilee', a dialogue between Jesus and his disciples after the Resurrection.

Edition: R. Beylot, *Testamentum Domini éthiopien: Édition et traduction* (Louvain 1984).

Literature: Hammerschmidt, 'Pseudo-apostolisches Schrifttum', 118–20; idem, *Äthiopische liturgische Texte der Bodleian Library in Oxford* (Berlin 1960) 48–72; idem, *Äthiopien* 55, 107, 131, 133, 146. R.-G. Coquin, 'Le Testamentum Domini: Problèmes de tradition textuelle', ParOr 5 (1974) 165–88 (especially 184–88). See also above the section on West Syrian canon law.

Pseudo-Clement (Qalēmentos)

The pseudo-Clementine 'Roll Book' (Kitāb al-Maǧāll), which has survived in several Arabic versions, was also translated in the fourteenth century into Ethiopian. The translator completely reorganized the second part (books 3–7) and in the place of prophecies he incorporated older legal sources and penitentials.

Translation: S. Grébaut, 'Littérature éthiopienne pseudo-clémentine, 3: Traduction du Qalēmentos', ROC 16 (1911) 72–88, 167–75, 225–33; 17 (1912), 16–31, 133–44, 244–52, 337–46; 18 (1913), 69–78; (Book 3:) 19 (1914), 324–33; 20 (1915–17), 33–37, 424–30; 21 (1918–19), 246–52; 22 (1920–21), 22–28, 113–17, 395–400; 26 (1927–28), 22–31 (not finished); A. Bausi, *Qalēmentos etiopico: La rivelazione di Pietro a Clemente: I libri 3–7: Traduzione e introduzione* (Istituto Universitario Orientale, Serie Etiopica 2; Naples 1992).

Literature: A. Dillmann, 'Bericht über das ethiopische Buch Clementiner Schriften', *Nachrichten von der Georg-August-Universität und der Königlichen Gesellschaft der Wissenschaften zu Göttingen* 1858) 185–99, 201–15, 217–26; Graf, *Geschichte* 1.287–88; Hammerschmidt, 'Pseudo-apostolisches Schrifttum', 120–211; G. Haile, 'Religious Controversies and the Growth of Ethiopic Literature in the Fourteenth and Fifteenth Centuries', Or-Chr 65 (1981) 102–36; A. Bausi, 'San Clemente' 13–55.

Nikon of the Black Mountain

The *Pandects of Nikon (Hāwī)*, originally composed in Greek by Nikon of the Black Mountain (see above, on the canon law of the Melkites), was transmitted, by an Arabic version known to the Melkites and Copts, to the Ethiopians. In 1583 a monk of the monastery of Dabra Libanos translated it.

Literature: Guidi, *Letteratura* 73–74.

The *Spiritual Medicine*

Also of Coptic-Arabic origin is the *Spiritual Medicine (Faus manfasawi)*. That work was translated in 1667 from Arabic to Ethiopian.

Literature: Guidi, *Letteratura* 78.

The *Fetha Nagašt*

The *Law of the Kings* (Fetha Nagašt) was translated into Ethiopian during the seventeenth century from the systematic thirteenth-century Arabic legal collection of the Copt Ibn al-ʿAssāl that contained both canon and civil law. It is disputed how much authority this work had in the legal practice of Ethiopia.

Editions (partial): J. Bachmann, *Corpus Iuris Abessinorum: Textem aethiopicum arabicumque ad manuscriptorum fidem cum versione latina et dissertatione iuridico-historica edidit,* Pars 1: *Jus connubii* (Berlin 1890); I. Guidi, *Il 'Fetha Nagast' o 'Legislazione dei Re.' Codice ecclesiastico e civile di Abessinia* (2 vols. Roma 1897–1899, Repr. of vol. 1: Napoli 1936).

Translation: *The Fetha Nagast: The Law of the Kings,* Translated from the Ge'ez by Abba Paulos Tzadua (Addis Ababa 1968).

Literature: Guidi, *Letteratura* 78; E. Cerulli, *La letteratura etiopica* (3rd ed. Milan 1968) 176–77; S. Euringer, 'Abessinien und der Heilige Stuhl', *Theologische Quartalschrift* 92 (1910) 339–99, 491–531; R. Rossi Canevari, *Fetha Nagast (il libro dei re) codice delle leggi abissine con note e riferimenti al diritto italiano* (Milan 1936); Abd el-Samei and Mohammad Ahmad, *Fetha Nagasht* (Cairo 1965) (Arabic); P. Tadzua, 'The Ancient Law of the Kings—the Fetha Nagast—in the actual practice of the Established Ethiopian Orthodox Church', *Kanon: Jahrbuch der Gesellschaft für das Recht der Ostkirchen* 1 (1973) 112–46; V. N. Durǎ, 'Nomocanone etiopian 'Feta Nagast'în lumine cercetarilor istoricilor şi cuniştilor etiopeni şi europeni', *Studi Teologice* 37 (1975) 96–108; F. A. Dombrowsji, 'Das Fetha Nagaśt—eine Richtschnur der Äthiopischer Kirche?' *Internationale Kirchliche Zeitschrift* 76 (1986) 218–29.

Monastic Rules

Ethiopian manuscripts preserve three 'rules' of the Egyptian monastic father Pachomius. The first is a translation of the chapter 'Pachomius and the Monks of Tabennēse' from the *Historia Lausiaca* of Palladios. The second is a true monastic rule that is also preserved in Coptic. The third consists of penitential canons and an allegorical monastic apocalypse. In this case it is uncertain whether it originated in Ethiopia or is of foreign origin.

Edition: A. Dillmann, *Chrestomathia Aethiopica* (1st ed., Leipzig 1866); the second, unaltered edition has addenda and corrigenda by E. Littmann (Berlin 1950, reprint, Darmstadt 1967) 57–69. Collation of more manuscripts: O. Löfgren, 'Zur Textkritik der äthiopischen Pachomiusregeln 1.2', *Le Monde oriental* 30 (Uppsala 1936) 171–87.

Translations: E. König, 'Die Regeln des Pachomius: Aus dem Aethiopischen übersetzt und mit Anmerkungen versehen', *Theologische Studien und Kritiken* 51 (1878) 323–37; G. H. Schodde, 'The Rules of Pachomius, translated from Ethiopic', *Presbyterian Review* 6 (1885) 678–89; R. Bassett, 'Les règles attribuées à Saint-Pakhôme', *Les Apocryphes éthiopiens traduits en français* 8 (Paris 1896); O. Löfgren, '"Pakomius" etiopiska klosterregler', *Kyrkohistorisk Årsskrift* (Stockholm 1948) 163–84.

Literature: ClavisG 2353; Guidi, *Letteratura* 17; E. Cerulli, *La letteratura etiopica* (3rd ed., Milan, 1968) 23–24; Graf, *Geschichte* 1.459–60.

Beyond those mentioned, there are elements of canon law in some theological works of the fifteenth century, such as the 'Book of Mysteries' [= Sacraments] (*Maṣḥafa mestir*), the 'Book of Light' (*Maṣḥafa berhān*) and the 'Book of the Birth [of Christ]' (*Maṣḥafa milād*).

Editions and translations: Y. Beyenne, *Giyorgia di Sagla: Il libro del Mistero (Mashafa mestir)* (CSCO 515–16; Louvain 1990); C. Conti Rossini and L. Ricci, *Il libro della luce del Negus Zar'a Yā'qob* (CSCO 250–51, 261–62; Louvain 1964–65); K. Wendt, *Das Mashafa Milād (Liber Nativitatis) . . . des Kaisers Zar'a Yā'qob* (CSCO 221–22, 235–36; Louvain 1962–63).

Literature: Guidi, *Letteratura* 51; Hammerschmidt, *Äthiopien* 56; R. Beylot, 'Langues et littérature éthiopiennes', *Christianismes orientaux* 244–45.

Eastern Syrians (Nestorians)

History of the Church

Christianity spread among the Aramaic population of southern Mesopotamia at a very early time, even if reports of a mission by apostles or followers of the apostles are legendary. The earliest congregations must have been established in the third century. Christians endured several persecutions under the Persian Sassanids (224–632). By the beginning of the fifth century there emerged an ecclesiastical organization with a supreme bishop in the capital of Seleucia-Ctesiphon (who later received the title 'Katholikos'), several metropolitans, and many bishops. In the course of the fifth century Nestorius's concepts of the relationship of the divine and human nature of Christ won support among the Eastern Syrians. Although this doctrine was condemned at the Ecumenical Council of Ephesus (431), the Eastern Syrian Church adopted it officially in 484 at a synod in Seleucia-Ctesiphon. After this synod, the Eastern Syrians stood alone against the rest of Christianity. Their church soon developed a zealous missionary activity, and further Nestorian congregations and bishoprics were established in Arabia, Persia, and Central Asia all the way to China and India. As happened with the other Eastern churches, the number of faithful declined with the spread of Islam, but the cultural life of the Eastern Syrians still blossomed for centuries. A rapid decline set in after the Mongol invasions in the thirteenth and fourteenth centuries, which practically obliterated the institutional church. Splits within the Nestorian church and the rise of a Chaldaean Church united with Rome weakened it even further.

Literature: Spuler, *Die morgenländischen Kirchen* 120–69; Heiler, *Ostkirchen* 303–30; Atiya, *Eastern Christianity* 237–88; Müller, *Orientalische Nationalkirchen* 294–311; G. Troupeau, 'L'église Nestorienne d'orient', *Histoire du Christianisme* 4.438–454 (*Geschichte des Christentums* 4.453–72); J. Richard, 'L'Église chaldéenne', *Histoire du Christianisme* 6.215–9 (*Geschichte des Christentums* 6.211–4); R. le Coz, *Histoire de l'Eglise d'Orient* (Paris 1995).

Eastern Syrian Literature

The Eastern Syrians spoke the same language as the Monophysite Western Syrians, namely Old Syriac. The literature that survives is exclusively from Christian authors and is considerable. Besides translations of the Bible and numerous Greek and Persian works, there is a significant original literature: theological, dogmatic, exegetical works, monastic literature, poetry, history, legal literature, medicine and much more. After the expansion of Islam Arabic gradually replaced Old Syriac, but Syriac survived as a literary language into the fourteenth century and beyond. As a liturgical language it remained in use until recent times. As among the Western Syrians, the Eastern Syrians still use modern Syriac dialects as colloquial languages in remote areas. Since the ninth century there has also evolved an important literature among the Eastern Syrians in Arabic.

Literature: see on the Syriac literature of the Western Syrians.

On Arabic literature: Graf, *Geschichte* 2.103–219, 4.94–113 (French translation of 2.103–219: *La littérature Nestorienne*, translated from the German by J. Sanders [sine loco 1985]).

Eastern Syrian Sources of Canon Law

The history of Eastern Syrian (Nestorian) canon law has already been relatively well researched. Most of the important sources exist in editions and translations. As was the case with the Western Syrians, the Maronite Joseph Simonius Assemani first studied the subject in the third volume of his *Biblioteca Orientalis*.[149] He not only dealt thoroughly with Eastern Syrian literature in part one but also described theology, history, the ecclesiastical constitution, ecclesiastical life, etc., from the sources (part two). In his catalogue of the Syriac manuscripts of the Biblioteca Vaticana he included those with legal contents. In 1828 Angelo Mai edited the most important systematic legal work of an Eastern Syrian, the *Nomokanon* of ʿAbdīšōʿ bar Brīkā (Ebedjesus of Nisibis) with a Latin translation. At the end of the nineteenth century and the beginning of the twentieth century editions of several texts of ecclesiastical and civil law were made. Most important of these were Oskar Braun and Jean-Baptiste Chabot (pseudo-Nicene canons, 1898; synods of the Eastern Syrian Church, 1900 and 1902), Eduard Sachau (Syrian law books of primarily civil law contents, 1907–14), Friedrich Schulthess (Greek synods, 1908) and Jacques-M. Vosté (Latin translation of another work of ʿAbdīšōʿ bar Brīkā, 1940). This activity resumed after the Second World War.

Jean Dauvillier wrote the first thorough discussion of Eastern Syrian canon law in his article in the *Dictionnaire du droit canonique* (1938). The contribution of Vosté to the *Studi storici sulle fonti del diritto canonico orientale* (1932) only offered a brief outline of the sources; a second essay in the same work by Cyrille Korolevskij (Charon), did not add much. He dealt chiefly with the newer sources of the Uniate Church. Walter Selb wrote a thorough summary of the sources and institutions of canon law using the latest literature and his own research in 1981.

Literature: J.-M. Vosté, 'Caldei', *Studi storici* 649–64; C. Korolevskij, 'Classification et valeur des sources connues de la discipline chaldéenne', ibid., 665–703; J. Dauvillier, 'Le droit de l'église chaldéenne au Moyen Age', *Actes du XXe Congrès International des*

---

149. (Rome 1725–1728).

Orientalistes (Bruxelles 1938; Louvain 1940) 351–52; W. de Vries, *Sakramententheologie bei den Nestorianern* (OCA 133; Rome 1947) (also drew upon many canon law sources); C. D. G. Müller, 'Die ältere Kirchenrechtsliteratur der Perserkirche', OrChr 59 (1975) 47–59; Selb, *Orientalisches Kirchenrecht* 1; H. Kaufhold, 'Römisch-byzantinisches Recht in den Kirchen syrischer Tradition', *Atti del congresso internazionale 'Incontro fra canoni d'oriente e d'occidente'* ed. R. Coppola (Bari 1994) 1.133–64; idem, 'Die syrische Rechtsliteratur', *Nos Sources: Arts et Littérature Syriaques* (Antelias, Lebanon 2005) 275–289; idem, 'La littérature pseudo-canonique syriaque', *Les Apocryphes syriaques*, ed. by A. Desreumaux et. al. (Études syriaques 2; Paris 2005).

Greek Synods

Authentic Synods

In the acts of the Eastern Syrian synod that was held in 410 under the Grand Metropolitan (Katholikos) Isaac of Seleucia-Ctesiphon (more on him, the texts, and authors mentioned below), Greek canons, particularly of the synod of Nicaea were often noted. The account is, however, not free of inconsistencies. Supposedly 'the volume within which the canons are written' was brought out and read before the synod in the presence of the representative of Antioch, Mārūtā of Maipherkat, and subscribed by the Fathers. We do not know whether it was a Greek text or a Syriac translation. It is remarkable, however, that several of the canons issued by the synod corresponded to canons of Nicaea, and probably others to those of Neocaesarea and Antioch.

A report on the synod of the Eastern Syrian Katholikos Yahballāhā (A.D. 420) declared that the bishops asked for the famous *taxeis*, 'which had been decreed by our dear fathers the Apostles for the guidance of the priesthood, along with the true laws and canons that had been passed by an episcopal synod in the West at various times.' The names of the councils were then given: Nicaea, Ancyra, Syria (that is, Caesaria) in Cappadocia, Neocaesarea, Gangra, Antioch and Laodiceia. This must be a reference to pseudo-apostolic canons and the *Corpus canonum* of Antioch, not yet supplemented by Constantinople (381). According to the report, each of the bishops received these canons, though we do not know whether they were in Greek or Syriac. Such an early Syriac translation has not survived among the Eastern Syrians, in any case.

We read in the introduction to the canons of Katholikos Mār Abā (middle of the sixth century) that they were taken in part from the canons of Nicaea, Ancyra, Neocaesarea, Gangra, Antioch, Laodiceia and Chalcedon. That makes sense. The Syriac text of Mār Abā does not, however, agree with either of the two Syriac translations of Greek canons. Whether it was a free reworking or was taken directly from the Greek text has still to be investigated.

Katholikos Timothy I (780–823) cited individual canons of the councils of Neocaesarea, Laodiceia and Gangra, but from the brief citations it cannot be determined whether he had a Syriac translation before him, and if so, which one it may have been.

It is surprising that canons of the Greek councils do not appear in the oldest systematic legal collection, the *Nomokanon* of Gabriel of Basra (end of the ninth century). His contemporary, Elias of Damascus (al-Ǧauharī), compiled a comprehensive chronological collection of canons in Arabic that contained Ancyra, Neocaesarea, Nicaea, and Constantinople. As bishop of Damascus he had easy access to these canons. In his eleventh-century Arabic chronological collection Ibn aṭ-Ṭaiyib included the usual Greek councils from Ancyra to Constantinople. Ibn aṭ-Ṭaiyib also compiled a systematic collection based on the *Nomokanon* of Gabriel of Basra but did not include these old Greek conciliar canons. He called both collections the *Law of Christianity*. In the thirteenth and fourteenth centuries ʿAḇdīšōʿ bar Brīkā (Ebedjesus of Nisibis), relied on the same source and included the canons to a limited extent. The citation of canon 24 of the Council of Antioch by ʿAḇdīšōʿ in his *Nomokanon* corresponded to the older translation (see above on the canon law of the Western Syrians). We do not know whether ʿAḇdīšōʿ took it from a chronological collection or found it somewhere as a citation. The extremely sparse use of Greek councils in Eastern Syrian legal literature is certainly surprising. Yet ʿAḇdīšōʿ enumerated the Greek canons from Ancyra to Chalcedon as authoritative in his *Ordo iudiciorum* (book 2, chapter 2).

The anonymous, extensive Syriac chronological collection in the manuscript, Baghdad, Chaldaean Monastery Syr. 509 (olim Notre-Dame des Semences 169) from the thirteenth or fourteenth centuries, included the translation of the *Corpus canonum* that originated around A.D. 501/2 in Hierapolis (Mabbug) and circulated among the Western Syrians. In view of the latest datable items, this compilation of canon law texts could not have been made before the eleventh century. We cannot know when the version of the Greek councils contained in the Baghdad manuscript reached the Eastern Syrians. As in the West Syrian tradition the four canons of the First Council of Constantinople are the same as the first six Greek canons that are included in the collection.[150] The Council of Ephesus was not included.

---

150. Chabot, *Synodicon*, 5–6, n. 5; Schulthess, *Die syrischen Kanones* 106–13 (Sigle F). The same divison of the canons is found in the first part of the *Law of Christianity* of Ibn aṭ-Ṭaiyib, that is his chronological collection; see the edition and translation of Hoenerbach-Spies (below) 71–2 (text), 64–66 (translation).

Editions: F. Schulthess, *Die syrischen Kanones der Synoden von Nicaea bis Chalkedon nebst einigen zugehörigen Dokumenten* (Abh. Göttingen, 2nd series, 10.2; Berlin 1908); O. Braun, 'Syrische Texte über die erste allgemeine Synode von Konstantinopel', *Orientalische Studien Th. Nöldeke gewidmet*, ed. C. Bezold (Leipzig 1906) 1.463–78.

Literature: W. Selb, 'Die Kanonessammlungen der orientalischen Kirchen und das griechische Corpus canonum der Reichskirche', *Festschrift für W. M. Plöchl zum 60. Geburtstag* (Vienna 1967) 371–83; idem, *Orientalisches Kirchenrecht* 1.197ff.; Kaufhold, *Gabriel von Basra* 8–24; idem, 'Griechisch-syrische Väterlisten der frühen griechischen Synoden', OrChr 77 (1993) 15–16; A. de Halleux, 'La falsification du symbole de Chalcédoine dans le Synodicon nestorien', *Mélanges offerts à Jean Dauvillier* (Toulouse 1979) 375–84.

The Pseudo-Nicene Mārūtā Canons ('Canons of the 318 Fathers')

While the genuine canons of the Greek councils play a minor role in Eastern Syrian legal literature, 73 putative 'Canons of the 318 Fathers' of Nicaea are widely distributed, just as we have already seen to be the case with the Melkites, Maronites and Copts (the 'Arabic canons'). According to Eastern Syrian sources, they were translated into Syriac by Mārūtā of Maipherkat and sent to the Eastern Syrian Grand Metropolitan Isaac. Katholikos Timothy I frequently cited these canons in his letters. Elias bar Šīnāyā referred to canon 17 in his letter on the election of Katholikos Īšōʿyahb (1023). The systematic works of Ibn aṭ-Ṭaiyib and the *Nomokanon* of ʿAbdīšōʿ bar Brīkā were based on the *Nomokanon* of Gabriel of Basra. The 73 putative 'Canons of the 318 Fathers' of Nicaea are completely incorporated into all three collections. They are excerpted and cited partially included in the *Ordo iudiciorum* of ʿAbdīšōʿ. There are epitomes of all the canons in book 2, chapter 6. A Syriac text is also preserved in the great chronological collection in the manuscript, Baghdad, Chald. Monastery Syr. 509.

Edition: A. Vööbus, *The Canons Ascribed to Mārūtā of Mapherqat and Related Sources* (CSCO 439; Louvain 1982).

Translations: O. Braun, *De Sancta Nicaena Synodo: Syrische Texte des Maratu von Maipherkat nach einer Handschrift der Propaganda zu Rom übersetzt* (Kirchengeschichtliche Studien 4.3; Münster 1898); Vööbus, *The Canons Ascribed to Mārūtā*.

Literature: Dauvillier, 'Chaldéen (Droit)' 299–304; W. de Vries, *Der Kirchenbegriff der von Rom getrennten Syrer* (Orientalia Christiana Analecta 145; Rome 1955) 54–59; Selb, *Orientalisches Kirchenrecht* 1.100–101.

The 'Letter of the Western Fathers' and the 'Correspondence of Pāpā'

A spurious 'Letter which was written by an assembly of Fathers in the West to their brethren in the East' played a certain role in Eastern Syrian collections as well as in the *Nomokanones*. In this letter the Fathers supposedly bestowed on the Grand Metropolitan of Seleucia-Ctesiphon the title of patriarch, thus holding the fifth rank among the patriarchs. This grant was confirmed by purported letters of Katholikos Pāpā later.

Edition of the 'Letter of the Western Fathers': Assemani, *Bibliotheca Orientalis* 3.1.52–54.

Translation of the 'Letter of the Western Fathers': Assemani, ibid., 54–55; G. P. Badger, *The Nestorians and Their Rituals* (London 1852) 1.137–42.

Literature: Baumstark, *Syrische Literatur* 29–30, 124; O. Braun, 'Der Briefwechsel des Katholikos Papa von Seleucia', *Zeitschrift für katholische Theologie* 18 (Innsbruck 1894) 163–82 and 546–65; Kaufhold, *Gabriel von Basra* 105–7; Selb, *Orientalisches Kirchenrecht* 1.61, 108–10.

Pseudo-Apostolic Texts

As we have seen, the synod of Yahbalāhā also asked for the *taxeis* of the apostles 'for the guidance of the priesthood.' This must have meant the text that is preserved as book 6 of the *Octateuchus Clementinus*.

In the synodal canons of Mār Abā, which rely partially on the Greek councils, we look in vain for references to pseudo-apostolic texts. On the other hand, Katholikos Timothy I described the title 'Canons of the Apostles' as being 'those which (were given) through Clement' in his letters. Although the canon cited in letter 9 (a man may not marry two sisters) and 'canon 13' in letter 12 (with the same theme) cannot be identified, nevertheless, 'Canon 18' in letter 12 is clearly canon 18 of the Apostolic Canons.

Elias bar Šīnāyā also cited what is certainly the parallel text to book 8 of the 'Apostolic Constitutions', which corresponds in turn to book 6 of the *Octateuchus Clementinus* ('Peter and Paul'), as well as canons 28 and 29 of the Apostolic Canons. In Gabriel of Basra and the *Nomokanones* dependent on him there are only two citations from these two texts.

In the Arabic chronological collections of Elias of Damascus and of Ibn aṭ-Ṭaiyib, three series of pseudo-apostolic canons appear: the 27 canons of the 'Teachings of the Apostles' (among the Western Syrians also called the 'Teachings of the Apostle Addai'), the (81 or 82) 'Apostolic Canons' and the text corresponding to book 6 of the *Octateuchus Clementinus*. The same is true of the *Ordo iudiciorum* of ʿAbdīšōʿ bar Brīkā, where a short version of these canons are in book 2, chapters 3–5. The great chronological collection in Baghdad, Chaldean Monastery, Syr. 509 is incomplete at the beginning; it only starts with Nicaea, but one may assume that the three texts were present in it.

In view of the sparse citations in the legal literature, the significance of the pseudo-apostolic canons for Eastern Syrian legal literature cannot be estimated as very high.

ʿAbdīšōʿ bar Brīkā in his *Ordo iudiciorum* made references to the 'Didascalia of the Apostles'. He did not use the Syriac text of the *Didascalia*, however, but rather that of his immediate source, the CoptiArabic *Nomokanon* of Ibn al-ʿAssāl (see below).

Literature: H. Kaufhold, 'Die "Lehre des Apostels Addai" ("Lehre der Apostel")', *Paul de Lagarde und die syrische Kirchengeschichte*, ed. Göttinger Arbeitskreis für syrische Kirchengeschichte, (Göttingen 1968) 105–28; Selb, *Orientalisches Kirchenrecht* 1.103–4. Cf. the other literature cited in the section on the Western Syrians concerning this text.

Eastern Syrian (Nestorian) Synods ('Synodicon orientale')

The acts or at least the canons of Eastern Syrian synods held in Seleucia-Ctesiphon under the authority of the Katholikos have been preserved from the beginning of the fifth century on. In most cases the names of the Fathers are also conserved.

1. Mention has already been made of the synod of Isaac (410). Their 21 canons agree largely with those of earlier Greek synods and deal with various questions, particularly rules for bishops and other clerics as well as for the divine service.

2. The synod of the Katholikos Yahbalāhā (420), which have also been mentioned, did not issue any canons but generally confirmed earlier ones.

3. No canons were issued at the next synod (424), which took place during a time of internal ecclesiastical turmoil. Bishops confirmed the legitimacy of Katholikos Dādīšōʿ and rejected the authority of the Western Syrian Church of Antioch over the Eastern Syrians.

4. The three long canons of the synod of Akakios (Aqaq, A.D. 485) forbade anchorites to enter cities and villages and permitted clergy to marry, even to remarry.

5. The Fathers of the synod of the Katholikos Bābai (497) only gave general approval to earlier rules concerning the first rank of the Katholikos as well as the twice-yearly synod of metropolitans, and otherwise they concerned themselves with current conflicts.

6. The 40 canons of the synod of the Katholikos Mār Abā I (542–43) was also already mentioned above. It repeated canons of Greek councils and of Katholikos Isaac. Of the six surviving letters of Mār Abā I, some of them badly preserved, three were recognized by numerous bishops with their signature, one of them at a synod at Bēt Lapaṭ; they deal with current disputes and schisms, the election of the Katholikos, dogmatic questions and moral teaching.

7. The 23 canons of Joseph (552.3) forbid bishops from acting in foreign dioceses, regulate rivalries and conflicts between ecclesiastical officers, deal with questions of the life and official function of clerics as well as the moral conduct of laymen. In addition, the canons of Mār Abā were reconfirmed.

8. Katholikos Ezechiel and his synod (567) issued 39 canons of quite varied contents.

9. The 31 canons of the Katholikos Īšōʿyahb (585) begin with a confession of faith, a confirmation of the teachings of Theodore of Mopsuestia and statements on the usefulness of laws and canons. Further decisions deal particularly with the moral conduct of clergy, monks, and laymen.

10. The synod of the Katholikos Sabrīšōʿ (596) decided internal ecclesiastical disputes but issued no canons.

11. At the synod of Gregory (605), the bishops dealt with dogmatic questions, and in four canons they dealt with the discipline of clerics and monks.

12. A synod held in 615, when the office of Katholikos was vacant, was also dedicated to dogmatic matters.

13. The synod of George (676) issued canons dealing particularly with the discipline of clerics and laymen and with marital law.

14. In 775–776 the synod of the Katholikos Ḥnānīšōʿ regulated the election of the Katholikos in light of current disputes.

15. A provincial synod of 782 and a general synod of 790 under Timothy I also dealt with the election of the Katholikos. Another synod took place under Timothy in 804, but we know nothing about it.

16. The 28 canons of the synod of John bar Abgārē (900) dealt with dogmatic matters, the relationship to members of other religions and confessions, liturgical questions, etc.

17. The last of the synods to be dealt with here took place under Timothy II in 1318. Of particular importance, it proclaimed the two legal works of ʿAbdīšōʿ bar Brīkā (see below) to be authoritative.

18. The synod held by Metropolitan Barsaumā of Nisibis in 484 in Bēt Lapat was not recognized.[151] Some of the canons were received into the *Ordo iudiciorum* anyway (according to the enumeration of legal sources in book 2, chapter 2, three synods took place under Barsaumā).

Besides these assemblies of which acts or canons are preserved, we know of many more synods of the Eastern Syrians from historical sources, particularly those that dealt with the election of the Katholikos.

Most of the canon law texts are preserved in what is called the 'Book of Synods' (Synodicon orientale). It was certainly preserved in the archives of the Katholikos, and at least excerpts from it were circulated among the bishops. The core of the compilation in the manuscript Baghdad Syr. 509 must have originated at the end of the eighth century, since it contained the synod of the Katholikos Ḥnānīšōʿ (775) but not that of Timothy I (790). Perhaps it goes back to Timothy, whose interest in juristic sources is doc-

---

151. See S. Gero, *Barsaumā of Nisibis and Persian Christianity in the Fifth Century* (CSCO 426; Leuven 1981) 41–53, 73–76.

umented. This collection embraces nos. 1–14 above, as well as letters of Barsaumā, in which he subjected himself to the Katholikos Acacius, as well as other texts to be considered in the following chapter. Later synodal canons have come to us in other manuscripts. The Arabic chronological collections of Elias of Damascus and also that of Ibn aṭ-Ṭaiyib contain only the synods from Isaac through George, and they exclude that of Ḥnānīšōʿ. The synod of Ḥnānīšōʿ also is missing from the index of legal sources in the *Ordo iudiciorum* of ʿAḇdīšōʿ bar Brīḵā (only the judicial decisions of Ḥnānīšōʿ are mentioned). They are also never cited in the systematic works. Perhaps this evidence points to an older model for those collections that have been preserved.

Editions and translations of the 'Book of Synods': Braun, *Synhados*; J. B. Chabot, *Synodicon Orientale ou Recueil des synodes nestoriennes, publié, traduit et annoté* (Paris 1902); J. Vosté, *Disciplina caldea: 1. Droit ancien: Synodes (Synodicon orientale); Collectio canonum synodicorum d'Ebed-Jesus de Nisibe* (Fonti, series 1, fasc. 4; Rome 1931). Translation in Malayalam: G. Chediath and K. V. Joseph (Vadavathoor, Kottayam-Kerala 1996).

Literature: Dauvillier, 'Chaldéen, Droit' 327–28, 333–35, 336, 343–45; J. Janin, 'Synodicon orientale', DDC 7 (1965) 1140–42; G. Wiessner, 'Zu den Subskriptionslisten der ältesten christlichen Synoden in Iran', *Festschrift für Wilhelm Eilers*, ed. G. Wiessner (Wiesbaden 1967) 288–98; Selb, *Orientalisches Kirchenrecht* 1.61–62, 111–15; Kaufhold, *Gabriel von Basra* 25–31.

On individual synods:

On 1: T. J. Lamy, *Concilium Seleuciae et Ctesiphonti habitum anno 410; Textum syriacum edidit, latine vertit notisque instruxit* (Louvain 1868).

On 6: Braun, *Synhados* 97–145; Chabot, *Synodicon orientale* 68–95, 318–51.

On 12: Chabot, *Synodicon orientale* 625–34.

On 15: Chabot, *Synodicon orientale* 599–608; O. Braun, 'Zwei Synoden des Katholikos Timotheos I.', OrChr 1 (1901) 283–311; H. Putman, *L'Église et l'Islam sous Timothée I* (Beirut 1975) 62–64.

On 16: Preserved in Syriac only as a citation in the *Nomokanon* of ʿAḇdīšōʿ bar Brīḵā. Arabic translation at the end of the chronological collection of Ibn aṭ-Ṭaiyib, see Hoenerbach and Spies (see below), 210–15 (text), 202–7 (translation). Cf. also Dauvillier, 350.

On 17: A. Mai, SVNC 10.260–68 (text), 96–105 (translation). Cf. also Dauvillier, 'Chaldéen (Droit)' 365–66.

On 18: Braun, *Synhados* 74–83; Chabot, *Synodicon orientale* 525–39; S. Gero, *Barsaumā of Nisibis and Persian Christianity in the Fifth Century* (CSCO 426; Louvain 1981), particularly pp. 2–4, 41–50, 73ff., 79ff.

Canons and Canon-Law Writings of Individual Persons

1. In the Book of Synods, 20 canons by Katholikos Īšōʿyahḇ, already mentioned, were accepted, written in response to questions by Jacob, Bishop of the island of Dārai. They deal with priests and concern divine service as well as things related to it, but also on the permissibility of oaths and the legality of usury.

Edition: Chabot, *Synodicon orientale* 165–96.

Translation: Chabot, *Synodicon orientale* 424–55; Braun, *Synhados* 237–72.

2. Katholikos Timothy I (780–823) composed many letters, of which 59 are an integral collection. They often dealt with themes of canon law.

Edition and translation: O. Braun, *Timothei patriarchae I epistulae* (CSCO 74–75; Louvain 1914–15). Edition of the first 38 letters: Thoma Darmo, *Letters of Patriarch Timothy I (778–820 A. D.)* (Trichur, Kerala [India] 1982).

Literature: Dauvillier, 'Chaldéen (Droit)' 344–45; R. J. Bidawid, *Les lettres du patriarche nestorien Timothée I* (ST 187; Vatican City 1956); Putman, *L'Église et l'Islam* 28ff., 66ff.

3. From Timothy's successor Īšōʿbarnūn (823–28) survive letters to a visitator Isaac and a deacon Makarios which deal with questions of canon law and responses primarily of a liturgical content.

Literature: Dauvillier, 'Chaldéen (Droit)' 349; W. C. van Unnik, *Nestorian Questions on the Administration of the Eucharist, by Isho'yabh IV* (Haarlem 1937, reprint Amsterdam 1970) 130–33.

4. From the Katholikos John bar Aḇgārē (900–905) we have 24 canons of liturgical content 'for the servants of the altar'.

Editions and translations: Assemani, *Bibliotheca orientalis* 3.1 pp. 238–48; J. A. Assemani, *De catholicis seu patriarchis Chaldaeorum et Nestorianorum commentarius historico-chronologicus* (Rome 1775; reprinted Piscataway 2004) 112–18. Arabic translation (the text ends incomplete in the last canon) at the end of the chronological collection of Ibn aṭ-Ṭaiyib (Hoenerbach and Spies, *Ibn aṭ-Ṭaiyib, Fiqh an-Naṣrānīya* 216–18, 208–11).

Literature: Dauvillier, 'Chaldéen (Droit)' DDC 350–51; van Unnik, *Nestorian Questions* 133–35.

5. There are 123 anonymous canons arranged in questions and answers regulating liturgical usage connected with the Eucharist. They probably come from Katholikos Īšōʿyahḇ IV (1020–25).

Edition, translation and commentary: van Unnik, *Nestorian Questions*.

Literature: Dauvillier, 'Chaldéen (Droit)' 353.

6. Katholikos Īšōʿyahḇ IV also probably wrote answers to 50 questions on the administration of Baptism.

Edition and translation: J. Isaak, 'Questions on the Administration of Baptism, by Iso'yahb IV' (in Arabic), *Bayn al-Nahrayn* 20 (1992), no. 80, pp. 52–87. (The Syrian text is taken from the manuscript in Notre-Dame des Semences 176, pp. 57–80, with an Arabic translation.)

Syrian Law Books

Under Islam, Christians (and Jews) possessed their own jurisdiction in civil matters, particularly in cases of marriage and inheritance. Among the Eastern Syrians we possess a large number of legal sources to aid ecclesiastical courts. These are usually private, not official works, and they were later accepted into chronological and systematic collections (particularly that in Baghdad, Chaldaean Monastery, Syr. 509).

Edition of several law books (with a German translation): E. Sachau, *Syrische Rechtsbücher*, 1–3; Selb-Kaufhold, *Rechtsbuch* vol. 2.

Literature: J. Partsch, 'Neue Rechtsquellen der nestorischen Kirchen', ZRG Rom. Abt. 30 (1909) 355–98; Selb, *Orientalisches Kirchenrecht* 1.63–64.

1. Katholikos Mār Aḇā I (539–52) composed a brief work on marital law according to the rules of the Old Testament (Lev. 18:6–23) and against the Persian practice of marriage with relatives.

Edition and translation: Sachau, *Syrische Rechtsbücher* 3.255–85.
Literature: Dauvillier, 'Chaldéen (Droit)' 343; Selb, *Orientalisches Kirchenrecht* 1.104–5.

2. Simeon of Rēvardašīr was metropolitan of Rēvardašīr in Persis in the mid-seventh century (or around the turn of the seventh and eighth centuries?). He composed his work in Persian, but only the Syriac translation, written no later than the ninth century, survives. Simeon begins with a long general introduction on why Christ issued no secular laws and why the Christians do not use the Law of Moses. He then discussed the source of orally transmitted, authoritative laws in the Church. Following that he responds to 22 anonymous questions dealing mainly with inheritance, but also to whether a cleric could marry a slave woman and whether the children of a slave could become clerics (question 11).

Editions and translations: A. Rücker, *Die Canones des Simeon von Rêvârdesîr* (Leipzig 1908); Sachau, *Syrische Rechtsbücher* 3.203–53.
Literature: Dauvillier, 'Chaldéen (Droit)' 331–32.

3. Īšōbōkt, like Simeon, was metropolitan of Rēvardašīr, and probably lived at the end of the eighth century. He also wrote in Persian. His extensive work, dealing primarily with civil law that was based on Persian law, consists of six books and also survives only in a Syriac translation, made at the command of Katholikos Timothy I. The first book deals with the question why neither Christ nor the Apostles did not discuss human laws. Books 2 and 3 are dedicated to marital law (impediments to marriage, ban on marriage with relatives and on levirate marriages, partial validity of the law of Moses, grounds for divorce, contracting of marriage, etc.).

Edition and translation: Sachau, *Syrische Rechtsbücher* 3.1–201.
Literature: Dauvillier, 'Chaldéen (Droit)' 340–43; N. Pigulevskaja, *Les villes de l'état Iranien aux époques Parthe et Sassanide* (Paris 1963) 106–11 ('Le recueil d'Ishobokt'); idem, 'Die Sammlung der syrischen Rechtsurkunden des Ishobocht und des Matikan', *Akten des 24. Internationalen Orientalistenkongresses* (Wiesbaden 1959) 219–20; M. Macuch, *Das*

sassanidische Rechtsbuch 'Mātakdān i hazār dātistān' (Wiesbaden 1981); idem, *Rechtskasuistik und Gerichtspraxis zu Beginn des siebenten Jahrhunderts in Iran* (Wiesbaden 1993).

4. The collection of practical decisions by Katholikos Ḥnānīšōʿ (686–700) is not a law book in the proper sense. The Katholikos resolved legal questions in letter form and gave ecclesiastical judges directions for the legal cases brought to him. The letters treat the ecclesiastical law of property, slavery, marriage and above all inheritance.

Edition and translation: Sachau, *Syrische Rechtsbücher* 2.1–51.

Literature: Dauvillier, 'Chaldéen (Droit)' 335–36.

5. Katholikos Timothy I (780–823) not only issued canons in conjunction with the synod of 790 and dealt with canon law questions in his letters, but also was responsible for the translation of the law books of Īšōbō*k*t and perhaps for the collection of Eastern Syrian synods. He also composed a law book consisting of 99 canons. It treats with various questions of canon and civil law, particularly with marital law (§§ 18–45) and inheritance law (§§ 46–99, occasionally interrupted by other decisions). The law book was also known among the Western Syrians and the Maronites.

Edition and translation: Sachau, *Syrische Rechtsbücher* 2.53–117.

Literature: Dauvillier, 'Chaldéen (Droit)' 345–47; H. Labourt, *De Timotheo I Nestorianorum Patriarcha (728–823) et christianorum orientalium condicione sub chaliphis Abbasidis* (Paris 1904); G. Furlani, 'Gli 'impedimenta matrimonii' secondo il patriarca nestoriano Timoteo I', *Accademia Nazionale dei Lincei, Rendiconti della Classe di Scienze morali, storiche e filologiche* (series 5, vol. 29; Rome 1920) 261–72. On the tradition in Western Syria: Vööbus, *Kanonessammlungen* 303, 464, 521. On the Maronite transmission: M. Breydy, 'La IIIᵉ apologie de Duwayhī et la tradition des Canons de Timothée Ier, d'Īšōʿbarnūn et autres', *Actes du premier congrès international d'études arabes chrétiennes* (OCA 218; Rome 1982) 241–50.

6. The successor of Timothy as Katholikos, Īšōʿbarnūn (823–28) composed a similar work in 130 paragraphs, in which he made somewhat differing rulings from Timothy's (marital law, §§ 1–33, 78–80 and elsewhere; magic, §§ 34–40; inheritance law, §§ 41–70, 81–86; monks and clerics, §§ 70–77; civil-law, penal and other rulings, §§ 78ff.).

Edition and translation: Sachau, *Syrische Rechtsbücher* 2.119–177; three paragraphs missing in Sachau at the beginning: J.-M. Sauget, 'Décisions canoniques du Patriarche Īšōʿbarnūn encore inédits', *Apollinaris* 35 (1962) 259–65 (reprint: J. M. Sauget, *Littératures et manuscrits des chrétientés syriaques et arabes. Recueil d'articles publié par L. Duval-Arnould et F. Rilliet* (ST 389; Vatican City 1998) 27–33). On the Maronite tradition: Breydy, 'La IIIᵉ apologie.'

Literature: Dauvillier, 'Chaldéen (Droit)' 348–49.

7. ʿAḇdīšōʿ bar Bahrīz was metropolitan of Mosul in the first half of the ninth century and wrote a law book which dealt first with marital law and then, in a very sizable segment, with inheritance law as well.

Edition and translation: W. Selb, *'Aḇdīšō' Bar Bahrīz: Ordnung der Ehe und der Erbschaften sowie Entscheidungen von Rechtsfällen* (Vienna 1970).

Literature: Dauvillier, 'Chaldéen (Droit)' 352–53; Kaufhold, *Gabriel von Basra* 44–49 (on dating); idem, 'Ein weiteres Rechtsbuch der Nestorianer—das Erbrecht des Johannes?' *Gedächtnisschrift für Wolfgang Kunkel,* ed. D. Nörr and D. Simon (Frankfurt am Main 1984) 103–16 (on another version).

8. George, metropolitan of Arbela and of the Adiabene (or of Assur = Mosul), who dates to the second half of the tenth century, composed a compendium on inheritance law. Only citations remain of his work on marital law (among others, in the *Ordo iudiciorum* of 'Aḇdīšō' bar Brīkā).

Literature: Selb, *Orientalisches Kirchenrecht* 1.71.

9. Assigning to Katholikos John bar Aḇgārē (900–925) authorship of a law book which relies almost entirely on Islamic inheritance law is very dubious. It is known in Syriac only in the Western Syrian tradition. It survives in Arabic fragments in the appendix to the second part of Ibn aṭ-Ṭaiyib's 'Law of Christianity'.

Literature: Baumstark, *Syrische Literatur* 235. See also the section on the canon law of the Western Syrians.

Other Legal Sources

1. One may gain an impression of the activities of the theological school of Nisibis, which existed from the fifth to the ninth centuries, from the statutes of the school.

Edition and translation: A. Vööbus, *The Statutes of the School of Nisibis* (Stockholm 1962).

2. Some of the sources already mentioned contain canons for monks (for example, the pseudo-Nicaean 'Canons of the 318 Fathers'and the law book of Īšōʻbarnūn). Specialized monastic rules also survive by Abraham of Kaškar († 588), the founder of the 'Grand Monastery' on Mount Izla, and his successors Dādīšō' († 604) and Baḇai († about 628; his rule survives in Arabic only). There are also rules for the school of the 'Upper Monastery' at Mosul (Arabic).

Edition and translation: J. Chabot, 'Regulae monasticae saeculo VI ab Abrahamo fundatore et Dadiesu rectore conventus Syrorum in monte Izla conditae', *Accademia Nazionale dei Lincei, Rendiconti della Classe di Scienze morali, storiche e filologiche* (5 series, vol. 7; Rome 1898) 39–50, 77–102; Vööbus, *Documents* 113–20; ; idem, *History of Asceticism in the Syrian Orient* (vol. 3, CSCO 500; Louvain 1988) passim (only in 'Monasticism in the light of the legislative sources'; only translations); S. Chiala, *Abramo di Kashkar e la sua communità* (Magnano 2005), 159–67 (rules of Abraham), 169–82 (rules of Dādīšō') (in Italian translation).

3. A long letter which has a canonical contents was written by Metropolitan Elias bar Šīnāyā of Nisibis (1008–56), in which he declares the elec-

tion of Katholikos Īšōʿyahḇ IV (1020–25) to be invalid on the grounds of simony, referring to numerous legal sources.

Translation: B. Vandenhoff, 'Ein Brief des Elias bar Šinaja über die Wahl des Katholikos Išoʿjahb IV. in Übersetzung bekanntgemacht', OrChr 11 (1913) 59–81, 236–62.

4. Even the 'Book of the Fathers' (Liber Patrum) can be considered a part of the canonical literature. It was attributed in the manuscripts to the Grand Metropolitan (Katholikos) Simeon bar Sabbāʿē († 344), but the tract was actually written in the thirteenth and fourteenth centuries. It describes the heavenly and earthly hierarchies, the ranks of the latter, their election, duties and obligations, their ecclesiastical garments, enumerates the metropolitan sees, and much more.

Translation: I.-M. Vosté, *Liber Patrum latine interpretatus est notis illustravit* . . . (Fonti, series 2, fasc. 16; Vatican City 1940).

Liturgical Sources

The rubrics of liturgical books as well as explications of the liturgy (among others, by Gabriel Qaṭrāyā, Abraham bar Līpe, pseudo-George of Arbela) are also of canonical significance.

Literature: Baumstark, *Syrische Literatur* 200–1, 239; Dauvillier, 'Chaldéen (Droit)' 328–29, 347, 353, 358; W. de Vries, *Sakramententheologie bei den Nestorianern* (OCA 133; Rome 1947); P. Yousif, *A Classified Bibliography on the East Syrian Liturgy* (Rome 1990) passim.

Canonical Collections

Gabriel of Basra

Metropolitan Gabriel of Basra compiled the first systematic legal collection of the Eastern Syrians at the end of the ninth century. This *Nomokanon* only survives in very fragmentary form (we do not even know the title), but it can be almost completely reconstructed because it is preserved in the Arabic reworking of Ibn aṭ-Ṭaiyib and because ʿAḇdīšōʿ bar Brīḵā also used it extensively for his *Nomokanon*. Gabriel of Basra's collection contains both civil and canon law. The first parts contains citations from the earlier legal literature. After dealing with marital and inheritance law, Gabriel included secular rules that he followed the organization of the law book of Īšōʿbōḵt. Gabriel's part one consisted of 48 'questions', but only questions 21–48 are preserved in the original Syriac text. The second part includes canon law in the narrower sense (rules for the clergy), consisting of citations from the Imperial and Eastern Syrian councils (of this part of the work only a few Syrian citations have survived). Between these parts, Gabriel included material on liturgical matters that he framed in the form of questions and answers. It may be that Gabriel had written this part himself. It is preserved in Syriac.

Gabriel used the 73 pseudo-Nicene 'Canons of the 318 Fathers', the canons of Eastern Syrian synods, the Eastern Syrian law books (without the collection of decisions by Ḥnānīšōʿ), the *Syro-Roman Lawbook*, letters of Katholikos Timothy, the letter of Katholikos Īšōʿbarnūn to Makarios and others. He did not use the Greek councils and hardly any pseudo-apostolic texts. Gabriel usually does not give his sources verbatim, and he shortens or alters them on occasion.

Edition: Kaufhold, *Gabriel von Basra*.
Literature: Dauvillier, 'Chaldéen (Droit)' 349–50; G. Graf, 'Das Rechtswerk des Nestorianers Gabriel, Bischofs von Basra, in arabischer Bearbeitung', OCP 6 (1940) 517–22; Selb, *Orientalisches Kirchenrecht* 1.73–75.

Elias of Damascus (al-Ǧauharī?)

The second-oldest collection is a chronological collection in Arabic. "Metropolitan Elias of Damascus," compiled it. He is perhaps identical with a Bishop Elias ibn ʿUbaid of Jerusalem who became metropolitan of Damascus in A.D. 893. An identification with a Bishop Elias al-Ǧauharī of Jerusalem, who was active literarily, is less probable. The collection could have originated about A.D. 900. The collection includes pseudo-apostolic texts and Western councils (excerpts from the canons of Ancyra and Neocaesarea, genuine canons and the bogus 'Canons of the 318 Fathers of Nicaea') as well as the Eastern Syrian synods from Isaac to George.

Literature: Dauvillier, 'Chaldéen (Droit)' 351–52; Graf, *Geschichte* 2.132–35; S. Jargy, 'Élie de Damas', DDC 5 (1953) 248–51; G. Fiaccadori, 'On the Dating of Īliyā al-Ǧawharī's *Collectio canonica*', OrChr 68 (1984) 213–14; H. Kaufhold, 'Nochmals zur Datierung der Kanonessammlung des Elias von Damaskus', ibid., 214–17 (reply by Fiaccadori in OrChr 70 [1986] 192–93); J. M. Fiey, Les insaissables nestoriens de Damas', *After Chalcedon: Studies in Theology and Church History offered to A. Van Roey*, ed. C. Laga et al. (Leuven 1985) 167–75; here, 173–75; Selb, *Orientalisches Kirchenrecht* 1.72–73.

Katholikos Elias I

Katholikos Elias I (1028–49) wrote an extensive Syriac collection on inheritance law, of which only chapters 6 to 12 survive. The conjecture that Elias is also responsible for the comprehensive collection of Eastern Syrian legal sources found in Baghdad, Chaldaean Monastery, Syr. 509, does not hold up under close examination. The collection on inheritance law has not yet been edited.

Literature: Dauvillier, 'Chaldéen (Droit)' 354–55; Kaufhold, *Gabriel von Basra* 93–95. On the collection of the Baghdad Syr. 509: H. Kaufhold, review of Selb, *Orientalisches Kirchenrecht*, 1 ZRG Rom. Abt. 100 (1983) 724–35 (especially 727–30).

Elias bar Šīnāyā (of Nisibis)

On the basis of the collection of inheritance law by Elias I, Metropolitan Elias bar Šīnāyā of Nisibis (1008–56), whose canonical letter has already been mentioned, fashioned a compendium on inheritance law in 25 chapters, in which he also dealt with the hereditary rights of monks. The work only survives in an Arabic translation. A Syriac re-translation from Arabic was undertaken by ʿAbdīšōʿ bar Brīkā as chapter 3 of his *Nomokanon*.

Literature: Dauvillier, 'Chaldéen (Droit)' 356–57; Graf, *Geschichte* 2.186–87; Kaufhold, *Gabriel von Basra* 95–97.

Ibn aṭ-Ṭaiyib, Law of Christianity

Abu ʾl-farağ ʿAbdallāh ibn aṭ-Ṭaiyib was a physician, a monk, and secretary of Katholikos Elias I, and, among many other works he composed a two-part legal collection in Arabic under the title, 'Law of Christianity'. The first part is a chronological collection which, like the work of Elias of Damascus, includes primarily pseudo-apostolic writings (the beginning is not preserved and commences at canon 39 of the pseudo-Nicene canons; there follows the parallel text to book 6 of the 'Apostolic Constitutions'), the canons of Ancyra, Neocaesarea, Nicaea (genuine and the 'Canons of the 318 Fathers'), Gangra, Antioch, Laodiceia, Constantinople, canons of Pope Damasus (see above in canon law of the Copts) and those of Cyprian of Carthage as well as those of Chalcedon. Lastly the Eastern Syrian synods from Isaac to George are included. These are followed by translations of law books: the version R I of the *Syro-Roman Lawbook*, Īšōʿbōkt, Timothy, and Īšōʿbarnūn. The canons of John bar Abgārē 'on fundamental doctrines' and 'for the servants of the altar' complete the work.

Ibn at-Tayyib's book is very regularly and well ordered, but much which does not seem practical or useful is abbreviated or left out . . . the contents of the canons are given but not infrequently in a severely abbreviated form. With Elias [of Damascus], in contrast, the old form was preserved, but much left out. Ibn at-Tayyib has produced, so to speak, a compendium, and Elias a sampling of the old Eastern Syrian collection.[152]

The second part of the work consists of an Arabic reworking of the collection of Gabriel of Basra, and it is preserved almost complete. In his systematic collection Ibn aṭ-Ṭaiyib had also abbreviated the canons but left none of them out.

Edition and translation: W. Hoenerbach and O. Spies, *Ibn aṭ-Ṭaiyib, Fiqh an-Naṣrānīya 'Das Recht der Christenheit'* (2 parts CSCO 161, 162, 167, 168; Louvain 1957).

---

152. Guidi, 'Ostsyrische Bischöfe' 389–90.

Literature: I. Guidi, 'Ostsyrische Bischöfe und Bischofsitze im V., VI. und VII. Jahrhundert', ZDMG 43 (1989) 388–414; Dauvillier, 'Chaldéen (Droit)' 355–56; G. Graf, 'Das Rechtswerk des Nestorianers Gabriel, Bischofs von Basra, in arabischer Bearbeitung', OCP 6 (1940) 517–22; Graf, *Geschichte* 2.160ff. (173–76); S. Jargy, 'Ibn aṭ-Ṭaiyib', DDC 5 (1953) 1242–44; Kaufhold, *Gabriel von Basra* 39–40, 57–63; Selb, *Orientalisches Kirchenrecht* 1.75–76. Selb-Kaufhold, *Rechtsbuch* 1.90, 122–23, 165–66.

ʿAbdīšōʿ bar Brīkā (Ebedjesus of Nisibis)

Metropolitan ʿAbdīšōʿ (Latinized form of the Western-Syrian pronunciation is Ebedjesus) bar Brīkā of Nisibis († 1318) stands at the apex but also the close of Eastern Syrian legal literature. Besides many other works, he wrote two Syriac legal compendia.[153]

He began writing on law as a monk before A.D. 1284/85 and composed a 'brief collection of synodal canons' in 9 sections, which is usually called the *Nomokanon*. The first section deals primarily with the synod of Nicaea (it includes the list of participants), the second with marital law, the third with inheritance (= the compendium of Elias bar Šīnāyā), and the third with purely civil-law matters. Part 5 treats various matters of canon law with more liturgical material, parts 6 and 7 considers clerics (through the rank of priest) and monks, part 8 with bishops and the last part with the Katholikos. The collection consists almost entirely of excerpts from earlier legal literature, particularly the pseudo-apostolic 'Canons of the 318 Fathers', the 'Book of Synods' and other Eastern Syrian synodal canons (such as those of John of Abgārē), the law books of Simeon of Rēvardašīr, of Īšōʿbōkt, of Ḥnānīšōʿ, of Timothy and of Īšōʿbarnūn as well as the *Syro-Roman Lawbook*. ʿAbdīšōʿ has referred to the originals only in part, since it appears that he cites them in most cases (where this can be established) according to the shortened version of Gabriel of Basra, so far as Gabriel's collections contained the texts. Other than a few transpositions, ʿAbdīšōʿ also follows the sequence of his model. As is the case with Gabriel, canons of the Greek councils are almost entirely omitted.

Editions: 'Ebediesu metropolitae Sobae et Armeniae Collectio Canonum Synodicorum ex chaldaicis Bibliothecae Vaticanae codicibus sumpta et in latinam linguam translata ab A. Assemani', SVNC vol. 10; J. E. H. Kellaita, *The Nomocanon or The Collection of Synodical Canons of Mar Abdisho bar Brikha Metropolitan of Nisibis and Armenia* 1290 A.D. (Urmia, Persia 1918); *The Nomocanon of Metropolitan Abdisho of Nisibis. A Facsimile Edition of MS 64 from the Collection of the Church of the East in Thrissur*, ed. I. Perczel. With a New Introduction by H. Kaufhold Piscataway 2005; 2nd ed. 2009).

Translation: Assemani, SVNC 10.21–168. Excerpts: J. Vosté, *Disciplina caldea* 1: *Droit ancien: Synodes (Synodicon orientale)*; *Collectio canonum synodicorum d'Ebed-Jesus de Nisibe* (Fonti, series 1, fasc. 4; Rome 1931); Mar Aprem, 'A Concise Collection of Synodical Can-

---

153. Baumstark, *Syrische Literatur* 323–25; J. Dauvillier, 'Ebedjesus de Nisibe', DDC 5 (1953) 91–134; H. Kaufhold, Introduction to the Facsimile Edition of the Nomokanon (see below in the text).

ons', *Voice of the East* 30 (Trichur 1983) no. 10, pp. 6–8; 31 (1984) no. 3, pp. 4–5 (= index of contents); idem, 'The Nestorian Canon Law', *Voice of the East* 38 (1991) no. 9–10, pp. 9–16, 39 (1992) no. 1, 2, 5–6, 11–12 (= excerpts from the Mēmrē 1–5).

Literature: Dauvillier, 'Chaldéen (Droit)' 361–64; idem, 'Ebedjésus de Nisibe', *DDC* 5 (1953) 93–118; Kaufhold, *Gabriel von Basra* 58–63; Selb, *Orientalisches Kirchenrecht* 1.76–77; Mar Aprem, Canon Law of Mar Abdisho', *The Harp: A Review of Syriac and Oriental Studies* 4 (Kottayam-Kerala) 85–102; idem, 'Codification of the Canon law by Mar Abdisho in 1290 A.D.', *VI Symposium Syriacum 1992*, ed. R. Lavenant (OCA 247; Rome 1994) 371–80; C. Gallagher, *Church Law and Church Order in Rome and Byzantium. A Comparative Study* (Aldershot 2002) (= Birmingham Byzantine and Ottoman Monographs, vol. 8) 187–226.

As the metropolitan of Nisibis, probably in A.D. 1314–15, Ebedjesus compiled a second, more original compendium in 10 parts under the title 'Order of Ecclesiastical Decisions' (known by its translated title as the *Ordo iudiciorum ecclesiasticorum*). It consists of sources of canon law with abbreviated excerpts from pseudo-apostolic and synodal canons (part 1), rules of a more moral nature (2), prayer hours and liturgy (3), explanation of Greek and Syriac technical expressions (4), ecclesiastical hierarchy (5), ecclesiastical jurisdiction (6), ecclesiastical judges and trials (7), marital law (8), norms of civil law (9) and the law of inheritance (10). Insofar as the author used older sources, he cited them normally in their original wording (alongside the sources used for the *Nomokanon*, he occasionally drew upon sources that have otherwise since disappeared). Essentially his exposition rests on the Coptic-Arabic *Nomokanon* of Ibn al-ʿAssāl without referring to him at any point. Through this source he drew citations from the *Didascalia*, Byzantine law books ('Books of the Kings') and, not least of all, Islamic law.

Edition and excerpts: J. E. Manna, *Morceaux choisis de littérature araméenne*, (Part 2; Mosul 1901) 400–409 (chapter 1.1. 7 and 8: synods of Isaac and of Yahḅallāhā).

Latin translation: I.-M. Vosté, *'Ordo iudiciorum ecclesiasticorum' collectus, dispositus, ordinatus et compositus a Mar 'Abdiso' metropolita Nisibis et Armeniae, latine interpretatus est notis illustravit* (Fonti, series 2, fasc. 15; Vatican City 1940).

Literature: Dauvillier, 'Chaldéen (Droit)', 364–65; idem, 'Ebedjésus de Nisibe', DDC 5 (1953) 118–27; Kaufhold, *Gabriel von Basra* 63–64; idem, 'Der Richter in den syrischen Rechtsquellen: Zum Einfluss islamischen Rechts auf die christlich-orientalische Rechtsliteratur', OrChr 68 (1984) 91–113 (here, 95–106, 111–13); Selb, *Orientalisches Kirchenrecht* 1.77–78.

The two legal works of ʿAḅdīšōʿ bar Brīḳā were recognized at the synod of Katholikos Timothy II (1318), in which ʿAḅdīšōʿ participated, and they (particularly the *Nomokanon*) to this day provide the foundation of the canon law of the Eastern Syrian Church not united with Rome. A theological work of ʿAḅdīšōʿ bar Brīkā, the 'Book of the Pearl', is a source for canon law to a limited extent.

Translation: G.-P. Badger, *The Nestorians and Their Rituals* (vol. 2, London 1852, Repr. Farnborough 1969) 380–422.

Literature: de Clercq, 'Ebedjésus de Nisibe' 127–30.

Collection of the Eleven Ecumenical Councils

The acts and canons of the eleven ecumenical councils from Nicaea to Florence were translated in 1662 into Arabic, and from the Arabic, Uniate Eastern Syrian (Chaldaean) Metropolitan and later Patriarch Joseph II (1694–1713) translated them into Syriac.

Edition: [P. Bedjan], *Compendium Conciliorum Oecumenicorum Undecim* (Paris 1888; reprint Piscataway 2007).

Literature: Graf, *Geschichte* 4.104, 247.

Legal Sources in Sogdian

The Sogdians in Northeastern Iran, who speak a middle-Iranian dialect, perhaps in part belong to the Eastern Syrian Church. The small remains of canonical writings (a fragment with pseudo-apostolic canons, namely the 'Teaching of the Apostles') in Sogdian are surely translations from Syriac.

Edition: O. Hansen, 'Berliner sogdische Texte, II: Bruchstücke der großen Sammelhandschrift C', *Abhandlungen der Akademie der Wissenschaften und der Literatur Mainz* 15 (Wiesbaden 1954) 75–85 (= 893–903); N. Sims-Williams, *The Christian Sogdian Manuscript C₂* (Berliner Turfantexte 12; Berlin 1985) 101–9.

On Sogdian literature: O. Hansen, 'Die christliche Literatur der Sogdier', HbOr 1.4.2 (Leiden 1968) 91–9; N. Sims-Williams, 'Christianity. IV. Christian Literature in Middle Iranic Languages', *Encyclopaedia Iranica* 5 (1991) 534–35; idem, 'Sogdian and Turkish Christians in the Turfan and Tun-Huang Manuscripts', *Turfan and Tun-Huang: The Texts*, ed. A. Cadonna (Orientalia Venetiana 4; Florence 1999) 43–61, especially 53.

India

According to tradition the beginnings of Christianity in southern India (Kerala, the Malabar Coast) go back to the Apostle Thomas. It may be assumed that India was proselytized by the Eastern Syrian Church. Consequently, Eastern Syrian legal sources would have been known there. The Indian Christians also had their own local customs. Nothing more precise may be said in the face of a lack of sources. Western concepts of canon law penetrated after colonization by the Portuguese. Southern Indian libraries preserve many Syriac manuscripts of Eastern and Western Syrian origins, including some canonical manuscripts.

Literature: J. P. Podipara, *The Canonical Sources of the Syro-Malabar Church*, ed. X. Koodapuzha (Kottayam, India 1986); A. Thazhath, *The Juridical Sources of the Syro-Malabar Church (A Historico-Juridical Study)* (Kottyam, India 1987); J. Kollaparambil, *The Archdeacon of All-India* (Kottyam, India 1972); Kaufhold, *Syrische Handschriften*.

Armenians

History of the Church

According to tradition, the Apostle Thaddeus and others founded the Armenian Church. It is certain that there was a very early mission. Their true founder and organizer was Gregory 'the Enlightener' (about A.D. 300). Since about the fifth century its head bears the title Katholikos. During the following centuries, Armenia was partitioned between Byzantium and Persia. At the synods of Dwin (506–7 and 552) the Armenian Church adopted Monophysitism. Around 600 the Georgian Church separated from it and turned to the Chalcedonian Byzantine Imperial Church. As a result of the invasion of the Seljuks beginning in the eleventh century, a large portion of Armenians emigrated, particularly to Cilicia, where the so-called Lesser Armenian kingdom arose. From 1166 onward, the Katholikos also resided in Cilicia. From 1441 there were two Katholikoi, in Cilicia (at Sis) and in Greater Armenia (Ējmiacin). In Lesser Armenia, the Armenians came into closer contact with the crusaders and the Latin Church, but also with the Byzantines. From the fourteenth century the Armenians suffered greatly from attacks of Mongols as well as of Turks and Persians. In 1828 a part of Armenia was incorporated into the Russian Empire. Because of emigrations that have been happening for centuries, many Armenians live today outside their historical homeland.

Literature: M. Ormanian, *L'église arménienne: Son histoire, sa doctrine, son regime, sa discipline, sa liturgie, sa littérature, son présent* (Paris 1910); Jean Mécérian, *Histoire et institutions de l'église arménienne: Evolution nationale et doctrinale—spiritualité—monachisme* (Beirut 1965); Spuler, *Die morgenländischen Kirchen* 240–68; Heiler, *Ostkirchen* 375–91; Atiya, *Eastern Christianity* 303–56; Müller, *Orientalische Nationalkirchen* 354–60; *Die Kirche Armeniens*, ed. Friedrich Heyer (Die Kirchen der Welt 18; Stuttgart 1978); K. Beledian, *Les Arméniens* (Turnhout 1994). J.-P. Mahé, 'L'Église arménienne de 611 à 1066', *Histoire du Christianisme* 4.457–547 (*Geschichte des Christentums* 4.473–542); J. Richard, 'L'Église arménienne', *Histoire du Christianisme* 6.227–33 (*Geschichte des Christentums* 6. 224–29).

Armenians sent missions to christianize the Caucasian Albanians (in the regions of the present Karabakh and Azerbaijan) during the fourth century. The Albanians established their own Katholikos but in communion with the Armenian Katholikos. From the eighth century onward, a large part of the Albanians were converted to Islam. The remaining Christians were absorbed into Georgia or Armenia, and the office of Katholikos disappeared. The canons of a synod under the Albanian king Vačagan (beginning of the fifth century) are only preserved in Armenian sources. David of Gandzak and Mechitar Goš also were active in the Albanian region (see below).

Literature: A. Manandian, *Beiträge zur albanischen Geschichte* (Leipzig 1897); J Rist, 'Albanier, Albanische Kirche', KLCO 7–10; A. Bozoyan and H. Ditten, *Klio* 72 (1990) 347–55 (review of A. A. Akopjan [= A. H. Hakobyan], *Albanija-Aluank w greko-latinskix i drevnearmjanskix istočnikax* (Yerevan 1987).

Armenian Literature

Soon after the creation of the Armenian alphabet at the beginning of the fifth century, many Greek and Syriac works were translated into Armenian, an Indo-European language; these translated works included canonical texts. Further, in the course of centuries a rich Armenian literature arose that was not just theological. In the Cilician realm an Old French legal text and Byzantine-Greek legal works were translated. In this period classical Armenian was transformed under the influence of vernacular into 'Middle Armenian'.

Very little has been preserved of Albanian literature.

Literature: F. N. Finck, 'Geschichte der armenischen Literatur', *Christliche Literaturen* 75–130; H. Thorossian, *Histoire de la littérature arménienne* (Paris [1951]); Vahan Inglisian, 'Die armenische Literatur', HbOr 1.7 pp. 156–250; N. Poğarean (Bogharian), *Hay grołner* (Jerusalem 1971) (Armenian); K. Sarkissian, *A Brief Introduction to Armenian Christian Literature* (London 1960, 2nd ed., Bergenfield, New Jersey 1974); M. Abegian, *Istorija drevearmjanskoj literatury* (Yerevan 1975); V. S. Nalbandian, V. S. Nersessian and H. G. Bakhchinian, *Histoire abregée de la littérature arménienne médiévale* (Yerevan 1986); L. Ter Petrossian, *Ancient Armenian Translations*, trans. K. Masoudian (New York 1992); C. Renoux, 'Langue et littératures arméniennes', *Christianismes orientaux* 107–66; R. W. Thomson, *A Bibliography of Classical Armenian Literature to 1500 AD* (Corpus Christianorum: Turnhout 1995).

Armenian Sources of Canon Law

Work on Armenian canon law began in Europe in the first half of the nineteenth century. In 1838 Angelo Mai published canons of the Armenian Church in Latin translation in his *Scriptorum veterum Nova Collectio*. In 1906–7 there appeared the still-significant essay *Grundriss der Geschichte des armenischen Rechts* by the philologist Joseph Karst, who also edited and translated the law book of the Cilician military chief Sembad. Knowledge of Armenian law was deepened by Armenians residing in Europe to study, particularly members of the Armenian-Catholic Mechitharist Order, founded in 1701, whose two branches had their seats in Venice and Vienna. The numerous editions, monographs, and essays published in Armenia during the last century were written in Armenian or Russian, and for that reason they have not received very wide circulation. To date the greatest comprehensive presentation of Armenian canon law is by Melik'-T'angean.

1. H. Kaufhold, 'Stand und Aufgaben der Erforschung des armenischen und georgischen Rechts', *Izvestija Akademii Nauk Gruzii: Serija istorii, etnografii i istorii iskusstva*

(Tbilisi 1991) 63–73 ; N. Sakayan, 'Der Beitrag von P. Joseph Katherdjian und der philologischen Schule der Wiener Mechitharisten-Kongregation zur Kanonistik der armenischen Kirche', *Kanon: Jahrbuch der Gesellschaft für das Recht der Ostkirchen* 18 (2004) 78–104.

2. Bibliographies: K. N. Yuzbashyan, *Droit armenien* (Introduction bibliographique à l'histoire du droit et à l'ethnologie juridique, E 17; Brussels 1972); *Bibliographie zur Rezeption des byzantinischen Rechts im alten Russland sowie zur Geschichte des armenischen und georgischen Rechts*, ed. L. Burgmann and H. Kaufhold (Frankfurt am Main 1992) 89–187; Thomson, Bibliography 265–67.

3. General surveys: N. Melik'-T'angean, *Hayoc ekeġecakan iravunk'e* [Armenian Canon Law] (2 vols. Shushi 1903–1905) (Armenian, with sources); J. Karst, 'Grundriss'; A. Abrahamian, *Die Grundlagen des armenischen Kirchenrechts* (Zürich 1917); V. Hatzuni, 'Disciplina armena', *Studi storici* 139–168; C. de Clercq, 'Arménien (Droit canonique)', DDC 1 (1935) 1043–1047; J. Doens, 'Armenian canon law', *The Eastern Churches Quarterly* 3 (1938–1939) 419–29, 460–73; J. Mécérian, 'Bulletin armenologique (Cahier 1–2)', *Mélanges de l'Université Saint Joseph* 27 (Beirut 1947/48) 177–311 [= fasc. 10] and 30 (1953) 63–310 [= fasc. 4]. Section 1 of Cahier 1 (pp. 181–249) and section 4 of Cahier 2 (pp. 238–46); G. Amaduni, 'Armenia', [section] 5: 'Il diritto canonico', *Enciclopedia cattolica* (Vatican City 1949) 1.1980–85; M. K. Krikorian, '<Ius Graeco-Romanum> and Canon Rules in the Tradition of the Armenian Church', *Atti del congresso internazionale Incontro fra canoni d'oriente e d'occidente*, ed. R. Coppola (Bari 1994) 1.165–91; idem, 'The Formation of Canon Law of the Armenian Church in the IVth Century', *Die Christianisierung des Kaukasus*, ed. by W. Seibt (Österreichische Akademie der Wissenschaften. Phil.-hist. Klasse, Denkschriften 296; Vienna 2002) 99–106; A. Bozoyan, 'Le development des lois ecclésiatiques en Arménie', *Kanon: Jahrbuch der Gesellschaft für das Recht der Ostkirchen* 18 (2004) 35–44.

Canon Book of the Armenians (Kanonagirk' Hayoc')

Since Armenian bishops participated in the Council of Nicaea,[154] one might assume that its canons were known among the Armenians and translated into Armenian.[155] We do not know with certainty when the canons of the other early councils and Fathers were translated from Greek. The foundation of the existing Armenian canonical collections is, as in almost all churches, the expanded *Corpus canonum* of Antioch, including the canons of Ephesus (the canons of the Council of Chalcedon are missing because its canons were not recognized by the Armenians on dogmatic grounds), so that the translation of the *Corpus canonum* could not have taken place before the middle of the fifth century.

The first collection of Armenian canon law is thought to have been composed in the Synod of Schahapivan (444 A.D.) and contained the

---

154. See Faustos of Buzand 3.10 (N. G. Garsoïan, *The Epic Histories attributed to P'awstos Buzand* (Cambridge, Mass. 1989) 79; Moses of Khoren 2.90 (Moses Khorenatsi', *History of the Armenians: Translation and Commentary* by R. W. Thomson (Harvard Armenian Texts and Studies 4; Cambridge, Mass. 1978) 246.

155. Thomson, Moses Khorenatsi's *History* 246: 'Then Aristakēs returned with the orthodox creed and the twenty canonical chapters of the council'.

'Teaching of the Apostles', the Antiochean 'Corpus Canonum' (Nicaea Ancyra, Neocaesaria, Gangra, Antioch, Laodicea) with the canons of Schahapivan. The collection may have been enlarged with numerous texts in the first half of the seventh century by the member of the Julian party, Johannes Mayragomecʻi. The collection could be the foundation for the compilation of Katholikos John of Odzum (Odznecʻi) 'the Philosopher' (718–29). His collection is not preserved in its original form.

The 'Canon Book of the Armenians' in the form in which it has survived is much more extensive. The oldest of the many manuscripts (Nor-Dshulfa 131) dates to A.D. 1038, and, along with a few other manuscripts, it comes the closest to the original version. The collection of John of Odzun is still the easiest to recognize in this manuscript, since it ends with the canons of John himself and a colophon. In the eleventh century many supplemental texts were added to John's collection, which were then passed on almost unchanged into later manuscripts. Afterwards, other canon law sources were no longer added to it but were preserved separately. A later editor significantly altered the sequence of the 'Canon Book'. He attempted to construct a better chronological order by inserting pieces from the appendix in the original collection of John of Odzun. Thus he incorporated the putative canons of the apostles Thaddeus and Philip into the other pseudo-apostolic texts. Then he placed the Council of Ancyra before that of Nicaea. This transposition were justified by a note in the manuscript. He made other chronological changes. This altered format has been preserved in many manuscripts.

General edition: V. Hakobyan, *Kanonagirkʻ Hayocʻ* (2 vols. Yerevan 1964–71).

Partial translations: 'Ecclesiae Armeniacae canones selecti', A. Mai, SCNC 10.269–316 [second pagination] *Editoris praefatio* [chapter] xiii–xiv, pp. xxi–xxiii (Latin translation by A. Angiarakianus); A. Balgy, *Historia doctrinae catholicae inter Armenos unionisque eorum cum Ecclesia Romana in concilio Florentino* (Vienna 1878) 203–19, 294–335 (translation of the Armenian edition: A. Palčean, *Patmoutʻiwn katʻoġike wardapetoutʻean i Hays* [Vienna 1878] 191–203, 267–98); [G. Amaduni], *Disciplina Armena: Testi vari di diritto canonico armeno secolo IV–XVII* (Fonti, series 1, fasc. 7; Vatican City 1932). Older editions in Burgmann and Kaufhold, *Bibliographie* 132–39.

Literature: É. Hermann, 'Jean d'Ozun', DDC 6 (1957) 115; T. Nersoyan, 'A Brief Outline of the Armenian Liber Canonum and its Status in Modern Times', *Kanon: Jahrbuch der Gesellschaft für das Recht der Ostkirchen* 1 (1973) 76–86; M. van Esbroeck, 'Die sog. Konziliengeschichte des Johannes von Odzun (717–728)', *Annuarium Historiae Conciliorum* 26 (1994) 31–60; M. E. Shirinian and G. Muradian, 'The Armenian Collection of the Ecclesiastical Canons', *Christianskij Vostok* 7 (New Series 1; 1999) 124–54; A. Mardirossian, *Le Livre des Canons arméniens (Kanonagirkʻ hayocʻ) de Yovhannês Awjnecʻi. Église, roit et société en Arménie du IVe au VIIIe siècle* (CSCO 606; Leuven 2004) especially 41–43, 264–88, 501–625.

Individual Texts

Pseudo-Apostolic Canons

As with the miscellaneous works of the Syrians, the collection of John of Odzun contains the 'Teaching of the Apostles' (with 30 canons), supplemented at the end by three other canons unknown in Syriac or Greek. The second pseudo-apostolic text is the 'Apostolic Canons' accepted by all the churches, which is divided into 85 canons as in the Greek collections. A third text with the title 'Canons of the Fathers who followed after the Apostles' in 27 canons is singular to the Armenians. It contains punishments, some mandating the death penalty, for various misdeeds (killing children, sexual crimes, theft, grave-robbing, killing thieves and robbers), marital rules (ban on repudiating wives and sequential marriages, marriage of monks, indecency of women before marriage), rules for treatment of priests' misconduct, and for nocturnal pollution. Two further canons are unusual. In the first, the wife of a priest is permitted to teach laymen, because 'just as the wife of a judge is called a "female judge", and the wife of a king a "queen", so also the wife of a priest is called a "priestess".' In the second, it is forbidden to eat or drink anything which has been polluted by a dead mouse. This is a theme that recurs with David of Gandzak (see below) and in later controversies between Armenians and Western Syrians over disciplinary questions. At the end, the books of the Old Testament are enumerated. This third pseudo-apostolic text followed the two others in the manuscript from A.D. 1038, so that it probably already existed in the collection of John of Odzun.

Editions (and translation): Y. Tašean (= Jacob Dashean), *Wardapetowt'iwn arakeloc'* (Nationalbibliothek 20; Vienna 1896); *Collectio canonum ecclesiae Armenae*, 1: *Canones apostolici, quos apparatu critico dotavit et latine interpretatus est,* ed. H. Ghedighian (Fonti, series 2, fasc. 21; S. Lazzaro-Venice 1941).

Literature: Mardirossian, *Le livre des canons arméniens* 529–32, 557–62, 603–8.

Greek Councils and Fathers

As usual Greek councils are combined in the following sequence: Nicaea (with the list of bishops, without the pseudo-Nicene canons), Ancyra, Neocaesarea, Gangra, Antioch, Laodiceia, Sardica, Constantinople and Ephesus. It is a peculiarity of the Armenian collection that the first 9 canons of Neocaesarea (as well as four additional) are attributed to a putative Council of Caesarea. The attempt of Joseph Lebon to prove the existence of such a council on the basis of this evidence is not convincing. There is otherwise no documentation for this Council of Caesarea. The Armenian tradition is explained, as Eduard Schwartz has demonstrated, by a scribal error in the Greek original. The Armenian translation of the early councils of the Church is not precise. It contains many differences from the Greek, so that the assumption cannot be made that the Armenian text is particularly close to the lost Greek *Corpus canonum* of Antioch. The collection contains the first four canons from the First Council of Constantinople. In the Armenian collection, the Greek canons two and three are combined as the third canon, for a total of three canons. The collection then included the first six canons from the Council of Ephesus.

The collection of John of Odzun has the following texts of the Fathers: questions and answers (at the most 88) attributed to Athanasius of Alexandria. However, the first questions correspond to the Greek questions and answers of Timothy of Alexandria, though in a slightly different sequence. They have, nevertheless, been expanded from an unknown source. The 51 canons of Basil of Caesarea sent to Amphilochius of Iconium (canons 1–50) and Diodorus of Tarsus (canon 51) might have belonged to the collection from the beginning. They are a selection from the Greek canons 1 to 87 of Basil (3 letters to Amphilochius and one letter to Diodorus).

Translations: B. R. Rackham, 'The Text of the Canons of Ancyra', *Studia biblica et ecclesiastica: Essays chiefly in Biblical and Patristic Criticism by Members of the University of Oxford* (Oxford 1891) 3.139–216 and on pp. 209–16 (Latin translation by F. C. Conybeare): 'Appendix II: "The Armenian Version"'; F. Macler, 'Une recension arménienne des canons du concile de Gangres', REA 9 (1929) 73–97; I. Rucker, *Ephesinische Konzilsakten in armenisch-georgischer Überlieferung* (Sb Munich, 1930, no. 3; München 1930); C. Mercier, 'Les canons des conciles oecuméniques et locaux en version arménienne: Avant-propos et notes additionelles par J.-P. Mahé', REA 2nd series 15 (1981) 187–262.

Literature: On the putative Council of Caesarea: J. Lebon, 'Sur un concile de Césarée', *Muséon* 51 (1938) 89ff.; E. Schwartz, 'Die Kanonessammlungen der alten Reichskirche', ZRG Kan. Abt. 25 (1936) 16–17 (= *Gesammelte Schriften* 4.174ff.); H. Kaufhold, *Gabriel von Basra* 11–15.

On the relationship between the Greek original and the Armenian translation: C. Hannick, 'Zur Rezeption des byzantinischen Kirchenrechts in Armenien', W. Diem and A. Falaturi, eds., ZDMG, Supplement 7: *XXIV. Deutscher Orientalistentag 1988 in Köln* (Stuttgart 1990) 116–22 ; Mardirossian, *Le livre des canons arméniens* 533–57, 570–75 (Kaisareia), 578–81 (Athanasios), 608–18 (Konstantinopel, Ephesus, Sardika), 618–23 (Basileios).

Armenian Synods and Fathers in John's Collection

Probably the following 5 Armenian texts belong to the original corpus of John of Odzun.[156]

1. 55 *Canons of St. Sahak* (= Isaac) Patriarch of the Armenians (387–439). Its authenticity is not certain.

---

156. Contents and other information in Hatzuni, 'Disciplina armena', in Fonti VII 158–66.

Literature: Mardirossian, *Le livre des canons arméniens* 582–88.

Translations: Mai, SVNC 10.276–77; F. C. Conybeare, 'The Armenian Canons of St. Sahak, Catholicos of Armenia (390–439 A.D.)', *American Journal of Theology* 2 (Chicago 1898) 828–48.

2. 20 canons of the Armenian synod of Shahapivan (A.D. 444).

Edition: N. Akinian, *Die Kanones der Synode von Schahapiwan: Text und Untersuchung* (2nd ed., Vienna 1950) (Armenian).

Translation: Mai, SVNC 10.290–96.

Literature: Mardirossian, *Le livre des canons arméniens* 501–10, 562.

3. Letter of an otherwise unknown Bishop Sevantos in 14 chapters.

Literature: Mardirossian, *Le livre des canons arméniens* 565–70.

4. 37 canons of Katholikos Narsai (Nersēs II Aštarakecʻi; A.D. 548–557), 9 canons of Katholikos John Mandakuni (end of the fifth century; presumably written by John Mairagomecʻi, seventh century), 3 canons of Abraham, bishop of the Mamiconians, 15 canons of Katholikos Sahak III 'the Last' (A.D. 677–703).

Translation: Mai, SVNC 273–6, 296–99, 299–300, 300. Canons of John Mairagomecʻi: van Esbroeck, 'Die sog. Konziliengeschichte', 56–60.

Literature: Mardirossian, *Le livre des canons arméniens* 589–603, 623–25.

5. 32 canons of Katholikos John of Odzun.

Translation: Mai, SVNC 10.302–7.

Literature: van Esbroeck, 'Die sog. Konziliengeschichte' 38.

6. It is improbable that the 30 spurious canons of Gregory the Enlightener, which are inserted in all the manuscripts between the councils of Laodiceia and Sardica, belong to John's collection. They were probably a later addition.

Edition and translation: N. Adontz, 'Le questionnaire de Saint Gregoire l'Illuminateur et ses rapports avec Eznik', ROC 25 (Paris 1925–1926) 309–57 (the text also contains two canons).

Translation: Mai, SVNC 10.269–70.

Literature: Mardirossian, *Le livre des canons arméniens* 575–78.

Later Additions to John's Collection

1. In the 'Canon Book of the Armenians' in its present form, there are 33 'Rulings of the Holy Apostle Thaddeus' (in two versions) and 9 'Canons of our Lord Philip the Apostle', which are not found in other churches and certainly were written in the Armenian region. The first part contains, in the form of questions and answers, regulations for clerics (quali-

fications for the office of bishop and conduct of office, married priests, oaths by priests), then punishments (for indecency and other sexual misdeeds, magic, apostasy, killing) and other matters (abstinence, marriage among foster children or among relatives, violation of boundaries). The second part deals with the forty-day fasting period, barren women, the sacrifice of animals, unclean animals, menstruating women, and the obligation to morning and evening prayer in the church.[157]

Edition and translation: Ghedighian, *Collectio canonum ecclesiae Armenae* 85–116. Edition of the canons of Thaddaios: Tašean, *Wardaetout'iwn* 392–425.

2. A purported second set of canons of Antioch, the Declaration (hostovanut'iwn) of the Council of Antioch and the 114 Second Nicaean Canons are further additions. The latter consist of the contents of the genuine 20 canons of Nicaea (canons 1–20) and a selection from the canons of Ancyra (21–32), Neocaesarea (33–45), Gangra (46–52 and 65–70), Laodiceia (53–64 and 82–113) as well as Antioch (71–81 and 114) in a different translation. We cannot determine why the canons of the councils are so out of order. The 'second canons of Antioch' cannot be attributed to other synods in the same way.

Literature: Hatzuni, 'Disciplina armena', *Fonti* 7.155–56, 165–66; Mardirossian, *Le livre des canons arméniens* 510–29.

3. In the beginning of the later version of John's collection, there are many, often very brief, and in part certainly spurious pieces, such as 5 chapters of Cyril of Alexandria, 5 canons of Epiphanius of Cyprus, 272 canons of Basil of Caesarea, 30 canons of Gregory of Nazianzus, the Epistle of Makarios of Jerusalem to the Armenians.

Editions of individual texts: F. C. Conybeare, *The Key of the Truth: A Manual of the Paulician Church of Armenia* (Oxford 1989) on pp. 178–86: 'Appendix IX: Macarius' Epistle to the Armenians'.
Literature: Hatzuni, 'Disciplina armena', *Fonti* 7.148 (Makarios), 164–66.

4. Original Armenian pieces from the time of John of Odzun are added, such as the canons of Katholikos Sion (synod of Partav, about A.D. 770) or of the synod of Karin (= Theodosiupolis, Erzurum; according to van Esbroeck: 693 A.D.).

Literature: Hatzuni, 'Disciplina armena', *Fonti* 7.164–66. For the synod of Karin: M. van Esbroeck, 'Le discours du Catholicus Sahak III en 691 et quelques documents arméniens annexes au Quinisexte', ed. G. Nedungatt and M. Featherstone, *The Council in Trullo Revisited* (Kanonika 6; Rome 1995) 323–454, especially 360–63, 439–44 (translation of the canons).

157. These works are listed by Mardirossian, *Le livre des canons arméniens* 696–97.

Translation: A. Mardirossian, 'Les Canons du synode de Partaw (768)', REA New Series 27 (1998–2000) 117–34.

Other Armenian texts can be found in a miscellaneous work, the Book of Letters (Girk' tġtoc'), which contains 5 canons of a synod of Dwin (A.D. 607) on penance and return of Chalcedonian bishops and priests.

Armenian text of the canons: Y. Izmireanc, Girk' tġtoc' (Tbilisi 1901) 146–48; with a Georgian translation: A. Aleksidze, *Liber epistolarum* (Tbilisi 1968) 53–56 (Georgian).

Literature: A. Schmidt, 'Das armenische "Buch der Briefe:" Seine Bedeutung als quellenkundliche Sammlung für die christologischen Streitigkeiten in Armenien im 6./7. Jh.', *Logos: Festschrift für Luise Abramowsky* (Berlin–New York 1993) 511–33, here 531.

Also preserved are 15 canons of a synod of Širakawan (A.D. 862).

Edition: Palčean, *Patmout'iwn* 202–3.

The later Armenian synods, particularly those of Cilicia, circulate outside the 'Canon Book'. Most significant to be named are the synods of Ani (970, 1036), Hromkla (1179), Sis (1204, 1246, 1307, 1342) and Adana (1316); the encyclicals of Nersēs IV Šnorhali (1166) also have canonical contents.

Edition: Palčean, *Patmout'iwn* 267–98.

Literature: N. Melik'-Tangean, *Hayoc' ekeġecakan iravunk'ē* 438–39; J. Partamian, *Un législateur arménien du XII siècle, le Patriarche S. Nerses IV le Gracieux (1165–73)* (Rome 1955).

Penitential of David, Son of Alavik (David of Ganjak)

It was probably in the 1130s that the Wardepet (= title of a monastic priest of high education) David, son of Alavik (Alawkayordi), from Ganjak in Causasian Albania, composed Canonistic Admonitions (or Counsels) (hratk' kanonakank') in 97 sections. In an unsystematic way, this remarkable work treats questions of religious practice and gives keen insight into Armenian daily life, usage and views, but also into the superstition of the times. The author begins with the distinction between pure (edible) and impure animals. He then discusses the pollution of food and utensils caused by dead mice and other animals as well as through infidels. Subsequently he considers the proper conduct toward infidels (Kurds). After turning to questions of baptism, reception of communion and conduct in church, he finally deals with all possible, in some cases peculiar, misconduct by clerics and laymen, including those of a sexual nature. Penalties consist of exclusion from the Church and sacraments for a specified time or—in the case of the most severe crimes—permanently, fasts and, for clerics, removal from office. In specific cases polluted food and utensils were to be cleaned or even destroyed, and animals had to be killed but could not then be eaten. Sources for the cases and decisions are largely unknown, but strong Old Testament, Jewish, or Islamic influence can be conjectured. Besides the work of David there are comparable works among the Armenians, but they are less extensive.

Edition and translation: *The Penitential of David of Ganjak*, ed. and trans. by C. J. F. Dowsett, (CSCO 216–217; Louvain 1961).

Literature: Thomson, *Bibliography* 111; J. Mécérian, 'Un précurseur des codificateurs du droit arménien', *Actes du XXIe Congrès International des Orientalistes, Paris, 23–31 Juillet 1948* (Paris 1949) 363–65; J. Mécérian, 'David fils d'Alavic', *Bulletin arménologique* (1947–48) 184–201; (1953) 243–44: Le recueil de David fils d'Alavic.

Datastanagirkʻ (Lawbook) of Mechitar Goš

Mechitar Goš, born in the middle of the twelfth century in the region of Ganjak, reached the rank of a Wardapet, resided for a time in Cilicia, and finally founded the monastery of Nor Getik in Caucasian Albania, where he died in 1213. Besides his works of theology, homilies, and parables, in 1184, he composed a 'Lawbook' (Datastanagirkʻ) at the request of the Albanian Katholikos Stephan, which contains an analytical introduction followed by 251 sections of canon and civil law. The sources upon which he based his work included the Old Testament and the 'Canon Book of the Armenians', particularly the 'Apostolic Canons', the 'Canons of the Fathers who came after the Apostles', the Greek councils, the canons of Athanasius and Basil, as well as the canons of the Armenian synods of Šahapiwan, Partav, and Dwin, and also unidentified sources, together with customary law and Islamic law.

The work survives in two versions. In the original version Mechitar first followed the Old Testament (Deuteronomy, with many additions), and from section 36 on the 'Canon Book'. In doing so, he preserved the sequence of the texts or the sequence of the canons within the texts, although he did not include all the rulings. Between canons 16 and 17 of the 'Fathers after the Apostles', he inserted a large text (about 80 sections) whose sources are the books of Exodus, Leviticus, and Deuteronomy. An editor later completely reordered the main part of the Law Book by placing 130 canon law sections at the beginning, but retaining their original order, and in a following part placed the 120 sections on civil law. This altered version survives in many manuscripts, and it is the basis of the first edition by Bastameancʻ as well as the literature that relies on it.

Editions: V. Bastameancʻ, *Mhitʻar Goši Datastanagirkʻ Hayocʻ* (Vaġaršapat 1880); H. Torosyan, *Mhitʻar Goš: Girkʻdatastani* (Russian title: *Mxitar Goš: Sudebnik*) (Yerevan 1975).

Translations: J. Karst (not as a complete text but scattered in the commentary of his edition of the lawbook of Sembad, see below); *Armjanskij sudebnik Mxitara Goša*, ed. A. Papovjan, and B. M. Arutjunjan (Yerevan 1954); R. W. Thomson, *The Lawcode [Datas-*

tanagirkʻ] of Mxitʻar Goš. Translated with Commentary and Indices (Dutch Studies in Armenian Language and Literature 6; Amsterdam–Atlanta, Georgia 2000). Excerpts: N. Akinian, *Testi vari di diritto canonico armeno (Secoli IV–XVII)* (*Fonti* I, VII; Vatican City 1932).

Literature: Thomson, *Bibliography* 170–73; M. F. Brosset, *Rapport sur un manuscrit armenien: Mekhitar Gosch: Livre de decision judiciaire* (St. Petersburg 1849); Karst, 'Grundriss' especially 368ff. (with a translation of excerpts from Mechitar's introduction); D. Ghijirighian, 'Un manuscrit arménien du code de Mekhitar Goch', *Studia et acta orientalia* 3 (Bucharest 1960) 47–63. J. Mécérian, 'Mekhitar Kosch', *Bulletin arménologique* (1947–48) 202–34.

The Lawbook of Smbad Sparaped

On the basis of the Lawbook of Mechitar Goš, which was written in Old Armenian, the Constable (Gundstapl) Smbat, a brother of the local king, Hetʻum I, composed a law book in Middle Armenian in A.D. 1256. It consists of 202 (according to the edition of Karst 177) chapters dealing with civil and canon law in a more or less systematic fashion. Following chapters 1–7 on the law of princes and state is the law of the Church in chapters 8–77 (Karst, 8–71) with rules for clerics and their conduct of office, for monasteries and ecclesiastical property, on hierarchical ranking, on laymen, etc. It closes with marital law (chapters 78–117 or 72–93), inheritance, family law, property law, the law of merchants, the law of testaments, the law of slavery, penalties for delicts, and the like. Besides this work, there is a history by Smbat from 951 to 1276, as well as another judicial work, a translation from the lost original Old French, the 'Assises of Antioch', dealing with feudal law.

Edition, translation and commentary: *Sempadscher Kodex aus dem 13. Jahrhundert oder Mittelarmenisches Rechtsbuch nach der Venediger und der Etschmiadziner Version unter Zurückführung auf seine Quellen herausgegeben und übersetzt von* J. Karst (Strasbourg 1905); idem, *Sempadscher Kodex aus dem 13. Jahrhundert: In Verbindung mit dem Grossarmenischen Rechtsbuch des Mechithar Gosch aus dem 12. Jahrhundert unter Berücksichtigung der jüngeren abgeleiteten Gesetzbücher erläutert von* J. Karst (Armenisches Rechtsbuch 1–2; Strasbourg 1905); A. G. Galstjan, *Smbat Sparapet. Sudebnik.* (Yerevan 1958) (text and Russian translation); A. Sukiasjan, *Sudebnik Smbata Sparapet* (Yerevan 1971).

Literature: Thomson, *Bibliography* 198–99; Karst, 'Grundriss' 346–47.

Further Reworkings of Datastanagirkʻ

The Lawbook of Mechitar Goš also circulated among the Armenians in Ukraine and Poland, and it survives in several versions and corresponding translations. At the beginning of the eighteenth century it was translated into Georgian.

Literature: F. Bischoff, 'Das alte Recht der Armenier in Polen: Aus Urkunden des Lemberger Stadtarchivs', *Österreichische Blätter für Literatur und Kunst: Beilage zur Oesterreichisch-Kaiserlichen Wiener Zeitung* (Wien1857) nos. 8, 33, 37, 39, = pp. 217–19, 257–60, 289–91, 305–7; idem, 'Das alte Recht der Armenier in Lemberg', *Sitzungsberichte der Kaiser-*

lichen Akademie der Wissenschaften 40 (Vienna 1862) 255–302 (printed separately, Vienna 1862); Karst, 'Grundriss' 348–67; M. Oleś, *The Armenian Law in the Polish Kingdom (1356–1519): A Juridical and Historical Study*. Foreword by C. de Clercq (Rome 1966)

Translations of Byzantine Law Books

In Cilicia during the twelfth century various Byzantine law books were translated into Armenian from Greek: the *Ekloge* of 726 with its appendix, the *Nomos Stratiotikos* and the *Nomos Mosaikos*; from Syriac the *Syro-Roman Lawbook* and the *Sentientiae Syriacae*.

Editions: K. G. Bruns and E. Sachau, *Syrisch-römisches Rechtsbuch aus dem fünften Jahrhundert* (Leipzig 1880) 95–141 (text) 115–50 (translation); *Die armenischen Übersetzungen byzantinischer Rechtsbücher, Erster Teil: Allgemeines. Zweiter Teil: Die 'Kurze Sammlung' ('Sententiae Syriacae')*, ed., trans., and commentary by H. Kaufhold (Forschungen zur byzantinischen Rechtsgeschichte 21; Frankfurt am Main 1997). Further editions: see Kaufhold in Burgmann and Kaufhold, *Bibliographie* 160–62 (nos. 294–96, 299, 301).

Literature: Karst, 'Grundriss' 340–45; G. Amaduni, 'Influsso del diritto romano giustineaneo sul diritto armeno e quantità di tale influsso', *Acta congressus juridici internationalis* (Rome 1935) 2.225–58; J. Mécérian, 'Note sur les documents juridiques arméniens d'origine romano-byzantine', *XIIe Congrès international des études byzantines, Ochrides 1961: Résumés des communications* (Belgrade-Ochrida 1961) 67–69; H. Kaufhold, 'Zur Übernahme byzantinischer Rechtsbücher durch die Armenier', *Handes Amsorya* 90 (1976) 591–614; B. Martin-Hisard, 'La version arménienne de l'Ecloga de Léon III', *REA* N. S. 21 (1988–1989) 145–58; Selb-Kaufhold, *Rechtsbuch* 1.64, 93–95, 172–73; H. Kaufhold, 'Armenische Übersetzungen byzantinischer Rechtsbücher', *Armenologie in Deutschland*, ed. A. Drost-Abgarjan and H. Goltz (Münster 2005) 47–55.

Monastic Rules

Monasticism also played an important role among the Armenians. The Rules of Basil were translated into Armenian and are still extant. Nersēs of Lambron translated the Rule of St. Benedict in the twelfth century. 'Syntagma Doctrinae' (see above, section on Coptic law) contained a monastic rule that is always attributed to Euagrios Pontikos, but falsely. Beyond that, other Armenian writings provide guidance for monks.

Editions and translations: J. Muyldermans, 'Une recension arménienne du Syntagma doctrinae', *Handes Amsorya* 41 (1927) 687–700; M.-A. van den Oudenrijn, *Les constitutions des Frères Arméniens de Saint Basile en Italie* (OCA 126; Rome 1940); G. Uluhogian, *Basilio di Cesarea: Il libro della 'Domande' (Le Regole)* (CSCO 536, 537; Louvain 1993). Systematic excerpts in translation: G. Amaduni, *Monachismo: Studio storico-canonico e fonti canoniche* (Fonti, series 2, fasc. 12; S. Lazzaro-Venice 1940).

Literature: G. Uluboghian, 'La tradizione medioevale armena sull'origine delle Regole di San Basilio', *Studi e ricerche sull'Oriente cristiano* 14 (1991) 341–46; Thomson, *Bibliography* 40 (St. Benedict).

Western Canon Law Sources

From the thirteenth century on, Dominicans were active in Armenia as missionaries, and Armenians soon joined the order. In 1330 a congregation was established that used the rule of the Dominicans. It consisted only of Armenian priests and was called the Fratres Unitores. They flourished in the middle of the fourteenth century and comprised about 700 monks residing in more than 50 houses. A bishop resided in Nakhichevan. The order died out at the beginning of the nineteenth century. Its members translated many works from Latin into Armenian, although, naturally, the works were primarily theological. In 1331 there was a translation of a canonical work that the Dominican Peter of Aragon compiled from writings of Raymond of Peñafort, Thomas Aquinas, Goffredus Tranensis, and others while he worked in Armenia. It had the following contents, which was modeled after the format of Pope Gregory IX's *Decretales*: De iudicibus (56 chapters), De iudiciis (26 chapters), De vita et discipina clericorum (42 chapters), De matrimonio (29 chapters), De poenis pro delictis (51 chapters). The Armenian text survives in several manuscripts but has never been edited.

Literature: M. A. van den Oudenrijn, 'Uniteurs et Dominicains d'Arménie', OrChr 42 (1958) 110–33 (here 113–14); idem, *Linguae Haicanae Scriptores* (Bern-Munich 1960) 192–94 (no. 463).

Causasian Albanians

The canons of a synod of the Albanian Church, which was held at the beginning of the fifth century under King Vačagan is contained in the 'Canon Book' as well as in the 'History of the Albanians' of Moses of Dasxuranc'i, originally written in Albanian but surviving only in Armenian (book 1, chapter 26). The canons deal with dues to the churches, commemoration of the dead, religious houses, marital law, fasts, suits against clerics, and the like.

Editions: V. Hakobyan, *Kanonagirk' hayoc' II* (Yerevan 1971) 91–100; *Movsēs Kagankatouac'i: Patmout'iwn Aguanic' ašharhi*, ed. V. Arakelyan (Yerevan 1983) 89–94.

Translation: Mai, 'Ecclesiae Armeniacae canones selecti', SVNC 10.314; A. Manandian, *Beiträge zur albanischen Geschichte* (Leipzig 1897), 44–48; C. J. F. Dowsett, *The History of the Caucasian Albanians by Movsēs Dasxuranci* (London 1961) 50–54.

Literature: A. A. Akopjan, *Abanija-Aluank v greko-latinskich i drevnearmjanskich istočnikach* (Yerevan 1987) 184–88.

The law books of David of Ganjak and of Mechitar Goš, which were compiled in the Albanian region, belong to the history of Armenian law.

Georgians

History of the Church

The Georgian Church was established in the first Christian centuries. The Armenians and Syrians sent missions from the south, the Greeks from the west. Christianity was already the state religion by the beginning of the fourth century. From the fifth century onward, the church was autocephalic, led by an archbishop and later by the Katholikos with a seat in Mcʰetʿa (near Tbilisi), who was still being consecrated by the patriarch of Antioch into the eighth century. Together with the Armenian Church, the Georgian Church received the Henotikon of Emperor Zeno at a synod in Dwin (505–6), but the Georgians separated from the Armenians about 600, recognized the creed of Chalcedon, and oriented itself toward Byzantium both ecclesiastically and culturally. From Melkʿisedek I (1012) the head of the Georgian Church has designated himself as Katholikos-patriarch. At the height of Georgian power under Queen Tamar († 1213) the Georgian Church was said to have had more than 30 bishoprics. At the end of the fourteenth century, during the political decline that resulted from the Mongol invasions, there arose a separate office of Katholikos in Western Georgia (Abkhazia). Following the annexation of Georgia by Russia at the beginning of the nineteenth century, the office of Katholikos was abolished and the Georgian Church was amalgamated with the Russian. It received its autonomy back in 1917, and since then it has again been led by a Katholikos-patriarch.

Literature: M. Džanašvili, *Sakʿartvelos saekʿlesio istʿoria* (Tbilisi 1886, reprinted 1990) (in Georgian); S. C. Malan, *A Short History of the Georgian Church* (London 1866); M. Tamarati, *L'église géorgienne* (Rome 1910); C. Toumanoff, 'Introduction to Christian Caucasian History', *Traditio* 15 (1959) 1–104; P. Hauptmann, 'Unter dem Weinrebenkreuz der heiligen Nino: Kirchengeschichte Georgiens im Überblick', *Kirche im Osten* 17 (Göttingen 1974) 9–41; J. Assfalg, 'Georgische Kirche', KLCO 167–70; Müller, *Orientalische Nationalkirchen* 361–67; B. Martin-Hisard, 'Christianisme et Église dans le monde géorgien', *Histoire du Christianisme* 4.549–603 (*Geschichte des Christentums* 4.543–99); J. Richard, 'L'Église géorgienne', *Histoire du Christianisme* 6.233–37 (*Geschichte des Christentums* 6.320–23).

Georgian Literature

Georgian belongs to a group of South Caucasian languages and developed at early date into an important literary language. The Georgian alphabet is documented from the fifth century onward. The predominant ecclesiastical literature from the fifth to the thirteenth century is composed in Old Georgian, which has survived into modern times as an ecclesiastical language. From the twelfth century, Modern Georgian, the current spoken language, developed. Until the seventh century, Georgian literature stood under strong Armenian and Syrian influence (the 'oriental period'). After the doctrinally driven schism from the Armenian Church there followed a national Georgian period. Its 'Golden Age' lasted from about 980 to the middle of the thirteenth century. In this period, particularly through Georgian monasteries in Byzantine cultural territories (Iviron on Mount Athos, houses on the Black Mountain near Antioch, the Petric'oni houses [Bačkovo, Bulgaria], Constantinople and in modern northeastern Turkey as well as Georgian monks on the Sinai) Greek influence was significant. Alongside many translations from Armenian, Syriac and later, above all, Greek (Bible, hagiography, philosophy, spiritual poetry, etc.), an extensive ecclesiastical and secular original literature in Georgian came into being. The Mongol incursions led to a decline of Georgian culture and to a temporary decline of its literature.

Literature: A. Baumstark, *Die christliche Literaturen des Orients* (Leipzig 1911) 2.99–110 on Georgian literature; J. Karst, *Littérature géorgienne chrétienne* (Paris 1934); Tarchnišvili, *Georgische Literatur*; G. Deeters, 'Georgische Literatur', HbOr 1.7: *Armenische und kaukasische Sprachen* (Leiden-Cologne 1963) 129–55; J. Assfalg, 'Georgische Literatur; Georgische Schrift; Georgische Sprache', all in KLCO 184–87; H. Fähnrich, *Die georgische Literatur* (Tbilisi 1981; 2nd ed. Aachen 1883); B. Outtier, 'Langue et littérature géorgiennes', *Christianismes orientaux* 263–300; D. Rayfield, *The Literature of Georgia: A History* (2nd ed. Richmond, Virginia 2000).

Georgian Sources of Canon Law

Scholarly study of the language, literature, and history of Georgia begins in the first half of the nineteenth century with the Frenchman Marie-Félicité Brosset (1802–80). The center of Georgian Studies was, besides Georgia itself, above all St. Petersburg. There were only a few scholars in Western Europe who included Georgia in their research.

That also applied to the study of the law of the Georgians. In 1829 Brosset published a report on a Georgian manuscript with the legal collection of King Vachtang VI (seventeenth century). A year later Friedrich August Biener published his essay in which he briefly discussed Vachtang's collection. August von Haxthausen (1792–1866) enriched our knowledge of Georgian law in his work *Transkaukasia,* which appeared in 1856, printing sources in translation. At the beginning of the twentieth century, works appeared by Felix Holldack and Friedrich Jessner, but real progress was made only by the linguist Joseph Karst. In 1934–40 he edited parts of the collection of Vachtang VI and translated them into French. In 1938–39 his *Recherches sur l'histoire du Droit ecclésiastique carthvélien* appeared, the first history of Georgian canon law, that is now partially antiquated.

In Georgia itself critical editions of the primary sources of canon and civil law were published, and many monographs and essays on legal history were written in Georgian and Russian. We have the noted Georgian historian Ivan Džavahišvili to thank for a two-volume history of Georgian law in which he also treated canon law. These works are not accessible to a larger circle of readers for linguistic reasons, and thus they have not yet received adequate recognition. In summary works on the law of the Eastern churches, the Georgians often do not appear[158] or if they do, only inadequately.[159]

History of research: H. Kaufhold, 'Stand und Aufgaben der Erforschung des georgischen und armenischen Rechts', *Sakart'velos Respublikis Mecnierabat'a Ak'ademils Mac'ne Istoriis . . . seria* [Izvestija Akademii Nauk Gruzii. Serija istorii . . .] 1991 no. 2 (Tbilisi 1991) 63–73.

Surveys: Džavahišvili, *Istoria*; Karst, 'Recherches'; Tarchnišvili, *Georgische Literatur* 429–38 (canon law).

Bibliography: *Bibliographie zur Rezeption des byzantinischen Rechts im alten Russland sowie zur Geschichte des armenischen und georgischen Rechts*, ed. L. Burgmann and H. Kaufhold, et al. (Frankfurt am Main 1992) 189–276.

Pseudo-Apostolic Sources

Didache

Little can be said about the Georgian translation of the *Didache* with any certainty. In 1932 Gregor Peradse published a list of the variants of the Georgian from the Greek text. He wrote that he used a transcription made in Constantinople in 1923. Neither this transcription nor the Constantinople original nor any other Georgian manuscript of the *Didache* has yet been found. The manuscript in Constantinople was supposed to be from the first half of the previous century and it contained other items besides the *Didache*, not only in Georgian but also in Armenian.[160] More is not known about this manuscript, and the Georgian text has never been printed. The combination of Georgian and Armenian pieces in one manuscript would be unusual. If Peradse is right, the translation would have been done before the tenth or eleventh centuries. The translator is supposed to have been a certain Jeremias, whom Peradse identifies as a bishop of the time of the Council of Ephesus. So long as no manuscripts are known, the assertions of Peradse remain unprovable and have inspired doubt. However, there are also grounds for accepting the authenticity of a Georgian translation, which closely follows the Greek text.[161]

---

158. Cf., for example, *Studi storici*; A. Coussa, *Epitome praelectionum de iure ecclesiastico orientali* (Grottaferrata 1948) 1.121–66 ('Disciplina Byzantina'); Saïd Elias Saïd, *Les églises orientales et leur droits* (Paris 1989) 37–82 ('Presentation des Églises orientales').
159. 'Byzantin (droit canonique)', DDC 1; C. de Clercq, *Fontes iurisdictionis ecclesiarum orientalium: Studium historicum* (Rome 1967) (see Indices).
160. Peradse, 'Die "Lehre der Zwölf Apostel"' 111.
161. Schöllgen, *Didache* 91. Peradse treats the Didache briefly in his autobiographical report: 'So fand ich ganz zufällig in den Papieren eines Georgiers die georgische Übersetzung der Lehre der 12 Apostel, die ich in der Zeitschrift der neutestamentlichen Wissenschaft herausgab', 'Im Dienste der georgischen Kultur (1926–1940), mit einer Einleitung von H. Kaufhold', OrChr 83 (1999) 200–225, at 216. Peradse was a serious scholar. The Georgian church declared him to be a saint. Both of these facts indicate that he probably did not falsify the translation of the *Didache*.

Literature: ClavisG 1735; G. Peradse, 'Die "Lehre der zwölf Apostel" in der georgischen Überlieferung', *Zeitschrift für die neutestamentliche Wissenschaft* 31 (1932) 111–16; Audet, *La Didaché* 45–50; Niederwimmer, *Didache* 44–45; Schöllgen, *Didache* 89–92.

Testamentum Domini nostri Jesu Christi

A part of the *Testamentum Domini* was used in the apocryphal work of Joseph of Arimathia; the Georgian version certainly rests on a Syriac or Arabic original.[162] It cannot be demonstrated that the Georgians knew the *Testamentum Domini* as a legal source; only some liturgical parts were known.

Literature: Carl Schmidt, 'Eine Benutzung des Testamentum Domini nostri Jesu Christi', *Harnack-Ehrung: Beiträge zur Kirchengeschichte* (Leipzig 1921) 263–67; H. Brakmann and T. Chronz, 'Fragmente des *Testamentum Domini* in georgischer Übersetzung', *Zeitschrift für Antikes Christentum* 13 (2009) 395–402; M. Kohlbacher, Georgische Paralleltexte zum Testament unseres Hernn Jesus Christus (CPG 1743), R. Voigt, ed., *Akten des 5. Symposiums zur Sprache, Geschichte, Theologie und Gegenwartslage der syrischen Kirchen* (Aachen 2010) 97–126.

Pseudo-Apostolic Canons and Clement of Rome

The 85 Apostolic Canons exist in a Georgian translation only as a part of the *Great Nomokanon* (see below). In two manuscripts of this collection (Tbilisi A-76 from the twelfth century and H-1670 from thirteenth and fourteenth centuries) the parallel text to the eighth book of the Apostolic Constitutions also appears, specifically 'Commands of the Most Holy Apostle Paul Concerning the Ecclesiastical Canons' and 'Commands of the Holy Apostles Peter and Paul'. They do not appear in the Greek *Nomokanon* in 14 titles, but they are separately preserved in Greek.[163]

Editions of the Greek text: Paul de Lagarde, *Reliquiae iuris ecclesiastici antiquissimae graece* (Leipzig 1856); J. B. Pitra, *Iuris ecclesiastici Graecorum historia et monumenta* (Rome 1864) 1.64–72.
Literature: introduction to the edition of Gabidzašvili (see below), 35–39 (in Georgian).

An obvious excerpt from the parallel text circulating under the title of 'Commission of the Apostles by Clement to all Apostolic Catholic Churches', deals with holidays and must have been translated in the seventh century at the latest.

Literature: Tarchnišvili, *Georgische Literatur* 382; J. Hofmann, *Unser heiliger Vater Klemens* (Trier 1992) 32–33. Manuscripts: Tbilisi A-19:9 and A-95:9.

General works on the Apostolic Tradition of Hippolytus and the pseudo-apostolic writings do not pay any attention the Georgian tradition.

---

162. Tarchnišvili, *Georgische Literatur* 163, 338.
163. The first text corresponds from p. 10, line 18 through p. 12, line 19, and the second text from p. 12, line 20, to page 15, line 23, of the Greek edition of Lagarde.

Canons of the Greek Synods and Fathers
Collection of the Greek Canons

Georgian had been used as a literary language since the fifth century. The vernacular had been enriched by translations from Armenian, Syriac and Greek. The Greek canons, however, were not translated. In spite of the collection's wide circulation among the Eastern churches, as far as we know no early Georgian translation of the *Corpus canonum* was ever made. Georgian scholars believe such a translation had been in existence from the beginning, but their proofs are unconvincing.[164]

Some scholars have claimed that the acts of the Eastern Syrian synod under Katholikos Yaḫballāhā in Seleucia-Ctesiphon (A.D. 420) had made available the canons issued by the Western Fathers; this synod had acted on behalf of the Georgian Church as well. A bishop of Gurzān participated in the synod, which is the region around the present-day Tbilisi, Χορζηνή in Greek.[165] Whether one should draw from this the evidence that the canons were translated into Georgian at that time is questionable.

In his response to a letter of the Armenian Katholikos Abraham, the Georgian Katholikos Kyrion (beginning of the seventh century), in which he discussed dogmatic questions, wrote:

> But since you test and wish to know our faith, I have had translated and acquired the book of the four synods that the Byzantines use, and which is read out in the Holy Anastasis, just as it is in Holy Zion.

He then reported on the councils of Nicaea, Constantinople, Ephesus, and Chalcedon, in which he gave brief accounts of these councils and their dogmatic decisions (such as the confessions of Nicaea and Constantinople). Tarchnišvili assumes that the 'Book of the Four Synods' 'probably means the conciliar acts in general and not simply their dogmatic definitions'.[166] Yet that conclusion cannot be drawn from the context of the letter nor from the citations in it; we must conclude that the conciliar acts of Nicaea and Constantinople were not yet available. This letter has no recognizable similarity to the canonical collections found in the other churches. Further, it is not certain that the translation mentioned was made from Georgian. Tarchnišvili believes Kyrion wrote his letters in Georgian, and they were later translated into Armenian. The report could also have been taken directly out of Greek and then most likely translated into Armenian.[167]

---

164. Džavahisvili, *Kart'uli samart'lis istoria* 1.3ff.; Tarchnišvili, *Georgische Literatur* 430–31.
165. See Braun, *Synhados* 35; Chabot, *Synodicon* 37.276, 672; see above in the canon law of the Eastern Syrians.
166. Tarchnišvili, *Georgische Literatur* 431; cf. also 89, 365.
167. The letters are included in the Armenian miscellaneous work 'Book of Letters' (Girk')

In the *Vita* of the monastic father Gregory of Ḥandzta († 861) which George Merčule wrote in the middle of the tenth century,[168] he reported that Guaram, a son of the Kuropalates Aschot, said to the assembled members of the monastery:

> Holy fathers, bishops and hermits, you all know from the canon of the law (kanoni šdžulisai) that it is unjust to install a bishop or a Katholikos by force.

Gregory responded, among other things, with:

> Know now that at the synod of the early holy Fathers together with the bishops and leaders of the monastic communities, the first faithful kings were (also) present. . . . Neither in the canon, which is from the Holy Apostles, nor approved by estimable hierarchs, has it ever been permitted for a layman to dare to exercise legislative authority over bishops and monastic leaders, or to introduce new things.

These statements are too imprecise for us to identify a source. Contrary to the opinion of Tarchnišvili, one cannot conclude with certainty that there was a Georgian translation of the collection of canons.

We have certain evidence of Georgian use of the Greek conciliar canons in the *Small Nomokanon* of Euthymios Mtʻacʻmi(n)deli (about 955–1028). It will be discussed in the following section. Since he included only the canons of the Synod of Trullo (691–92), one may probably assume that the canons of the older synods were already available in Georgian translation. Nothing more certain may be said.

Parts of the acts of the Council of Ephesus were translated from Armenian only in 1776 by Katholikos Anton I with the assistance of a priest.

Some manuscripts preserve the canons of Carthage and those of the second council of Nicaea as individual texts. These might be excerpts from the Great *Nomokanon* (see below).

Literature: Tarchnišvili, *Georgische Literatur* 284; Beck, *Kirche* 45–46; I. Rucker, *Ephesinische Konzilsakten in armenisch-georgischer Überlieferung* (Sb Munich 1930, no. 3; Munich 1930) S. P. Cowe, 'The Armeno-Georgian Acts of Ephesus—A Reconsideration', JTS 2nd series 40 (1989) 125–29.

The 'Small Nomokanon' (Mcire sdžuliskanoni)

At the end of the tenth century, the Georgian John Varazvače founded the monastery of the Georgians (τῶν Ἰβήρων, Iviron) on the Holy Mount

---

Tġtocʻ), cf. Schmidt, 'Das armenische "Buch der Briefe",' 533. The Armenian text of the letter in the edition of Y. Izmireanc, *Girkʻ Tġtocʻ* (Tiflis 1901) 185–88, in the second edition of Jerusalem 1994; with a Georgian translation in A. Aleksidze, *Liber epistolarum* (in Georgian) (Tbilisi 1968) 102–11; an excerpt (without the report on the synods) is also found in chapter 51 of the history of Uḫtanes (probably composed in 987), edition (with Georgian translation): Z. Aleksidze, *Uḫtanes. Historia seperationis Iberorum ex Armeniis* (Tbilisi 1975) 142–43.

168. Latin translation in P. Peeters, *Histoire monastique géorgienne* (Brussels-Paris 1922) 268–69 (reprint from *Analecta Bollandiana* [1917–19]).

Athos. After his death (1002) his son Euthymius Mtʻacʻmi(n)deli (that is, 'from the holy mountain') took over the leadership of the house. He was one of the most important translators of Greek writings into Georgian.

Among his translations was the '*Small Nomokanon*', which survives in many manuscripts. Euthymius himself declared that he translated the book on the command of his father and other holy fathers for the purpose of instruction and for the use of the souls of people. The title is 'Order and Gathering and (ecclesiastical) Legislation (sdžuliskanoni) of the sixth synod of the 168 holy fathers who gathered in Constantinople, the new Rome, before Constantine, the God-loving emperor, the son of Emperor Heraclius'. We may conclude from this evidence that the canons circulated under the name of the Sixth Ecumenical Council of Constantinople, which actually met in 680 during the reign of Emperor Constantine IV (668–85), the grandson (!) of Emperor Heraclius (610–41). Whether this false attribution went back to Euthymius or was found by him in his Greek original must remain unresolved. According to the Greek text, not 168 but 165 bishops took part.[169]

The contents of Euthymius's *Small Nomokanon* is: First comes the preface (pp. 15–23 of the edition of Giunašvili), which actually belongs to the synod of 680, and then follow the canons of the Trullo (pp. 23–85 of the edition). There are 100 canons in the Georgian version. Of the 102 Greek canons, numbers 16, 26, 29, 34, 39, 45, 48, 52, 63, 64, 71, 80, 99, 100, and 101 are missing. In their place the translator placed texts of other fathers in some cases; in others he wrote some sections himself (introduction to the edition by Giunašvili, 5–6; Russian summary, 135).

Edition with a Georgian introduction (pp. 3–14) and a Russian summary (pp. 134–36): *Mcire sdžuliskanoni, gamosacemad moamzada E. Giunašvili* (= The *Small Nomokanon*, prepared for edition by E. Giunašvili) (Tbilisi 1972).

Literature: [M. F.] Brossei, 'Notice sur un Nomocanon géorgien [sdžulis-kanoni], manuscrit du Musée asiatique de l'Académie Impériale des Sciences, no. 103a', *Bulletin de l'Acadamie des Sciences de St. Pétersbourg* 19 (St. Petersburg 1874) 337–74 (printed in *Mélanges Asiatiques, tirés du Bulletin Historico-Philologique de l'Académie Imperiale des Sciences* 7 [St. Petersburg 1876] 113–66); Džavahišvili, *Istoria* 1.46–47; Karst, 'Recherches' 322–24; Tarchnišvili, *Georgische Literatur* 152–54; M. van Esbroeck, 'Euthyme l'Hagiorite: Le traducteur et ses traductions', *Revue des Études Géorgiennes et Caucasiennes* 4 (1988) 73–107 (pp. 76–80: 'Le Petit Nomocanon').

Additional Material

The next pieces in Giunašvili's edition, which usually are found in Georgian manuscripts with the '*Small Nomokanon*', were probably also translated by Euthymius. Whether someone had gathered them together

---

169. Joannou, CPG 1.101.

in a Greek manuscript of whether he compiled them himself needs further study.

Two series of penitential canons are preserved under the name, but spuriously, of John the Faster (Ioannes Nesteutes), the patriarch of Constantinople (582–95).[170] The first is entitled 'Canons for Sins (šecʻodebultʻa) written by our Blessed Father John, Archbishop of Constantinople, called "the Faster".' The fact that these canons could not have been taken from the patriarch of the sixth century is made clear at the beginning of the introduction, where it says: 'Know that this Blessed John the Faster was the last of all those writing ordinances of (ecclesiastical) legislation; that was long after the sixth synod'. Today the author is believed to be a monk and deacon named John with the nickname 'Son of Obedience'.[171]

The second text bears the title, 'Canons for Sinners (šecʻodebultʻa), commanded by our blessed father John the Faster the patriarch of Constantinople'.

The next section is entitled: 'Canons for daily misdeeds (ctomatani), as our Holy Father Basil commanded'.[172] They have nothing to do with Basil the Great. In the Munich, Staatsbibl. Greek 498 there are also penitential canons of a Basil, 'Son of Obedience'. It is obvious that the name Basil had been put in the place of John the 'Son of Obedience.' In all likelihood this is also the case with the Georgian canons that circulate under the name of John the Faster.

The next part can be identified certainly. It is a translation of the 'Synodicon of Orthodoxy' from 843. The title reads, 'Pillar inscription of the faith which those holy fathers gathered in Constantinople inscribed for the veneration of holy pictures, and which was read out in the Hagia Sophia on the first Sunday of holy lent.' The Georgian translation has a version of the text that differs from the Greek, which must be closer to the original. For example, in the title, Hagia Sophia is given as the site of the council, the Imperial couple Michael and Theodora are mentioned at the beginning, a long citation from the 'Horos' of 787 is given *verbatim*, and a passage unclear in Greek is made understandable.

Edition: Giunašvili, *The Small Nomokanon* 124–33.

---

170. Editions by N. A. Zaozerskij and A. S. Xaxanov, *Nomokanon'Ioanna Postnika b ego redakziax: gruzinskoj, grečeskoj i slavjanskoj* (Moscow 1902); Giunašvili, *The Small Nomokanon* 86–99 and 100–117. See ClavisG 7555; Beck, *Kirche* 423–24; Džavahišvili, *Istoria* 1.49–50; Karst, 'Recherches' 324, 331–32; Tarchnišvili, *Georgische Literatur* 152–53; E. Herman, 'Il piu antico penitenziale greco', OCP 19 (1953) 71–127 (also on the Georgian version); M. Arranz, *I penitenziali bizantini* (Kanonika 3; Rome 1993); review by Kohlbacher, OrChr 1995, 236–40.

171. Beck, *Kirche* 424.

172. Edition by Giunašvili, *The Small Nomokanon* 118–23.

German translation: M. van Esbroeck and N. Karadeniz, 'Das Synodikon vom Jahre 843 in georgischer Übersetzung', *Annuarium Historiae Conciliorum* 19 (Paderborn 1987) 304–13.
Literature: Beck, *Kirche* 497; Tarchnišvili, *Georgische Literatur* 151.

The Great Nomokanon

About 100 years after the translation of the *Small Nomokanon*, Arsen of Iqaltʻo (Iqaltʻoeli) translated a second, substantially more extensive work of canon law from Greek into Georgian, the so-called *Great Nomokanon*. Arsen obviously had received a thorough education in Byzantium, lived at first as a monk on the Black Mountain near Antioch, and returned to Georgia in 1114, settling in the house of Gelati, a cultural center in Western Georgia. He is thought to have returned to his home town of Iqaltʻo in Eastern Georgia, where he founded a famous academy. As with Euthymius Mtʻacʻmindeli, he is particularly noted as a translator.[173]

The *Great Nomokanon* also consists of various parts. It lacks a title for the whole work in the manuscripts.

The first part (pp. 100–103 in the edition) bears the title 'Collection of ecclesiastical canons, divided into 14 parts.' In fact this is the preface to the *Nomokanon* of John Scholasticus in 50 titles, with the number 50 simply replaced by 14.[174]

The second part (pp. 103–7), the 'preface to the chapter index', is a combination of the preface to the original collection in 14 titles and the reworking from 843, the *Syntagma*.[175]

The next part (pp. 107–9) is entitled, "From which synods and persons or how many canons are assembled in the present book." Here the various synods and patristic texts are listed and the number of canons in each given.[176]

Then follows on pp. 110–215 the Syntagma of the canons with the title 'Excerpts of the canonical rulings and titles and the relevant chapters'. First there is an index of titles and chapters (pp. 110–24), followed by the work itself, divided into 14 titles, in which, along with the chapter headings, are given only the sources and the number of canons, as in its Greek original. In some cases scholia follow.[177]

The next part (pp. 216–542) contains the full text of the canons of the

---

173. Cf. Tarchnišvili, *Georgische Literatur* 201–11. It is a matter of dispute when he translated the *Great Nomokanon*. According to Tarchnišvili (210–11), it was written in Gelati, but according to Gabidzašvili, the editor of the work (see introduction, 17–23, Russian summary, 93) the work had already been presented to the Georgian synod of Ruis-Urbnisi (see below).
174. Beck, *Kirche* 422–23; Gabidzašvili, *Didi sdžuliskanoni* Introduction 35–39; summary 95.
175. Beck, *Kirche* 146; Gabidzašvili, *Didi sdžuliskanoni* Introduction, 41–43, summary, 95.
176. Cf. Gabidzašvili, *Didi sdžuliskanoni* Introduction, 43–48, summary, 95–96.
177. Cf. ibid. 48–64, 72–74, summary 96.

Greek councils and Fathers. It is arranged in chronological order as in the Greek manuscripts and the 'Nomokanon in 14 Titles'.[178] They are as follows (the numbers of the canons are given in parentheses):

1. Pseudo-apostolic texts: (85) Apostolic Canons. In two manuscripts there are also the previously mentioned 'Commands of the Most Holy Apostle Paul Concerning the Ecclesiastical Canons' (17) and 'Commands of the Holy Apostles Peter and Paul' (17). Both of these texts were obviously inserted later.

2. Greek councils: Nicaea (20 canons); Ancyra (25); Neocaesarea (15); Gangra (21); Antioch (25); Laodiceia (59); Constantinople (Address to Emperor Theodosius, 7 canons); Ephesus (6 canons, Speech on accepting the confession of Nicaea, decision for the bishops of Cyprus, Letter to the synod in Pamphylia); Chalcedon (27 canons, decision for the priests in Constantinople, On Photius of Tyros, On the bishops of Egypt); Sardica (20); Carthage (217 Fathers; A.D. 419; 158 canons); Constantinople II; Council in Trullo) 102 canons and list of bishops;[179] Nicaea II (20); the letter of Tarasius (see below); Constantinople (Prima-Secunda or Πρωτοδευτέρα, A.D. 861; 17 canons); synod in the church of Hagia Sophia (A.D. 879; 3 canons).

3. Fathers of the Church: Tarasius (letter to Pope Hadrian I, placed after Nicaea II); Dionysius of Alexandria (Letter to Basileides, 4 canons); Peter of Alexandria (14 canons, excerpts from an Easter letter = canon 15); Gregory Thaumaturgos of Neocaesarea (canonical letter); Athanasius (letter to Ammun and an excerpt from the 39th Easter letter); Basil of Caesarea (4 letters to Amphilochius of Iconium, letter to Diodorus of Tarsus, to Gregory the priest, the *chorepiscopi,* his suffragan bishops, excerpts from chapters 27 and 28 of his letter to Amphilochius); Gregory of Nyssa (letter to Litaeus of Melitene); Gregory the Theologian [= of Nazianzus] (poem on the books of the Bible); Amphilochius of Iconium (from the iambs to Seleucus); Timothy of Alexandria (15 responses); Theophilos of Alexandria (address, exhortation to Ammon, letters to Aphyngius, Agatho, Menas); Kyrillos of Alexandria (letters to Domnus, the bishops of Libya and of the Pentapolis); Gennadius of Constantinople (letter to the metropolitans, letter to Martyrius of Antioch,[180] written in Constantinople); Athanasius of Alexandria (letter to Rufinianus). This collection is also found in Greek;

---

178. Cf. ibid. 64–72, summary 96

179. Cf. H. Kaufhold, 'Die Bischofsliste der Trullanischen Synode in georgischer Überlieferung', OrChr 78 (1994) 1–9.

180. Gennadius is not mentioned as the author in the Georgian text. The text also appears as canon 7 of Constantinople and canon 95 of the Trullanum (the wording of these texts do not completely agree in the Georgian text). The letter also appears as a letter to Martyrius in the Syriac tradition, see the section above on the canon law of the Western Syrians.

in that version the collection begins with the letter of Tarasius and ends with the letters of Gennadius and the letter of Athanasius to Rufinianus.[181]

The end of almost all manuscripts of the 'Great *Nomokanon*' is the "Inscription on the Column of the Georgian national synod of Ruis-Urbnisi" (see below).

Edition with a thorough Georgian introduction (pp. 3–91) and Russian summary (pp. 92–99): E. P. Gabidzašvili, *Didi sdžuliskanoni, gamosacemad moamzades* B. Gabidzašvila, E. Giunašvila, M. Dolakidzem, G. Ninuam (*Velikij gruzinskij Nomokanon* [= *The Great Nomokanon*]. Edition prepared by E. Gabidzašvili, E. Giunašvili, M. Dolakʻidze, G. Ninua] (Tbilisi 1975).

Literature: V. N. Beneševič, 'Gruzinkij Nomokanon' po spiskam' Tiflisskogo Cerkovnago Muzeja', *Christianskij Vostok* 2 (1914) 349–77; 5 (1917) 112–27; Džavahišvili, *Istoria*; Karst, 'Recherches' 332–34.

Other Texts Translated from Greek

Both in the manuscripts of the '*Small Nomokanon*' and in many other manuscripts with canon law texts, there are still unpublished texts that were translated from Greek. No one can know when the translations were made. They show the strong influence of Greek-Byzantine canon law on the Georgians. Among others, these texts include:

1. Several series of canons by Basil the Great are preserved, including the 'Admonitions to Priests and Deacons' and 'Rules for Venerating Martyrs'. It remains to be seen what they have to do with the '*Nomokanon* (sdžulis kanoni) of Basil, Gregory and John the Merciful'.[182]

2. John Chrysostom's 'Inquiries', dealing particularly with the slave trade.[183]

3. The 'Book of Judges' of Eusebius of Dorylaeum (fourth century) appears to be otherwise entirely unknown.[184]

4. Germanus of Constantinople (715–30), 'Order of the Mysteries' (sacraments) of the Catholic Church.[185]

5. Writing of Patriarch Methodius of Constantinople (843–47) on the reconciliation of those who have left the Christian faith.[186]

6. Canonical response of Peter Chartophylax (second half of the eleventh century) to a monk.[187]

---

181. Cf. Joannou, CPG, introduction, p. xx (with the manuscripts).
182. Mocʻqale, Greek, Eleimon, died about 620, cf. Beck, *Kirche* 459. Manuscripts: Tbilisi H-405:2; H-899:10; H-3027:22.
183. Tarchnišvili, *Georgische Literatur* 431.
184. Manuscript: Tbilisi, A-226, fol. 173–74.
185. Beck, *Kirche* 474; Tarchnišvili, *Georgische Literatur* 353, n. 1, no. 5.
186. Edition of the Greek text in J.-B. Pitra, *Iuris ecclesiastici Graecorum historia et monumenta* 2.362–63. There are numerous Georgian manuscripts. See Beck, *Kirche* 497; Tarchnišvili, *Georgische Literatur* 453 (footnote).
187. Manuscript: Tbilisi, A-450, no. 166. See Beck, *Kirche* 659.

7. Questions and answers of John Chartophylax (of Chalcedon? twelfth century).[188]

8. Works of Symeon of Thessalonike († 1429).[189]

9. By what route the certainly spurious writing of Gennadius of Constantinople (1405–72), 'On Christian Faith and Life', reached the Georgians is in doubt. It appears not to have survived in Greek, but it is also known among the Slavs. A late manuscript from 1847 (Tbilisi A-323), which also has the letter of the three patriarchs Jeremiah of Constantinople, Athanasius of Antioch, and Chrysanthus of Jerusalem and their synod of 1722, contains the text. The texts were probably translated from Russian.[190]

10. The work of Manuel Xantios, deacon and chartophylax of Constantinople (sixteenth century) on marital law, which relied extensively on the *Syntagma* of Matthew Blastares (fourteenth century), is found in many manuscripts.[191]

11. Brief descriptions of the old Greek councils, probably part of the old genre of the conciliar synopses. There are obviously different versions in circulation that should be studied.

12. Further there are many other anonymous treatises on marital law, monasticism, tracts for priests and deacons, on prayer, penance and communion, alms, etc., which are in most cases probably of Greek origin.[192]

Original Georgian Literature

A series of liturgical-canonical responses to a Georgian questioner by Euthymius Mtʻacʻmindeli (around 1000), dealing with apocryphal books, festivals of the Lord, dreams as a hindrance to the reception of communion, teachers and pupils, the eating of fish, masses for the living, and other matters is preserved. It might have been composed or summarized in Georgian. Here as well 'the Byzantine and occidental practice which Euthymius follows' is reflected in the work.[193]

Synods of the Georgian Church

The Georgian Church's first synod of which acts survive is the Synod of Ruis-Urbnisi. It assembled at the command of the King David II (IV) 'the

---

188. Manuscript: Tbilisi, H-405: 9. Beck, *Kirche* 658; Tarchnišvili, *Georgische Literatur* 431.
189. Manuscripts: Tbilisi, A-1155:1; H-405: 1, 4; Q-828:1; S-4963:5. Beck, *Kirche* 752–53.
190. Beck, *Kirche* 76; Joannou, CPG 291 (Gennadius); Graf, *Geschichte* 3.133 (letter of the patriarchs).
191. K. E. Zachariae von Lingenthal, *Geschichte des griechisch-römischen Rechts* (3rd ed. Berlin 1892) 46; Tarchnišvili, *Georgische Literatur* 299.
192. Tarchnišvili, *Georgische Literatur* 353, n. 1.
193. Most recent edition (of two versions): I. Dolidze, *Kartʻuli samartʻis dzeglebi* (Tbilisi 1970) 3.5–11 and 12–18. Tarchnišvili, *Georgische Literatur* 153 (4), 330–31.

Builder' (1089–1125) in 1103 and 1105. It was a dedicated reforming synod, where abuses in the Church were to be eliminated.[194] Their acts, called the 'column inscription' (Dzeglis-cerai) of the synod, begin with an introduction that mentions, among other things, that the synod was not concerned with dogmatic questions, for Georgians had always been orthodox, but with canonical matters on discipline. The sources of canon law are also enumerated in this introduction. These are entirely Greek: native sources and the '*Small Nomokanon*' were not used.

Ruis-Urbnisi incorporated the following councils and Fathers (in parentheses, the number of canons): Nicaea (20), Ancyra (24), Neocaesarea (14), Gangra (20), Antioch (25), Laodiceia (21), Constantinople (7), Ephesus (8), Chalcedon (28), Carthage (118), Constantinople II, Synod 'in the royal palace' (102 canons = Trullo), Nicaea II (18), Constantinople (= Prima-Secunda) (17); Constantinople A.D. 879 (3).

Fathers: Dionysius of Alexandria (4), Peter of Alexandria (15), Gregory Thaumaturgos of Neocaesarea (canonical letter), Basil the Great (85 canons, letters to Diodoros, Gregory [= Paregorios], the chorepiscopi, the suffragan bishops, to Amphilochios), Gregory of Nyssa (8), Timothy of Alexandria (15), Philotheos (= Theophilus) of Alexandria (10 canons, letters to Aphyngios, Agathon, and Menas), Kyrillos of Alexandria (7), Gennadios of Constantinople and his synod (letter to all metropolitans).

In contrast to the sources enumerated in the 'Great *Nomokanon*', the Council of Sardica, and that of the Hagia Sophia are missing, as well as a series of canons of Fathers (including Athanasius and Gregory of Nazianzus).

The editor of the text, E. Gabidzašvili, thinks that the principal source of the canons of Ruis-Urbnisi is the Great *Nomokanon*, which must already have been available in translation. The author of the acts of Ruis-Urbnisi could have been the translator of the *Nomokanon*, Arsen of Iqaltʻo.[195]

The canons of the synod of Ruis-Urbnisi deal with the following themes:[196]

1. Clergy: Canon 1 ordained that unworthy bishops are to be deposed. The Katholikos and bishops must know the divine laws, and priests must adhere to ecclesiastical discipline (canon 8). The minimum age for the consecration of a bishop was set at 35, 30 for a priest, 25 for a deacon, and 8 for a lector. Several consecrations may not be performed on the same day for the same person (canon 2). Simony is also forbidden (canon 4).

---

194. G. Pätsch, *Das Leben Kartʻlis: Eine Chronik aus Georgien, 300–1200* (Leipzig 1985) 404–5; Karst, 'Recherches' 339–40.
195. Tarchnisvili, *Georgische Literatur* 229.
196. Cf. Karst, 'Recherches' 337–38.

2. Monasteries: Several superiors may not reside in one and the same house. No assembly of pilgrims may take place in monasteries (canon 10).

3. Sacraments: Their bestowal is to take place in keeping with the *Euchologion*, which George Mt'ac'mi(n)deli (c. 1009–1065) translated from Greek into Georgian (canon 3). A mass may not be celebrated by several priests for several souls, and a simple priest may not celebrate in a cathedral or a monastic church (canon 11). Baptism and marriage must take place in a church (canon 6). It is forbidden to marry heretics and infidels (canon 13). The minimum age for marriage is 12 for women (canon 7). Marriages may not take place by proxy (canon 14). Heretics must be rebaptized (canon 12). The sale of ecclesiastical vessels is forbidden (canon 5).

4. Penal Law (canon 15).

Editions: E. Gabidzašvili, et al., ['Great Nomokanon', see above], 543–59; idem, *Ruis-Urbnisis krebis dzegliscer̄aj* [= Column Inscription of the Synod of Ruis-Urbnisi] (Tbilisi 1978) 176–96; Column Inscription of the Synod of Ruis-Urbnisi, 1103 also in I. Dolidze, *Kart'uli samart'lis dzeglebi* (Tbilisi 1970) 3.106–27.

Literature: Tamarati, *L'église géorgienne* 274–79; Džavaḫišvili, *Istoria* 53–58; Karst, 'Recherches' 335–40; Tarchnišvili, *Georgische Literatur* 436–37.

Later Synods

In the biography of King David the Builder the author described a later synod which was to bring about a union with the Armenians. A second such synod took place under Queen Tamar (1184–1213). Acts or canons are unknown.[197]

In contrast, there is an incompletely preserved text of a synod held around 1263 that deals with the administration of ecclesiastical properties by high-ranking laymen.[198]

Further, rulings of several synods from the twelfth and thirteenth centuries have been preserved in the monastery of Šio-Mġvime.[199]

The Law of the Katholikoi

In the first half of the eighteenth century King Vaḫtang VI ordered an extensive collection of legal sources. Among these was a brief text from the middle of the sixteenth century entitled 'Law (samart'ali) of the Katholikoi'. The short introduction states:

In the name of God, I Malachia, blessed by Christ as Katholikos-patriarch of all Georgia (Sak'art'velo), (and) I, blessed by Christ as Katholikos and head of the

---

197. Tamarati, 'L'église géorgienne', 286–87, 291–92; Pätsch, *Das Leben Kartlis* 436–37.
198. Most recent edition is Dolidze, *Kart'uli samart'lis dzeglebi* 3.161–64. Džavaḫišvili, *Istoria* 1.58–61; 2.363–69 (idem, *Kart'uli eris istoria* [Tbilisi 1966]) 3.491–97; Karst, 'Recherches' 340–41.
199. Edition is Dolidze, *Kart'uli samart'lis dzeglebi* 3.128–32, 160–64, 165–68, 174–76.

Fathers (= patriarch) of Abkhazia, Eudaimon have taken counsel and gathered together all the bishops of Abkhazia. And a great famine came as a result of our sins, and disorder and unjust things happened: killing, slave-trade, plundering of churches and illegality. We have turned to the book of the law (sdžulis kanoni) and have taken out what is relevant. And that which we did not take out, we have from there . . .

The text listed punishments for the sale of human beings, for the devastation of churches, for theft of ecclesiastical goods, for the killing of persons, for theft, for the abandonment of wives, for the abuse of office by bishops, priests, and *chorepiscopi*, as well as for disrespect to bishops and to the Katholikos.[200]

The Law of Moses

King Vaḫtang included in his collection norms from the Old Testament (Law of Moses): extracts from Deuteronomy, chapters 5 and 13–26. Its relation to texts of this genre in other languages, such as the Greek *Nomos Mosaikos*, is not yet clear.[201]

Monastic Rules (Typica)

The best known of the monastic rules is that from 1084 by Gregory Pakurianos (Bakurianisdze) for the Georgian Petric'oni house in what is now Bulgaria (Bačkovo). Also preserved are the 'typica' of the Vahani house in Georgia (thirteenth century) and of another, unnamed house.

Editions and translations: *Typicon Gregorii Pacuriani*, Edidit (Interpretatus est) M. Tarchnišvili (CSCO 143–144; Louvain 1954); A. Šanidze, *Kart'uli monasteri da misi tipik'oni* (Tbilisi 1971) (with a Russian translation); Dolidze, *Kart'uli samart'lis dzeglebi* 3.35–105 (Petric'oni house), 132–34 (unknown house), 135–53 (Vahani house); L. Mushelišvili, *Vahanis kvabt'a gangeba (XIII s.)* (Tbilisi 1939).

Literature: Džavaḫišvili, *Istoria* 1.69–70; A. Chanidze, 'Le Grand Domestique de l'Occident, Gregorii Bakurianis-dzé, et le monastère fondé par lui en Bulgarie', *Bedi Kartlisa* 38 (Paris 1971) 133–66; P. Gautier, 'Le Typikon du Sébaste Grégoire Pakourianos', *Revue des Études Byzantines* 42 (1984) 5–146. H. Métrévéli deals with questions of monastic constitutions: 'Les normes pour l'installation d'un supérieur au monastère d'Ibères au Mont Athos (X^e–XIe siècles)', *Festgabe für J. Assfalg* (Wiesbaden 1990) 211–19.

Charters

In addition to these sources, Georgian kings and representatives of the Church granted a whole series of charters that have been preserved. They deal with contracts of purchase, donations, bequests, and other matters,

---

200. Most recent edition is I. Dolidze, *Kart'uli samart'lis dzeglebi* 1.391–97. A French translation in Karst, 'Recherches' 346–53. See Džavaḫišvili, *Istoria* 1.62–67; Karst, 'Recherches' 342–46; Tarchnišvili, *Georgische Literatur* 437.
201. An edition in Dolidze, *Kart'uli samart'lis dzeglebi* 1.103–25.

usually to the benefit of religious houses. Their significance for the history of Georgian canon law remains to be investigated.

Edition: Dolidze, *Kart'uli samart'lis dzeglebi* (vol. 2; Tbilisi 1965) (secular charters from the tenth to the nineteenth centuries) (vol. 3; Tbilisi 1970) (ecclesiastical charters from the eleventh to nineteenth centuries). Some of the charters are also in Russian translation: *Gruzinskie dokumenty IX–XV vv,* perevod i kommentarii S. S. Kakabadze (Moscow 1982). See also Karst, 'Recherches' 365–66.

The Greek charters dealing with the Georgian Iviron house on Mount Athos are in the course of publication.

Edition, translation and commentary: J. Lefort, et al., *Actes d'Iviron.* 1: *Des origines au milieu du XIe siècle,* 2: *Du milieu du XIe siècle à 1204,* 3: *De 1204, à 1328,* 4: *De 1328 au début du XVI siècle* (Archives de l'Athos 14, 16, 18, 19; Paris 1985–95).

Index of Councils and Synods

Akakios (485), 301
Ancyra (314), 17–20, 25, 39–41, 44, 114, 116, 121–23, 163, 182, 216, 226, 229–30, 258, 273–74, 291, 298, 309, 317–18, 321, 336, 339
Ani (970), 322
Ani (1036), 322
Ankyra. *See* Ancyra
Antioch (328), 29
Antioch (ca.330/341?), 25–26, 44–48, 116–17, 119, 123, 188, 216, 226–27, 229, 258, 271–273, 291, 297, 310, 318, 321, 336, 339
Antioch (341), 67–68, 76,
Aqaq. *See* Akakios
Arles (314) 35

Bēt Lapat, (484), 301–302

Caesaria. *See* Syria
Carthage (255), 113
Carthage (256), 224, 244
Carthage (258,) 25
Carthage (419), 25, 74–75, 82, 122, 124, 188, 227 233, 236, 339
Chalcedon (451), 17, 26, 47, 52, 57–66, 82, 86, 111, 116–17, 119, 121–22, 128, 162, 181, 215, 226–27, 229–30, 234, 244, 258, 297, 310, 316, 331, 336, 339
Chalkedon. *See* Chalcedon
Constantinople (330–331/334–335?), 68
Constantinople I (381), 25, 26, 31, 49–53, 82, 106–8, 112, 113, 116–17, 122–23, 128, 216, 226–27, 229, 233, 244, 258, 273–74, 297–98, 310, 318–19, 331, 336, 339
Constantinople (382), 50
Constantinople (394), 25, 75–77, 106, 124, 189

Constantinople (536), 223
Constantinople II (553), 78, 223, 226–27, 229, 233, 336, 339
Constantinople (571), 223
Constantinople III (681/82) 78, 79, 226–27, 229, 233, 333, 336
Constantinople (691/92). *See* Quinisext
Constantinople (861). *See* Primasecunda
Constantinople (869), 232
Constantinople (879/80), 149–50, 188, 207, 232, 336, 339
Constantinople (Endemousa), 163–65, 170

Dai'i Mūsā (1598), 262
Dwin (506/07), 314, 322–23, 327
Dqin (552), 314

Ephesos. *See* Ephesus
Ephesus (431), 53–57, 60, 116, 118, 123, 128, 229, 233, 244–45, 258, 271–73, 316, 318, 331–32, 336, 339
Ephesus (449), 58–59, 61
Erzurum. *See* Karin

Gangra (ca.340–42), 25, 26, 42–44, 116–17, 119, 121–22, 216, 227, 229–30, 234, 258, 273, 291, 297–98, 310, 318, 321, 336, 339

Hagia Sophia (879/880). *See* Constantinople (879/80)
Harran (794), 1
Harran (812/13), 245
Harrāš (1644), 262
Hromkla (1179), 322

343

344 Index of Councils and Synods

Jerusalem (50/52), 17

Karin (693), 321
Kallinikos (817/18), 246
Kefartūta, 246

Laodicea (363/64?), 25–26, 29–30, 44, 47–49, 116–17, 119, 216, 226–27, 230, 234, 258, 271–74, 291, 297–98, 310, 318, 321, 339
Laodikeia. *See* Laodicea
Lateran IV (1215) 53

Mar Mattai (629), 246
Mount Lebanon (1596), 262

Neocaesarea (318, ca. 315/19), 17, 20, 25, 26, 39, 41–42, 44, 116, 121–22, 177, 216, 226, 229–30, 233–34, 258, 273–74, 297–98, 309–10, 318, 321, 336, 339
Neokaisareia. *See* Neocaesarea
Nicaea I (325), 1, 17, 20, 25, 29–30, 34–38, 39, 41, 45, 46, 48, 51–52, 56, 65, 72, 74, 96, 113, 116–17, 119, 121–23, 128, 147, 226, 230, 233–34, 258, 271–74, 297–98, 310, 316, 318, 321, 331, 339
Nicaea II (787), 24, 122, 124, 143–46, 150, 154, 163, 226, 228–29, 233, 336, 339

Partav (770), 321, 323
Penthekte. *See* Quinisext
Primasecunda (861), 123, 146–48, 188, 232, 336, 339
Protodeutera. *See* Primasecunda

Qannūbin (1580), 262
Quinisext (691/692), 24, 75, 77–84, 85, 113, 122–24, 130, 145, 148, 154, 164, 166, 181, 226–29, 332–33, 339

Rome (340), 67
Rome (869), 150
Ruis-Urbinsi (1103/05), 337–40
Sardica. *See* Serdica

Sarug (785), 245
Sarug (846), 246
Sarug (896), 246
Seleucia-Ctesiphon (410), 252, 254, 301
Seleucia-Ctesiphon (420), 301, 331
Seleucia-Ctesiphon (484), 295
Serdica (342), 43, 45, 47, 66–74, 77, 78, 117–19, 122–23, 227, 229, 245, 273, 291, 318, 339
Šahapiwan, 323
Schahapivan (444), 316–17, 320
Širakawan (862), 322
Sis (1204), 322
Sis (1246), 322
Sis (1307), 322
Sis (1342), 322
St. Sophia, 123
Synod of George (676), 302
Synod in the Royal Palace. *See* Quinisext
Synod of John bar Aḇgārē (900), 302
Synod of Katholikos Bābai (497), 301
Synod of Katholikos Ezechiel (567), 301
Synod of Katholikos Ḥnānīšōʿ (775/76), 302–3
Synod of Katholikos Isaac (410). *See* Seleucia-Ctesiphon (410)
Synod of Katholikos Īšōʿyahḇ (585), 302–3
Synod of Katholikos Mār Aḇā I (542–543), 301
Synod of Katholikos Saḇrīšōʿ (596), 302
Synod of Katholikos Yahḇalāhā. *See* Seleucia-Ctesiphon, (420)
'Synod of the Oak' (403), 108
'Synod of the Persian Bishops'. *See* Seleucia-Ctesiphon (410)
Synod of Timothy I (782), 302
Synod of Timothy I (790), 302
Synod of Timothy I (804), 302
Synod of Timothy II (1318), 302, 312
Syria, 297

Theodosiupolis, Karin
Trullanum. *See* Quinisext
Tyre (341), 76

General Index

ʿAbdallāh al-Qarāʾali, 286
ʿAbdallāh ibn aṭ-Ṭaiyib, See Ibn aṭ-Ṭaiyib
ʿAḇdīšōʿ bar Bahrīz, metropolitan of Mosul, 307–08
ʿAḇdīšōʿ bar Brīḵā, metropolitan of Nisbis, 302; 'Book of the Pearl', 312, *Nomokanon*, 296, 298–99, 308, 310–11; *Ordo iudiciorum ecclesiasticorum*, –19, 286, 298–300, 303, 307, 312
Abéla, Charles, 22–223
Abraham bar Lipe, 308
Abraham of Kaškar, 307
Abū Isḥāq ibn Faḍlallāh, 266, 270, 292
Abū Naṣr Yaḥyā ibn Ǧarīr: 'Book of the Guide' ('Kitāb al-Mursid') 254
Abū Ṣāliḥ Yūwannīs ibn ʿAbdallāh, See Abū Ṣulḥ Yūnus ibn ʿAbdallāh
Abū Ṣulḥ Yūnus ibn ʿAbdallāh, *nomokanon*, 283
Abulfaraǧ ʿAbdallāh ibn aṭ-Ṭaiyib, See Ibn aṭ-Ṭaiyib
Abūʾl-Barakāt ibn Kabar, 245; *Encyclopedia*, 271–74, 276, 282–84; 'Lamp of Darkness for Performing (ecclesiastical) Services'
Acacius, katholikos, 303
Acta conciliorum oecumenicorum, 79
ad-dasqalīya, See Didascalia
ad-dusqūlīya, See Didascalia
Agapius of Bostra, 77
Alexander, emperor, 150
Alexandria, Church, 38, 51–52, 65, 89, 91, 108, 225, 263, 270
Alexios Aristenos, scholia, 27, 121–23, 161, 163, 177–180 191, 238; 'Synopsis', 163
Alexios I, emperor, 171, 174–76
Alexios II, emperor, 184

Alexios I the Studite, patriarch of Constantinople, 167
Alexius Aristenos, See Alexios Aristenos
Amphilochius, bishop of Iconium, 76, 85–86, 88, 99, 106–7, 123, 336
Anastasios, metropolitan of Caesarea, 225
Anastasius, emperor, 126
Anatolius, patriarch of Constantinople, 65, 111
Andronikus II, emperor, 175–76
Anonymous of Codex Sinaiticus 1117, 183–85, 205
Anonymous Enantiophanes, 135, 139
Anonymous Syrian Treatise on the Priesthood, 262
Anthimos, patriarch of Constantinople, letters, 248
Antioch, Church, 40, 45, 56, 60, 77, 96, 110, 220–21, 239, 255, 301
Antiochean corpus canonum, See *corpus canonum*
Anton I, katholikos of Georgia, 332
Antonios, 'Rules and Commands', 281
Antonius III, patriarch of Constantinople, 166
Antony IV, patriarch of Constantinople, 196
Apiarius, priest of Sicca, 74–75
Apostolic canons, See *Canons of the Apostles*
Apostolic Church Order, 241–42, 267–69, 290
Apostolic Constitutions, 28–33, 116, 224, 242, 232, 258, 266–67, 269, 282, 290–92, 310, 330
'Apostolic Tradition of Hippolytus', 14–17, 29, 267, 269–70, 330
appendix Eclogae, 131–32
Arethas, metropolitan of Caesarea, 169
Armenian Church, 80, 216, 219, 314–26

345

General Index

Arsen of Iqalt'o (Iqalt'oeli), *Great Nomokanon*, 330, 332, 335–37, 339
Arsenios, *Synopsis of Canons*, 188
Arsenios Autorianos, patriarch of Constantinople, 188
Arcadius, emperor, 76
Arabianus, bishop of Ancyra, 77
Arianism, 35, 52, 67, 116, 144
aṣ-Ṣafī abu'l-Faḍā'il ibn al-'Assāl, *Nomokanon*, 218, 273, 275–76, 282–87, 300, 312
Assemani, Joseph Simonius, 240, 296
Assizes of Antioch, 219, 324
Athanasios Philanthropenos: typikon, 211
Athanasios of Balad, Syrian patriarch of Antioch, 249
Athenasios, bishop of Alexandria, *See* Athanasius, bishop of Alexandria
Athanasios the Athonite, 162; typika, 211
Athanasios of Emesa, *Epitome novellorum*, 135–38
Athenasios bishop of Alexandria, *See* Athanasius, bishop of Alexandria
Athanasius (the Great), bishop of Alexandria, 45, 67, 68, 73, 85–88, 94–97, 123, 162, 189, 217, 284, 323; *Epistula ad Amunem*, 95; *Epistula ad Rufinanum*, 95, 337; Letters, 248; *Tomus ad Antiochenos*, 96
Atiya, Aziz A., 265
Aurelius, bishop of Carthage, 75

Babai, rule, 307
Badr al-Ǧamālī, vezir, 277
Ballerini, Pietro and Girolamo, 39, 45, 71
Bar Hebraeus: 'Book of Direction', *See Nomokanon*; *Ethicon*, 253; Ktōbō d-Ētiqōn, *See Ethicon*; Ktōbō d-Hudōyō, *See Nomokanon*; *Nomokanon*, 240, 245–246, 252–53;
Barlaam, 207
Barsaumā, metropolitan of Nisibis, 63, 302–3
Basil I, emperor, 149–50, 155
Basil II Bulgarslayer, emperor, 157
Basil Archidenos, archbishop of Thessalonike, *responsa*, 200–201
Basil of Gortyna, metropolitan of Crete, 79
Basil (the Great), bishop of Caesarea, 43, 86, 97–103,104–6, 113, 119, 124, 159, 163, 166, 217, 229, 234, 237, 248, 284–85, 321, 323; 'Canons of Basil', 86, 97, 230, 234, 237, 248, 258, 282, 284, 319, 321; Letters, 87, 98–99, 102–3 179, 248, 254, 319, 336; Rules, 325; Rules for Venerating Martyrs', 337 *Sermo ob Sacerdotum instructionem*, 98; *De Spiritu Sancto*, 88, 98, 102–3
Basilides, bishop of Pentapolis, 89–90
Basilika, 155, 178, 182, 184, 186
Basilius, 85
Bassianus, bishop of Ephesus, 61
Bastameanc', V., 323
Batiffol, P., 70
Bausi, Alessandro, 291
Bedjan, Paul, 240
Beneševič, Vladimir N., 26
Benjamin I, patriarch, 281
Bickell, J.W., 32
'Book of the Birth [of Christ]' (Maṣḥafa milād), 294
'Book of [33] Chapters' (Kitāb ar-Ru'ūs), 279
'Book of Correct Guidance', *See Kitāb al-Hudā*
'Book of the Fathers', 308
'Book of Letters', 322
'Book of Light' (Maṣḥafa berhān), 294
'Book of Mysteries' (Maṣḥafa mestir), 294
Book of Spiritual Medicine (*Kitāb aṭ-Ṭibb ar-Ruḥānī*), *See* Michael, Bishop of Aṭrīb and Maliǧ
'Book of Synods', 301–3, 311
'Books of the Canons of the Kings', *See* 'Canons of the Kings
Braun, Oskar, 296
Brennecke, Hans Christof, 68
Breydy, Michael, 256, 258–60
Brosset, Marie-Félicité, 328
Bruns, Hermann Theodor, 27

Caelestine, *See* Celestine
Caelestius, 55
Celestine I, pope, 7, 54
Candidianus, 54
Canons of the Apostles, 24–26, 28–33, 77, 85–86, 117–19, 121–23, 154, 177, 179, 188, 216, 224, 226, 229–30, 234, 242, 258, 260, 267–69, 271, 290–92, 300, 318, 323, 330, 336
'Canons of the Church', 267
'Canons of Clement', 258, 260
'Canons of Epiphanius', 227–29, 234, 237
Canons of the Fathers, 26–27, 84–89, 113–14, 117, 120, 154, 260
'Canons of the Fathers who followed after the Apostles', 318, 323
'Canons of John the Deacon', 237
'Canons of Hippolytus', 269, 282, 284–85
'Canons of our Holy Fathers the Apostles', 267

'Canons of the Kings', *See* 234–36, 276, 284–86, 312
'Canons of Our Lord Philip the Apostle', 321–22
'Canons of the 318 Fathers', 233, 245, 299, 307, 309–11
'Canons of Simon the Canaanite', 291
'Canons of Theodosios of Alexandria', 247
Canones Apiarii causae, 75
Cathars, *See* Novations
Chabot, Jean-Baptiste, 296
'Chapters written out of the Orient', 247
Charisius, priest of Philadelphia, 55
Charon, Cyril, 222, 296
Christodulos, metropolitan of Damietta, 279
Christodulos, patriarch of Alexandria, 277, 285
Chrysos, E., 59, 65
'Church Order of Hippolytus', *See* 'Egyptian Church Order'
Clement of Alexandria, 9–10
Clement, pope, 6
De Clerq, Charles, 256, 265
Codex of Lucca, 50
Codex of Trebezond, 103
Collatio legum Mosaicarum et Romanarum, 218, 235
Collectio Ambrosiana, 136–37
Collectio Atheniensis, 55–56
Collectio XXV capitulorum, 118, 132, 136
Collectio LXXXVII capitulorum, *See* John Scholasticus
Collectio LXXXVII titulorum, *See* John Scholasticus
Collectio constitutionum ecclesiasticarum, See *Collectio tripartita*
Collectio tripartita, 120, 135–36, 139, 182
'Collection of Theodosius Diaconus', 87
The Collection of the Sixty Titles, 117–18, 132
Cöln, Franz Joseph, 265, 286
'Commands of Holy Apostles Peter and Paul', 330, 336
'Commands of the Most Holy Apostle Paul Concerning the Ecclesiastical Canons', 330, 336
'Commission of the Apostles by Clement to all Apostolic Catholic Churches', 330
'Concerning the transfer of bishops', 205
'Confession of Hierotheos', 229, 235
Constable Smbat. *See* Smbat
Constantine I, emperor, 21, 35, 126–27
Constantine I Doukas, emperor, 141, 157
Constantine IV, emperor, 333
Constantine V, emperor, 129, 132
Constantine VI, 144
Constantine VII Porphyrogennetos, emperor, 157
Constantine VIII, emperor, 167
Constantine, bishop of Pamphilia, 199
Constantine Akropolites, typikon, 214
Constantine Harmenopoulos, 206; 'Concerning the fasts', 207; 'Concerning heresies' 207; 'Concerning the orthodox faith', 207; *Epitome of Holy and Divine Canons*, 188–190; *Hexabiblos*, 189–90
Constantine Manasses, metropolitan of Naupaktos, 194
Constantinople, Church, 45, 52, 63, 65, 152, 176, 222, 238
Constans, emperor, 67
Constantinus I, pope, 82–83
Constantius II, emperor, 67, 96
Copts, 215, 263–87, 289, 293, 299
Coquin, René-Georges
Corpus canonum, 48, 115–19, 216, 224, 226, 244, 270–71, 297–98, 316–17, 319, 331
corpus canonum Ecclesiae Africanae, *See* materies Africana
Corpus iuris civilis, 33, 125, 131, 155; *Codex Justinianus*, 125–28, 132–33, 135; *Collectio CLXVIII novellarum* (*Collection of the 168 Novellae*) 33, 57, 127–28, 132–34, 136–37, 164, 182, 233, 276; *Digest* (*Pandects*) 125, 135, 138, 140 ; *Institutes*, 135
Coussa, Acace, 223
Crum, W.E., 265
Cyriacus, Syriac patriarch of Antioch, 284
Cyprian, bishop of Carthage, 85, 112–114, 310
Cyril, bishop of Koila and Kallipolis, 56
Cyril, patriarch of Alexandria, 53–4, 85–86, 109–11, 123, 321, 339; letters, 336
Cyril II, patriarch of Alexandria, 277
Cyril III ibn Laqlaq, patriarch of Alexandria, 278–79; 'Dialogue between the teacher and the pupil'; Penance Book, 279
Cyril, bishop of Jerusalem, 77

Dādīšōʿ, 307
Damasus, 310
Darblade, Jean Baptiste, 223, 234
Darrouzès, J., 203
Dauvillier, Jean, 296
David II (IV) the Builder, Georgian king, 338–339
David Alawkayordi, *See* David of Ganjak

David of Gandzak, *See* David of Ganjak
David of Ganjak, 314, 318; 'Canonistic Admonitions (Counsels)' 322–23, 326
'Declaration of the Council of Antioch', 321
Decisions of the Patriarchal Court, 196–97
Decretales of Gregory IX, 326
Demetrios, metropolitan of Kyzikos, 169
Demetrios Chomatenos, *See* Demetrios Chomatianos
Demetrios Chomatianos, archbishop of Ohrid, 193–194; 'Concerning the degrees of marriages with impediment and without', 206; 'Concerning degrees of relationship', 206; 'Concerning the degrees of relationship from marriage and from blood', 206; 'Concerning illegal and forbidden marriages', 206; Court Decisions, 194–95; *responsa*, 202–3
Dib, Pierre, 256
Didachè, 4–6, 7, 16, 22, 29, 95, 224, 266, 292, 329
Didascalia, 10–14, 29–30, 224, 241–42, 266, 270, 282, 284–85, 287, 292, 300, 310
Didaskalia, *See* Didascalia
Diem, Werner, 265
Diocletian, bishop of Oriens, 89
Diocletian, emperor, 37, 39
Dionysiana secunda, 75
Dionysius, bishop of Alexandria, 85–86, 88, 123, 285, 339; letters, 336
Dionysius, proconsul of Antioch, 56
Dionysius bar Ṣalībī, metropolitan of Amida, 250
Dionysius of Tel-Maḥrē, Syrian patriarch, 245–246, 254
Dionysius Exiguus, 32–33, 39, 50, 57, 69, 74, 75, 117
Dioscorus, patriarch of Alexandria, 58–60, 89–90; *Letter to Basilides*, 89–90; *Letter to Kolon*, 90
'Discourse ascribed to St. John the Evangelist delivered at Constantinople', 251
'Doctrine of Addai the Apostle', *See* 'Teaching of the Apostles'
'Doctrine of the Apostles', *See* 'Teaching of the Apostles'
Dominicans, 326
Domninos, *See* Domnus II
Domnus II, patriarch of Antioch, 110
Drey, Johann S. von, 28, 32
Duchesne, Louis, 76
Džavahišvili, Ivan, 328

Eastern Syrians, 215–18, 252–54, 269, 295–314
Ebedjesus of Nisibis. *See* ʿAḇdīšōʿ bar Brīḵā
'Ecclesiastical canons issued by the Holy Fathers in the time of persecution', 247
Ecloga, 129–32, 153, 186, 217, 234, 325; *See* also appendix *Eclogae*
Ecloga private aucta, 190
Edict of Toleration, 39, 41
'Egyptian Church Order', 267, 269
Eisagoge, 151–53, 156, 186
Eisagoge aucta, 190
Ekloge, *See Ecloga*
Eliano, Giambattista, legate, 257, 259–62
Elias I, katholikos, 309–310
Elias al-Ǧauharī, bishop of Jerusalem, 309, *See* also Elias, metropolitan of Damascus
Elias ibn ʿUbaid, bishop of Jerusalem, 309 *See* also Elias, metropolitan of Damascus
Elias, metropolitan of Crete, *responsa*, 198, 200
Elias, metropolitan of Damascus, 218, 298, 300, 303, 310
Elias bar Šināyā, metropolitan of Nisibis, 257, 287, 300, 308–11; *See* also *Kitāb al-Hudā*
Encratites, *See* Enkratites
Enkratites, 99
Epanagoge, *See Eisagoge*
Epanagoge aucta, *See Eisagoge aucta*
Epiphanius of Constantinople, 285
Epiphanios of Cyprus, *See* Epiphanius of Cyprus
Epiphanius of Cyprus, 321
Epiphanius of Salamis, 92 letters, 271
Epistle of Barnabas, 5, 9, 11–12, 17, 22
'Epistle of Peter to Clement', *See* 'Letter of Peter to Clement
Epitome legume, 190
van Esbroeck, Michel, 321
Ethiopian Church, 215, 217, 263, 288–94
Euagrios Pontikos, 325
Eunomius, patriarch of Nicomedia, 61
Euphemianos, metropolitan of Thessalonike, *responsa*, 200
Euphrosyne Palaeogina, typikon, 213
Euprepius, bishop of Bizye and Arkadiopolis, 56
Eusebius, 17
Eusebius, bishop of Ankara, 64
Eusebius, bishop of Caesarea, 45; *Ecclesiastical History*, 17, 39, 89–90
Eusebius, bishop of Dorylaeum; 'Book of Judges', 337
Eusebius, bishop of Nicomedia, 67, 71

General Index

Eustathius, patriarch of Antioch, 68
Eustathius, bishop of Berytus, 66
Eustathius bishop of Sebaste, 43, 45
Euthymios Mt'ac'mi(n)deli, 333–35; *responsa*, 338; *Small Nomokanon*, 332–33, 339
Eutyches, 58, 63
Eutychius, patriarch of Constantinople, 119–20
Excerpta ex registro ecclesiae Carthaginiensis, 75
'Ezana, king of Aksum, 288

Farağallāh al-Akhmīmī', *Nomokanon*, 287–288
Feghali, Joseph, 256
Fetha Nagašt (Laws of the Kings), 285, 293–294
Flavian, patriarch of Antioch, 76, 77
'From a letter which the Holy Fathers wrote to the priests and abbots Paulos and Paulos and the village of Lisos in the region of Cilicia', 247
'From a letter which one of the holy bishops wrote to his friend', 247
'From the letter of the Holy Konstantinos, Metropolitan of Laodiceia, to Abbot Markos from Isauria', 247
Funk, F.X., 28

Gabidzašvili, Enriko, 339
Gabriel of Basra, *Nomokanon*, 298–300, 308–10
Gabriel ibn al-Qulā'ī, 'Nomos of the Holy Church of Antioch', 262
Gabriel II ibn Tarīk, *See* Gabriel II ibn Turaik
Gabriel II ibn Turaik, Coptic patriarch of Alexandria, 278; *Nomokanon*, 283, 285
Gabriel V, Coptic patriarch of Alexandria, Kitāb Tartīb, 280
Gabriel Qaṭrāyā, 308
Gebadius of Bostra, 77
Gelasius I, Pope, 33
Gelasius, bishop of Caesarea Maritima, 76
Gelasius of Cyzicus, 36
Gelzer, Heinrich, 70
Gennadius I, patriarch of Constantinople, 50, 85, 111–12, 123, 190; *Epistula encyclical*, 111, 336, 339; letters, 336–37
George, metropolitan of Arbela and Adiabene, 307
George, Syrian patriarch, 245, 254
George Bardanes, metropolitan of Kerkyra, 202
George the Bishop of Arabs, 251
George Drazionos, 203
George Merčule, *Vita of Gregory of Ḥandzta*, 332

George Mt'ac'mi(n)deli: *Euchologion*, 340
George II Xiphilinos, patriarch of Constantinople, 173, 201
Georgian Church, 215, 217, 220, 326–42
Gerasimos I, patriarch of Constantinople, 196
Gerasimos of the Holy Mountain, monk, 200
Germanos II, patriarch of Constantinople, 173; 'Order of Mysteries of the Catholic Church', 337
Germanus of Constantinople, *See* Germanos II, patriarch of Constantinople
Gesta de nomine Apiarii, 75
Ğirğis of Ehden, 'Book of Canons' (Kitāb al-qawānīn), 260–261
Giunašvili, E., 333
Gnosticism, 17, 264
Goffredus Tranensis, 326
'Good Friday Mystagogy', 229, 234
Gozman, Francis, 265
Graf, Georg, 223, 230, 234, 237, 256–59, 262
Gratian; *Decretum*, 33, 44, 47
'Great Book', *See* Nikon of the Black Mountains, *Pandects*
Gregorian, 21
Gregory I, pope, 53
Gregory II, pope, 82
Gregory, bishop of Nazianzus, 50, 85–86, 88, 105–06, 107, 123, 190, 217, 321; *Carmina dogmatia*, 106, 336
Gregory, bishop of Nyssa, 76, 85, 103–5, 123, 217, 285, 339; letters, 248, 336
Gregory Doxapatres, *See* Gregory Doxopatres
Gregory Doxopatres, Epitome of the *Nomokanon of Fourteen Titles*, 191
Gregory the Enlightener, 320
Gregory Pakourianos, typika, 211
Gregory Palamas, 207, bishop of Neocaesarea, 85, 86, 88, 93–94; *Epistola canonica*, 93, 336, 339
Gregory the Theologian, *See* Gregory, bishop of Nazianzus
Gregory the Wonder-Worker, *See* Gregory Thaumaturgus
Grohmann, Adolf, 265
Guidi, I., 289
Gundstapl Smbat, *See* Constable Smbat

Hadrian, 21
Hadrian II, pope, 149
Hammerschmidt, Ernst, 289
Haneberg, Daniel Bonifatius, 264
Hankiewicz, Gregor R. von, 71

Haxthausen, August von, 328
Hegesippus, 6
Herakleios, emperor, 129, 137, 139
Hermogenes, 21
Hess, Hamilton, 70–71
Het'um I, king, 324
Hibatallāh ibn Yūnus ibn abi 'l-Fath, 230
History of the Patriarchs, 277, 281
Holldack, Felix, 328
Ḥnānīšōʿ, katholikos, 306, 309, 311
Honorius, emperor, 76
Horsiesios: monastic rule, 280
Hormisdas, Pope, 33, 53
Horner, George William, 264
Humbert, cardinal of Silva Candida, 84

Ibas, bishop of Edessa, 61, 63
Ibn al-ʿAssāl, *See* Ṣafi abu'l-Faḍāʾil ibn al-ʿAssāl
Ibn aṭ-Ṭayib, 218, 257, 273, 287, 303, 308; 'Law of Christianity', 253, 298, 307, 310–11
Ibn Faḫr, Elias, 238
iconoclasm, 143–44, 150
Ignatios, *See* Ignatius
Ignatius, patriarch of Antioch, 7–8, 13, 15, 22, 87, 224, 248, 254
Ignatius, patriarch of Constantinople, 146–49
India, 253–5, 295, 313
Innocent I, pope, 45
'Inscription on the column off the Georgian national synod of Ruis-Urbnisi', *See* Index of Councils and Synods, Ruis-Urbinsi
Ioakeim, metropolitan of Zichnai: typikon, 214
Ioasaph, metropolitan of Ephesus: *responsa*, 203
Irenaeus, 6, 10
Irene, empress, 132, 144
Irene Choumnaena: typikon, 213
Isaac, katholikos of Seleucia-Ctesiphon, 252, 297, 299
Isaac I Comnenos, emperor, 157, 180, 212
Isaac II Angelos, emperor, 175, 180–81
Isaac, patriarch of the Armenians, *See* Sahak, patriarch of the Armenians
Isaiah, patriarch of Constantinople, 196
Isaias, anchorite, 281
Isidoriana, 39
Isidore, 50
Islamic law, 252–53, 285, 312, 323
Īšōʿbarnūn, katholikos, 252, 306, 307; letters, 304, 309–11

Īšōbōḵt, metropolitan of Rēvardašīr, 305–306, 308, 310–11
Īšōʿyahḇ IV, katholikos, 304, 308

Jacob Baradaios, bishop, 239
Jacob of Edessa, 242, 244–45, 247, 249–52
Jacobites, *See* Western Syrians
Jarawan, Elias, 223, 231
Jessner, Friedrich, 328
Jews, 131, 145
Joannou, Perikles-Petros, 26, 28, 47, 86, 96–97, 108–9, 111
Johannes bar Aḇgārē, katholikos, 253, 304
Johannes bar Qursos, bishop of Tella, 249, 251; letters, 254
Johannes Maron, *See* Anonymous Syrian Treatise on the Priesthood
John I Comnenus, emperor, 179
John II Comnenus, emperor, 211
John II, pope, 126
John VII, pope, 82–83
John VIII, pope, 150
John I, patriarch of Antioch, 54–56, 110
John III, patriarch of Antioch, 204, 225
John IV(V), patriarch of Antioch, 'On Monastic Teaching', 225
John Kastamonites, metropolitan of Chalcedon, 184, 205–6, responsa, 200–2
John III Scholasticus, patriarch of Constantinople 26, 33, 50, 118–20, 134, 224; Collectio LXXXVII Capitulorum, 120, 133–34, 136, 138, 188, 228, 233; Nomokanon in fourteen titles, 238; Nomokanon in fifty titles, 137–38, 140, 191, 335; Synagogue of Fifty Titles (Synagoga, Synagogue of Ecclesiastical Canons Divided into 50 Titles), 36, 66, 74, 86, 118–20, 137, 191
John Chrysostom, archbishop of Constantinople, 44–45, 108, 162, 260, 276, 282, 284–85, 291
John IV Nesteutes, patriarch of Constantinople, 85, 120, 142
John VIII Xiphilinus, patriarch of Constantinople, 86, 166–67
John IX Agapetos, patriarch of Constantinople, 171
John XI Bekkos, patriarch of Constantinople, responsa, 202
John XIII Glykes, patriarch of Constantinople, 196
John, bishop of Cyprus, letters; 248 (look into)
John, metropolitan of Kitros, responsa, 186, 202

John, metropolitan of Mardin, 246, 251
John, monk of Monacheion, 212
John Apokaukos, metropolitan of Naupaktos, 192–93; Court Decisions, 193–94; responsa, 202
John, bishop of Nikiu, 108
John Comnenos, archbishop of Ohrid, 191
John of Odzun, katholikos: 'Canon Book of the Armenians', 316–23
John, Syrian patriarch, 246, 250
John bar Abgārē, 307, 310–11
John of Dārā, See Anonymous Syrian Treatise on the Priesthood
John the Faster, See John IV Nesteutes
John Malalas, 119
John Pantechnes, chartophylax, responsa, 200, 338
John Pediasimos, chartophylax, 'Concerning marriages', 206
John Scholastikos, See John Scholasticus
John Tarchaneiotes, protos of Mt. Athos, 204
John Zonaras, 20, 27, 84, 103, 176–78, 183–84, 238; 'Concerning that two second cousins should not be married', 205; Homily to those who believe that natural human excretion is unclean', 205
Jonah, monk 203
Joseph of Egypt, 230
Joseph II, patriarch, 313
Julian the Apostate, emperor, 96
Julius I, pope, 67, 68
Justin II, emperor, 130, 137
Justinian, 119, 125–30, 133, 155; Epistola adversus Theodorum Mopsuestenum, 75 See also Corpus iuris civilis
Justinian II, emperor, 78, 82, 145
Juvenal, patriarch of Jerusalem, 54, 58, 60

Kallistos I, patriarch of Constantinople, 196
Kallistos II Xanthopoulos, patriarch of Constantinople, 196
Karalevsky, Cyril See Charon, Cyril
Karst, Joseph, 315, 328
Kitāb al-Hudā, 233–234, 256–59, 261
Kitāb al-Kamāl, See Kitāb al-Hudā
Kitāb al-Qawānīn, See Kitāb al-Hudā
Kitāb an-Namūs, See Kitāb al-Hudā
Kolon, bishop of Hermopolis, 90
Konon, See Kolon
Korolevskij, Cyrille, See Charon, Cyril
Kosmas I, patriarch of Constantinople, 166

Kosmas II Attikos, patriarch of Constantinople: *responsa*, 200
Kounales, Kritopoulos: paraphrase of the *Syntagma*, 186
Krasnožen, Michail E., 121–22
Kyriakos, Syrian patriarch, 245–246, 251, 254; *responsa*, 250
Kyrillos ibn Laqlaq, See Cyril III ibn Laqlaq
Kyrion, katholilos of Georgia

de Lagarde, Paul, 240, 264
Lauchert, Friedrich, 27
'Law of the Katholikoi', 340–41
Lebon, Joseph, 41, 42, 318
Leo I, emperor, 126, 133
Leo III, emperor, 129, 143
Leo V, emperor, 132
Leo VI (the Wise), emperor, 129, 150, 153–56
Leo I (the Great), pope, 6, 7, 53, 59, 65
Leo, archbishop of Ohrid, 206
Leontios, bishop of Nauplia, typikon, 212
Letoius, bishop of Melitene, 104
'Letter of Peter to Clement', 229, 235, 237, 270, 282, 285, 291
'Letter of the Western Fathers' 299
'Letter which was written by an assembly of Father in the West to their Brethren in the East', See 'Letter of the Western Fathers'
Libanius, 106
Libellus synodicus, 40
Liber Patrum, 308
Liber Pontificalis, 78, 82
Licinius, 39
'List of the 72 Disciples', 229, 234
'List of Heresies', 229, 232
'List of Synods', 229, 232
Logos Prosphoneticus, 50–51, 78
Loofs, F., 43
Loukas, abbot of Christ the Savior, 212
Loukas Chrysoberges, patriarch of Constantinople, 171, *responsa*, 200–201
Ludolf, Hiob, 288

Mai, Angelo, 240, 296, 315
Makarios, metropolitan of Ankyra, See Makarios, *Syntagma*
Makarios, patriarch of Constantinople, 196, 203
Makarios, bishop of Jerusalem, letters, 321
Makarios Chrysokephalos, metropolitan of Philadelphia, See Makarios, *Syntagma*

Makarios, *Syntagma*: 187–88, 267–68, 272–273, 275–276, 278, 282–284
Makarios Choumnos: typikon, 214
Manichaeism 131, 264
Mansi, Giovan Domenico, 27
Manuel I Comnenos, emperor, 174–75, 177, 181
Manuel II, patriarch of Constantinople, 172; *responsa*, 202
Manuel Xantios, deacon and chartophylax, 338
'Maphrian', 239, 246
Mār Abā, katholikos, 297, 300, 305
Mār Ignatios, 254
Mār Johannes, 254
Marcian, emperor, 58–60, 65, 126
Marcellus, bishop of Ancyra, 40, 45, 68
Mark, patriarch of Alexandria, 201, 225
Markos of Alexandria, *See* Mark, patriarch of Alexandria
Markos ibn Zurʿa, Coptic patriarch, 271
Markus ibn al-Qanbar, 286 'Book of Chapters' (Kitāb ar-Ruʾūs), 279
Maronites, 216–17, 219, 255–63, 270, 299
Martyrius of Antioch, 50, 248
Martyros of Antioch, *See* Martyrius of Antioch
Mārūtā, bishop of Maipherkat, 233, 297, 299
materies Africana, 117–18, 120
Matthew I, patriarch of Constantinople, 174, 196; typika, 214
Matthew Blastares, 183, 206, 238; *Adnoumion Lexikon*, 187; Synopsis of the canons of Pseudo Nikephorouous, 186; Synopsis of the *Kanonikon* of 'John Nesteutes', 186; *Syntagma*, 27, 84, 103, 185–87, 338
Maurice, emperor, 137
Maximinus, 18
Maximos, monk, 199,
Maximos, monk of Theotokos Skoteine, typikon, 213
Maximus, patriarch of Antioch, 60, 61
Maximinus Daia, emperor, 39
Mechitar Goš, 314; Datastanagirkʿ, 323–324
Melchites, *See* Melkites
Melkʿisedk I, katholikos-patriarch, 327
Melitus of Lycopolis, 35–36, 91–92
Melkites, 215, 217–218, 220–238, 263, 269–70, 273, 275–76, 286, 289, 293, 299
Memnon, bishop of Ephesus, 54
Methodius, patriarch of Constantinople, 337
Metzger, Marcel, 28
Miaphysites, *See* Monophysites
Michael III, emperor, 147, 149

Michael VII Doukas, emperor 191
Michael VIII Palaeologus, emperor, 176; typika, 213
Michael, Bishop of Atrīb and Maliğ: 'Book of Spiritual Medicine', 237, 261, 275, 286–87, 293
Michael II, patriarch of Constantinople, 172, 201
Michael III Anchialos, patriarch of Constantinople, 171–72, 174
Michael, metropolitan of Damietta, 273, 275, 278, 282; Nomokanon, 276, 284–85
Michael Choumnos, patriarch of Thessalonike, 205; *responsa*, 200
Michael the Syrian, Syrian patriarch, 246
Michael Attaleiates, Ponema Nomikon, 190
Michael Psellus, 86; 'Concerning the Nomokanon', 191; Synopsis of Laws, 191
Milasch, Nikodim, 168
Monophysites, 144, 215, 220, 211 227, 263, 288, 314
Monothelite, 216, 257
Montanists, 49, 99, 131
Mount Athos, 188, 193, 197, 328, 342
Moses of Abydos: rule, 280
Moses of Dasxuranc'i; 'History of the Albanians', 326
Moses bar Kepha, *See* Anonymous Syrian Treatise on the Priesthood
Mūsā al-ʿAkkarī, *See* Petros, Maronite patriarch

Nallino, Carlo Alphonso, 240
Nasrallah, Joseph, 223, 230
Nau, François, 240
Nectarius of Constantinople, 32, 76
Neilos, bishop of Constantinople: typikon, 213
Neilos, patriarch of Constantinople, 174, 196
Neilos Damilas: typikon, 214
Neilos Diasorenos, metropolitan of Rhodes: *responsa*, 203; 'A synoptic account of the holy and ecumenical councils', 207
Neilos Doxopatres: *responsa*, 200–1
Neophytos, monk, 200
Neophytos VII, Patriarch, 27
Neophytos Enkleistos: *Enkomion*, 112
Nersēs of Lambron, archbishop of Tarsus, 325
Nersēs IV Šnorhali, patriarch of Armenia, 322
Nestorianism, 111; *See* also Eastern Syrians
Nestorius, patriarch of Constantinople, 53–55, 58, 61, 110–11, 295
New Rome, *See* Constantinople
Nicaenum, 37

Nicholas I, patriarch of Constantinople, 165–66
Nicholas III Grammatikos, patriarch of Constantinople, 171–72, 189, 199; 'Concerning fasting', 204; 'Concerning the fasts', 204; reponsa, 198–199
Nicholas IV Mouzalon, patriarch of Constantinople, responsa, 200–201
Nicholas I, pope, 147, 149
Nicholas, abbot of St. Nicholas, typikon, 212
Nicholas Mystikos: typikon, 212
Nicholas Skrivas, 169
Nikephoros I, emperor, 132
Nikephoros II Phokas, 157
Nikephoros III Botaneiatis, emperor, 157
Nikephorus II, patriarch of Constantinople, 199
Nikephorus Blemmydes, typikon, 213
Nikephorus, cartophylax, responsa, 198–99
Niketas II, patriarch of Constantinople, 181
Niketas, metropolitan of Amasea, 204–5
Niketas, metropolitan of Ankyra, 204
Niketas, metropolitan of Heraclea, responsa, 186, 198–99
Niketas of Herakleia, See Niketas, metropolitan of Heraclea
Niketas, metropolitan of Thessalonike, respona, 198–99
Niketas Stethatos, 84, 206
Nikodemos the Hagiorite, *Pedalion*, 27, 77, 85, 90, 103, 107
Nikodemos Hagiotites, See Nikodemos the Hagiorite
Nikon of the Black Mountains: *Pandects* ('Interpretations of the divine injunctions of the Lord', *al-Ḥāwī al-kabīr*) 141, 225, 237, 293; *Taktikon*, 142–43, 212, 225; Typikon, See *Taktikon*
Niphon I, patriarch of Constantinople, 172
Nomokanon of 14 Titles, 27, 85–86, 120, 123–24, 135, 137, 138–42, 181–82, 184, 188, 191, 330, 336
Nomokanon of 50 Titles, See John III Scholasticus
Nomokanon of Basil, Gregory, and John the Merciful, 337
Nomokanon of Photius, See *Nomokanon of 14 Titles*
Nomokanon of Pseudo-Photius, See *Nomokanon of 14 Titles*
Nomos Mosaikos, 235, 325, 341
Nomos Stratiotikos, 325
Novations, 48, 55, 99
Nubian Church, 263, 287–288

Octateuchus Clementinus, 241–43, 268, 291, 300
Optimus of Antioch, 106
Origen, 10; Origenism, 67, 69, 108–9
Orlandi, T., 273
Ossius, bishop of Cordoba, 67, 71

Pachomius, rule, 280
Palladios: *Historia Lausiaca*, 294
Palladius; *Vita* of John Chrysostom, 45
Paul, apostle, 2–4, 7 11, 21–22
Paul IV, patriarch of Constantinople, 143
Paul of Samosata, 17, 36
Payne-Smith, Robert, 259
Pedalion, See Nikodemos the Hagiorite
Pelagianism, 55
Pelagius I, pope, 76
Peña, Francisco, 240
Peradse, Gregor, 329
Peter of Aragon, 326
Peter, chartophylax, *reponsa*, 198, 337
Peter, bishop of Alexandria, 51, 85–86, 88, 90–93, 123, 248, 275, 339; letters, 336; 'Logos' 87; *Epistola canonica*, 91
Peter the Fuller, patriarch of Antioch, 111
Petros, Maronite patriarch, 259
Petros II al-Ḥadatī, 259
Philotheos of Alexandria, See Theophilus, bishop of Alexandria
Philotheos Kokkinos, patriarch of Constantinople, 173, 196
Philoxenos of Hieropolis, 251
Photinians, 48
Photinus of Sirmium, 48
Photios, See Photius
Photius, patriarch of Constantinople, 140, 146–48, 150, 153, 163, 169
Photius, bishop of Tyre, 66
Phritilas, bishop of Herakleia, 56
Pitra, J.B. Cardinal, 27, 35, 162
Polycarp of Smyrna, 8
Primasecunda, See Councils and Synods, Constantinople (861)
Prinzing, Günter, 195
Prisca, 39, 50, 69
Procheiron, See *Procheiros nomos*
Procheiros Nomos, 156, 186, 217, 229, 236, 263, 276
Prochiron auctum, 190, 206
Prochoros, metropolitan of Stauroupolis, *responsa*, 203
'Pseudo-Apostolic Canons', See 'Teaching of the Apostles'

Pseudo-Athanasius, 236–37, 275–76 *Quaestiones ad Antiochum ducem*, 96
Pseudo-Basil Canons, 229, 235, 275; 'Canons for daily misdeeds', 334
Pseudo-Clement, 'Roll Book' (Kitāb al-Mağāll) 292
Pseudo-Ephrem the Syrian, 251
Pseudo-Epiphanios, 226, 276
Pseudo-Epiphanius, *See* Pseudo-Epiphanios
Pseudo-Gennadius of Constantinople, 'On Christian Faith and Life', 338
Pseudo-George of Arbela, 308
Pseudo-Gregory of Nyssa, 276
Pseudo-John IV Nesteutes, 158–160, 237; 'Canons for Sinners', 334; 'Canons for Sins', 334; 'Homily to One About to Confess to His Spiritual Father', 160; 'Instruction for Nuns', 160; 'Kanonarion', 159–60; 'Nomonikon', 160; 'Service and Order of Confession', 160; 'Teaching of the Fathers Concerning Those Who Ought to Confess Their Sins', 160
Pseudo-Nicene canons, 227, 245, 258, 287
Pseudo-Nikephorus I, 160–61, 189
Pseudo-Isidorian Decretals, 33
Pulcheria, empress, 59, 65

Quartodecimians, 48, 55
'Qawānīn ar-rusul', *See Canons of the Apostles*

Rabbūlā, bishop of Edessa, 248, 251, 260–61
Rahmani, Ignatius Ephrem, 240
Raymond of Peñafort, 326
Renaudot, Eusebius, 264
Rhalles, George A., 26–27
Rhalles, George A. and Potles, Michael, 85, 90, 103, 107, 163
Rheginus of Constantia, bishop of Cyprus, 56
Riedel, Wilhelm, 264–265
Ritter, Adolf M., 51
Romanos, metropolitan of Dyrrachion, 202
Romanos I Lakapenos, emperor, 157
Rome, Church, 51–52, 63, 73, 82; New Rome, *See* Constantinople
Rufinus of Aquileia: *Ecclesiastical History*, 37, 96
Rufinus, pretorian prefect, 76
'Rules of Christianity', 260
'Ruling of the Holy Apostle Thaddeus', 321
Rusticus, deacon, 57

Saban, typikon, 210
Sabianus, bishop of Perre, 61
Sachau, Eduard, 296
Sahak, patriarch of the Armenians, 319–20
Sahidic, 272
Samir Khalil, 257
Sava, archbishop of Serbia, typikon, 212
Schiller, Arthur, 265
Schulthess, Friedrich, 240, 296
Schwartz, Eduard, 28, 33, 45, 48, 59, 70–71, 73, 86–87, 101–2, 318
'Second canons of Antioch', *See* 'Declaration of the Council of Antioch'
Selb, Walter, 240, 296
Senodos, *See Synodos*
Sententiae Syricae, 217, 219, 248, 325
Sergios Amphiator, letters, 248
Sergius I, pope, 82
Sevantos, bishop, letter, 320
Severos ibn al Muqaffaʾ: 'The Order of the Priesthood', 277
Severus, Monophysite patriarch of Antioch, 224; letters, 248
Shenoute the Great, 'Canons' 280
Shepherd of Hermas, 9–10, 17, 22, 95
Silvester, patriarch of Antioch, 238
Simeon, metropolitan of Rēvardašīr, 305, 311
Simeon bar Sabbāʿē, katholikos, 308
Siricius I, pope, 77
Sisinnios II, patriarch of Constantinople, 162, 166–67, 170
Small Nomokanon, *See* Euthymios Mtʿacʿmi(n)deli
Smbat, 219; Lawbook, 324
Socrates of Constantinople: *Historia Ecclesiastica*, 43, 57 107
Sozomenus: *Historia ecclesiastica*, 43
Spiritual Canons, 227, 229, 234
'Statutes of the Old Testament', 229, 234, 282, 284
Steindorff, Georg, 265
Steinwenter, Arthur, 70, 265
Stephan, katholikos of Albania, 323
Stephan I, pope, 113
Stephan ad-Duwaihi, Maronite patriarch, 257–260
Stephanos, *See* Stephanus
Stephanus of Salona, Bishop, 32
Stephanus, bishop of Ephesus, 61, 121–22
Stolte, B. H., 135
Symeon, metropolitan of Thessalonike, 338; *responsa*, 203

Symeon Stylites, 248
Synaxarion, 108
Synodicon orientale, *See* 'Book of Synods'
'Synodicon of Orthodoxy', 334
Synodos, 289–292, 310
Synopsis of Canons, 120–124, 179
Syntagma XIV titulorum, 25–27, 66, 74, 75, 76, 111, 113, 120, 122, 135, 139, 179
Syntagma of Canons of 14 Titles, See Syntagma XIV titulorum
'Syntagma Doctrinae', 274, 325
Syriac, 231, 256
Syrian Orthodox Church, *See* Western Syrians
Syrian Roman Lawbook, See Syro-Roman Lawbook
Syro-Malankaya Church, *See* India
Syro-Roman Lawbook, 217, 219, 227, 229, 235, 248, 252, 258, 263, 276, 284–85, 309–11, 325

Ta'alīm ar-rusul, *See* 'Teachings of the Apostles'
Tamar, queen, 327, 340
Tarasios, patriarch of Constantinople, 144–45, letters, 336–37
Tarasius, *See* Tarasios, patriarch of Constantinople
'Tartīb al-kahanūt', 277
Tarchnišvili, Michael, 331–32
Tattam, Henry, 264
'Teaching of the Apostles', 232, 243–44, 266, 269, 313, 318
'Teaching of the Apostle Addai', *See* 'Teaching of the Apostles'
Testament of Our Lord Jesus Christ, 224, 242, 268, 270, 292, 330
Testamentum Domini Nostri Jesu Christi, See Testament of our Lord Jesus Christ
Thalassus, bishop of Caesarea
Theodora, empress of Michael VIII Palaeologus, typikon 213
Theodora, wife of John Synadenos, typikon, 213
Theodore Balsamon, patriarch of Antioch 27, 79, 84, 103, 178, 180–84, 225, 238; 'annotations of *Nomokanon of Fourteen Titles*', 181; 'Concerning novices', 205; 'Concerning the offering of incense', 205; *responsa*, 200–201; A study concerning the patriarchal privileges', 205; 'A study concerning the two offices of *chartophylax* and *protekdikos*', 205 'That one should not be reading books on mathematics', 205;

Theodore Bestes, 123–24, 140; *Nomokanon*, 181
Theodore I Doukas, emperor, 195
Theodore, bishop of Mopsuestia, 76, 302
Theodore abū Qurra, bishop of Harran, 230
Theodore of Studios, *See* Theodore the Studite
Theodore the Studite, abbot of Stoudios,162; canons, 237; typikon, 210–211
Theodoret, bishop of Cyrrhus, 36, 47–48, 60–61
Theodosios, *See* Theodosius
Theodosius I, emperor, 50, 76, 105, 107, 116, 126
Theodosius II, emperor, 53, 126, 133
Theodoule, *See* Theodroa
Theophilus, bishop of Alexandria, 44, 76–77, 85, 88, 108–9, 190; letters, 336, 339
Theodosius of Corinth, monk, 199
Thomas Aquinas, 326
Tiberius II, emperor, 127
Till, Walter 265
Timotheus I, *See* Timothy I, katholikos
Timothy I, bishop of Alexandria, 85–86, 123, 285, 339; 'Erotapokriseis', 87–88, 107–8; 'Fifteen Questions', 246 *reponsa*, 217, 224, 271, 274–75, 291, 319, 336
Timothy II Ailurus, patriarch of Alexandria, 111–12
Timothy I, katholikos, 252, 298, 300, 305–6, 311; letters, 304, 309–10
Traditio Apostolica, See Apostolic Tradition
'Traditions of the Apostles', 269, 285, 291
Trajan, Emperor, 7
Tribonian, 128
Turner, C.H., 28, 69, 70, 72
Typika of Christ Panoiktirmon, 211
Typika of Kosmosoteira, 212
Typika of Pantokrator, 211
Typika of St. John Prodromos, 212
Typika of St. John the Theologian, 212
Typika of Theotokos Eleousa, 211–212
Typika of Theotokos Euergetis, 211
Typika of Theotokos Kecharitomene, 211

'Ubaid ibn Sa'āda, Michael, 263

Vačagan, king, 326
Vaḫtang VI, 219, 328, 340–41
Valens, emperor, 61
Valens of Mursa, 71
Valentinian, emperor, 61
Vansleb, Johann M, 289
Vitalis of Antioch, bishop, 39, 41

Voel, Guillaume and Justel Henri 121
Vööbus, Arthur, 240, 245
Vosté, Jacques-M., 296
Van der Wal, Nicolaas, 153–54
van der Wal-Lokin, 139

Wansleben, Johann Michael, 264
Western Syrians, 215, 238–55, 269, 275, 285–86

Yahḇallāhā, katholikos, 297, 300
Yūḥannā ibn Zindah, 263

Zanetti, Ugo, 287
Zeno, emperor, 126
Zosimus, pope, 74

The History of Byzantine and Eastern Canon Law to 1500 was designed in Dante and typeset by Kachergis Book Design of Pittsboro, North Carolina. It was printed on 55-pound Natures Book Natural and bound by Thomson-Shore of Dexter, Michigan.